MASTERING™
HTML 4.0

Deborah S. Ray
Eric J. Ray

SYBEX®

San Francisco • Paris • Düsseldorf • Soest

Associate Publisher: Gary Masters
Acquisitions Manager: Kristine Plachy
Acquisitions & Developmental Editor: Dan Brodnitz
Editor: Pat Coleman
Project Editor: Davina Baum
Technical Editor: Matthew Fiedler
Book Designers: Patrick Dintino and Catalin Dulfu
Graphic Illustrators: Steve Brooks and Andrew Benzie
Electronic Publishing Specialists: Nathan Johanson and
Kate Kaminski
Production Coordinator: Amy Eoff
Proofreaders: Katherine Cooley, Charles Mathews, Eryn
Osterhaus, and Duncan Watson
Indexer: Lori Lathrop
Companion CD: Molly Sharp and John D. Wright
Cover Designer: Design Site
Cover Illustrator/Photographer: Design Site

Library of Congress Card Number: 97-68719
ISBN: 0-7821-2102-0

Manufactured in the United States of America

10 9 8 7 6 5 4 3 2 1

To each other…
and Ashleigh.

Acknowledgments

We'd like to thank the many folks who helped bring this book together. First, a big thanks to Pat Coleman, Editor, for applying her superlative talents and experience to this book. Never before have we learned so much from a book project, and we have Pat to thank for helping us become better authors.

Also, a big thanks goes to Dan Brodnitz, Acquisitions and Developmental Editor, for his confidence in us to take on such a monstrous project.

We'd also like to thank some folks for helping with chapter content:

- Thanks to Terry "Wassat?" Zambon for reviewing, editing, and commenting on chapters before we submitted them.

- Thanks to David Hailey for researching and providing content for the HTML Help chapter.

- Thanks to Wanda Jane Phillips for compiling the JavaScript and Style Sheets reference sections and for providing content for the JavaScript chapter.

- Thanks to Randy Jay Yarger for providing content for the chapters on creating searchable HTML and generating HTML from a database.

We'd also like to thank the "behind the scenes" folks who brought this book together. First, thanks to Davina Baum for making submitting a 1000-page book a well-coordinated process—also known as bringing order out of chaos. Also, many thanks to the technical editor, Matt Fiedler, who helped make this book as timely and as accurate as possible. Thanks also to Nathan Johanson and Kate Kaminski, Electronic Publishing Specialists, for putting this book together—they did a wonderful job, particularly with the special stuff we threw at them. Thanks also to Amy Eoff, the Production Coordinator, and to the proofreaders, Katherine Cooley, Charles Mathews, Eryn Osterhaus, and Duncan Watson, who made this book usable and readable, and to Molly Sharp and Dale Wright, for all their help with the CD.

Last but not least, thanks to Holly Foht, without whom we'd never have gotten it done.

Contents at a Glance

TABLE OF CONTENTS

PART II • ADVANCING YOUR SKILLS

INTRODUCTION

Welcome to *Mastering HTML*—your one-stop comprehensive guide to HyperText Markup Language! In it, you'll find:

- Comprehensive information about the latest and greatest HTML 4 specification—what it includes and how to use it

- Advice and ideas about developing Web pages to accommodate multiple browsers

- Easy-to-follow instructions, which help you build HTML documents one step at a time

- Examples of how you can enhance your Web pages with various technologies, including multimedia and JavaScript

- Design guidelines to help you use HTML effectively

- Expert advice about choosing HTML development tools that meet your needs

- Special uses for HTML, such as creating searchable HTML and generating HTML from a database

- Cutting-edge HTML technologies, such as Dynamic HTML and push technologies

- A comprehensive reference on HTML, Style Sheets, JavaScript, special characters, and browser-safe colors

- Sample software and files, located on the Companion CD

We developed this book so that any HTML author—whether you're a newbie or seasoned professional—can learn and effectively use HTML. For example, if you're new to HTML, you can start at the beginning and work your way forward as you advance your skills. You'll find the step-by-step instructions and examples easy to follow and understand.

Or, if you've already created a few (or several!) HTML documents, scan the chapters for HTML 4 information, thumb through later chapters and pick up new skills, or use the Master's Reference to find the specific information you want. You'll find complete information about Dynamic HTML, push technologies, Style Sheets, HTML help, JavaScript, and frames.

Mastering HTML is platform independent. You'll find it a valuable resource regardless of whether you are developing for Windows, Macintosh, or Unix.

What's in This Book?

This book contains five parts, a Master's Reference, and the Companion CD. Here's what to expect in each.

Part One: Getting Started

In this part, you'll learn about HTML and its uses. We'll introduce you to a few essential HTML tools, discuss the HTML document-development process, and walk you through developing your first HTML page. We'll look at all the common page elements and even a few perks such as links, more elaborate formatting, and Style Sheets.

In this part and the next two, we focus on hand-coding HTML. Although many Web publishing tools do a good job of applying HTML code, the only way to really master HTML and to be able to make the most of the available tools is to know how to hand-code.

Part Two: Advancing Your Skills

In this part, you'll move on to some of the more fun and impressive HTML effects such as including images, tables, forms, and frames. These effects can really enliven your pages and give them the "up-with-technology" look and feel.

Part Three: Moving Beyond Pure HTML

In this part, you'll learn how to include JavaScript, multimedia, Dynamic HTML, and push technologies. These technologies are out near the cutting edge and can add great power and pizzazz to your HTML pages when wielded properly.

Part Four: More Tools for the HTML Pro

In this part, you'll get acquainted with a whole slew of HTML-related tools. For example, you'll see how conversion tools and validation services can help ease the document-development process. And, you'll also see how to generate HTML from a database and learn about creating searchable HTML pages.

Part Five: Developing Web Sites

In this part, you'll learn the ins and outs of developing functional Web sites that your visitors will want to return to again and again. Also, you'll find tips and tricks for developing specific types of Web sites—public, personal, and intranet sites. These chapters show you how to develop and design your pages and sites according to what they'll be used for and who will be viewing them. Finally, you'll learn about HTML help files—a hot new technology for creating cross-platform help files.

Master's Reference

The Master's Reference includes five sections:

- Part 1 provides a comprehensive catalog of HTML tags and attributes, shows which HTML standard they belong to (HTML 4, 3.2, and so on), and gives you examples of how to apply them.
- Part 2 provides a comprehensive catalog of Style Sheet tags and attributes and gives you examples of how to apply them.
- Part 3 provides a comprehensive catalog of JavaScript objects, properties, methods, and functions and shows examples of how to use them.
- Part 4 gives you a list of special characters, such as copyright symbols and diacritics, and shows you how to include them in your documents.
- Part 5 provides a list of browser-safe color descriptions and the appropriate RGB numbers that you'll use to include these colors in your documents.

Companion CD

The Companion CD provides you with scads of sample files and software. Using the sample files is a great way to learn how to achieve HTML effects—you can either take a peek at the code in the files or copy and paste the code into your own documents. The software provides you with all the programs you need to get started—and then some! You'll find freeware, shareware, and some commercial demos to use and experiment with (subject to the licensing agreements with each package, of course). You can use these packages to do real work and to determine which work best for your needs!

Conventions in This Book

Throughout this book, we've used several conventions intended to help you find and use the information more easily.

Text Conventions

The following text conventions will help you easily identify new words, show you how to follow along with the examples, and help you use menu commands.

The first time a new word is used, it appears in *italics* and is followed by a brief definition or example.

HTML code appears in a special font, like this. If an example requires that you type in new code in each step, the new code appears in boldface type, like this:

```
A line of code from a previous step
Another line of code from a previous step
The new line of code you enter in the current step
```

Finally, where instructions indicate that you use a menu command, the menu sequence appears like this:

1. Choose File ➢ Save As to open the Save As dialog box, and then choose Options.

This sequence means that you go to the File menu and then choose Save As from the drop-down list. In the Save As dialog box, you choose Options.

Icon Conventions

The following icons will provide you with helpful notes, tips, and warnings.

Tips include time-saving information to help make your HTML authoring easier and faster.

Notes provide information to help you better understand the surrounding text.

Warnings highlight potential trouble spots.

Visit the Examples and Web Sites

Throughout this book, you'll find plenty of examples that help illustrate how to develop code or that show the results of steps you follow. Most of these examples are on the Companion CD—simply look in the appropriate chapter folder.

Also, we point you to lots of Web sites—some show you examples of how companies apply HTML code to their needs, some offer software for you to download, and some are information resources to help keep you up-to-date with HTML and related technologies. Keep in mind that Web site content changes frequently and that you might not find exactly what we describe or even find the pages at the right location. We verified everything just before the book went to press, but we can't guarantee specific content at each Web address.

Contact Us

We're glad you chose *Mastering HTML* as your one-stop HTML resource. Please let us know how it goes—we're always happy to hear comments and answer questions. You can contact us at `mastering.html@raycomm.com`. We look forward to hearing from you!

PART I

Getting Started

LEARN TO:

- Understand HTML, related tools, and the Web

- Plan HTML documents

- Create HTML documents

- Link HTML documents

- Develop and apply Style Sheets

- Post your Web site on a server

Chapter

1

Getting Acquainted
with HTML, Related
Tools, and the Web

Getting Acquainted with HTML, Related Tools, and the Web

HyperText Markup Language, or HTML, is a system of codes that you use to create active documents—that is, documents with which you and others can interact. HTML's popularity has brought hypertext technology—the technology that lets you jump from topic to topic, rather than finding and reading information linearly—to the fingertips of people worldwide, particularly in the context of the World Wide Web. Now, instead of slogging through page after page of information, you can click links and connect to the information you want, contact people via e-mail with a click of the mouse, fill out forms and submit them online, and access huge databases and information sources. The result is that those who access, read, and use your HTML documents can do so quickly and efficiently.

NOTE

Throughout this book, we use the term *visitors* to describe the people who use the HTML documents you develop.

The uses for HTML have expanded dramatically over the past few years. The most common HTML application continues to be pages and sites that can be published on the Internet (or, specifically, on the World Wide Web) or on a corporate intranet. Other applications for HTML, such as creating online help files and developing kiosk applications (stand-alone computers you see in malls, museums, or your local grocery store), are also becoming popular.

This chapter introduces you to specific HTML applications, provides information about HTML components, gives you a brief history of HTML, and shows you how to keep up with this progressive technology.

Publishing on the Internet

The Web—and, by extension, HTML—is invading a significant part of our lives. At work, the Web serves as an advertising medium, as a communication tool, and even as a message center. At home, the Web has become integral to our offices, television sets, and homework time.

Coincidence? Probably not. It's a sign that HTML and Web technologies are here to stay.

Throughout the world, companies, individuals, and organizations are providing, retrieving, and publishing information with the help of HTML. Whether a Web page consists of only text or also includes intricate graphics, elaborate animations, and sophisticated formatting, underlying it is HTML.

Communicating via the Web

For companies and organizations, the Web is an effective, interactive means of advertising products and services while providing essential contact information. By using the Web, service-oriented organizations can effectively communicate with customers, give the impression that they're technologically with it, and—above all else—let their constituents know that they're keeping up with (or surpassing!) the competition.

As an advertising tool, the Web is an effective way to provide information. Some Web sites merely list the company's products, while others actually let potential customers test their products—interactive technology at its best! For example, at some Web sites you can send online greeting cards to your friends and family. Visitors select an online card, fill in some information, and then send the card with a click of the mouse (of course, the recipient has to be connected to the Internet).

As a contact and information resource, the Web provides companies, organizations, and individuals with an easy way to request or submit information. For example, most Web sites provide e-mail links and online forms.

Individuals are using the Web to provide information about themselves—as in personal home pages or résumés. Personal home pages often include information about hobbies and interests or the latest photos of the family. The Web helps people stay in touch with a large number of people. And, Web page résumés are quickly becoming a means of reaching potential employers. In this sense, the Web serves as a worldwide employment bulletin board.

Retrieving Information from the Web

As the Web has grown to an enormous size, it has also become a vast repository for information on just about any topic under the sun. For example, you can find out which baby car seat is rated highest, find a prime vacation spot, find a Brady Bunch fan club, or even find an attorney specializing in patents.

The Web is not, however, a panacea for information seekers. The enormous amount of information available on the Web in itself poses a problem. Looking for a specific tidbit on the Web puts you in mind of the proverbial needle in the haystack. Fortunately, we now have directories and search engines to help with this ever-increasing mound. Figure 1.1 shows one of the many Internet directories.

FIGURE 1.1

The flood of information on the Internet has led to a variety of information retrieval tools.

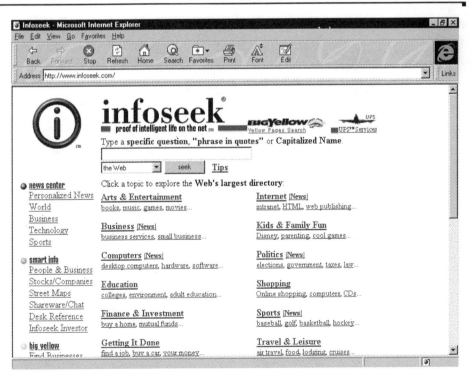

The nature of the Web also poses another problem: With all its interesting topics and tangential information, it often tempts you to wander off the topic. A link to related information often turns up another and another, and suddenly you're off on a different topic entirely.

As a developer of Web pages, you must remember how easy it is to lose your visitors to the wealth of information out there.

Publishing on the Web

The Web has helped revolutionize the publishing industry, making it possible to easily and quickly publish valuable research, lengthy documents, and a variety of other materials that probably would never have been circulated without the ease and low cost of Web-based publishing.

Schools and universities use the Web to publish course descriptions, materials, syllabi, and assignments, as shown in Figure 1.2. In this capacity, the Web provides the information and becomes a tool in itself as students learn to use it effectively. Given a Web page full of links, images, and information, children and adults alike gravitate to the information they need and learn the ins and outs of the Web as they search.

FIGURE 1.2

Providing timely information, for any purpose, is a key role for HTML.

Timely information

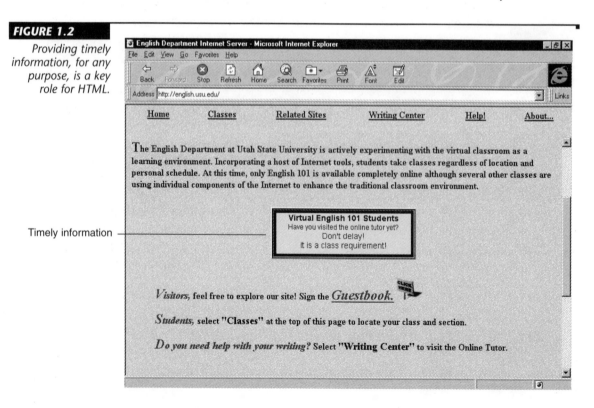

Finally, many scientific journals—in which up-to-date information is key—are published only or primarily on the Web. Researchers can now prepare articles using HTML and then easily publish the information directly on the Web, making it instantly available to the entire world without the several-month lag of getting published through traditional means. The downside, though, is that the critical peer review process can be bypassed. On the Web, as elsewhere, check the reliability of your sources.

Publishing on Intranets

An intranet uses the tools and standards of the Internet to create an infrastructure that can only be accessed by those within a corporate enterprise or an organization. It consists of Web servers connected to a local network.

Intranets have helped improve corporate communication, eliminating (or reducing) the need for memos, bulletin boards, and hardcopy documentation. The result is, in theory, that employees communicate and access company information, instructions, and policies more easily and effectively.

Intranets have changed corporate communications in three ways. First, intranets allow companies to easily provide information to all employees without the hassles and expense of paper, snail mail, faxes, or telex—a real advantage for companies that have offices scattered over wide geographical areas. Intranets provide essential information, for example, internal job openings, new contracts awarded, the latest technological advances, or even an invitation to the boss's 50th birthday bash. In this sense, intranets have replaced mounds of paper with information easily accessible by everyone in the company.

Second, intranets allow companies to publish internal information with only a minimal risk of nonemployees seeing it. A properly configured intranet is not accessible to people outside the company or organization. In some cases, intranet users have access to the Internet, but users of the Internet can't access a corporate intranet.

Third, intranets allow companies to provide all this information using any computer platform or workgroup. For example, employees using PCs, Macs, or Unix can access information on an intranet. One of the intranet's most valued features is its *cross-platform compatibility*: the ability to connect all kinds of hardware running all kinds of software.

Of course, the resulting flood of information has introduced its own set of information issues, but the overall influence of intranet sites has been positive.

Developing Help Files

One of the real benefits of HTML is that it's cross-platform compatible, which means that you can view an HTML document on any computer that has a browser installed on it. This flexibility makes HTML invaluable to anyone dealing with a variety of computer platforms, but particularly to developers, who have long been stymied by the difficulty of providing useful help information without developing separate help applications for each platform.

Before HTML, developers had to completely reinvent the wheel and code their own help systems (which has a plethora of disadvantages besides the time and money expended), use a specialized help application, or find a help system resident on the destination platform. Unfortunately, many of the target platforms had distinctly different help systems.

HTML has surmounted many cross-platform obstacles associated with creating online help files and has allowed developers to readily and inexpensively produce documentation that is accessible on any platform. However, HTML extensions, specialized browsers, and progressive technologies, such as video and sound files, have eroded the original advantages of HTML somewhat. In particular, these technologies introduced features that are only supported by specific browsers on specified platforms.

Each competing standard has advantages and disadvantages, thus requiring that authors who are developing HTML-based online help files overlook some portion of their audience, just as with most of the older technologies.

Microsoft's HTML Help requires a browser, such as Internet Explorer, that supports ActiveX—a Microsoft technology used to enhance HTML documents. HTML Help is planned to be a cross-platform solution, but will be initially released for Windows 95/NT. When Macintosh, Unix, and Windows 3.1 platforms will be supported is an open question. On the other hand, Netscape's NetHelp application is nearly cross-platform, but far less full-featured and standardized. However, as a more purely HTML-based solution, NetHelp is much easier to develop and implement. See Figure 1.3 for an example of NetHelp in action.

Netscape's NetHelp looks different from most HTML documents you see on the Web, but it's really just another HTML document in a fancy wrapper.

Developing Kiosk Applications

As a standard cross-platform means of generating hypertext, HTML's popularity as a vehicle for kiosk applications—those stand-alone computers with the neat touch-screen capabilities—is growing. Kiosk technology is even supported by a few of the latest browser versions, such as the Netscape browser, Navigator. Using Navigator, you can eliminate all standard window elements—menus, toolbars, title bars, and so on—and display only the document window portion of the screen, as shown in Figure 1.4.

Because kiosk applications run without additional software support, you can use them to develop effective (and inexpensive) cross-platform applications. For example, you can use HTML, in conjunction with Java or JavaScript or another programming or scripting language, to develop a Computer-Based Training (CBT) application or product demonstration.

FIGURE 1.4

Kiosk applications, featuring a browser window without menus or toolbars, are an increasingly popular HTML application.

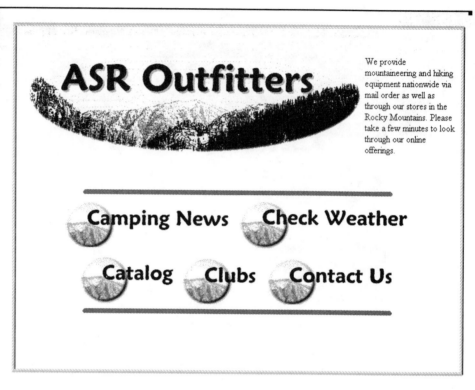

Kiosk applications have a few downsides, though. For example, without the standard Windows elements such as the title bar and menu bar, you have fewer points of reference on the screen. In other words, rather than looking in a toolbar for the Back button, you have to search the screen. Likewise, without these menus and buttons, kiosk applications often use graphics as the primary navigation tools, meaning that pages often take longer to download.

Developing Network-Based Applications

A growing number of network-based applications rely on HTML to provide the user interface. For example, rather than providing a separate program to administer Web servers, a set of HTML documents and forms provide the user interface and connect to the configuration settings, as shown in Figure 1.5.

FIGURE 1.5

The Microsoft Personal Web Server uses HTML forms to configure the server.

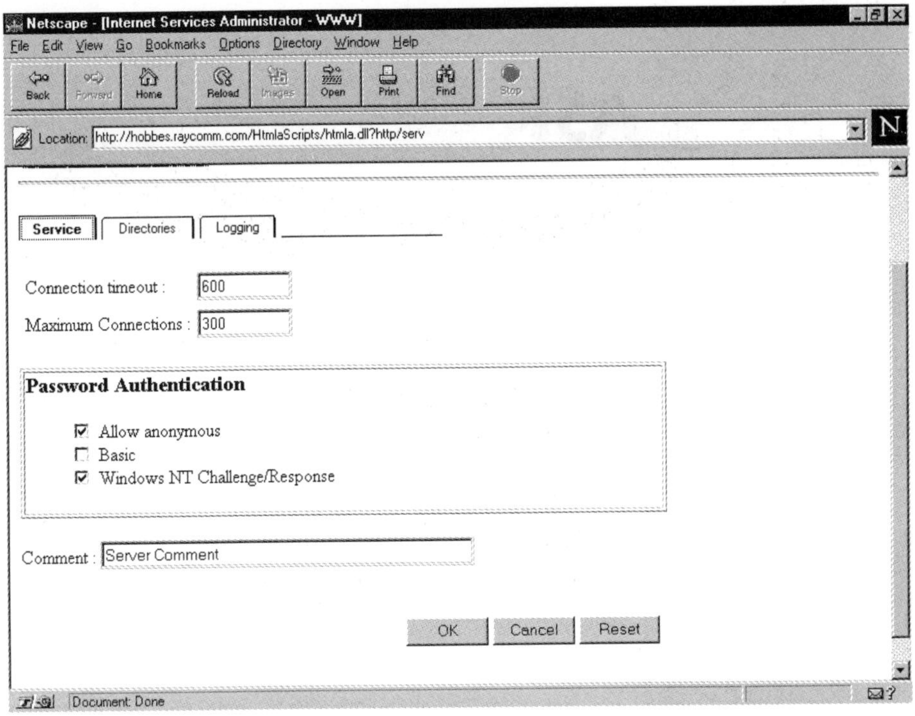

Increasingly, companies are using HTML to record and track information over the Web. These Web-based applications have several advantages. For example, they eliminate the need to train employees on software, they make updating software to accommodate new uses and features unnecessary, and they keep users' hard drives available for other resources.

The Components of HTML

HTML documents are essentially plain text files. They contain no images, no sounds, videos, and no animations; however, they can include "pointers," or links, to these other file types, which is how Web pages end up looking as if they contain nontext elements.

HTML itself is a system of codes made up of *tags* and *attributes* that serve to identify parts and characteristics of HTML documents. Some tags provide document structure; others reference other files. Attributes provide additional information within tags.

TIP

You'll find more information about tags and attributes, including what they look like and how to use them, in Chapter 3.

Tags Identify Logical Document Parts

HTML tags identify logical document parts—that is, the major structural components in documents such as headings, lists, and paragraphs. These structural components are part of the HTML document. For example, if you want to include a heading, a paragraph, and a list in your document, you type the text and apply the appropriate tags to the text, as shown in Figure 1.6.

FIGURE 1.6

HTML tags specify generally how various document parts—headings or body text, for example—should appear.

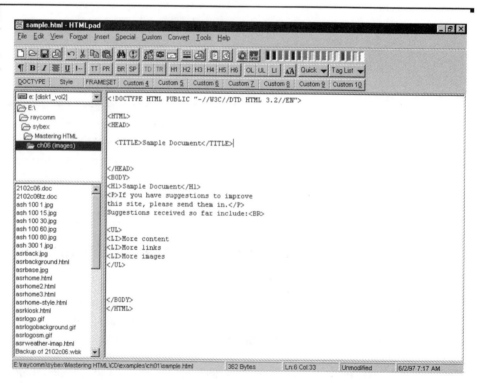

Exactly how structural components appear on your computer screen depends on the browser. For example, one browser might display a first-level heading as 15-point Times

New Roman bold, whereas another browser might display the same heading as 14-point Arial italic. In both cases, the browser displays the heading as bigger and more emphasized than regular text, but the specific text characteristics vary. Figures 1.7, 1.8, and 1.9 show how different browsers display the same HTML document.

FIGURE 1.7

The NCSA Mosaic browser displays a sample HTML document.

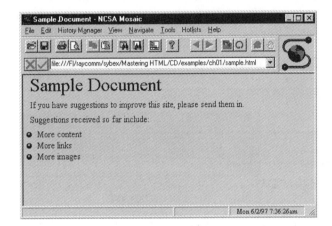

Some tags work in conjunction with attributes, which provide additional information about an element, such as how elements should align (left, center, or right), what other file should be accessed, or even the color of an element. For example, an attribute might indicate that a heading should appear centered in the browser window, that the browser should load an image file from the Web, or that the Web page background should appear sky blue.

FIGURE 1.8

The Opera browser shows the same document with slightly different formatting.

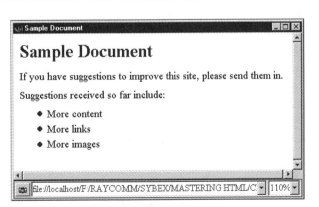

Recent HTML developments include *Cascading Style Sheets* (*CSS1*), which you can use to specify text formatting for logical document parts. For example, you can format a line of text as a first-level heading, and you can further specify that the heading (and optionally subsequent first-level headings in the document) appear in a particular font, size, emphasis, and color. Furthermore, after you set up style sheets, you can easily use the same styles in other HTML documents, without completely retagging the documents. Style Sheets also provide for somewhat fancier formatting options than plain HTML.

The only real disadvantage to using Style Sheets is that older browsers do not support them; they simply disregard them.

FIGURE 1.9

Internet Explorer formats the document yet again slightly differently.

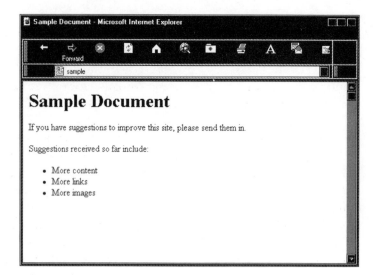

Tags Include Other Items by Reference

Tags also include other elements in HTML documents by *reference*—that is, tags can include pointers and links to other HTML documents, images, sound files, video files, multimedia applications, animations, applets, and so on. For example, if you want to include an image of your company's product in your HTML document, rather than applying a tag to text, you include a tag that points to the image file name, as shown below:

```
<IMG SRC="company-logo.gif"?
```

Tags and Attributes Change over Time

The *World Wide Web Consortium (W3C)* was founded in 1994 at the Massachusetts Institute of Technology (MIT) to oversee the development of Web standards, including the HTML standard. This consortium defines and publishes HTML standards, the tags and attributes within HTML documents.

The HTML standard is an *open standard*, meaning that any browser developer—and everyone else—has complete access to the HTML specification. Microsoft and Netscape, however, have introduced a variety of *extensions* to HTML that enhance design and layout control. These "improvements" have taken HTML from a practical, information-based means of communication to a marketing tool filled with effects designed to dazzle Web page visitors.

Some of these extensions are useful, and some less so, but as a whole any nonstandard tags introduced into HTML cause problems both for Web developers and for visitors. For developers, the issue is which tags to include in a document. At one end of the extreme are the strictly readable-by-every-browser, often visually boring pages, and at the other are the bleeding edge, visually exciting, readable-by-only-the-newest-browsers-of-a-certain brand, "Oh, wow" pages. For visitors, the issue becomes which browser to use.

The larger problem with these differing HTML extensions is that they don't advance evenly on all browsers and on all systems. Some visitors, using certain browsers, will have a completely different experience from other visitors using less "enhanced" browsers. For example, if you use, say, Navigator-specific extensions in your documents, you may not be able to reach all your visitors; those using Internet Explorer won't be able to view the Navigator-specific extensions you've added. And, visitors using less popular platforms, such as the Amiga, won't be able to view any enhancements—they'll see only the HTML effects—and not necessarily the newest HTML effects at that. In fact, many of the cutting-edge features are only available on Windows or, at best, on Windows now and Mac and Unix later, if at all.

At the time of this writing, about 60 percent of Net surfers used Netscape Navigator, about 25 percent used Internet Explorer, and the remaining 15 percent used a variety of other browsers. Realistically, about 75 to 80 percent of all Web users can access the majority of sites incorporating the latest HTML tags and recent enhancements.

A Short History of HTML and the World Wide Web

The evolution of HTML involved more than changes to the tags and attributes. You'll see that its variety of uses and resulting popularity have changed the nature of HTML from a functional information resource to a marketing tool. HTML did not evolve as an entity on its own; it took the efforts of many people to bring the technology to what it is today.

HTML Is Born

Although the concept of hypertext is hardly new—Vaneever Bush originated the term, if not the concept, in the late 1940s—the technology to implement it is a recent development. Additionally, merging the network and hypertext to provide linked information from a distributed set of computers was not practical until only a few years ago.

Physicists at CERN (Centre Europeen pour la Recherche Nucleaire), a European particle physics laboratory, needed an easy way to share information over their network. In 1980, Tim Berners-Lee developed the initial program that allowed pages to links to one another. A decade later, development moved into the realm of text-only hypertext browsers, and the World Wide Web was born. In 1992, CERN made the system and the software available to the rest of the world through the Internet. At that time, the Internet was used primarily for academic research, and so the fledgling Web was extended to other academic research centers and universities throughout the world, including the National Center for Supercomputing Applications (NCSA) at the University of Illinois at Urbana-Champaign. The World-Wide Web (with a hyphen) was named in late 1990 by Berners-Lee.

Browser Technologies Develop

One of the first text-only browsers, Lynx, was developed at the University of Kansas, and it ran under the Unix and VMS operating systems. Figure 1.10 shows how a Web page looks when viewed with Lynx. As you can see, it contains no splashy graphics.

By the end of 1992, the first graphical browser appeared for use on Unix workstations running the X Window System. The next major development was the advent of Mosaic, which has been called the "killer application of the 1990s." Originally designed and programmed by Marc Andreesen and Eric Bina at NCSA, Mosaic was the first truly graphical browser and, when first released in April 1993, also ran on the X Window System. By December 1993, however, versions were released for the Apple Macintosh and Microsoft Windows. NCSA Mosaic, as it was called, was distributed freely over the Internet. Anyone could download and use it at no charge. The distribution of NCSA Mosaic marked the beginning of the rapid, exponential growth of the World Wide Web.

By today's standards, though, these early browsers were rather primitive in form and function. They could display images and text, but little else—certainly the animations, colors, and multimedia effects of today's Web were far from anyone's mind. Figure 1.11 shows a Web page viewed with NCSA Mosaic.

FIGURE 1.10

The Lynx browser and an old screen from the World Wide Web Consortium

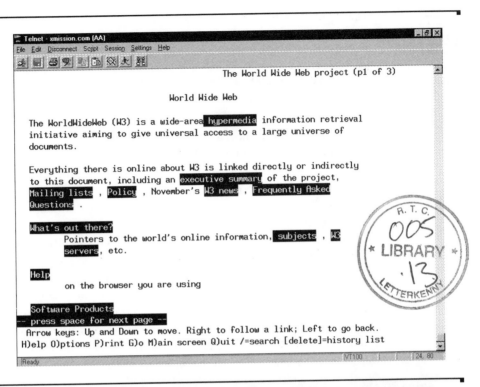

FIGURE 1.11

Old versions of Web browsers can display text, but not the attractive formatting we have come to expect.

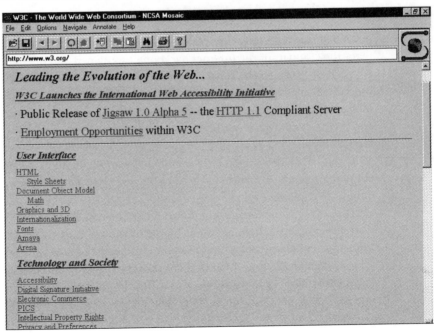

NOTE

By October 1993, approximately 200 Web servers existed. Contrast that number with the approximately 500,000 Web servers that are active on the Internet today, according to a recent survey by Netcraft.

In January 1994, Spry, now a division of CompuServe, Inc., released Internet in a Box, a commercial product that included software for accessing the Internet through one of the first Internet service providers. Until this point, the only access to the Internet was through corporate or, more commonly, university networks. The U.S. portion of the Internet was funded by the federal government to support academic research, and commercial access and Internet service providers were almost unheard of.

Two months later, in March 1994, Marc Andreesen and others left NCSA to form their own company to market and sell Web browsers and related products. This company, originally called Mosaic Communications Corporation, is now Netscape Communications, Inc., the developer of the wildly popular Netscape Navigator. Although NCSA continued until recently to produce new versions of the Mosaic Web browser, most of the innovation and advanced development took place at Netscape. In August 1995, however, Microsoft entered the competition with the first release of Internet Explorer, and the war of the browsers began.

Internet Technologies Mature

Internet growth, initially slow because of federal regulation, took off in 1995. Until then, the U.S. part of the Internet backbone was owned and operated by the federal government through the NSFnet (National Science Foundation Network). Because of the role government and tax dollars played in the infrastructure, strict policies prohibited commercial use. As the network was privatized, these restrictions were relaxed and finally discarded in April 1995. Scores of companies formed to provide Internet services for all.

At this point, Internet use beyond the scope of academia and larger (usually computer-related) companies started to blossom. All the pieces were in place: freedom from regulatory restrictions, software, access, and interest. Since then, Web watchers have seen heated competition to produce the best Web browsers, servers, search engines, and literally dozens of related products. By 1996, the Web moved from a secret held by those "in the know" to the hot topic on the evening news.

Today, there are some 40 million users of the Internet, and there are more Web pages than anyone can actually count. Unfortunately, this astronomical growth has also led to competition for the "latest and greatest" tags—even at the cost of negating

some of the most significant advantages of HTML (such as cross
ity)—and to making HTML less useful for many purposes, such
lishing information.

Keeping Up with HTML Standards, Extensions, and Differences

Even after you've mastered HTML and are creating Web sites without looking back,
you'll still have to keep up with HTML changes. Knowing HTML 4.0 (the current standard) doesn't mean that you've got HTML 5.23 down cold. In this section, we'll tell
you about some of the best places to go to keep up with the latest and greatest.

Visit the W3C

The best way to monitor HTML changes is to visit the W3C site:

    www.w3.org/

Here, you'll find new releases of HTML standards, proposed standards, and other
developments in Web-related specifications (such as the PNG graphic format). (You'll
find details about PNG in Chapter 7.)

Can you use new tags and attributes as they become available? For the most part,
yes. By the time most tags and attributes become part of the standard, they already
have browsers' support. Some tags and attributes, however, such as some that were
introduced with HTML 4.0, did not have wide or stable browser support when the
specification was released. We'll point these out throughout this book and show you
how they differ from the previous version of HTML.

Monitor Netscape and Microsoft Sites

Each time that Netscape and Microsoft release a new browser version, look for new
HTML extensions. Following a new release, each will pick up many (but not all) of the
other's extensions and keep going. Whew. However, take heart—the pace of HTML
change seems to be slowing somewhat.

You can find Netscape's extensions at:

    home.netscape.com/

And you will find Microsoft's extensions at:

    www.microsoft.com/ie/

Know what's new and trendy, but don't hop on the bandwagon too quickly. New
tags and extensions are generally unstable and not widely supported. At the least, if
you've got to be at the cutting edge, give your visitors a break, and be sure that you

provide alternatives so that those with older browsers can easily view the most important content at your site. You'll find that developing HTML documents quickly becomes a challenging effort to be simultaneously inclusive and cutting edge.

For example, our site—at least at the time of this writing—is easily accessible to anyone with a browser that accommodates tables, which means most potential visitors. A link from the home page directs visitors who are interested to a more cutting edge presentation. It's not an ideal solution, particularly because we have twice the development effort, but it meets the needs of most visitors.

Monitor Other Sites

Although definitive information on the newest developments will always come from the innovators, it's a good idea to keep up with other sites too. Monitoring all sites that attempt to provide information about HTML and related topics is a practical impossibility, but Table 1.1 gives you a list of some to check regularly.

TABLE 1.1: SOME SITES THAT PROVIDE UP-TO-DATE HTML INFORMATION

Organization	URL
Web Design Group	www.htmlhelp.com/
Web Developer's Virtual Library	www.stars.com/
HTML Writer's Guild	www.hwg.org/
NetscapeWorld	www.netscapeworld.com/

Deviate at Your Own Risk

Deviating from HTML standards often results in unreadable pages, crashes, and unpredictable behavior. Remember that what looks great on your computer could appear unreadable on your visitors' computers. You can spend lots of time tweaking pages to look great, with no guarantee of what they'll look like on your visitors' computers. Your best bet is to balance the effects available through the HTML standard with what your visitors' browsers can display.

Know thy audience. If all your visitors are using Netscape 3, you have a good idea which rules and standards you can disregard (anything from Microsoft, for example). If you're writing for a varied audience, you need to stick with the basic approach and not include any fancy stuff.

Preparing multiple paths to information is time consuming. But before you expend the time and the effort, be sure that it's necessary. A variety of Web services report on the browsers that visitors use. For example, check out Browser Watch at:

`browserwatch.iworld.com/`

Additionally, if you can contact your visitors or provide them with a browser, you can also reduce the uncertainty of not knowing what your pages will look like in their hands. Accommodating all your visitors and striking a balance between hot layout and universal access is one of your primary responsibilities as a Web developer.

Where to Go from Here

This chapter gave you a brief overview of HTML—what it is, what it's used for, and how it came about. Although you haven't yet done any HTML coding, you should have a good grasp of HTML's limitations and of the challenges you'll face in determining which HTML features to include and which to disregard.

From here, you have several options:

- If you are an HTML beginner, move on to Chapter 2 for information about planning HTML documents or to Chapter 3 to learn how to enter basic HTML tags.
- If you are an intermediate HTML user, you might move on to Chapter 4, which addresses linking HTML documents, or you might select topics from Part II.
- If you are an advanced user, you can select from several topics, including frames, layers, Style Sheets, enhancements, JavaScript, Java applets and ActiveX, and searchable HTML.

Chapter

2

Understanding the HTML Document Life Cycle

FEATURING

Understanding the HTML Document Life Cycle

The life cycle of an HTML document includes developing, publishing, testing, and maintaining it— whether its ultimate home is on an intranet, on the Internet, in a kiosk, or in a help file. Because a single HTML document is usually the foundation for sets of documents, we are going to look at the document life cycle in a step-by-step fashion.

Most of the examples focus on developing *Web pages* (single HTML documents) and *sites* (collections of HTML documents) in a corporate environment. To illustrate parts of the HTML document life cycle, we'll follow the process for WAMMI, Inc., a mythical, smaller version of General Motors. If you're developing HTML documents for nonprofit organizations, corporate intranets, or departmental sites, you'll still need to go through this same process. The only substantive difference might be that the "meeting with the marketing guru" in a one- or two-person office might be a meeting with yourself over breakfast.

The task of developing HTML documents often falls (or gets assigned) to those with specific technical skills or to those who have a knack for marketing and sales, but not necessarily to those who have HTML-related experience. Thus, we are going to take a linear approach (you'll see more about this later in this chapter) and give you a development plan that starts with conception and concludes with maintenance.

We recommend that you start at the beginning and read through the sections in order. Along the way, you'll find numerous tips and advice to help you make decisions that will positively affect the applications you develop.

TIP

Specific information about choosing and using software, coding documents, or applying HTML effects is located in other chapters throughout this book.

The following sections present a four-phase process, and within each of these phases are subprocesses. If you follow along, applying the examples and guidelines to your situation, you will be in a position to create HTML documents that are easy for you to maintain and useful to your visitors.

Phase 1: Developing Documents

Within the development phase are four subprocesses:

- Planning
- Organizing
- Creating
- Testing

Within these phases are several smaller processes, as shown in Figure 2.1. As you work through the process in this chapter, you may find it helpful to refer to this chart from time to time.

Planning Documents

As originally conceived, HTML focused on making information easily available. The resulting World Wide Web and corporate intranets were primarily used to provide information to those who needed it. In this capacity, HTML authoring was *visitor-centered*—that is, authors focused on determining what their audience wanted and then provided that information.

However, as HTML and other Web technologies became popular, they evolved into a marketing tool for millions of companies, organizations, and individuals worldwide. Rather than strictly providing information, the purpose of many Web sites is now to tell visitors what the company wants them to know, to persuade them to purchase a product or service, and to keep them coming back for more. As a result, HTML development has shifted to being simultaneously visitor-centered and *author-centered*. Now, you not only need to consider what your visitors want to know, you need to consider what information your organization wants to provide.

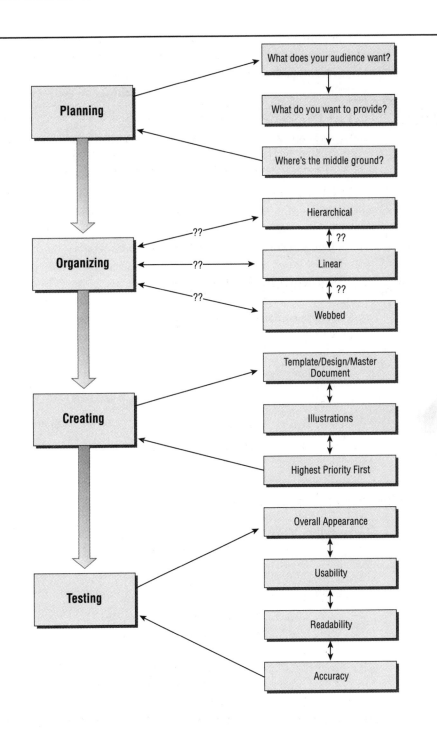

FIGURE 2.1

*The HTML docu-
ment development
process*

Therefore, before you start willy-nilly producing HTML, you need to do some planning. In particular, you need to determine what information your visitors want and what your organization wants to provide. Your goal is to reconcile these "wants" into a single list that accommodates both your visitors and your organization.

What Do Your Visitors Want?

When you visit a Web site, you usually have a reason for going there. Although you often stumble onto a site that interests you while you're browsing, you normally have something specific in mind when you start.

Thus, as you begin the planning phase, you'll want to think about what visitors expect to see at your site. A great place to start is with your customers (or co-workers, if you're developing an intranet). For example, they might want general information about you, your company, or your products and services. Or they might want specific information, such as contact names, troubleshooting advice, safety information, prices, schedules, order forms, and so on.

At WAMMI, Inc., a survey revealed that visitors were interested in knowing what models were available, their cost, and their reliability and safety records. They also wanted to be able to request brochures and locate local dealerships. Their list of wants looked like this:

- Available models
- Cost
- Safety record
- Reliability record
- Contact information
- Request brochure
- List of dealerships

What Do You Want to Provide?

Ideally, your Web site would provide all the information that your visitors want; however, what they want isn't necessarily what you can or want to provide. For example, you might not want to publicize a product's unstable repair history—or at the very least, you might want to downplay it. Or, if you're developing pages for a corporate intranet—say, the R&D department—you wouldn't publish *all* the information the department has available. You probably would want to include information about upcoming projects, recent successes and failures, and planned product improvements.

A great way to start figuring out what you want to include is to take a look at materials you already have on hand. For example, marketing materials often include information about the company, products, and services suitable for use on a Web site. Even if you're developing pages for an intranet, marketing materials often provide a jumping-off place.

If you don't have access to marketing materials (or the marketing guru), ask yourself a few questions:

- What do I want people to know about my organization? What is the corporate mission statement? What are my company's goals?

- What are my company's products or services? How do they help people? How do people use them?

- How do customers order our products?

- Is repair history or safety information so positive that I want to publicize it?

- Can I include product specifications?

- What product information can I send to people if they request it?

- Can I provide answers to frequently asked questions?

- Do I want to include information about employees? Do their skills and experience play a big part in how well our products are made or sold?

- Can I provide information that is more timely, useful, or effective than other marketing materials, such as brochures or pamphlets, provide?

After you answer these and any other questions that are helpful in your situation, you should be able to develop a list of what you want to provide. WAMMI, Inc. decided to provide general information about the company, tell potential customers about the various models, show a few snazzy pictures, and brag about the cars' reliability records. They were unsure about discussing prices because they were higher than those of their competitors, and likewise they were unsure whether to publicize safety records—they were only average. The final list looks like this:

Definite:

- Company information

- Car models

- Photos

- Contact information

Maybe:

- Prices

- Safety records

Reconciling the Want Lists

You may well find that visitors want information that you simply can't provide. For example, they might want to know product release dates or be privy to product previews, which is probably information your company doesn't want to disclose. And, other times, you might want to provide your audience with information that they don't necessarily care about. For example, you might want to tell people that your company received a big award or just reached one million in sales this year—certainly interesting information that's good for marketing, but it's not on your visitors' priority list.

As you can see, what WAMMI wanted and what their visitors wanted didn't necessarily coincide:

Visitors Want	Company Wants
company information	company information
car selection	car selection
reliability records	
contact information	contact information
	photos
car cost	prices
safety records	safety records
request brochure	
list of dealerships	

Although these two lists have items in common, each list also contains unique items. At the very least, we wanted to include all the items common to both lists. At WAMMI, the reconciled list included the following:

- Company information
- Car selection
- Safety records
- Contact information

Now, what do you do about the items that are unique to each list? We suggest that you consult some of your colleagues, perhaps those in marketing or public relations, and see what they think.

NOTE

Getting a consensus before you start to build your Web site is always a good rule to follow. The last thing you want after your site goes public is some vice-president announcing that you can't publish information that's blaring off your Web site.

At WAMMI, we decided to classify the items common to both lists as primary Web site information and to classify unique items as secondary information.

Planning for Maintenance

Although maintaining your documents after you create them and throughout their existence on your site is a separate phase in the life cycle of documents (see the later section, "Developing a Plan"), you also need to include maintenance in the planning phase. This is particularly the case if you answer yes to any of the following questions:

- Will more than one person be involved in developing the content?
- Will more than one person play an active role in maintaining the site?
- Will your site include more than about 20 HTML documents?
- Will you frequently add or modify a significant numbers of pages—say, more than 20–25 percent of the total number of documents?

As you can see, you need to plan for both content and site maintenance.

Planning for Content Maintenance

If you will be depending on others for content, you need to make arrangements at the outset for how you will obtain updates. Will content providers actually develop and update the Web pages, or will they simply send you new information via e-mail? You need to plan accordingly if they are going to merely send you a publication (for example, the annual report) and expect you to figure out what has changed. Planning now how you will handle content revisions and updates will save you time (and grief) later.

Planning for Site Maintenance

Regardless of whether you or someone else will maintain the site you develop, you need to carefully document the development process and include the following information:

- The site's purpose and goals

- The process whereby you determined content
- Who provides content

Documenting the development process will help those who maintain the site (or fill your position when you leave) keep everything up-to-date.

Organizing Your Documents

After you decide what information to include in your site, you need to determine how you will arrange individual HTML documents. Taking the time to organize the information carefully is often the difference between having frequent visitors to your site and having none at all. How often do you return to a site that's not well organized? If you can't find what you need easily and quickly, you have no reason to go there, and the same will be true of visitors to your site.

You have three types of organization at your disposal:

- Hierarchical
- Linear
- Webbed

You can use each type individually or combine them as needed.

Hierarchical Organization

When you organize information in a hierarchical structure, you present a first group of equally important topics, followed by another group of equally important topics, and so on. You're familiar with this technique if you've ever created or used an organization chart. The hierarchy starts with top officials, then shows the managers who work for them, the employees who work for those managers, and so on.

A document outline is another example of hierarchical organization. Multiple main points are followed by subpoints, which are followed by more subpoints. In both an organization chart and a document outline, using hierarchical organization allows you to provide multiple levels of structured information.

You can do the same with a Web site. You can provide several main points, and under each point, you can include subpoints. For example, the WAMMI Web site uses hierarchical organization to structure the main pages according to the major topics, as shown in Figure 2.2.

FIGURE 2.2

*Hierarchical organi-
zation accommo-
dates several main
topics and
subtopics.*

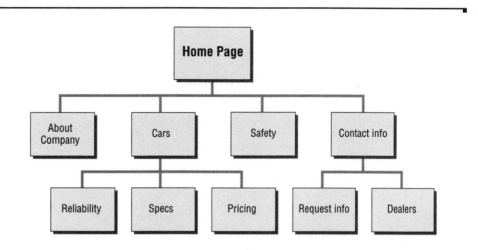

If you choose hierarchical organization, remember to keep it simple. Visitors to your site will dig through two or three levels of information, but after that they are likely to give up.

Linear Organization

When you organize information in a linear structure, you impose a particular order on it. Instructions and procedures are examples of this type of organization. If you've ever used a Microsoft Wizard, you've seen linear organization in action. You start the Wizard, and then you proceed in a linear fashion from one screen to the next until you click Finish. You can back up a step or two if necessary, but if you don't complete all the steps, you terminate the procedure.

At a Web site that uses linear organization, a visitor can move forward and backward within a sequence of pages but cannot jump to other pages. Because this can occasionally frustrate a visitor who wants to get to other pages, you need to use linear organization only when it's necessary. For example, at our WAMMI site, we used linear organization to walk a visitor through requesting a brochure, as shown in Figure 2.3.

FIGURE 2.3

Linear organization works well when you want visitors to your site to perform actions in a specific order.

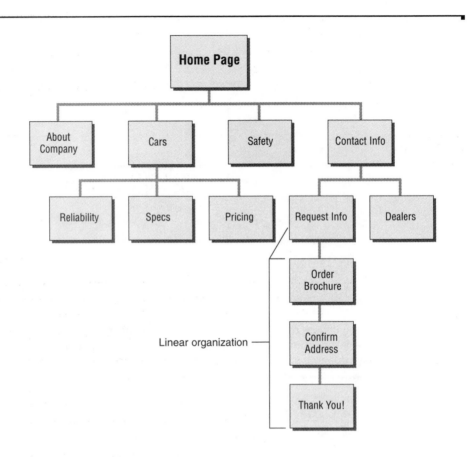

Here are some guidelines to keep in mind when you employ linear organization:

- When visitors to your site are working through pages that are organized in a linear fashion, they can't roam to other pages. Therefore, be sure the linear process is essential to the task at hand.

- Keep the linear sequence as short as possible so that visitors focus on the process and complete it successfully.

Webbed Organization

Webbed organization is a fairly new type of organization that has evolved with online technology and provides visitors with multiple, unorganized paths to resources at a site. A visitor can link from one Web page to many other pages at the same Web site or at another Web site. You often hear stories about Web surfers becoming disoriented or lost—they don't know where they are or where they've been. Webbed organization is the culprit.

An example of effective webbed organization, though, is an online index that's extensively cross-referenced. At the WAMMI site, they provided an index of the available models and cross-referenced each model to its specific features and to other models. Figure 2.4 shows how this works.

FIGURE 2.4

Webbed organization is a good technique to use when you want to cross-reference information.

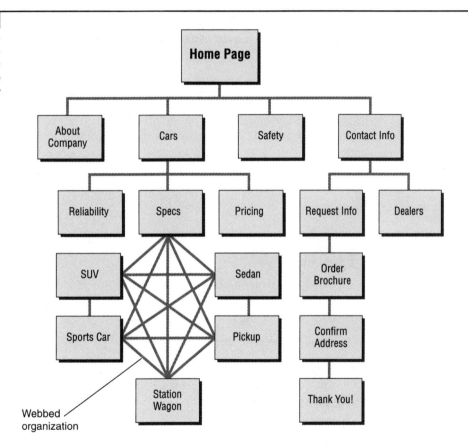

Here are some guidelines to keep in mind when you are using webbed organization:

- Provide information on each page that helps readers orient themselves. For example, include a running footer or company logo (keep it small) on each page.
- Provide a link to your home page on all pages. If you do so, visitors can easily return to a familiar page.

Storyboards: An Essential Organizational Tool

Storyboarding is the process of breaking information into discrete chunks and then reassembling it. It's a technique that Web authors borrowed from the film industry, and it's a great way to help you determine the best organizational approach for your site.

Here's one way to do it (and the way the WAMMI site was storyboarded):

1. Write each topic or group of information on a separate note card.
2. Pin the note cards to a wall or spread them out on a table or the floor.
3. Group and rank related information.
4. Continue moving cards around until all the information is organized and ranked to your satisfaction.
5. When you've decided what should link to what, connect those notecards with string.

The resulting groups of information should follow one of the three organization approaches discussed above or some combination thereof.

Creating Documents

After you've adequately planned your HTML documents, deciding which information to include and how to organize it, you're ready to start creating HTML documents. Much of the rest of this book is about how to create HTML documents, including which software to use, how to use tags, how to add links and images, and how to include more advanced effects such as video, sound, frames, JavaScript, and applets. Before we get to the specifics, however, let's take a brief look at the overall process.

Create a Master Document

A master HTML document contains the necessary structure tags as well as the general document format you want to use. When you create a master HTML document, you establish the look of the site even before you start adding content. Include the elements that you want to appear on every page, such as the following:

- The background
- Repeating images
- The corporate logo

- Icons
- Footer information

If you place these elements in your master document, you will need to develop them only once, not every time you start a new document.

After you create a master document, test it (as described in the section, "Testing Documents Before Publication") to be sure that it appears as you want, that it is usable and readable, and that it is error free. Finding and solving problems early on will save you lots of time in the overall process.

Select Images

Determine which images (graphics) or illustrations are available before you start developing individual pages. Having an idea of what images you can include will help you determine page layout, and you can avoid rearranging pages later.

Create Important Pages First

Web sites, by nature, are always "under construction." You'll find that you're constantly updating content, adding new pages, or removing pages. If you create a few of the most important pages first, test them, and publish them, you can eliminate the tedious task of polishing many pages later. You can then add and modify pages as needed, after you create an initial few.

TIP

For a much closer look at this process, see Chapter 3.

Testing Documents Before Publication

Testing an HTML document involves viewing your documents in multiple browsers with a variety of system settings. The purpose is to see how your documents will appear to your visitors, to check readability and usability, and to root out any layout or formatting problems.

You'll want to test for these issues on your local computer *before* you publish your pages on the World Wide Web or on an intranet. In doing so, you can get a general idea of what your visitor is likely to see; however, your visitor's browser and computer settings could alter a document's appearance. You can check this out if you view a document using Internet Explorer on a computer with a low-resolution monitor and then look at it using a Netscape browser on a computer with a high-resolution monitor.

See Chapter 3 for more information about browsers.

Remember, Web pages are similar to the marketing materials your company uses. Just as an editor checks corporate brochures closely for layout, design, organization, and accuracy, carefully check your Web pages.

Getting Ready to Test

Before you start testing, manually expire all the links. Most browsers are set by default to remember links that you've visited for about 30 days, and they color those links differently from unvisited links. You can easily see which sites you've visited, which is handy if you'd rather not browse in circles. By expiring links before you test your pages, you can see, for example, that the link colors (for links, active links, and visited links) appear as they should, and you can tell which links you haven't yet followed in your testing process.

Exactly how you expire links varies from browser to browser. The following steps give you the general procedure:

1. Look for a menu option that lets you change browser settings. For example, in the Navigator browser, choose Edit ➤ Preferences. In Internet Explorer, choose View ➤ Options.

2. In the resulting dialog box, look for an option that lets you change document "history."

3. Expire the links by clicking the Clear History button.

4. Click OK when you're done.

Testing for Overall Appearance

With your links expired, open your pages in your browser, and ask yourself the following questions:

- Is the layout and design aesthetically appealing? Do page elements align as planned?

- Is all the content visible? All text? All images?

- Do all colors appear as they should? Are there any odd patterns or colors?

- Do all pages contain navigation tools?

- Do all frames, applets, and other objects appear as planned?

After you've answered these questions and are satisfied with the results, change the size of your display window and test the overall appearance again. For example, make your display window smaller. You'll find that some elements may not appear on the screen or align as intended. Make any necessary adjustments. Figure 2.5 shows a page that didn't resize well.

FIGURE 2.5

Reducing window size can wreck the appearance of your Web page.

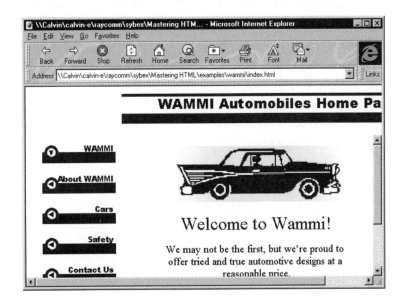

To quickly and easily evaluate different page sizes in Windows, create wallpaper with rectangles at 640 x 480 (VGA), 800 x 600 (SVGA), and 1024 x 768 (high-resolution). Then, assuming your display is set to at least 1024 x 768, you can simply resize the browser window to exactly overlap one of the rectangles. If you want to try this out, copy `ruler.bmp` from `\examples\ch02` on the Companion CD into your Windows folder or to your Macintosh, and then choose it for your wallpaper. In Windows 95, right-click the desktop, choose Properties ➤ Appearance, and then select the wallpaper.

TIP

Windows, Windows 95, Macintosh, and Unix users can all use built-in operating system functions to reset display characteristics. But if you are a Windows 95 user, go to www.microsoft.com and download the Microsoft Power Toys. Now you can use the Quick Res Powertoy to change display settings quickly and easily.

Now, change the color depth and see what happens to your pages. (Color depth is number of colors being displayed.) View your pages in millions of colors, in 256 colors, and in 16 colors in all your browsers. Check what happens to background and image color when you reduce the color depth. Yes, it's an incredible hassle—but, with some practice, you'll learn how HTML effects appear at various resolutions, and you can improve your pages accordingly.

Testing for Usability

Usability refers to how easily a visitor to your site can find and use information. The information may well be there, but will visitors find it, wait for it to download, or go through layers of links to get to it? In testing for usability, consider the following:

- How long do the pages take to download? Remember, you're testing your pages on your local computer; therefore, you can expect the pages to download *much* slower when a visitor accesses them over a dial-up Internet connection. Using tools such as Bandwidth Buster from Sausage Software can help you get a feel for how long the page might take to download over an Internet connection.

- Do the benefits of the enhancements outweigh the extra download time? For example, do images or the JavaScript you've added merit the added time required to download?

- How easily can you find navigation tools? Are they readily available, or do you have to scroll to find them? Are they consistent from page to page?

- Do *all* links work—links to information within the site as well as to information outside the site?

- Are the levels of links appropriate for the information provided? For example, is the information located in a third-level link clearly subordinate to information in the first- and second-level links? Also, if you've provided many link levels, is the information important enough that your visitors will take the time to wade through the other links?

Pilot Testing Your Documents

When you *pilot test* your documents, you ask real people to look at them and to identify problems and areas for improvement. The two main methods for pilot testing are contextual inquiry and the talking aloud protocol, which are often used in combination.

When you use *contextual inquiry*, you observe visitors in their own environment. One of the best ways to get started is to simply sit with a notebook and quietly watch your visitors. Pay attention to everything they do, including which information they refer to, which links they use most, and in what order they visit pages. Make a note about when they refer to your site for information, when they appear to get lost or frustrated, and when they head down the hall to ask someone else. Although this method is time consuming, it can be a real eye-opening experience, particularly if most of your information about your visitors' needs is based more on conjecture than on observation.

When you use the *talking aloud protocol*, you listen to visitors describe what they're doing and why they're doing it as they navigate your site. Follow this process:

1. Make a list of five or fewer items that you want a visitor to find at your Web site.

2. Give your visitor the list and ask him or her to find each item.

3. Insist that your visitors talk out loud throughout the test, saying anything that pops into their heads about the search, the site, or overall tasks.

If possible, record the session. In all likelihood, you'll end up with a transcript that is fairly disjointed but rich in information. For example: "Let's see, I'm supposed to find safety information about this particular car model. Hmmm. No menu items for safety. Maybe it'll be under the reliability menu. Nope, don't see it. Lessee. Search. No search items. It's gotta be under reliability. Aha, there it is, hiding under Protection. I saw Protection the first time, but thought that had something to do with undercoating or paint."

Pilot testing your site can identify how people *really* find information at your site and can indicate exactly where you need to make improvements.

Testing for Readability

Readability refers to how easily visitors can read information—text and images. Because a number of readability issues—fonts, font sizes, emphases, and colors— contribute to a document's overall appearance, you may have addressed some of them already. However, you need to look at these same issues from a visitor's point of view.

To test readability, search for a specific piece of information on your site. Observe which information you are drawn to on the page—usually images and headings stand out. Be sure that important information stands out adequately and that you can easily read all text, headings, captions, addresses, and so on.

Reading Online

By nature, reading on a computer screen is more difficult than reading the printed page. Hindrances include the size of the monitor, screen glare, and difficulty in navigating different windows. In addition, a computer screen has much coarser resolution than the printed page (72 to 100 dots per linear inch as compared with 600 to 2650 dots for laser printed or typeset ink on paper). Consequently, readers get tired quickly, read more slowly, and frequently skip information.

As an HTML author, you can improve readability somewhat with a few design techniques:

- Use headings and subheadings to break up long sections of text and to announce to a reader what information is on the page.
- Use bulleted and numbered lists, which give readers at-a-glance information.
- Use short paragraphs to encourage reading.
- Use text and background colors that adequately contrast.
- Use images to illustrate difficult concepts, rather than describing concepts in words.

Always test readability after changing the size of your display window or decreasing the color depth settings. Often, decreasing the window size or color depth makes pages much more difficult to read. For example, a Web site with a nice menu down the left side, banner on the top, and black text on the right looks great at 1024 × 768. At lower resolutions, however, the black text ends up over the dark background, as Figure 2.6 shows, and it's impossible to read.

FIGURE 2.6

Reducing window size can hinder readability.

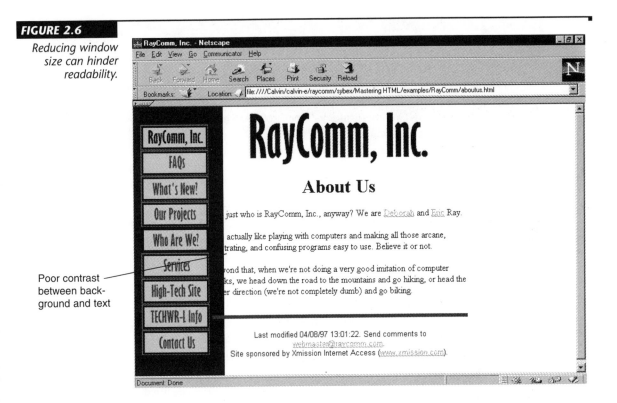

Poor contrast between background and text

Testing for Accuracy

Finally, if the content at your site isn't accurate, you might as well fold up your HTML documents and take a hike. In particular, a site littered with typos has just about zero credibility. Your accuracy checklist also needs to ensure that:

- The content is correct and up-to-date.
- Headings summarize the content that follows.
- Any references to figures or illustrations are correct.
- The *date last modified* information is current. The date last modified, as the name indicates, tells your visitors how current the information is and helps them decide whether it's usable.

Can Validation Services Help?

Validation services, accessed either through the Internet or from a program on your local computer, help ensure that you've used standard HTML or an HTML variant, such as HTML for Netscape Communicator or Microsoft Internet Explorer. For example, you might check to see that you're using HTML 4 correctly or that you really are providing HTML 2 code to your visitors with old browsers. Although validation services are not a panacea for solving HTML coding problems, you can use them to ensure that your code is complete, that it is more or less accurate, and that it is more or less standard. You'll find more information about using validation services in Chapter 17.

Phase 2: Publishing Documents

Publishing means putting HTML documents on a Web server and telling people where to look for them. The information in this section applies specifically to publishing your documents on the Internet or on an intranet.

The exact process you'll use for publishing documents depends on your situation. Some large organizations have well-defined publishing procedures; in these cases, you might simply fill out an HTML form and save your files in a specified folder. If your organization doesn't have procedures or if you're publishing on the Internet, you'll need to *upload* your files (which means to copy files from your computer to a server).

Before you can upload your files, you need to obtain the following information from your system administrator or your Internet service provider (ISP):

- The address of the Web server (for example, `www.raycomm.com`, `hobbes.raycomm.com`).

- The address of the FTP server, if required (for example, `ftp://ftp.xmission.com/`). Otherwise, you'll need a location to which to mail the files or the location on the Local Area Network (LAN) where you will place the files.

- A password and any access restrictions.

While you're at it, you might also ask the following:

- What kind of server (Apache, NCSA, WebStar, Netscape, and so on) is it, and on which platform does the server run?

- Can I restrict access to my pages?

- Can I install and run my own scripts?

- What's the default index file name?
- Are access logs maintained? How can I find out how many hits my site gets?

TIP

Chapter 6 provides specific information about using a server to publish your documents on an intranet or on the Internet.

QUICK LOOKUP

The *default index* is the file that automatically appears when you specify the address without a specific filename. For example, if you specify www.raycomm.com/news.html, the server displays the news page. However, if you specify www.raycomm.com/, the server displays the file index.html because that's how the server is configured.

On another server, the same address might display the default.htm file or the home.htm file. If you don't identify the index file correctly, your visitors will be able to view the entire list of files and browse according to their whim—not according to your plan.

Phase 3: Testing Published Documents

Earlier in this chapter, we discussed testing documents on your local computer. Now it's time to test them in the real world, looking for the same issues addressed previously, as well as making sure that all the links work and that the documents all transferred properly to the server. Additionally, at this stage, your goal is not only to look for layout, formatting, and proofreading errors, but also to get an accurate idea of what visitors will see when they access your pages. In particular, find out how fast pages load, how pages appear at various screen sizes and color depths, and how different browsers display page elements.

When you're testing, you want to do the following:

- Check how fast pages load using several connection types and speeds. Ask a few friends or colleagues to look at your pages and to report problems with layout, links, colors, download time, and so on.

- Check to see that the server displays the pages properly. As a rule, everything will look fine, but it's not unheard of to have a misconfigured server that displays nothing but HTML code in the browser.

If you find that browsers are displaying documents as HTML code, try changing the file extension to `html` (rather than `htm`). If that doesn't work, contact the server administrator ASAP.

- Test your pages using different computers, operating systems, and configurations. Remember to resize your document window and change color depth.

Phase 4: Maintaining Documents

Maintaining HTML documents is the process of updating and revising existing pages, adding new pages, and deleting outdated pages. Regularly maintaining HTML documents is essential if you want visitors to keep returning to your site. Also, regular maintenance helps make long-term maintenance less cumbersome.

HTML documents contain two types of information:

- Static
- Dynamic

Static information remains constant. The company logo, most menus, and even product descriptions are examples of static information. *Dynamic* information, on the other hand, must be changed or updated regularly. Prices, schedules, specific or timely information, and product lists are examples of dynamic information. Figure 2.7 shows a Web page that includes both types.

Developing a Plan

Back in the HTML document planning stages, you might have taken a few steps to make maintenance easier. In particular, you might have made update arrangements with content providers. Or, you might have developed some sort of documentation to help focus pages as the content changes. If you took either of these steps, you have a head start.

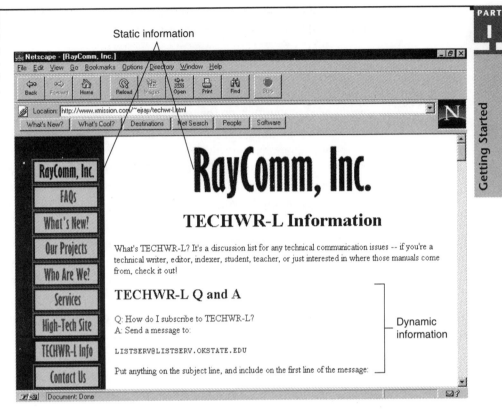

FIGURE 2.7

Static information remains constant; dynamic information changes frequently.

If you didn't plan adequately for maintenance—for example, if you didn't realize how much content you'd have or how difficult it would be to get updated information from your providers—you can still make maintenance a fairly straightforward process. First, devise a maintenance schedule. Set a time every day, every few days, or every few weeks (depending on how frequently the dynamic information changes) to update your documents.

Second, devise a maintenance plan. For example, if you know that you'll only be adding tidbits of information every few weeks, you can probably do that without much problem. If you're likely to receive pages and pages of information to add or if you're likely to make significant changes, however, you'll need to determine how to make the additions and changes most effectively. In these cases, hand-coding the information probably isn't the most effective way; conversion software, which does a lot of the coding for you, might be a better idea. In either case, determine how much you'll be changing and decide how best to handle it. (Yes, the rest of this book will provide all kinds of good information to help you along.)

Keeping Up

As you're adding, deleting, and updating information in your HTML documents, you'll need to routinely do the following:

- Check for links that don't work or that go to outdated information (also known as *link rot*). As you add and remove information from your site, you'll find that some pages suddenly have no links to them, and other existing links don't go anywhere. Manually browse all your links, and take advantage of link-checking programs on the Web. (Check this book's Web site for the latest addresses—they tend to change quickly.)

- Balance the latest HTML specification capabilities with what visitors' browsers can display. You probably won't want to develop a totally HTML 4–enhanced document if your visitors' browsers don't support all the version 4 effects.

- Ensure that older pages still look good in new versions of browsers. Often changes in browser software affect how some elements—such as images, tables, and forms—are displayed.

- Check older pages for references to outdated information. For example, you might want to update present-tense references to past presidential elections, sports records, or even products, prices, and schedules.

Where to Go from Here

This chapter provided an overview of the HTML document life cycle. In particular, it covered planning and organizing issues as well as issues about creating, publishing, publicizing, and maintaining HTML documents. If you understand these planning issues, you'll be able to develop HTML documents and use them for a variety of applications, including Web pages and sites, intranet sites, help files, and kiosks.

From here, you can refer to several chapters, depending on your HTML proficiency and the specific application you're developing:

- Chapters 3 and 4 get you started creating your first HTML document.
- Chapter 6 explains how to publish HTML documents on a server.
- Chapter 20 gives you general tips and advice to apply to all Web sites.
- Chapter 21 gives you tips and advice geared toward specific Web site types: public, personal, and intranet.

Chapter

3

Creating Your First
HTML Document

Creating Your First HTML Document

The overall HTML document development process starts with planning and ends with maintenance, as we discussed in the previous chapter. This chapter focuses on the part of that process you'll spend most of your time on—creating HTML documents. We'll explain the essential HTML authoring tools, show you how to enter HTML code, and introduce you to structure tags and tags for adding headings, different kinds of body text, character formatting, lists, and horizontal rules.

You'll find examples of HTML code and figures that show you what this code looks like in a browser. Follow along with the examples—try them out, verify that you're getting the expected results, and get comfortable with coding HTML. As explained below, all you'll need is a plain text editor, such as Notepad, Simple Text, or Vi (depending on your platform), and a Web browser, such as the Netscape browser or Microsoft Internet Explorer.

After you work through this chapter, you'll have developed your first HTML document, complete with text, headings, horizontal rules, and even some character-level formatting. With these basic skills, you can master any other HTML-related topic.

Understanding Basic HTML Tools

For your first documents, you need only two basic tools: an HTML editor and a Web browser.

- An *HTML editor* is the program you use to create and save your HTML documents.
- A *Web browser* is the program you use to view and test your HTML documents.

HTML Editors

In general, HTML editors fall into two categories:

- *Text-* or *code-based*, which allow you to see the HTML code as you're creating documents.
- *WYSIWYG* (What You See Is What You Get), which show the results of code, similar to the way it will appear in a browser, as you're formatting your document.

Although dozens of excellent WYSIWYG editors are available, learn to code HTML using a standard text editor. Text editors force you to *hand-code* HTML, meaning that you, not the software, enter tags and attributes. Hand-coding helps you learn HTML tags and structure and lets you see where you've made mistakes. Also, with hand-coding, you can easily include the newest HTML enhancements in your documents. Notepad for all Windows versions, Vi or pico for Unix, and TeachText or SimpleText for Macintosh are good choices.

MASTERING THE OPPORTUNITIES

HTML 4 Opportunity

Learning to hand-code is essential for using the latest-and-greatest HTML effects. For example, if you'd like to include any HTML 4 effects, you'll need to do some hand-coding because most editors don't support (at least at the time of writing) all the HTML 4 tags and attributes.

WARNING

Using a word-processing program such as Word, WordPerfect, or even WordPad to create HTML documents introduces extra formatting and control characters, which will cause problems. HTML requires plain text with no formatting at all.

Simple WYSIWYG editors, such as Netscape Composer and Microsoft FrontPad (included in Internet Explorer 4), are good for quickly generating HTML documents. They do not, however, give you, the author, as much control over the final appearance of your document as code-based editors do. Also, WYSIWYG editors lag behind HTML specifications and often don't support newer enhancements.

After you've developed a few HTML documents and understand basic HTML principles, you may choose to use both a WYSIWYG editor and a code-based editor. For example, you can get a good start on your document using a WYSIWYG editor and then polish it using an HTML editor. For now, though, use a code-based editor.

Creating a New HTML Document

You create an HTML document in much same way that you create any plain text document. Here's the general process:

1. Open your text editor.

2. Start a new document. If you're using Windows or Macintosh, choose File ➤ New. If you're using Unix, type **vi** or **pico** to start the editor.

3. Enter the HTML code and text you want to include. (In later sections of this chapter, you'll see how to enter code, and you'll find plenty of examples.)

4. Save your document. If you're using Windows or Macintosh, choose File ➤ Save or File ➤ Save As.

Guidelines for Saving Files

If you follow a few simple rules when saving HTML files, you'll find Web-authoring a more pleasant experience:

- If you aren't using a text-only editor such as Notepad or TeachText, verify that the file type is set to Text or ASCII (or HTML, if that's an option). If you use word-processing programs to create HTML documents (and remember our caveat about this), save your documents as HTML, Text Only, ASCII, DOS Text, or Text with Line Breaks (the specific options *will* vary with your word processor).

- Name the file with an htm or html extension. Windows 3.1*x* doesn't recognize four-character extensions, so you are limited to htm on that platform. (Of course, Windows 3.1*x* users can still open files from the Web that have four-character extensions such as html, but not from a local drive.)

CONTINUED

- Use only letters, numbers, hyphens (-), underscores (_), and periods (.) in your file-name. Many browsers also accept spaces in file names; however, spaces often make creating links difficult, as you will see in Chapter 4.

- Save the document (and the rest of the documents and files associated with a particular project) in one folder. You'll find that this makes using links, images, and other advanced effects easier.

Web Browsers

If you've ever surfed the Web, you've used a Web browser to view HTML documents. The most common browsers are Netscape Navigator and Microsoft Internet Explorer, although a variety of browsers are available for virtually all computer platforms, online services, and Internet service providers.

How your documents appear in browsers varies not only from browser to browser, but also from computer to computer. For example, most browsers in use today are *graphical browsers*: They can display elements other than text. A *text-only* browser can display—you guessed it—only text. How your HTML documents appear in each of these types of browsers differs significantly, as shown in Figures 3.1 and 3.2.

FIGURE 3.1

An HTML document displayed in Netscape Navigator

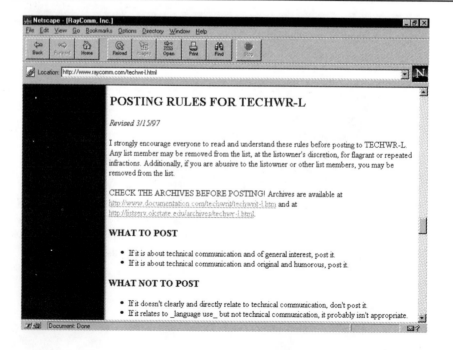

FIGURE 3.2

The same HTML document viewed in Lynx, a text-only browser

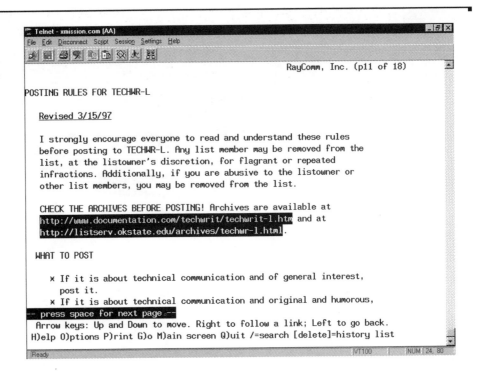

Your visitor's computer settings can also make a big difference in how your HTML documents appear. For example, the computer's resolution and specific browser settings can alter a document's appearance, as shown in Figures 3.3 and 3.4.

If you have a fairly recent browser—say, Internet Explorer 3.02 or Netscape Navigator 3—you'll be able to try out most of the examples in this book. However, you'll need Internet Explorer 4 and Netscape Communicator to experiment with many of the fancier effects such as Style Sheets, layers, and Dynamic HTML.

Viewing Documents

Viewing the HTML documents that you develop is as simple as opening them from your local hard drive in your browser. Here are the general steps:

1. Choose File ➤ Open and type the local file name or browse your hard drive until you find the file you want to open. Your particular menu commands might be File ➤ Open Page or File ➤ Open File, but it's all the same thing.

2. Select the file, and click OK to open it in your browser.

FIGURE 3.3

With the right settings, most HTML documents can be attractive.

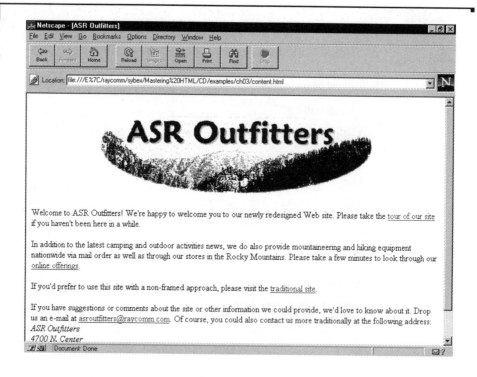

FIGURE 3.4

Different settings, different browsers, and system configuration can waylay page design.

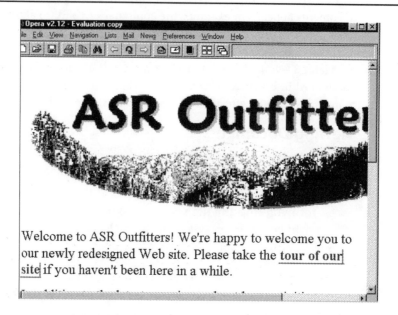

Alternative Ways To Open Files

Most browsers provide some clever features that can make developing HTML files easier.

You can easily see your editing changes in a file by *reloading* it. For example, after you've viewed a document and then saved some editing changes, you can reload the document and see the latest changes. Clicking a Reload button is obviously much easier than going back through the File ➤ Open and browse sequence. Generally, you reload documents by clicking a Refresh or Reload button or by choosing options from the View menu.

In addition, you can open a file by selecting it from a *bookmarked list* (or from a Favorites list, in Microsoft parlance). Bookmarking a file means adding a pointer to the file so that you can open the file quickly, just as a bookmark makes it easier to open a book to a specific page. Creating bookmarks (or Favorites) is as easy as clicking a menu option while viewing a page. Whenever you want to go back to that page, simply click the bookmark rather than choosing File ➤ Open and opening the file as you usually would. Most browsers have bookmark options; just look for a button or a menu command.

Entering Tags and Attributes

HTML is made up of tags and attributes, which work together to identify document parts and tell browsers how to display them. Tags identify document parts by specifying, for example, that a chunk of information be displayed as a paragraph or that another chunk of information be displayed as a heading. Attributes are optional parts of tags and modify or more thoroughly specify information in tags, such as color, alignment, height, or width.

Adding Tags

Tags are easy to read and use once you become familiar with their components. First, all tags are composed of *elements* that are contained within *angle brackets* (< >). The angle brackets simply tell browsers that the text between them is an HTML command. A tag with its angle brackets looks like this:

```
<TAG>
```

Second, most tags are paired, with an opening tag (<TAG>) and a closing tag (</TAG>). Both tags look alike, except the closing tag also includes a forward slash (/). To apply tags to information in your document, place the opening tag before the information, and place the closing tag after the information, like this:

```
<TAG>information that the tags apply to</TAG>
```

Enter both the opening and closing tag at the same time so that you don't forget the closing tag. If you happen to forget it, most paired tags will run on and on until the browser finds a matching closing tag.

NOTE

You'll learn more about nonpaired tags in the section "Paragraph-Level Formatting," later in this chapter.

To apply more than one tag to a chunk of information, you nest them. *Nesting* means placing one set of tags inside another set. For example, to apply both bold and italic to text, you can nest the tags, like this:

```
<B><I>information that the tags apply to</I></B>
```

When you nest tags, the first tag is also the last tag, and the second tag is also the second to last tag, and so on.

Typing Tags Correctly

When typing tags, be particularly careful not to include extra spaces. If you do so, a browser may not recognize the tag and will thus not display the information correctly. In addition, the browser might display the tag itself.

For example, a title should look like this:

```
<TITLE>Correctly Formed Title</TITLE>
```

Do *not* include spaces within the tags, like this:

```
< TITLE >Incorrectly Formed Title< /TITLE >
```

Improving Readability

You'll find it easier to read and use tags if you follow a few conventions. In particular, type tags using all caps, and use hard returns to create shorter lines. These conventions do not affect how browsers display code—they just make it easier for you to read it.

The following two examples show you how using caps and hard returns can improve readability.

```
<!doctype HTML public "-//w3c//dtd HTML 4.0 Final//en"><html><head>
<title>Mastering HTML Document Title</title></head><body>Mastering HTML
Document Body</body></html>
```

or

```
<!DOCTYPE HTML PUBLIC "-//W3C//DTD HTML 4.0 Final//EN">
<HTML>
<HEAD>
```

```
<TITLE>Mastering HTML Document Title</TITLE>
</HEAD>
<BODY>
 Mastering HTML Document Body
</BODY>
</HTML>
```

No question, right?

Including Attributes

Attributes provide extra information about a tag. For example, if you apply a heading tag (<H1>) to a line of text, like this:

```
<H1>A heading goes here</H1>
```

you can further specify that it should be centered by using an attribute, like this:

```
<H1 ALIGN="center">A centered heading goes here</H1>
```

All attributes go in the opening tag and are separated from other attributes and the tag itself by a space. Some attributes require quotes; some don't. As a general rule, most attributes—those that include only letters, digits, hyphens, or periods—work fine without quotes. For example, you can type ALIGN=CENTER or ALIGN="CENTER"; all browsers should display these in the same way.

Attributes that have other characters, such as spaces, % signs, or # signs, however, do require quotes. For example, if you use the WIDTH= attribute to indicate a percentage of the document window, type WIDTH="75%".

TIP

When in doubt, use quotes with attributes. Although they aren't always necessary, they never hurt. Throughout this book, we've included the quotes—for good practice and good example.

You can include multiple attributes in a tag by using one space between each attribute, like this:

```
<H1 ALIGN="center" SIZE="+2" COLOR="#FF0000">A wildly formatted heading goes
here</H1>
```

NOTE

In HTML tags, the attributes can go in any order after the element, but the element must always go first.

Applying Structure Tags

Structure tags provide browsers with information about document characteristics, such as the version of HTML used, introductory information about the document, and the title. Most structure tags, although part of the HTML document, do not appear in the browser window. Instead, structure tags work "behind the scenes" and essentially tell the browser which elements to include and how to display them. Although these tags do not produce the snazzy results you see in Web pages or help files, they are essential for telling browsers how to interpret the document.

NOTE

Most browsers, including Netscape Navigator and Microsoft Internet Explorer, usually correctly display documents that do not include structure tags. However, there is no guarantee that future versions will continue to do so or that your results will be consistent. We strongly advise using structure tags.

All HTML documents should include five structure tags, nested and ordered as in the following example code:

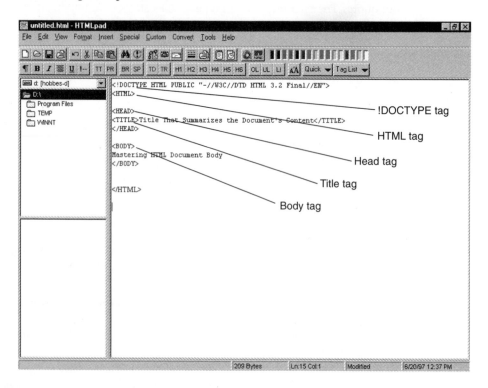

△ TIP

As we mentioned in Chapter 2, a great way to save time is to create a master document that includes all the required structure tags so that you can reuse them in other HTML documents. We've included a sample document containing these structure tags on the CD. You'll find it in this chapter's folder; it's /examples/ch03/minimal.htm.

The <!DOCTYPE ...> Tag

The <!DOCTYPE...> tag tells browsers (and validation services) the HTML version with which the document complies. The HTML 3.2 and 4 specifications require this non-paired tag, and, therefore, you should use it in all your documents. Enter it at the top of your document, like this:

```
<!DOCTYPE HTML PUBLIC "-//W3C//DTD HTML 3.2 Final//EN">
```

or, like this:

```
<!DOCTYPE HTML PUBLIC "-//W3C//DTD HTML 4.0 Final//EN">
```

The key part of the <!DOCTYPE...> tag is the DTD element (*Document Type Definition*), which tells browsers that the document complies with a particular HTML version—the first example complies with HTML 3.2, and the second, with HTML 4. A DTD specifies the organization that issues the specification (W3C, in these cases) and the exact version of the specification.

As new HTML standards evolve, you can expect this tag to change to indicate new versions. For example, in a year or so, the <!DOCTYPE...> tag might look like this:

```
<!DOCTYPE HTML PUBLIC "-//W3C//DTD HTML 5.23 Final//EN">
```

Even after new standards appear, you don't need to revise the <!DOCTYPE...> tag in existing documents. If your document conforms to the HTML 3.2 standard, it'll conform to that standard, regardless of more recent HTML versions.

The <HTML> Tag

The <HTML> tag identifies the document as an HTML document. Technically, this tag is superfluous after the !DOCTYPE tag, but it is necessary for older browsers that do not support the <!DOCTYPE...> tag. It is also helpful to people who read the HTML code. To use the <HTML> tag, enter it in your document below the <!DOCTYPE...> tag, like this:

```
<!DOCTYPE HTML PUBLIC "-//W3C//DTD HTML 4.0 Final//EN">
<HTML>
</HTML>
```

The <HEAD> Tag

The <HEAD> tag contains information about the document, including its title, scripts used, style definitions, and document descriptions. Not all browsers require this tag, but most browsers expect to find any available additional information about the document within the <HEAD> tag. Additionally, the <HEAD> tag can contain other tags that have information for search engines and indexing programs. To add the <HEAD> tag, enter it between the <HTML> tags, like this:

```
<!DOCTYPE HTML PUBLIC "-//W3C//DTD HTML 4.0 Final//EN">
<HTML>
<HEAD>
</HEAD>
</HTML>
```

Don't confuse this document heading tag, which is a structure tag, with heading tags such as <H1> that create heading text in a document body. We discuss heading tags later in this chapter in the "Headings" section.

The <TITLE> Tag

The <TITLE> tag, which the HTML 3.2 and 4 specifications require, contains the document title. The title does not appear within the browser window, although it is usually visible in the browser's title bar. Between the opening and closing tags, include a title that briefly summarizes your document's content. To use the <TITLE> tag, enter it between the opening and closing <HEAD> tags, like this:

```
<!DOCTYPE HTML PUBLIC "-//W3C//DTD HTML 4.0 Final//EN">
<HTML>
<HEAD>
<TITLE>
Title That Summarizes the Document's Content
</TITLE>
</HEAD>
</HTML>
-
```

Titles should represent the document, even if the document is taken out of context. Some good titles include the following:

- Sample HTML Code
- Learning to Ride a Bicycle
- Television Viewing for Fun and Profit

Less useful titles, particularly taken out of context, include the following:

- Examples
- Chapter 2
- Continued

The <BODY> Tag

The <BODY> tag encloses all the tags, attributes, and information that you want a visitor's browser to display. Almost everything else in this entire book takes place between the <BODY> tags. To use the <BODY> tag, enter it below the closing </HEAD> tag and above the closing </HTML> tag, like this:

```
<!DOCTYPE HTML PUBLIC "-//W3C//DTD HTML 4.0 Final//EN">
<HTML>
<HEAD>
<TITLE>
Title That Summarizes the Document's Content
</TITLE>
</HEAD>
<BODY>
All the tags, attributes, and information in the document body go here.
</BODY>
</HTML>
```

If you've been following along, save your document, view it in a browser, and compare it with Figure 3.5 to confirm that you're on the right track. The title appears in the title bar, and some text appears in the document window.

FIGURE 3.5

Your first HTML document, including all structure tags

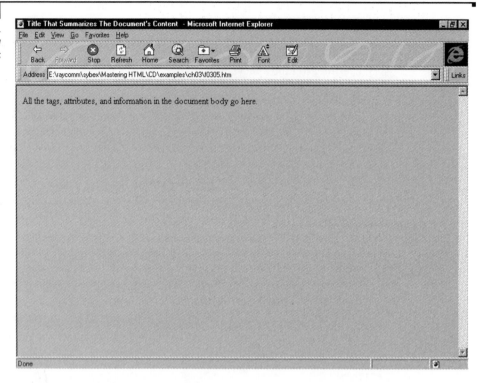

Minimal Compliance for Structure Tags

As shown in the previous sections, the HTML 4 specification does not require all structure tags. In fact, only two: the <!DOCTYPE...> tag and the <TITLE> tag. If you choose to use only these two tags, the code would look like this:

```
<!DOCTYPE HTML PUBLIC "-//W3C//DTD HTML 4.0 Final//EN">
<TITLE>The name of a minimal and content free document</TITLE>
```

Of course, there's no purpose in creating a document with nothing but the minimal tags—the document doesn't say anything and doesn't present any information. (We don't recommend it, but it's possible.) If you use these two tags as a starting point, however, you can create a standard compliant document and save yourself a few keystrokes on each new document you create.

Applying Common Tags and Attributes

After you've included the structure tags, you're ready to start placing basic content in the document body. The following sections show you how to include headings, paragraphs, lists, and rules (horizontal lines). These elements constitute the basic HTML document components and, unlike the structure tags, do appear in the browser window. Learning to apply these basic tags and attributes will prepare you to apply practically any HTML tag or attribute.

As you create your content, keep in mind that its exact appearance will vary from browser to browser. For example, a first-level heading in one browser might appear as approximately 16-point Times New Roman Bold, whereas another browser might display it as 14-point Arial Bold Italic. Both browsers display the heading bigger and bolder than other heading and body text, but the specific font, size, and emphasis will vary.

Headings

Headings break up large areas of text, announce topics to follow, and arrange information according to a logical hierarchy. HTML provides six levels of headings; <H1> is the largest of the headings, and <H6> is the smallest:

```
<H1> ... </H1>
<H2> ... </H2>
<H3> ... </H3>
<H4> ... </H4>
<H5> ... </H5>
<H6> ... </H6>
```

 TIP

For most documents, limit yourself to two or three heading levels. After three heading levels, many readers begin to lose track of your hierarchy. If you find that you're using several heading levels, consider reorganizing your document—too many heading levels often indicates a larger organizational problem.

To use heading tags, enter them around the heading text, like this:

```
<!DOCTYPE HTML PUBLIC "-//W3C//DTD HTML 4.0 Final//EN">
<HTML>
<HEAD>
<TITLE>Sample Headings</TITLE>
```

```
</HEAD>
<BODY>
<H1>First Level Heading</H1>
<H2>Second Level Heading</H2>
<H3>Third Level Heading</H3>
</BODY>
</HTML>
```

Figure 3.6 shows how Internet Explorer displays a few heading levels.

FIGURE 3.6

Heading levels provide visitors with a hierarchy of information.

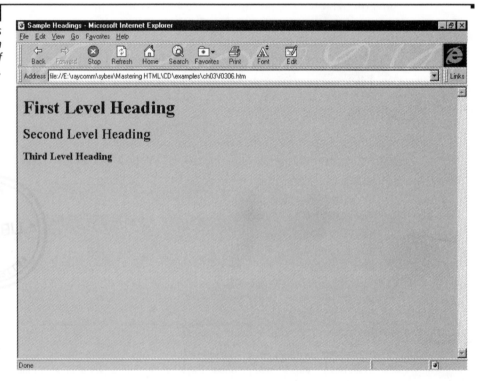

Use heading tags only for document headings—that is, don't use heading tags for figure captions or to emphasize information within text. Why? First, you don't always know how browsers will display the heading. It might not create the visual effect you intend. Second, some indexing and editing programs use headings to generate tables of contents and other information about your document. These programs won't exclude headings from the table of contents or other information just because you used them as, say, figure captions.

By default, all browsers align headings on the left. Most browsers, however, support alignment attributes, which also let you right-align and center headings. Table 3.1 shows the alignment attributes.

TABLE 3.1: ALIGNMENT ATTRIBUTES	
Heading Attribute	**Effect**
ALIGN=LEFT	Aligns the heading on the left (default).
ALIGN=CENTER	Aligns the heading in the center.
ALIGN=RIGHT	Aligns the heading on the right.

To use the alignment attributes, include them in the initial heading tag, like this:

```
<H1 ALIGN=LEFT>Left-aligned Heading</H1>
<H1 ALIGN=CENTER>Centered Heading</H1>
<H1 ALIGN=RIGHT>Right-aligned Heading</H1>
```

Figure 3.7 shows headings aligned left, center, and right.

FIGURE 3.7

Headings can be aligned left, center, or right.

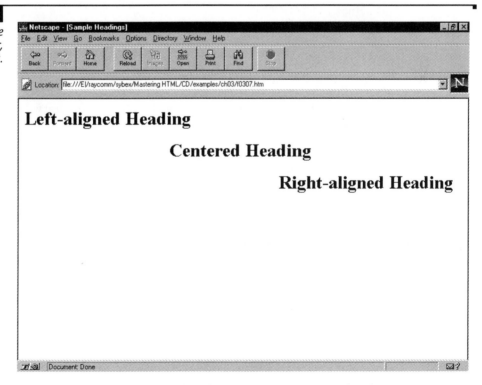

MASTERING THE OPPORTUNITIES

HTML 4 Opportunity

Although most browsers support the ALIGN= attribute, consider using Style Sheets to create the same effect. The HTML 4 specification deprecates (strongly discourages) using the ALIGN= attribute in favor of using Style Sheets. So, although this attribute has wide support, if your visitors will be using very new browsers, you might consider moving toward Style Sheets for your formatting needs. You'll find how-to information about Style Sheets in Chapter 5 and a comprehensive list of Style Sheet options in the Master's Reference.

NOTE

If you're writing for a wide audience, some of whom might be using older browsers, surround the ALIGN=CENTER attributes with <CENTER> tags to ensure that the text actually appears centered, yielding something like <CENTER><H1 ALIGN=CENTER>Centered Heading</H1></CENTER>.

Body Text

Earlier in this chapter, you learned about <BODY> tags, which identify the part of the document that appears in browsers. Body text is text that you use within the <BODY> tags. Body text tags and attributes are divided into two categories:

- Paragraph-level tags and attributes, which apply formatting to sections of text
- Character-level tags and attributes, which apply formatting to individual letters or words

Paragraph-Level Formatting

Paragraph-level formatting applies formatting to an entire section of text. The most common format is a paragraph, <P>, which is appropriate for regular body text. The paragraph tag does not have to be paired (it's called a *nonpaired tag*)—you can simply use the opening tag, <P>, where you want to start a paragraph. As with many tags, however, it's easier to identify where the tag begins and ends if you use both opening and closing tags.

To use the paragraph tags, enter them around the text you want to format as a paragraph, like this:

```
<P>
A whole paragraph goes right here.
</P>
```

Figure 3.8 shows a sample paragraph.

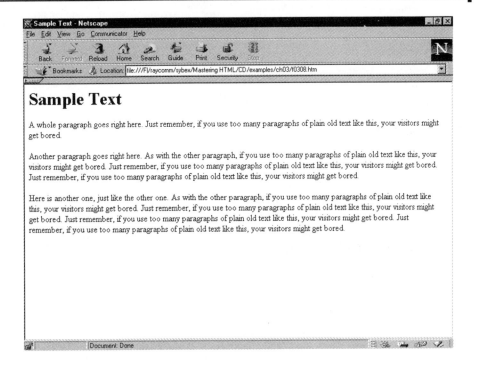

You can also apply other paragraph formats instead of the <P> tag to achieve some slightly different paragraph formats, as explained in Table 3.2.

Alignment attributes are often used with these paragraph formatting tags, including ALIGN=LEFT, ALIGN=CENTER, and ALIGN=RIGHT. To apply these attributes, include them in any of the opening paragraph tags, like this:

```
<P ALIGN=CENTER>
Paragraph of information goes here.
</P>
```

TABLE 3.2: OTHER PARAGRAPH FORMATTING TAGS

Paragraph Format	Effect
<ADDRESS>	Used for address and contact information. Often appears in italics.
<BLOCKQUOTE>	Used for formatting a quotation. Usually appears indented from both sides and with less space between lines than does a regular paragraph.
<PRE>	Effective for formatting program code or similar information. Usually appears in a fixed-width font with ample space between words and lines.

Figure 3.9 shows how the <ADDRESS> and <PRE> tags appear in Internet Explorer.

FIGURE 3.9

Special paragraph-level tags make information stand out.

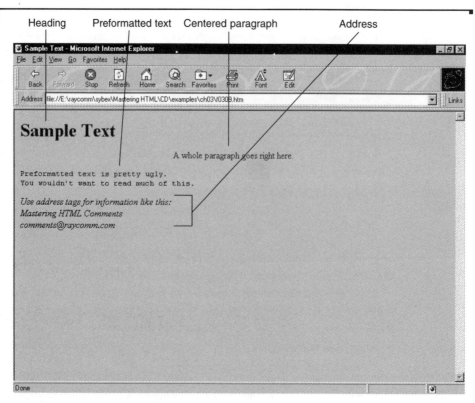

Specifying Line Breaks

Sometimes you need to break a line in a specific place, but you don't want to start a new paragraph (with the extra space). For example, you might not want lines of poetry text to go all the way across the document; instead, you might want to break them into several shorter lines that look better. You can easily break paragraph lines by inserting the <BR> tag where you want the lines to break, like this:

```
<P>
There once was an HTML writer,<BR>
Who tried to make paragraphs wider.<BR>
He found with a shock<BR>
All the tags did mock<BR>
The attempt to move that text outside-r.<BR>
Mercifully Anonymous</P>
```

The <BR> tag is completely standard, and you can use it in any context.

Character-Level Formatting

Character-level formatting applies emphases to individual letters or words. For example, you can make a word appear *italic,* **bold**, underlined, or superscript, as in e^2. You use character-level formatting tags within paragraph-level tags—that is, you can't put a <P> tag within a character-level tag such as <B>. You have to close the character-level formatting before you close the paragraph-level formatting.

Correct:

```
<P><B>This is the end of a paragraph that also uses boldface.</B></P>
<P>This is the beginning of the following paragraph.
```

Incorrect:

```
This text <B>is boldface.</P>
<P>As is this </B></P>
```

Although many character formatting tags are available, you'll probably use <B> (for **boldface**) and <I> (for *italics*) most often. Table 3.3 shows a list of the most common character formatting tags.

TABLE 3.3: COMMON CHARACTER-FORMATTING TAGS

Character Tag	Effect
<B>	Applies boldface.
<BLINK>	Makes text blink, usually considered highly unprofessional.

Continued

TABLE 3.3: (CONTINUED) COMMON CHARACTER-FORMATTING TAGS

<CITE>	Indicates citations or references.
<CODE>	Displays program code. Similar to the <PRE> tag.
<EM>	Applies emphasis; usually displayed as italic.
<I>	Applies italics.
<S>, <STRIKE>	Applies strikethrough to text. These tags are deprecated in the HTML 4 specification.
<STRONG>	Applies stronger emphasis; usually displayed as bold.
<SUB>	Formats text as subscript.
<SUP>	Formats text as superscript.
<TT>	Applies a fixed-width font.
<U>	Applies underline. This tag is deprecated in the HTML specification.
<VAR>	Displays variables or arguments.

To use these tags, enter them around the individual letters or words you want to emphasize, like this:

```
Making some text <B>bold</B> or <I>italic</I> is
a useful technique, more so than <STRIKE>strikethrough</STRIKE> or
<BLINK>blinking</BLINK>.
```

Figure 3.10 shows some sample character formatting. (The blinking word doesn't appear in this figure so you can see that it disappears.)

TIP

Spend a few minutes trying out these character-formatting tags to see how they work and how they look in your favorite browser.

MASTERING THE OPPORTUNITIES

HTML 4 Opportunity

The HTML 4 specification strongly encourages using Style Sheets for your formatting needs. Although the specification still supports many individual formatting tags, it is moving toward Style Sheets as the recommended way to include formatting in your HTML documents. Using Style Sheets, you can apply the following:

• Character-level formatting such as strikethrough and underline

MASTERING THE OPPORTUNITIES CONTINUED

- Paragraph-level formatting such as indents and margins
- Other formatting such as background colors and images

See Chapter 5 and the Master's Reference for Style Sheet information.

FIGURE 3.10

Character formatting helps you emphasize words or letters.

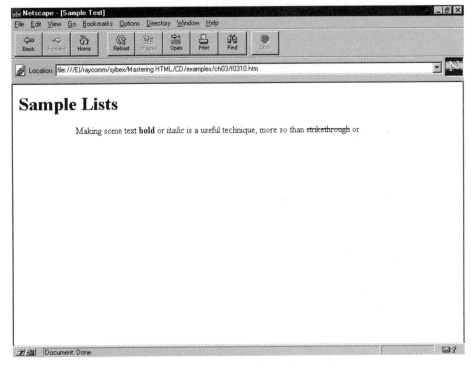

Lists

Lists are a great way to provide information in a structured, easy-to-read format. They help your visitor easily spot information, and they draw attention to important information. A list is a good form for a procedure. Figure 3.11 shows the same content formatted as both a paragraph and a list.

Lists come in two varieties:

- Numbered (*ordered*)
- Bulleted (*unordered*)

To create either kind, you first specify that you want information to appear as a list, and then you identify each line item in the list. Table 3.4 shows the list and line item tags.

FIGURE 3.11

Lists are often easier to read than paragraphs.

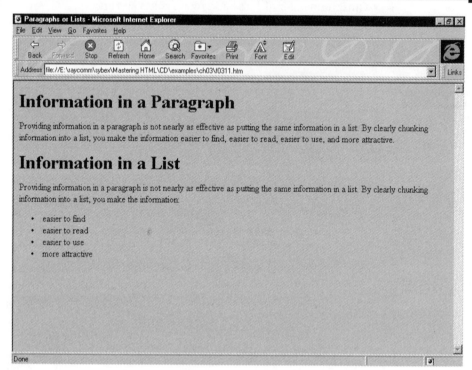

TABLE 3.4: LIST AND LINE ITEM TAGS

List Tag	Effect
<OL>	Specifies that the information appear as an ordered (numbered) list.
<UL>	Specifies that the information appear as an unordered (bulleted) list.
<LI>	Specifies a line item in either ordered or unordered lists.

The following steps show you how to create a bulleted list; use the same steps to create a numbered list.

1. Start with text you want to format as a list.

```
Lions
Tigers
```

Bears

Oh, My!

2. Insert the <UL>tags around the list text.

<UL>

Lions

Tigers

Bears

Oh, My!

</UL>

3. Type the <LI> tag for each list item.

<UL>

<LI>Lions

<LI>Tigers

<LI>Bears

<LI>Oh, My!

</UL>

The resulting list, viewed in a browser, looks like that shown in Figure 3.12.

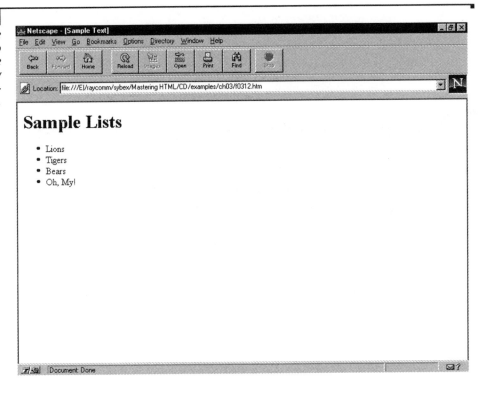

To change your list from unordered (bulleted) to ordered (numbered), change the <UL> to <OL> (and </UL> to </OL>). The resulting numbered list is shown in Figure 3.13.

FIGURE 3.13

Numbered lists provide sequential information.

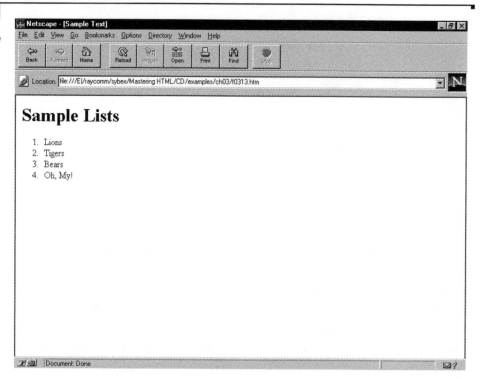

Other less commonly used list tags include <DIR>, to create a directory list and <MENU>, to create a menu list. You use these tags just as you use the <UL> and <OL> tags. For more information about these tags and their uses, see the Master's Reference.

Setting List Appearance

By default, numbered lists use arabic numerals, and bulleted lists use small, round bullets. You can change the appearance of these by using the attributes listed in Table 3.5.

TABLE 3.5: LIST ATTRIBUTES	
List Tag	**Effect**
For numbered lists:	
TYPE=A	Specifies the number (or letter) with which the list should start: A, a, I, i, or 1 (default).
TYPE=a	
TYPE=I	
TYPE=i	
TYPE=1	
For bulleted lists:	
TYPE=DISC	Specifies the bullet shape.
TYPE=SQUARE	
TYPE=CIRCLE	

To use any of these attributes, include them in the initial <OL> or <UL> tag or in the <LI> tag, like this:

```
<OL TYPE=A>
<LI>Outlines use sequential lists with letters.
<LI>So do some (unpopular) numbering schemes for documentation.
</OL>
```

Or, like this:

```
<UL TYPE=SQUARE>
<LI>Use bullets for non-sequential items.
<LI>Use numbers for sequential items.
</UL>
```

Or this:

```
<UL>
<LI TYPE=CIRCLE> Use bullets for non-sequential items.
<LI TYPE=SQUARE> Use different bullets for visual interest.
</UL>
```

Figure 3.14 shows how these attributes appear in a browser.

FIGURE 3.14

You can change the appearance of numbers and bullets using list attributes.

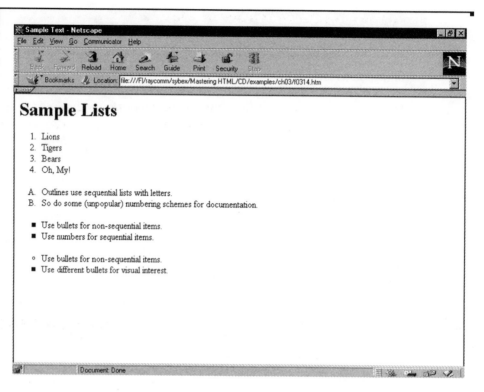

You can add the COMPACT attribute to initial <OL> or <UL> tags to tell browsers to display the list as compactly as possible. Generally, this setting will make little difference, as most browsers render lists this way by default.

Type attributes for unordered lists are currently (at the time of writing) supported by only a few browsers, although support is expected to grow over time.

More Options for Ordered Lists

Ordered lists have additional attributes that you can use to specify the first number in the list, as well as to create hierarchical information.

First, you can start a numbered list with a value other than 1 (or A, a, I, or i). Simply include the START= attribute in the initial <OL> tag, as in <OL START=51>. Or, you can even change specific numbers within a list by using the VALUE= attribute in the <LI> tag, as in <LI VALUE=7>. To use these attributes, include them in the <OL> tag, like this:

```
<OL START=51>
<LI>This is the fifty-first item.
<LI>This is the fifty second.
<LI TYPE=i VALUE=7>This item was renumbered to be the seventh, using
lowercase roman numerals, just because we can.
</OL>
```

Figure 3.15 shows how this code appears in a browser.

FIGURE 3.15

Attributes let you customize ordered lists in a number of ways.

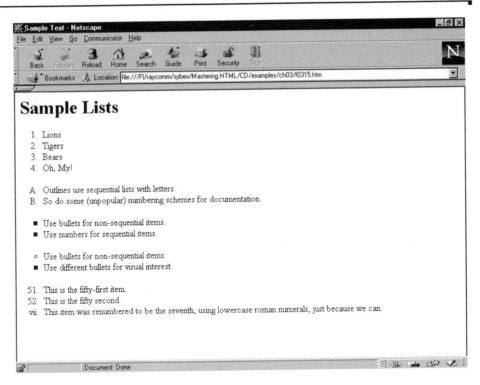

Second, you can use nested ordered lists and different TYPE= attributes to create outlines. The numbering continues past each lower-level section without the need to manually renumber with a VALUE= attribute. The results are visible in Figure 3.16.

```
<OL TYPE=I>
<LI>Top Level Item
<LI>Another Top Level Item
<OL TYPE=A>
   <LI>A Second Level Item
   <LI>Another Second Level Item
   <OL TYPE=1>
           <LI>A Third Level Item
           <LI>Another Third Level Item
   </OL>
   <LI>Another Second Level Item
</OL>
<LI>A Top Level Item
</OL>
```

FIGURE 3.16

Ordered lists are even flexible enough to format outlines.

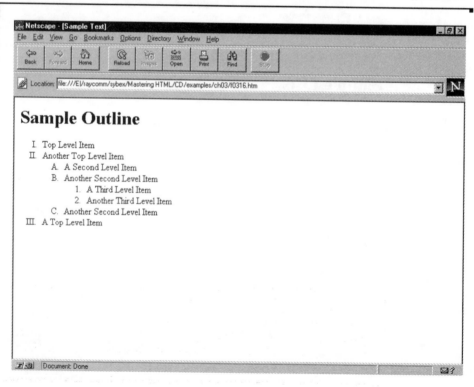

Using Definition Lists

Finally, one special list variant, *definition lists*, can be useful for providing two levels of information. You can think of definition lists as dictionary entries—you have two levels of information: the entry, followed by a definition. You can use these lists to provide glossary-type information, or you can use them to provide two-level lists. Table 3.6 lists the tages and their effects.

TABLE 3.6: DEFINITION LIST AND ITEM TAGS.

List Tag	Effect
<DL>	Specifies that the information appear as a definition list.
<DT>	Identifies definition terms.
<DD>	Identifies definitions.

To create a definition list, as shown in Figure 3.17, follow these steps:

1. Enter the <DL> tags to start the definition list.

```
<DL>
</DL>
```

2. Add the <DT> tag to identify definition terms.

```
<DL>
<DT>HTML
<DT>Maestro
</DL>
```

3. Add the <DD> tag to identify individual definitions.

```
<DL>
<DT>HTML
<DD>Hypertext Markup Language is used to create Web pages.
<DT>Maestro
<DD>An expert in some field. See "Readers of <I>Mastering HTML</I>" for examples.
</DL>
```

TIP

A great way to apply definition lists is in "What's New" lists—a special page that tells people what's new and exciting on your site or at your organization. Try putting the dates in the <DT> tag (maybe with boldface and italics) and the information in the <DD> tag.

FIGURE 3.17

Definition lists are a formatting option that is useful when presenting dictionary-like information.

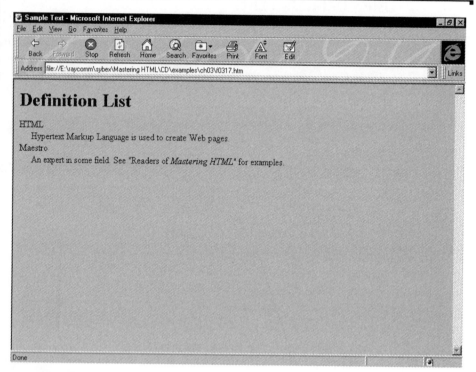

Horizontal Rules

Horizontal rules are lines that break up long sections of text, indicate a shift in information, or help improve the overall document design. To use a horizontal rule, include the <HR> tag where you want the rule to appear, like this:

```
<P>Long passages of text should often be broken into sections with headings
and, optionally, horizontal rules.</P>
<HR>
<H3>A Heading Also Breaks Up Text</H3>
<P>A new long passage can continue here. </P>
```

By default, horizontal rules appear shaded, span the width of the browser window, and are a few pixels high. You can change a rule's shading, width, height, and alignment by including the appropriate attributes. Table 3.7 shows horizontal rule attributes.

QUICK LOOKUP

Pixels are the little dots on your screen that, taken together, produce an image. Pixel is actually an abbreviation for Picture Element. If your display is set to 800 × 600, you have 800 pixels horizontally and 600 pixels vertically.

TABLE 3.7: HORIZONTAL RULE ATTRIBUTES

Rule Attribute	Effect
SIZE=n	Specifies rule height; measured in pixels.
WIDTH=n	Specifies rule width (length); measured in pixels.
WIDTH="n%"	Specifies rule width (length); measured as a percentage of the document width.
ALIGN=LEFT	Specifies left alignment.
ALIGN=CENTER	Specifies center alignment.
ALIGN=RIGHT	Specifies right alignment.
NOSHADE	Specifies that the rule has no shading.

To use any of these attributes, include them in the <HR> tag, like this:

```
<HR WIDTH="80%" SIZE=8>
<HR WIDTH="50%">
<HR WIDTH=400 ALIGN=RIGHT>
<HR NOSHADE ALIGN=CENTER WIDTH=200>
```

Figure 3.18 shows some sample horizontal rules, with height, width, alignment, and shading attributes added.

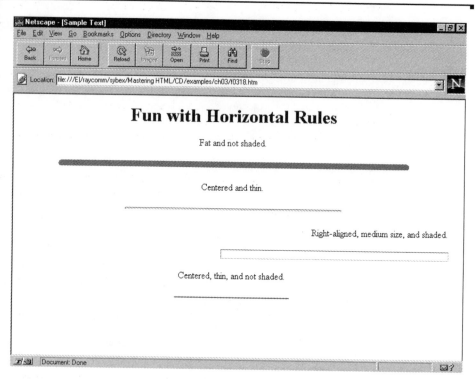

FIGURE 3.18

Horizontal rules can help separate information, improve page design, and simply add visual interest to the page.

Including Fancier Formatting

Now that you have a firm grip on using the basic HTML formatting options, you can dive into some of the fancier formatting effects. In the following sections, we'll show you how to add colors and specify fonts and sizes. Although most newer browsers support these effects, not all browsers do; your fancier effects might not reach all visitors. Also, the HTML 4 specification deprecates many of these effects in favor of Style Sheets. If your visitors use Style Sheet–capable browsers, you might consider using Style Sheets instead of the tags and attributes mentioned here.

Adding Colors

One of the easiest ways to jazz up your documents is to add colors to the background or text. You can enliven an otherwise dull Web page with a splash of color or an entire color scheme. For example, add a background color and change the text colors to coordinate with the background. Or highlight a word or two with color and make the words leap off the page. Or, if you're developing a corporate site, adhere to the company's color scheme to ensure a consistent look.

TIP

As you'll see later in Chapter 20, developing a color scheme is a great way to help unite your pages into a cohesive Web site.

The drawback to setting colors is that you really don't have control over what your visitors see. Visitors might set their browsers to display colors they like, or they might be using a text-only browser, which generally displays only black, white, and gray.

You specify colors using hexadecimal numbers, which combine proportions of Red, Green, and Blue—called RGB numbers. RGB numbers use six digits, two for each proportion of red, green, and blue. As you're choosing colors, remember that not all RGB numbers display well in browsers; some colors *dither*, meaning that they appear spotty or splotchy. We recommend that you select RGB values that are appropriate for Web page use, as listed in Table 3.8. Although you'll never go wrong with these "safe" colors, it's most important to use these colors in page backgrounds or in places with large patches of color, where dithering will occur if you don't use these number combinations.

TABLE 3.8: RECOMMENDED RGB VALUES

R	G	B
00	00	00
33	33	33
66	66	66
99	99	99
CC	CC	CC
FF	FF	FF

To create an RGB number from the values in this table, simply select one number from each column. For example, choose FF from the Red column, 00 from the Green column, and 00 from the Blue column to create the RGB number FF0000, which has the largest possible red component but no blue and no green, therefore appearing as a pure, bright red. You'll find a complete list of appropriate RGB numbers and corresponding descriptions in the Master's Reference.

Setting Background Colors

Using a *background color*, which is simply a color that fills the entire browser window, is a great way to add flair to your Web pages. By default, browsers display a white or gray background color, which may be adequate if you're developing pages for an intranet site where flashy elements aren't essential. If you're developing a public or personal site, however, you'll probably want to make your site more interesting and visually appealing. For example, if you're developing a public corporate Web site, you might want to use your company's standard colors—ones that appear on letterhead, logos, or marketing materials. Or, you might want to use your favorite color if you're developing a personal site. In either case, using a background color can improve the overall page appearance and help develop a theme among pages.

 **TIP**

Check out Chapters 20 and 21 for tips and information about developing coherent public, personal, and intranet sites.

As you'll see in the next section, pay careful attention to how well text contrasts with the background color. If you specify a dark background color, use a light text color. Likewise, if you specify a light background color, use a dark text color. Contrast is key for ensuring that visitors can read information on your pages.

To specify a background color for your documents, include the BGCOLOR=#"..." attribute in the opening <BODY> tag, like this:

```
<BODY BGCOLOR="#FFFFFF">
```

Setting Text Colors

Like background colors, text colors can enhance your Web pages. In particular, you can specify the color of the following:

- Body text, which appears throughout the document body

- Unvisited links, which are links not yet followed

- Active links, which are links as they're being selected

- Visited links, which are links previously followed

Changing body text is sometimes essential—for example, if you've added a background color or an image. If you've added a dark background color, the default black body text color won't adequately contrast with the background, making the text difficult or impossible to read. In this case, you'd want to change the text color to one that's lighter so that it contrasts with the background sufficiently.

Changing link colors helps keep your color scheme intact—for unvisited as well as visited links. Set the visited and unvisited links to different colors to help visitors know which links they've followed and which ones they haven't.

To change body text and link colors, simply add the attributes listed in Table 3.9 to the opening <BODY> tag.

TABLE 3.9: TEXT AND LINK COLOR ATTRIBUTES

Attribute	Description
TEXT="…"	Sets the color for all text within the document with a color name or a #RRGGBB value
ALINK="…"	Sets the color for active links, which are the links at the time the visitor clicks on them, with a color name or a #RRGGBB value
VLINK="…"	Sets the color for links the visitor has recently followed with a color name or a #RRGGBB value (how recently depends on browser settings)
LINK="…"	Sets the color for unvisited links with a color name or a #RRGGBB value

We recommend setting all Web page colors at one time—that way you can see how background, text, and link colors appear as a unit.

To change text and link colors, follow these steps:

1. Within the <BODY> tag, add the TEXT= attribute to set the color for text within the document. This example makes the text black.

When setting text colors, using a "safe" color is less important for text than for backgrounds. Dithering is less apparent in small areas, such as text.

```
<BODY TEXT="#FFFFFF">
```

2. Add the LINK= attribute to set the link color. This example uses blue (#0000FF) for the links.

```
<BODY TEXT="#FFFFFF" LINK="#0000FF">
```

3. Add the VLINK= attribute to set the color for visited links. If you set the VLINK= to the same as the link, links will not change colors even after visitors follow them. This could be confusing, but also serves to make it look like there is always new material available. This example sets the visited link to a different shade of blue.

```
<BODY TEXT="#FFFFFF" LINK="#0000FF" VLINK="#000099">
```

4. Finally, set the ALINK= or active link color. This is the color of a link while visitors are clicking on it and will not necessarily be visible in Internet Explorer 4, depending on visitor settings. This example sets ALINK= to red.

```
<BODY TEXT="#FFFFFF" LINK="#0000FF" VLINK="#000099" ALINK="#FF0000">
```

TIP

Specify fonts and increase font sizes to improve readability with dark backgrounds and light colored text.

Specifying Fonts and Font Sizes

If your visitors will be using fairly new browsers, you can use the <FONT> tag to specify font characteristics for your document, including color, size, and typeface. Table 3.10 describes the tag and attributes you'll use to set font characteristics.

TABLE 3.10: FONT CHARACTERISTICS

Tag/Attribute	Description
<FONT>	Sets font characteristics for text.
SIZE="…"	Specifies relative font size on a scale of 1 through 7. Three (3) is the default or normal size. You can also specify the relative size by using + or −, for example, +2.
COLOR="…"	Specifies font color in #RRGGBB numbers or with color names. This color applies only to the text surrounded by the <FONT> tags.
FACE="…"	Specifies type faces as a list of possible type faces, in order of preference, separated by commas—for example, "Technical, Times New Roman".
<BASEFONT>	Sets the text characteristics for the document.

As you're determining which font face to use, keep in mind that the font must be available on your visitors' computers for them to view the fonts you specify. For example, if you specify Technical as the font to use and your visitors do not have Technical, their computer will substitute a font, which might not be a font you'd consider an acceptable substitute. As a partial way of overcoming this problem, you can list multiple faces in order of preference; the machine displays the first available. For example, a list of "Comic Sans MS, Technical, Tekton, Times, Arial" will display Comic Sans MS if available, then try Technical, then Tekton, and so forth.

So, which fonts should you choose? Table 3.11 lists fonts that are commonly available on PC, Mac, and Unix platforms.

TABLE 3.11: FONTS COMMONLY AVAILABLE ON PC, MAC, AND UNIX

Windows	Macintosh	Unix
Arial	Helvetica	Helvetica
Times New Roman	Times	Times
Courier New	Courier	Courier

TIP

You might check out Microsoft's selection of fonts, which you can easily download (go to www.microsoft.com). These fonts, which are cool, are available only to visitors who have also downloaded the fonts to their computers.

To specify font characteristics, follow these steps. You can set some or all of the characteristics used in this example.

1. Identify the text to format with the <FONT> tag.

   <FONT>Look at this!**</FONT>**

2. Select a specific font using the FACE= attribute. See Table 3.11 for a list of commonly available fonts.

   <FONT FACE="Technical, Times New Roman, Times">Look at this!</FONT>

3. Change the font size using the SIZE= attribute. You set the size of text on a relative scale—from 1 to 7, with the default size being 3. Either set the size absolutely, with a number from 1 to 7, or relatively, with + or – to change the size. Almost all newer browsers (and all HTML 3.2 and 4–compliant browsers) support SIZE= to set font size. The only significant downside to setting the font

PART

1

Getting Started

size is that your visitor might already have increased (or decreased) the default font size, so your size change might have more of an effect than you would have expected.

```
<FONT FACE="Technical, Times New Roman, Times" SIZE="+2">Look at
this!</FONT>
```

4. Add a COLOR= attribute to set the color, using a color name or a #RRGGBB value.

```
<FONT FACE="Technical, Times New Roman, Times" SIZE="+2"
COLOR="#FF0000">Look at this!</FONT>
```

Figure 3.19 shows the resulting appearance.

FIGURE 3.19

Setting font characteristics can spiff up your pages and help you achieve the visual effect you want.

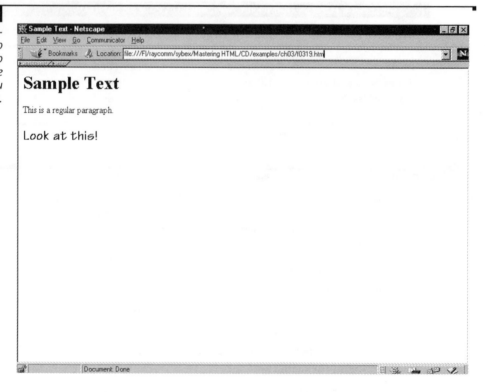

Where to Go from Here

Congratulations! You've just learned the basics of HTML, learned to apply HTML code, and even learned some of the most common tags and attributes. From here, you can jump to just about any chapter in the book. Here are a few suggestions:

- If you've just created your first page during this chapter, check out Chapter 4 to learn how to link HTML documents.
- If you want to include images in your documents, go to Chapter 7.
- If you want to add some advanced document features, such as tables, forms, frames, Java, JavaScript, or multimedia, check out Chapters 8 though 14.

Chapter

4

Linking Your Documents

Linking Your Documents

inks are the "hyper" part of hypertext—
that is, the part that you use to jump from
one document to another. Links differen-
tiate HTML documents from other electronic documents. They connect your HTML
documents to create a unified Web site as well as connect them to other information
on the Internet.

In this chapter, we discuss the structure of links and their uses and show you how to
include various kinds of links in your HTML documents. Through the examples and
instructions, you'll see that links are made up of nothing more than a Web address and
a few HTML tags, which are easy to include in your Web pages. Specifically, you'll learn
to link to pages within your site, to pages at other sites, and to specific places within
pages. In addition, you'll learn how to include e-mail links.

Links (also called *anchors*) mark text or images as elements that point to other HTML
documents, images, applets, multimedia effects, or specific places within an HTML document. Links are made up of three parts:

- An *anchor tag*, <A>, which marks the text or image as a link.

- An attribute, HREF="...", which is located within the opening anchor tag, like <A
  HREF="...">...</A>.

- An address (called a *URL*), which tells browsers the file to link to. URLs identify file locations (addresses) on the Web or on your local hard drive. These addresses can be HTML documents or elements referenced by documents, such as images, applets, scripts, and other files. The URL is always enclosed in quotes, for example, `"address.html"`.

Put these together, and a basic link looks like this:

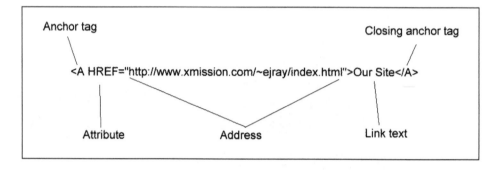

The "link text" part of this example actually appears in the document. Text links usually appear as blue and underlined text, but this depends on your visitor's computer and browser settings. Image links generally appear in a border. Figure 4.1 shows text and an image used as links.

See Chapter 8 for information about setting link colors.

All links include an anchor tag, an attribute, and a URL. The specific address you use, however, depends on where the documents you link to are located.

Throughout this chapter, *originating document* refers to the document that is linked *from* and contains the anchor tag; *linked document* refers to the document linked *to*.

FIGURE 4.1

Text links usually appear underlined; image links usually have a border around them.

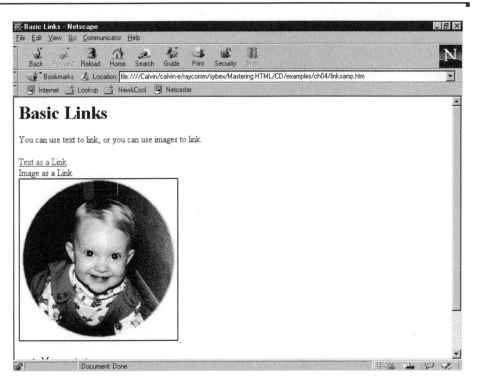

URL Anatomy

URL (pronounced U-R-ell) stands for *Uniform Resource Locator*, which is simply an address of a document on the Web or, more accurately, on the Internet. Although a URL can look complex and long, it's made up of four basic parts—protocols, hostname, folder name, and file name—each of which has a specific function. Depending on the application, a URL can include additional information, to specify user names or input to a server-side script, but fundamentally these four parts cover the basics.

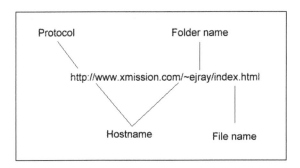

Protocol

The protocol specifies the computer language used to transfer information. Specifically, a protocol tells the browser where the information is located (for example, on a Web server, an FTP (File Tranfer Protocol) server, a local hard drive, and so on) and tells the browser what to expect from the document retrieval process (for example, whether a logon is required, what information about the document will be provided by the server, and so on).

The protocol you use depends on where the file is. For example, if you are working with an HTML document in a specific location on your local computer, you'd use `file:///` as the protocol indicator to specify that a browser should look for the file on its local computer. Or, if within your HTML document you include a link to information located on an FTP server, you'd use `ftp://` as the protocol indicator. This protocol tells the browser that it will have to provide certain logon information to retrieve it.

One of the most common protocols is HTTP, or *hypertext transfer protocol*, which indicates that information is located on an http server, more commonly known as a World Wide Web server. HTTP provides basic information about the content of documents based on their file name extensions. For example, `gif` or `jpg` extensions tell browsers that the file contains a graphic, and a `zip` extension tells the browser to save the file or run a special program to handle the file (or to ask the visitor what to do).

Although it's possible to retrieve HTML documents from other servers, particularly FTP servers, HTTP servers are nearly always a better choice because they're easier on the server than other protocols. In addition, they support features that help enhance Web pages with extra features, as discussed in Chapter 5.

About HTTP

HTTP is easier on servers than other protocols, but significantly harder on the network. HTTP generates more traffic for transferring files than most other protocols because a new connection is opened for each file. The extra traffic is in the form of the multiple packets that server and client exchange to initiate the connection. Furthermore, each and every HTTP connection wastes bandwidth while it comes up to speed for each transfer. Conversely, when FTP is not transferring files, it isn't using any network resources.

When browsers use HTTP to retrieve documents, they connect, retrieve the document, and then disconnect, meaning that while a page is being viewed, the browser is not connected to the Web server. When you click a link within a page, the browser again makes a connection, retrieves the information, and breaks the connection.

Reconnecting each time a page is accessed makes HTTP efficient from a server standpoint. These separate connections, however, also cause some difficulty from the Web author's perspective. You have no way of knowing that a visitor has been viewing your pages for the past two hours and has seen every page in the site. (If you knew that, you might provide a "you seem to be lost, can we help?" page.)

Table 4.1 lists the most common protocols you can use in HTML documents.

TABLE 4.1: COMMON PROTOCOLS

Protocol Indicator	Use
`http://`	For documents on the Web, including HTML documents and associated files.
`file:///`	For documents on the local hard drive. The third slash replaces the hostname, so you can simply type the folder and file name.
`ftp://`	For documents on an FTP server.
`gopher://`	For documents on a Gopher server.
`telnet://`	To open a telnet connection to a specific host. Good for connecting to library catalogs. This protocol indicator is chancy, however, because you don't know that telnet applications are installed or configured on the visitor's end.
`wais://`	To connect to a WAIS (Wide Area Information Server) database. This is seldom used because forms and CGI scripts offer a better way to process searches and because few visitors have WAIS clients installed and properly configured.
`mailto:`	For providing a window in which readers can send an e-mail message to the specified address. Most newer browsers support `mailto:`, although it is not a standard or an officially accepted protocol. This indicator does not include //.
`news:`	To connect to a newsgroup or a specific article in a group. This is not guaranteed, though, because you don't know which newsgroups your visitors might have access to. Also, before using the `news:` protocol, consider that articles periodically expire and disappear from the server. This indicator does not include //.

Hostname

The hostname is the name of the server that holds HTML documents and related files. Each server has a specific address, and all documents stored in the server share the same hostname. For example, if your Internet service provider's server name is xmission, your hostname would be something like `www.xmission.com`.

As an information provider, you are not limited to using the server name as the hostname portion of your URL. Instead, you can use a *virtual domain*, which gives you a hostname of your own, but your files still reside on a host computer. Virtual domains are becoming a popular way for small companies and organizations to look bigger than they really are.

For example, if you put your files on a server called `xmission.com`, your Web address might look something like the following:

```
http://www.xmission.com/~accountname/filename.html
```

In this example, the address includes the protocol indicator, a special folder on the server (indicated by the tilde [~]), an account name, and a file name.

A virtual domain changes the address to eliminate the special folder and account names and replaces these with a new host (domain) name. For example, a Web address using a virtual domain (ours, actually) might look like this:

```
http://www.raycomm.com/index.html
```

This example includes the protocol indicator, the domain name (`www.raycomm.com`), and the file name (`index.html`).

The easiest way to get a virtual domain is to ask your Internet service provider to set it up for you. It might charge in the neighborhood of $50 to $100 to set it up, plus a $100 charge for registering your domain name with InterNIC, the main domain name registration service, for two years. If you do a little homework with your Internet service provider, however, you can set up a virtual domain yourself and save a few dollars. Go to `www.internic.net/`, click the Registration Services link, and follow the on-screen instructions.

Folder Names

Folder names are the next chunk of information in a URL, indicating the folder in which files are located. Folders perform the same function on a Web server that they perform on your PC: They organize documents. There's virtually no limit to how deep you can nest folders, and there's no limit as to what files the folders can contain. For that matter, you don't even need a folder—everything in a site could be at the top level.

NOTE

The terms *folder* and *directory* are interchangeable. Folders are more commonly used in the context of desktop computers; directories are more common for older versions of Windows and for Unix.

When naming folders and files, include only the following:

- Alphabetic characters (upper- and lowercase)
- Numbers
- Symbols, including the dollar sign ($), hyphen (-), underscore (_), and period (.)

If the folder name contains characters other than these, you need to include the hexadecimal (hex) representations of those characters. For example, some operating systems support spaces in file names. To include spaces in URLs, you need to use the corresponding hex characters in the link name. If someone tells you to link to a document named Document B.html, you would include the hex characters %20 in the URL where the space appears. So, rather than your link looking like this:

```
<A HREF="Document B.html">link text goes here</A>
```

it would look like this:

```
<A HREF="Document%20B.html">link text goes here</A>
```

We strongly recommend not using special characters in folder or file names to ensure that anyone using any operating system can access your files.

File Names

File names are the names of specific HTML documents and consist of two pieces of information:

- A name, which identifies the file to display
- A file extension, which specifies the file type—an HTML document, an image, a text file, and so on

If you're creating links to other documents and other locations on the Internet, you might see a wide range of file names. Some will be short and cryptic—frntmter .htm, mynewhmp.htm—as a result of either the developer using Windows 3.1x or (far less likely) as a result of the server using Windows 3.1x. You might, however, also see much longer file names if both the server and the developer use Windows 95 or NT, Macintosh, Unix, or some combination. Regardless of the platform or platforms that you use, you'll need to use the file name as it was provided to you. That is, even if you're using Windows 3.1*x*, you still won't have any difficulty pointing to a long file name on a Web server, like:

```
http://www.xmission.com/~ejray/very_long_filename_example.html
```

On many Web servers, certain files are retrieved by default if a folder name but no file name is specified in the URL. For example, on the server we use, `index.html` is the default file name. If you point to a relative URL such as `<A HREF="services/">link text</A>`, the server automatically displays the `index.html` file if it exists. If it does not exist, the server might display only the folder listing.

This explains why many URLs have only a hostname, for example, `http://www.yahoo.com/`. The main document is named with the default file from that server. This naming technique makes the URL shorter and easier to remember. Additionally, by serving a specific file automatically when no name is specified, you can prevent visitors from just browsing through all the files in the folder.

Ask your server administrator for the default file name for the server (or read the instructions your server administration provides). Most ISPs provide this sort of information in a visible help page immediately off their home pages.

File Name Extensions Matter

File name extensions are significant because they identify the type of information that the file contains. For example, your browser recognizes a perfectly valid HTML document with an extension of `html` and displays it as you might expect. If you rename an HTML document with a `txt` extension and then try to view it in your browser, you'll see the actual HTML code, not the formatted HTML document.

If your documents are on a Web server, browsers must recognize the extension and display the information appropriately. However, in between the recognizing and displaying stages is an intermediate step. The Web server recognizes the document with an `htm` or `html` extension as having a MIME type of `text/html`, which, in this case, tells the browser that it's an HTML document. (MIME stands for Multipurpose Internet Mail Extensions and is the standard used to identify the content of documents on the Internet.) If you rename the file with a `txt` extension, the MIME type indicates that it's a text document and tells the browser to display it as such. In this case, the browser displays the un-interpreted source code.

CONTINUED

File name extensions become more significant if you provide documents other than HTML files or basic images on your site. Web browsers use MIME-type identifiers for all documents. On occasion, a server will be misconfigured and will need to have additional MIME types added or have existing definitions changed. For example, if you placed Word documents with a doc extension on a server, you might need to ask the server administrator to tell the server to send those documents out with a MIME type of application/ms-word or application/octet-stream. You do this so that visitors' browsers display the document in a word processor program or prompt them to save the file to disk.

See Chapter 5 for a more comprehensive discussion of MIME types and how servers send files.

Types of URLs

URLs vary depending on the location of the document to which you're linking. For example, a URL will be longer and include more information if the file is on the World Wide Web. A URL will be shorter and include less information if the file is on your local computer or server. Basically, URLs fall into two categories:

- Absolute
- Relative

An absolute URL contains all the information necessary to identify files on the Internet. A relative URL points to files in the same folder or on the same server. In other words, the file linked to is relative to the originating document. Figure 4.2 illustrates absolute and relative URLs.

Absolute URLs

An absolute URL contains the protocol indicator, hostname, folder name, and file name. Absolute URLs are similar to addresses used by the U.S. Postal Service, which include a name, street address, apartment number (if applicable), city, state, and zip code. If some of the information is missing—say, the street number or house number—the carrier can't deliver the mail to the right person.

Similarly, if the protocol indicator or hostname is missing from a URL, browsers cannot link to a specific file because they won't know where or how to look for the file. Likewise, if the folder or file name is missing, browsers won't know which piece of information to pull up off the server.

FIGURE 4.2

Relative URLs point only to documents near the originating document, and absolute URLs point to documents on the Web.

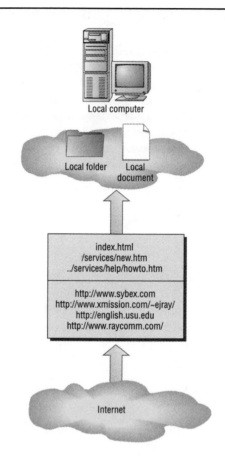

Here are some absolute URLs:

```
http://www.xmission.com/services/index.html
http://www.altavista.digital.com/
ftp://ftp.raycomm.com/download/readme.txt
```

Relative URLs

A relative URL usually contains only the folder name and file name or even just the file name. You can use these partial URLs when you're pointing to a file that's located within the same folder or on the same server as the originating file. In these cases, a browser doesn't need the server name or protocol indicator because it assumes the files are located in a folder or on a server that's relative to the originating document.

Using a relative URL is similar to instructing someone to look "next door" for a piece of information. In this case, next door is relative to where you are; it's accurate and complete only if you originate the request from a place that has a next door neighbor with the correct information.

You can use relative URLs to refer to documents in relation to the originating document (called a document-relative URL) or to the server on which the originating document resides (called a server-relative URL).

Document-Relative URLs

Figure 4.3 illustrates how relative folders and files relate.

FIGURE 4.3

You can indicate each of these locations with a relative URL when linking from other nearby documents.

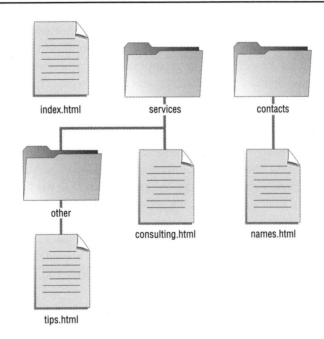

You'll often use a document-relative URL when you're developing or testing a set of HTML documents. As we developed examples for this book, we used document-relative URLs and put all the files in a single folder. In fact, in most cases, we included only the file name.

When linking from `index.html`, use the following URLs:

```
services/consulting.html
services/other/tips.html
```

When linking from `consulting.html` to `tips.html`, use the following URLs:

`other/tips.html`

If you're familiar with the Unix and DOS convention of using a ".." to move up a directory in the hierarchy, you can use that as well to link to documents in other folders. For example, to link from `consulting.html` to `names.html` (see Figure 4.3, earlier in this chapter), you could use a link like this:

`<A HREF="../contacts/names.html>link text</A>`

The address indicates moving up a level (the .. part), then into the `contacts` folder, and then into the `names.html` document. Likewise, a link within `tips.html` to the `names.html` file would look like this:

`<A HREF="../../contacts/names.html>link text</A>`

Nested folders that lie deep within the server hierarchy or sets of folders that might be used and moved as a unit can benefit from these links. These relative URLs can link all the documents within the unit (say, everything within the drawing), and then you can move the unit to other servers or even to other locations within the specific server hierarchy. All the links among the documents will continue to work.

Server-relative URLs

A server-relative URL is relative to the *server root*—that is, relative to the hostname part of the URL. Figure 4.4 illustrates how documents and folders relate to servers.

Server-relative URLs have a forward slash (/) at the beginning of the file name, which indicates that you interpret the path of the document from the top of the current server (the server root), rather than from the current document location. For example, from anywhere in our site, we could use a server-relative URL to display our home page with a link to `/index.html`, which would display the `index.html` file right under the top of the server. Some server-relative URLs include:

`/index.html`

`/contacts/names.html`

Likewise, you can link to folders and file names with a server-relative URL. From the `tips.html` document, you can link to the `names.html` document within the contacts folder with a link to a URL like the preceding example.

Server-relative URLs are useful when you are linking to a specific location on the server (such as contact information) that isn't likely to change and that isn't clearly relative to the current document. For example, you might use a server-relative URL if you're working on a document that does not yet have a specific home on the server but still links to specific pages (such as the home page). If you don't use a server-relative URL, you'd have to code the server name into the URL, and then if you had to change servers or move the documents to a different server, the links would no longer work.

FIGURE 4.4

The same set of files as in Figure 4.3, positioned in relation to the server

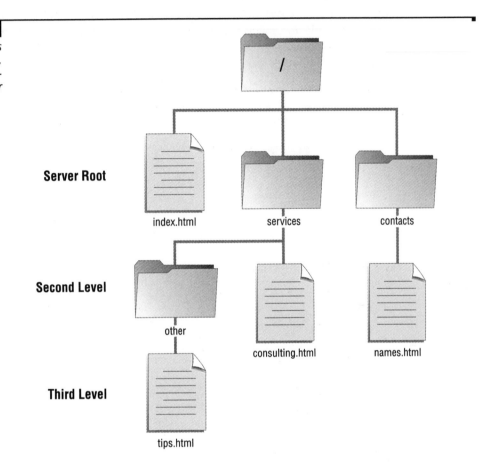

Server Root

index.html   services   contacts

Second Level

other   consulting.html   names.html

Third Level

tips.html

 **TIP**

Use relative URLs whenever possible because relative URLs let you move your documents around without breaking too many links. If you link all your documents with absolute URLs, you'll break all those links each time you move the documents around on a server or move them to a different server.

Setting the Base Location for a Document

A lot of times, you'll develop HTML documents and put them in one folder, only to later move some of the documents to a different folder. When you move documents to new folders, all the document-relative links will be broken. Rather than changing all the relative URLs, you can use the BASE HREF= attribute in the <HEAD> tag to specify what the relative URLs are relative to.

For example, suppose you want to move a document called www.raycomm.com/test/long.html out of the "test" folder into the server root. Rather than editing all the links, you can just add <BASE HREF="http://www.raycomm.com/test/long.htm"> within the <HEAD> tag, like this:

```
<HEAD><TITLE>Document Title</TITLE>
<BASE HREF="http://www.raycomm.com/test/long.htm">
</HEAD>
```

Including the BASE HREF= in the head tag resets all relative links in the document so that all relative URLs point correctly into the test folder to the real locations of the documents. Without the BASE HREF= tag, all relative URLs from the long.html document would point to (nonexistent) documents within the server root.

Constructing Link Anchors

Link anchors are the glue that holds the Web together. Fortunately, they are simple to construct—they require only a single tag and careful use of the URL. In this section, we'll look at how to link to documents in the same folder, in different folders, and on different servers.

Linking to Documents in the Same Folder

The basic link connects one document to another file in the same folder. Figure 4.5 shows two documents within the same folder.

To create a link from DocumentA.html to DocumentB.html, you include the anchor tag (<A>), the HREF= attribute, and a URL that points to the file name of DocumentB. In this case, the link from the originating document (DocumentA) might look like this:

```
<A HREF="DocumentB.html">link text goes here</A>
```

FIGURE 4.5

DocumentA.html
and DocumentB
.html *both reside
in a folder called
FatFolder.*

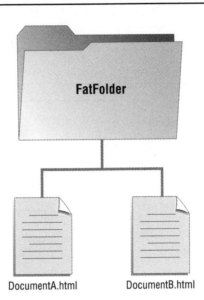

When linking to documents within the same folder, you need include only the file name. Without additional information, browsers will look in the same folder as the originating document. In this sense, both the locations of DocumentA and DocumentB are indicated relative to the folder in which they reside.

Linking to Documents in a Different Folder

Figure 4.6 shows two documents located in separate folders.

To create a link from Aboutus.html to consulting.html, you include a URL that contains two pieces of information:

- A folder name, which specifies the folder on the server
- A file name and extension, which specifies the exact file to display

In this case, the link might look like this:

```
<A HREF="services/consulting.html">link text</A>
```

The folder (services) and file name (consulting.html) are separated by a forward slash (/), which indicates the end of the folder name and the beginning of the file name.

FIGURE 4.6

Aboutus.html *resides in a folder called* ACMEInc; consulting.html *resides in a subfolder called* services.

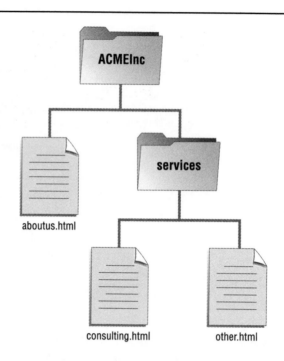

Linking to Documents on the Web

When you link from one document to another document on the Web, the documents might reside on different servers. Figure 4.7 shows an originating document with a link to a document on the Web.

To create a link to futile.html in the attempts folder of the www.coyote.org server, you need to include the following information:

- The protocol indicator, which specifies how the server and browser communicate
- The hostname, which tells the browser the name of the server that holds the information
- The folder name, if necessary, which specifies the folder on the server
- The file name, if necessary, which specifies the exact file to display

So, your URL might look like this:

```
http://www.coyote.org/attempts/futile.html
```

and the full link text would look like this:

```
<A HREF=" http://www.coyote.org/attempts/futile.html">Last Try</A>
```

FIGURE 4.7

The acmeinfo
.html *file resides
on a server called*
www.acme.com;
futile.html
*resides on a server
called* www.coyote
.org *in the*
attempts *folder.*

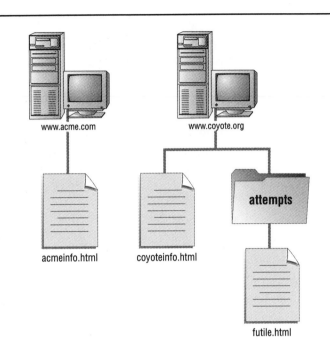

Linking to a Specific Location in a Document

Whereas a link anchor connects to an HTML document, a *name anchor* connects to a specific location within an HTML document. Thus, using a name anchor gives you more precise control over your links.

For example, you can use a name anchor to link to a subheading. In a document about your organization's services, you might have a Proposals subheading. When you link to that subheading with a name anchor, a visitor can go directly to that section of the document.

Forming Name Anchors

Name anchors are made up of three parts:

- An anchor tag, <A>, which marks the text or the location within a document as a target
- An attribute, NAME=, which identifies the anchor as a name anchor
- A name, enclosed in quotes, which identifies the specific location

Put these together, and a basic name anchor looks like this:

```
<A NAME="location">A location goes here</A>
```

The text between the opening and closing name anchor tags ("A location goes here" in this example) is visible in your document, but, unlike link anchors, it is not highlighted nor is any other specific visual indicator associated with it. You can use the name anchor tag in combination with other tags in your document.

Here's the process for creating a name anchor:

1. Start with a subheading.

```
<H2>Proposals</H2>
```

2. Add the anchor tag.

```
<H2><A>Proposals</A></H2>
```

3. Add the name attribute (use something specific that you'll be able to remember).

```
<H2><A NAME="proposals">Proposals</A></H2>
```

That's all there is to it. You will see nothing different in your document when you view it with your browser, but you have just provided the tools necessary to link directly to a subsection of your document, as described in the next section.

Linking to Name Anchors

After you create a name anchor, you can link to it. To continue with our example, the Proposals section is in a document that has the file name `services.html`, which is in the `information` folder on the `www.xmission.com` server.

A link to that document looks like this:

```
<A HREF="http://www.xmission.com/information/services.html">Link</A>
```

A link to the Proposals section, using an absolute URL, looks like this:

```
<A HREF="http://www.xmission.com/information/services.html#proposals">
Link</A>
```

How much information you include in a URL that links to a place within a document depends on where the linked document is located, as shown in Table 4.2.

You can't link to NAME= anchors that don't exist, and you can't add them to other documents on the Web. To ensure that visitors can link to specific places within your documents, include NAME= anchors in places likely to be visited.

PART

I

Getting Started

TABLE 4.2: URLS FOR VARIOUS DOCUMENT LOCATIONS	
From Within	**Link Looks Like**
The same document	`<A HREF="#proposals">`
The same folder, different document	`<A HREF="services.html#proposals">`
The same server (different folder and document, server-relative URL)	`<A HREF="information/services.html#proposals">`
A different server	`<A HREF="http://www.xmission.com/information/services.html#proposals">Link</A>`

Inserting E-mail Links

An e-mail link uses the `mailto:` protocol and gives visitors an easy way to communicate with you. As we mentioned, the `mailto:` protocol is not an HTML standard, but it is widely used and recognized.

To create an e-mail link, simply add an anchor link with the `mailto:` protocol indicator and the e-mail address. For example, you might include a link to send the authors of this book e-mail with a link like this:

```
<A HREF="mailto:info@raycomm.com">Send Feedback</A>
```

MASTERING THE OPPORTUNITIES

HTML 4 Opportunity

The HTML 4 specification lets you add link descriptions that pop up on the screen when visitors move their mouse over the link, as shown here:

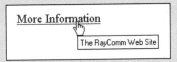

To add pop-up descriptions to your links, simply include the TITLE= attribute in the anchor tag, like this:

```
<A HREF="http://www.raycomm.com" TITLE="The RayComm Web Site">More
Information</A>
```

Where to Go from Here

In this chapter, you've learned about the various flavors of URLs and how to use them to construct links. You also learned how to label locations within your documents with name anchors and link to those locations. Armed with this information, you are now ready to tackle just about any HTML task.

- Next up in Chapter 5, you'll learn to develop Style Sheets—the newest and most comprehensive way to add formatting to your HTML documents.

- See Chapter 6 for information about publishing HTML documents on a Web server and for information about MIME types.

- Check out Chapter 2, specifically the sections on testing, for reminders about how to test your documents—before and after publishing them.

- See Part II, starting with Chapter 6, for information about adding images, tables, forms, frames, and multimedia.

- See Chapter 8 for information about setting link colors and other advanced formatting.

- See Chapter 23 for information about developing marketing sites and Chapter 24 for information about developing intranet sites.

Chapter

5

Using Style Sheets

FEATURING

Using Style Sheets

Using Style Sheets—formally known as the World Wide Web Consortium *Cascading Style Sheets* recommendation, level 1 (or *CSS1*)—is one of the best ways to format HTML documents easily and consistently. Adopted by the W3 Consortium in December 1996, Style Sheets take a step toward separating presentation from content, returning HTML to its function-oriented roots yet allowing you almost total control over page presentation.

Are Style Sheets here to stay? Yes. In fact, the HTML 4 specification deprecates many formatting tags and attributes (such as <FONT> and ALIGN=) in favor of Style Sheets.

In this chapter, you'll see how Style Sheets enhance the effectiveness of HTML and how you can benefit from using them. You'll learn how to apply Style Sheets to your HTML documents and how to develop the Style Sheet. We include some examples that illustrate how to implement Style Sheets, but you'll want to take a look at the Cascading Style Sheets section of the Master's Reference to get all the specifics. You'll find that Style Sheets give you an enormous number of formatting options.

How Do Style Sheets Work?

As we mentioned in Chapter 1, HTML is a markup language that you use to identify structural elements in a document. For example, you can specify that this element is a first-level heading, this one is a bullet point, this one is a block quotation, and so on by manually inserting formatting tags and attributes. The browser (with input from the visitor) controls formatting and layout.

Manually inserting all these formatting tags can quickly become a tedious process. With Style Sheets, however, you specify formatting only once, and it is applied throughout the document. If you've used styles in a word processor, you're familiar with this concept.

Style Sheets give you nearly the layout and format control you may be accustomed to in programs such as PageMaker or Quark. You can control how page elements look, where they appear, their color and size, the font they use, and so on. Now, you—rather than browsers and visitors—can determine page appearance.

Browsers, Visitors, and Style Sheets

Unfortunately, Style Sheets are available only to visitors using Internet Explorer 3 (or later) and Netscape Navigator 4 (or later). Visitors using earlier versions of these browsers or other browsers will see a plain HTML document that includes little more than the logical formatting elements—headings, paragraphs, tables, and lists, with no colors.

In addition, because Style Sheet technology is new, browsers don't yet provide stable or consistent support. Pages that use Style Sheets will appear differently in different browsers.

Also, your visitors still have some control over the document appearance, regardless of the formatting you supply in the Style Sheet. They can disable Style Sheets or override them with their personal preferences for colors and fonts.

Some Advantages of Using Style Sheets

In addition to giving you more control over how your documents appear to visitors, Style Sheets let you manage HTML documents more easily than if they were filled with formatting tags. When you place these tags in the Style Sheet, your document is less cluttered.

Style Sheets also reduce the time you spend developing and maintaining HTML documents. Rather than manually formatting paragraphs of text, you simply change the style definition in one place—the Style Sheet—and the Style Sheet applies the definition to all occurrences in the HTML document. No muss, no fuss.

Finally, Style Sheets give you flexibility from document to document within a Web site. Even if you set up a Style Sheet that applies to all pages in the site, you can set up individual Style Sheets to apply to individual HTML documents. The individual Style Sheet overrides the global one. And, you can further tweak individual Style Sheets to accommodate special text formatting, such as a document in which certain paragraphs should appear in a different color.

Implementing Style Sheets

As you're perusing the rest of this chapter, remember that your HTML documents and the associated Style Sheets work as a team. HTML documents carry the content, and Style Sheets carry the formatting information. As you'll see, developing Style Sheets is a two-part process:

- You connect (or associate) the Style Sheet to the HTML document.

- Then you develop the actual Style Sheet, complete with all the formatting options.

Associating Style Sheets with HTML Documents

You can associate Style Sheets with your HTML documents in four ways:

- You can embed the Style Sheet in the HTML document by defining it between the opening and closing <HEAD> tags.

- You can store the Style Sheet in a separate document and either link or import the Style Sheet to associate it with the HTML document.

- You can apply style definitions to specified parts of an HTML document.

- You can use inline style definitions.

Embedding the Style Sheet in the HTML Document

Embedding the Style Sheet, which is the easiest of the four methods, means inserting the <STYLE> tags, along with style information, between the <HEAD> tags. Figure 5.1 shows how you do this.

FIGURE 5.1

An HTML document with inserted <STYLE> tags

Embedded Style Sheet

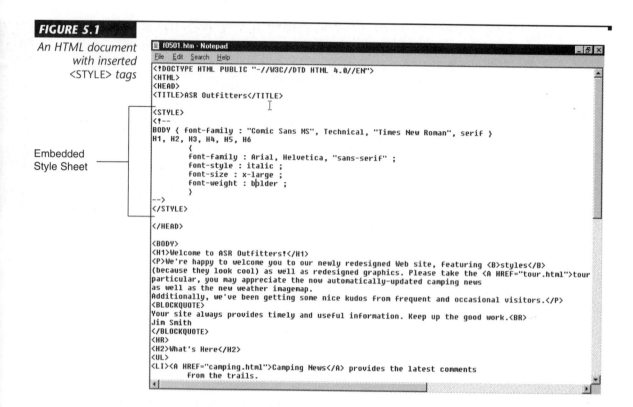

```
<!DOCTYPE HTML PUBLIC "-//W3C//DTD HTML 4.0//EN">
<HTML>
<HEAD>
<TITLE>ASR Outfitters</TITLE>

<STYLE>
<!--
BODY { font-family : "Comic Sans MS", Technical, "Times New Roman", serif }
H1, H2, H3, H4, H5, H6
        {
        font-family : Arial, Helvetica, "sans-serif" ;
        font-style : italic ;
        font-size : x-large ;
        font-weight : bolder ;
        }
-->
</STYLE>

</HEAD>

<BODY>
<H1>Welcome to ASR Outfitters!</H1>
<P>We're happy to welcome you to our newly redesigned Web site, featuring <B>styles</B>
(because they look cool) as well as redesigned graphics. Please take the <A HREF="tour.html">tour
particular, you may appreciate the now automatically-updated camping news
as well as the new weather imagemap.
Additionally, we've been getting some nice kudos from frequent and occasional visitors.</P>
<BLOCKQUOTE>
Your site always provides timely and useful information. Keep up the good work.<BR>
Jim Smith
</BLOCKQUOTE>
<HR>
<H2>What's Here</H2>
<UL>
<LI><A HREF="camping.html">Camping News</A> provides the latest comments
        from the trails.
```

Embedding Style Sheets makes maintaining or updating styles easy because you don't have to work with two or more documents (the Style Sheet document and the HTML document)—you simply open the HTML document and adjust the Style Sheet code. If you are working with multiple documents or documents that you'll update frequently, however, you'll probably want to use another method. If you embed the Style Sheet in every document, you'll have to adjust it in every document.

 **TIP**

At the time of writing, embedding is the only method that works reliably in both Microsoft Internet Explorer 4 and Netscape Navigator 4.

To embed a Style Sheet in an HTML document, apply the tags and attributes shown in Table 5.1 between the <HEAD> tags.

TABLE 5.1: STYLE SHEET TAGS AND ATTRIBUTES

Tag/Attribute	Description
`<STYLE>`	Specifies the Style Sheet area within an HTML document. Within this section, you can define or import formatting.
`<!-- ... -->`	A comment tag that hides Style Sheet contents from non–style-capable browsers.
`TYPE="text/css"`	Specifies the type of Style Sheet. Valid choices, at the time of writing, include `text/css`, for Cascading Style Sheets (standard and covered in this chapter), and `text/jss`, for JavaScript Style Sheets.

To embed a minimal Style Sheet (that, in this example, colors paragraphs red) in an existing document, follow these steps:

1. Start with a functional document header.

```
<!DOCTYPE HTML PUBLIC "-//W3C//DTD HTML 4.0//EN">
<HTML>
<HEAD>
<TITLE>ASR Outfitters</TITLE>
</HEAD>
```

NOTE

In practice, style definitions also work within the document body, but the HTML 3.2 and 4 specifications require that the style definition block goes between the document <HEAD> tags.

2. Add opening and closing <STYLE> tags.

```
<!DOCTYPE HTML PUBLIC "-//W3C//DTD HTML 4.0//EN">
<HTML>
<HEAD>
<TITLE>ASR Outfitters</TITLE>
<STYLE>
</STYLE>
</HEAD>
```

3. Add the comment (`<!-- -->`) tag to hide the contents from non–style-capable browsers.

```
<!DOCTYPE HTML PUBLIC "-//W3C//DTD HTML 4.0//EN">
<HTML>
<HEAD>
<TITLE>ASR Outfitters</TITLE>
<STYLE>
<!--


-->
</STYLE>
</HEAD>
```

Browsers that do not support Style Sheets ignore the tags but display the text that appears between them. Adding comment tags within the <STYLE> tags ensures that the styles will not appear as content in older or less-capable browsers.

4. Add style definitions within the comment tags. In this (minimal) example, we specify that paragraph text is red.

```
<!DOCTYPE HTML PUBLIC "-//W3C//DTD HTML 4.0//EN">
<HTML>
<HEAD>
<TITLE>ASR Outfitters</TITLE>
<STYLE>
<!-
P {color: red}
-->
</STYLE>
</HEAD>
```

That's it! To test your embedded Style Sheet, simply open the HTML document in Internet Explorer or Netscape Navigator.

Storing Style Sheets Separately

A separate Style Sheet is simply a plain text file and includes only the style definitions. Develop a separate Style Sheet any time you're working with several HTML documents, particularly if they share similar formatting. In this case, you develop a single Style Sheet and apply it to all the HTML documents, as shown in Figure 5.2. You can then make a formatting change in all the documents by simply changing the Style Sheet.

FIGURE 5.2

When you develop a separate Style Sheet, you can easily apply styles to many HTML documents.

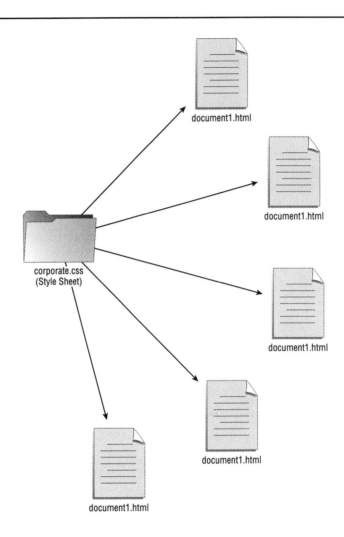

document1.html

document1.html

document1.html

corporate.css
(Style Sheet)

document1.html

document1.html

 TIP

Even if you're only working with a few HTML documents, consider developing a separate Style Sheet. You never know how many HTML documents your site will eventually include.

After you develop the separate Style Sheet document, you associate it with the HTML document(s) using either of these methods:

- Importing
- Linking

Both methods work only with Internet Explorer.

Importing This method is handy when you are developing multiple Style Sheet pages that each has a particular function. For example, as illustrated in Figure 5.3, you can develop a page that applies corporate styles, one that applies styles for your department, and another that specifies particular document formatting. Rather than wading through a 10-page Style Sheet, you work with multiple smaller ones.

FIGURE 5.3

Importing allows you to easily maintain a detailed Style Sheet.

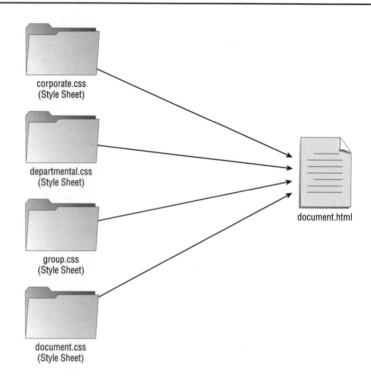

corporate.css
(Style Sheet)

departmental.css
(Style Sheet)

group.css
(Style Sheet)

document.css
(Style Sheet)

document.html

Table 5.2 describes the tags and attributes you use to import Style Sheets.

TABLE 5.2: TAGS AND ATTRIBUTES FOR IMPORTING STYLE SHEETS	
Tag/Attribute	**Description**
`<STYLE>`	Specifies the Style Sheet area within an HTML document. Within this section, you can define or import formatting.
`<!-- ... -->`	A comment tag that hides contents from non–style-capable browsers.
`TYPE="text/css"`	Specifies the type of a Style Sheet. Valid choices, at the time of writing, include `text/css`, for Cascading Style Sheets (standard and covered in this chapter), and `text/jss`, for JavaScript Style Sheets.
`@import url(...)`	Imports a Style Sheet. Usage is `url(http://mystyles.com/new.css)`.

To import a Style Sheet, follow these steps:

1. Start with a complete style block, such as the following code:

```
<!DOCTYPE HTML PUBLIC "-//W3C//DTD HTML 4.0//EN">
<HTML>
<HEAD>
<TITLE>ASR Outfitters</TITLE>
<STYLE>
<!--

-->
</STYLE>
</HEAD>
```

2. Within a style block or Style Sheet, add a line similar to the following:

```
<STYLE>
<!--
@import url('red.css');
-->
</STYLE>
```

A complete style block that does nothing but import two Style Sheets would look like the following:

```
<STYLE>
<!--
```

```
@import url('red.css');
@import url('redder.css');
-->
</STYLE>
```

Linking   This method has a distinct advantage over the other methods: It gives visitors a choice of Style Sheets to use for a specific page. For example, you can link one Style Sheet to a page that visitors will read online and link a different Style Sheet to a page that visitors will print, as shown in Figure 5.4. Theoretically, you could even develop a style sheet (as browsers implement this functionality) optimized for aural presentation. Although you could do this with importing, linking the Style Sheet is a better long-term choice because future browser versions should offer visitors the option to select from among multiple Style Sheets.

FIGURE 5.4

Linking lets you apply Style Sheets for specific uses.

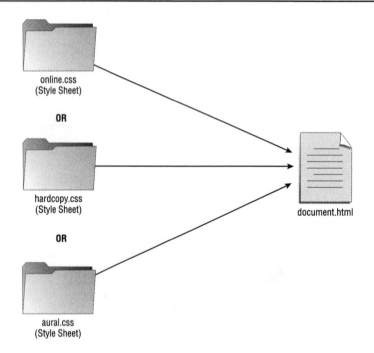

online.css
(Style Sheet)

OR

hardcopy.css
(Style Sheet)

OR

aural.css
(Style Sheet)

document.html

Table 5.3 explains the tags and attributes you use to link Style Sheets to HTML documents.

TABLE 5.3: TAGS AND ATTRIBUTES FOR LINKING STYLE SHEETS	
Tag/Attribute	**Description**
`<LINK>`	References a Style Sheet.
`REL=StyleSheet`	Specifies that the referenced file is a Style Sheet. You can also use `Alternate Style Sheet` to reference optional Style Sheets.
`TYPE="text/css"`	Specifies the type of a Style Sheet. Valid choices, at the time of writing, include `text/css`, for Cascading Style Sheets (standard and covered in this chapter), and `text/jss`, for JavaScript Style Sheets.
`HREF="URL"`	Identifies the Style Sheet source as a standard URL.
`TITLE="..."`	Names the Style Sheet. Unnamed Style Sheets are always applied. Named Style Sheets are applied by default or provided as options, depending on the `REL` attribute used.

TIP

At the time of writing, only Internet Explorer 4 supports linking.

To link a Style Sheet to an HTML document, follow these steps:

1. Start with a complete HTML `<HEAD>` section, such as the following code:

```
<!DOCTYPE HTML PUBLIC "-//W3C//DTD HTML 4.0//EN">
<HTML>
<HEAD>
<TITLE>ASR Outfitters</TITLE>
</HEAD>
```

2. Add the `<LINK>` tag.

```
<!DOCTYPE HTML PUBLIC "-//W3C//DTD HTML 4.0//EN">
<HTML>
<HEAD>
<TITLE>ASR Outfitters</TITLE>
<LINK>
</HEAD>
```

3. Specify the `REL` and `TYPE` values of Style Sheet and `text/css` to link to a standard Style Sheet.

```
<LINK REL="StyleSheet" TYPE="text/css">
```

4. Specify the address of the Style Sheet with the HREF= attribute. Specify either a relative URL, as in the sample code, or an absolute URL.

```
<LINK REL="StyleSheet" HREF="blue.css" TYPE="text/css">
```

There you go! To link your HTML document to more than one Style Sheet, simply include multiple <LINK> tags complete with each of the Style Sheets to which they link. For example, you might link an HTML document to a generic Style Sheet that contains basic style definitions and then also link it to a more specific Style Sheet that contains definitions suitable to a particular style of document—instructions, marketing, and so on. If you link to multiple Style Sheets, all take effect. If you define the same element in multiple sheets, however, the later links override the previous links.

The HTML specification indicates that you can also link your HTML documents to optional Style Sheets using the REV="Alternate Style Sheet" attribute so that visitors can choose which styles to use. Theoretically, you can provide optional Style Sheets that let visitors choose a low-bandwidth style for viewing over a modem connection or a high-bandwidth style with lots of cool images for viewing over a high-speed connection. Or, you can present choices for high-resolution and high color depth monitors and provide alternatives for standard monitors at lower color depth. At the time of writing, however, neither Internet Explorer nor Netscape Navigator support optional Style Sheets, and only Internet Explorer supports linking.

Applying Style Sheets to Parts of Documents

So far, you've seen how to apply Style Sheets to entire HTML documents. You can also apply styles included in a Style Sheet to specific parts of HTML documents, as shown in Figure 5.5. This is called applying *style classes*, which you define in your Style Sheet. For example, suppose you specify in a Style Sheet that the first line of all paragraphs is indented. You might find though that paragraphs after a bulleted list should not be indented because they continue the information from the paragraph above the list. To address this issue, you can manually format the paragraph, which might be appropriate for a one-time occurrence. A better solution, however, is to set up a new class of paragraph tag within your style definition called, say, continue. You can use this new paragraph class whenever the first line of a paragraph should not be indented.

FIGURE 5.5

Applying style classes, you can specify how parts of HTML documents appear.

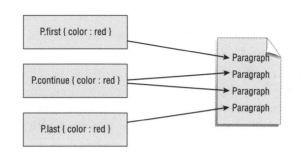

Table 5.4 describes the tags and attributes you use to apply classes.

TABLE 5.4: TAGS AND ATTRIBUTES FOR APPLYING CLASSES

Tag/Attribute	Description
<SPAN>	Holds style attributes and applies them to the HTML code between the opening and closing tags. Surround letters and words with these tags.
<DIV>	Holds style attributes and applies them to the HTML code between the opening and closing tags. Surround paragraphs or other block-level elements with these.
CLASS="..."	References a style class to apply to a specified part of an HTML document.
ID="uniquen"	Specifies a unique name associated with a specific style definition. You can use this only once within a Style Sheet.

You can apply a class to an existing HTML tag, or you can use the <DIV> and <SPAN> tags to specify that the class apply to other elements—such as specific letters or words—not individually specified by an HTML tag.

Applying Classes to an HTML Tag   You apply a class to an existing HTML tag— such as <P>, <H1>, <UL>, and so on—to specify formatting for a group of items. To apply classes within an HTML document, follow these steps:

1. Start with an existing paragraph within an HTML document.

```
<P>Many people buy ASR products despite the higher cost.</P>
```

2. Add the CLASS= attribute to the opening <P> tag, like this:

```
<P CLASS="">Many people buy ASR products despite the higher cost.</P>
```

3. Add the name of the paragraph class. (You'll see how to define and name classes when you develop the Style Sheet later in this chapter.)

```
<P CLASS="continue">Many people buy ASR products despite the higher
cost.</P>
```

That's it!

If you have a specific formatting need—a one-time need—you can define a style ID and then apply the ID= attribute in the place of the CLASS= attribute in the preceding example. You would end up with something like this:

```
<P ID="538fv1">Many people buy ASR products despite the higher cost.</P>
```

We don't generally recommend this one-time formatting use, but it can be appropriate in some cases, including in particular Microsoft's Dynamic HTML implementation, covered in Chapter 13.

Applying Classes to Other Document Parts   You can also apply classes to specific parts of an HTML document that do not have existing tags. For example, suppose you want to make the first letter in the document body a drop cap (like the first letter of each chapter in this book). Because no drop cap tag exists to designate the first letter, you must specify the letter to which the style applies.

To apply classes to specific parts of an HTML document, use the <DIV> and <SPAN> tags, described earlier in Table 5.4. These tags provide a place to apply class formatting when there's no existing HTML tag.

You use the <DIV> tag to apply classes to block-level sections of a document. Here are the steps:

1. Start with an existing HTML document and text.

```
<P>Many people buy ASR products despite the higher cost.</P>
```

2. Add the <DIV> tags around the section.

```
<DIV>
<P>Many people buy ASR products despite the higher cost.</P>
</DIV>
```

3. Add the appropriate CLASS= attribute.

```
<DIV CLASS="notice">
<P>Many people buy ASR products despite the higher cost.</P>
</DIV>
```

Use the <SPAN> tag to apply classes to characters or words. For example, to apply the firstuse class (that you define elsewhere) to a word, follow these steps:

1. Start with an existing HTML document and text.

```
<P>Many people buy ASR products despite the higher cost.</P>
```

2. Add the <SPAN> opening and closing tags.

<P>Many people buy **<SPAN>**ASR products**</SPAN>** despite the higher cost.</P>

3. Add the appropriate CLASS= attribute.

<P>Many people buy <SPAN **CLASS="firstuse"**>ASR products</SPAN> despite the higher cost.</P>

TIP

You might use classes in conjunction with HTML 4 Tables (covered in Chapter 8). Table tags accept CLASS= attributes, to apply formatting to the table sections you specify rather than to individual cells, rows, and columns or to the table as a whole.

Applying Inline Style Definitions

Applying inline style definitions throughout an HTML document is similar to adding formatting extensions. For example, just as you can apply an alignment attribute to a paragraph, you can apply a style definition within the <P> tag, as Figure 5.6 shows. Of course, with Style Sheets you have far more formatting possibilities than with simple HTML formatting commands.

Although you wouldn't use this method to apply styles throughout an HTML document—it's time-consuming—you might use it to make exceptions to an existing Style Sheet. For example, your Style Sheet might specify that paragraphs appear in blue text. You can apply an inline style to specify that one specific paragraph appears in red. Table 5.5 lists the tags and attributes you use to apply inline styles.

TABLE 5.5: TAGS AND ATTRIBUTES FOR INLINE STYLE SHEETS	
Tag/Attribute	**Description**
Any HTML tag	All HTML tags within and including <BODY> can support style definitions.
STYLE="..."	Used for inline style definitions, which you apply as an attribute to HTML tags. Provide the style definition within quotes, and provide quoted elements within the STYLE="..." attribute within single quotes.

FIGURE 5.6

*You apply inline
style definitions
within HTML code.*

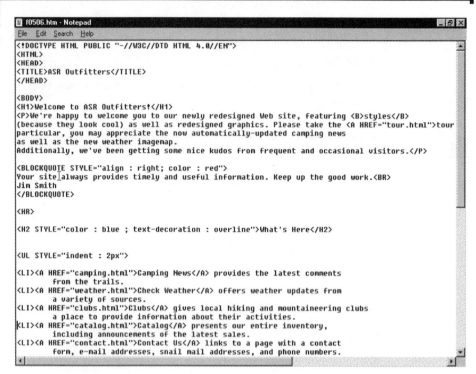

To add a style definition to an existing HTML tag, follow these steps:

1. Start with an existing HTML tag.

```
<P>Many people buy ASR products despite the higher cost.</P>
```

2. Add the STYLE= attribute.

```
<P STYLE="">Many people buy ASR products despite the higher cost.</P>
```

3. Add the style definition(s), separated by semicolons. Substitute single quotes for double quotes within the attribute; otherwise, you'll bring the attribute to a premature end.

```
<P STYLE="color : blue; font-family: 'Times New Roman', Arial">Many people buy ASR products despite the higher cost.</P>
```

Developing a Style Sheet

In the previous sections, you learned how to associate a Style Sheet with an HTML document. Your goal now is to develop the Style Sheet—that is, to specify the style definitions you want to include. A *style definition* specifies formatting characteristics.

You can choose from any combination of the five categories of style properties.

- Font properties specify character-level (inline) formatting such as the type face.
- Text properties specify display characteristics for text, such as alignment or letter spacing.
- Box properties specify characteristics for sections of text, at the paragraph (or block) level.
- Color and Background properties specify color and background images at the paragraph (or block) level.
- Classification properties specify display characteristics of lists and elements (such as P or H1) as inline or block level.

When developing a Style Sheet, simplicity is key. You can easily get carried away with formatting options, but keep things simple. Take a glance through the Style Sheet section in the Master's Reference to get an idea of the vast number of options. And, as you might guess, using even some of these options can quickly get complex.

Before we dive into developing a Style Sheet, let's take a look at some Style Sheet code:

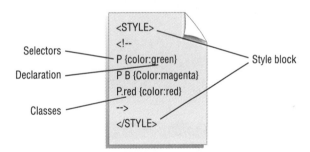

Here's what each part does:

- The style block includes style and comment tags, plus style definitions (or rules).
- Selectors are HTML elements. In this example, the P—as in a paragraph tag—is a selector.
- Declarations are the properties of the HTML elements, such as color, background, alignment, and font. In this example color:red is the declaration. The style block is enclosed within brackets, {}.
- Classes specify an additional style definition associated with specific occuurences of the HTML element. For example, paragraphs tagged with <P CLASS=red> would use this style class.
- Each style definition can define the formatting associated with a specific HTML tag, with a specific CLASS, or with a specific ID. The formatting associated with

HTML tags appears in the document without any special action on your part. Style definitions for CLASSes or IDs also require that you add the CLASS= or ID= attribute to the appropriate HTML document section before the formatting can appear in the HTML document.

To add these elements, follow these steps:

1. Be sure the style block is in place, like this.

```
<STYLE>
<!--
-->
</STYLE>
```

2. Add a selector and brackets, as shown here:

```
<STYLE>
<!--
P { }
-->
</STYLE>
```

3. Add the declaration between the brackets.

```
<STYLE>
<!--
P { color : aqua }
-->
</STYLE>
```

Style Sheet Tips

As you're building a Style Sheet, the process will be easier if you follow these guidelines:

- To include multiple selectors, place them on separate lines, like this:

```
<STYLE>
<!--
P {color: red}
H1 {color: blue}
BLOCKQUOTE {color: green}
-->
</STYLE>
```

- To provide multiple declarations for a single selector, group the declarations within the brackets, separated by a semicolon. For example, to define P as red with a yellow background, use the following code:

```
<STYLE>
<!--
P {color: red ; background: yellow}
-->
</STYLE>
```

- You might find the style definitions easier to read if you space them out somewhat, as in this example, and put only one declaration on a single line:

```
<STYLE>
<!--
P       {color: red ;
          background: yellow}
-->
</STYLE>
```

- Start at the highest level—the most general level—within your document, which is probably the body. Format the <BODY> as you want most of the document to appear, and then use specific style rules to override the <BODY> settings.

In addition, become familiar with ways to specify measurements and value which are discussed in the next two sections.

Specifying Measurements

When specifying locations of elements, you might also want to specify their size. For example, when specifying that the first line of paragraphs indent, you can also specify the size of the indention. In general, provide measurements in the units shown in Table 5.6. You can also express most measurements as a percentage of the browser window.

Your measurement might look like this:

```
P { text-indent : 2px }
```

or like this:

```
P { text-indent : 1em }
```

Unit	What It Is	Description
TABLE 5.6: UNITS OF MEASURE IN STYLE SHEETS		
em	Em space	The width of a capital M in the typeface being used.
ex	X-height	The height of a lowercase letter x in the typeface being used.
in	Inch	
cm	Centimeter	
mm	Millimeter	
px	Pixel	The individual screen dots are one pixel.
pt	Point	A typographical measurement that equals ½ inch.
pc	Pica	A typographical measurement that equals ⅙ inch.

Specifying Colors in Style Rules

Using Style Sheets, you can specify colors in the standard HTML ways (as a #rrggbb value and as a color name), as well as in two other ways, which use a slightly different approach to specify proportions of red, green, and blue. The following four lines show how to specify red in each method.

```
P { color : #FF0000 }
P { color : red }
P { color : rgb(255,0,0) }
P { color : rgb(100%,0%,0%) }
```

Although each of these is equally easy to use, we recommend using the #rrggbb option because it's likely to be more familiar, as it matches HTML color statements.

In the following sections, we'll show you how to develop an embedded Style Sheet. After you complete an embedded Style Sheet, you can move it to a separate document and import it or link it.

If you're following along with the example, have ready an HTML document with the complete structure tags, or use the following sample code, which you'll find on the Companion CD in the /examples/ch5 folder under the name of sampsty.htm.

Listing 5.1

```
<!DOCTYPE HTML PUBLIC "-//W3C//DTD HTML 4.0//EN">
<HTML>
<HEAD>
<TITLE>ASR Outfitters</TITLE>
</HEAD>

<BODY>
<H1>Welcome to ASR Outfitters!</H1>
<P>We're happy to welcome you to our newly redesigned Web site, featuring
<B>styles</B>
(because they look cool) as well as redesigned graphics. Please take the <A
HREF="tour.html">tour of our site</A> if you haven't been here in a while.
In
particular, you may appreciate the now automatically-updated camping news
as well as the new weather imagemap.
Additionally, we've been getting some nice kudos from frequent and
occasional visitors.</P>
<BLOCKQUOTE>
Your site always provides timely and useful information. Keep up the good
work.<BR>
Jim Smith
</BLOCKQUOTE>
<HR>
<H2>What's Here</H2>
<UL>
<LI><A HREF="camping.html">Camping News</A> provides the latest comments
   from the trails.
<LI><A HREF="weather.html">Check Weather</A> offers weather updates from
   a variety of sources.
<LI><A HREF="clubs.html">Clubs</A> gives local hiking and mountaineering
clubs
   a place to provide information about their activities.
<LI><A HREF="catalog.html">Catalog</A> presents our entire inventory,
   including announcements of the latest sales.
<LI><A HREF="contact.html">Contact Us</A> links to a page with a contact
   form, e-mail addresses, snail mail addresses, and phone numbers.
   If it isn't here, you can't find us.
</UL>
```

```
<H2>What We Do</H2>
<P>In addition to providing the latest camping and outdoor activities news,
we do
also provide mountaineering and hiking equipment nationwide via mail order
as well as through our stores in the Rocky Mountains.
Please take a few minutes to look through our <A HREF="catalog.html">online
offerings</A>.</P>
<H2>Other Issues</H2>
<UL>
<LI>As you may know, our URL was misprinted in the latest <I>Hiking
News</I>. Please
tell your hiking friends that the correct URL is
<TT>http://www.asroutfitters.com/</TT>.
<LI>To collect a $1000 reward, turn in the name of the person who set the
fire in the Bear Lake area last weekend.
<OL>
<LI>Call 888-555-1212.
<LI>Leave the name on the recording.
<LI>Provide contact information so we can send you the reward.
</OL>
</UL>
<H2>What Would You Like To See?</H2>
<P>If you have suggestions or comments about the site or other information
we could provide, we'd love to know about it. Drop us an e-mail at
<A HREF="mailto:asroutfitters@raycomm.com">asroutfitters@raycomm.com</A>.
Of course, you could also contact us more traditionally at the following
address: </P>
<ADDRESS>ASR Outfitters
<BR>
4700 N. Center <BR>
South Logan, UT 87654<BR>
801-555-3422</ADDRESS>
</BODY>
</HTML>
```

Without any styles or formatting other than the standard HTML/browser defaults, this document looks something like that in Figure 5.7.

FIGURE 5.7

An HTML document without any special formatting or Style Sheets.

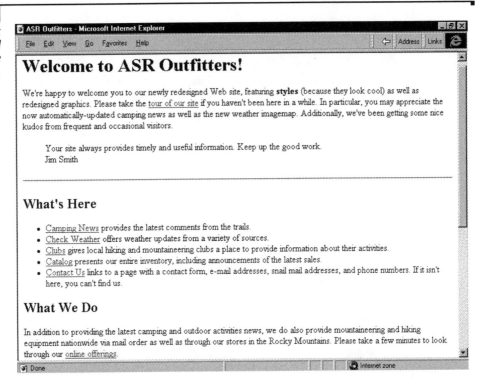

To add a style block to the document, follow these steps.

1. Add a pair of opening and closing <STYLE> tags within the document head, as shown in the following code.

```
<!DOCTYPE HTML PUBLIC "-//W3C//DTD HTML 4.0//EN">
<HTML>
<HEAD>
<TITLE>ASR Outfitters</TITLE>
<STYLE>

</STYLE>
</HEAD>
```

2. Add an opening and closing comment (<!-- -->) tag within the <STYLE> tags, as shown here:

```
<STYLE>
<!--
```

```
-->
</STYLE>
```

After the `<STYLE>` and comment tags are in place, define the Style Sheet. Think of defining styles as specifying rules for what each element should look like. For example, specify that you want all text blue, all bullets indented, all headings centered, and so on.

Next, you specify style properties, such as fonts, text, boxes, colors, backgrounds, and classifications. The following sections do not build on one another; instead, they show you how to set each of the properties separately, based on the sample ASR Outfitters page. Through these examples, you'll see *some* of the Style Sheet effects you can achieve. For a complete list of Style Sheet options, see the Cascading Style Sheets section in the Master's Reference.

Setting Font Properties

If the font properties you specify are not available on your visitors' computers, the browser will display text in a font that is available. To ensure that one of your preferred fonts is used, choose multiple font properties. Table 5.7 shows some of the basic font properties and values.

TABLE 5.7: FONT PROPERTIES

Property	Value
font-family	Times New Roman, Arial, serif, sans-serif, monospace
font-style	normal, italic, oblique
font-variant	normal small-caps
font-weight	normal, bold, bolder, lighter, 100, 200, 300, 400, 500, 600, 700, 800, 900
font-size	xx-small, x-small, small, medium, large, x-large, xx-large, or size measurement
font	any or all of the above properties

The following example sets a basic font for the whole document—everything between the opening and closing `<BODY>` tags. It sets the basic font for a document to Comic Sans MS, with Technical and Times New Roman as other choices and with a generic serif font as the last choice.

1. Within the style block, add a `BODY` selector.

```
<STYLE>
<!--
```

```
BODY
-->
</STYLE>
```

2. Add brackets.

```
<STYLE>
<!--
BODY {}
-->
</STYLE>
```

3. Add the property. To set only the typeface, use `font-family`.

```
<STYLE>
<!--
BODY { font-family }
-->
</STYLE>
```

4. Add a colon to separate the property from the value.

```
<STYLE>
<!--
BODY { font-family : }
-->
</STYLE>
```

5. Add the value `"Comic Sans MS"` (the first choice typeface).

```
<STYLE>
<!--
BODY { font-family : "Comic Sans MS" }
-->
</STYLE>
```

6. Add additional values, as you choose, separated by commas. If the font family name contains a space, put the name in quotes. Otherwise, quotes are optional. Conclude your list of fonts with either a serif or sans-serif font that's bound to match something on the visitor's computer.

```
<STYLE>
<!--
BODY { font-family : "Comic Sans MS", Technical, "Times New Roman",
serif }
-->
</STYLE>
```

Here is the resulting page, complete with the new font for the document body.

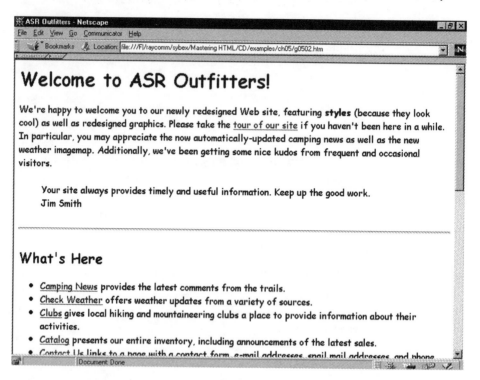

 **TIP**

See Chapter 3 for a list of fonts commonly available on various platforms.

Setting Link Characteristics

You use three special style classes (and font style rules) to control the colors of links in your document:

- A:link
- A:active
- A:visited

CONTINUED

Use these within your Style Sheet definition to specify the rules that apply to links, active links, and visited links. For example, to set unvisited links to blue, active links to red, and visited links to magenta, your style block would look like this:

```
<STYLE>
<!--
A:link { color : blue }
A:active { color : red }
A:visited { color : magenta }
-->
</STYLE>
```

You can also define additional text styles within the document. For example, to set all headings to Arial italic, follow these steps:

1. Add a comma-separated list of all headings to the existing style block, as selectors. The comma-separated list specifies that the style rule applies to each selector individually.

```
<STYLE>
<!--
BODY { font-family : "Comic Sans MS", Technical, "Times New Roman",
serif }
H1, H2, H3, H4, H5, H6
-->
</STYLE>
```

2. Add brackets.

```
<STYLE>
<!--
BODY { font-family : "Comic Sans MS", Technical, "Times New Roman",
serif }
H1, H2, H3, H4, H5, H6 { }
-->
</STYLE>
```

3. Add the font-family property, with Arial as the first choice, Helvetica as the second choice, and sans-serif as the third choice.

```
<STYLE>
<!--
```

```
BODY { font-family : "Comic Sans MS", Technical, "Times New Roman",
serif }
H1, H2, H3, H4, H5, H6 { font-family : Arial, Helvetica, "sans-serif" }
-->
</STYLE>
```

4. After the font-family values, add a semicolon and a new line so that you can easily enter (and read) the font-style rule.

```
<STYLE>
<!--
BODY { font-family : "Comic Sans MS", Technical, "Times New Roman",
serif }
H1, H2, H3, H4, H5, H6 { font-family : Arial, Helvetica, "sans-serif" ;
}
-->
</STYLE>
```

5. Add the font-style property, a colon, and the italic value.

```
<STYLE>
<!--
BODY { font-family : "Comic Sans MS", Technical, "Times New Roman",
serif }
H1, H2, H3, H4, H5, H6 { font-family : Arial, Helvetica, "sans-serif" ;
font-style : italic }
-->
</STYLE>
```

6. Continue adding font properties, separated by a semicolon, if you want to define other aspects, such as font size or weight. The following lines of code show the headings set to a larger size and weight than usual. You'll see the results in Figure 5.8.

```
<STYLE>
<!--
BODY { font-family : "Comic Sans MS", Technical, "Times New Roman",
serif }
H1, H2, H3, H4, H5, H6 {
                font-family : Arial, Helvetica, "sans-serif" ;
                font-style : italic ;
                font-size : x-large ;
                font-weight : bolder ;
                }
-->
</STYLE>
```

FIGURE 5.8

The results of setting the font-family, style, size, and weight for headings

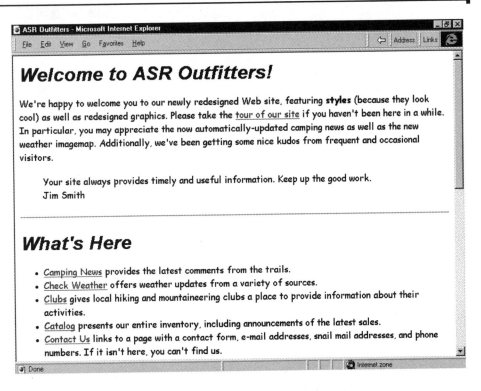

Combining Multiple Characteristics

With font properties, you can combine multiple characteristics into a single line—kind of like using shorthand. For example, you could reduce the sample heading definition to:

```
H1, H2, H3, H4, H5, H6 { font: Arial, Helvetica, "sans-serif" italic x-
large bolder }
```

Using this shorter definition has a few disadvantages. First, the reduced code is more difficult to interpret—particular for those just learning Style Sheets. Also, browser support is even sketchier for the shorter version than for the longer version, so visitors may not be able to view the effects.

Setting Text Properties

Text properties specify the characteristics of text blocks (sections of text, not individual characters). Table 5.8 shows some of the most common text properties.

TABLE 5.8: TEXT PROPERTIES	
Property	**Value**
word-spacing	measurement
letter-spacing	measurement
text-decoration	none, underline, overline, line-through, blink
vertical-align	baseline, super, sub, top, text-top, middle-bottom, text-bottom
text-transform	none, capitalize, uppercase, lowercase
text-align	left, right, center, justify
text-indent	measurement or %

You apply these properties to selectors in the same way you apply font-level properties. To indent paragraphs and set up a special, nonindented paragraph class, follow these steps:

1. Within the style block, add a P selector.

   ```
   <STYLE>
   <!--
   P
   -->
   </STYLE>
   ```

2. Add brackets.

   ```
   <STYLE>
   <!--
   P {}
   -->
   </STYLE>
   ```

3. Add the text-indent property, with a value of 5% to indent all regular paragraphs by 5 percent of the total window width.

   ```
   <STYLE>
   <!--
   P { text-indent : 5% }
   -->
   </STYLE>
   ```

4. Add the `P.noindent` selector on a new line within the style block. Using a standard selection, in conjunction with a descriptive term (that you make up), you create a new style class within the style sheet.

```
<STYLE>
<!--
P { text-indent : 5% }
P.noindent
-->
</STYLE>
```

5. Add brackets and the `text-indent` property, with a value of 0% to specify no indent.

```
<STYLE>
<!--
P { text-indent : 5% }
P.noindent { text-indent : 0% }
-->
</STYLE>
```

6. To specify which text should be formatted without an indent, add a new <P> tag with a `CLASS="noindent"` attribute, as shown here.

```
<P>We're happy to welcome you to our newly redesigned Web site,
featuring <B>styles</B>
(because they look cool) as well as redesigned graphics. Please take the
<A HREF="tour.html">tour of our site</A> if you haven't been here in a
while. In
particular, you may appreciate the now automatically-updated camping
news
as well as the new weather imagemap. </P>
<P CLASS="noindent">Additionally, we've been getting some nice kudos
from frequent and occasional visitors.</P>
```

Figure 5.9 shows the results. All text tagged with <P> in the HTML document is indented by 5 percent of the window width, and special formatting, set up with the CLASS= attribute, does not indent.

FIGURE 5.9

Setting text properties lets you customize your documents—the second paragraph is not indented, while the first one is, because of a style class.

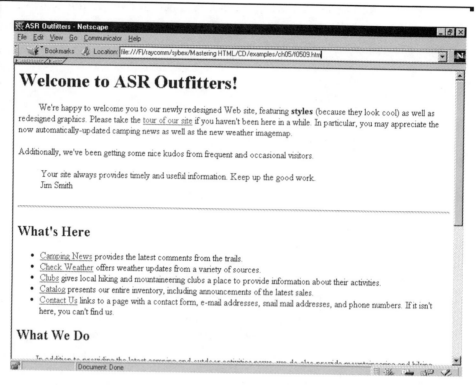

Specifying Generic Style Classes

You can also specify a class without a selector, as in the following style block:

```
<STYLE>
<!-
.red { color : red }
->
</STYLE>
```

You can use a generic class, such as red in this example, with any HTML tags in your document. If you specify an element with the class (P.red, for example), you can only use that class with <P> tags.

You can also use text properties to apply special formatting to headings. To format all headings with a line below them, centered, and with extra spacing between the letters, follow these steps:

1. Add the list of heading selectors you want to format to your basic Style Sheet. To apply these formats to headings 1 through 3, for example, list H1, H2, H3.

```
<STYLE>
<!--
H1, H2, H3
-->
</STYLE>
```

2. Add brackets following the selector.

```
<STYLE>
<!--
H1, H2, H3 {  }
-->
</STYLE>
```

3. Add the text-decoration property with underline as the value to place a line above each heading.

```
<STYLE>
<!--
H1, H2, H3 { text-decoration : underline }
-->
</STYLE>
```

4. Add a semicolon (to separate the rules) and the text-align property with a value of center.

```
<STYLE>
<!--
H1, H2, H3 { text-decoration : underline ;
text-align : center}
-->
</STYLE>
```

5. Finally, add another separation semicolon and the letter-spacing property with a value of 5px (5 pixels).

```
<STYLE>
<!--
H1, H2, H3 { text-decoration : underline ;
text-align : center ;
```

```
letter-spacing : 5px }
-->
</STYLE>
```

The sample page looks like this:

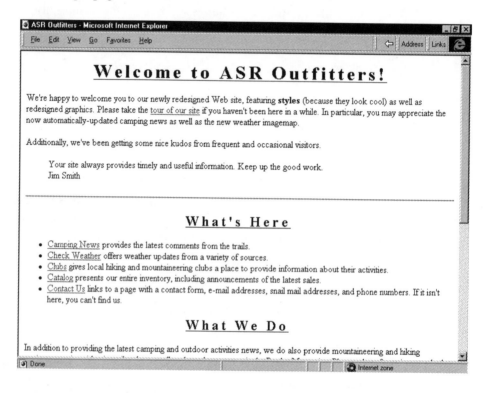

Specifying Style IDs

You can specify an ID for a one-time use—for example, if you're developing a Dynamic HTML document. Use a # at the beginning of the ID selector, as in the following style block:

```
<STYLE>
<!--
#firstusered { color : red }
-->
</STYLE>
```

CONTINUED

You can use an ID, such as `firstusered` in this example, with any single ID= attribute in your document. If you specify an element with the ID (`<P ID=firstusered>`, for example), you can only use that ID once in the document.

Setting Box Properties

You use box properties to create all sorts of box designs—a feature that's not available in standard HTML. You can box text, such as cautions or contact information, to call attention to it, as shown in Figure 5.10. You can adjust the margins to control how close text is to the border, and you can also remove the border to create floating text.

FIGURE 5.10

Floating boxes are handy for calling attention to information or making the page design more interesting.

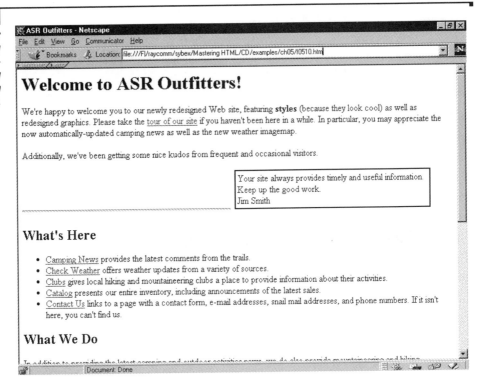

TIP

At the time of writing, Internet Explorer and Netscape Navigator support box properties differently—in particular, the relationship between the surrounding text and the box, and the size of the box around text is quite inconsistent.

Table 5.9 lists some commonly used box properties.

TABLE 5.9: BOX PROPERTIES

Property	Value
margin-top	measurement, percentage of parent
margin-right	measurement, percentage of parent
margin-bottom	measurement, percentage of parent
margin-left	measurement, percentage of parent
margin	measurement, percentage of parent
border-width	measurement, thick, medium, thin
border-color	#rrggbb
border-style	none, dotted dashed, solid, double, groove, ridge, inset, outset
border	any or all of the above attributes
width	measurement or %
height	measurement or %
float	right, left, none
clear	right, left, none, both

To create a box, apply these box-level characteristics to existing text in an HTML document, including, for example, paragraphs, block quotes, or headings. The following steps show you how to create a box using an existing block quote. This box will float close to the right margin with a 2-pixel border and will occupy only 50 percent of the window width.

1. Within the style block, add a BLOCKQUOTE selector.

```
<STYLE>
<!--
BLOCKQUOTE
-->
</STYLE>
```

2. Add brackets.

```
<STYLE>
<!--
BLOCKQUOTE {}
-->
</STYLE>
```

3. Add a WIDTH property, with a value of 50%.

```
<STYLE>
<!--
BLOCKQUOTE { width : 50% }
-->
</STYLE>
```

4. Add a semicolon as a separator and the FLOAT property with a value of right.

```
<STYLE>
<!--
BLOCKQUOTE { width : 50% ;
float : right }
-->
</STYLE>
```

5. Add another semicolon as a separator and the BORDER property. In this example, we provided the individual border properties together, rather than as individual entities.

```
<STYLE>
<!--
BLOCKQUOTE { width : 50% ;
float : right ;
border : 2px solid black }
-->
</STYLE>
```

Figure 5.11 shows the results.

Setting Color and Background Properties

To establish color and background properties for the sample document or for any block-level elements, use the properties and values shown in Table 5.10.

FIGURE 5.11

Using boxes is an excellent way to call attention to information.

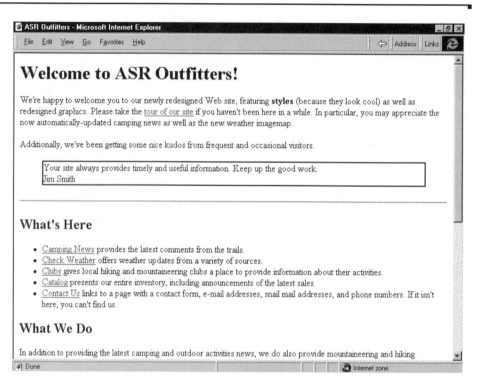

TABLE 5.10: COLOR AND BACKGROUND

Property	Value
color	#rrggbb
background-color	#rrggbb, transparent
background-image	url(http://sampleurl.com)
background-repeat	repeat, repeat-x, repeat-y, no-repeat
background	any or all of the above properties

To include a background color, add the properties to the <BODY> element, as shown in the following steps, which add #FFFFCC (light yellow) to the background:

1. Within the style block, add a BODY selector.

```
<STYLE>
<!--
BODY
```

```
-->
</STYLE>
```

2. Add brackets and the `background-color` attribute and the #FFFFCC value, which specifies the light yellow color.

```
<STYLE>
<!--
BODY    {background-color: #FFFFCC}
-->
</STYLE>
```

When·viewed in a browser, the background will appear lightly colored, just as it would if the BGCOLOR= attribute were applied to the <BODY> tag. Each element within the document inherits the background color from the body.

You can also add a background image to the <BODY> tag or other block elements. Remember, block elements are any elements with a line break before and after, such as <BODY>, <P>, or <H1>.

As shown in the following steps, you can tile the background image either vertically or horizontally:

1. To add a background image to the document body, add the `background-image` property, separated from the previous property with a semicolon.

```
<STYLE>
<!--
BODY    {background-color: #FFFFCC ;
background-image : }
-->
</STYLE>
```

2. Add the value for the background image as `url(pattern.gif)`. Use any absolute or relative URL in the parenthesis.

```
<STYLE>
<!--
BODY    {background-color: #FFFFCC ;
background-image : url(pattern.gif) }
-->
</STYLE>
```

3. Add `background-repeat: repeat-x` to specify that the background image repeat horizontally (in the direction of the x-axis). To repeat only vertically, use `repeat-y`; use `no-repeat` if you don't want a repeat.

```
<STYLE>
<!--
```

```
BODY    {background-color: #FFFFCC ;
        background-image : url(pattern.gif) ;
        background-repeat: repeat-x ; }
        }
        -->
        </STYLE>
```

Figure 5.12 shows this effect in Netscape Navigator.

FIGURE 5.12

Style Sheets let you easily add a background image.

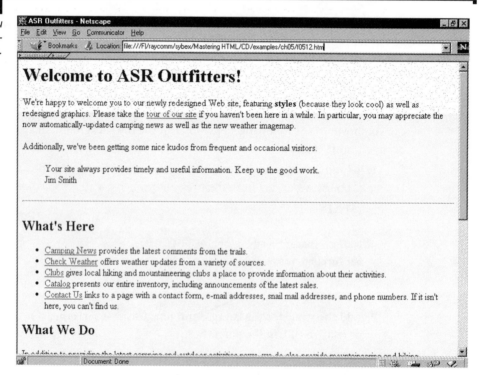

Setting Classification Properties

You use classification properties to change specific elements from inline (such as I or B) to block elements with line breaks before and after (such as P and H1), as well as to control the display of lists. Table 5.11 lists some classification properties and their values.

TABLE 5.11: CLASSIFICATION PROPERTIES	
Property	**Value**
display	inline, block, list-item
line-height	measurement or %
list-style-type	disc, circle, square, decimal, lower-roman, upper-roman, lower-alpha, upper-alpha, none
list-style-image	url(http://someurl.com/image.gif)

To specify that an unordered list use square bullets, follow these steps:

1. Within the style block, add a UL selector followed immediately by an LI selector on the same line. By combining these, the style rule will apply only to an <LI> within a <UL>. Setting a rule for only <LI> affects all numbered and bulleted lists.

```
<STYLE>
<!--
UL LI
-->
</STYLE>
```

2. Add brackets.

```
<STYLE>
<!--
UL LI {}
-->
</STYLE>
```

3. Add a list-style-type property with the value of square.

```
<STYLE>
<!--
UL LI { list-style-type : square }
-->
</STYLE>
```

You can also set a specific image for use as a bullet by using list-style-image : url(figure.gif), as shown here:

```
<STYLE>
<!--
UL LI { list-style-image : url(figure.gif) }
-->
</STYLE>
```

By changing the display property, you can change a list from displaying as a vertical list, as is customary, to an inline list in which each item appears within a line of text. Use the following style rule.

```
<STYLE>
<!--
UL LI { display : inline }
-->
</STYLE>
```

Where to Go from Here

In this chapter, you learned how Style Sheets and HTML documents relate and how to develop Style Sheets for your own needs. As you can see, Style Sheets are certainly more comprehensive than any formatting option previously available in HTML.

You might check out some of these chapters:

- See Chapter 3 for more information about standard HTML tags and formatting options.
- See Chapter 8 to find out more about HTML 4 tables.
- Check out Chapter 10 to learn about frames.

Chapter

6

Understanding and Using Web Servers

A Web server is a computer that supplies Web pages to requesting computers. In a sense, a server acts as a central clearinghouse for information made available to other computers on a network. For the most part, Web servers (we'll just call them *servers*) wait for visitors to request a Web page; they then find the requested page and send it to the requesting computer.

Throughout this chapter, you'll read about Web server computers (the physical machines) and Web server software (the program on the computer that makes it function as a Web server). Unless we specify that we're talking about the physical you-can-kick-it computer, we're discussing the software.

Not only do servers store and serve Web pages, but they also process forms, direct links from image maps, run programs, and provide the basis for interactive Web sites and extended Web capabilities, such as Web-based chat rooms. In this chapter, we'll give you some background about networks and servers, explain your options for getting access to a server, talk about how you can run your own server, and show you how to use some specific server applications to upload your Web page files and run a counter (which tracks the number of visits to your site).

An Overview of Networking

Server computers are located on *networks*, which are groups of connected computers that can communicate and share information and files. Although many kinds of networks exist, for the purposes of this discussion only a couple are critical:

- Peer-to-peer or server-based networks
- Client-server networks

You may be familiar with peer-to-peer or server-based networks. If you are part of a workgroup and use Microsoft Windows networking or Lantastic networking, you're using a peer-to-peer network. Or, if you use Novell or Banyan Vines networks, you're using a server-based network. Both differ fundamentally from the technologies used on the Internet. In general, if you use these server-based networks, you log on to a file server or to a network and are dependent on the server to be functional. If the server (holding the data or the logon information or the program you want to run) is not functional, you can do little or nothing.

Client-server networks are more flexible than peer-to-peer or server-based networks. In a client-server environment, individual computers (called *workstations*) have all the software and data necessary to function, but also have the resources to connect to servers for other information. The Internet is the most common (but certainly not the only) example of this technology. In contrast to peer-to-peer or server-based networks, client workstations continue to function normally even if the network goes down (although they won't have access to the resources on the network).

These two types of networks are not mutually exclusive; they coexist all the time. If you're on a Novell Netware network and can also use your Web browser, you're on both a corporate server-based network and a client-server network (probably the Internet, possibly only a corporate intranet). The remaining information in this chapter concerns client-server networks because that's the kind of network that supports Web servers, Web browsers, and myriad other HTML-related technologies.

The Internet

The Internet is the world's largest network. Specifically, it's a client-server network, including millions of computers that are physically connected and speak the same networking language, *TCP/IP* (*Transmission Control Protocol/Internet Protocol*). A variety of computers and operating systems understand TCP/IP, which is one reason the Internet has become so popular. TCP/IP provides the foundation for other computer communication protocols, such as HTTP.

Because the Internet is a client-server network, you don't have to "log on to" a server to get on the network. If you're connected to the network and your computer is configured to speak TCP/IP, you're on the network. "Access" to specific computers or resources occurs on a server-by-server basis.

NOTE

Having to log on to your Internet service provider's computer before you get on the Internet is a special case—you're actually logging on to your ISP's server to make the connection to the network.

Any computer in a client-server environment can function as a client, as a server, or as both. Unlike a Novell network, for example, in which a computer is dedicated to being a server and the others are dedicated to being workstations, any computer in a client-server environment (such as the Internet) can function in either capacity. Figure 6.1 gives you an idea of how computers on the Internet connect.

FIGURE 6.1

*The Internet is just
a huge network
that contains a
multitude of smaller
networks.*

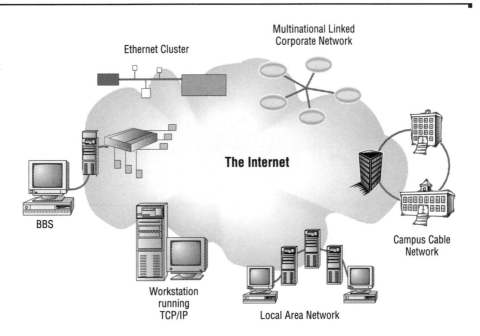

If your workstation somewhere in the corporate or academic world is connected to the Internet, you could install Web server software and let your personal workstation also serve documents. That's why Windows NT, for example, comes with a Web server right out of the box. (Of course, the security implications make system administrators more than a little jumpy.) Likewise, even huge servers, such as those at Netscape

Communications, Inc. (`home.netscape.com`), can be clients. If Marc Andreessen sits down at the console of `home.netscape.com` and launches a browser application (any browser application), his computer is acting as a client. If Marc connects to `home.netscape.com` to find out what's happening with his company, his computer will be simultaneously acting as a client and as a server (and talking to itself).

So all these millions of computers on the Internet can be either servers or clients or both. Most are only clients, some are servers, and a few are both. It all depends on the software they're running.

Intranets

Intranets are similar to the Internet—technologically speaking, they're identical. The difference is that intranets are either not connected to the Internet or are shielded from the Internet with a device called a *firewall*, which keeps people outside the firewall from accessing information on the intranet. As Figure 6.2 shows, an intranet can include one or more groups of computers , all joined together in much the same way that your computer connects to the Internet—with dedicated, private lines.

FIGURE 6.2

An intranet includes multiple computers joined together through direct connections.

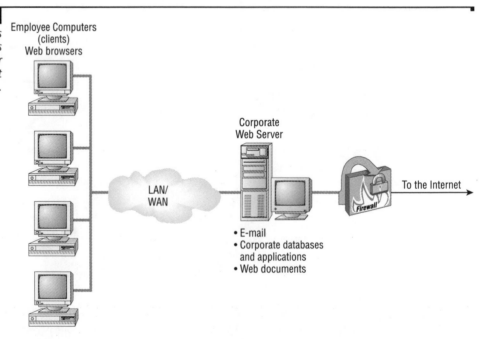

You'll notice in Figure 6.2 that the connection between the computers doesn't have to be in the same location—the network is not geographically constrained.

NOTE

The term *intranet* might seem a little confusing or redundant if you're familiar with a *LAN (Local Area Network)* or a *WAN (Wide Area Network)*. An intranet can be either a LAN—if it's all in one location—or a WAN, if it's geographically dispersed.

Extranets

Extranets are intranets that allow people outside the company to access some company-specific information. Extranets can connect through the Internet (with appropriate security provisions) or can connect together through a dedicated line. Functionally, for the purposes of HTML and Web development, they're the same as intranets—that is, they join computers separated geographically.

Extranet, the buzzword, just refers to a different way of joining networks at different locations. Piggy-backing a connection through the Internet requires a far smaller investment in telecommunications resources (but a higher investment in security provisions) than providing a dedicated circuit between the same two points. Either way, your work as a Web developer will be the same.

Web Servers

A Web server's main function is to distribute HTML documents on request. When a visitor accesses your site, the Web server finds the specific file and serves it to the computer requesting it.

Web servers—and by necessity clients—all speak a common "language" called *HTTP*, which stands for *Hypertext Transfer Protocol*. Whereas computers on the Internet speak TCP/IP, which provides the communication foundation between computers, HTTP is the language that Web servers and Web browsers use to communicate. And, yes, the TCP/IP protocol must be in place for the HTTP communication to occur between the server and browser.

NOTE

HTTP servers are commonly called *HTTPD* servers—the *D*, in Unix terms, stands for *Daemon*, which refers to programs that run whenever the computer is running.

When a Web browser connects to a Web server to retrieve a page, the browser connects, retrieves the page, and then disconnects. After the visitor selects a link, the browser connects to the server again, retrieves the next page, and then disconnects. This process of connecting, transferring information, and disconnecting is different from remote logon protocols (such as Telnet) or file transfer protocols (FTP); with those protocols, the established connection remains open even when idle.

From the perspective of a server administrator, the HTTP protocol is quite efficient—it doesn't tie up network resources when nothing is happening. From the perspective of a Web developer, however, HTTP is problematic because it doesn't "maintain state." When a browser connects to a server and retrieves a page, the server has no way of knowing which other pages the browser has retrieved in the same session or at different times. From the server's perspective, each retrieval is a separate transaction.

TIP

The casual visitor might not even be aware that the connection is not maintained the entire time that he or she is viewing the page.

This *statelessness* means that you, as a Web developer, can't tell directly from the Web server exactly what your visitors are doing or have done at your site. You have to go to extraordinary measures to even know what your visitors' names are from one visit to the next. Although new, promising proposals for advances in the HTTP protocol are under consideration, it will be several years before any changes in the protocol address this issue.

TIP

You can overcome problems with the ability to maintain state through multiple HTTP connections. Of the ways to do so, the most popular are *cookies*, which we discuss in Chapter 11.

In addition to serving files, servers also perform other functions that let you tailor your Web pages. For example, servers process forms by taking the data that a visitor submits and forwarding it to you via e-mail or saving it in a database that processes the information as you specify.

Servers also run programs to support the Web site. They can maintain a counter to track the number of times a specific Web page has been accessed, and they can run a server-side image map, which allows a single image to be linked to multiple files, depending on which part of the image the visitor clicks.

TIP

You'll find more information about adding a counter later in this chapter. And, you can find information about image maps—both client-side and server-side in Chapter 7. Ceilidh, the chat room to end all chat rooms, is available on the Companion CD.

Finally, servers can also help control access to your Web documents. If you don't want certain files universally available, you can use the security functions of your Web server to restrict access based on domain, user name and password, or other characteristics.

WARNING

If you have documents that should not be available to everyone on the Internet, don't put them on a server. Even if you don't have links to the documents, your documents could still be indexed or directly accessed.

Getting Access to a Server

In general, you can access a server in three ways:

- Through your ISP
- Through your corporate IS department
- By installing and running your own server

Regardless of which type you use, be sure to address server-access issues as soon as you start developing a site. If you wait until you've completed the site, you might find out that you could have taken advantage of server-specific capabilities, that your site will be too large for the allotted space on the server, or that the server just won't support what you thought it would.

Accessing a Server through Your ISP

ISP access is one of the most common types of access, both for individuals and for businesses. If you're looking for an ISP, you can find one in several ways, including:

- On the Web
- In a local or regional newspaper or magazine
- By word of mouth

For a comprehensive list of ISPs, along with contact information and services, visit:

`www.yahoo.com/Business_and_Economy/Companies/Internet_Services/`
`Access_Providers/Directories/`

or:

`thelist.internet.com/`

Local and regional publications are also a good source. Often, you'll find ads for local ISPs in the Technology or Business section of your daily newspaper.

Also, ask friends, neighbors, business associates, or folks at your local computer store about the services they use and their experiences. The quality, reliability, and service of both ISPs and Web hosting services vary; so get all the advice and input you can before you commit.

TIP

Once you find an ISP that appears to suit your needs, start by signing a short contract—say, no longer than six months—until you know that the service is satisfactory.

Finding a Web-Hosting Service

Another option—one that's not quite an ISP, but similar—is a Web-hosting service. A Web-hosting service does not provide dial-up Internet access but simply provides a home from which you can serve your sites.

Generally, you use Web-hosting services in conjunction with an ISP, thus combining the best Web-hosting deal with reliable dial-up access. Although it's possible that a single company could meet all your needs, shopping for these services separately can be useful. For a fairly comprehensive list of Web-hosting services, check out:

`www.yahoo.com/Business_and_Economy/Companies/Internet_Services/`
`Web_Services/Hosting/`

Getting an Individual ISP Account

Generally, ISPs provide individual subscribers—as opposed to business subscribers—with access to the Internet, to e-mail, and to a small amount of space on a Web server.

Many ISPs also provide some other services, such as sending you the results of a form via e-mail.

The process for obtaining an account depends on the server and the ISP. For example, at our last ISP, we could publish Web pages, but could not install or run programs (such as a counter or chat room) on the server, nor could we control which programs were available. At our current ISP, we can request specific programs, and we can install and run them ourselves if we're feeling ambitious.

If you're not able to do everything you want on your ISP's server, shop around. If you can't do everything you want at your company, either appeal to the powers that be, install your own server, or deal with it. In either case, as a visitor on someone else's system, you're at the mercy of whoever is running the show.

Getting a Business Account

If you are actually running a business and using the Internet (or if you're moving in that direction), consider getting a business account with an ISP. Business accounts, although somewhat more expensive than individual accounts, usually include more Web space, better access to server-side programs, and more comprehensive services, with guaranteed uptime, backups, and more attention to individual needs.

Most ISPs require a business account to have its own *domain name*, which replaces the ISP's name in the URL. For example, instead of our business's URL being:

```
www.xmission.com/~ejray/index.html
```

(which includes the ISP name and a folder designated to us), it simply reads:

```
www.raycomm.com
```

Having your own domain name enhances your professional appearance and can help make your business appear bigger than it really is.

Having your own domain name also offers a few practical advantages. First, you can keep a consistent address even if you move or change ISPs. Visitors (who may be your customers or potential customers) will always be able to find you because your address remains constant.

Second, you can easily expand your Web site as your needs grow. If you start by having your service provider host your domain (called a *virtual domain*), you can easily expand your capacity or add services, without changing your address or revising your advertising materials.

Virtual Domains

If you have a regular domain—for example, `microsoft.com`—the computers on that network have unique names in that domain, for example:

```
billg.microsoft.com
www.microsoft.com
nt.microsoft.com
```

If your domain shares space on a server with other domains (as `raycomm.com` does on the `xmission.com` system), it's a virtual domain and does not have a computer to itself.

Finally, using a domain name helps establish your identity. Each domain name is unique and can include the business name itself or other names. For example, our business name is RayComm, Inc., but we probably could have extended the domain name to say `raycommunications.com` (or something to that effect).

There is a catch, though. If you don't claim your domain name, someone else will. If you have a company name under which you operate, get a domain name immediately, even if you're not likely to use it in the near future. Many of the most popular names are already taken. For example, we originally wanted `ray.com`. Since that was already taken by Raytheon, we settled for `raycomm.com`.

If you have a small business and aren't incorporated or are thinking of incorporating, consider getting the domain name first and then incorporating under that name. It seems a little backward, but a domain name must be unique, and competition for good names is stiff. After you obtain your domain name, take care of registering to do business under that name.

At the time of writing, a company called Network Solutions, Inc., or InterNIC, controlled all registration for `.com`, `.org`, and `.net` names.

To register a domain name, follow this process:

1. Go to `rs.internic.net/` and choose Registration services.

2. Select Whois from the menu, and then enter your prospective domain name in the query field and press Enter. For example, you might enter `joesburgers.com` or `breakfastbuffet.com`.

If you're lucky, you will see a No Match message, which means that your domain name is available. If you're less fortunate, you'll see the InterNIC records for whoever does own the name you entered. If you want, you can contact them and see if they want to sell it or give it to you, but you're likely to have more success if you simply look for another name.

3. Either register the name yourself or pass the buck to your ISP. Many ISPs will register domain names for free if they'll be hosting them, or they charge a reasonable ($100 or less) fee for the service, plus hosting charges. If your ISP attempts to charge significantly more than $100, it's trying to take you for a ride. Either do it yourself or find another ISP.

If you really want to do it yourself, all the information and instructions you'll need are available at the InterNIC site, although you'll need to get a little information and cooperation from your ISP to fill out all the forms correctly.

Accessing a Corporate Server

If you work for a large company or an educational institution or if you work with an organization or group that handles system administration tasks, you'll probably have little to do when it comes to accessing a Web server. All the necessary pieces—access, administration, security—are likely to be in place, and you'll simply step in and start using the server. This situation can be either the ideal or the worst possible case, depending on the group that actually runs the Web server.

What access and control you have at the corporate level varies from company to company. In the ideal situation, someone else takes care of running the server, but lets you do anything you want, within reason. You get help setting up and running server-side programs and can essentially do anything you need to provide information. At the other extreme, a rigid process exists to submit information to the intranet. You'll submit HTML documents and then have little control over where they're placed or how they're linked.

In all likelihood, your company will be somewhere in the middle, with an established procedure for accessing the corporate intranet but a substantial amount of freedom to do what you need to do. If not, or if the process of providing content is tightly controlled, you may want to see about running your own server.

In any event, you'll need to find out how to contact the server administrators, get emergency contact numbers, find out about the corporate intranet policies, and go from there.

Running Your Own Server

If you have the technical savvy and existing infrastructure to run your own Web server, this option affords you the most flexibility and best range of resources. One good reason to run your own server is that it's a more authentic environment for developing and testing pages. For example, if you have server-relative URLs in links, they'll work properly if you're loading the files from a server, but not if you're loading the same file locally. (See Chapter 4 for more about links and server-relative URLs.)

If you have a fairly powerful desktop machine, you can certainly use it as a Web server. A 486 computer with 16MB of RAM can run an adequate Windows or Windows NT server for testing purposes. It can also run a rather speedy and spiffy Linux (freeware Unix) Web server.

A Great Example of a Local Test Server

Any figures you see in this book that have a URL of hobbes.raycomm.com/ were developed on a server running on our local network, which is isolated from the Internet. The server software running on hobbes—at various times—includes the Netscape FastTrack Server, Windows NT built-in Internet Information Server, OmniHTTPd, and Microsoft's Personal Web Server. The hobbes server is a 486 computer with 16MB of RAM. The performance isn't great, but it's more than adequate for testing purposes. The client and server software were both on the local machine during testing.

Although we could have loaded all the files onto our real Web site, that would have put a lot of very under-development garbage out on the Internet under our URL. By testing locally, we keep the stuff that doesn't work right yet to ourselves.

Although we could have opened all the files directly from the hard drive, that wouldn't have let us test server-side programs, server-relative URLs, or given us the sense of working on a real server.

Considering that it only took about 10 minutes each to install the server software packages (on an existing network), it's worth it.

Particularly in a corporate or educational environment, where a network infrastructure exists, installing and running a server is straightforward. To run a public server, whether at home or at work, you'll need a dedicated network connection—anything from a full-time ISDN line from your ISP to a direct connection will work.

If you're just setting up a local server for your own testing purposes, you can even run the server on a stand-alone machine.

Server Considerations

Windows NT comes with Internet Information Server, and the Personal Web Server for Windows 95 or Macintosh is available at no charge from Microsoft at:

`www.microsoft.com/msdownload/`

A feature-rich server called OmniHTTPd, in both a freeware and a shareware version, is available for Windows 95 and NT at:

`www.fas.harvard.edu/~glau/httpd/`

Macintosh users can find httpd4Mac, which is available at no charge, at:

`sodium.ch.man.ac.uk/pages/httpd4Mac/home.html`

If your desktop machine is a Unix box, Apache is the most popular UNIX-based server software, and it is also free from `www.apache.org`.

If running your own server proves a good choice and you need more capabilities or power, check out the following:

- WebStar (`www.starnine.com`) for the Mac
- WebSite (`software.oreilly.com`)
- Netscape's variety of server choices for Windows and Unix (`home.netscape.com`)

If you're considering running your own server, here are some issues to consider:

Security: Web servers do present a security risk, although not a huge one. Letting other people access files on your computer, through any means, is inherently a little iffy. If you're paranoid about security, you don't want to run a server on your desktop machine. On an intranet, assuming you don't have highly confidential material on the server machine, you should be fine.

Uptime and access: If you're going to set up and publicize a server, you must ensure that it stays up and available. If you don't have a full-time Internet connection or if you like to turn your computer off on occasion, don't use it for a Web server. Similarly, if your machine crashes often, is heavily taxed by other software, or experiences slowdowns when local network traffic is heavy, consider other alternatives, such as a secondary computer or simply putting your site on a dedicated server.

Time: Running a Web server takes some time. If all you're doing is serving pages, it doesn't take much, but expect a certain investment. If you'll be generating pages from a database (see Chapter 18) or installing and running other add-in programs, it'll take more time, both to keep the server going and to monitor security issues.

Capacity: If your Web server provides only plain HTML documents and a few graphics to others on an intranet or if it's just for testing purposes, almost any computer will do. If you expect heavy traffic or lots of access, however, be sure that the computer you use can handle the load or can easily be upgraded.

Backups: If you're running your own server, you're responsible for backups. If the hard drive on your server dies, will you be in a position to restore everything and get it all back up?

Installing Your Own Server

Installing your own server, as with installing any software, varies depending on the computer platform. If you're comfortable installing software on your computer, setting up and configuring a Web server should pose no particular challenges—although setting up a Unix-based server is substantially more complex than setting up Windows or Macintosh servers.

The following steps walk through the process of installing and running OmniHTTPd on a Windows 95 or NT computer. Although the specific steps differ, depending on the platform, the configuration options and considerations are the same.

1. Download the server software from `www.fas.harvard.edu/~glau/httpd/`.

2. Use Windows Explorer to browse to the downloaded files (they are probably in `ohttpd101.exe`) and double-click.

3. You'll see a message asking if you really want to install the program. Choose OK.

4. Follow the Wizard through the installation process, making selections and clicking Next until you're finished.

5. Launch the server and try out your new site.

You can put the program in any location you choose. The typical installation will probably be your best choice. We usually accept that option or the Custom option. That's all there is to it. Not bad so far, huh? Now, all that's left is to configure it.

NOTE

If your computer will be usually acting as a Web server, choose Yes when asked if OmniHTTPd should be run automatically at startup.

Local Networking

If you're installing your new Web server on an existing network that supports TCP/IP, you'll have few headaches as far as networking is concerned—talk with your administrator about getting your computer up on the network if it isn't already. However, if you're considering setting up your own Web server at home or on a network that isn't currently running TCP/IP, you'll have a little more to think about.

If you're on a corporate network, talk to your network administrator—there's nothing you personally can do.

If you have a network—say, in a small business or at home—that's not connected to a network, you could either set up the network with a never-to-be-connected-to-the-Internet setup or with one that would allow you to eventually link to the Internet.

For safety's sake, we recommend taking the open-ended approach and requesting IP numbers from your Internet service provider. However, if you are absolutely sure that you won't ever be connecting to the Internet or if you have only a couple of computers to configure, you can use the IP numbers 192.0.2.1 through 192.0.2.255.0 for your local network. Simply use a unique number (1 through 255 in the final set of numbers) for each computer.

While actually getting the network going is beyond the scope of this book, the online help in Windows 95 and NT effectively covers the basics. If you need a little more information, check out *Mastering Windows NT Server,* by Mark Minasi, and *Networking Windows 95 with IntranetWare and NT Server,* by Jeff Bankston. Both are available from Sybex.

Configuring Your Server

After installing your new server, you'll need to configure it. As you would expect, how you do this depends on the server. OmniHTTPd has its own little program, and Microsoft's Personal Web Server and Netscape servers use HTML forms to handle the configuration. Of course, traditional Unix servers such as Apache have huge, long conf files that you have to edit manually. For example purposes, in this section we'll configure OmniHTTPd.

You'll find the icons to start the Administration portion of a Web server either in the Control Panel, in the System Extensions (on Macs), or hanging out in the icon tray at the right edge of the Windows taskbar. Double-click the icon, and, if necessary, look for a Properties or Setup choice. For example, OmniHTTPd has a Properties item on the Admin menu. Browse through the menus, dialog boxes, and tabs to see what's going on. The server should start out functional, so any changes you make will be for your convenience, to improve the features supported, or to improve security.

Use the following information to get your Web server up and running. The exact commands and their locations will differ from server to server, but the principles are the same.

Port   The port specifies where the server will listen for HTTP connections. By default (both with your personal server and on the Internet as a whole), the listening port is 80. By choosing a different port, you make it more difficult for people to find you (the URL would look like www.me.com:911 if you choose port 911), but the different port also lets you run multiple Web servers on the same machine. For example, you could have the OmniHTTPd server at port 80, Microsoft's Personal Web Server at port 8080, and a Netscape FastTrack Server at port 8888, thus letting you test out multiple servers with the same data.

Site Address   This is the IP number or domain name for the server. If you're on a network, enter either your domain name (if you have one) or the IP number (if you don't have a domain name) for your computer here. If you installed a server on a stand-alone machine for testing or if you don't care about accessing the server remotely, you can use 127.0.0.1, which always specifies the local machine.

NOTE

A DNS (Domain Name Service) server on most TCP/IP networks provides the computers on the network with the equivalent numbers (such as 139.78.200.19) for each domain name (such as raycomm.com). Although the computers require the numbers, the names are—obviously—far easier for mere mortals to remember.

Server Root   This is the top-level folder and contains your Web documents. If you specify the server root of hobbes.raycomm.com as c:\mydocs\, the directory listing of c:\mydocs will be visible at hobbes.raycomm.com/. You can use any folder you want as the server root—many of the examples in this book use a server root buried many levels deep in our Mastering HTML folders.

Default Index   This specifies which file opens automatically if the URL does not specify a file name. For example, if you connect to www.xmission.com//, you'll see the index.html file because you didn't specify a file and the index.html file is the default index for that server. Were that file missing, you'd probably see the listing of all files in that folder.

Logging   This specifies which logs (or records) of Web server activity will be kept. This item is much more important if you're connected to a network or running an intranet server on your local computer than it might be if you're running a personal Web server for the heck of it. You can store the logs anywhere on the server, but we recommend keeping them with the rest of your Web materials.

Aliases   You can use aliases to make it appear that other folders are located within your Web "tree" (subfolders from the document root) without actually moving them there. For example, if you want your graphics files from c:\graphics to be accessible through the Web, you can set an alias so that they're accessed through the Web, even if your document root is in c:\httpd\htdocs. It would look something like Figure 6.3.

FIGURE 6.3

Aliased folders are accessible through the Web, even though they are not within the main documents folder.

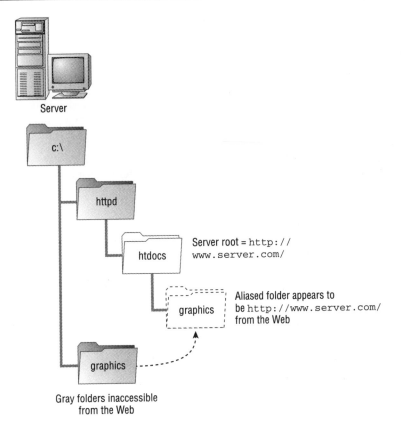

Server

c:\

httpd

htdocs

Server root = http://www.server.com/

graphics

Aliased folder appears to be http://www.server.com/ from the Web

graphics

Gray folders inaccessible from the Web

CGI You use CGI settings to specify which folders contain programs that visitors can run through the Web. You must list any folders containing counters, form processors, or similar applications here. For your protection, however, you should probably ensure that all applications to be run from the Web end up in the same folder and make that your only CGI folder. CGI can open a large security hole in your system, and you should be aware of the programs that are available to be run, particularly if your server is on the Internet.

MIME MIME, which stands for *Multipurpose Internet Mail Extensions*, specifies how files are sent out from the Web server. The MIME type of a file, in conjunction with browser settings, determines how the server handles the file. For example, from the MIME table (a sample is shown in Table 6.1), the server determines that files with the extension of htm or html will be sent out with the MIME type identification of text/html. When a browser receives a file of text/html type, the browser promptly displays the file because the browser can display an HTML document. Browsers also display other types, such as image/gif, while they pass off less common or easily handled files such as application/rtf to whatever program usually takes care of those files.

Again, the browser dictates which programs handle which files—all the server does is specify the MIME type for a specific extension. The most likely change you'd make to the list of MIME types on the server would be to specify that unconventional extensions be sent as specific file types. For example, Cold Fusion (which helps generate HTML from a database), uses a file extension of cfm, but the CFM files are really HTML documents. Therefore, you'd add cfm as a legitimate extension that should be sent to the browser as an HTML document.

TABLE 6.1: MIME TYPES

MIME Type	Typical File Extensions
application/mac-binhex40	hqx
application/octet-stream	bin
application/oda	oda
application/pdf	pdf
application/postscript	ai eps ps
application/rtf	rtf
application/x-mif	mif
application/x-csh	csh
application/x-dvi	dvi
application/x-hdf	hdf
application/x-netcdf	nc cdf

Continued ▶

TABLE 6.1 CONTINUED: MIME TYPES

MIME Type	Typical File Extensions
application/x-latex	latex
application/x-sh	sh
application/x-tcl	tcl
application/x-tex	tex
application/x-texinfo	texinfo texi
application/x-troff	t tr roff
application/x-troff-man	man
application/x-troff-me	me
application/x-troff-ms	ms
application/x-wais-source	src
application/zip	zip
application/x-bcpio	bcpio
application/x-cpio	cpio
application/x-gtar	gtar
application/x-shar	shar
application/x-sv4cpio	sv4cpio
application/x-sv4crc	sv4crc
application/x-tar	tar
application/x-ustar	ustar
audio/basic	au snd
audio/x-aiff	aif aiff aifc
audio/x-wav	wav
image/gif	gif
image/ief	ief
image/jpeg	jpeg jpg jpe
image/tiff	tiff tif
image/x-cmu-raster	ras
image/x-portable-anymap	pnm
image/x-portable-bitmap	pbm
image/x-portable-graymap	pgm
image/x-portable-pixmap	ppm
image/x-rgb	rgb
image/x-xbitmap	xbm
image/x-xpixmap	xpm
image/x-xwindowdump	xwd
text/html	html htm htl
text/plain	txt c cc h
text/richtext	rtx

Continued ▶

TABLE 6.1 CONTINUED: MIME TYPES	
MIME Type	**Typical File Extensions**
text/tab-separated-values	`tsv`
text/x-setext	`etx`
video/mpeg	`mpeg mpg mpe`
video/quicktime	`qt mov moov`
video/x-msvideo	`avi`
video/x-sgi-movie	`movie`

Indexing or Directory Listing   The Indexing or Directory Listing specifies whether the server should send the directory listing to the browser (assuming that no specific file is requested and that no file of the Default Index name exists). If you're working on your local computer and simply testing pages, you'll probably want to enable this option (either as a table or as a list, whichever is most convenient). If your Web server is on the Internet, however, or even on an intranet but needs to look presentable, consider disabling this so that your visitors can't freely roam through your site and see all of the not-for-public-consumption documents out there.

Server-Side Includes   These allow you to tell the server to include information, commands, or files when the server sends the file back to the browser. Precisely which includes are available depends greatly on the server, but some examples are the date and time, the server name, the last date on which a file was modified, and the address the browser came from, plus the ability to include other files. Although items such as the date and time and the server name aren't particularly useful (although passing that information back to a JavaScript application in a Web page can be handy), including last modified dates automatically can be a time saver, and can help your visitors know what's current and what's not.

Using a Server

Regardless of the server or servers you choose to install, you'll need to get the following information from your system administrator if you're accessing through an ISP or a corporate server:

> **The address of the HTTP server** (for example, www.raycomm.com, hobbes.raycomm.com): Depending on your situation, you may need to know

the folder name from which your files will be accessed. For example, the following URL was necessary to access files at our site: www.xmission.com/~ejray/.

The address of the FTP server, if required (for example, `ftp://ftp.xmission.com/`): Depending on how you get your files onto the server, you might have to use FTP (*File Transfer Protocol*). Of course, it's also possible, particularly in a corporate or educational environment, that you would simply copy the files to a specific folder on a network drive, and that would be that.

Password and access restrictions: You probably (almost certainly) need a userid and password to upload files to the server.

Here are some additional questions you'll want to ask:

What kind of server is it, and what platform does the server run on? If you know the server and the platform, you can find the documentation on the Web, which should tell you which scripts you can easily add. For example, if an Apache server is running on a Sun Sparcstation (a likely ISP scenario), you can reasonably request that your server administrator install specific Perl scripts. However, if you're on an intranet with a Windows NT-based Netscape server and you hear of a cool enhancement to the WebStar server on a Macintosh, you can save yourself some embarrassment and just not ask for it.

Can I restrict access to my pages? When testing pages on the server, you don't want the whole world to see them—setting a password-restricted access to the whole site helps with this. Additionally, if you have some pages that you want to make available to only a few people (or to everyone except a few people), you need to be able to set passwords.

TIP

Not making obvious links to a page is by no means a guarantee that nobody will be able to find it. See Chapter 19 to learn about searchable HTML.

Can I install and run my own scripts? If you can, you'll have a lot more flexibility and capabilities than you would otherwise. If you're limited to what your ISP has already installed for your use, you are likely to have access to special capabilities, such as chat rooms.

Do you maintain access logs? How can I find out how many hits my site gets? If you're selling services, promoting your company, or doing anything else where the number of people who see your message is significant, you'll need to be sure that accesses are logged and you'll need to learn how to get to those logs.

Ask your server administrator what kinds of tools are available to view and sort Web server access logs—the "raw" (unprocessed) logs are an ugly mess, but lots of neat programs exist to parse the logs into something useful. Although your server administrator might well have some of these programs installed, the access instructions might not be publicized.

Who do I call if the server fails to respond at 2 PM? How about 2 AM?

Do you make backups or do I need to back up my own site personally? Under what circumstances will you restore backup files—only if the server crashes or also if I make a mistake and delete my files?

Uploading Your HTML Documents to a Server

The process involved in uploading (copying) your documents to a server will be different for most servers and installations. It can be as easy as copying a file to a folder (on a corporate intranet) or as idiosyncratic as completing multiple page online forms and copying files to a folder (on intranets in Dilbert-esque companies—yes, we have examples). It can also be a straightforward process involving an FTP application (the common process on intranets and with ISPs).

The easiest way to upload files to a server is with a program such as the Microsoft Web Publishing Wizard or the one-button publishing tools included in Netscape Communicator and in many higher-end HTML editing applications. The one-button tools work well if all the files belong in one folder and if you're comfortable letting the programs (particularly Communicator) "adjust" links as the files are uploaded.

The best way, however, is probably to use a more traditional FTP application, which is scarcely more complex, but infinitely more powerful and flexible. Literally dozens of FTP applications exist and work equally well. We'll walk you through traditional FTP in the next section and then show you what to expect from a graphical FTP application in the following section.

Uploading Using FTP

FTP is the Internet standard mechanism for transferring files. Although the specific folders will depend on your server setup, you'll need to know the information outlined in Table 6.2 (make a copy of this table and put your specific information in column 3).

TABLE 6.2: INFORMATION YOU'LL NEED TO KNOW BEFORE USING FTP

Information	Example	Your Information
FTP Server Address	`ftp.xmission.com`	
Userid	`foobar`	
Password	`********`	Don't write it down!
Folder on server to use	`public_html`	

Table 6.3 lists most of the FTP commands you'll need to upload files with a traditional FTP application.

TABLE 6.3: FTP COMMANDS USED FOR TRANSFERRING FILES

Command	Description
`ftp`	Starts an FTP application.
`open "…"`	Opens an FTP connection to the ftp server name specified.
`close`	Closes an FTP connection without exiting the FTP application.
`quit`	Closes an FTP connection and the application.
`put`	Uploads files to the server computer.
`get`	Downloads files from the server computer.
`ascii`	Sets the file type to ASCII, to upload HTML or other text documents.
`binary`	Sets the file type to binary, to upload image or class files and other binary documents.
`cd`	Changes directory on the server. Follow cd with the folder name to change into the folder, and follow cd with a .. to move out of the folder.
`pwd`	Print Working Directory, which tells you what folder you're in.
`quit`	Exits the FTP applicaation.

Uploading Files Using a Text-Based FTP Application   Before you get started, you'll need the information specified in Table 6.2, and you'll need to have your HTML documents and related files at hand. Follow these steps:

1. At a text prompt (a DOS prompt or the Unix shell), change into the folder that contains the files you want to upload. For example, if you are at a `c:` prompt and your files are in the TestWeb subfolder, type **cd testweb**.

2. Type **FTP** to start the FTP application.

3. At the FTP> prompt, type **open** and the address of the FTP server, for example:

`open ftp.xmission.com`

4. When prompted, enter your userid and then your password. Remember that the userid and password are case-sensitive.

5. Change to the folder where you want to store the files. If you're uploading files to an ISP, your folder name will probably be `public_html` or `www` or something similar.

`cd public_html`

6. To upload HTML documents, first set the file type to ASCII. Type **ascii**.

7. Now, upload the documents with the `put` command. For example, type:

`put filename.htm`

If you have multiple files to upload, you can use the `mput` command and a wildcard. For example, to upload all files in the folder that have a filename ending with `htm`, type:

`mput *.htm`

8. To upload binary files (such as graphics), first set the file type to binary. Type **binary**.

9. Now, upload the documents with the `put` command. For example, type:

`put image.gif`

If you have multiple files to upload, use the `mput` command and a wildcard. For example, to upload all files in the folder that have a name ending with `gif`, type:

`mput *.gif`

10. When you're finished, type **quit**.

Now, open your Web browser and try to access the files you just uploaded. If you find broken image icons, odds are that you didn't specify binary before you uploaded the files (a common problem). Try again, being careful to specify binary.

If you used a WYSIWYG editor and your links do not work correctly, check out the raw HTML code to verify that the links were not "helpfully" changed. Netscape Composer and Gold (Composer's predecessor) are notorious for fixing links that then don't work.

Uploading Files Using Graphical FTP Applications An arguably easier procedure is available if you have a graphical FTP application (such as WS-FTP, for Windows) or Fetch (available from fetch.dartmouth .com). The specific procedure depends on the software, but generally resembles the following. Before you start, have at hand the same information you gathered for the text-based FTP application.

Use the following procedure to upload files with WS-FTP, a Windows application:

1. Start the application, probably by double-clicking its icon.

2. Fill in the essential blanks in the Session Properties dialog box.

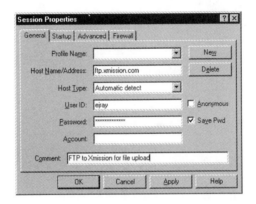

Host Name/Address: Enter the address of the FTP server.

Host Type: Choose Automatic or the specific type if you know it. Generally, Automatic works fine.

User ID: Enter the id that the system administrator or ISP provided.

Password: Enter the password that the system administrator or ISP provided.

Leave the other fields blank unless your system administrator gave you that information.

Both userid and password are case-sensitive—if you substitute uppercase for lowercase or vice versa, it won't work.

3. Click OK. You'll see a connecting message as your FTP client connects to the FTP server.

4. Select the appropriate local folder on the left side of the window and the appropriate remote folder on the right side of the window. You select folders by double-clicking them or by selecting them and clicking the ChgDir button.

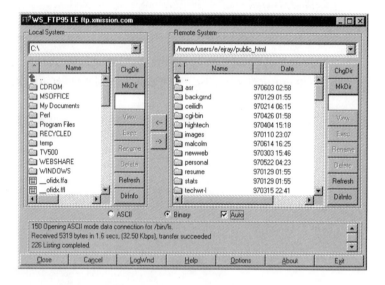

5. When you have the correct folders open on both sides, check the Auto checkbox to specify how the computers exchange files. Automatic is usually fine. HTML files transfer as ASCII (because they're plain text), and images transfer as binary (because they're binary, not text, files). If you try automatic and uploaded files don't work properly, set the transfer manually to binary for graphics and ASCII for HTML and other text documents.

If you can't open and read the file in Notepad, Simple Text, or vi, it's not a text file. You must transfer all word-processed documents, spreadsheets, and multimedia files as binary.

6. Select the files to transfer, and then click either the arrow (pointing from your local drive to the server drive) or the Copy button.

That's all there is to it. Now, test all your uploaded files.

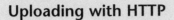

Uploading with HTTP

Some automatic publishing tools offer the option of uploading via HTTP instead of FTP. However, relatively few ISPs support HTTP uploads because of security considerations and because it's a fairly new technology.

The primary difference is that with HTTP you need provide only the Web address at which your files should end up, rather than the FTP server address.

For you, the Web developer, there's no real benefit to either approach as long as the files transfer correctly.

Uploading through Your Browser

If you use a fairly recent version of the Navigator browser, you can upload files by entering `ftp://yourid@yourftpserver.com/` in the Location line. You'll be prompted for your password. The only drawback to this approach is that you must be familiar with the structure of the files on the server. For example, at our ISP, we have to browse through the following folders to get into the folder to upload files to our Web site:

```
ftp://ejray@ftp.xmission.com/home/users/e/ejray/public_html
```

(We can also enter that whole long line into the location window directly.) After you browse to the correct folder, choose File ➣ Upload File to select the file to upload (you can upload only one file at a time).

TIP

If you upload through your browser, take a second to bookmark that long URL location of your files so that you won't have to browse to it again.

Including Server-Specific Capabilities

Different Web servers offer different—often drastically so—capabilities and strengths. It's in your best interest, particularly if you're working on a large site or complex material, to learn your server's particular strengths and how to take advantage of them.

Using Server-Side Includes

Server-side includes (SSIs) are commands to the Web server that are embedded in HTML documents. The server scans all files as it sends them out, and when it sees a server-side include, it replaces the command with the actual text. Some of the most obvious and commonly used SSI commands include the date on which a file was last modified (giving an automatic last modified date that works for all browsers, not just JavaScript capable browsers) and the current date and time. JavaScript and Java applets can also use data from server-side includes.

See Chapters 11 and 12 for information about JavaScript and Java applets.

Although these uses are valid, one of the truly useful applications of server-side includes is to automatically add boilerplate text to documents. For example, if you want a footer on every page, you can simply place the `include` command in each file and keep a master footer file on the server. By separating documents from boilerplate headers and footers, you can maintain a single copy of the boilerplate text and require that all pages on the server include the `include` directive.

What good does this do? It allows you to develop a footer once—with, for example, copyright information, a `mailto:` link to contact the Webmaster, and a tiny version of your corporate logo. The server can then automatically insert that material in every document. If you need to change the footer for any reason, you change the `include` directive, and the change takes place automatically on all pages served thereafter. You don't have to worry about getting *all* your files updated and revised with the new information, nor do you have to worry about making sure that all pages are identical throughout the server.

The downside to using SSIs is that you really have to test everything on a Web server—you can't see how it will look unless you have the server to fill in the `include` directive. When you open a document locally with an `include`, the server is out of the picture, and the browser ignores the `include` statement.

Check out the documentation for the Web server you're using to find out how to use server-side includes on your server and to learn what includes are available.

To include a file with standard SSI commands, use the following process. This particular example shows you how to include a file with a server-side include, although the steps apply to any SSI.

1. Develop the file to include. This can be as complex or as simple as you want, but should be generic enough to be identical on all pages. Omit the HTML structural tags. You'll have something like the following code:

```
<HR WIDTH=70% SIZE=8 NOSHADE>
<IMG SRC="asrlogosm.gif" ALIGN="LEFT" WIDTH="200" HEIGHT="84" BORDER="0"
ALT="ASR Small Logo">
<P ALIGN=RIGHT>Copyright &copy; 1997 ASR Outfitters, Inc.<BR>
ASR Outfitters,
<A HREF="mailto:info@asroutfitters.com">info@asroutfitters.com</A><BR>
4700 N. Center,
South Logan, UT 87654<BR>
801-555-3422</P>
```

2. Develop the main document—or one of them.

NOTE

If you are inserting a file into only one document, you should probably not be using a server-side include.

3. Place the `include` statement at the bottom of the main document, above the closing </BODY> and </HTML> tags, like this:

```
<!--#include virtual="/footer.htm"-->
</BODY>
</HTML>
```

This `include` statement tells the server to replace the statement with the file called footer.htm found in the root folder of the Web server. (The footer.htm file could as easily be in a subfolder of the server—just adjust the path accordingly.) When you open the main document through a Web server, the server fills in the footer automatically.

Understanding CGI

CGI (an abbreviation for *Common Gateway Interface*) defines how Web pages interact with programs on the server. CGI programs can be anything from simple scripts to show what time it is wherever the server is, to complex chat programs or redirection scripts that send you off to a different page automatically. Writing CGI programs is beyond the scope of this book, but you will likely have occasion to use some scripts. This section will give you some background.

You can write CGI scripts in any programming or scripting language that the server computer supports, but C, C++, and Perl scripts are by far the most common. The functionality of the script is completely independent of the programming language in which it was written, so don't be concerned about using the "right" language.

Unless you have something particular and idiosyncratic in mind, you probably won't need to write many scripts or CGI programs anyway—almost anything you'd ever want exists and is readily available. Check out the Companion CD (or the Web sites for the latest versions) for:

- Selena Sol's Public Domain CGI Script Archive at `selena.mcp.com/`
- Matt's Script Archive at `www.worldwidemart.com/scripts/`

Both sites offer plenty of ideas, examples, functional scripts, and starting points.

In addition to the complex scripts available from Matt and Selena's archives, more simple scripts exist as a good starting place for your CGI ventures. In this section, we'll briefly examine the process of including a simple script—for a counter—in your page. Because the script is already complete, including a reference to it in your Web site is simple and straightforward.

A counter is one of the first CGI programs that most Web developers install, more because of the availability of counters than for any other reason. Installing a CGI program on the server and then adding the lines of HTML code to access the program (or just doing the HTML code part) is straightforward for all programs, from counters to chat rooms.

For many of you, tracking the number of *hits* (the number of times your site is accessed) provides useful information. For example, if you advertise a product on your Web site and you seem to be getting a lot of hits, you might consider letting visitors order your products online. Also, knowing how much traffic your site gets can help you budget time and money for developing, enhancing, and updating it.

Keep in mind, though, that a counter shows the number of hits, which could be embarrassing if you have a completely underwhelming number, such as 000000021. Additionally, because many counters can easily be reset (quite unlike a car odometer), they're not a reliable indicator. In this case in particular, if visitors' browsers are set not to load images, the server will not add to the counter.

To set up a counter for your Web site, check with your server administrator for the specific commands to use. In the case of our ISP, there is already a counter program installed—they told us that. Because the program is already in place on the server, we just have to add a bit of HTML code to access it. This particular counter produces an image that looks vaguely like a car odometer.

Because the counter program produces an image, the actual Web page must include a reference to the image. Thus, we include a simple command like this:

```
<IMG SRC="/cgi-bin/counter.cgi">
```

The server runs the `counter.cgi` program whenever anyone accesses the page. The program generates the image and sends it back through the server, to the browser, just like any other image. Slick, huh? As you can imagine, CGI programs don't speed up your pages, but they do add a neat touch.

Where to Go from Here

In this chapter, you learned how large a role servers can play in the HTML development process. You not only use a server to publish your pages on the Web or on an intranet, but you also use them to process forms and track hits.

From here, you have lots of options. Here are a few suggestions:

- Head to Chapter 7 to learn how to include images.

- See Chapter 9 to learn how to include forms (remember, you'll need to get the server to process the form for you!).

- Check out Chapter 11 for a little information about using cookies, which allow you to track visitor information from one visit to another.

PART II

Advancing Your Skills

LEARN TO:

- *Incorporate images and image maps*

- *Develop tables*

- *Work with forms*

- *Create and use frames*

Chapter

7

Including Images

Including Images

lthough the original HTML implementation did not provide for images, the specification has evolved to allow you to include images and also to control them to some extent. Images (graphics, pictures, or illustrations) have become obligatory for most Web sites because they are an excellent way to communicate and because, let's face it, they're a lot more fun to look at than plain text.

Using images in HTML documents is a double-edged sword. On the one hand, using attractive, professional images is important if you want your site to be recognized and used. On the other hand, the more elaborate your images, the longer it takes for the page to load and the more likely your audience is to tire of waiting and head elsewhere. Your objective is to provide high-quality images in the smallest number of bits and bytes.

In this chapter, we'll look at how to select, prepare, and manipulate images, how to choose colors, and how to create image maps.

Developing Images

Although images add life to your Web pages, they can become a liability if not developed properly. As you select and develop images, consider three issues:

- File size
- Physical dimensions
- File type

Determining File Size

The file size of an image is the number of kilobytes, megabytes, or gigabytes it occupies on disk. Think of image files as being three-dimensional, having height and width as well as a number of colors. For example, a 16-color image not only has height and width, which you can see on the screen, but it also has 16 *layers*, one for each color. Therefore, the image's basic file size equals width × height × color depth.

You can effectively reduce file size with the following techniques:

- Reduce the number of colors. For example, you can reduce the color depth of an image that has millions of colors to only 256 colors with surprisingly little degradation in quality.

- Reduce the physical image size. For example, you can reduce an image from 600 × 400 pixels to 300 × 200 pixels. The resulting smaller image includes the details and clarity of the larger size, yet it occupies significantly less disk space. (You'll find guidelines for sizing images in the following section, "Dealing with Physical Size.")

- Use a format that *compresses* the file to cram more data into less space. (You'll find more details about suitable images formats in the section "Image Formats," later in this chapter.)

Dealing with Physical Size

The physical size of an image is its height and width and affects not only how it appears in a browser, but also how quickly it loads. Just how big should images be? If you browse the Web for a while, you'll notice that most professional-looking Web sites use small graphics, particularly for navigation buttons, icons, and highlights. As a rule, images can be smaller than you think and still be effective. For example, the ubiquitous Download Microsoft Internet Explorer button is approximately 88 × 31 pixels. Although this image is quite small, it is nevertheless effective.

Several factors are influential in determining the size of an image:

- The image's purpose
- The overall page design
- Your visitors' computer settings

Consider Image Purpose

Every time you add an image to a page, you need a good reason for doing so—to illustrate a point, to show a person or a location, to outline a process, or simply to add some color and zest to an otherwise hum-drum document. Be sure that every image enhances content, design, or both.

When determining the size of an image, consider its importance. For example, if your visitors need an image to understand a concept, the image should be larger. On the other hand, an image that adds a splash of color should probably be a bit smaller. If you're not sure how important an image is, lean toward smaller.

Consider Page Design

Images are visually "weighty" objects—that is, they attract attention faster than other page elements. Images that are too large often overwhelm page contents and obscure the message. When determining image size, in particular, consider how the image will appear relative to other page elements. Here are some questions to ask yourself:

- Will the page include multiple graphics?
- Will the page incorporate borders and shading, which are also weightier than text?
- Will the page contain a substantive amount of text or only a few words? Text can make up in volume what it lacks in visual weight. A lot of text balances a graphic more effectively than a small amount of text.

Consider Visitors' Computer Settings

If you have a smallish browser window, say 640×480 pixels, you will be overwhelmed by an image that will seem small to someone who has a 1280×1024 browser window. A good rule of thumb is to limit image size to no more than 600×400 pixels. An image of this size will fit completely within the browser window on Windows computers using the smallest (and, unfortunately, most common) screen resolution of 640×480 pixels.

When you encounter an image larger than 600×400, you will have to scroll vertically or horizontally to see it in its entirety, and, of course, it won't download quickly.

To convey content adequately, few images need to be larger than 600 × 400. Something in the 300 × 200 pixels range is usually a good size for photographs, and buttons are generally 50 × 50 pixels or smaller.

Understanding Image Formats

The information contained in an image file and how that file is stored define the image format. Two image formats now predominate on the Web and are widely accepted by graphical browsers:

- GIF
- JPG

A third image format, PNG, is new. It combines the best of both GIF and JPG formats and is likely to become a popular and widely accepted format in the near future.

Understanding GIFs

GIF, which is pronounced like *jiffy*, is an acronym formed from Graphics Interchange Format. All graphical browsers recognize the GIF format; in fact, some browsers recognize only GIF images. (CompuServe developed this format specifically for use online.) All GIF images have a file name extension of gif. Two main GIF formats exist: 87a and 89a. Only the 89a version offers the advantages we look at next.

GIF supports *transparency*. Transparency sets an image's background color to the browser's background color, thereby making the image appear as if it has no background. This transparent color blends into the background of the browser and can create the effect of an image that is not rectangular. For example, the ASR Outfitters logo is a transparent image—the corner areas are a different color and set to be transparent. Figure 7.1 shows this image as it appears in an image-editing program (Paint-Shop Pro); even if you set the background as transparent, you can still see it. Figure 7.2 shows this image as it appears in a browser (Netscape Navigator).

FIGURE 7.1

Viewed in an image-editing program, the transparent background is still visible.

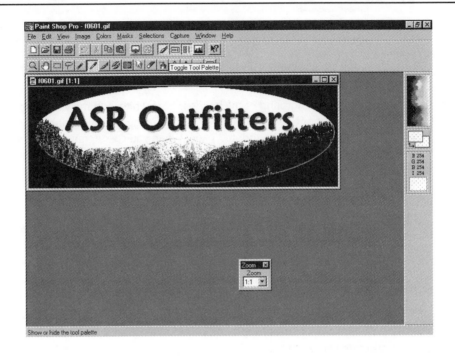

FIGURE 7.2

Viewed in a browser, the transparent background is not visible.

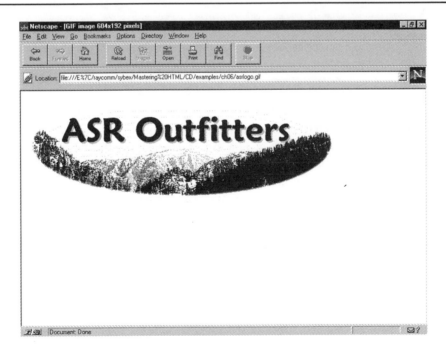

PART

II

Advancing Your Skills

About These Images

First, the image shown in Figures 7.1 and 7.2 is about 600 pixels wide, and it is almost overwhelming when viewed in a browser.

Second, the background of the image is pure white, and the visible area within the oval is almost, but not quite, white. We had to change the background color to make transparency apparent on the printed page. When you create transparent images, you might find it useful to set the transparent color to an unusual color, thus making it easier to see at a glance what is supposed to be transparent.

GIF supports *animation*.   Some image-editing programs and specialized programs can combine several GIF images into a single file, which then displays each image or panel in turn. The effect is rather like that in cartoon flip books—you flip the pages and see an illusion of motion.

Not all browsers display animated GIFs, although the newest browsers support them. Using animated GIFs is a simple way to provide animation without resorting to Java applets or to more sophisticated plug-ins. You'll find more information about animated GIFs in Chapter 12.

Animated GIFs are much larger than non-animated GIFs, containing the equivalent of an additional image for each panel of animation.

GIF supports *progressive rendering*.   Progressive rendering is also known as *interlacing*, which refers to how an image comes up on the screen. A browser displays a non-interlaced image line by line, as it is received over the network or loaded off a disk. The complete image is not visible until it has all been loaded. A browser displays interlaced images in passes, filling in every eighth line until the entire image is displayed.

The effects of interlacing vary from browser to browser. Some browsers display the downloading image as slowly coming into focus. Other browsers display it as venetian blinds slowly being opened until the entire image is displayed. Either way, interlaced images begin to appear on the screen faster than noninterlaced images and allow visitors who are familiar with the image to get the gist before the whole image appears.

GIF supports *lossless compression.* Lossless compression is an efficient way to save files without losing image details. When GIFs are saved, they are compressed to take less space on the disk and less time to download. Roughly speaking, the compression algorithm notices broad expanses of single colors, and, instead of recording the color for each individual pixel in the image, it indicates the color and the number of times to repeat the color. The image is not changed; it is simply saved more efficiently. Because GIF compression is lossless, GIF images are best for line art, icons, and drawings.

NOTE

GIFs do have one significant disadvantage—they can only include 256 colors, which is not sufficient for true photographic quality. Although for many purposes 256 colors is adequate, you may want to use the JPG file format for images requiring higher quality.

Understanding JPG/JPEG

JPEG, which is pronounced *jay-peg*, is an acronym formed from Joint Photographic Experts Group. This image format (often written as JPG) is the second most popular for images on the Web. As a whole, JPG images are less flexible than GIF images, and most significantly, they do not support the variety of rendering options that GIFs support.

As a whole, JPG images are less flexible than GIF images, and most significantly, they do not support the variety of rendering options that GIFs support.

TIP

We expect JPG to support progressive rendering sometime in the near future.

The most significant advantage of JPG is that it supports millions of colors, thereby providing much more realistic photographic reproduction. Additionally, because JPG images use a more effective—but lossy—compression algorithm, they are much smaller and download faster. *Lossy* compression discards some details of the image to decrease the file size. JPG images are best for photographs because the loss of detail is less noticeable with photographs than with line art; plus, the compression ratio and resulting quality are much better with photographs.

Setting JPG options in your image-editing program helps control both the eventual file size and the quality. In most image editing programs, you can set the number of dots per inch (DPI) and the level of JPG compression. If the images are only for Web use—they won't be used for print publications—a DPI of 100 is more than adequate.

PART

II

Advancing Your Skills

Depending on the image, the application, and the eventual purpose for the image, you can often increase the compression substantially without losing much detail.

The samples in this chapter's folder (jpgcomp.htm) on the Companion CD show the same image saved in JPG format at compression levels of 1, 15, 30, 60, and 80. The sizes range from 130K all the way down to 11K, and the difference in quality is barely discernible except at very high compression levels.

Understanding PNG

PNG, pronounced *ping*, stands for Portable Network Graphics. This new image file format is the wave of the future for the Web. PNG images combine most of the advantages of GIF, including transparency and interlacing, plus the ability to accommodate millions of colors and a tight, lossless compression technique. At this time, only Internet Explorer 4 supports PNG, and it could be quite some time before PNG images are supported widely enough to be considered a primary graphic in Web pages.

NOTE

Plug-ins are available, at the time of writing, for Netscape Communicator to support PNG graphics. However, direct support, as for JPG or GIF, is not in the immediate plans.

Which Image Format Is Right For You?

Which image format you choose depends on the features you want to include. Table 7.1 compares the relative features of the three graphic formats examined.

TABLE 7.1: FEATURES OF GIF, JPG, AND PNG

Features	GIF	JPG	PNG
Transparency	Yes	No	Yes
Interlacing/progressive rendering	Yes	Qualified Yes	Yes
Millions of colors	No	Yes	Yes
Lossless compression	Yes	No	Yes
Good for line art	Yes	No	Yes
Good for photographs	No	Yes	Yes
Accepted on most browsers	Yes	Yes	No

As you can see, GIF and JPG have complimentary advantages and disadvantages. As more browsers support PNG, however, it will probably become the first choice.

Adding Images

In this section, we're going to create some Web pages for ASR Outfitters, a mountaineering and hiking supply company that is a mythical, miniversion of REI, the recreation equipment retailer. In the process, you'll learn how to include images in an HTML document. Although this may seem like putting the cart before the horse, knowing how to include images makes learning to develop them easier.

TIP

If you want to experiment with the examples, you'll find the files on the CD in the /examples/ch07 folder.

Table 7.2 shows the main image tags and attributes used to insert images in Web pages.

TABLE 7.2: IMAGE TAGS AND ATTRIBUTES

Tag	Use
`<IMG>`	Marks an image within an HTML document
`ALT="..."`	Specifies alternative text to display if an image is not displayed
`SRC="..."`	Points to an image file (URL) to include
`HEIGHT=n`	Specifies the final height of an image in pixels
`WIDTH=n`	Specifies the final width of an image in pixels
`BORDER=n`	Specifies the width of a border around an image, in pixels
`ALIGN="..."`	Specifies image alignment as TOP, MIDDLE, BOTTOM, LEFT, or RIGHT

Adding an Image

To add an image to an HTML document, you include a single tag with a reference to the image. The image reference is called the *source*, indicated by the SRC= attribute, which points to the image file.

Although you'll probably be linking to another file within the same folder—at least initially—and thus using only the file name, you can use any valid URL within the SRC= attribute. For example, if you are developing a Web site for a local organization and the headquarters provides a standard logo at its Web site, you might consider linking to this source. Or, if ASR Outfitters franchises a new outlet, the franchisee can use an <IMG> tag such as the following to include the logo:

```
<IMG SRC="http://www.asroutfitters.com/gifs/asrlogo.gif"
ALT="ASR Outfitters Logo">
```

A URL used in the SRC= attribute is called a *remote reference*. Referencing logos and images remotely has certain advantages and some significant drawbacks. One advantage is that remote references to images ensure that you're always using the current logo. For example, if ASR Outfitters hires a graphic design company to change its corporate image, the franchisee's site will reflect the changes as soon as the main site changes. Additionally, remote references lighten the load on your server and reduce the number of files you must manage and manipulate.

On the down side, changes that are out of your control can easily break links from your site. If the ASR Outfitters Webmaster decides to move the images from a GIFs subdirectory into an images subdirectory, the franchisee's images will no longer work, because the SRC= attribute points to the subdirectory that no longer contains the image files. From the visitor's perspective, the franchisee simply has a nonfunctional site—the visitor really doesn't know or care about the reason.

Additionally, network glitches or server problems can also render your images inoperative if you link to them remotely. If the load on your own site is significant and you use remote image, the other site may be swamped with the demand and not even know why. Overall, you're probably better off copying the images to your local folder or at least to a different folder on your server, rather than relying on remote servers.

Copyright Laws Apply to Images

It is entirely possible to engage in copyright infringement without physically copying the images. For example, if Bad Karma Hiking Equipment decided that the ASR Outfitters images were cool and linked to them remotely without permission, you can bet that the ASR lawyers would be all over Bad Karma. This also applies to background images (covered later in this chapter) and any other content in any document. Be careful!

To add images to your document, start with a basic HTML document that, along with content, includes the following tags:

```
!DOCTYPE

<HTML>
```

```
<HEAD>

<BODY>
```

We used this basic document for ASR Outfitters:

```
<!DOCTYPE HTML PUBLIC "-//W3C//DTD HTML 4.0//EN">
<HTML>
<HEAD>
<TITLE>ASR Outfitters</TITLE>
</HEAD>
<BODY>
<H1 ALIGN=CENTER>ASR Outfitters</H1>
<P>We provide mountaineering and hiking equipment nationwide via mail order
as well as through our stores in the Rocky Mountains. </P>
<HR WIDTH=70% SIZE=8 NOSHADE>
<P>Please select from the following links:</P>
<UL>
<LI><A HREF="camping.html">Camping News</A>
<LI><A HREF="catalog.html">Catalog</A>
<LI><A HREF="clubs.html">Clubs</A>
<LI><A HREF="contact.html">Contact Us</A>
<LI><A HREF="weather.html">Check Weather</A>
</UL>
<HR WIDTH=70% SIZE=8 NOSHADE>
<CENTER>
<ADDRESS ALIGN=CENTER>ASR Outfitters<BR>
<A HREF="mailto:info@asroutfitters.com">info@asroutfitters.com</A><BR>
4700 N. Center<BR>
South Logan, UT 87654<BR>
801-555-3422<BR>
</ADDRESS>
</CENTER>
</BODY>
</HTML>
```

To add an image to this basic document, follow these steps:

1. Insert an <IMG> tag where you want the image to appear.

```
<H1 ALIGN=CENTER>ASR Outfitters</H1>
<IMG>
```

<P>We provide mountaineering and hiking equipment nationwide via mail order as well as through our stores in the Rocky Mountains.</P>

2. Add an SRC="..." attribute pointing to the image file name. In this example, the file name is `asrlogo.gif`, and it's in the same folder as the document; so that's all that's required.

`<IMG SRC="asrlogo.gif">`

3. In this case, add a line break tag <BR> after the <IMG> tag so that the next text starts on the following line (and not in any available space behind the image).

`<IMG SRC="asrlogo.gif">`**`<BR>`**

4. Because the image duplicates the content of the first-level heading, consider removing the first-level heading.

5. The first-level heading was centered, so consider adding a <CENTER> tag around the logo to center it.

`<CENTER>``<IMG SRC="asrlogo.gif"><BR></CENTER>`

NOTE

The <IMG> tag supports ALIGN= attributes with values of TOP, MIDDLE, BOTTOM, LEFT, and RIGHT, but does not support horizontal centering. If you want to use horizontal centering, use the <CENTER> tag. See the "Aligning the Image" section, later in this chapter, for more information.

You can see the resulting image in the ASR Web page shown in Figure 7.3.

Including Alternative Text

Alternative text describes an image that you have inserted. You include alternative text for the following reasons:

• Some of your visitors may be using text-only browsers.

• A visitor may have turned off images so that a file will load faster.

• Sometimes browsers don't display images correctly.

• Sometimes images don't display because the links aren't working properly.

• Sometimes browsers display alternative text while images load.

FIGURE 7.3

An image in the ASR Web page

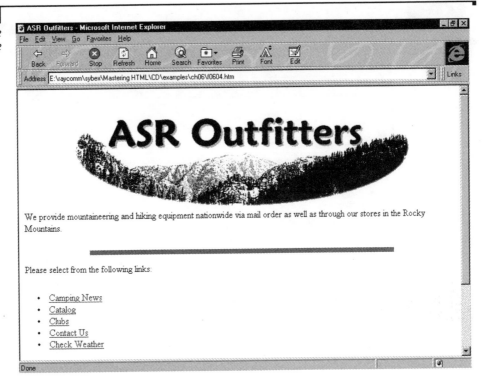

Alternative text should be clear and concise. Provide your visitors with enough information so they can understand the image content without viewing it. For example, alternative text for a logo can be as simple as the company name and the word *logo*. Even text as simple as "ASR Sample Photograph" or "ASR Content-Free Image" is helpful to visitors. If they see only the word *Image* (as they would if you omit the ALT= attribute), they'll have to load the images to see the content.

To add alternative text to your images, simply add the ALT= attribute to the <IMG> tag, like this:

```
<IMG SRC="asrlogo.gif" ALT="ASR Outfitters Logo">
```

The resulting alternative text is shown in Figure 7.4.

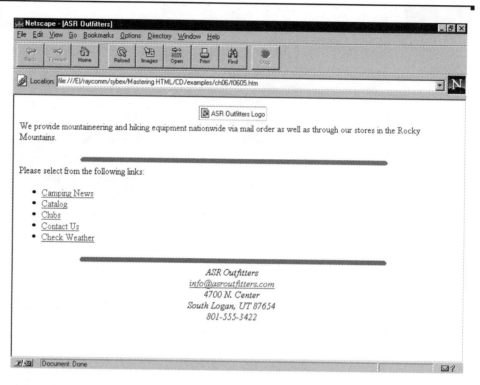

Speeding Perceived Image-Loading Time with Netscape

A Netscape-specific tag, LOWSRC=, works in conjunction with the SRC= attribute; it tells the browser to load a smaller version of the image first and then load the full image.

The idea is to use a small image (in terms of file size) for the LOWSRC= image. For example, use a JPG image that is compressed as much as possible but that retains the dimensions of the original image. This image appears quickly, and, if the visitor stays on the page long enough, the full image then loads.

This attribute, although not universally recognized, causes no adverse effects in browsers that don't support it—they simply ignore it.

Specifying Height and Width

You can speed the loading time of images by specifying an image's height and width. As the browser loads the page, it notes the height and width attributes and leaves that much space for the image. Next, it lays out the remaining text, and then it goes back and fills in the image. If you do not include these attributes, the browser has to load enough of the image to get the dimensions before it can lay out the rest of the text, thereby slowing the display of text.

To specify image height and width, add the HEIGHT= and WIDTH= attributes in the <IMG> tag, like this:

```
<IMG SRC="asrlogo.gif" ALT="ASR Outfitters Logo" HEIGHT="192" WIDTH="604">
```

As a rule, use the actual height and width of the image. To get the dimensions, open the image in an image-editing program, and look at the status bar. You will see something like 604 x 192 x 256, which indicates, in this example, that the asrlogo.gif image is 604 pixels wide, 192 pixels high, and 256 colors deep. With this information, you can then add the width (604) and height (192) attributes to the <IMG> tag.

PART

II

Advancing Your Skills

Formatting Using the Transparent GIF Trick

You can use transparent images to help force specific spacing in your documents. Suppose you want a blank space between two paragraphs. Because you can't insert a carriage return like you would in a word processor, you have to put in the blank space some other way—inserting a transparent GIF works really well in this case. A transparent GIF could also ensure that text appears a specific distance from the left margin—a transparent GIF works here, too.

To add spacing in a document with a transparent GIF, simply create a 1 x 1 pixel transparent GIF in your image-editing software and then insert that GIF into your HTML document.

Does the space have to be 1 pixel wide or 1 pixel high? Not necessarily. You can insert the itty-bitty (and thus very fast to download) image in the document and specify the size it will appear in a Web browser by adding the HEIGHT= and WIDTH= attributes. For example, your code might look like this:

```
<IMG SRC="trans.gif" HEIGHT="10" WIDTH="1">
```

CONTINUED

This example results in a blank space that's 10 pixels high and 1 pixel wide—ideal for ensuring spacing between paragraphs! Or, set the height to 1 and the width to 10, to indent text.

We present this option to you because, well, lots of people use it and if you have really specific formatting needs, it works. Keep in mind, though, that it's not standard, nor do we recommend it. HTML doesn't pretend to provide exact layout control, and attempting to get it is likely to prove frustrating.

If you really need to control the formatting exactly and your visitors have new browsers, your best bet is to try Style Sheets, which is the up-and-coming way to format your pages (see Chapter 5).

Aligning the Image

HTML provides several alignment options:

- Three vertical options align the image with respect to a line of text.
- Two options align the image to the left or to the right of the window (with corresponding text wrap).

The alignment options within the `<IMG>` tag override other alignment settings within the HTML document (for example, the `<CENTER>` tags surrounding the `<IMG>` tag).

By default, images align on the left, with accompanying text appearing on the same line; however, long text wraps to the following line. To ensure that accompanying text appears on the same line as the image, specify `ALIGN="LEFT"` in the `<IMG>` tag, like this:

```
<IMG SRC="asrlogo.gif" ALT="ASR Outfitters Logo" WIDTH="604" HEIGHT="192"
ALIGN="LEFT">
```

The text appears to the right of the left-aligned image, as shown in Figure 7.5.

You can create attractive effects by combining image alignment and text alignment. For example, setting an image to `ALIGN="RIGHT"` and then setting the accompanying text to `ALIGN="RIGHT"` forces the text to be flush against the image with a ragged left margin, as shown in Figure 7.6.

The remaining alignment options—`TOP`, `MIDDLE`, and `BOTTOM`—offer more in the context of small images. You use them to align the image within the text. For example, using `ALIGN="TOP"` aligns the top of the image with the top of the surrounding text, and the remainder of the image hangs below the text line. Using `ALIGN="MIDDLE"` places the middle of an image at the baselineof surrounding text. Similarly, using `ALIGN="BOTTOM"` places the bottom of an image on the same line as the text, and the remainder of the image extends considerably higher than the surrounding text. The effect of these options is shown in Figure 7.7.

MASTERING THE OPPORTUNITIES

HTML 4 Opportunities

Though any of these image-formatting tags will appear fine in HTML 3.2-compliant browsers, you might consider using Style Sheets for your formatting needs—including image formatting. The HTML 4 specification deprecated formatting tags, including alignment options, in favor of Style Sheets. See Chapter 5 for information about developing Style Sheets and see the Master's Reference for a comprehensive list of Style Sheet options.

FIGURE 7.5

Specifying left alignment ensures that accompanying text appears to the right of the image.

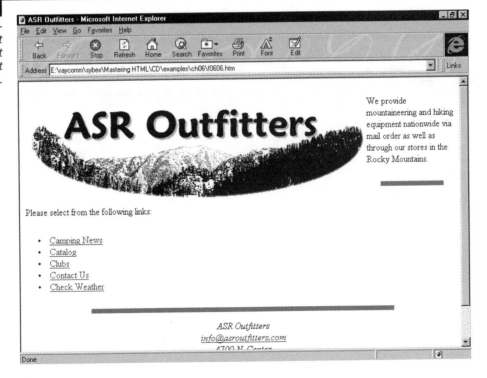

FIGURE 7.6

Specifying right alignment for the image and text produces appealing results.

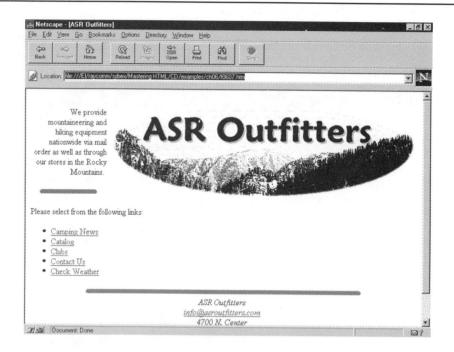

FIGURE 7.7

Top, middle, and bottom alignment float the image differently in relationship to the surrounding text.

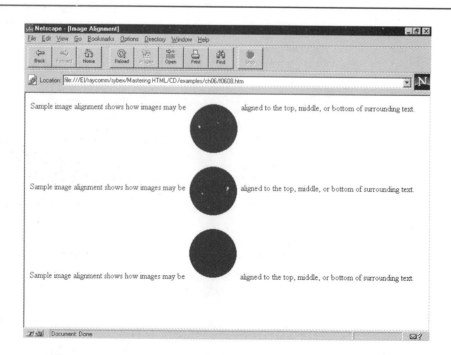

Controlling the Border

You control the border around an image with the BORDER= attribute. In most browsers, by default, the border is visible only on images that are used as links. To turn the border off for all images, add the BORDER="0" attribute to the <IMG> tag, resulting in a complete image tag:

```
<IMG SRC="asrlogo.gif" ALT="ASR Outfitters Logo" WIDTH="604"
HEIGHT="192" BORDER="0">
```

TIP

Remember, placing quotes around numeric values, such as 0, 192, or 604, is optional in attributes.

Likewise, you can increase the border width around an image by increasing the value in the BORDER= attribute, like this:

```
<IMG SRC="asrlogo.gif" ALT="ASR Outfitters Logo" WIDTH="604"
HEIGHT="192" BORDER="7">
```

The resulting border looks like that in Figure 7.8.

PART

II

Advancing Your Skills

FIGURE 7.8

Setting a large border width frames your images.

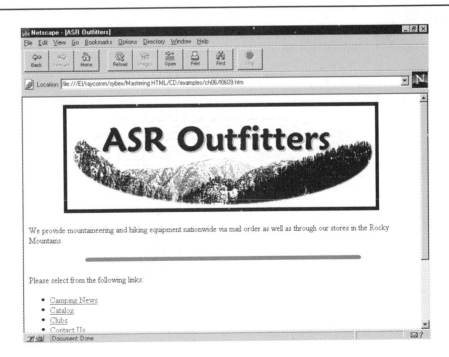

Choosing Suitable Colors

When creating your own images—or choosing colors for Web page or table backgrounds—you obviously want to choose colors that look good in most browsers, most of the time. If you're selecting colors for text or for small swatches of color, choose anything that appeals to you. However, if you're selecting a background color or a color that will appear in broad expanses of your HTML documents, be careful.

If you choose a color that is not available on a viewer's system, the browser will dither the color to approximate its appearance. *Dithering* is the technical term for substituting other colors, partially or wholly, to minimize the impact of not having the correct color. Dithering in photographs or small images is rarely noticeable, but dithering in large single-color areas results in blotchy or mottled appearances.

Now, consider that a large number of your visitors—or, at least, a large number of Web users in general—have computers set to display 256 colors. Sounds like the solution is to choose one of those 256 colors, doesn't it? Not quite. Macintosh, Unix, and Windows each use a different set of colors for system functions, and those colors—up to 40—are taken from the available 256, leaving only 216 colors for general use. If you choose one of these 216 colors, however, you can be fairly certain that the colors will look as good as they can in all browsers on all platforms. These remaining 216 colors are evenly distributed over the color spectrum, giving you a wide range of colors from which to choose.

In computer-ese, colors are represented as proportions of Red, Green, and Blue (RGB) and are specified by an RGB number. These RGB numbers combine to produce all available colors.

To specify a color, you provide numeric values to represent the proportions of red, green, and blue. In most image-editing programs, you can provide values in decimal numbers. However, when you're specifying colors in some image-editing programs and for colors within a Web page, you use hexadecimal numbers.

What are these numbers? They are the decimal values 0, 51, 102, 153, 204, 255 for each color. That is, a good (preferred) color might be 51, 51, 51 for the red, green, and blue values. In hexadecimal, the good values are 00, 33, 66, 99, CC, FF, so the corresponding sample color would be #333333. Where do these good values come from?

Table 7.3 lists the preferred (good) RGB values using hexadecimal numbers; Table 7.4 lists the values using decimal numbers. To create a safe (nondithering) color, choose one value from each column. For example, choose 66 from the first column, 33 from the second, and 00 from the third to create an RGB color of 663300.

TABLE 7.3: PREFERRED RGB VALUES IN HEXADECIMAL		
Red	**Green**	**Blue**
00	00	00
33	33	33
66	66	66
99	99	99
CC	CC	CC
FF	FF	FF

TABLE 7.4: PREFERRED RGB VALUES IN DECIMAL		
Red	**Green**	**Blue**
0	0	0
51	51	51
102	102	102
153	153	153
204	204	204
255	255	255

As a rule, colors close to these colors will also not dither, but there's no hard and fast rule on how "close" is close enough. For example, we tried 000001 and found that it didn't visibly dither on our computers...this time.

You'll find a complete list of browser-safe colors in the Master's Reference.

Using Images As Links

Using images as links offers two distinct advantages to both you and your visitors. First, images really can be as good as a thousand words. Often, including an image link can replace several words or lines of text, leaving valuable space for other page elements.

Small image links (called *thumbnails,* a term borrowed from the graphic arts world) representing larger images can decrease loading time. A visitor can view the thumbnail, which takes minimal time to download, and then choose to wait for the larger version to download or pursue some other avenue. (You'll find details about thumbnails in a following section, "Creating Thumbnails.")

Creating Image Links

To add an image as a link, start by adding an image tag. In this example, we are adding a fancy button to the ASR Outfitters page to replace the more prosaic Camping News bulleted list item. The name of the image is camping.gif, and the file it should link to is camping.html.

NOTE

When you use images as links, the alternative text is critical. If clicking the image is the only way visitors can connect to the other page, the alternative text is their only clue if the image is not displayed (because of technical difficulties, because they've turned off images, because they have a text-only browser, and so on).

Here are the steps for adding an image link:

1. Add an image tag and an SRC= attribute to the document.

   ```
   <IMG SRC="camping.gif">
   ```

2. Include alternative text using the ALT= attribute.

   ```
   <IMG SRC="camping.gif" ALT="Camping News">
   ```

3. Add the remaining attributes you want to include, like the HEIGHT= and WIDTH= and BORDER= attributes. If you choose to use BORDER=0 and turn off the border completely, be sure that the image is visually identified as a link. Otherwise, your visitors might not know it's a link unless they pass their mouse over it and see the pointing-hand cursor.

   ```
   <IMG SRC="camping.gif" WIDTH="300" HEIGHT="82" BORDER="0"
   ALT="Camping News">
   ```

4. Add the link anchor tag, <A>, before and after the image.

   ```
   <A><IMG SRC="camping.gif" WIDTH="300" HEIGHT="82" BORDER="0"
   ALT="Camping News"></A>
   ```

5. Add the HREF= attribute to the opening anchor tag to specify the image file name.

   ```
   <A HREF="camping.html"><IMG SRC="camping.gif" WIDTH="300" HEIGHT="82"
   BORDER="0" ALT="Camping News"></A>
   ```

Now you have an image that acts as a link to the camping.html file. After adding a couple more images and surrounding them all with the <CENTER> tags, the ASR Outfitters page is similar to Figure 7.9.

FIGURE 7.9

Image links can make a page much more attractive (and slower to load).

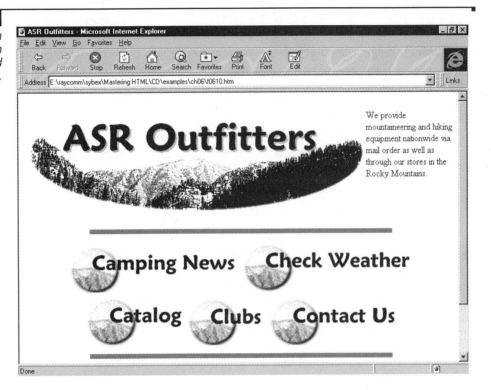

PART

II

Advancing Your Skills

Creating Thumbnails

As we mentioned earlier, a thumbnail is a smaller version of an image, but it is also a link to the larger version. Thumbnails can also link to multimedia applets or to other content that is time-consuming to download or not universally accessible.

For example, ASR Outfitters included a thumbnail of the original photograph that inspired its logo. This thumbnail links to the original photograph, a larger image.

To add a thumbnail image, start by having both images—the thumbnail and the larger version—available. You can use samples from the /examples/ch07 folder on the CD, or you can create your own. Make a thumbnail by starting with the full-size version (from an image library on the CD, scanned from your private collection, or from any other source). Then, use your image-editing software to resize or resample the image to a much smaller size—as small as possible while still retaining the gist of the image. Save this second image under a different name. Then follow these steps:

1. Include the thumbnail image in your document as you'd include any other image. For example, the code might look like this:

```
<IMG SRC="photo-thumbnail.jpg" HEIGHT="78" WIDTH="193" ALIGN="RIGHT"
BORDER="1" ALT="Thumbnail of Original Photo">
```

2. Add a link from the thumbnail to the larger image.

```
<A HREF="photo.jpg"><IMG SRC="photo-thumbnail.jpg" HEIGHT="78"
WIDTH="193" ALIGN="RIGHT" BORDER="1" ALT="Thumbnail of Original
Photo"></A>
```

If you set the border to 0, be sure that the supporting text or other cues in the HTML document make it clear that the image is, in fact, a link to a larger photograph. Alternatively, do as we did and simply set BORDER=1 to make clear that an image is a link. Here's the result from the bottom corner of the ASR Outfitters home page:

Although you can achieve the same visual effect in your document by using the original image and setting a smaller display size with the HEIGHT= and WIDTH= attributes, this technique defeats the purpose of thumbnails. Even if you reset the display size with HEIGHT= and WIDTH=, the entire (full-size) image will have to be downloaded to your computer. The trick to effective thumbnails is to reduce both the dimensions and the actual file size to the smallest possible value so the page will load quickly.

Creating Image Maps

An image map, also called a *clickable image*, is a single image that contains multiple links. In your Web travels, you may have used image maps without knowing it. Clicking on a portion of an image map takes you to the link connected with that part of the visual presentation. For example, a physician might present an image map of the human body to a patient, with instructions for the patient to "click where it hurts." Another good use replaces individual images (that browsers could realign depending on the window width) with a single *graphical menu*. Figure 7.10 shows a sample image map from the ASR Outfitter's Web site. (Visitors can click on each area for weather conditions—weather at the high peaks and lower elevations—and even the ultraviolet index.)

FIGURE 7.10

Image maps are single images with multiple links to other information or graphics.

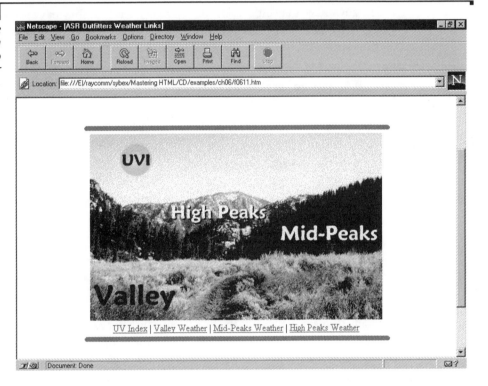

Understanding Image Map Types

The two types of image maps are:

- Server-side
- Client-side

The feature distinguishing the two types is where the processing takes place (where a visitor's mouse-click is translated into a link to another document). The processing can occur either on the server (hence, server-side image map) or on the visitor's computer (hence, client-side image map).

Server-Side Image Maps

In a server-side image map, the coordinates of the click are transmitted to the server computer, which determines what instructions apply to that click. The server then sends that information back to the client, which then sends a request for the appropriate document. The server computer does the calculating and tells the client what to do.

The advantage to using server-side image maps is that they have been around longer than client-side maps and that they are widely supported. The disadvantages to using server-side image maps include the following:

- Because a server-side image map requires input from the server, it generally responds slower than a client-side image map, depending on network traffic.
- The server may need supplemental software to process the image map.
- The server administrator may have to specify how the image map is processed.

Client-Side Image Maps

Generally, you'll want to use client-side image maps for several reasons. To start with, they're faster (because there's no need for back and forth communication between client and server to process the map) and more reliable, for those browsers that support client-side maps. For example, if a document with a client-side image map comes from Server A and points to a document on Server B, the client can do the calculations and request the document directly from Server B.

Client-side image maps are more user-friendly than server-side image maps. When a visitor moves the cursors over an image-map link within a document, the status bar generally displays the URL of the link. Newer browsers, including the latest versions of Netscape Navigator and Internet Explorer, also show information about the link in a small pop-up window. In contrast, when a visitor places the cursor over a server-side image-map link, the status bar displays only the coordinates of the cursor.

Finally, client-side image maps are better for you, the Web author, because you can use and test them before you put the image map on the server. In contrast, server-side maps do not work until they have been installed on the server, making testing much more difficult.

For best results, use both client-side and server-side image maps. If browsers see a client-side map, they'll use it. If they don't recognize the client-side image map, they'll revert to the server-side map. The only disadvantage to this approach is that you have to do twice as much work.

Making Appropriate Image Maps

Poorly constructed or carelessly selected image maps can be much worse than no image map at all. The inherent disadvantages of images (for example, their download time and their inaccessibility for text-only browsers) apply in spades to image maps. When determining whether an image map is appropriate for your needs, ask the following questions:

Is the image map linking to a stable navigational structure? If the links will be changing or if the overall site navigation structure isn't completely worked out, it's not time for an image map. Revising image maps is possible, but generally a real hassle. Often it's easier to completely redo an image map than to update it.

Is the image final? If the image hasn't passed all levels of review and isn't polished, you're not ready to make an image map. Changes as trivial as cropping the image slightly or rescaling the image by a few percentage points can completely break your map.

Is the image function appropriate to an image map? Flashy images on a home page are good candidates for image maps, particularly if the design reflects the corporate image. In many cases, an intricate design must be a single image—browsers cannot always accurately assemble individual images into the arrangement the designer intends. However, pages buried within an intranet site or that have a technical and practical focus are less likely to benefit from an image map.

Is the image content appropriate to an image map? Artificial or gratuitous use of image maps can be a real drawback to otherwise fine Web pages. Is clicking certain spots in an image really the best way for your visitors to link to the information they need? For example, in a Web site about automobile repair and diagnosis for the layperson, a picture of a car and the instructions to click where the funny sound seems to originate is completely appropriate. In a site directed at experienced mechanics, however, a list of parts (hood, trunk, dashboard, tire) would be much faster and more appropriate.

Does the function or content merit an image map? If both do, that's great. If one does, you can probably proceed with an image map. If, however, the links on a page don't need to be flashy and the content is not substantially clarified with an image map, omit the image map entirely.

Can the image map be completely reused? If you are planning to use an image map on several pages (you will use exactly the same image and code), its value increases. In this case, it's more likely to be worth the download time than if it's a one-time use.

If you answered no to one or more of these questions, consider using traditional, individual images or navigation aids. For example, if you can easily break the content or image into multiple smaller images with no significant problems, strongly consider doing so. The AltaVista Public Search home page (www.altavista.digital.com), shown here, is a good example of this.

The AltaVista designers could have chosen to make this one entire image map, with each button separately defined. Doing so would have closed the (admittedly small) space between each of the links (buttons) and tightened the logo. By using multiple smaller images, however, the designers made a small sacrifice in the visual appearance, but improved the stability, reliability, and universal accessibility of the navigation logo. The potential problems with image maps did not, in the AltaVista designer's eyes, justify the minor visual improvement. Think about it.

Selecting an Image

When you select a suitable image to use as an image map, follow the same guidelines as you would for choosing other images:

- Be sure that the image supports the content.
- Ensure that the physical size is as small as possible, but large enough to convey the content.
- Be sure that the file size is as small as possible.

For example, if you are creating an auto-repair image map for lay persons, use a simple drawing or schematic. At the other extreme, however, is the ASR Outfitters image map, which is primarily a visual attraction with only a tangential function. The image map shown in Figure 7.10, earlier in this chapter, is part of a localized weather page. Visitors can click on an area to get the weather for that region.

Setting Alternate Navigation

Unless you know beyond a doubt that *all* your visitors have graphical browsers and will choose to view images, you must provide alternate navigation options. Those who don't see the images—for whatever reason—won't be able to link to the information via your image map so provide text-based alternatives. An easy solution is to create a list of links. For example, alternate navigation for the image shown in Figure 7.10, earlier in this chapter, might look like the following code:

```
<BR>
<A HREF="uvi.html">UV Index</A> |
<A HREF="valley.html">Valley Weather</A> |
<A HREF="midpeaks.html">Mid-Peaks Weather</A> |
<A HREF="highpeaks.html">High Peaks Weather</A>
```

In this code, the vertical line (|) separates the links and creates the menu effect, as shown at the bottom of in Figure 7.10, earlier in this chapter.

Creating the alternate navigation before you develop the image map helps remind you of the links to include.

Creating Client-Side Image Maps

Creating a client-side image map involves three steps:

1. Defining the image area
2. Creating the image map
3. Activating the image map

Defining Image Areas

All image maps are simply a combination of three shapes:

- Circles
- Rectangles
- Polygons (any shapes other then circles and rectangles)

You can create almost any image by combining these shapes. Figure 7.11 shows the ASR Outfitters image map from within a map-editing program (available on the CD). The UVI link is a circle, the valley temperatures link is a rectangle, and the mid- and high-peak links are triangles.

You don't have to be precise with most map definitions. You can assume that most visitors will click somewhere in the middle of the link area; if not, they're likely to try again.

The next three sections show you how to define these three shapes. Before you get started, open an image in an image-editing or a mapping program.

FIGURE 7.11

This image map includes a circle, a rectangle, and two polygons.

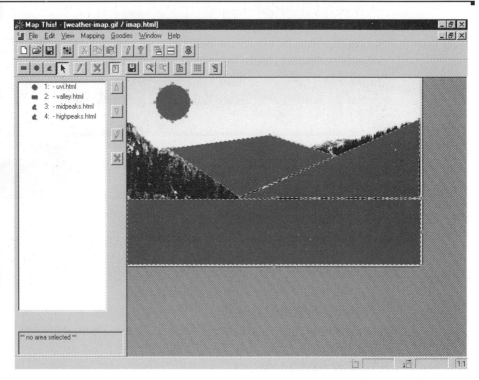

TIP

If you'll be developing several image maps, we recommend installing Map This or checking out some of the software available on the Internet. If you're creating simple maps or if you're only doing a few, however, creating them manually is almost as easy.

Defining Circles   To define a circle, follow these steps:

1. Identify the center and the radius. Use the pointer tool to point at the center of the circle, and note the coordinates in the status bar of your paint program. For example, in Paint Shop Pro (available on the CD), the pointer tool looks like a magnifying glass, and the x,y coordinates are at the bottom of the window. The x is the number of pixels from the edge of the image, while the y is the number of pixels from the top.

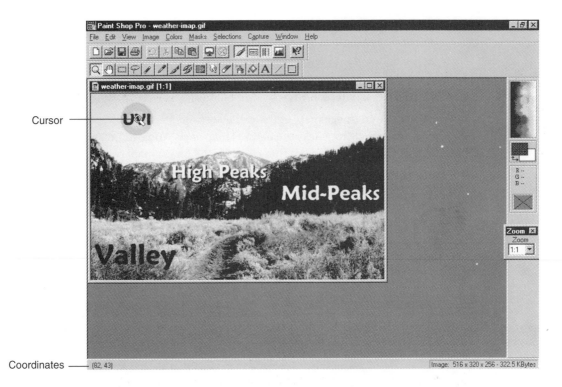

Cursor

Coordinates

2. Move the cursor horizontally to the edge of the circle, and note the coordinates.

3. Subtract the first x coordinate from the second x coordinate to get the radius of the circle.

4. Make a note of these coordinates.

Defining Rectangles   To define a rectangle, follow these steps:

1. Identify the upper left corner and the lower right corner. Point your mouse at the upper left corner of the rectangle and record the coordinates; then point at the lower right and record the coordinates.

2. Make a note of these coordinates.

Defining Polygons   To define a polygon, follow these steps:

1. Identify each point on the shape, moving in order around the shape. You can start at any point on the perimeter and proceed clockwise or counterclockwise, as long as you don't skip points. For example, in the ASR Outfitters map, the Mid-Peaks area can be defined with three points—making a right triangle with the long side running between the Mid-Peaks and High Peaks areas. The High

PART II

Advancing Your Skills

Peaks area might include several points across the top of the mountains, or it might be as simple as another triangle.

2. Make a note of these coordinates.

Creating the Image Map

When you create an image map, you include tags and attributes that tell a browser what to do when a visitor clicks the defined map areas. You can include this information within the HTML document that contains the image map, or you can include it in a separate document. The first is more common, but if you'll be using the image map (say, as a navigation aid) in several documents, consider storing it in a separate file and referencing it from each of the documents.

You can place the map definition block anywhere within the body of your HTML document, but it is easier to update and maintain if you place it either immediately after the opening <BODY> tag or immediately before the closing </BODY> tag. Table 7.5 explains image map tags and attributes.

TABLE 7.5: IMAGE MAP TAGS AND ATTRIBUTES

Tag/Attribute	Use
USEMAP="..."	Names the client-side map definition to use. Attribute of <IMG> tag.
ISMAP	Specifies that the image uses a server-side image map. Attribute of <IMG> tag.
<MAP>	Marks the map definition block within the HTML document.
NAME="..."	Provides a name for the map definition block.
<AREA>	Defines an area within the map.
SHAPE="..."	Identifies the shape of an area as RECT, CIRCLE, or POLY.
HREF="..."	Specifies a target for area. A click in the area link to this URL.
NOHREF	Specifies that a click in this area will not link anywhere.
COORDS="x,y, x1,y1,x2,y2"	Identifies the shape of an area.
ALT="..."	Provides alternate text (or pop-up text) describing each link.

To include a client-side image map, follow these steps (we'll use the ASR Outfitters page in this example):

1. Within your HTML document, add opening and closing <MAP> tags.

```
<MAP>
</MAP>
</BODY>
```

2. Give the map a clear, descriptive name with a NAME= attribute. This name is comparable to the NAME= attribute of the <A> tag. It provides an internal anchor of sorts that you can link to from either the same document or from other documents.

```
<MAP NAME="weather_zones">
```

3. Add an <AREA> tag for one of the shapes.

```
<MAP NAME="weather_zones">
<AREA>
```

4. Add a SHAPE= attribute to the <AREA> tag. In this example, CIRCLE represents the UVI area in the ASR example map.

```
<AREA SHAPE=CIRCLE>
```

5. Add the COORDS= attribute with the x,y coordinates of the center of the circle and with the radius of the circle.

```
<AREA SHAPE=CIRCLE COORDS="82,43,30">
```

6. Add an HREF= attribute pointing to the target file. You can use relative or absolute URLs in client-side image maps, but, as with other links, using relative URLs is a good idea. In this case, the area links to a file called uvi.html in the same folder.

```
<AREA SHAPE=CIRCLE COORDS="82,43,30" HREF="uvi.html">
```

7. Add the ALT= attribute describing the link for use in pop-ups.

```
<AREA SHAPE=CIRCLE COORDS="82,43,30" HREF="uvi.html" ALT="UV Index">
```

NOTE

As you add areas, some may overlap others. The first area defined overrides overlapping areas.

8. Add additional <AREA> tags, one at a time. In this example, the next <AREA> tag is for the Valley area, so it is a RECT (or RECTANGLE). The coordinates for the top left and lower right are required to link to valley.html.

```
<AREA SHAPE=CIRCLE COORDS="82,43,30" HREF="uvi.html" ALT="UV Index">
<AREA SHAPE=RECT COORDS="1,209,516,320" HREF="valley.html" ALT="Valley
Weather">
```

9. For the Mid-Peaks area, a triangle will suffice to define the area; so the shape is a POLYGON with three pairs of coordinates. This links to midpeaks.html.

```
<AREA SHAPE=CIRCLE COORDS="82,43,30" HREF="uvi.html" ALT="UV Index">
<AREA SHAPE=RECT COORDS="1,209,516,320" HREF="valley.html" ALT="Valley
Weather">
```

```
<AREA SHAPE=POLY COORDS="199,207,513,205,514,71" HREF="midpeaks.html"
ALT="Mid-Peaks Weather">
```

10. The High Peaks area is easily defined with a figure containing four corners—vaguely diamond shaped, as in the following example.

```
<AREA SHAPE=CIRCLE COORDS="82,43,30" HREF="uvi.html" ALT="UV Index">
<AREA SHAPE=RECT COORDS="1,209,516,320" HREF="valley.html" ALT="Valley
Weather">
<AREA SHAPE=POLY COORDS="199,207,513,205,514,71" HREF="midpeaks.html"
ALT="Mid-Peaks Weather">
<AREA SHAPE=POLY COORDS="63,123,251,98,365,134,198,204,73,121"
HREF="highpeaks.html" ALT="High Peaks Weather">
```

Refer to Figure 7.11 for a reminder of what this shape looks like.

11. Set the HREF= attribute for the remaining areas. You could set the remaining area so that nothing at all will happen when a visitor clicks there.

```
<AREA SHAPE=default NOHREF>
```

That's all there is to it. The final map looks something like the following code:

```
<MAP NAME="weather_zones">
<AREA SHAPE=CIRCLE COORDS="82,43,30" HREF="uvi.html" ALT="UV Index">
<AREA SHAPE=RECT COORDS="1,209,516,320" HREF="valley.html" ALT="Valley
Weather">
<AREA SHAPE=POLY COORDS="199,207,513,205,514,71" HREF="midpeaks.html"
ALT="Mid-Peaks Weather">
<AREA SHAPE=POLY COORDS="63,123,251,98,365,134,198,204,73,121"
HREF="highpeaks.html" ALT="High Peaks Weather">
<AREA SHAPE=default NOHREF>
</MAP>
```

Activating the Map

Before you can activate the map, you must place the map image in your document. The image tag (in a new document from the ASR site), looks like this.

```
<CENTER>
<IMG SRC="weather-imap.gif" ALIGN="" WIDTH="516" HEIGHT="320" BORDER="0"
ALT="Weather Zones in the Mountains">
</CENTER>
```

To connect the image to the map definition created in the previous section, simply add the USEMAP= attribute, as in the following example.

```
<IMG SRC="weather-imap.gif" ALIGN="" WIDTH="516" HEIGHT="320" BORDER="0"
ALT="Weather Zones in the Mountains" USEMAP="#weather_zones">
```

TIP

The USEMAP= attribute requires a pound sign (#) in the value to indicate that the link goes to a place within a document.

If you want to link to a map definition in another document, add an absolute URL to the USEMAP= attribute. If you do this, test thoroughly because not all browsers support this feature. The final map looks like that shown in Figure 7.12.

FIGURE 7.12

The ASR Outfitters image map

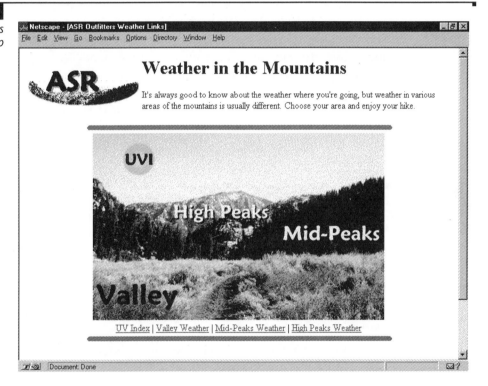

Creating Server-Side Image Maps

The process for making server-side maps is virtually identical to that of making client-side image maps. The only real differences are in map file format. Each type of server can have a different type of image map configuration.

In practice, however, only two main server-side map formats exist: NCSA (National Center for Supercomputing Applications) and CERN (Centre Européen pour la

Recherche Nucléaire). They function in similar ways, but each requires a slightly different format for map definitions. Each format represents an implementation of server-side image maps from the earliest server software these organizations produced.

NOTE

Ask your server administrator which image map format you'll need to use for a server-side image map. Additionally, check on what the URL is for using a server-side image map.

The only real issue with converting your client-side image map to a server-side image map is that you must know more about (be sure of) the URLs. For example, everything in the ASR example was located initially in one folder. To properly set up a server-side map, we need to determine the full path to the information. Because of limitations in the NCSA image map implementation, the map should be contained in a subdirectory, not in the server root. ASR will put the image map document, the map file, and the associated (linked) files together in the weather subdirectory on www.asroutfitters .com. Therefore, the complete URL to the main file is:

```
http://www.asroutfitters.com/weather/asrweather-imap.html
```

NOTE

You must use server-relative URLs or absolute URLs to ensure that everything works properly. See Chapter 4 for more about URLs.

Creating an NCSA Image Map

In general, the NCSA image map format is

method URL coordinates

The code for the sample client-side image map looks like this:

```
<MAP NAME="weather_zones">
<AREA SHAPE=CIRCLE COORDS="82,43,30" HREF="uvi.html" ALT="UV Index">
<AREA SHAPE=RECT COORDS="1,209,516,320" HREF="valley.html" ALT="Valley
Weather">
<AREA SHAPE=POLY COORDS="199,207,513,205,514,71" HREF="midpeaks.html"
ALT="Mid-Peaks Weather">
<AREA SHAPE=POLY COORDS="63,123,251,98,365,134,198,204,73,121"
HREF="highpeaks.html" ALT="High Peaks Weather">
```

```
<AREA SHAPE=default NOHREF>
</MAP>
```

You use an NCSA server side map file like this:

```
default /weather/asrweather-imap.html
circle /weather/uvi.html 82,43,30
rect /weather/valley.html 1,209,516,320
poly /weather/midpeaks.html 199,207,513,205,514,71
poly /weather/highpeaks.html 63,123,251,98,365,134,198,204,73,121
```

The default item points explicitly back to the file containing the map; so clicks outside active areas will not link to other pages. The remaining lines include the shape, URL, and coordinates, just as the client-side map definition file did, but using a slightly different format.

NOTE

The NCSA server-side format also supports a point "shape" (in addition to the circle, rectangle, and polygon) with a single pair of coordinates. A click "near" the point takes a visitor to that URL. If you provide multiple points, the server chooses the closest one to your click. Because other image map formats do not support the point, we recommend using only the existing shapes.

After you create this map file, save it with a map extension. ASR places the map file in the same folder as the rest of the files—that is, in the /weather folder, just below the server root.

Activating NCSA-Style Server-Side Image Maps

Activating the server-side image map makes much more sense if you think of it as making the image a link (though one with an added level of complexity). Follow these steps:

1. Start with the map in your document (the client-side map, if you choose).

```
<IMG SRC="weather-imap.gif" ALIGN="" WIDTH="516" HEIGHT="320" BORDER="0"
ALT="Weather Zones in the Mountains" USEMAP="#weather_zones">
```

2. Add the ISMAP attribute to the <IMG> tag, as shown here:

```
<IMG SRC="weather-imap.gif" ALIGN="" WIDTH="516" HEIGHT="320" BORDER="0"
ALT="Weather Zones in the Mountains" USEMAP="#weather_zones" ISMAP>
```

3. Add a link around the image.

```
<A>
```

```
<IMG SRC="weather-imap.gif" ALIGN="" WIDTH="516" HEIGHT="320" BORDER="0"
ALT="Weather Zones in the Mountains" USEMAP="#weather_zones" ISMAP>
</A>
```

4. Add the HREF= attribute specified by the network administrator. In all probability, it will look something like this:

```
<A HREF="http://www.asroutfitters.com/cgi-bin/imagemap/weather/weather-
imap.map">
<IMG SRC="weather-imap.gif" ALIGN="" WIDTH="516" HEIGHT="320" BORDER="0"
ALT="Weather Zones in the Mountains" USEMAP="#weather_zones" ISMAP>
</A>
```

If the client recognizes a client-side image map, it disregards the server-side map. If the client cannot recognize the client-side map, it uses the server-side map.

When you've finished creating the map, be sure to upload the map file at the same time you upload the rest of your files. That's an easy one to forget.

Implementing CERN-Style Image Maps

CERN-style maps are considerably less common than NCSA-style maps. Again, the same basic information is included, but slightly reshuffled. The original client-side map format is:

```
<MAP NAME="weather_zones">
<AREA SHAPE=CIRCLE COORDS="82,43,30" HREF="uvi.html" ALT="UV Index">
<AREA SHAPE=RECT COORDS="1,209,516,320" HREF="valley.html" ALT="Valley
Weather">
<AREA SHAPE=POLY COORDS="199,207,513,205,514,71" HREF="midpeaks.html"
ALT="Mid-Peaks Weather">
<AREA SHAPE=POLY COORDS="63,123,251,98,365,134,198,204,73,121"
HREF="highpeaks.html" ALT="High Peaks Weather">
<AREA SHAPE=default NOHREF>
</MAP>
```

After converting it, you end up with a CERN map file of

```
default /weather/asrweather-imap.html

circle (82,43) 30 /weather/uvi.html
```

```
rect (1,209) (516,320) /weather/valley.html
poly (199,207) (513,205) (514,71) /weather/midpeaks.html
poly (63,123) (251,98) (365,134) (198,204) (73,121) /weather/highpeaks.html
```

The major differences are that the coordinate pairs are enclosed in parentheses, the coordinates go before the URLs, and the rectangle can use any two opposite coordinates, rather than the top left and lower right. The URLs can be either absolute or server-relative.

Other types of servers exist, and administrators configure their servers differently. Asking up-front how to implement a server-side image map will reduce frustration.

Using Background Images

Most browsers support background images, the patterns or images behind the text in HTML documents. As a rule, background images are *tiled* throughout the available space, meaning that they are multiple copies of one image placed side by side to fill the screen.

Tiling offers two main advantages. First, you can produce a *seamless background*, meaning that the casual viewer cannot see where individual images start and stop. Figure 7.13 shows a seamless background.

Second, you can develop more visually interesting backgrounds by ensuring that background images tile either horizontally or vertically. For example, an image that is only 10 pixels high and 1280 pixels wide is as wide or wider than any browser window is likely to be. Therefore, the image will repeat vertically, but not horizontally. This can produce a vertical band, as shown in Figure 7.14.

The magic number 1280 ensures that no browser can be wider than the image. If you use a narrower image, you might have an attractive image when viewed at 800 × 600 resolution, but with two vertical bands (on the left and near the right) at 1024 × 768 resolution, for example.

FIGURE 7.13

In seamless back-
grounds, the tiled
images blend
together.

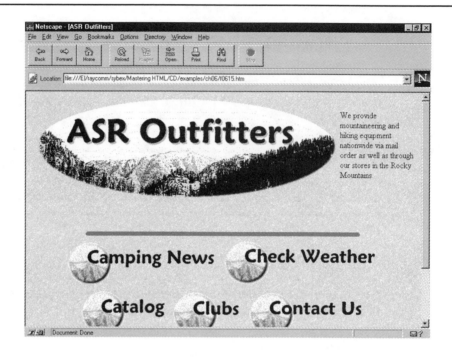

FIGURE 7.14

Wide images tile
only vertically.

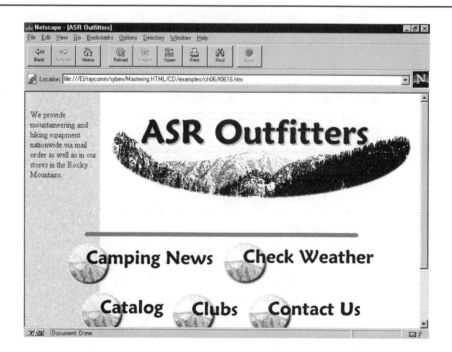

PART

II

Advancing Your Skills

Similarly, you can use a tall image to produce a tiled horizontal band, as shown in Figure 7.15. Pay careful attention to making the image taller than your page could possibly be; otherwise, the background will repeat. A good technique is also to make the image fade into the background color of the document.

If you use background images in your document and the color of the image does not adequately contrast with the text color, reset your document colors. You might also want to set the colors to complement your background image.

To add a background image, use the attributes in Table 7.6 in the opening <BODY> tag.

TABLE 7.6: BACKGROUND ATTRIBUTES

Tag	Use
BACKGROUND="..."	Uses URL to identify an image for the background of an HTML document.
BGPROPERTIES=FIXED	Sets the background image as nontiled, nonscrolling for use with Internet Explorer.

To specify a background image, add the BACKGROUND= attribute to your opening <BODY> tag.

```
<BODY BACKGROUND="asrback.jpg">
```

You can use Style Sheets to include background images behind individual page elements, rather than placing a background image behind the entire page.

When you develop background images, you will find that creating a seamless image is difficult. Although some programs, such as Paint Shop Pro, offer a menu option to create a seamless image, you still often see a vague repeating pattern. If you must have a seamless background, consider using samples from the clip art libraries on the Companion CD.

If you have a background image that you want to use as a watermark of sorts for your pages—and if your visitors will use Internet Explorer—add the BGPROPERTIES=FIXED attribute. This attribute prevents the image from tiling throughout the background. The full code for the <BODY> tag is:

```
<BODY BACKGROUND="asrbackfull.jpg" BGPROPERTIES=FIXED>
```

This produces the effect shown in Figure 7.16.

FIGURE 7.15

A horizontal band looks like this in a browser.

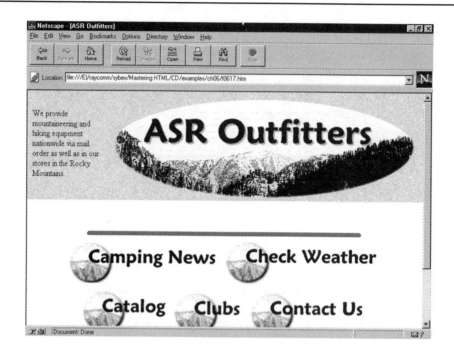

FIGURE 7.16

A fixed background acts as a watermark.

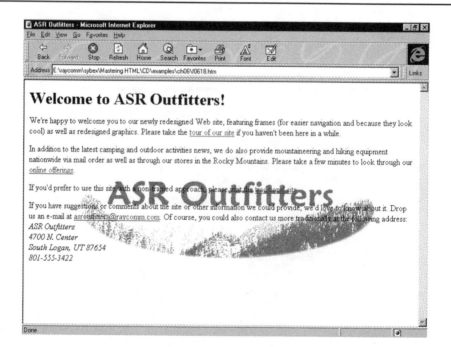

Where to Go from Here

In this chapter, you learned how to select appropriate images, include them in your HTML documents, and format them to make them appear as you want. You also learned about two image map types, client-side and server-side, which give you a useful way to provide multiple links from a single image.

From here, you could move on to one of several chapters, but here are a few suggestions:

- Check out Chapter 3 for more formatting information.
- See Chapter 5 and the Master's Reference for information about Style Sheets.
- See Chapter 8 to see how to include images in tables.

Chapter

8

Developing Tables

Developing Tables

This chapter introduces HTML *tables*, which are grids made up of rows and columns. These rows and columns create individual *cells* that can contain either text or images. Tables serve two functions. First, they help present complex data in a readable format. Traditionally, you use tables when information can more effectively be portrayed visually than described in paragraph form, as shown in Figure 8.1.

Second, you can use tables to incorporate more sophisticated design elements into Web pages. For example, HTML does not support columns, side headings, column widths, or precisely juxtaposed text and graphics. Using tables, however, you can create all these effects and more—with little concern about how this might affect your visitor's computer or browser settings. Figure 8.2 shows an example of formatting using tables—in this case, we used tables to create sideheads, headings that appear to the side of paragraphs rather than above them.

FIGURE 8.1

At a fundamental level, tables present some information more effectively than plain text can.

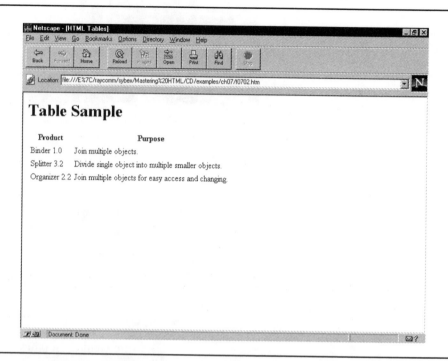

FIGURE 8.2

Tables help you develop interesting page designs, such as the sideheads shown here.

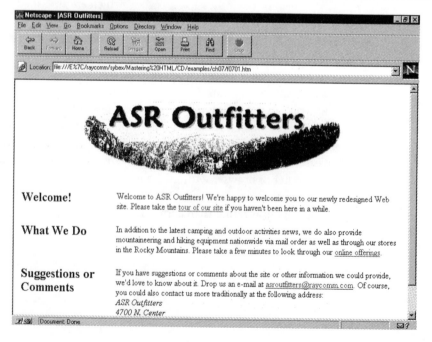

TIP

If your visitors are not all using browsers that support HTML 4 tags, using tables for formatting is a good way to go; however, as you'll see in many places throughout this chapter, the HTML 4 specification moves away from using this formatting technique in favor of Style Sheets. Find out how to develop Style Sheets in Chapter 5, and find a complete Style Sheet reference in the Master's Reference.

Not all browsers support tables, but most versions of Netscape Navigator, Internet Explorer, and many other browsers do. Furthermore, not all browsers that support tables support all table features. For example, Netscape supports tables, but does not support extended features such as the table footers from the "Using HTML 4 Table Features" section later in this chapter. Table 8.1 lists browsers that support tables and extended table features.

TABLE 8.1: BROWSERS THAT SUPPORT STANDARD TABLES AND HTML 4 TABLES

Browser Version	Tables	HTML 4 Tables
Netscape Navigator	Yes	No
Internet Explorer	Yes	Yes (in 4 and later versions)
Lynx	No	No

Before including tables in an HTML document, be sure your visitors use a browser that supports tables. If they don't, the table will not appear properly, if at all.

NOTE

Table features commonly not supported are noted throughout this chapter.

Creating Basic Tables

Creating tables is a two-step process:

1. Create the table structure—that is, enter the <TABLE> tags, specify rows and columns, and specify column headings.

2. Enter the data in table cells.

By first creating the table structure and then entering the data, you can avoid tagging errors. Most commonly, Web authors forget the closing </TABLE> tag or omit an entire paired tag. These errors result in an odd-looking table or no table at all. Ensuring that the basic table structure is in place before you start adding text can help you troubleshoot problems. Table 8.2 describes the basic table tags.

Table tags become complex quickly! Be sure that you open and close tags as needed and that you don't omit tags. Debugging problems in a table can be tedious and frustrating.

TABLE 8.2: BASIC TABLE TAGS

Tag	Use
<TABLE>	Marks a table within an HTML document.
<TR>	Marks a row within a table. The closing tag is optional.
<TD>	Marks a cell (table data) within a row. The closing tag is optional.
<TH>	Marks a heading cell within a row. The closing tag is optional.

Although closing tags </TR>, </TD>, and </TH> are optional, including them can help you see where one tag ends and another begins. Also, including these closing tags might increase compatibility with older table-capable browsers.

The following steps show you how to build a table and enter information into it. The sample table, shown below, represents a product summary on a corporate Web site. The sample table looks like this:

Product	Purpose
Binder 1.0	Join multiple objects.
Splitter 3.2	Divide single object into multiple smaller objects.
Organizer 2.2	Join multiple objects for easy access and changing.

1. Start with a functional HTML document containing the appropriate structure tags and any additional information you want to include.

2. Add the <TABLE> tags where you want the table boundaries to appear.

<TABLE>
</TABLE>

3. Add <TR> tags between the boundaries noted above for each row. The sample table includes four <TR> tags, one for each row.

<TABLE>
<TR>
</TR>
<TR>
</TR>
<TR>
</TR>
<TR>
</TR>
</TABLE>

4. Add <TH> tags in the first row where you want to include table headings. The sample table includes two <TH> tags. You might include some spaces or tabs to set off the table heading (and data) tags so that you can easily see which text is associated with each row and cell.

<TABLE>
<TR>
       <TH></TH>
       <TH></TH>
</TR>
<TR>
</TR>
<TR>
</TR>
<TR>
</TR>
</TABLE>

5. Add <TD> tags to create individual cells in which to include information. The sample table includes six data cells.

<TABLE>
<TR>
       <TH></TH>
       <TH></TH>
</TR>

```
<TR>
        <TD></TD>
        <TD></TD>
</TR>
<TR>
        <TD></TD>
        <TD></TD>
</TR>
<TR>
        <TD></TD>
        <TD></TD>
</TR>
</TABLE>
```

6. Add the content for each cell. Place table heading information between the <TH> tags, and enter data between <TD> tags.

```
<TABLE>
<TR>
        <TH>Product</TH>
        <TH>Purpose</TH>
</TR>
<TR>
        <TD>Binder 1.0</TD>
        <TD>Join multiple objects.</TD>
</TR>
<TR>
        <TD>Splitter 3.2</TD>
        <TD>Divide single object into multiple smaller objects.</TD>
</TR>
<TR>
        <TD>Organizer 2.2</TD>
        <TD>Join multiple objects for easy access and changing.</TD>
</TR>
</TABLE>
```

TIP

If you chose to omit the closing tags, place the content after the opening tag and before the next tag. (Browsers interpret the next <TH>, <TD>, <TR>, or closing </TABLE> tag as implicitly closing the current tag.)

Figure 8.3 shows the results. Notice that the content is present, but that the table does not include any formatting or borders.

FIGURE 8.3

A basic table includes content, but it does not include formatting or borders—yet.

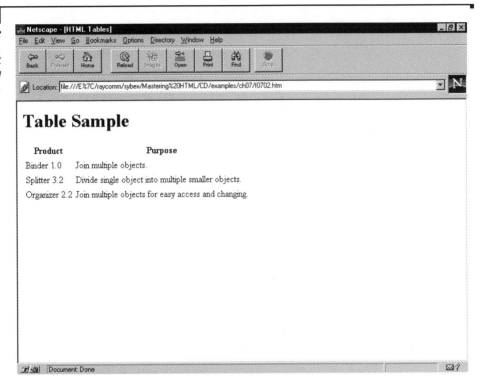

Adding or Removing Rows and Columns

After you create a table, you can easily add to it or delete from it as your information needs change. The following sections show you how to add and remove rows and columns. The example results in a table that has one more column and one more row than the previous example:

Product	Purpose	Industry standard term
Binder 1.0	Join multiple objects.	Stapler
Organizer 2.2	Join multiple objects for easy access and changing.	Ring binder
Combiner 0.9	Join multiple objects at the edges.	Tape
Splitter 3.2	Divide single object into multiple smaller objects.	Scissors

PART

II

Advancing Your Skills

Adding Rows

To add a row to your table, insert additional <TR> and <TD> tags where you want the new row to appear. For example, you can add a new row at the bottom of a table like this:

```
<TABLE>
<TR>
    <TH>Product</TH>
    <TH>Purpose</TH>
</TR>
<TR>
    <TD>Binder 1.0</TD>
    <TD>Join multiple objects.</TD>
</TR>
<TR>
    <TD>Splitter 3.2</TD>
    <TD>Divide single object into multiple smaller objects.</TD>
</TR>
<TR>
    <TD>Organizer 2.2</TD>
    <TD>Join multiple objects for easy access and changing.</TD>
<TR>
    <TD>Combiner 0.9</TD>
    <TD>Join multiple objects at the edges.</TD>
</TR>
</TABLE>
```

The resulting table looks like that shown in Figure 8.4.

Adding Columns

Adding columns is somewhat more difficult than adding rows because you have to add a cell to each row. The general process, however, is the same—you insert the tags where you want the new column to appear, either to the left or to the right of existing columns or somewhere in between.

FIGURE 8.4

The sample table now has four rows.

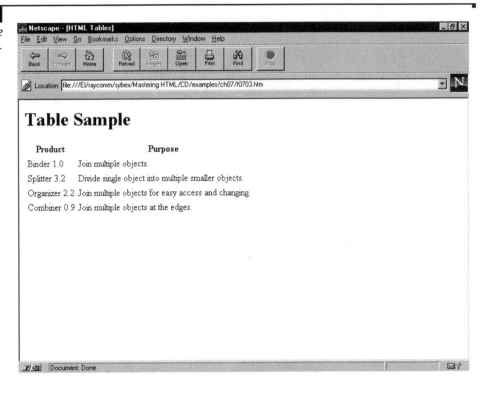

For example, you can add a new column at the right end of the sample table by adding <TH> tags to the top row and by adding <TD> tags to each of the other rows. The sample code would look like this:

```
<TABLE>
<TR>
    <TH>Product</TH>
    <TH>Purpose</TH>
    <TH>Industry standard term</TH>
</TR>
<TR>
    <TD>Binder 1.0</TD>
    <TD>Join multiple objects.</TD>
    <TD>Stapler</TD>
</TR>
<TR>
```

```
    <TD>Organizer 2.2</TD>
    <TD>Join multiple objects for easy access and changing.</TD>
    <TD>Ring binder</TD>
</TR>
<TR>
    <TD>Combiner 0.9</TD>
    <TD>Join multiple objects at the edges.</TD>
    <TD>Tape</TD>
</TR>
<TR>
    <TD>Splitter 3.2</TD>
    <TD>Divide single object into multiple smaller objects.</TD>
    <TD>Scissors</TD>
</TR>
</TABLE>
```

The resulting table looks like that shown in Figure 8.5.

FIGURE 8.5

Adding columns allows you to provide additional information.

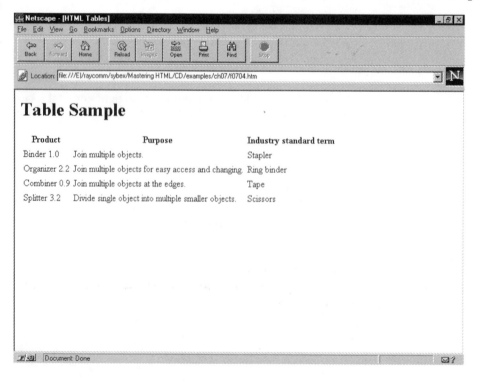

Deleting Rows and Columns

Deleting rows and columns is easier than adding them. You have to be careful, though, to delete all the tags associated with a row or a column.

- When deleting a row, be sure to delete the <TD> tags and the <TR> tags that enclose it.
- When deleting a column, be sure to delete the <TH> tags as well as the <TD> tags from each row.

For example, to delete the bottom row in the sample table, you delete the tags in strikethrough in the following code:

```
<TABLE>
<TR>
    <TH>Product</TH>
    <TH>Purpose</TH>
    <TH>Industry standard term</TH>
</TR>
<TR>
    <TD>Binder 1.0</TD>
    <TD>Join multiple objects.</TD>
    <TD>Stapler</TD>
</TR>
<TR>
    <TD>Organizer 2.2</TD>
    <TD>Join multiple objects for easy access and changing.</TD>
    <TD>Ring binder</TD>
</TR>
<TR>
    <TD>Combiner 0.9</TD>
    <TD>Join multiple objects at the edges.</TD>
    <TD>Tape</TD>
</TR>
<TR>
    <TD>Splitter 3.2</TD>
    <TD>Divide single object into multiple smaller objects.</TD>
    <TD>Scissors</TD>
</TR>
</TABLE>
```

To delete the final column in the sample table, delete the last tag from each table row, like this:

```
<TABLE>
<TR>
   <TH>Product</TH>
   <TH>Purpose</TH>
   <TH>Industry standard term</TH>
</TR>
<TR>
   <TD>Binder 1.0</TD>
   <TD>Join multiple objects.</TD>
   <TD>Stapler</TD>
</TR>
<TR>
   <TD>Organizer 2.2</TD>
   <TD>Join multiple objects for easy access and changing.</TD>
   <TD>Ring binder</TD>
</TR>
<TR>
   <TD>Combiner 0.9</TD>
   <TD>Join multiple objects at the edges.</TD>
   <TD>Tape</TD>
</TR>
<TR>
   <TD>Splitter 3.2</TD>
   <TD>Divide single object into multiple smaller objects.</TD>
   <TD>Scissors</TD>
</TR>
</TR>
</TABLE>
```

WARNING

The HTML editor and Web browser have no concept of columns within a table. If you delete the final cell from each row, your revised table will look just fine. If you delete a random cell from each row, your table will still look just fine, but the data will be corrupted. Be careful to delete the tags and content consistently from each row.

Spanning Rows and Columns

Spanning refers to stretching a cell over multiple rows or columns. Figure 8.6 shows a sample table in which the cells labeled Merchandise and Descriptive Information span two columns each, indicating that they apply to the multiple columns they span. The Joining Tools cell spans three rows to show which rows apply to that category.

FIGURE 8.6

This sample table features a cell (Joining Tools) that spans three rows.

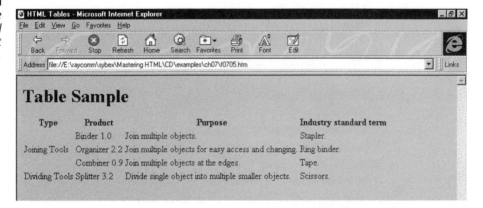

To specify column and row spans, use the attributes listed in Table 8.3.

TABLE 8.3: ROW AND COLUMN SPAN ATTRIBUTES

Attribute	Use
ROWSPAN=n	Used in <TH> or <TD> tags, ROWSPAN= indicates how many rows the cell should span. For example, ROWSPAN=3 spans three rows.
COLSPAN=n	Used in either <TH> or <TD> tags, COLSPAN= indicates how many columns the cell should cover. For example, COLSPAN=3 spans three columns.

PART

II

Advancing Your Skills

Spanning Rows

You can span rows using either the <TH> or <TD> tag, depending on whether you're spanning a table heading or table data. The following example shows you how to span one cell over three rows, as shown in the Joining Tools cell in Figure 8.6, earlier in this chapter. The steps build on this sample code:

```
<TABLE>
<TR>
   <TH>Product</TH>
   <TH>Purpose</TH>
   <TH>Industry standard term</TH>
</TR>
<TR>
   <TD>Binder 1.0</TD>
   <TD>Join multiple objects.</TD>
   <TD>Stapler</TD>
</TR>
<TR>
   <TD>Organizer 2.2</TD>
   <TD>Join multiple objects for easy access and changing.</TD>
   <TD>Ring binder</TD>
</TR>
<TR>
   <TD>Combiner 0.9</TD>
   <TD>Join multiple objects at the edges.</TD>
   <TD>Tape</TD>
</TR>
<TR>
   <TD>Splitter 3.2</TD>
   <TD>Divide single object into multiple smaller objects.</TD>
   <TD>Scissors</TD>
</TR>
</TABLE>
```

1. Add a new column for the tool categories, as shown in Figure 8.6, earlier in this chapter. Place **Type** in the top left cell with a <TH> tag. Place **Joining Tools** in the second cell (with a <TD> tag), which will eventually span three rows. Place **Dividing Tools** in the third cell but in the fifth row with a <TD> tag.

```
<TABLE>
<TR>
        <TH>Type</TH>
        <TH>Product</TH>
        <TH>Purpose</TH>
        <TH>Industry standard term</TH>
</TR>
<TR>
        <TD>Joining Tools</TD>
        <TD>Binder 1.0</TD>
        <TD>Join multiple objects.</TD>
        <TD>Stapler.</TD>
</TR>
<TR>
        <TD>Organizer 2.2</TD>
        <TD>Join multiple objects for easy access and changing.</TD>
        <TD>Ring binder.</TD>
</TR>
<TR>
        <TD>Combiner 0.9</TD>
        <TD>Join multiple objects at the edges.</TD>
        <TD>Tape.</TD>
</TR>
<TR>
        <TD>Dividing Tools</TD>
        <TD>Splitter 3.2</TD>
        <TD>Divide single object into multiple smaller objects.</TD>
        <TD>Scissors.</TD>
</TR>
</TABLE>
```

NOTE

Three of the rows now have too many cells. If you display the table in a browser, you'll see that the cells appear out of alignment.

PART

II

Advancing Your Skills

2. Add the ROWSPAN= attribute to a <TH> or <TD> tag that affects the cell you want to span. In the sample table, add the ROWSPAN=3 attribute to the Joining Tools <TD> tag (which should affect rows 2 through 4), like this:

```
<TD ROWSPAN=3>Joining Tools</TD>
```

The resulting table, complete with a spanned row, looks like that shown in Figure 8.7.

FIGURE 8.7

Use spanned rows to create more interesting table layouts.

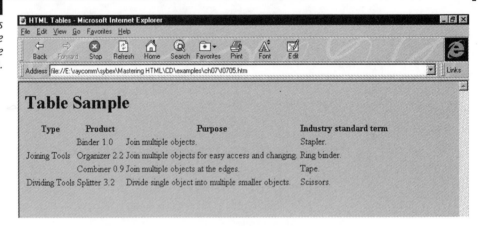

Spanning Columns

You can span columns using either the <TH> or <TD> tag, depending on whether you're spanning a table heading or a table cell. The following example shows how to add two cells that each span two columns. Start with the following code, which includes the spanned row from the previous section:

```
<TABLE>
<TR>
   <TH>Type</TH>
   <TH>Product</TH>
   <TH>Purpose</TH>
   <TH>Industry standard term</TH>
</TR>
<TR>
   <TD ROWSPAN=3>Joining Tools</TD>
   <TD>Binder 1.0</TD>
```

```
  <TD>Join multiple objects.</TD>
  <TD>Stapler.</TD>
</TR>
<TR>
  <TD>Organizer 2.2</TD>
  <TD>Join multiple objects for easy access and changing.</TD>
  <TD>Ring binder.</TD>
</TR>
<TR>
  <TD>Combiner 0.9</TD>
  <TD>Join multiple objects at the edges.</TD>
  <TD>Tape.</TD>
</TR>
<TR>
  <TD>Dividing Tools</TD>
  <TD>Splitter 3.2</TD>
  <TD>Divide single object into multiple smaller objects.</TD>
  <TD>Scissors.</TD>
</TR>
</TABLE>
```

1. Add a <TR> tag for the new row.

   ```
   <TR>
   </TR>
   ```

2. Add <TH> or <TD> cells that you want to span. In the sample table, add two <TH> cells—one with the word *Merchandise* and one with the phrase *Descriptive Information*.

   ```
   <TABLE>
   <TR>
           <TH>Merchandise</TH>
           <TH>Descriptive Information</TH>
   </TR>
   <TR>
           <TH>Type</TH>
           <TH>Product</TH>
           <TH>Purpose</TH>
           <TH>Industry standard term</TH>
   </TR>
   ```

3. Add the COLSPAN= attribute to a <TH> or <TD> tag that affects the cell you want to span. In the sample table, add COLSPAN=2 to the <TH> tag because each cell should span two columns.

```
<TR>
    <TH COLSPAN=2>Merchandise</TH>
    <TH COLSPAN=2>Descriptive Information</TH>
</TR>
```

The resulting table, complete with row and column spans, should look like that in Figure 8.8.

FIGURE 8.8

Spanning rows and columns helps you provide complex information.

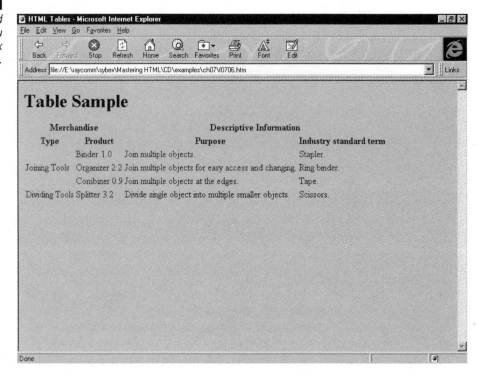

Design Workshop

You can include both the ROWSPAN= and COLSPAN= attributes in one <TH> or <TD> tag. For example, a large or complex table might have two heading rows and two columns with descriptive information, such as the following:

		Top Heading	
		Heading	Heading
Top Category	Category	Content	Content
	Category	Content	Content

The first cell in the table spans two columns (COLSPAN=2) to cover both category columns. It simultaneously spans two rows (ROWSPAN=2) to cover both heading rows. No content necessarily fits in this area of the table, so you might use a logo or some sort of graphic to fill the space attractively.

Adding Captions

A caption is explanatory or descriptive text that usually appears above the table. A caption serves two purposes:

- To summarize table contents
- To provide at-a-glance information about table contents

Although HTML allows you to place captions above or below tables, place the caption above the table to ensure that your visitor sees it. If tables are more than one screen full, a visitor might not scroll down to read the caption.

To add a caption to your table, use the tag and attribute provided in Table 8.4.

TABLE 8.4: CAPTION TAG AND ATTRIBUTE

Tag/Attribute	Use
<CAPTION>	Used within a table to identify the text of the table caption.
ALIGN="..."	Places the caption at the TOP or BOTTOM of the table.

HTML 4 has added LEFT and RIGHT to the possible caption alignment options. If you choose ALIGN="LEFT", the caption appears on the left side of the table. If you choose ALIGN="RIGHT", the caption appears on the right side of the table.

To add a caption to the sample table, follow these steps:

1. Add the <CAPTION> tag between the opening and closing <TABLE> tags. In the sample table, place the <CAPTION> tag below the opening <TABLE> tag.

   ```
   <TABLE>
   <CAPTION>
   </CAPTION>
   ```

2. Add caption text, like this:

   ```
   <CAPTION>
   Office Product Merchandise and Category Information
   </CAPTION>
   ```

3. Specify whether the caption should appear above or below the table by using the ALIGN=TOP or ALIGN=BOTTOM attribute, like this:

   ```
   <CAPTION ALIGN=TOP>
   Office Product Merchandise and Category Information
   </CAPTION>
   ```

4. Optionally, add character-level formatting tags to the caption. The caption, without boldface or italics, often gets buried in the table.

   ```
   <CAPTION ALIGN=TOP><B>Office Product Merchandise and Category
   Information</B></CAPTION>
   ```

The resulting caption looks like that shown in Figure 8.9.

See Chapter 3 for a review of character-level formatting tags.

Remember that the ALIGN= attribute controls where the caption appears. Where you insert the ALIGN= attribute within the <TABLE> tags has no effect on where the caption appears.

FIGURE 8.9

*Table captions pro-
vide an at-a-glance
summary of table
contents.*

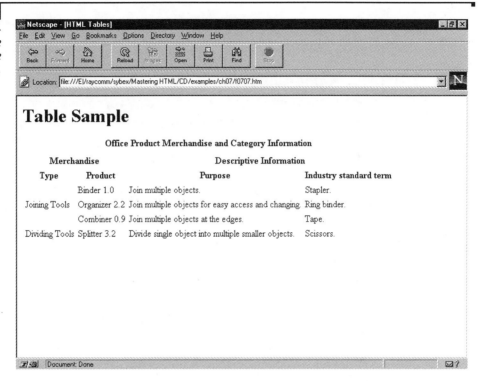

Formatting Tables

Once you set up a table, you can add a number of formatting options that improve its
overall appearance. In particular, you can do the following:

- Add borders
- Include background colors and images
- Adjust cell spacing and padding
- Adjust cell alignment
- Specify cell size
- Specify table alignment

HTML 4 Opportunities

As you'll see in the next several sections in this chapter, you can add a lot of formatting to tables—backgrounds, borders, colors, alignment, and so on. Keep in mind that many of these options are not standard HTML and that not all browsers support them. Additionally, HTML 4 strongly encourages you to use Style Sheets to apply formatting options.

If you're certain your visitors use browsers that support HTML 4 tags, consider using Style Sheets to format your tables. Style Sheets, which are supported by the HTML 4 specification, are the up-and-coming way to apply styles throughout your HTML documents—tables included! See Chapter 5 and the Master's Reference to learn to use Style Sheets.

Adding and Formatting Borders

Borders are the lines that enclose tables and that clearly separate rows, columns, and cells. By default, most browsers display tables without borders; however, tables that have borders are much easier to read and more attractive. For example, the sample tables shown thus far in this chapter have not had borders and have been rather difficult to read—it's hard to tell where one cell stops and the next begins. Without borders, the cells visually run together, and the columns and rows are somewhat obscured. Figure 8.10 shows the table in Figure 8.9, earlier in this chapter, with borders as viewed in Netscape Navigator.

Creating Table Borders

You specify table borders using an attribute and a number, measured in pixels, that tell browsers the width of the border. As shown in Figure 8.10, most browsers display borders as lines with a 3-D effect. Table 8.5 lists border attributes that newer versions of Netscape Navigator and Internet Explorer support.

PART

II

Advancing Your Skills

FIGURE 8.10

Borders often improve table readability and appearance.

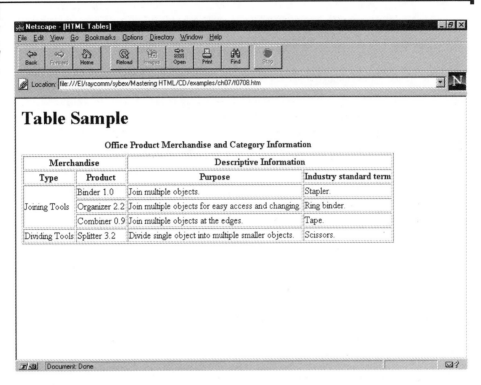

TABLE 8.5: BORDER ATTRIBUTES

Attribute	Use
BORDER=n	Specifies a table border width, which is measured in pixels. The larger the number, the wider the border. BORDER=0 removes borders (generally also the default setting).
BORDERCOLOR= "#rrggbb"	Specifies a color for the table border as #rrggbb number or name; supported by newer versions of Netscape Navigator and Internet Explorer.

To create a table border and specify its color, follow these steps:

1. Add the BORDER= attribute to the opening table tag.

```
<TABLE BORDER=2>
```

2. Specify the border color by using the BORDERCOLOR= attribute and either an RGB number or an accepted color name. Specifying the border color is not essential—the border will be wider because of the BORDER=2 attribute, and the color is simply another formatting characteristic that you can add if you choose.

`<TABLE BORDER=2 `**`BORDERCOLOR="#FF0000">`**

Figure 8.11 shows the results of using BORDER=2 in the table tag.

FIGURE 8.11

A 2-pixel border added around table cells

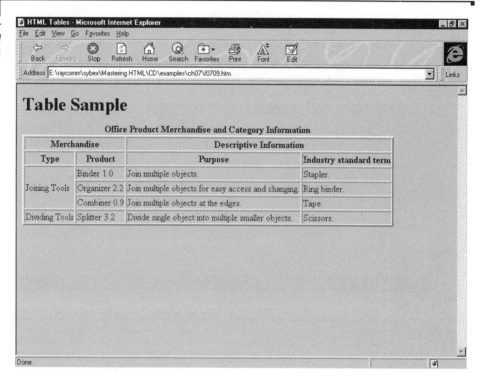

See Chapter 7 for more information about RGB numbers and accepted color names.

Specifying No Table Borders

Although most browsers display tables without borders by default, you can specify no borders to ensure that no borders display. For example, if you're using tables for advanced formatting such as columns, side headings, or juxtaposed text and graphics, you want to ensure that the table appears without borders. Figure 8.12 shows an example of advanced formatting using tables that have no borders.

FIGURE 8.12

The RayComm, Inc. site relies on tables to format two columns.

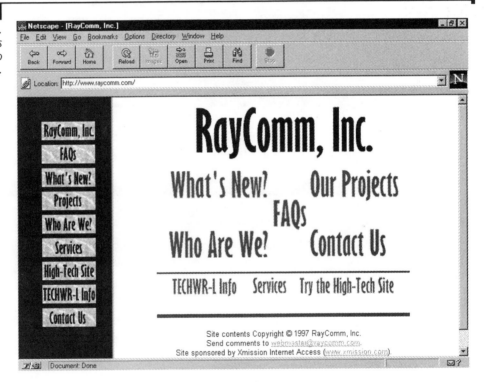

PART

II

Advancing Your Skills

The buttons on the left of the browser window are in one table cell, and the graphic and content on the right are in another cell. To specify no table borders, set the BORDER= attribute to zero (0), like this:

```
<TABLE BORDER=0>
```

Using Internet Explorer–Specific Border Attributes

Microsoft has implemented two additional tags in Internet Explorer to control border color. In many browsers, the table borders are presented in 3-D—that is, a darker color at the bottom and right edges, with a lighter color at the top and left, as shown here:

Table Sample

Office Product Merchandise and Category Information

Merchandise		Descriptive Information	
Type	Product	Purpose	Industry standard term
Joining Tools	Binder 1.0	Join multiple objects.	Stapler.
	Organizer 2.2	Join multiple objects for easy access and changing.	Ring binder.
	Combiner 0.9	Join multiple objects at the edges.	Tape.
Dividing Tools	Splitter 3.2	Divide single object into multiple smaller objects.	Scissors.

Internet Explorer recognizes attributes to set the darker and lighter color of the 3-D effect. Table 8.6 lists these attributes.

TABLE 8.6: INTERNET EXPLORER BORDER ATTRIBUTES

Attribute	Use
BORDERCOLORLIGHT="#rrggbb"	Specifies a light border color for 3-D effect on tables.
BORDERCOLORDARK="#rrggbb"	Specifies a dark border color for 3-D effect on tables.

To apply these attributes, insert them in the initial <TABLE> tag, just as you insert standard border attributes, like this:

```
<TABLE BORDERCOLORLIGHT="CCCCCC">
```

or

```
<TABLE BORDERCOLORDARK="33FF33">
```

TIP

If you have specific border color needs and you know that your visitors will be using Internet Explorer, you can further customize border colors by applying the same attributes to individual table cells.

Setting Table Background Options

In addition to specifying border color, you can specify that the table background appear as a particular color or image. Using a background color or image enhances table appearance, makes the table more interesting, provides a place for corporate logos, and helps contrast text and image colors.

TIP

The HTML 4 specification deprecates table background options in favor of Style Sheets. Although these background options will still work in Netscape Navigator and Internet Explorer, consider setting table background colors using Style Sheets.

Setting a Table Background Color

Only the newer versions of Netscape Navigator and Internet Explorer support table background colors. You can, however, provide table background colors and images for Netscape Navigator and Internet Explorer visitors with no adverse effects on those who use other browsers. For example, Figure 8.13 shows a table that uses a background color viewed in Internet Explorer. If you display this table in an older browser, the background color will be the same as the background color of the browser.

FIGURE 8.13

A color background can enhance a table's appearance when viewed in a browser that supports background colors.

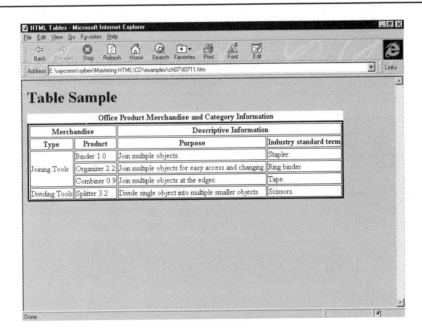

For background colors to be effective, they must adequately contrast with text color(s); otherwise, the text becomes virtually unreadable, as you can see here:

To ensure that your table background color(s) are effective, follow these guidelines:

- Choose a light background color if your text color(s) are dark; choose a dark background color if your text color(s) are light.

- Choose colors that are aesthetically pleasing and suit the purpose of your document. For example, if your topic is fast-paced, choose bright colors; if your topic is slower-paced, choose paler colors.

- View your HTML documents in a few different browsers.

- Choose from one of the 216 nondithering colors.

As we mentioned in Chapter 7, nondithering colors appear solid (not splotchy or spotted) in browsers. See Chapter 7 for more information.

The table background color attribute is BGCOLOR="#rrggbb", and it is used in the opening <TABLE> tag.

To use a color throughout the background of the table, add BGCOLOR= followed by the RGB number or color name, as in the following:

```
<TABLE BGCOLOR="#CCFFFF">
```

The table background (not including the borders) will be colored, as in Figure 8.14.

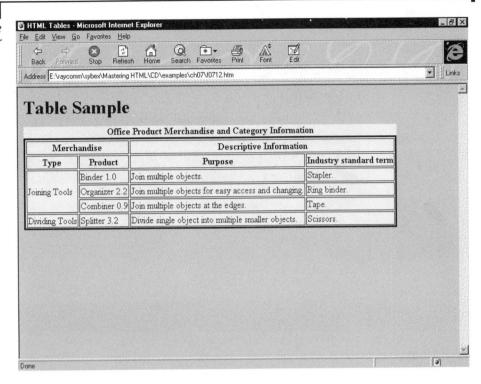

FIGURE 8.14

The resulting table background color

Setting a Table Background Image

Only the newer versions of Netscape Navigator and Internet Explorer support table background images. Other browsers display the browser's default background color instead of the background image.

> To accommodate visitors who are using browsers that do not support background images and visitors who have image options turned off, use background images and background colors. Visitors can, then, view a table enhanced with color, rather than one that uses the browser's default background color.

Table background images are *tiled*—that is, they are repeated on the screen until the available background space is filled. Not all browsers tile images in the same way. For example, Figures 8.15 and 8.16 show how Netscape Navigator and Internet Explorer display a table that uses a small pair of scissors as the background image.

PART

II

Advancing Your Skills

FIGURE 8.15

A table background
image viewed in
Navigator

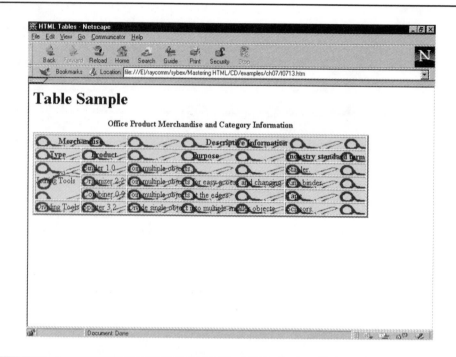

FIGURE 8.16

A table background
image viewed in
Internet Explorer

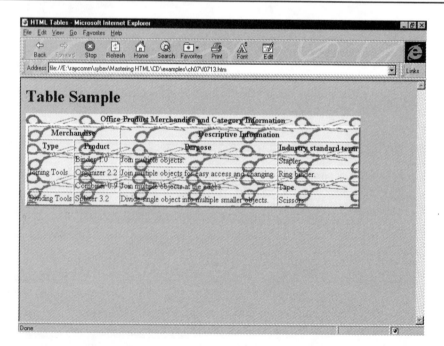

Although the image is inappropriately dark and the text is unreadable, the overall effect is quite different in each browser. In Figure 8.15, the tiling restarts at the upper-left corner of each cell, and the caption is not considered part of the table for the purpose of background. In Figure 8.16, the image is rendered slightly larger, fills behind the caption, and is tiled throughout the table without consideration for individual cells.

TIP

To ensure that the whole image is visible in a table cell (and only once), include the <IMG> tag in the table cell, not as a background image.

Also, as Figures 8.15 and 8.16 show, table background images can easily overpower table content if you use too many shapes, patterns, or colors. The resulting text becomes virtually unreadable.

To ensure that you choose a suitable background image, follow these guidelines:

- Choose small, subtle images that are not essential for conveying information.
- Choose simple background images—ones with few shapes, patterns, or colors.
- Choose background images that enhance the purpose of the document.
- View your HTML documents in as many browsers as possible.

To indicate background image in a table, you use the background image attribute BACKGROUND=" . . . ".

Internet Explorer 3 and newer plus Netscape Navigator 4 both support these tags on individual cells as well as for the table as a whole. Add the attribute to the <TD> or <TH> tag, just as you would add it to the <TABLE> tag.

To use a table background image, add BACKGROUND= followed by the URL, as in the following code:

```
<TABLE BACKGROUND="coolimage.gif">
```

Figure 8.17 shows an effective background image.

Specifying Cell Alignment

Cell alignment refers to the horizontal or vertical alignment of cell contents. Most browsers have the following default cell alignment settings:

- Table headings are aligned in the center (horizontally) and center (vertically) in the cell.
- Table contents are aligned on the left (horizontally) and center (vertically) in the cell.

PART
II

Advancing Your Skills

Using the attributes described in Table 8.7, however, you can change the default horizontal and vertical alignment in table cells.

An effective table background image enhances the table content.

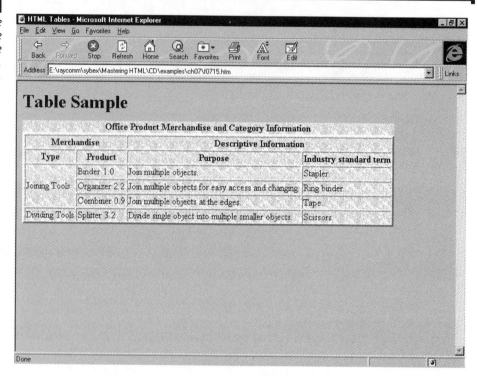

TABLE 8.7: CELL ALIGNMENT ATTRIBUTES

Attribute	Use
ALIGN=n	Specifies the horizontal alignment of cell contents as LEFT, CENTER, or RIGHT.
VALIGN=n	Specifies the vertical alignment of cell contents as TOP, MIDDLE, BOTTOM, or BASELINE.

To use these alignment attributes, include them within any <TR>, <TD>, or <TH> tag, like this:

```
<TR ALIGN=RIGHT>
```

or

```
<TD VALIGN=TOP>
```

or

```
<TH ALIGN=CENTER VALIGN=MIDDLE>
```

You can save some typing by setting the alignment for a row in the <TR> tag, rather than in each individual cell. If you set the alignment in the <TR> tag, you can override it on a cell by cell basis in the <TD> or <TH> tags.

Specifying Cell Size

Most browsers make cells as large as necessary to hold the contents and wrap text to a new line only after the table is as wide as the browser window and table width settings permit. You can, however, specify cell size to keep the text from wrapping to a new line or to make content easier to read.

Specifying all cell widths decreases perceived download time by allowing some browsers to lay out the table as it arrives, rather than waiting for the whole table to download. The table still takes the same time to download; however, it appears to load faster because it arrives gradually, rather than in one big chunk.

You can specify cell size in two ways:

- As a percentage of the browser window
- As a specific size, measured in pixels

Although most browsers support alignment attributes, how they display attributes depends on the table size and other table or cell settings. For example, a cell size that is 50 percent of the browser window will be wider or narrower, depending on the screen resolution and on the size of the browser window. Likewise, if you set cell width to 100 pixels, it will be exactly that wide in browsers that support cell width tags, regardless of what that does to the overall page layout.

PART

II

Advancing Your Skills

TIP

If you can avoid setting specific cell widths in your tables, do so. The more restrictively you set the table formatting, the less leeway the browser has to reformat the table to fit and the more unpredictable the results.

Use the attributes in Table 8.8 in either the <TH> or <TD> tags to control the table width and text wrap.

TABLE 8.8: TABLE WIDTH AND TEXT WRAP ATTRIBUTES

Attribute	Use
WIDTH="n" NOWRAP	Specifies the width of a cell in either pixels or as a percentage of table width. Prohibits text wrapping within the cell, thus requiring all text to appear on one line.

Specifying Cell Width

To specify cell width, simply add the WIDTH="n" attribute to the <TD> or <TH> tags. For example, you can specify that a header cell (and, therefore, the cells below it) occupy 15 percent of the table width, like this:

```
<TR>
    <TH>Type</TH>
    <TH>Product</TH>
    <TH>Purpose</TH>
    <TH WIDTH="15%">Industry standard term</TH>
</TR>
```

If you set the WIDTH in a cell with a COLSPAN attribute, like the Descriptive Information cell shown in a Figure 8.18, the attributes affect individual columns below proportionately. For example, if you add a WIDTH="50%" to the Descriptive Information cell, the browser attempts to make the columns starting with Purpose and with Industry Standard Term together total approximately 50 percent.

```
<TR>
    <TH COLSPAN=2>Merchandise</TH>
    <TH COLSPAN=2 WIDTH="50%">Descriptive Information</TH>
</TR>
```

Figure 8.19 shows the resulting table.

FIGURE 8.18

The browser determined the sizes of the cells in this table automatically.

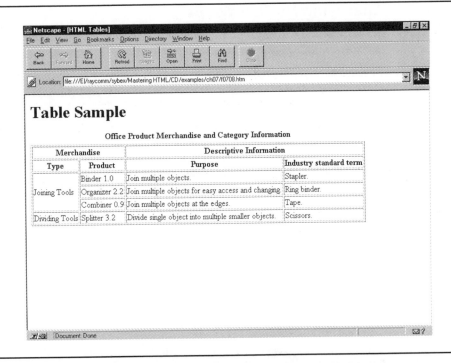

FIGURE 8.19

Combine cell size and column span attributes to customize your tables.

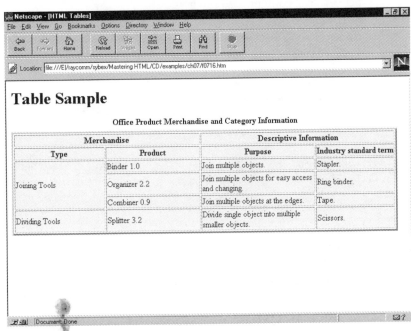

PART

II

Advancing Your Skills

Specifying No Text Wraps

If you reset the width of certain cells, you may want to ensure that the contents do not wrap to multiple lines. Add the NOWRAP attribute, as in the following example, to encourage the browser not to break the line.

```
<TH COLSPAN=2 WIDTH="30%" NOWRAP>Descriptive Information</TH>
```

NOTE

HTML 4 deprecates the NOWRAP attribute. You guessed it—if your visitors will have browsers that recognize Style Sheets, use them to format tables.

To set a minimum size for a cell, smaller than which it cannot be displayed, use a transparent GIF image 1 pixel × 1 pixel in size with HEIGHT and WIDTH attributes set to the size necessary. (See Chapter 7 for more on using transparent GIF images for size control.)

Adding Cell Spacing and Padding

Cell spacing and padding refer to how much white space appears in a table. In particular, *cell spacing* refers to the spacing between cells, and *cell padding* refers to spacing between cell contents and cell borders.

For many tables, open space around cell contents makes the table much easier to read and more aesthetically pleasing. For example, the contents in Figure 8.20 are somewhat difficult to read.

Table 8.9 describes cell spacing and cell padding attributes.

TABLE 8.9: CELL SPACING AND PADDING ATTRIBUTES

Attribute	Use
CELLSPACING=n	Specifies, in pixels, the amount of space between cells.
CELLPADDING=n	Specifies, in pixels, the amount of space between cell contents and cell borders.

TIP

If the table has a border, the CELLSPACING= attribute enlarges the rule between cells. If there is no border, the space between adjacent cells will simply be somewhat larger.

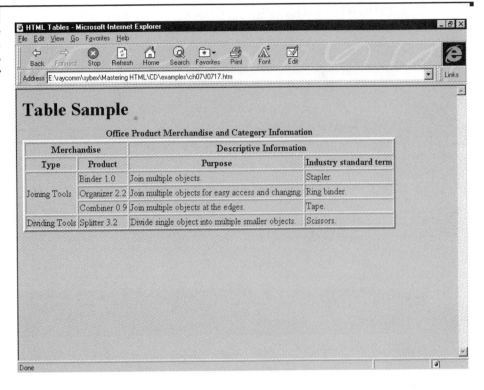

To add cell spacing and padding, include the attributes in the <TABLE> tag, like this:

<TABLE **CELLSPACING=5 CELLPADDING=5** BORDER=3>

The resulting table will look like this:

PART

II

Advancing Your Skills

Specifying Table Alignment, Width, and Text Wrap

Up to now in this chapter, most of the tags and attributes have specified the relationship of the table contents to each other or to other table components. Table width, alignment, and wrap settings, however, specify how the table fits into the HTML document as a whole.

These settings are important for two reasons:

- Browser and computer settings vary significantly from computer to computer. By using width, alignment, and wrap attributes, you help ensure that your visitors can easily view your tables.

- By default, text that surrounds tables does not wrap—it stops above the table and starts below the table. The table itself takes up the full browser width. These attributes narrow the space that the table uses and allow the text to wrap around the table.

Table 8.10 describes the table width, alignment, and wrap attributes.

TABLE 8.10: TABLE WIDTH, ALIGNMENT, AND WRAP ATTRIBUTES	
Attribute	**Use**
WIDTH=n	Specifies table width in pixels or as a percentage of the window width.
ALIGN="..."	Specifies table alignment as LEFT, CENTER, RIGHT and, for Internet Explorer only, BLEEDLEFT, BLEEDRIGHT, and JUSTIFY.
CLEAR=	Specifies that new text following the table should appear below the table, when the LEFT, RIGHT, ALL, or NO margins are clear (unobstructed by the table).

To use any of these attributes, insert them in the opening <TABLE> tag. The following code uses the WIDTH= attribute to set the table width to 600 pixels:

```
<TABLE BORDER=3 WIDTH=600>
```

As a rule, however, setting your table width to a percentage of the browser window—not to a fixed number of pixels—results in a more reliable display. For example, if you set the table width to a size wider than visitors have available, the table could easily run off the edge of the browser window and require them to scroll horizontally. The table in Figure 8.21 requires horizontal scrolling.

FIGURE 8.21

When visitors must scroll horizontally, they have to work harder to get information.

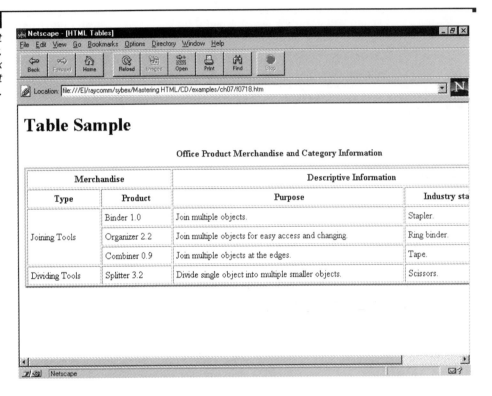

To restrict the width of the table (for example, to allow text to wrap around it), use percentages, as in the following example:

```
<TABLE BORDER=3 WIDTH="70%">
```

NOTE

All percentage values in attributes require quotation marks.

Aligning the table to the left, right, or center is as easy as adding another attribute to the table, as in the following:

```
<TABLE BORDER=3 WIDTH="70%" ALIGN=RIGHT>
```

When you use these attributes and make the table substantially narrower than the window, you may also have to contend with unwanted text wrapping. For example, the preceding line of code causes text following the table to wind up on the left of the right-aligned table, as in Figure 8.22.

FIGURE 8.22

Text wrapping sometimes causes unusual effects.

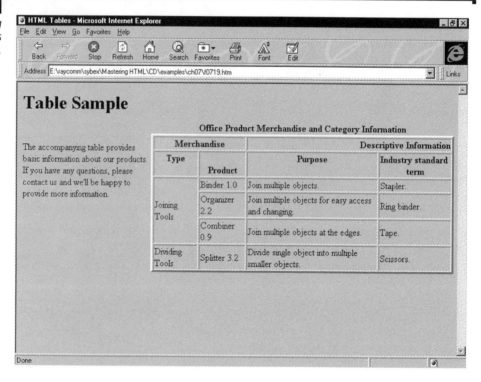

Design Workshop: Creating Newspaper-Style Headings

Here's a handy formatting trick. Use tables to set up a heading with several columns of text below it—like a newspaper:

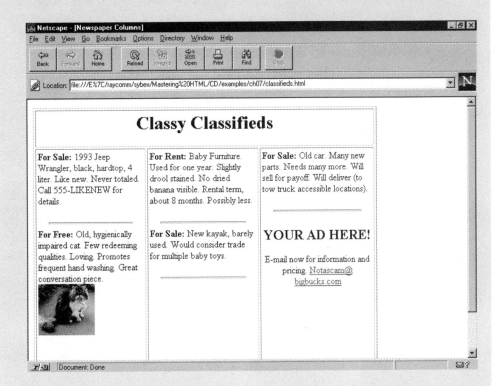

The HTML that produces this effect follows (and is on the CD in the /examples/ch07 folder).

```
<!DOCTYPE HTML PUBLIC "-//W3C//DTD HTML 3.2//EN">

<HTML>

<HEAD><TITLE>Newspaper Columns</TITLE></HEAD>

<BODY BGCOLOR="FFFFFF" TEXT="000000" LINK="0000FF" VLINK="800080"
  ALINK="FF0000">

<TABLE CELLPADDING=3 CELLSPACING=3 BORDER=1 WIDTH="80%">

<TR><TD VALIGN=MIDDLE ALIGN=CENTER COLSPAN=3><H1>Classy Classifieds</H1>
```

CONTINUED

```
<TR><TD VALIGN=TOP WIDTH="120"><B>For Sale:</B> 1993 Jeep Wrangler,
  black, hardtop, 4 liter. Like new. Never totaled. Call 555-LIKENEW for
  details.<P>

<HR WIDTH="80%">

<B>For Free: </B>Old, hygienically impaired cat. Few redeeming qualities.
  Loving. Promotes frequent hand washing. Great conversation piece.

<IMG SRC="winthumb.gif" ALIGN="" WIDTH="100" HEIGHT="88" BORDER="0"
  ALT="Winchester">

<TD VALIGN=TOP WIDTH="120"><B>For Rent:</B> Baby Furniture. Used for one
  year. Slightly drool stained. No dried banana visible. Rental term,
  about 8 months. Possibly less. <P>

<HR WIDTH="80%">

<B>For Sale:</B> New kayak, barely used. Would consider trade for
  multiple baby toys. <P>

<HR WIDTH="80%">

<TD VALIGN=TOP WIDTH="120"><B>For Sale:</B> Old car. Many new parts.
  Needs many more.

  Will sell for payoff. Will deliver (to tow truck accessible locations).
<P>

<HR WIDTH="80%">

<CENTER><H2>YOUR AD HERE!</H2>

  E-mail now for information and pricing.

<A HREF="mailto:Notascam@bigbucks.com">

  Notascam@<BR>bigbucks.com</A></CENTER>

</TABLE>
```

Feel free to take this example and adapt it for your own needs. It contains many of the tags and concepts discussed in this chapter.

Using HTML 4 Table Features

With the advent of HTML 4, you now have many new table tags at your fingertips. In particular, HTML 4 table features give you added control over formatting tables. Instead of formatting the table as a whole, you can format specific table parts, such as the table head, body, footer, and column groups.

At the time of writing, only Internet Explorer supports these tags; however, because they are part of the most recent specification, it's likely that other browsers will soon also support them.

You can use HTML 4 tables to format portions of the table separately—as sections, rather than as individual cells. For example, you can do the following:

- Group similar areas of tables and add borders around the areas.

- Add lines or text formatting to table headings.

- Include a table footer, which is handy if a table has totals at the bottom of the columns.

- Use these additional tags as hooks for Style Sheets to get into more sophisticated formatting. All style tags can be used with these tags.

TIP

See Chapter 5 for more about Style Sheets.

For example, Figure 8.23 uses HTML 4 table tags and attributes to group two main columns (Merchandise and Descriptive Information) and to include a two-line header.

HTML 4 tables work in conjunction with standard table tags—that is, you develop tables using the standard tags, and then you add the version 4 tags and attributes. The result is that visitors using the newest browsers can view the HTML 4 effects and users of other browsers can still view the basic table.

To apply HTML 4 table tags and attributes, follow these general steps, which are described in detail in the next two sections:

1. Identify table sections.

2. Apply frames and rules to table sections.

PART

II

Advancing Your Skills

FIGURE 8.23

You can use advanced table tags to group table parts.

Main column groups —
Header —

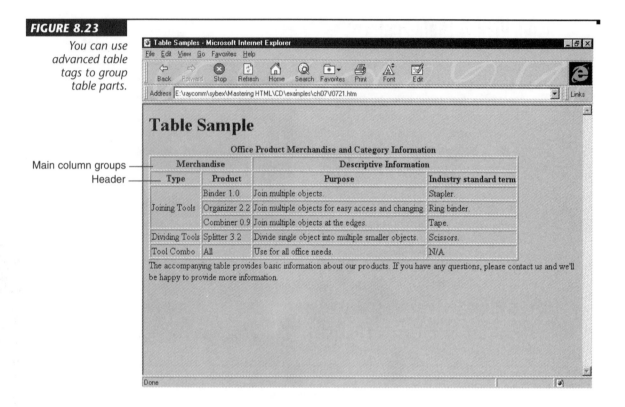

Identifying Table Sections

The first step in using HTML 4 tables is identifying table sections by grouping similar table parts and identifying each part as being part of the table heading, body, footer, or columns. Table 8.11 describes advanced table tags.

TABLE 8.11: ADVANCED TABLE TAGS

Tag	Use
<THEAD>	Labels the header area of a table.
<TBODY>	Labels the body area of table.
<TFOOT>	Labels the footer area of table.
<COLGROUP>	Identifies column groups within a table.

Identifying Row Groups

Row groups include parts such as the header, body, and footer—the table parts that contain table rows. To identify row groups, start with the standard table tags and then include the HTML 4 table tags around them. Take a look at the following code, which nests the standard table tags within the table header tags (<THEAD> ... </THEAD>):

```
<THEAD>
<TR>
    <TH COLSPAN=2>Merchandise</TH>
    <TH COLSPAN=2>Descriptive Information</TH>
</TR>
<TR>
    <TH>Type</TH>
    <TH>Product</TH>
    <TH>Purpose</TH>
    <TH>Industry standard term</TH>
</TR>
</THEAD>
```

You can also identify table body parts by using the <TBODY> tags, like this:

```
<TBODY>
<TR>
    <TD ROWSPAN=3>Joining Tools</TD>
    <TD>Binder 1.0</TD>
    <TD>Join multiple objects.</TD>
    <TD>Stapler.</TD>
</TR>
<TR>
    <TD>Organizer 2.2</TD>
    <TD>Join multiple objects for easy access and changing.</TD>
    <TD>Ring binder.</TD>
</TR>
<TR>
    <TD>Combiner 0.9</TD>
    <TD>Join multiple objects at the edges.</TD>
    <TD>Tape.</TD>
</TR>
<TR>
    <TD>Dividing Tools</TD>
```

PART

II

Advancing Your Skills

```
      <TD>Splitter 3.2</TD>
      <TD>Divide single object into multiple smaller objects.</TD>
      <TD>Scissors.</TD>
   </TR>
   </TBODY>
```

Finally, you can identify a table footer by using the <TFOOT> tags in the same way. The <TFOOT> tags must follow the <THEAD> tag and *precede* the <TBODY> tag.

```
   <TFOOT>
   <TR>
      <TD>Tool Combo</TD>
      <TD>All</TD>
      <TD>Use for all office needs.</TD>
      <TD>N/A</TD>
   </TR>
   </TFOOT>
   </TABLE>
```

At this point, the advanced table won't look any different from the standard table. After you've tagged your table with these additional table tags, you can either identify column groups or format the tagged parts with the advanced formatting tags.

Identifying Column Groups

In addition to identifying table headers, body, and footers, you can identify column groups. The <COLGROUP> tags, which are used in conjunction with the SPAN= attribute, are located at the beginning of the table and announce the columns to which they apply.

The table shown in Figure 8.23, earlier in this chapter, contains two distinct groups of columns, with two columns in each. Therefore, there will be two <COLGROUP> tags with SPAN=2 attributes in each, as in the following example:

```
   <CAPTION ALIGN=TOP><B>Office Product Merchandise and Category
   Information</B></CAPTION>
   <COLGROUP SPAN=2>
   <COLGROUP SPAN=2>
   <THEAD>
```

If there were three groups—two of one column and one of two columns—you would include three <COLGROUP> tags, the third with a SPAN=2 attribute, as in the following:

```
   <COLGROUP>
   <COLGROUP>
   <COLGROUP SPAN=2>
```

You won't see anything different about your table now when you view it in a browser. After you identify column groups, you need to format them.

HTML 4 Table Borders

You can use HTML 4's formatting capabilities to create custom table borders—called *rules*—which apply to specified sections of the table. Rather than applying borders to an entire table, which is all you can do with standard table capabilities, you can apply borders just to the table heading, body, footer, or specific columns. Table 8.12 shows HTML 4's table formatting options. Table 8.12 describes the advanced table formatting attributes.

TABLE 8.12: ADVANCED TABLE FORMATTING ATTRIBUTES

Attribute	Use
FRAME=	Specifies the outside edges of the table that will have a border. Possible choices include BORDER (the default), VOID (no borders), ABOVE, BELOW, HSIDES (top and bottom), LHS (left hand side), RHS (right hand side), VSIDES (left and right), and BOX (all sides).
RULES=	Specifies which internal borders of the table are displayed. NONE, GROUPS (rules between table groups), THEAD, TBODY, TFOOT, COLGROUP, ROWS (rules between table rows), COLS (rules between table columns), ALL.
COLS=	Specifies the number of columns in the table.

To format the identified table parts, include these attributes in the <TABLE> tag by following these general steps:

1. Add an outside border (the frame) by adding the FRAME= attribute to the <TABLE> tag, like this:

```
<TABLE FRAME=BOX>
```

NOTE

You can still control the border width with the BORDER=n attribute, covered earlier in this chapter. For example, to set the outside border to 3 pixels wide, the opening <TABLE> tag would look like this:<TABLE FRAME=BOX BORDER=3>. The BORDER= attribute in the <TABLE> tag affects only the width of the outside border, not the width of the internal rules.

2. Add inside borders (called rules) by adding the RULES= attribute to the <TABLE> tag, like this:

```
<TABLE FRAME=HSIDES RULES=NONE BORDER=3>
```

If you look carefully, you'll notice a thin line above the table footer—that's part of the footer formatting, just as the boldface is part of the <TH> formatting.

TIP

To insert a rule between the groups you defined in the table, add RULES=GROUPS. This is an effective technique, as is RULES=ROWS.

The resulting table looks like that shown in Figure 8.24, as viewed in Internet Explorer.

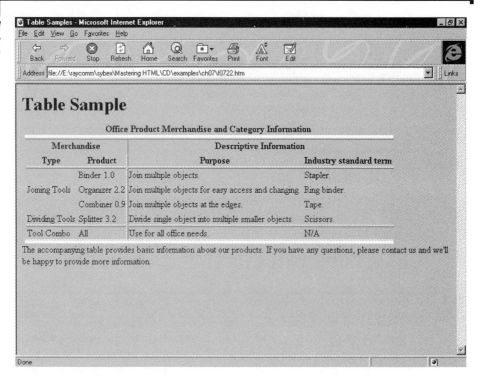

Additionally, as a step toward speeding the perceived download and redraw time, you can specify the number of columns in the table. Doing so has no effect on the visual appearance of the table, but allows the browser to lay out the table more quickly. Add the COLS= attribute to the <TABLE> tag, like this:

<TABLE **COLS=4**>

Because tables are laid out as soon as the whole table is downloaded to the browser (rather than line by line as with regular text), using multiple, smaller tables will improve the perceived download time.

Where to Go from Here

This chapter showed you how to develop and format standard HTML tables plus tables built with HTML 4 tags and attributes. Knowing how to develop tables, you can effectively present complex data and create interesting page layouts. From here, check out these chapters:

- Check out Chapter 3 for general formatting and design topics.
- See Chapter 5 and the Master's Reference for complete information about creating and applying Style Sheets.
- Look at Chapter 7 to see how to include images and use colors wisely.
- See Chapter 10 to see how to create HTML frames.
- See the Master's Reference for more table options.

PART

II

Advancing Your Skills

Chapter

9

Developing
HTML Forms

Developing HTML Forms

When you submit credit card information to purchase something
online, search the Web with
AltaVista or HotBot, participate in a Web-based chat room, or even select a line from a
drop-down menu, you're using a form. Within the scope of plain HTML—as opposed
to extensions such as JavaScript, Java applets, and other embedded programs—forms
are the only method of two-way communication between Web pages and Web sites.

Perhaps because of the name, HTML developers tend to assume that forms are for
collecting pages of data. Actually, you can use forms to get information from visitors
without giving them the feeling of "filling out a form."

In this chapter, we'll look at how to develop forms using standard tags and attributes, which virtually all browsers support. We'll develop a form for ASR Outfitters
piece by piece.

Check out the Master's Reference for a comprehensive list of form tags and attributes.

You can create forms using any HTML development tools—alone or in combination. For example, if you plan to develop a lot of forms, you might consider using a WYSIWYG editor to create the basic form. These editors don't produce consistently good results, but they help ensure that you don't leave out any tags or necessary attributes. You can then manually modify the formatting as necessary. If you'll only be doing one or two forms, however, creating them manually or with the help of a code-based editor is more than adequate and is probably easier than learning how to use a WYSIWYG editor effectively.

Determining Form Content

The first step in developing a form is determining which information to include and how to present it, that is, how to break it down into manageable pieces. You then need to ensure that visitors can easily provide the information you want from them, which means that your form needs to be both functional and visually appealing.

Information Issues

When deciding which information to include and how to break it down, consider your purposes for creating the form. You might begin by answering these questions:

- What information do I want? Customer contact information? Only e-mail addresses so that I can contact visitors later? Opinions about the site?

- Why will visitors access the form? To order something online? To request information? To submit comments or questions about products or services?

- What information can visitors readily provide? Contact information? Description of their product use? Previous purchases?

- How much time will visitors be willing to spend filling out the form? Would they be willing to describe something in a paragraph or two, or would they just want to select from a list?

After determining what information you want and what information your visitors can provide, break the information into the smallest chunks possible. For example, if you want visitors to provide contact information, divide contact information into name, street address, and city/state/zip. Go a step further, however, and collect the city, state, and zip code as separate items so that you can later sort data according to, say, customers in a particular city, state, or zip code. If you don't collect these items separately, you won't be able to sort on them individually.

Although it's possible to go back and change forms after you implement them, careful planning will save a lot of trouble and work later. For example, if you complete and implement a form and then discover that you forgot to request key information, the initial responses to the form will be less useful or skew the resulting data. Fixing the form takes nearly as much time as doing it carefully at first.

ASR Outfitters includes a form on its Web site to collect targeted addresses for future product and sale announcements. Although ASR could just as easily (but not as cheaply) use regular mailings by purchasing mailing lists, a Web site form avoids the cost of traditional mailings, collects information from specifically interested visitors, and keeps the Internet-based company focused on the Net.

Because filling out a Web page form takes some time, ASR created a form that includes only the essentials—in this case, a little demographic information:

First name: This is necessary to help personalize responses.

Last name: This is also necessary to help personalize responses.

E-mail address: Collecting this information is the main purpose of the form.

Company, street address, city, state, zip: All are necessary for future snail mailings and for later demographic analysis. Collecting the address, even with no immediate intent to use it, is probably a wise move, because it would be difficult to ask customers for more information later.

Referral: The marketing department wants to know how the audience found the Web site.

Online purchasing habits: ASR wants to learn about the possible acceptance rate for taking orders over the Net.

Areas of interest: ASR wants to find out about the customer's interests to determine areas in which to expand its online offerings.

Other comments: It's always important to give visitors an opportunitye to provide additional information.

The form ASR Outfitters eventually developed is shown in Figure 9.1.

PART

II

Advancing Your Skills

ASR Outfitters' form collects only the basic demographic and marketing information.

Thank you for your interest in getting e-mailed information from ASR Outfitters. We assure you that we do not resell or distribute these addresses in any form. We use this information exclusively to provide you with better service.

Information Request

First Name
Last Name
E-mail Address
Address
City State Zip or Postal Code
Country

Please choose the most appropriate statement.
- ○ I regularly purchase items online.
- ○ I have on occasion purchased items online.
- ● I have not purchased anything online, but I would consider it.
- ○ I prefer to shop in real stores.

I'm interested in (choose all that apply):
- ☐ Hiking
- ☐ Mountain Biking
- ☐ Camping
- ☐ Rock Climbing
- ☐ Off-Road 4WD
- ☐ Cross-country Skiing

I learned about this site from:
Print Ads ▼

Comments:
Please type any additional comments here

Submit   Start Over

ASR Outfitters
info@asroutfitters.com
4700 N. Center
South Logan, UT 87654
801-555-3422

Usability Issues

Usability, as it applies to forms, refers to how easily your visitors can answer your questions. Most online forms require some action of visitors and usually offer no concrete benefit or reward for their efforts. Therefore, if forms are not easy to use, you won't get many (or any) responses. Here are some usability guidelines to consider when you are creating forms.

Group Similar Categories

When you group similar categories, as you can see from Figure 9.1, the form appears less daunting, and visitors are more likely to fill it out and submit it. ASR can group the information it's soliciting from visitors into three main categories:

- Contact information
- Purchasing habits and areas of interest
- Referrals and other information

Make the Form Easy

If you've ever completed a long form, you know how tedious it can be. Think tax form for an example of how not to do it. Although the specifics depend greatly on the information you'll be collecting, some principles remain constant:

- Whenever possible, provide a list from which visitors can choose one or more items. Lists are easy to use, and they result in easy-to-process information.

- If you can't provide a list, ask visitors to fill in only a small amount of text. Again, this takes minimal time, and it provides you with data that is fairly easy to process.

- If you absolutely must, ask visitors to fill in large areas of text. Keep in mind, though, that this takes a lot of time—both for the visitor and for you. Additionally, many visitors are likely to ignore a request that requires them to enter lots of text.

TIP

For more information about how to create lists and areas to fill in, see the section "Creating Forms," later in this chapter.

Provide Incentives

Provide visitors with incentives to fill out the form and submit it. Offer them something, even if its value is marginal. Studies show that a penny or a stamp included in mailed surveys often significantly improves the response rate. Consider offering a chance in a drawing for a free product, an e-mailed list of tips and tricks, or a discount on services.

ASR Outfitters might have offered anything from a free tote bag to an e-mailed collection of hiking tips or a discount on the next purchase, but chose to settle for a small coupon book available on the next visit to the store.

Design Issues

Perhaps because of the need to address all the technical issues, Web authors often neglect design issues. A well-designed form, however, helps and encourages visitors to give you the information you want.

What constitutes good form design? Something visually appealing, graphically helpful, and consistent with the remainder of the site. A form at an intranet site that has a white background and minimal graphics and that is managed by conservative supervisors would likely have a simple, vertical design and be none the worse for it. A visually interesting or highly graphical Web site, however, calls for a form in keeping with the overall theme.

Although the visual interest of the form should not overwhelm the rest of the page, you'll want to make judicious use of color, alignment, small images, and font characteristics. Here are some guidelines:

- Use headings to announce each new group of information. This helps visitors move easily through the form.

- Be sure to visually separate groups. This makes the forms easier to use because sections become shorter and easier to wade through. You can use horizontal rules or the <FIELDSET> tage in HTML 4 to do this.

- Use text emphases to draw the audience to important information. You might recall from Chapter 3 that you should use emphases sparingly; emphasize only a few words so that they stand out on the page.

- Specify how visitors are to move through the form. Don't make your visitors scroll horizontally to access information. Consider making a narrow, longer form rather than a wider, shorter form to accommodate those who have lower monitor resolution. If your survey is in multiple columns, make different categories visually obvious.

- Use arrows to direct visitors through the page. This can help visitors move through the page in a specified order.

- Be sure that it's clear which checkboxes and fields go with the associated descriptive information. For example, if you have a long row of checkboxes and labels, it's fairly confusing to figure out whether the checkbox goes with the text on the right or the text on the left. Use line breaks and spacing to clearly differentiate.

- Specify which fields are optional (and required). Some browsers and processing programs reject forms that are incorrectly or not completely filled out.

- Use a background image. Forms with some texture tend to be less form-ish and more friendly. Be sure, though, that the image doesn't outweigh the content and that the text adequately contrasts with the image.

- Make all the text entry fields the same width and put them on the left if you have a vertical column of name and address information—that way all the text will align vertically and look much better. If the text labels go on the left, the fields will not (cannot) align vertically and will therefore look more random and less professional.

Creating Forms

Forms have two basic parts:

- The part you can see (that a visitor fills out)
- The part you can't see (that specifies how the server should process the information)

In this section, we'll show you how to create the part that you can see. We'll show you how to create the other part later in the section "Processing Forms."

Understanding Widgets

Forms consist of several types of widgets (they're also called controls), which are fields you can use to collect data:

- Submit and reset buttons send the form information to the server for processing and return the form to its original settings.

- Text fields are areas for brief text input. Use these for several word responses, such as names, search terms, or addresses.

- Select lists are lists from which visitors can choose one or more items. Use them to present a long but finite list of choices, for example, choose your state from this list, or choose one of these 17 options.

- Checkboxes allow visitors to select none, one, or several items from a list. Use them to elicit multiple answers. For example, ASR Outfitters used checkboxes to get information about the activities of its customers.

- Radio buttons give visitors an opportunity to choose only one item, for example, gender, a preference, or anything else that can be only one way.

- Textareas are areas for lengthy text input, as in open-ended comments or free-form responses.

Figure 9.2 shows a sample form that includes these widgets.

FIGURE 9.2

Forms give visitors different ways of entering information.

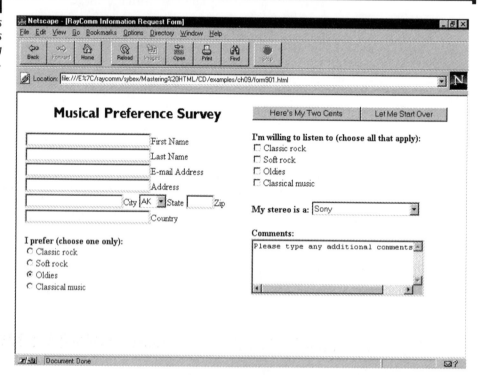

Which Widgets Are Best?

When deciding which widget to use, consider the information you want to collect. For example, start by seeing whether you can collect pieces of information using check-boxes and radio buttons. These are generally the easiest for your visitors to use because they specify the options and require only the click of a mouse. Then, look for places you can use select lists, which are also easy to use. Finally, include textareas only if audiences need to respond in their own words.

CONTINUED

In general, radio buttons, checkboxes, and select lists are all better choices for accepting input than textareas. If visitors are selecting choices from a list, you need not be concerned with misspellings, inconsistent answers, or free-form answers that don't fit the categories. If you can provide choices and let visitors choose from among them, do so.

Creating a Form and Adding Submit and Reset Buttons

The first step in creating a form is to insert the <FORM> tags and add submit and reset buttons. Submit and reset buttons are essential components because they allow visitors to submit information and, if necessary, clear selections. Although you must add other form fields before the form will do anything worthwhile, the submit button is the key that makes the form go somewhere.

NOTE

Forms require two other attributes in the <FORM> tag to specify what happens to the form results and which program on the server will process them. We'll look at those in the section "Processing Forms," later in this chapter.

Table 9.1 lists and describes the basic form tags as well as the submit and reset buttons.

TABLE 9.1: BASIC FORM TAGS

Tag/Attribute	Use
<FORM>	Marks a form within an HTML document.
<INPUT TYPE= "SUBMIT" VALUE="...">	Provides a submit button for a form. The Value= attribute produces text on the button.
<INPUT TYPE= "IMAGE" NAME="POINT" SRC="..." BORDER=0>	Provides a graphical submit button. The SRC= attribute indicates the image source file, and the BORDER= attribute turns off the image border.
<INPUT TYPE= "RESET" VALUE="...">	Provides a reset button for a form. The Value= attribute produces text on the button.

In the following example, we'll create a form for the ASR Outfitters site as we show you how to start a form and then add submit and reset buttons. The following code produces the page shown in Figure 9.3.

```
<!DOCTYPE HTML PUBLIC "-//W3C//DTD HTML 4.0//EN">
<HTML>
<HEAD>
<TITLE>ASR Outfitters Information Request Form</TITLE>
</HEAD>
<BODY BACKGROUND="" BGCOLOR="#ffffff" TEXT="#000000" LINK="#0000ff"
VLINK="#800080" ALINK="#ff0000">
<TABLE>
<TR>
<TD VALIGN=TOP>
<CENTER><IMG SRC="asrlogo.gif" ALT="ASR Outfitters Logo" WIDTH="604"
HEIGHT="192" BORDER="0" ALIGN=""><BR>
<FONT SIZE="7" FACE="Gill Sans">
<H2>Information Request</H2>
</FONT>
</CENTER>
<TD>
<FONT SIZE="3" FACE="Gill Sans">
Thank you for your interest in getting e-mailed information from
ASR Outfitters. We assure you that we do not resell or distribute
these addresses in any form. We use this information exclusively
to provide you with better service. <P></FONT>
</TABLE>
<HR WIDTH=80% SIZE=8 NOSHADE>

<HR WIDTH=80% SIZE=8 NOSHADE>
<IMG SRC="asrlogosm.gif" ALIGN="LEFT" WIDTH="200" HEIGHT="84" BORDER="0"
ALT="ASR Small Logo">

<DIV ALIGN=RIGHT>
<ADDRESS ALIGN=RIGHT>
<FONT FACE="Gill Sans">
<BR>ASR Outfitters<BR>
<A HREF="mailto:info@asroutfitters.com">info@asroutfitters.com</A>
<BR>
```

```
4700 N. Center<BR>
South Logan, UT 87654<BR>
801-555-3422<BR>
</FONT>
</ADDRESS>
</DIV>
</BODY>
</HTML>
```

FIGURE 9.3

The ASR Outfitters form page, sans form

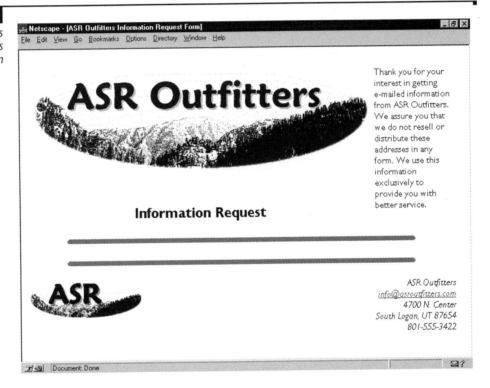

To add a form to the page, follow these steps:

1. Add the <FORM> tags where you want the form to be.

```
<HR WIDTH=80% SIZE=8 NOSHADE>
<FORM>
</FORM>
```

TIP

You can avoid problems with your forms by properly nesting your form within other objects in the form. Be careful to place the form outside paragraphs, lists, and other structural elements. For example, you do not want to open a table within the form and close it after the end of the form. Be sure to test your forms carefully.

2. Create a submit button by adding the <INPUT> tag, the TYPE= attribute, and the VALUE= attribute. Although the submit button traditionally goes at the bottom of the form, immediately above the </FORM> tag, it can go anywhere in the form. You can set the text on the face of the submit button to anything you want—simply substitute your text for the text in the VALUE= attribute:

```
<HR WIDTH=80% SIZE=8 NOSHADE>
<FORM>
<INPUT TYPE="SUBMIT" VALUE="Submit">
</FORM>
```

3. Create a reset button by adding the <INPUT> tag, the TYPE= attribute, and the VALUE= attribute. Again, although the reset button traditionally goes at the bottom of the form with the submit button, immediately above the closing </FORM> tag, it can go anywhere in the form. The reset button can have any text on its face, based on the VALUE= attribute. The following example has Start Over on the face.

```
<HR WIDTH=80% SIZE=8 NOSHADE>
<FORM>
<INPUT TYPE="SUBMIT" VALUE="Submit">
<INPUT TYPE="RESET" VALUE="Start Over">
</FORM>
```

Figure 9.4 shows what the buttons look like in a completed form.

NOTE

You cannot control button size directly—the length of the text determines the size of the button.

FIGURE 9.4

The submit and reset (Start Over) buttons are added to the form.

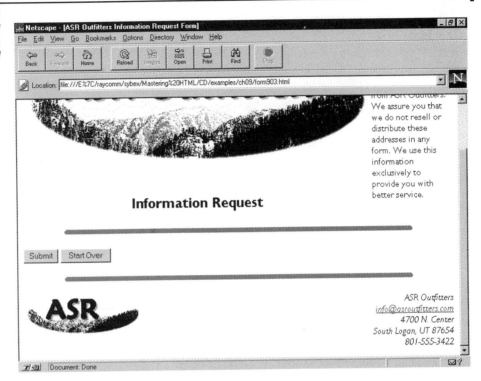

If the appearance of your form is extremely important to you, consider using a graphical submit button. Be sure, however, that your visitors will be using browsers that can handle these buttons.

Using images for submit buttons can cause unexpected or unwanted results in old browsers. For example, they crash old versions of Netscape Navigator. Consider using browser detection scripts to improve your success with image-based submit buttons. (See Chapter 7 for information about including images.)

If you want to use an image for your submit button, substitute the following code for the submit button (substituting your own image for submitbutton.gif):

```
<INPUT TYPE="IMAGE" NAME="POINT" SRC="submitbutton.gif" BORDER=0>
```

The TYPE="IMAGE" attribute specifies that an image will be used to click on and submit the form. The NAME="POINT" attribute specifies that the x,y coordinates where the mouse is located will be returned to the server when the image is clicked. Finally, the SRC= and BORDER= attributes work just as they do with regular images—they specify the URL of the image and turn off the border.

Figure 9.5 shows the complete ASR Outfitters form with a graphical submit button.

FIGURE 9.5

Graphical submit
buttons can make
your form more
interesting.

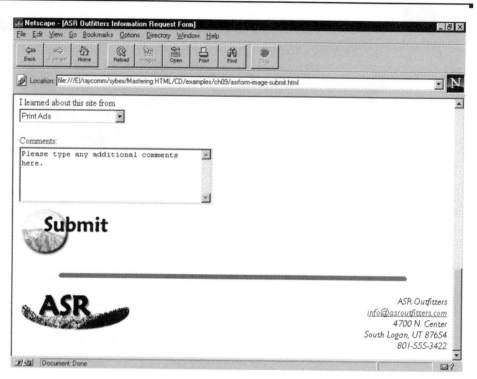

The submit button is in the same style as the images from the ASR Outfitters home page, developed in Chapter 7. Using similar images throughout helps maintain coherence and cohesion at a Web site. For more information on both, see Chapter 2.

HTML makes no provision for a reset button with an image; so if you choose to use an image for your submit button, dispense with a reset button. If you don't, you'll have to deal with the potentially poor combination of an image and a standard reset button.

HTML 4 Opportunities

If your visitors will be using HTML 4–compliant browsers, you can use the paired <BUT-TON> tag, which creates a button that you can include instead of or in conjunction with submit and reset buttons. Buttons created with the <BUTTON> tag have no specific action associated with them, as do the submit and reset buttons. If you're so inclined, you can link the button to a JavaScript script. Doing so, gives you all sorts of functional and flashy possibilities (see Chapter 11).

To provide a submit button, use code similar to the following:

```
<BUTTON TYPE="SUBMIT" VALUE="SUBMIT" NAME="SUBMIT">
Click to Submit Form
</BUTTON>
```

To provide a graphical reset button, use code similar to the following:

```
<BUTTON TYPE="RESET" VALUE="RESET" NAME="RESET">
<IMG SRC="gifs/resetbuttonnew.gif" ALT="Reset Button">
</BUTTON>
```

If you want to use a <BUTTON> to call a script that, for example, verifies a form's contents, you might use something like this, which creates a button that runs a verify script:

```
<BUTTON TYPE="BUTTON" VALUE="VERIFY" NAME="VERIFY"
onClick="verify(this.form)">
Click to Verify Form
</BUTTON>
```

Including General Input Fields

You can also develop other types of input fields using various attributes in the <INPUT> field. Table 9.2 shows the input field tags and attributes most often used.

Tag/Attribute	Use
TABLE 9.2: INPUT FIELD TAG AND ATTRIBUTES	
`<INPUT>`	Sets an area in a form for visitor input.
`TYPE="..."`	Sets the type of input field. Possible values are TEXT, PASSWORD, CHECKBOX, RADIO, FILE, HIDDEN, IMAGE, SUBMIT, and RESET.
`NAME="..."`	Processes form results.
`VALUE="..."`	Provides content associated with `NAME="..."`. Use this attribute with radio buttons and checkboxes because they do not accept other input. You can also use this attribute with text fields to provide initial input.
`SIZE="n"`	Sets the visible size for a field. Use this attribute with text input fields.
`MAXLENGTH="n"`	Sets the longest set of characters that can be submitted. Use this attribute with text fields.
`SELECTED`	Indicates the default selection to be presented when the form is initially loaded or reset.
`ACCEPT="..."`	Specifies the acceptable MIME types for file uploads. Wildcards are acceptable, as in `image/*`.

Text Fields

A text field is a blank area within a form and is the place for visitor-supplied information. As you can see below, text fields are commonly used for a name, an e-mail address, and so on:

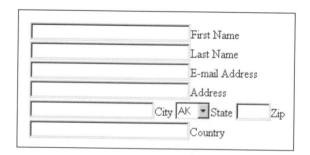

To add a text field to an existing form, follow these steps: .

1. Add an <INPUT> tag where you want the field.

```
<FORM>
<INPUT>
</FORM>
```

2. Specify the type of input field. In this case, use TYPE="TEXT".

```
<FORM>
<INPUT TYPE="TEXT">
</FORM>
```

3. Add the NAME= attribute to label the content. For example, one of the first fields in the ASR Outfitters form is for the first name of a visitor, so the field name is "firstname."

```
<INPUT TYPE="TEXT" NAME="firstname">
```

The values for NAME= should be unique within the form. Multiple forms on the same site (or even on the same page) can share values, but if different fields share a name value, the results will be unpredictable.

4. Specify the size of the field in the form by including the SIZE= attribute. Although this is optional, you can ensure your audience has ample space and can make similar text fields the same size. For example, 30 is a generous size for a name, but still not overwhelmingly large, even on a low-resolution monitor.

```
<INPUT TYPE="TEXT" NAME="firstname" SIZE="30">
```

5. Add the MAXLENGTH= attribute if you want to limit the number of characters your visitors can provide (for example, if the field passes into an existing database with length restrictions). Keep in mind that any MAXLENGTH= setting should not be less than the SIZE= attribute; otherwise, your visitors will be confused when they can't continue typing to the end of the field.

```
<INPUT TYPE="TEXT" NAME="firstname" SIZE="30" MAXLENGTH="30">
```

6. Add text outside the <INPUT> field to indicate the information your visitor should provide. Remember that the name of the field is not visible in the browser; up to this point, you've created a blank area within the form, but you have not labeled that area in any way.

```
<INPUT TYPE="TEXT" NAME="firstname" SIZE="30" MAXLENGTH="30">
First Name<BR>
```

Figure 9.6 shows the resulting text field in the context of the form. Use the same process to add other text fields.

PART

II

Advancing Your Skills

FIGURE 9.6

Visitors can enter information in text fields.

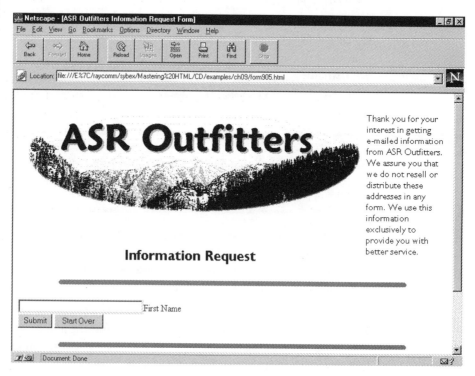

Guidelines for Including Multiple Text Fields

As a rule, forms are much more attractive if the fields are aligned. If they are nearly, but not exactly, aligned, the form looks sloppy, just as a misaligned paper form looks sloppy.

Here are some guidelines to follow when you include multiple text fields in your form:

- Place the fields at the left margin of your page, followed by the descriptive text. If you place the descriptive text (such as "First Name" or "Last Name") to the left of the fields, they will not line up correctly.

- Set the text fields to the same size, when appropriate. Of course, you wouldn't set the field for entering the official state abbreviation to 30 characters, but there's no reason that first name, last name, and company name couldn't all be the same length.

CONTINUED

- As you add descriptive labels, remember to also add line breaks (
 or <P>) in appropriate places. None of the form tags force a line break, so your form tags will all run together on a single line. In many cases, this is fine, but it can also look a little off.

- Optionally, add a VALUE= attribute to the text input tag to "seed" the field with a value or to provide an example of the content you want. For example, you could add VALUE="First Name Here" to the input field used for the first name to let your visitors know what to type.

If you are taking a survey, seeding a field is of questionable value. If your visitors can't figure out what to put in a field, you probably have a design problem. If you include some text, your visitors are likely not to complete the field (and submit your sample) or to accidentally leave part of your sample text in the field, thereby corrupting your data.

The best—possibly only—time to seed a field is if you do not have space on the form for descriptive labels.

Radio Buttons

A radio button is a type of input field that allows visitors to choose one option from a list. Radio buttons are so named because you can choose only one of them, just as you can select only one button (one station) at a time on your car radio. When viewed in a browser, radio buttons are usually small circles, as shown here.

I prefer (choose one only):
- ○ Classic rock
- ○ Soft rock
- ● Oldies
- ○ Classical music

In the ASR Outfitters questionnaire, we wanted to find out if visitors were inclined to make purchases online; the choices range from refusing to purchase to regularly purchasing online. Each choice is mutually exclusive—choosing one excludes the remainder. Radio buttons were our obvious choice.

PART

II

Advancing Your Skills

To add radio buttons to a form, follow these steps:

1. Add any introductory text to lead into the buttons, at the point where the buttons should appear. Also put in the descriptive text and formatting commands as appropriate. The text of the ASR Outfitters example looks like the following:

   ```
   <P>
   Please choose the most appropriate statement.
   <BR>I regularly purchase items online.
   <BR>I have on occasion purchased items online.
   <BR>I have not purchased anything online, but I would consider it.
   <BR>I prefer to shop in real stores.
   ```

2. Add the <INPUT> tag where the first radio button will go.

   ```
   <BR><INPUT>I regularly purchase items online.
   ```

3. Add the TYPE="RADIO" attribute.

   ```
   <BR><INPUT TYPE="RADIO">I regularly purchase items online.
   ```

4. Add the NAME= attribute. The name applies to the collection of buttons, not just to this item, so be sure the NAME= attribute is generic enough to apply to all items in the set.

   ```
   <BR><INPUT TYPE="RADIO" NAME="buying"> I regularly purchase items
   online.
   ```

5. Add the VALUE= attribute. In text input areas, the value is what the visitor types; however, you must supply the value for radio buttons (and checkboxes). Choose highly descriptive values (such as "regular" rather than "yes").

   ```
   <BR><INPUT TYPE="RADIO" NAME="buying" VALUE="regular"> I regularly
   purchase items online.
   ```

6. Add the attribute CHECKED to one of the items to indicate the default selection. Remember, only one radio button can be selected, so only one button can carry the CHECKED attribute.

   ```
   <BR><INPUT TYPE="RADIO" NAME="buying" VALUE="regular" CHECKED>I
   regularly purchase items online.
   ```

TIP

In general, make the most likely choice the default option, both to make a visitor's job easier and to minimize the impact of their not checking and verifying the entry for that question. Although adding the CHECKED attribute is optional, it ensures that the list records a response.

7. Add the remaining radio buttons.

CREATING FORMS | **317**

Use the same NAME= attribute for all radio buttons in a set. Browsers use the name attribute on radio buttons to specify which buttons are related and therefore which ones are set and unset as a group. Different sets of radio buttons within a page use different NAME attributes.

The completed set of radio buttons for the ASR Outfitters form looks like the following:

```
<P>
Please choose the most appropriate statement.
<BR><INPUT TYPE="RADIO" NAME="buying" VALUE="regular">I regularly purchase
items online.
<BR><INPUT TYPE="RADIO" NAME="buying" VALUE="sometimes">I have on occasion
purchased items online.
<BR><INPUT TYPE="RADIO" NAME="buying" VALUE="might" CHECKED>I have not
purchased anything online, but I would consider it.
<BR><INPUT TYPE="RADIO" NAME="buying" VALUE="willnot">I prefer to shop in
real stores.
```

When viewed in a browser, the radio buttons look like those in Figure 9.7.

FIGURE 9.7

A visitor can select a radio button to choose an item from a list.

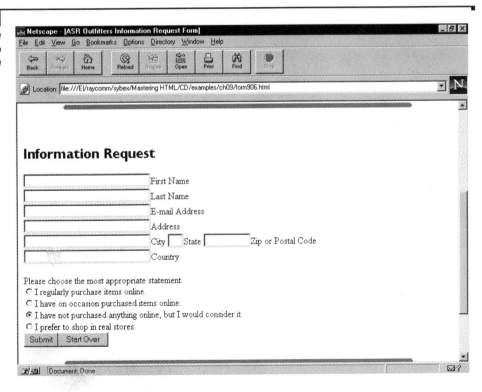

PART

II

Advancing Your Skills

MASTERING THE OPPORTUNITIES

HTML 4 Opportunities

HTML 4 lets you easily group related items using the <FIELDSET> tag. For example, in the ASR Outfitters form, several fields collect personal information, and you could group them within a <FIELDSET> tag, like this:

```
<FIELDSET>

...various input fields for personal information go here.

</FIELDSET>
```

Additionally, by adding <LEGEND> tags (aligned to the TOP, BOTTOM, LEFT, or RIGHT), you can clearly label content:

```
<FIELDSET>

<LEGEND ALIGN="TOP">Personal Information</LEGEND>

...various input fields for personal information go here.

</FIELDSET>
```

Checkboxes

Visitors can also use checkboxes to select an item from a list. Each checkbox works independently from the others; visitors can select or deselect any combination of checkboxes. Using checkboxes is appropriate for open questions or questions that have more than one "right" answer.

In most browsers, checkboxes appear as little squares that contain a checkmark when selected:

> **I'm willing to listen to (choose all that apply):**
> ☐ Classic rock
> ☐ Soft rock
> ☐ Oldies
> ☐ Classical music

The ASR Outfitters form is designed to find out about activities that interest customers. Any combination of answers from none to all might be possible, so this is a good place to use checkboxes.

To add checkboxes to your form, follow these steps:

1. Enter the lead-in text and textual cues for each item, as in the following code sample.

```
<P>I'm interested in (choose all that apply):
<BR>Hiking
<BR>Mountain Biking
<BR>Camping
<BR>Rock Climbing
<BR>Off-Road 4WD
<BR>Cross-country Skiing
```

TIP

The <BR> tags could just as easily go at the end of the lines, but after entering the form tags, placing the <BR> tags at the beginning of the lines will make the code easier to read.

2. Add an <INPUT> tag between the <BR> and the first choice from the list.

```
<BR><INPUT>Hiking
```

3. Add the TYPE="CHECKBOX" attribute to set the input field as a checkbox.

```
<BR><INPUT TYPE="CHECKBOX">Hiking
```

4. Add the NAME= attribute to label the item. For checkboxes, unlike radio buttons, each item has a separate label. Although the checkboxes visually appear as a set, logically the items are completely separate.

```
<BR><INPUT TYPE="CHECKBOX" NAME="hiking">Hiking
```

5. Add the VALUE= attribute for the item. In the ASR Outfitters form, the value could be yes or no—indicating that hiking is or is not an activity of interest. However, when the form is returned through e-mail, it's useful to have a more descriptive value. If the value here is hiking, the word *hiking* returns for a checkmark, and nothing returns for no checkmark. The e-mail recipient can decipher this easier than a yes or a no.

```
<BR><INPUT TYPE="CHECKBOX" NAME="hiking" VALUE="hiking">Hiking
```

6. Add a CHECKED attribute to specify default selections. Although you can, with checkboxes, include a CHECKED attribute for multiple items, be careful not to overdo. Each CHECKED attribute that you include is an additional possible false positive response to a question.

```
<BR><INPUT TYPE="CHECKBOX" NAME="hiking" VALUE="hiking" CHECKED>Hiking
```

7. Repeat this process for each of the remaining checkboxes, remembering to use different NAME= attributes for each one (unlike radio buttons).

In the ASR Outfitters form, the final code looks like this:

```
<P>I'm interested in (choose all that apply):
<BR><INPUT TYPE="CHECKBOX" NAME="hiking" VALUE="hiking">Hiking
<BR><INPUT TYPE="CHECKBOX" NAME="mbiking" VALUE="mbiking">Mountain Biking
<BR><INPUT TYPE="CHECKBOX" NAME="camping" VALUE="camping">Camping
<BR><INPUT TYPE="CHECKBOX" NAME="rock" VALUE="rock">Rock Climbing
<BR><INPUT TYPE="CHECKBOX" NAME="4wd" VALUE="4wd">Off-Road 4WD
<BR><INPUT TYPE="CHECKBOX" NAME="ccskiing" VALUE="ccskiing">Cross-country
Skiing
```

When viewed in a browser, the checkboxes look like those in Figure 9.8.

FIGURE 9.8

Visitors can use checkboxes to choose multiple items from a list.

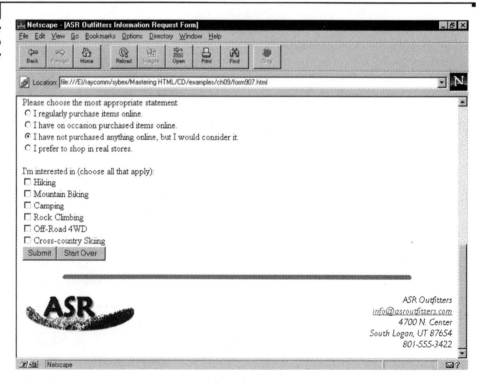

Password Fields

Password fields are similar to text fields, except the contents of the field are not visible on the screen. Password fields are appropriate whenever the content of the field might be confidential—as in passwords, but also in some cases for Social Security numbers or the mother's maiden name. For example, if a site is accessed from a public place and requires confidential information, a visitor will appreciate your using a password field. Of course, because your visitors cannot see the text they type, the error rate and problems with the data rise dramatically.

To establish a password field, follow these steps.

1. Add the <INPUT> field.

   `<INPUT>`

2. Set the TYPE="PASSWORD" attribute.

   `<INPUT `**`TYPE="password"`**`>`

3. Add the NAME= attribute.

   `<INPUT TYPE="password" `**`NAME="newpass"`**`>`

4. Specify the visible size and, if appropriate, the maximum size for the input text by using the MAXLENGTH= attribute.

   `<INPUT TYPE="password" NAME="newpass" SIZE="10" `**`MAXLENGTH="10"`**`>`

Viewed in the browser, each typed character appears as an asterisk (*):

Hidden Fields

Hidden fields are—obviously—not visible to your visitors. They are, however, recognized by the program receiving the input from the form and can provide useful additional information. ASR Outfitters uses the program cgiemail to process the form; it accepts a hidden field to reference a page shown after the customer completes and submits the form, as shown in Figure 9.9.

NOTE

The cgiemail program, which is software for a Unix Web server to return form results with e-mail, is discussed at length in the final section of this chapter, "One Solution: Processing Using Results with cgiemail."

If you need hidden fields, the program that requires them usually includes specific documentation for the exact values. The cgiemail program that ASR Outfitters uses requires a hidden field such as the following:

```
<INPUT TYPE="hidden" NAME="success"
VALUE="http://www.xmission.com/~ejray/asr/asrmaildone.html">
```

FIGURE 9.9

A hidden field can tell the server to send a reference page to the visitor.

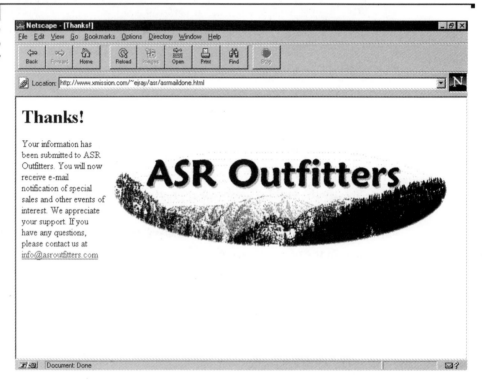

The `TYPE="HIDDEN"` attribute keeps it from being shown, and the `NAME=` and `VALUE=` attributes provide the information that cgiemail expects.

Hidden fields can go anywhere in your form, but it's usually best to place them at the top, immediately after the opening `<FORM>` tag, so that they aren't misplaced or accidentally deleted when you edit the form.

File Fields

HTML also supports a special input field, a file field, to allow visitors to upload files. For example, if you want visitors to submit information—say, a picture, a scanned document, a spreadsheet, or a word-processed document—they can use this field to simply upload the file without the hassle of using FTP or e-mailing the file.

TIP

You can specify which types of files to accept using MIME types. See Chapter 6 for a MIME type list.

This feature must be implemented both in the Web browser and in the Web server, because of the additional processing involved in uploading and manipulating uploaded files. After verifying that the server on which you'll process your form supports file uploads, you can implement this feature by following these steps:

1. Add the appropriate lead-in text to your HTML document.

   ```
   Please post this photo I took in your gallery!
   ```

2. Add an <INPUT> field.

   ```
   Please post this photo I took in your gallery!
   <INPUT>
   ```

3. Add the TYPE="FILE" attribute.

   ```
   Please post this photo I took in your gallery!
   <INPUT TYPE="FILE">
   ```

4. Add an appropriate NAME= attribute to label the field.

   ```
   Please post this photo I took in your gallery!
   <INPUT TYPE="FILE" NAME="filenew">
   ```

5. Optionally, specify the field's visible and maximum length with the SIZE= and MAXLENGTH= attributes.

   ```
   Please post this photo I took in your gallery!
   <INPUT TYPE="FILE" NAME="filenew" SIZE="30" MAXLENGTH="200">
   ```

6. Optionally, specify which file types can be uploaded by using the ACCEPT= attribute. For example, add ACCEPT="image/*" to accept any image file.

   ```
   Please post this photo I took in your gallery!
   <INPUT TYPE="FILE" NAME="filenew" SIZE="20" ACCEPT="image/*">
   ```

The values for the ACCEPT= attribute are MIME types. If you accept only a specific type, such as image/gif, you can specify that. If you'll take any image file, but no other files, you could use image/* as ASR Outfitters did. Finally, if you will accept only a few types, you can provide a list of possible types, separated by commas:

```
<INPUT TYPE="FILE" NAME="filenew" SIZE="20" ACCEPT="image/gif, image/jpeg">
```

PART

II

Advancing Your Skills

This code results in a text area plus a button that allows visitors to browse to a file, when rendered in most browsers, as shown in Figure 9.10.

Including Textareas

Textareas are places within a form for extensive text input. One of the primary uses for textareas is to solicit comments or free-form feedback from visitors, as shown here:

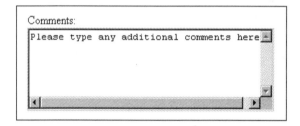

Table 9.3 lists and describes the tags and attributes used for textareas within HTML forms.

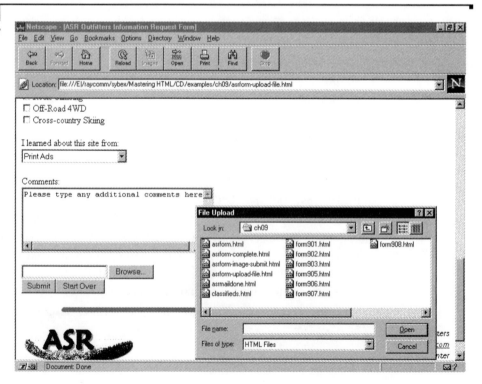

TABLE 9.3: TEXTAREA TAGS AND ATTRIBUTES	
Tag/Attribute	**Use**
<TEXTAREA>	Sets an area in a form for lengthy visitor input. Initial content for the textarea goes between the opening and closing tags.
NAME="..."	Establishes a label for an input field. The Name= attribute is used for form processing.
ROWS="*n*"	Sets the number of rows for the visible field.
COLS="*n*"	Sets the number of columns for the visible field.

TIP

Don't confuse text fields with textareas. *Text fields* are appropriate for shorter input; *textareas* are appropriate for longer input.

To include a textarea in a form, follow these steps.

1. Enter any lead-in text to set up the textarea.

```
<P>Comments:<BR>
```

2. Add an opening and closing <TEXTAREA> tag.

```
<P>Comments:<BR>
<TEXTAREA></TEXTAREA>
```

3. Add a NAME= attribute to label the field.

```
<TEXTAREA NAME="comments"></TEXTAREA>
```

4. Add ROWS= and COLS= attributes to set the dimensions of the textarea. The ROWS= attribute sets the height of the text area in rows, and COLS= sets the width of the textarea in characters.

```
<TEXTAREA NAME="comments" ROWS="5" COLS="40"></TEXTAREA>
```

5. Enter some sample information to let the audience know what to type by adding the text between the opening and closing <TEXTAREA> tags.

```
<TEXTAREA NAME="comments" COLS="40" ROWS="5">
Please type any additional comments here.</TEXTAREA>
```

This <TEXTAREA> code produces a text area field in the HTML document like the one shown in Figure 9.11.

PART

II

Advancing Your Skills

Including Select Fields

Select fields are some of the most flexible fields used in developing forms because you can let visitors select single and multiple responses. For example, suppose you need visitors to tell you the state in which they live. You could list the states as a series of radio buttons, but that would take up tons of page space. Or, you could provide a text field, but visitors could make a typing mistake or spelling error.

Your best bet is to use a select field, which lets you list all 50 states in a minimal amount of space. Visitors simply select a state from the list without introducing spelling errors or typos.

Select fields, as shown here, can either provide a long (visible) list of items or a highly compact listing, similar to the fonts drop-down list in a word-processing program.

 State

Table 9.4 lists and describes the tags and attributes used to create select fields.

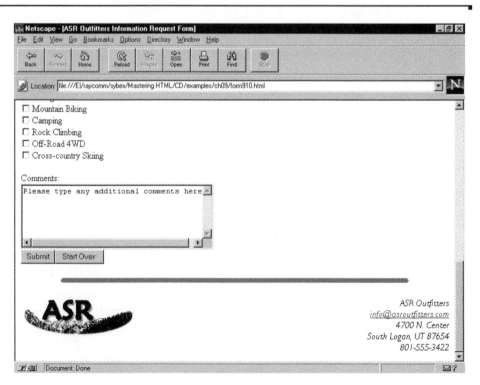

TABLE 9.4: SELECT FIELD TAGS AND ATTRIBUTES

Tag/Attribute	Use
`<SELECT>`	Sets an area in a form for a select field that can look like a drop-down list or a larger select field.
`NAME="..."`	Establishes a label for an input field. The `NAME=` attribute is used for form processing.
`SIZE="n"`	Sets the visible size for the select field. The default (1) creates a drop-down list. You can change the default (to 2 or higher) if you want more options to be visible.
`MULTIPLE`	Sets the select field to accept more than one selection. Use this attribute along with the `SIZE=` attribute to set to a number as large as the maximum number of likely selections.
`<OPTION>`	Marks the items included in the select field. You'll have an `<OPTION>` tag for each item you include. The closing tag is optional.
`VALUE="..."`	Provides the content associated with the `NAME=` attribute.
`SELECTED`	Lets you specify a default selection, which will appear when the form is loaded or reset.

Use a select field any time you need to list many items or ensure that visitors don't make spelling or typing errors. To include a select field in a form, follow these steps:

1. Enter the lead-in text for the select field.

   ```
   I learned about this site from:<BR>
   ```

2. Add an opening and closing <SELECT> tag.

   ```
   I learned about this site from:<BR>
   <SELECT>
   </SELECT>
   ```

3. Enter a NAME= attribute to label the select field.

   ```
   <SELECT NAME="referral">
   </SELECT>
   ```

4. Add the choices that your visitors should see. Because the select field takes care of line breaks and other formatting, do not include any line break tags.

   ```
   I learned about this site from:<BR>
   <SELECT NAME="referral">
   Print Ads
   In-Store Visit
   ```

```
Friend's Recommendation
Sources on the Internet
Other
</SELECT>
```

5. Add an <OPTION> tag for each possible selection. The closing </OPTION> tag is optional.

```
<SELECT NAME="referral">
<OPTION>Print Ads
<OPTION>In-Store Visit
<OPTION>Friend's Recommendation
<OPTION>Sources on the Internet
<OPTION>Other
</SELECT>
```

6. Provide a VALUE= attribute for each option tag. These values are what you will see when the form is submitted, so make them as logical and descriptive as possible.

```
I learned about this site from:<BR>
<SELECT NAME="referral">
<OPTION VALUE="print">Print Ads
<OPTION VALUE="visit"> In-Store Visit
<OPTION VALUE="rec"> Friend's Recommendation
<OPTION VALUE="internet"> Sources on the Internet
<OPTION VALUE="other"> Other
</SELECT>
```

7. Optionally, let visitors select multiple items from the list by including the MULTIPLE attribute in the opening <SELECT> tag.

```
I learned about this site from:<BR>
<SELECT NAME="referral" MULTIPLE>
<OPTION VALUE="print">Print Ads
<OPTION VALUE="visit"> In-Store Visit
<OPTION VALUE="rec"> Friend's Recommendation
<OPTION VALUE="internet"> Sources on the Internet
<OPTION VALUE="other"> Other
</SELECT>
```

If you choose to include MULTIPLE, your visitor can select one or all options; you cannot restrict the choices to only, say, two of four items.

8. Optionally, add the SELECTED attribute to the option tag to specify a default selection. You can offer more than one default setting if you used the MULTIPLE attribute.

```
I learned about this site from:<BR>
<SELECT NAME="referral" MULTIPLE>
 <OPTION VALUE="print" SELECTED>Print Ads
 <OPTION VALUE="visit"> In-Store Visit
 <OPTION VALUE="rec"> Friend's Recommendation
 <OPTION VALUE="internet"> Sources on the Internet
 <OPTION VALUE="other"> Other
</SELECT>
```

With this, the basic select field is complete. Browsers display this select field as a drop-down list, as in Figure 9.12.

FIGURE 9.12

Select fields let you provide many choices in a compact format.

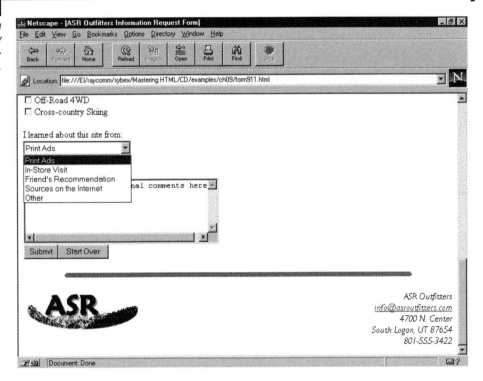

Designing Long Select Fields

When developing particularly long select fields—ones that include many items—be sure to make the area as easy to use as possible. Here are some guidelines:

- Be sure that the select field appears within one screen; don't make visitors scroll to see the entire select field.

- Add a SIZE= attribute to the opening <SELECT> tag to expand the drop-down list to a list box, like this:

    `<SELECT NAME="referral" MULTIPLE SIZE="5">`

The list box can have a vertical scrollbar, if necessary, to provide access to all items, as shown below. (Select boxes are horizontally fixed, meaning that they cannot scroll horizontally.)

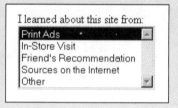

NOTE

You can use JavaScript to validate form input. For example, you can ensure that visitors fill out necessary contact information or credit card numbers you need to process their information or requests. See Chapter 11 for details.

Processing Forms

In general, after a visitor clicks the submit button on a form, the information is sent to the Web server and to the program indicated by the ACTION= attribute in the form. What that program then does with the data is up to you. In this section, we'll look at some, though not nearly all, of your options.

Here are some of your choices:

- The server can send the information back to you via e-mail.
- The server can enter the information into a database.
- The server can post the information to a newsgroup or a Web page.
- The server can use the input to search a database.

When you're working out what to do with the data you collect or if you're just checking out what others have done to get some inspiration, your first stop should always be your Web server administrator. In particular, ask which programs are installed to process form input. Depending on what's available, you might be able to take advantage of those capabilities.

Regardless of how you want the information processed, you include specific attributes in the opening <FORM> tag, as explained in Table 9.5.

TABLE 9.5: ATTRIBUTES FOR THE <FORM> TAG

Attribute	Use
ACTION="..."	Indicates the program on the HTTP server that will process the output from the form.
METHOD="..."	Tells the browser how to send the data to the server, with either the POST method or the GET method.

The ACTION= and METHOD= attributes depend on the server-side program that processes the form.

In general, the documentation that came with your form-processing script or with your Web server will tell you what to use for POST and GET. For example, ASR Outfitter's ISP (www.xmission.com) publishes information on its Web site about how to set up a form to mail the results (using a CGI script called cgiemail, discussed later in this chapter). In this case, the proper opening <FORM> tag is:

```
<FORM METHOD="POST" ACTION="http://www.xmission.com/
cgi-bin/cgiemail/~user/user-mail.txt">
```

Of course, the attributes you use depend on the program processing the information. By changing the attributes, you can also specify a different program. Because this single line of code within an HTML form determines how the information is processed, you can change what happens to the data without significantly changing the form itself.

Why would you want to change what happens to the data? You'd do so primarily because you discover better ways to manipulate the data. For example, if you're looking for feedback about your company's new product, you want the quickest way to get started collecting the data, which is probably having it e-mailed to you. Later on, after the crisis is over, you might investigate ways to have the data written directly into an automated database—which isn't as speedy to set up as e-mail, but can save you some work.

Some Web servers have built-in scripts or commands to process form results; others, particularly Unix servers, require additional programs.

In the following sections, we discuss your form-processing options—sending with e-mail, writing to a database, posting to a Web page, and other possibilities. Because your ISP's particular setup can vary significantly, we've provided general information that you can apply to your specific situation—probably with the help of your server administrator. The final section in this chapter, though, gives you a specific example of setting up an e-mail return—an option you're likely to encounter.

NOTE

To learn your form-processing options, check with your server administrator or visit your ISP's Web site.

About Using Form Data

Getting a good response rate is the single biggest challenge to survey takers. Using an HTML form to collect information puts you in a similar role, with the added complication that your visitors must find your Web site to complete it. Once you get the data, however, you need to use it wisely. Here are some guidelines:

- Carefully consider the source, and don't read more into the data than you should. It's quite tempting to assume that the available information is representative of what you might collect from an entire population (customers, users, and so on).

- Take the time to analyze your data carefully, determining what it does and doesn't tell you.

For example, after ASR Outfitters implements its form and receives a few hundred responses, it will have a general idea of how many customers would be willing to make purchases online, how many are located in specific areas, how many have certain interests, and even how many use online services. Much of this information will not have been previously available to ASR, and it will be tempting to assume that the data is representative of all ASR customers.

CONTINUED

The results of ASR's online survey reflect only the preferences and opinions of that small set of customers who use the Internet, and visited the site, and took the time to fill out the survey. Even if 95 percent of the people who complete the survey express interest in more rock-climbing gear, that might not reflect the interests of the overall ASR customer base.

Processing Forms via E-mail

Having the server return form results to you via e-mail isn't always ideal (although it can be), but it is often useful, it is nearly always expedient, and it is cheap. Using e-mail to accept form responses simply sends the information the visitor submits to you (or someone you designate) in an e-mail message. At that point, you have the information and can enter it (manually) in a database, send a response (manually), or do anything else you want with the data.

If you're collecting open comments from a relatively small number of people, using a program to e-mail the results is a reasonable, long-term solution. That is, it's a reasonable solution if you—or whoever gets the e-mail—can easily address the volume of form responses. E-mail is also a good solution if you do not know what level of response to expect. If the volume turns out to be manageable, continue. If the volume is high, consider other solutions, such as databases.

Database Processing

Writing the information that respondents submit into a database is a good solution to a potentially enormous data management problem. If you are collecting information about current or potential customers or clients, for example, you will probably want to quickly call up these lists and send letters, send e-mail, or provide demographic information about your customers to potential Web site advertisers. To do that, you'll want to use a database.

Although the specifics of putting form data into a database depend on the server and the software, we can make some generalizations. If you work in a fairly large company that has its own Web server on site, you'll encounter fewer problems with tasks such as putting form results directly into a database or sending automatic responses via e-mail. If you represent a small company and rely on an Internet service provider for Web hosting, you may have more of a challenge.

If your Web server uses the same platform on which you work—that is, if you're a Windows person and your Web server is a Windows NT Web server, feeding the form results directly into a database is manageable. However, if your Web server is, for example, on a Unix platform but you work on a Macintosh as a rule, you may face some additional challenges in getting the information from a form into a readily usable database.

Posting to a Web Page

Depending on the information you're collecting, you might want to post the responses to a Web page or to a discussion group. For example, if ASR Outfitters sets up a form to collect information about hiking conditions, the natural output might be a Web page.

A program called Ceilidh (pronounced kay-lee), which is available on the Companion CD, offers a good environment for online discussion or teaching applications, as shown in Figure 9.13.

Ceilidh offers outstanding online discussion or teaching applications.

Other Options

If you find that the options available on your system do not meet your needs, check out Matt's Script Archive (www.worldwidemart.com or on the Companion CD) or Selena Sol's Public Domain CGI Scripts (at selena.mcp.com and on the Companion CD).

These scripts offer a starting point, for either you or your server administrator, to handle form processing effectively. In particular, the form-processing script from Selena's archive offers everything from database logging to giving audiences the opportunity to verify the accuracy of the data they enter.

Keep in mind, if you choose to install and set up these scripts yourself, that the installation and debugging of a server-side script is considerably more complex and time consuming than installing a new Windows program. Not that it isn't possible for the novice to do it, and do it successfully, but set aside some time.

See Chapter 6 for more information about CGI programs and how they collect information from forms and other sources.

If you do choose to download and use scripts from the Net, be sure that you get them from a reliable source and that you or your server administrator scan the scripts for possible security holes. Form-processing programs must take some special steps to ensure that a malicious visitor does not use the form to crash the server or worse. Without taking precautions, forms can pass commands directly to the server, which will then execute them, with potentially disastrous results.

One Solution: Processing Using cgiemail

Because you will likely choose—at least initially—to have form results e-mailed to you, we will walk you through a form-to-e-mail program. The cgiemail program is produced and distributed for free by MIT, but it is only available for Unix servers. Check out:

```
web.mit.edu/wwwdev/cgiemail/index.html
```

for the latest news about this version, or grab it off the Companion CD. This program is a good example because many ISPs offer access to it and because it is also commonly found on corporate Internet and intranet servers.

PART

II

Advancing Your Skills

TIP

Comparable programs exist for both Macintosh and Windows 95/NT. You can find MailPost for the Macintosh at www.mcenter.com/mailpost/, and you can find wcgi-mail for Windows 95/NT at www.spacey.net/rickoz/wcgimail.stm.

Here is the general process for using cgiemail:

1. Start with a complete form—the one developed earlier in this chapter or a different one. Without a functional form, you cannot get the results sent to you via e-mail.

2. Add the ACTION= and METHOD= attributes with values you get from your server administrator. (See the "Processing Forms" section, earlier in this chapter, for more information about the ACTION= and METHOD= attributes.)

3. Develop a template for the e-mail message to you. This template includes the names of each of your fields and basic e-mail addressing information.

4. Develop a response page that the visitor sees after completing the form.

Now, let's look at how ASR Outfitters can use cgiemail to implement its form.

1. The Form

You don't need to do anything special to forms to use them with cgiemail. You have the option of requiring some fields to be completed, but that is not essential. For example, because the purpose of the ASR Outfitters form is to collect e-mail addresses, ASR would do well to make the e-mail address required.

The solution? Rename the name field from emailaddr to required-emailaddr. The cgiemail program will then check the form and reject it if that field is not complete. The actual code for that line of the form would look like this:

```
<BR><INPUT TYPE="TEXT" NAME="required-emailaddr" SIZE="30">E-mail Address
```

Optionally, add required- to each field name that must be completed.

2. The *ACTION*= and *METHOD*= Attributes

The server administrator provided ASR Outfitters with the ACTION= and METHOD= attributes shown in the following code:

```
<FORM METHOD="POST" ACTION="http://www.xmission.com/
cgi-bin/cgiemail/~ejray/asr/ejray-asr-mail.txt">
```

The file referenced in the ACTION= line is the template for an e-mail message. In this case, the http://www.xmission.com/cgi-bin/cgiemail part of the ACTION= line points to the program itself, and the following part (/~ejray/asr/ejray-asr-mail.txt) is the server-relative path to the file. (Remember, with a server-relative path, you can add the name of the server to the front of the path and open the document in a Web browser.)

3. The Template

The plain text template includes the bare essentials for an e-mail message, fields in square brackets for the form field values, and any line breaks or spacing needed to make it easier to read.

In general, you can be flexible in setting up the template, but you must set up the e-mail headers exactly as shown here. Don't use leading spaces, but do capitalize and use colons as shown. The parts after the colons are fields for the From e-mail address, your e-mail address (in both the To: line and in the Errors-To: line), and any subject field you choose.

```
From: [emailaddr]
To: ASR Webmaster <webmaster@asroutfitters.com>
Subject: Web Form Submission
Errors-To: ASR Webmaster <webmaster@asroutfitters.com>
```

Format the rest of the template as you choose—within the constraints of plain text files. If you want to include information from the form, put in a field name (the content of a NAME= attribute). The resulting e-mail will contain the value of that field (either what a visitor enters or the VALUE= attribute you specify in the case of checkboxes and radio buttons).

Be liberal with line breaks, and enter descriptive values as you set up the template. E-mail generated by forms may make sense when you're up to your ears in developing the form, but later on it's likely to be so cryptic that you can't understand it.

Following is the complete content of the ejray-asr-mail.txt file.

```
From: [emailaddr]
To: ASR Webmaster <webmaster@asroutfitters.com>
Subject: Web Form Submission
Errors-To: ASR Webmaster <webmaster@asroutfitters.com>


Results from Information Request Web Form:


[firstname] [lastname]
[emailaddr]
[address]
[city], [state] [zip]
[country]
```

PART

II

Advancing Your Skills

```
Online Purchasing:
[buying]

Interested In:
[hiking]
[mbiking]
[camping]
[rock]
[4wd]
[ccskiing]

Referral:
[referral]

Comments:
[comments]
```

The cgiemail program completes this template with the values from the form, resulting in an e-mail message like the following:

```
Return-path: <www@krunk1.xmission.com>
Envelope-to: asroutfitters@raycomm.com
Delivery-date: Sat, 24 May 1997 10:03:55 -0600
Date: Sat, 24 May 1997 10:03:51 -0600 (MDT)
X-Template: /home/users/e/ejray/public_html/asr/ejray-asr-mail.txt
From: hjones@raycomm.com
To: ASR Webmaster <asroutfitters@raycomm.com>
Subject: Web Form Submission
Errors-To: ASR Webmaster <asroutfitters@raycomm.com>

Results from Information Request Web Form:

Holly Jones
hjones@raycomm.com
402 E 4th
South Logan, UT 84341
USA

Online Purchasing:
might
```

```
Interested In:
hiking

camping
rock



Referral:
rec

Comments:
I'd also like information about
outdoor gear.
Thanks!
```

4. Success Page

The only remaining step is to set up a success page, a document that is returned to the visitor indicating that the form has been received. Although a success page is optional, we recommend that you use one. In the form code, a "success" field is actually a hidden <INPUT> field that looks like this:

```
<INPUT TYPE="hidden" NAME="success"
VALUE="http://www.xmission.com/~ejray/asr/asrmaildone.html">
```

A success page can contain any content you choose. If you want, you can point the success page back to your home page or to any other page on your site. On the other hand, many HTML developers use the success page as a place to thank the visitor for taking the time to fill out the form and to offer an opportunity to ask questions or make comments.

WARNING

A highly nonstandard way of returning forms is to use a mailto: URL in the ACTION= line. This hack works only with Netscape, and not with all versions at that. A much better solution, unless you can closely control the browsers your visitors use, is a server-based e-mail program.

Where to Go from Here

In this chapter, you learned how to determine what information to include in forms and to develop them using a variety of widgets. Additionally, you learned about the different ways to process forms and to get the data back.

What now? Following is a list of chapters that include related topics:

- For more information about WYSIWYG editors, see Chapter 3.
- For more information about using JavaScript to help control forms, see Chapter 11.
- For more information about planning HTML documents, check out Chapter 2.
- To learn more about character-level formatting, see Chapter 3.
- For an overview of server capabilities and CGI programs, see Chapter 6.

Chapter

10

Creating Frames

Creating Frames

Frames divide browser windows into several independent sections that can each contain a separate HTML document. Subdividing browser windows can dramatically improve both the appearance and the usability of a site. For example, because frames group information, visitors can more easily find what they want.

Frames can, however, make navigation difficult. For example, if followed links seem to appear randomly in different frames, your visitors will become confused.

In this chapter, we'll discuss framing principles, create a framed site, and look at navigation issues that arise when you use frames. We'll also discuss floating frames, an Internet Explorer–specific (and HTML 4 standard) option. Throughout, we'll use a few new terms:

- *Framed pages* or *sites* are HTML documents that use frames.

- *Nonframed pages* or *sites* are documents that do not use frames.

- *Nonframed browsers* are browsers that do not support frames.

- *Parent documents* are documents that contain frames.

Understanding Frames

Framed sites use a combination of HTML documents, displayed together in the browser. Most commonly, frames divide the window into two or more sections, with one larger section containing content and the smaller section(s) containing a logo, navigation links, or both. Figure 10.1 shows a framed site; one section contains content, and the other contains a logo and navigation links.

FIGURE 10.1

Frames usually contain either the main content or peripheral content such as a navigation menu or a logo.

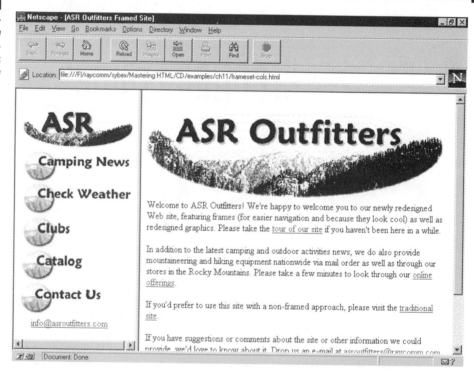

The appearance of frames depends on how you design them. For example, the frames in Figure 10.1 are vertical frames, meaning that the border between them runs vertically in the window. You can also create horizontal frames, in which the border runs horizontally, as shown in Figure 10.2.

FIGURE 10.2

This horizontal frame divides the window into top and bottom sections.

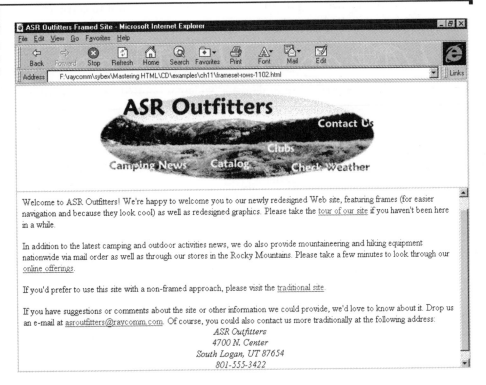

Because of the limited space in most browser windows—the result of limited screen resolution—using more than two or three frames is rarely a good choice. Use additional frames only if they are small and unobtrusive.

Deciding to Use Frames

The decision to frame your site will have long-range implications, particularly in terms of development effort. (If you create a complete framed site, you may also need to create a complete nonframed site to accommodate visitors that have nonframed browsers.)

When deciding whether to use frames, you'll want to consider both the advantages and the disadvantages of doing so.

Some Advantages of Using Frames

Frames, an HTML 4 standard and widely supported by popular browsers, offer a number of advantages, both to users and developers.

- Frames are widely used on the Internet and are perceived as a hallmark of a technically sophisticated site. If your site requires a "techie" face, strongly consider using frames.

- Frames can be implemented to accommodate older browsers that can't actually display frames, so if you're willing to take the time and effort, you can effectively serve all visitors to your site.

- Frames reduce downloading time. Visitors can download only the content pages–and not static elements such as logos and navigation menus.

- Frames improve site usability. Navigation remains visible as content changes in a separate frame.

- Because frames separate content from navigation elements and structural elements, you can easily and quickly update pages and provide new content. For example, if a framed site uses a top banner and a bottom banner, with scrolling content in the middle, you can replace the content—and only the content— without compromising appearance or navigation.

A Caution about Linking to Outside Sites

Unfortunately, frames have introduced the potential for legal problems, as evidenced in recent lawsuits by CNN and Time-Warner.

A standard framed site, for example, might use a banner frame at the top, a navigation frame on the left, and a content frame on the right. A visitor clicks a link in the left frame and views the content in the right frame—the top (banner) and left (navigation) frames remain the same, as shown on the next page.

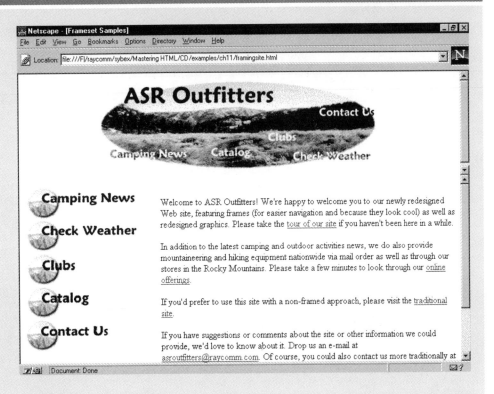

This layout works well as long as the links all point to HTML documents within the site. Problems occur, however, when the links point to documents outside the site. For example, one company used this type of frame layout and included a link to a CNN Web page. A visitor could click the News link in the left frame, and the news content—generated by CNN but not labeled as such—displayed in the right frame. This "borrowed" content appeared to belong to the company, not to CNN.

Similarly, in the screen below, ASR Outfitters frames content from RayComm, Inc. As you can see, it's not at all apparent that the content in the frame on the lower right belongs to someone other than ASR Outfitters.

PART
II

Advancing Your Skills

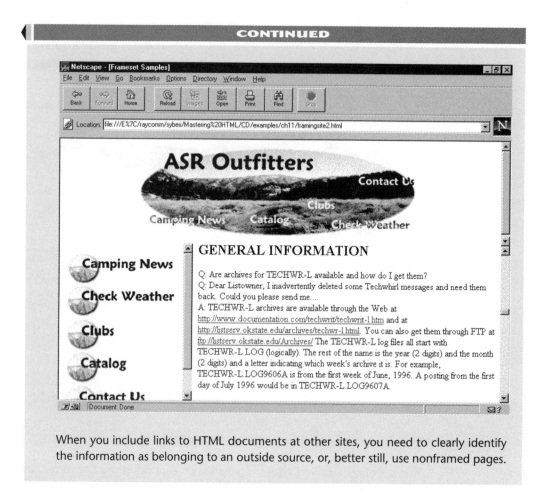

When you include links to HTML documents at other sites, you need to clearly identify the information as belonging to an outside source, or, better still, use nonframed pages.

Some Disadvantages of Using Frames

Despite the advantages of using frames, a number of drawbacks are associated with using frames as a result of early implementation problems and site design issues. For example, frames have an inconsistent usability record. For the first several months after frames were introduced, the Back button in some browsers returned to the last nonframed page, even if the visitor had been browsing through multiple pages within a framed site. This inability to move backward through visited pages was frustrating and caused many visitors to completely reject framed sites. To accommodate all visitors, provide a highly visible link, possibly at the top of your site, that will take visitors to an equivalent, nonframed site. Alternatively, start your visitors at the nonframed site and then allow them to choose the framed site if they want it.

Frame navigation is a mystery to many, and the mystery is compounded because many framed sites have links that seem to appear randomly. You need to ensure that your visitors can easily find what they want.

Frames may take up more space than they are worth. For example, the ASR Outfitters framed site was designed specifically for 800 × 600 or better resolution and looks good in Figure 10.1, at the proper resolution. When the site is viewed at 640 × 480, as shown in Figure 10.3, appearance degrades drastically. Not only do the graphics appear improperly, but the scrollbars obscure yet more of the page.

FIGURE 10.3:

Lower resolution in browsers can wreak havoc on framed sites.

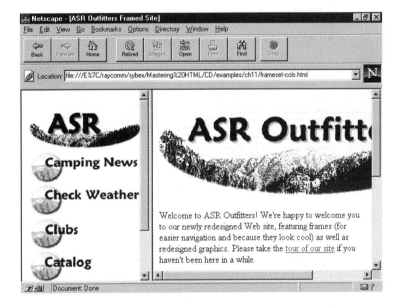

Frames are an HTML 4 standard, and most newer browsers, including the last several versions of Netscape Navigator and Internet Explorer, support frames.

Because frame technology—as with the rest of HTML—continues to improve and evolve, both the specification and its implementation could change somewhat.

PART

II

Advancing Your Skills

Creating Frames

Creating frames requires relatively few steps:

1. Create a frameset (or layout) document that determines the location and characteristics of the frames.

QUICK LOOKUP

A *frameset* specifies the layout for frames, including the locations and characteristics of the frames. The frameset acts as a holder for frame information.

2. Designate the frames and their contents.

3. Format the frames.

4. Make provisions for frames when viewed in nonframed browsers.

Table 10.1 lists and describes the frame tags and attributes used in creating frames.

TABLE 10.1: FRAMESET TAGS AND ATTRIBUTES

Tag/Attribute	Use
<FRAMESET>	Establishes frames within an HTML document.
ROWS="n1, n2, ..."	Sets the size for rows—horizontal frames—in pixels, as a percentage, or as a proportion of the remaining space with "*".
COLS="n1, n2, ..."	Sets the size for columns—vertical frames—in pixels, as a percentage, or as a proportion of the remaining space with "*".
<FRAME>	Identifies frame characteristics and initial content.
SRC="URL"	Identifies the source for the frame content as a standard URL.
NAME="..."	Labels a frame so that it can be targeted or referred to from other frames or windows.
<NOFRAMES>	Sets a section of an HTML document to be visible to nonframed browsers (and invisible to framed browsers).

Determining Frame Size

As you make decisions about how to frame your site, keep in mind size and scaling.

Size

The size at which frames display depends on the resolution of your visitor's monitor and the size at which the browser window is displayed. If a site is designed for a high-resolution monitor, it will be unreadable on a low-resolution monitor even if it has only a couple of frames.

For example, you have two columns. The first is set to a width of 200 pixels for your logo and navigation buttons; the other column fills the remaining space. At high resolution, you have a potentially attractive page. At 800 × 600, your logo will take about 25 percent of the window width, and at 1024 × 768 it will take about 20 percent. Not really a problem. At a resolution of 640 × 480, however, your logo will fill 30 percent of the window width, leaving precious little space for your content. Figure 10.3, earlier in this chapter, shows a two-frame page viewed at 640 × 480 resolution.

You can improve this page by setting the columns to 25 percent each, but the logo will still require horizontal scrolling.

The only real solution is to think small, particularly if you do much of your development at a high resolution. Test extensively at lower resolutions, and provide links that visitors can click to break out of the frames into a full-screen view.

Scaling

Scaling refers to how different screen resolutions and the size of browser windows affect the display of frames. By default, frames are resizable and automatically appear with scrollbars as needed to allow a visitor to view everything in the frame.

Depending on the layout, however, some frames might be more effective if they cannot be scrolled or resized. In particular, if frames contain only images—either image maps or regular images—set them to a fixed size and disable scrollbars and resizing. Doing so forces frames to accommodate the images and prevents visitors from resizing them. Your layout is thus preserved.

In general, simpler frames and sizes are better than fancy ones. Just because two frames are good doesn't mean that four frames are twice as good. Besides being insufferably ugly, the use of more than two frames leads to frames that are so small that even audiences using a high-resolution monitor must scroll both horizontally and vertically to read the content. Figure 10.4 shows a page with too many frames.

FIGURE 10.4

When you use too many frames, your Web pages become difficult to read.

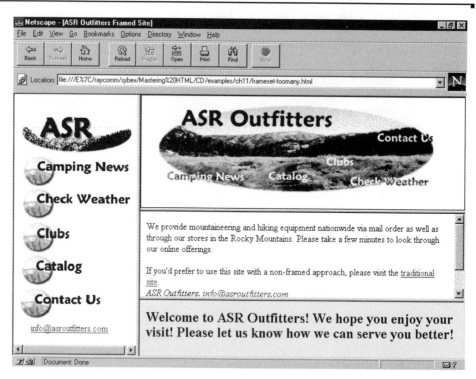

Creating a Frameset

A frameset is the foundation for individual frames and their content, and in it you specify the general frame layout—either vertical (using columns) or horizontal (using rows). The basic frameset closely resembles a standard HTML document, but often lacks the <BODY> tag.

The following example sets up a basic frameset document with two columns. Other examples in this section will develop this sample document further.

Before you start, prepare several HTML documents with minimal content, but possibly different background colors, so that you can easily experiment with and view various frameset combinations. Feel free to use the color named documents on the Companion CD in the /examples/ch10/folder. Follow these steps:

1. Start with a basic HTML document, including <HTML>, <HEAD>, and <TITLE> tags and <META> tags of your choice. Your code should look something like this:

   ```
   <HTML>
   <HEAD>
   ```

```
   <TITLE>Frameset Samples</TITLE>
</HEAD>
</HTML>
```

2. Add <FRAMESET> tags to establish the frameset:

```
<HTML>
<HEAD>
   <TITLE>Frameset Samples</TITLE>
</HEAD>
<FRAMESET>
</FRAMESET>
</HTML>
```

3. Add a COLS= or ROWS= attribute, depending on whether you want vertical or horizontal frames. We used the COLS= attribute with values of 50 % and * to get two columns, one at 50% and one filling the remaining space:

```
<FRAMESET COLS="50%, *>
</FRAMESET>
```

Here we could also use 50%, because we know how much space remains, but using the * is a better long-range choice because we can add columns without changing the existing values. If you change the first 50% value, you don't have to make any other changes. If you specify all values, you must then change all values when you want to add columns.

NOTE

If you view the document at this point, you will not see anything because you haven't specified any content. That comes when you add frames.

Within a frameset, you can specify either rows or columns, but not both. To divide your browser window into columns and then subdivide each column into rows, you nest frameset tags, like this.

```
<FRAMESET COLS="200,50%,*">
<FRAMESET ROWS="100,*">
</FRAMESET>
</FRAMESET>
```

Just How Are Frame Sizes Calculated?

When you specify frame sizes within your frameset, the visitor's browser must accommodate both your specifications and the browser size and resolution. The browser calculates the actual sizes as shown here:

- Browsers apply percentages, which indicate a percentage of the entire browser window first, if specified in the frameset.
- Browsers apply pixel values, which specify an exact size, second, if specified in the frameset.
- Browsers use wildcard (*) settings to fill the remaining space.

In general, you can use the * to set up proportional columns or rows. For example, the following frameset tag has three values after COLS=; therefore, the space is divided into three parts. To allocate those proportionately (evenly), use an * as shown here:

```
<FRAMESET COLS="*, *, *">
```

To make the middle frame twice as large as the other two, add a 2 to the *, as in the following:

```
<FRAMESET COLS="*, 2*, *">
```

The middle frame fills half the space, and the other two columns fill one-quarter each. If you add a 2 to the third space, the first column fills one-fifth and the remaining two fill two-fifths each, as shown below.

```
<FRAMESET COLS="*, 2*, 2*">
```

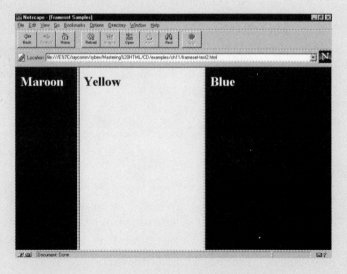

As we mentioned earlier, you can specify frame width in percentages, in pixels, and as a proportion of the remaining space. You can also combine these specifications. For example, a frameset might require one section that is 100 pixels wide, another that is 50% of the window, another that fills two parts of the remaining space, and a final section that is one part of the remaining space. That code (including the frame tags) looks like this:

```
<FRAMESET COLS="100, 50%, 2*, *">
FRAME NAME="third" SRC="z-maroon.html">
<FRAME NAME="first" SRC="z-yellow.html">
<FRAME NAME="second" SRC="z-blue.html">
<FRAME NAME="fourth" SRC="z-green.html">
</FRAMESET>
```

This code results in the frames shown below:

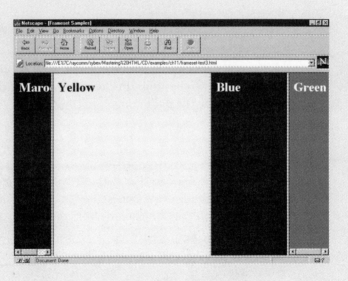

Adding Frames

Adding frames to an existing frameset document is straightforward. You add a frame tag for each column or row in the frameset document, specify the content for each frame, and then name each frame.

In the following example, we are going to add vertical frames. The process for adding horizontal frames is the same except for the ROWS= or COLS= attribute in the <FRAMESET> tag.

We'll start with the existing frameset document that we created in the last section, and then we'll add two frame tags and the content for each frame. The starting document looks like this:

```
<!DOCTYPE HTML PUBLIC "-//W3C//DTD HTML 4.0//EN">
<HTML>
<HEAD>
  <TITLE>Frameset Samples</TITLE>
</HEAD>
<FRAMESET COLS="50%, *">
</FRAMESET>
</HTML>
```

Now, follow these steps:

1. Add a <FRAME> tag within the <FRAMESET>.

   ```
   <FRAMESET COLS="50%, *">
   <FRAME>
   </FRAMESET>
   ```

2. Add the NAME= attribute to label the frame. Because browsers fill frames from left to right and top to bottom, this frame name is for the left frame. The second frame name is for the right frame.

   ```
   <FRAMESET COLS="50%, *">
   <FRAME NAME="first">
   </FRAMESET>
   ```

3. Add the SRC= attribute to specify the HTML document that will fill the frame. The document filling this frame is z-yellow.html. (You'll find an array of colorful documents on the Companion CD in the /examples/ch10 folder.)

   ```
   <FRAMESET COLS="50%, *">
   <FRAME NAME="first" SRC="z-yellow.html">
   </FRAMESET>
   ```

NOTE

The URL you use depends on where the file is located. If you're using a file in the same folder as the frameset document or in an adjacent folder, you can use a relative URL, as we are doing here. If the file is located elsewhere, you will need to adjust the URL accordingly.

4. Add the second frame tag, with the name *second* and source of z-blue.html.

```
<FRAMESET COLS="50%, *">
<FRAME NAME="first" SRC="z-yellow.html">
<FRAME NAME="second" SRC="z-blue.html">
</FRAMESET>
```

This step completes the frameset document. The frames, which include the yellow and blue documents, look like those in Figure 10.5.

FIGURE 10.5

Two frames, each with a separate document

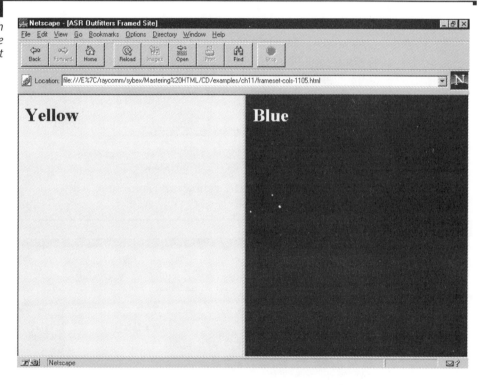

PART

II

Advancing Your Skills

As you test your documents, you may find that reloading framed documents looks a little random—sometimes the whole thing reloads, while at other times only a certain frame reloads. The easiest way to control how browsers reload is to ensure that the item you want to reload is active. To reload a single frame, click in the frame and then click the Reload button. To reload the entire frameset, click in the location line or in the address line (depending on the browser you use), and then click the Reload button.

To add another column, alter your frameset to make space and then add another <FRAME> tag. The current frameset looks like this:

<FRAMESET COLS="50%, *">

The 50% specifies that the first column fill 50% of the window. The * specifies that the second column fill the remaining space. To add an additional column, follow these steps:

1. Specify the amount of space for the additional column. For example, if you add a 200-pixel column after the 50% columns, the <FRAMESET> tag looks like this:

   <FRAMESET COLS="50%, **200**, *">

2. Add another <FRAME> tag. If you add the <FRAME> tag before the two existing tags, the new frame appears on the left, and the other two appear in the center and on the right. If you add the frame tag after the two existing tags, the new frame appears on the right, and the other two appear on the left and in the center. The frame columns fill in order from left to right. If you add the new frame tag at the beginning, the code looks like this:

   <FRAME NAME="third" SRC="z-maroon.html">
   <FRAME NAME="first" SRC="z-yellow.html">
   <FRAME NAME="second" SRC="z-blue.html">

The framed page looks like that shown in Figure 10.6.

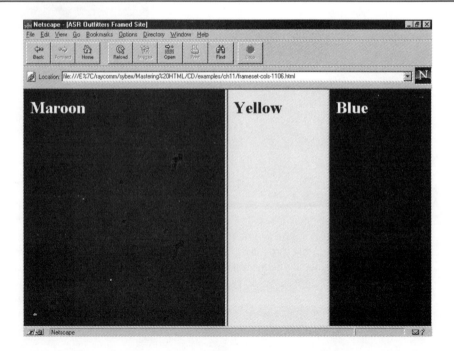

NOTE

You can follow these same steps to add horizontal frames.

Combining Horizontal and Vertical Framesets

Although many of your framing needs probably require only a pair of horizontal or vertical frames, you can easily nest frameset tags to combine vertical and horizontal frames within a single document. Each frame area in a frameset tag can contain either a <FRAME> tag, as in the preceding examples, or another <FRAMESET> tag.

TIP

The source documents in these examples are virtually blank documents, containing different colored backgrounds to make it easier to see different frames. These sample files are in the /examples/ch10 folder on the CD. Feel free to use them as you develop your framed site.

In the next example, we will set up a simple frameset with two columns and then divide the columns into two rows each. Follow these steps:

1. Start with a blank HTML document, similar to the following:

```
<HTML>
<HEAD>
  <TITLE>Frameset Samples</TITLE>
</HEAD>

</HTML>
```

2. Add the <FRAMESET> tags.

```
<HTML>
<HEAD>
  <TITLE>Frameset Samples</TITLE>
</HEAD>
<FRAMESET>
</FRAMESET>
</HTML>
```

3. Create two columns by adding the COLS= attribute. In this example, one column fills 30% of the window, and the other fills the remaining space.

```
<HTML>
<HEAD>
  <TITLE>Frameset Samples</TITLE>
</HEAD>
<FRAMESET COLS="30%, *">
</FRAMESET>
</HTML>
```

4. Add a second frameset tag pair, for two rows, each at 50% of the window, as shown in the following code. Within the first frameset tag pair, you could place two frames, two framesets, or one frame and one frameset (as this example shows):

```
<FRAMESET COLS="30%, *">
    <FRAMESET ROWS="50%, 50%">
    </FRAMESET>
</FRAMESET>
```

5. Add the three necessary <FRAME> tags so that you can view your document. The second frameset requires two <FRAME> tags, and the primary frameset tag requires only one (because the second frameset is taking one of the two available columns). Be sure to include both the NAME= and SRC= attributes with the <FRAME> tags. Your code should look like the following:

```
<FRAMESET COLS="30%, *">
    <FRAMESET ROWS="50%, 50%">
        <FRAME NAME="topleft" SRC="z-maroon.html">
        <FRAME NAME="lowerleft" SRC="z-blue.html">
    </FRAMESET>
    <FRAME NAME="right" SRC="z-white.html">
</FRAMESET>
```

Your frames should look like those in Figure 10.7.

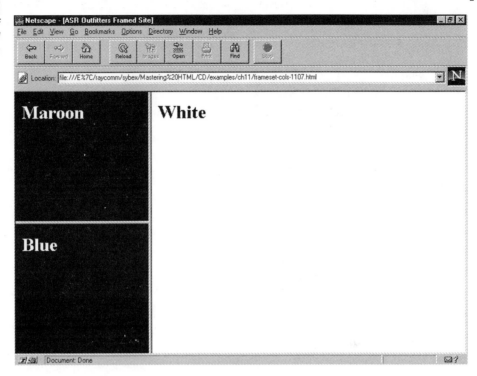

PART

II

Advancing Your Skills

FIGURE 10.7

A combination of horizontal and vertical frames is often effective.

To set a second pair of frames on the right side, replace the final <FRAME> tag with an additional <FRAMESET> tag pair, as well as two <FRAMES> to fill it. The final code looks like this:

```
<FRAMESET COLS="30%, *">
    <FRAMESET ROWS="50%, 50%">
        <FRAME NAME="topleft" SRC="z-maroon.html">
        <FRAME NAME="lowerleft" SRC="z-blue.html">
    </FRAMESET>
    <FRAMESET ROWS="100, *">
    <FRAME NAME="topright" SRC="z-yellow.html">
    <FRAME NAME="lowerright" SRC="z-white.html">
    </FRAMESET>
</FRAMESET>
```

When you view the results of this code in a browser, you'll see the frames as shown in Figure 10.8.

FIGURE 10.8

This paragraph comes after the picture box paragraph. Four frames are easy to create, but visually a little much.

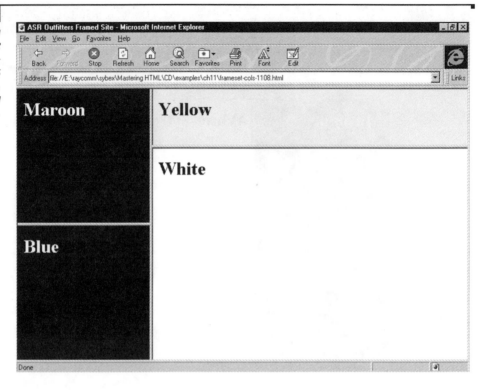

If your document does not appear in the browser, double-check that you have the correct number of frames and that every <FRAMESET> tag that you opened has an accompanying closing tag. An omitted closing <FRAMESET> tag is usually the villain, particularly if you are nesting multiple framesets.

Formatting Frames

Formatting a frame primarily involves changing its borders and adjusting its margins. You use the attributes shown in Table 10.2 to do so. These tags generally apply either to a <FRAMESET> tag—and thus to all <FRAME> tags within the frameset—or to individual <FRAME> tags, although the HTML 4 specification only supports using these attributes with individual <FRAME> tags.

TABLE 10.2: FRAME FORMATTING ATTRIBUTES

Attribute	Use
FRAMEBORDER=n	Sets or removes the border around a frame (per HTML 4 standard and Microsoft usage). For uniform results in all browsers, use in conjunction with the BORDER= attribute.
BORDER=n	Sets or removes the border around a frame (per Netscape usage). For uniform results in all browsers, use in conjunction with the FRAMEBORDER= attribute.
NORESIZE	Prohibits visitors from resizing a frame. In the absence of this attribute, visitors can click and drag the mouse to move the frame borders.
SCROLLING="..."	Prohibits scrollbars, requires scrollbars, or lets the browser provide scrollbars if required (the default). Possible values are YES, NO, and AUTO(matic).
MARGINHEIGHT=n	Sets the number of pixels of the margin above and below the content of the frame.
MARGINWIDTH=n	Sets the number of pixels of the margin to the left and the right of frame content.
BORDERCOLOR="..."	Sets the color of the frame border as either a #RRGGBB value or a color name.

NOTE

These options apply to actual frames, not to the content of the frames. Remember, frame content is simply a standard HTML document and is formatted accordingly.

Removing Borders

By default, all frames have borders. You can, however, remove them to give your pages a more streamlined appearance. To remove borders from your frames, follow these steps:

1. Start with a functional frameset document, such as the following.

```
<HTML>
<HEAD>
  <TITLE>Frameset Samples</TITLE>
</HEAD>
<FRAMESET COLS="30%, *">
```

```
<FRAMESET ROWS="50%, 50%">
    <FRAME NAME="topleft" SRC="z-maroon.html">
    <FRAME NAME="lowerleft" SRC="z-blue.html">
</FRAMESET>
<FRAMESET ROWS="100, *">
<FRAME NAME="topright" SRC="z-yellow.html">
<FRAME NAME="lowerright" SRC="z-white.html">
</FRAMESET>
</FRAMESET>
</HTML>
```

2. To remove all borders from your frames, add both a BORDER=0 and a FRAMEBORDER=0 attribute to the <FRAME> tags.

```
<FRAMESET COLS="30%, *">
    <FRAMESET ROWS="50%, 50%">
        <FRAME NAME="topleft" SRC="z-maroon.html" BORDER=0 FRAMEBORDER=0>
        <FRAME NAME="lowerleft" SRC="z-blue.html" BORDER=0 FRAMEBORDER=0>
    </FRAMESET>
    <FRAMESET ROWS="100, *">
<FRAME NAME="topright" SRC="z-yellow.html" BORDER=0 FRAMEBORDER=0>
<FRAME NAME="lowerright" SRC="z-white.html" BORDER=0 FRAMEBORDER=0>
</FRAMESET>
</FRAMESET>
```

These attributes result in the document shown in Figure 10.9.

NOTE

Because of the conflicting tags proposed and supported by Microsoft and Netscape, you must use both the BORDER= and the FRAMEBORDER= attributes to turn off borders in all browsers. If your visitors use a Netscape browser exclusively, use only the BORDER= attribute. If your visitors use Internet Explorer exclusively, use only the FRAMEBORDER= attribute.

If you remove or set borders in individual frames, remember that the borders that frames share must both be set to 0 to completely remove the border. If one frame is set to no borders and an adjacent frame has borders, you will see borders in the browser.

PART

II

Advancing Your Skills

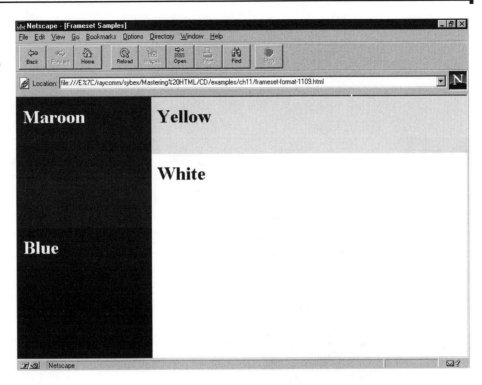

FIGURE 10.9

Frames without borders often look more attractive than bordered frames.

Specifying Border Width

Adding borders of a specific size gets a little more complex because of the conflicting attributes supported by the HTML 4 specification, Internet Explorer, and Netscape Navigator. To turn on borders, set FRAMEBORDER=1 (for Internet Explorer) and BORDER=1 (for Netscape Navigator). To set the border width, increase the value of BORDER= for both browsers.

The HTML 4 specification does not support the BORDER= attribute.

For example, to turn on borders at the default value, use the following:

`<FRAMESET COLS="30%, *" `**`BORDER=1 FRAMEBORDER=1`**`>`

To set the borders to a width of 20 pixels (excessively wide, but easy to see if you're following the example), use the following:

`<FRAMESET COLS="30%, *" `**`BORDER=20`**` FRAMEBORDER=1>`

The resulting screen looks like that shown in Figure 10.10.

FIGURE 10.10

A 20-pixel width is excessive, but it makes the change in border width apparent.

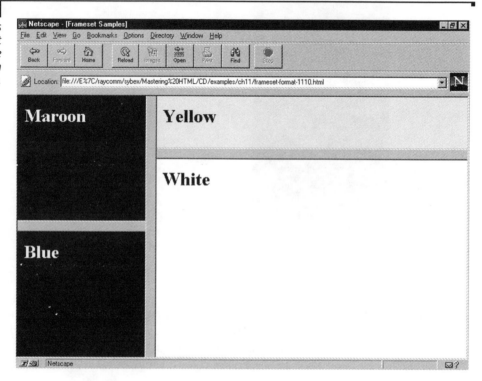

NOTE

Internet Explorer supports a FRAMESPACING=*n* attribute, which should increase the space between frames (in addition to the border width). However, because of Netscape's lack of support for this attribute and because this attribute is not included in the HTML 4 Frames specification, we don't recommend using it.

Specifying Border Color

Colored borders can enhance or complement the color schemes of the documents in the frames. However, only the latest versions of Netscape Navigator and Internet Explorer support them, and they are not part of the HTML 4 specification.

To color frame borders, add the BORDERCOLOR= attribute to the <FRAMESET> or <FRAME> tag, as in the following example.

```
<FRAMESET COLS="30%, *" BORDER=20 FRAMEBORDER=1 BORDERCOLOR="#008000">
```

When coloring borders, add the color to the individual frames for more consistent results. Although you can often add colors to frameset tags, not all browsers consistently support that usage.

Controlling Frames

Depending on your layout, you might want to exercise a little extra control over how frames appear. In particular, you can:

- Prevent visitors from resizing the frame
- Determine whether scrollbars appear on framed pages
- Set frame margins

Controlling these aspects will help keep your site predictable and thus more usable for your visitors.

Controlling Frame Size

If you have content of a known size, you might want to establish a fixed size for a frame and choose not to let visitors resize it. For example, if a frame encloses an image map that is used for site-wide navigation, you would probably size the frame to the image map. If the image map is 390 pixels wide and 90 pixels high, you might set the frame to 400 × 100 pixels with the following code:

```
<FRAMESET COLS="400, *">
  <FRAMESET ROWS="100, *">
```

You know the exact size of only the first frame; it will be 400 pixels wide and 100 pixels high. All other frames on the page will be resized according to the size of the browser window. If the browser window is set to 800 × 600, the second (variable) column will be about 400 pixels wide. If the browser window is 1024 × 768, however, the variable column will be about 600 pixels wide.

You can also set a frame to NORESIZE to prevent visitors from resizing it. Although many Web surfers do not know that they can resize frames by simply clicking and dragging the borders, some do and will rearrange the borders to suit themselves. If,

PART

II

Advancing Your Skills

however, visitors resize a frameset to not scroll, they might obscure some content without realizing it. To avoid this, simply add the NORESIZE attribute to the <FRAME> tag, like this:

```
<FRAME NAME="menu" SRC="imagemap.html" NORESIZE>
```

Setting one frame to NORESIZE also prohibits other frames from resizing. For example, if the maroon frame in Figure 10.10 is set to NORESIZE, visitors cannot horizontally resize the yellow frame or vertically resize the blue frame.

Controlling Scrollbars

Although scrollbars are essential to allow visitors to see all the content in most frames, they can be superfluous and visually distracting. For instance, depending on the margin that a browser inserts around an image, scrollbars might appear in some browsers on some platforms and not in others. If the entire image map fits within the frame, little scrolling is necessary, and scrollbars would probably obscure more of the image map than might be lost through the margins. Therefore, you might set this frame to SCROLLING=NO to prohibit scrollbars, like this:

```
<FRAME NAME="menu" SRC="imagemap.html" SCROLLING="NO" NORESIZE>
```

You can also put SCROLLING=NO in the <FRAMESET> tag if you want to prohibit scrolling in all frames within the frameset document. Keep in mind, though, that if you turn off the scrollbars in a frame containing more content than will fit in the window, your visitors will have no way to view the page.

Set SCROLLING=NO only if the frame contains an image or an object of a known size. Because browser settings, available fonts, and monitor resolution vary, you cannot predict what text might or might not fit within a frame.

Conversely, you might also set SCROLLING=YES in some cases. For example, if you have a contents page that contains most of the links from your navigation frame, you might set scrolling to yes so that the frame always has a scrollbar. If you have shorter documents, the scrollbar will be nonfunctional, but it will appear consistently and make your site look just a wee bit more professional. If you set scrolling to automatic (the default), some pages may have a scrollbar and some may not, which can be distracting to a visitor.

As a rule, apply the formatting tags to the <FRAMESET> tag, but apply the control tags to the <FRAME> tags. The tags will all work in either location, but you'll generally want the formatting to apply to all frames in a page, while the control tags will be specific to a single frame.

Setting Frame Margins

A frame margin is the space between the edge of the frame and the visible content of the HTML document. Adjusting the frame margin affects the framed document itself and keeps documents from appearing to nearly touch each other; in other words, adjusting the frame margins gives your documents a little "breathing room."

To set frame margins, add the MARGINHEIGHT= (for vertical margins) and MARGIN-WIDTH= (for horizontal margins) attributes to the <FRAME> tag as shown in the following code:

```
<FRAME NAME="topleft" SRC="z-maroon.html" MARGINWIDTH="100"
MARGINHEIGHT="100">
```

This code moves the document 100 pixels from the top and left margins, as shown in Figure 10.11.

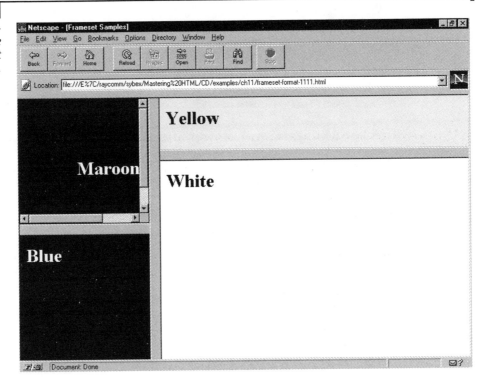

PART

II

Advancing Your Skills

FIGURE 10.11

The Maroon document's margins are a little big, but clearly different.

Accommodating Nonframed Browsers

As we mentioned earlier, not all browsers support frames. If a visitor to your framed site has a nonframed browser, what does he or she see? Nothing. Since that's the last thing you want, you need to accommodate visitors that are using nonframed browsers. This probably means supplying text that replicates the information in the framed document.

If you're developing a framed intranet site and your company has standardized on using only the latest version of Internet Explorer, you really don't need to worry about this. But if you are developing a Web site for general use, you need to give careful thought to how you will supply information to visitors using nonframed browsers. Here are some guidelines.

Provide some amount of nonframed information. Even if you decide not to accommodate nonframed browsers, display a courtesy message stating (positively) that your site requires the newest graphical browsers and that it is inaccessible with other browsers.

Use a browser-detection script that automatically redirects nonframe browsers to the nonframe pages. This option requires slightly more work than the previous guideline; however, it makes the browser do the work, not the visitor.

Include alternate text within the <NOFRAMES> section. If you do this carefully, your visitors may not even know that your site has other content. This option, however, increases your workload substantially. You must maintain two complete documents—the content within the frames and the content within the <NOFRAMES> section.

Tips for Maintaining Framed and Nonframed Documents

One way to lighten your workload is to make extensive use of server-side includes (discussed in Chapter 6) so that your content and presentation are essentially separate. You include the content in framed pages. In the nonframed pages, you include the content and another document that has navigation links.

Another alternative is to include the navigation links in your document and then use JavaScript to hide the links from framed browsers. This is not an elegant solution, but it works. Almost all browsers that support JavaScript also support frames, and vice versa.

Create your home page using frames, but provide a link to the nonframed version. Visitors thus have the option to use frames, but they aren't forced to do so. This option also doubles your work.

Develop your home page without frames, and then provide links to the framed version. Again, this is a double-your-work option.

At the time of writing, the RayComm, Inc., Web site (real, not hypothetical) used this final solution. The home page, at www.raycomm.com/, as in Figure 10.12, looks like a framed site, but is actually a fancy background and a table to separate the navigation buttons from the content. The High-Tech Site link goes to a roughly parallel site that looks the same, but uses frames.

FIGURE 10.12

A table can masquerade as a set of framed documents.

Are Tables or Frames Better for Your Design Needs?

You can use both tables and frames to create interesting page layouts and work around the limitations of HTML. For example, you can place navigation information beside the text of a document or array two columns of text side by side, using either tables or frames.

So how do you decide which to use? The advantages of tables include the following:

- Tables are more widely recognized by browsers than frames.
- Tables create fewer site navigation difficulties than frames.
- Tables are standard HTML 3.2 and 4.

The advantages of frames include the following:

- Frames are easier to update and maintain because the individual documents are shorter and simpler.
- Framed pages tend to download faster than tables because repeated information doesn't have to be downloaded repeatedly.
- Frames are more flexible for complex layouts. For example, they allow you to have information across the top of a page and scroll other information under that banner.
- Frames offer some useful bells and whistles, such as being able to call up a document in a specific part of the browser window—an effect that can be simulated with tables only at the cost of incredible effort.
- Frames are standard HTML 4.

For more information about tables, see Chapter 8.

Providing Nonframed Content

To accommodate visitors using nonframed browsers, use the <NOFRAMES> tags and include the alternate text. Start with an existing HTML frameset document such as the following:

```
<!DOCTYPE HTML PUBLIC "-//W3C//DTD HTML 4.0//EN">
<HTML>
<HEAD>
```

```
    <TITLE>Frameset Samples</TITLE>
</HEAD>
<FRAMESET COLS="30%, *" BORDER=0 FRAMEBORDER=0 BORDERCOLOR="#008000">
    <FRAMESET ROWS="50%, 50%" >
        <FRAME NAME="topleft" SRC="z-maroon.html">
        <FRAME NAME="lowerleft" SRC="z-blue.html">
    </FRAMESET>
    <FRAMESET ROWS="100, *">
<FRAME NAME="topright" SRC="z-yellow.html">
<FRAME NAME="lowerright" SRC="z-white.html">
</FRAMESET>
</FRAMESET>
</HTML>
```

Now, follow these steps:

1. Add the <NOFRAMES> tag pair somewhere in the document. The best choices—for ease of development—are either at the beginning, above the first <FRAMESET> tag, or at the end, just before the closing HTML tag.

```
<NOFRAMES>
</NOFRAMES>
</HTML>
```

2. Add any appropriate content within the <NOFRAMES> tags. The approach you take, as mentioned previously, will vary. For an intranet site for a company that has standardized on the latest version of Internet Explorer, you might choose something like the following.

```
<NOFRAMES>
<H1 ALIGN=CENTER>Intranet Access Problem</H1>
WAMMI, Inc., has standardized on the newest version of Internet
Explorer. You seem to be using an older version or a different browser
entirely. Please see your network administrator or check with the Help
Desk to get the proper browser. With the newest browser, you will be
able to access the corporate intranet.
</NOFRAMES>
```

When viewed in a nonframed browser, this page looks like that shown in Figure 10.13.

PART

II

Advancing Your Skills

The <NOFRAMES> content is visible only in browsers that cannot accommodate frames, as shown here.

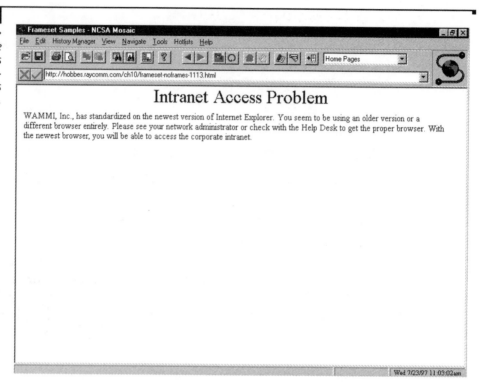

Some nonframed browsers support only a limited set of formatting tags. Keep this in mind if you're tempted to get fancy with your nonframes formatting.

Enabling Effective Navigation

Designing with frames and helping your visitors navigate your site effectively requires moderation and simplicity. The following sections explain the navigation types and show you how to implement navigation.

Choosing Navigation Types

You can design frames so that visitors can navigate in two ways:

- Visitors can click in one frame and view the resulting document in another frame (as shown in Figure 10.14).

- Visitors can click in one frame and view the resulting document in that same frame.

FIGURE 10.14

Navigation links can lead to a document in the same frame or in another frame.

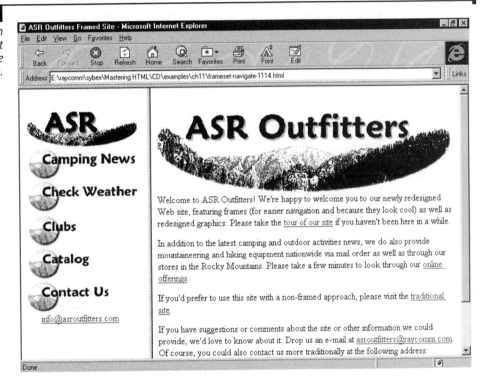

When you use the first option, navigation tools remain visible at all times in one frame, and the content appears and changes in another frame. In Figure 10.14, clicking a link on the left changes the content in the frame on the right.

When you use the second option, clicking a link changes the content in the frame that contains the link. For example, in Figure 10.14, clicking a link in the frame on the right changes the content of that frame.

You normally use the second option when content is logically cross-referenced to other documents at the site. All frames can, however, contain links, whether they are navigation links or cross-references.

Implementing Navigation

Linking to specific frames requires only one new attribute, TARGET=. When used in an anchor tag, this attribute directs the content of the link into a different frame.

The frameset document for Figure 10.14 looks like this:

```
<!DOCTYPE HTML PUBLIC "-//W3C//DTD HTML 4.0//EN">
<HTML>
<HEAD>
   <TITLE>ASR Outfitters Framed Site</TITLE>
</HEAD>


<FRAMESET COLS="230, *">
  <FRAME NAME="left" SRC="lefttoc1.html">
  <FRAME NAME="main" SRC="content.html">
    <NOFRAMES>
If you can see this, your browser is not capable of displaying
frames.
    </NOFRAMES>
</FRAMESET>
</HTML>
```

The first (left) <FRAME> tag carries the attribute NAME="left", and the other frame has the attribute NAME="main". These attributes allow the frames to be specifically addressed.

The basic code for the left frame is as follows.

```
<!DOCTYPE HTML PUBLIC "-//W3C//DTD HTML 4.0//EN">
<HTML>
<HEAD>
<TITLE>ASR Outfitters</TITLE>
</HEAD>
<BODY BACKGROUND="" BGCOLOR="#ffffff" TEXT="#000000" LINK="#0000ff"
VLINK="#800080" ALINK="#ff0000">
<IMG SRC="asrlogosm.gif" ALIGN="" WIDTH="200" HEIGHT="84" BORDER="0" ALT="">
<UL>
<LI><A HREF="camping.html">Camping News</A>
<LI><A HREF="weather.html">Check Weather</A>
<LI><A HREF="clubs.html">Clubs</A>
```

```
<LI><A HREF="catalog.html">Catalog</A>
<LI><A HREF="contact.html">Contact Us</A>
</UL>
</BODY>
</HTML>
```

As the document currently stands, clicking a link—say, Camping News—in the left frame displays the new document in the left (same) frame because frame links, by default, land in the same frame. If you want the linked document to appear in the right frame, follow these steps:

1. Add the TARGET= attribute to the anchor tag.

   ```
   <LI><A HREF="camping.html" TARGET="">Camping News</A>
   ```

2. Add the name of the frame to which you want to link. The initial frameset names right frames "main" frames, so that's the name you use.

   ```
   <LI><A HREF="camping.html" TARGET="main">Camping News</A>
   ```

When you click the Camping News link, the file appears in the right frame, as shown in Figure 10.15.

PART

II

Advancing Your Skills

FIGURE 10.15

The TARGET= attribute controls which frame receives the content of a link. The Camping News link was directed into the "main" frame.

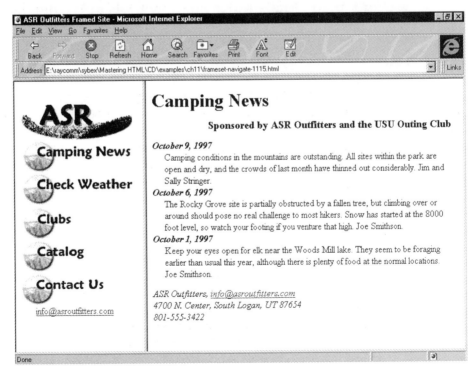

Of course, in this particular scenario, each link from this document should open in the main frame. To save time and reduce the possibility of error, you can add the TARGET="main" attribute to the <BASE> tag and force it to affect the entire document.

The <BASE> tag goes in the document head and sets the rules for the whole document. To set all links from the document in the left frame to open in the main frame, add the tag and attribute to the document head as in the following example:

```
<!DOCTYPE HTML PUBLIC "-//W3C//DTD HTML 4.0//EN">
<HTML>
<HEAD>
<TITLE>ASR Outfitters</TITLE>
<BASE TARGET="main">
</HEAD>
```

With the base target defined, the only need for TARGET= attributes in the document will be to link to other locations. The following section discusses some special target locations and names.

Using Image Maps As Navigation Tools in Framed Documents

The TARGET= attribute works in all contexts where links occur. For example, you can use an image map in a frame to provide navigation for an entire site. The following code and example show how to include an image map in a framed page:

```
<MAP NAME="frame-imagemap">
<AREA SHAPE=RECT COORDS="4,4,190,51" HREF="camping.html">
<AREA SHAPE=RECT COORDS="5,57,191,110" HREF="weather.html">
<AREA SHAPE=RECT COORDS="4,112,191,165" HREF="clubs.html">
<AREA SHAPE=RECT COORDS="3,167,191,220" HREF="catalog.html">
<AREA SHAPE=RECT COORDS="3,222,191,277" HREF="contact.html">
<AREA SHAPE=default HREF="lefttoc1.html">
</MAP>
```

To force each area, except the last, to open in the main frame, add the TARGET="main" attribute to each one, as in the following code:

```
<MAP NAME="frame-imagemap">
<AREA SHAPE=RECT COORDS="4,4,190,51" HREF="camping.html" TARGET="main">
<AREA SHAPE=RECT COORDS="5,57,191,110" HREF="weather.html" TARGET="main">
<AREA SHAPE=RECT COORDS="4,112,191,165" HREF="clubs.html" TARGET="main">
```

```
<AREA SHAPE=RECT COORDS="3,167,191,220" HREF="catalog.html" TARGET="main">

<AREA SHAPE=RECT COORDS="3,222,191,277" HREF="contact.html" TARGET="main">

<AREA SHAPE=default HREF="lefttoc1.html">

</MAP>
```

Using Special Target Names

In addition to the target names that you define in <FRAME> tags within the frameset document, you can use other, special target names in all tags that link HTML documents, such as <A>, <FORM>, and <AREA>. Table 10.3 explains these target names and their functions.

TABLE 10.3: SPECIAL TARGET NAMES

Target Attribute	Use
TARGET="..."	Sets the link to open in the frame named between the quotes.
TARGET="_self"	Sets the link to open in the current frame.
TARGET="_blank"	Sets the link to open in a new window.
TARGET="_parent"	Sets the link to open in the parent frameset of the current document. If only one frameset is present, this removes the frameset.
TARGET="_top"	Sets the link to open in the browser window, breaking out of all frames.

By using these special TARGET= attributes, in any context, you control the location where the linked file appears. In general, you can keep the targets predictable and usable by following these guidelines:

- Keep your pages together. If you're linking a closely related page from your site, direct the link into an adjacent frame, not into a separate window, so that your site remains visually cohesive.

- Keep your navigation content and regular content in a consistent location. If your navigation links appear in a frame that spans the top of the browser window, the content to which the objects in that frame link should appear in a different frame. Similarly, if a link within your Web content displays related content, use TARGET="_self" to ensure that the link appears in the same window, because your visitors will expect content in that particular frame.

- Llink to nonframed pages using TARGET="_top" to ensure that your nonframed documents really aren't framed.

- Keep your pages visible. If you link to another site, use TARGET="_blank" to open a new browser window for the other site, while keeping your window open and visible. That way, if your visitor tires of the other site, your site is still easily accessible.

- Don't frame other pages. By setting TARGET="_blank" or TARGET="_top" for external links, you can ensure that other people's content doesn't appear within your frames. Why? First, if you display content on your site that was created by someone else, that's potentially plagiarism. Second, you don't necessarily want your site associated with content from another site. (See the "A Caution about Linking to Outside Sites" sidebar earlier in this chapter for more information.)

- Don't frame yourself. If your framed site includes an active link to the home page (likely the frameset document for the site), be sure that the link includes TARGET="_top". If you accidentally point the link to your main frameset into a frame within the site, your home page will appear within your home page within your home page and so on. See Figure 10.16 for an example.

FIGURE 10.16:

Framing your own site, even accidentally, can look odd at best.

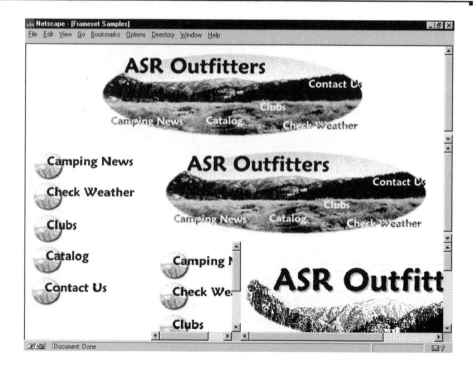

TIP

A little creativity in TARGET= attributes is a good thing, but a lot of creativity will either scare off visitors or entice them to click on every link you have just to see where it goes.

The Order of Target Attributes

If TARGET= attributes appear in more than one place—or don't appear at all—the order of precedence is as follows:

- No target attributes means that the link will appear in the same frame.
- Target attributes in the <BASE> tag apply to all links in the document.
- Target attributes in an anchor tag override the <BASE> tag.

Creating Inline Frames

Inline frames, often called *floating frames*, appear as part of an HTML document in much the same way that an image appears in an HTML document. They allow you to insert an HTML document into an area within another document. In this sense, inline frames blend traditional HTML documents with framed documents. At the time of writing, only Internet Explorer supported inline frames, although they are part of the HTML 4 specification. Figure 10.17 shows a sample inline frame from an ASR Outfitters page.

The basic tags you'll use for your inline frames are a combination of frame tags and image tags, as explained in Table 10.4.

FIGURE 10.17

Inline frames can contain any HTML document and can float within another document.

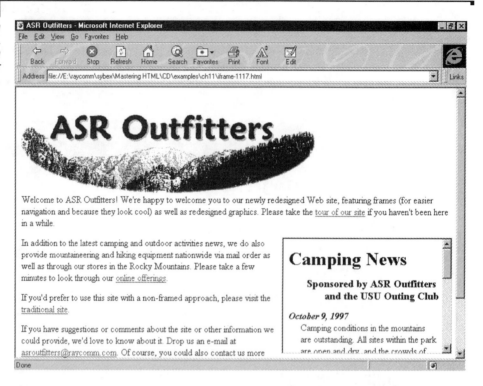

TABLE 10.4: INLINE FRAME TAGS AND ATTRIBUTES

Tag/Attribute	Description
`<IFRAME>`	Identifies frame characteristics and initial content.
`SRC="URL"`	Identifies the source for the frame content as a standard URL.
`NAME="..."`	Labels a frame so that it can be targeted or referred to from other frames or windows.
`FRAMEBORDER=n`	Sets or removes borders around frames.
`SCROLLING=`	Prohibits scrollbars, requires scrollbars, or, the default, lets the browser provide scrollbars if required. Possible values are YES, NO, and AUTO(matic).
`MARGINHEIGHT=n`	Sets the number of pixels in the margin above and below the content of a frame.
`MARGINWIDTH=`	Sets the number of pixels in the margin to the left and right of the frame.

TABLE 10.4: INLINE FRAME TAGS AND ATTRIBUTES (CONTINUED)

Tag/Attribute	Description
HEIGHT=*n*	Specifies the height of an inline frame in pixels.
WIDTH=*n*	Specifies the width of an inline frame in pixels.
ALIGN="..."	Specifies the alignment as LEFT, MIDDLE, RIGHT, TOP, or BOTTOM.

To add an inline frame to your document, start with a functional HTML document.

```
<!DOCTYPE HTML PUBLIC "-//W3C//DTD HTML 4.0//EN">
<HTML>
<HEAD>
  <TITLE>Floating Frame Samples</TITLE>
</HEAD>
<BODY BACKGROUND="" BGCOLOR="FFFFFF" TEXT="000000" LINK="0000FF"
VLINK="800080" ALINK="FF0000">
<H1>Floating Frames</H1>
Documents with floating frames look really cool, but only in Internet
Explorer.
</BODY>
</HTML>
```

Now, follow these steps:

1. Add an <IFRAME> tag pair.

```
<HTML>
<HEAD>
  <TITLE>Floating Frame Samples</TITLE>
</HEAD>
<BODY BACKGROUND="" BGCOLOR="FFFFFF" TEXT="000000" LINK="0000FF"
VLINK="800080" ALINK="FF0000">
<H1>Floating Frames</H1>
<IFRAME>
</IFRAME>
Documents with floating frames look really cool, but only in Internet
Explorer.
</BODY>
</HTML>
```

PART

II

Advancing Your Skills

2. Add the NAME= attribute to the <IFRAME> tag. Just as with traditional frames, the NAME= attribute labels the frame so that it can be targeted by links.

```
<IFRAME NAME="float1">
</IFRAME>
```

3. Add the SRC= attribute to specify the HTML document that will fill the frame. Technically, an image could also fill a frame, but that would rather defeat the purpose of a floating frame where an HTML document can be placed.

```
<IFRAME SRC="z-maroon.html" NAME="float1">
</IFRAME>
```

4. Include the HEIGHT= and WIDTH= attributes to specify the dimensions of the floating frame in pixels. These values are analogous to the HEIGHT= and WIDTH= attributes for an image, but are required with the <IFRAME> tag.

```
<IFRAME SRC="z-maroon.html" NAME="float1" HEIGHT=200 WIDTH=300>
</IFRAME>
```

5. Provide alternate text to accommodate visitors using browsers other than recent versions of Internet Explorer. This text is similar to the ALT= text from images except that you do not use an attribute with the alternate text here.

```
<IFRAME SRC="z-maroon.html" NAME="float1" HEIGHT=200 WIDTH=300>
Netscape Navigator users get to see this message.
</IFRAME>
```

6. Optionally, add an alignment attribute. Generally, you'll use either LEFT or RIGHT, but any alignment attribute that you'd use with images will also work with floating frames.

```
<IFRAME SRC="z-maroon.html" NAME="float1" HEIGHT=200 WIDTH=300
ALIGN="RIGHT">
Netscape Navigator users get to see this message.
</IFRAME>
```

If you're using a newer version of Internet Explorer (version 3 or later), you'll see something like Figure 10.18.

Because floating frames closely resemble images in the way they are implemented and manipulated within the parent document, you can often treat floating frames in similar ways. For example, you can array them within table cells to force a specific layout scheme. You can also wrap text around the floating frame just as you wrap text around an image, as ASR Outfitters did in Figure 10.17, earlier in this chapter.

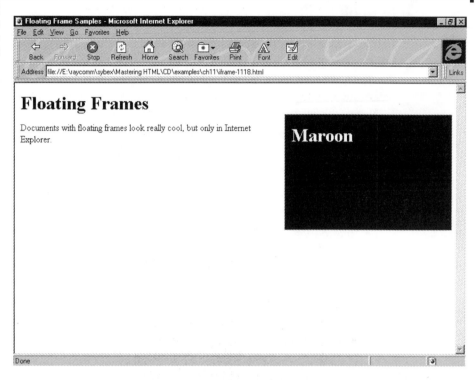

FIGURE 10.18

Floating frames can be visually interesting and make pages more attractive.

NOTE

Floating frames—as implemented by <IFRAME>—are skeptically regarded by the World Wide Web Consortium and will possibly not remain in the final Frames standard. The argument against <IFRAME> is that the <OBJECT> tag places any objects in an HTML document, and an HTML document is just another kind of object. Check out www.w3.org for the latest information.

Navigating in and among floating frames is similar to navigating in regular frames. The NAME= and TARGET= attributes serve the same purposes, and you use them the same way whether you're dealing with inline frames or regular frames. For example, use the following code to force a document to appear in a floating frame.

```
<A HREF="z-blue" TARGET="float1">Click to put the blue document in the
floating frame.</A>
```

Where to Go from Here

In this chapter, you learned about frames—their uses, advantages, and disadvantages—and about how to include them in your HTML documents. Keep in mind that not all browsers support frames; so use the guidelines throughout this chapter to determine when and how to include them effectively.

Also in this chapter, you learned how frames relate to other HTML components and about some of the unique uses. Following is a list of related information you might find useful:

- For information about computer and browser settings, see Chapter 2.
- If you want information about keeping up with standards, refer to Chapter 1.
- To find out more about images and image maps, see Chapter 7.
- To read more about tables, see Chapter 8.
- For more information about URLs, see Chapter 4.

PART III

Moving Beyond Pure HTML

LEARN TO:

- *Work with JavaScript*

- *Include multimedia elements in Web pages*

- *Use Dynamic HTML*

- *Implement push technologies*

Chapter

11

Adding JavaScript

FEATURING

Adding JavaScript

U sing JavaScript, you can add some pizzazz to your pages. HTML documents that include JavaScript can react to visitor actions, process and check information that visitors provide, and even deliver information appropriate to each visitor. With the increasingly sophisticated nature of the Web, you often need these kinds of attractions to hold visitors' attention and to keep them coming back.

For example, you can use JavaScript to change a button's color when the mouse cursor moves over it. This draws visitors' eyes to the button and indicates that they can follow this link to something new. Or, you can display a message in the status bar to give visitors more information about the link, such as "Follow this to our new catalog!" Highlighted links help visitors know what to expect at the end of the link.

You can also use JavaScript to validate forms before visitors submit them. For example, you can use JavaScript to ensure that a visitor completes an e-mail field before actually submitting the form, as shown in Figure 11.1. In addition, you can use JavaScript to change images based on visitor action or to provide fancy, form-based navigation links.

FIGURE 11.1

You can use JavaScript to validate form input.

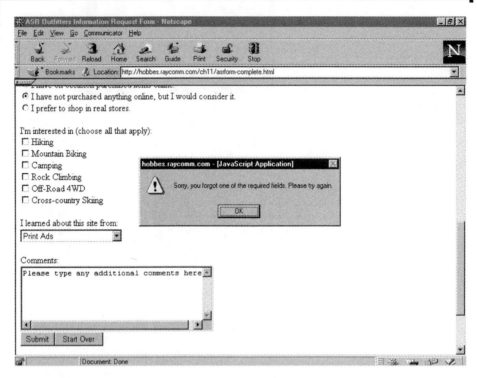

In this chapter, we'll look at what JavaScript is and how to use it, and, with some examples, we'll show you how to include JavaScript scripts in your HTML documents. We'll start with simple scripts and then build on them. We will concentrate on basic JavaScript capabilities (JavaScript 1.1 and some of 1.2), which is a good compromise between high functionality and broad browser acceptance. You'll find some sample scripts on the Companion CD, and you can easily use and modify them to meet your needs.

NOTE

The Master's Reference includes a comprehensive guide to JavaScript, which you can use to expand on the basics in this chapter.

What Is JavaScript?

JavaScript is a scripting language that Netscape created, and it resembles Sun's Java language. Most popular browsers, including Netscape Navigator 2 and later and Internet Explorer 3 and later, support JavaScript.

 NOTE

Microsoft also supports VBScript, a competing scripting approach. We recommend JavaScript (or the Microsoft equivalent called Jscript) for most purposes because JavaScript is much more widely supported.

 **TIP**

You'll find lots of scripts available for public use on the Web. For starters, search for JavaScript at www.yahoo.com or visit the Gamelan site at www.gamelan.com.

JavaScript is powerful enough to be truly useful, even though it isn't a full-fledged programming language. What's more, JavaScript is relatively easy and fun to use. JavaScript is simpler and less sophisticated (therefore less complex) than a "real" programming language. Many of the statements—sentences for JavaScript scripts—are remarkably natural in their structure and terminology.

To work with JavaScript, though, you need to be familiar with these concepts:

Object: An object is a thing—a checkbox on a form, the form itself, an image, a document, a link, or even a browser window. Some objects are built into JavaScript and are not necessarily part of your Web page. For example, the Date object provides a wide range of date information. You can think of objects as the nouns in the JavaScript language.

Property: A property describes an object. Properties can be anything from the color to the number of items, such as radio buttons, within an object. When visitors select an item in a form, they change the form's properties. You can think of properties as the adjectives in the JavaScript language.

Method: A method is an instruction. The methods available for each object describe what you can do with the object. For example, using a method, you can convert text in an object to all uppercase or all lowercase letters. Every

PART

III

Moving Beyond
Pure HTML

object has a collection of methods, and every method belongs to at least one object. You can think of methods as the verbs in the JavaScript language.

Statement: A statement is a JavaScript language sentence. Statements combine the objects, properties, and methods (nouns, adjectives, and verbs).

Function: A function is a collection of statements that perform actions. Functions contain one or more statements and thus can be considered the paragraphs of the JavaScript language.

Event: An event occurs when something happens on your page, such as a visitor submitting a form or moving the mouse cursor over an object.

Event Handler: An event handler waits for something to happen—such as the mouse moving over a link—and then launches a script based on that event. For example, the onMouseOver event handler performs an action when the visitor moves the mouse pointer over the object. You can think of an event handler as posing questions or directing the action of a story.

Before we get started, let's take a look at some JavaScript code. Once you identify the pieces, JavaScript is as easy to read as HTML code:

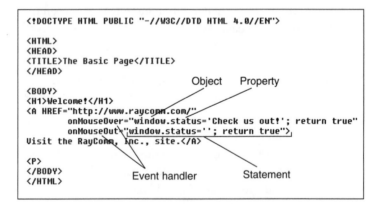

The JavaScript discussed in this chapter is exclusively client-side JavaScript. That simply means that the visitor's browser does the work and the server is not involved. Although server-side JavaScript exists, it is outside the scope of this book.

Adding JavaScript to Your Document

You can add JavaScript to your page in three ways:

- Embed the JavaScript in the page.
- Place the JavaScript in the document head.
- Link to JavaScript stored in another file.

TIP

The options for placing JavaScript closely resemble the options for placing Style Sheets, discussed in Chapter 5.

Table 11.1 lists and describes the HTML tags and attributes you use to add a JavaScript script.

TABLE 11.1: JAVASCRIPT TAGS AND ATTRIBUTES	
Tag/Attribute	**Description**
`<SCRIPT>`	Identifies the script section in the document.
`LANGUAGE="JavaScript"`	Specifies the scripting language. This attribute is deprecated but often used.
`TYPE="text/javascript"`	Provides the script MIME type.
`SRC="..."`	Optionally specifies the location of an external script.
`<NOSCRIPT>`	Provides content for nonscript-capable browsers.
`<!-- //-->`	Comment tags hide the contents of the script from non-script-capable browsers.

Embedding JavaScript

If you're adding a fairly short JavaScript script, your best bet is to embed it in the HTML document, in the code that the JavaScript affects. For example, you can embed a JavaScript script that adds the current date to your document because this particular script is only a few lines long.

PART

III

Moving Beyond
Pure HTML

Embedding works like this: When visitors open your page, their browser "reads" your HTML source document line by line. If your HTML code includes JavaScript within the document body, the browser performs the actions as it reads the page. For example, if the <BODY> tag includes a JavaScript script, the first task the browser completes is running the script. Or, if you include a JavaScript script in the first actual text of the document, the browser runs the script as soon as it gets to the text.

Let's embed a JavaScript script that prints the current time and date as the page loads. The JavaScript statement—in this case, the whole script—is `document .write(Date())`. Here are the steps:

1. Start with the following HTML code:

```
<!DOCTYPE HTML PUBLIC "-//W3C//DTD HTML 4.0//EN">
<HTML>
<HEAD>
<TITLE>The Date Page</TITLE>
</HEAD>
<BODY>
<H1>Welcome!</H1>
</BODY>
</HTML>
```

2. Add an introductory sentence, like this:

```
<!DOCTYPE HTML PUBLIC "-//W3C//DTD HTML 4.0//EN">
<HTML>
<HEAD>
<TITLE>The Date Page</TITLE>
</HEAD>
<BODY>
<H1>Welcome!</H1>
<P>Today's date is:
</P>
</BODY>
</HTML>
```

3. Add <SCRIPT> tags where you want the script:

```
<BODY>
<H1>Welcome!</H1>
```

```
<P>Today's date is:
<SCRIPT>

</SCRIPT>
</P>
```

4. Add the TYPE= attribute to specify the kind of script:

```
<BODY>
<H1>Welcome!</H1>
<P>Today's date is:
<SCRIPT TYPE="text/javascript">

</SCRIPT>
</P>
```

5. Add comment tags to hide the script from browsers that do not recognize scripting. Include the standard HTML comment tags (<!-- and -->), and preface the closing HTML comment tag with a // to hide the comment from the JavaScript interpreter. The complete comment tag looks like this:

```
<BODY>
<H1>Welcome!</H1>
<P>Today's date is:
<SCRIPT TYPE="text/javascript">
<!--

// -->
</SCRIPT>
</P>
```

6. Add the actual JavaScript statement:

```
<SCRIPT TYPE="text/javascript">
<!--
document.write(Date());
// -->
</SCRIPT>
```

That's it! The resulting page looks like this:

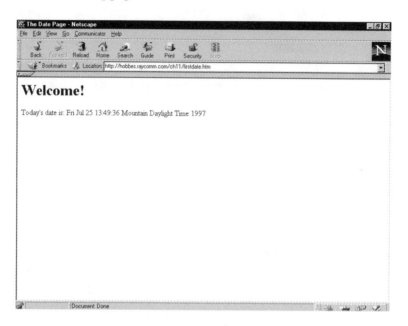

Using this method, the initial "Today's date is" text appears in all browsers, regardless of whether they support JavaScript. Browsers that don't support JavaScript display Today's Date Is and a blank. To hide the script from browsers that don't support JavaScript, simply replace the JavaScript statement with the following statement. In this way, visitors will either see it or not, but they won't see a lead-in with an unfulfilled promise. You get the same effect in JavaScript-capable browsers and nothing at all in non-JavaScript browsers.

```
<SCRIPT TYPE="text/javascript">
<!--
document.write("Today's date is: " + Date());
// -->
</SCRIPT>
```

You are not restricted to a single JavaScript statement, and you can embed several statements through the page source. These additional statements display information about the visitor's browser in the document:

```
<!DOCTYPE HTML PUBLIC "-//W3C//DTD HTML 4.0//EN">
<HTML>
<HEAD>
<TITLE>The Date Page</TITLE>
```

```
</HEAD>
<BODY>
<H1>Welcome!</H1>
<P>
<SCRIPT TYPE="text/javascript">
<!-
document.write("Today's date is: " + Date());
// ->
</SCRIPT>
</P>
<P>
<SCRIPT TYPE="text/javascript">
<!--
document.write("You appear to be using " + navigator.appName + " version " +
   navigator.appVersion + ".")
// -->
</SCRIPT></P>

</BODY>
</HTML>
```

In this script as well, the JavaScript is interpreted line by line as it appears in the HTML source. The resulting page look like this:

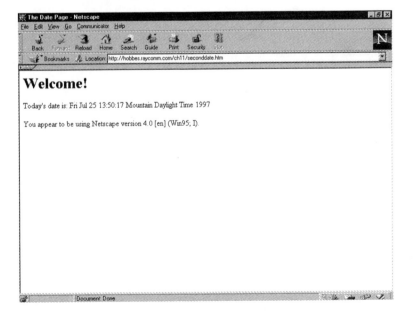

PART

III

Moving Beyond
Pure HTML

Embedding is a great way to start adding JavaScript to your page. You can use this technique alone or combine it with others.

Adding a JavaScript Block in the *<HEAD>*

If you repeatedly use JavaScript within documents, consider placing it in the document <HEAD> tag. Collecting individual statements together in one place creates a function; creating functions in the <HEAD> tag is convenient and easy to troubleshoot.

In the following examples, we'll show you how to move the JavaScript statements in the preceding example from the body of the document into the document head. Here's the code to start with:

```
<!DOCTYPE HTML PUBLIC "-//W3C//DTD HTML 4.0//EN">
<HTML>
<HEAD>
<TITLE>The Date Page</TITLE>
</HEAD>
<BODY>
<H1>Welcome!</H1>
<P>
<SCRIPT TYPE="text/javascript">
<!--
document.write("Today's date is: " + Date());
// -->
</SCRIPT>
</P>
<P>
<SCRIPT TYPE="text/javascript">
<!--
document.write("You appear to be using " + navigator.appName + " version " +
    navigator.appVersion + ".")
// -->
</SCRIPT></P>

</BODY>
</HTML>
```

This HTML document includes two JavaScript sections. One displays the current date and time, and the other displays the name and version number of the visitor's browser. You include the command in the document <HEAD> tag and then run the function from the document body. Here are the steps:

1. Add the script tags to the document <HEAD>, like this:

```
<HEAD>
<TITLE>The Date Page</TITLE>
<SCRIPT>

</SCRIPT>
</HEAD>
```

2. Add the TYPE= attribute to specify that the script is a JavaScript:

```
<HEAD>
<TITLE>The Date Page</TITLE>
<SCRIPT TYPE="text/javascript">

</SCRIPT>
</HEAD>
```

3. Add comment tags (<!-- //-->)to hide the script from other browsers. Don't forget the //!

```
<HEAD>
<TITLE>The Date Page</TITLE>
<SCRIPT TYPE="text/javascript">
<!--

// -->
</SCRIPT>
</HEAD>
```

Remember, we're putting the script in the document head, so it will not display anything in the browser window. You have to place instructions within the document body to do anything with the script.

4. To make the JavaScript statement that displays the date into a function, name it and place it in inside brackets ({ }). In this example, the name is printDate.

```
Add the function name (printDate) and {}.
<SCRIPT TYPE="text/javascript">
<!--
function printDate() {}
```

```
// -->
</SCRIPT>
```

5. Add the JavaScript statement within the brackets. Use what you used within the document body, which was document.write("Today's date is: " + Date();.

```
<SCRIPT TYPE="text/javascript">
<!--
function printDate() {document.write("Today\'s date is: " + Date());}
// -->
</SCRIPT>
```

6. To call (activate or run) the function from the document body, add your <SCRIPT> tags within the <BODY> tags, as shown here:

```
<BODY>
<H1>Welcome!</H1>
<P>
<SCRIPT TYPE="text/javascript">
<!--

// -->
</SCRIPT>
</P>
</BODY>
```

7. Add printDate(), which is the name you gave the function, within the tags.

```
<BODY>
<H1>Welcome!</H1>
<P>
<SCRIPT TYPE="text/javascript">
<!--
printDate()
// -->
</SCRIPT>
</P>
</BODY>
```

The resulting page looks similar to the following:

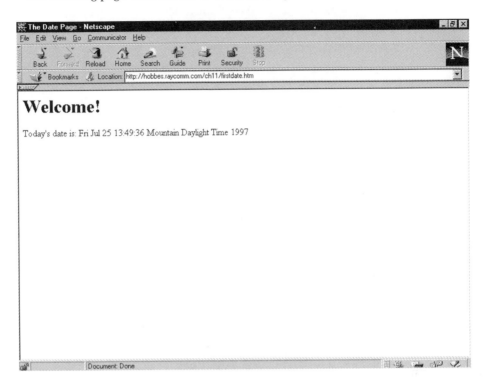

If you separate out the JavaScript into its own section, enclose it with comment marks `<!--` and `//-->`. Not all browsers can interpret JavaScript, and the comment marks instruct these browsers to ignore the JavaScript section. JavaScript-enabled browsers will see past the comment marks and recognize the `<SCRIPT>` tags.

Linking JavaScript

If you plan to use script functions in several documents, consider placing them in a separate file and refer to that file from your document. You can build, test, and store working JavaScript code in one location and use it in several Web pages. You can also share this code with others who can link it into their documents.

The linked document is simply a text file that includes all your variable definitions and functions. You can even copy the functions from the headers of your existing HTML documents if you want. If this document also includes variables and functions that you don't need for the Web page; the browser uses what it needs, as it is called.

To continue with our date example, you can make a `functions.js` document that contains the following text:

```
function printDate() { document.write(Date()) }
```

This linked document does not need any special headings or tags. It simply includes the definitions for the variables and functions. You can then link to the script with the following code from the document <HEAD> (including all the surrounding tags):

```
<HEAD>
<TITLE>The Date Page</TITLE>
<SCRIPT SRC="functions.js" TYPE="text/javascript">
<!--
// -->
</SCRIPT>
</HEAD>
```

Now, by including this reference to your functions document, you can access any functions from any document you create.

You can include as many functions or variable definitions within your functions document as you like. Alternatively, you can reference multiple external scripts by including additional <SCRIPT> tags.

Providing for Older Browsers

As you add JavaScript to your pages, you must accommodate older browsers that cannot interpret JavaScript as well as browsers in which JavaScript is not enabled. If you include a JavaScript script in the <HEAD> tag or if you link the JavaScript from a separate document, you've already provided for older browsers because these don't show up in the document body.

If you embed the JavaScript script, however, you must make sure the script doesn't show up. The best way to accommodate older browsers is to make sure that text dependent on the JavaScript (such as "Today's date is") is part of the JavaScript statement. You might recall from the example that the embedded code looks like this:

```
<SCRIPT TYPE="text/javascript">
<!-
document.write("Today\'s date is: " + Date());
// ->
</SCRIPT>
```

However, if you want to give additional information to nonscript-capable browsers (rather than just hiding information from them), you can also use the <NOSCRIPT> tag and include alternate text. For example, if you have a form that uses JavaScript to validate input, you might add a statement to the top of the form, within a <NOSCRIPT> tag, that warns users of non-JavaScript browsers that their responses won't be validated and that they should be particularly careful to proofread their responses:

```
<H2>Personal Information Form</H2>
<NOSCRIPT>
<P>Please be very careful to proofread your responses. If any information is
incorrect (particularly your e-mail address), we'll be unable to contact
you.</P>
</NOSCRIPT>
Please enter your name and address below:<BR>
```

In this example, the JavaScript-enabled browser displays only the Personal Information Form heading, followed by "Please enter your name and address below"; other browsers will also display the "Please be very careful to proofread your responses. If any information is incorrect (particularly your e-mail address), we'll be unable to contact you."

For a small amount of JavaScript or for JavaScript that isn't essential to the content of your document, using the <NOSCRIPT> tag is a convenient way to deal with both situations. If you have more complex JavaScript applications on your page, you'll need to identify visitors' browsers and automatically direct them to the correct page.

TIP

See Matt's Script Archive on the CD or on the Web at www.worldwidemart .com/scripts/ for server-side means of identifying browsers and redirecting them appropriately.

Adding Event Handlers

JavaScript relies heavily on event handlers, which react to visitor actions by running statements or calling JavaScript functions. Event handlers provide visitors with additional information by reacting to what they're doing on the page—moving their mouse, clicking a button, or selecting options on a form. JavaScript's event handlers react to these events by doing whatever you tell them to do. For example, with the onMouseOver and onMouseOut event handlers, you can change the information in your status bar, flash an alert box, or change an illustration. Figure 11.2 shows an Alert box triggered by an onMouseOver event.

FIGURE 11.2

One of the most common JavaScript event handlers is onMouseOver.

NOTE

JavaScript provides a variety of event handlers that can react to visitor actions. In this chapter, we discuss only a couple of them, but the Master's Reference explains all of them.

Using *onMouseOver* and *onMouseOut* Events

You commonly use an onMouseOver event with anchor tags (<A>) to provide additional information about the link. The onMouseOut event, then, generally undoes what the onMouseOver event does.

Using these event handlers, you can, among other things, implement timed status bar events, swap images, and alert visitors. We'll show you how in the next few sections. First, though, let's look at how to add the onMouseOver and onMouseOut event handlers.

TIP

Unfortunately, neither Internet Explorer 3 or earlier, or Netscape Navigator 2 or earlier recognize the onMouseOut event. If your visitors use these browsers, consider using a separate function to clear the status bar, as described below.

Let's now add the onMouseOver and onMouseOut event handlers to display a new message in the status bar and then remove it. This is handy for displaying information in the status bar that is more descriptive than the URL that the browser automatically displays there. Here are the steps:

1. Start with an HTML document that includes a link, like this:

```
<!DOCTYPE HTML PUBLIC "-//W3C//DTD HTML 4.0//EN">
<HTML>
<HEAD>
<TITLE>Status Bar</TITLE>
</HEAD>
<BODY>
<H1>Welcome!</H1>
<A HREF="http://www.raycomm.com/">
Visit the RayComm, Inc., site.</A>
<P>
</BODY>
</HTML>
```

2. Add the onMouseOver event handler to the <A> tag:

```
<A HREF="http://www.raycomm.com/" onMouseOver=" ">
Visit the RayComm, Inc., site.</A>
```

3. Add window.status= to the event handler. The window.status= property specifies what appears in the status bar.

```
<A HREF="http://www.raycomm.com/" onMouseOver="window.status= ">
Visit the RayComm, Inc., site.</A>
```

4. Add the text that will appear in the status bar, enclosed in single quotes (''). You use single quotes because the window status statement itself is enclosed in double-quotes, and you must nest unlike quotes within each other.

```
<A HREF="http://www.raycomm.com/" onMouseOver="window.status='Check us
out!' ">
Visit the RayComm, Inc., site.</A>
```

5. Add a semicolon (to indicate the end of the statement), and add `return true` to the end (just before the closing quotes). This essentially tells the JavaScript interpreter that the function is complete and to do it.

```
<A HREF="http://www.raycomm.com/"
onMouseOver="window.status='Check us out!'; return true">
Visit the RayComm, Inc., site.</A>
```

If you try this, you'll see that the "Check us out!" statement appears in the browser status bar after you move the cursor over the link. The statement stays in the status bar, which probably isn't what you want.

To restore the status bar after the cursor moves away from the link, simply add the `onMouseOut` event handler, like this:

```
<A HREF="http://www.raycomm.com/"
onMouseOver="window.status='Check us out!'; return true"
onMouseOut="window.status=''; return true">
Visit the RayComm, Inc., site.</A>
```

Using Timed Status Bar Text Events

JavaScript includes a `timer` method that allows you to set up timed events. For example, you can use it in conjunction with the `onMouseOver` event handler to display the status bar text for a period of time and then clear it. Although the timer is a bit more complicated than the `onMouseOut` event handler, it is more universal. It keeps the status bar text you set from remaining in the status bar, even with older browsers. More browsers will understand the `timer` method than will understand the `onMouseOut` event handler.

In general, the function we need to clear the status bar text should do two things:

- Set the status bar text to a specific text string.

- Wait for a specified time and then clear the status bar again.

Because this function is slightly more involved than resetting the status bar onMouseOver event, we create the script in the document head, as shown earlier in this chapter. Here's how:

1. In an HTML document, add the <SCRIPT> and comment tags in the document head:

```
<!DOCTYPE HTML PUBLIC "-//W3C//DTD HTML 4.0//EN">
<HTML>
<HEAD>
<TITLE>Status Bar</TITLE>
<SCRIPT TYPE="text/javascript">
<!--

// -->
</SCRIPT>
</HEAD>
<BODY>
<H1>Welcome!</H1>
<A HREF="http://www.raycomm.com/">
Visit the RayComm, Inc., site.</A>
<P>
</BODY>
</HTML>
```

2. Name the function SalesPitch and add the needed brackets:

```
<SCRIPT>
<!--
function SalesPitch() {  }
//-->
</SCRIPT>
```

3. Add the window.status statement to set the status bar. The return true won't strictly be needed, but it also won't hurt anything and might be useful later.

```
<SCRIPT>
<!--
function SalesPitch() {
    window.status="Check us out!"; return true;
}
//-->
</SCRIPT>
```

4. Add the new method, `setTimeout`. Within the parenthesis, the first parameter sets the window status to null (''), and the second specifies to wait 3000 milliseconds (3 seconds). The `return true` is, in this case, needed to tell the JavaScript interpreter that it's done.

```
<SCRIPT>
<!--
function SalesPitch() {
    window.status="Check us out!";
    setTimeout("window.status=''",3000); return true;
}
//-->
</SCRIPT>
```

That's it! With this SalesPitch script in the document header, you need only call the script from the link in the document with an `onMouseOver` statement, as shown here.

```
<A HREF="http://www.raycomm.com/" onMouseOver="SalesPitch(); return true">
```

The `return true` business at the end serves only to tell the JavaScript interpreter that the statement is done and the interpreter should act on it. In this example, the function displays the required text in the status bar, waits 3 seconds, and then clears the status bar.

NOTE

In most of these examples, we show fairly generic JavaScript. If you are using objects, methods, properties, or event handlers from early versions of JavaScript, you don't need to add the version to the JavaScript language attribute. But, if you are using a later version with expanded capabilities, such as `onMouseOut`, and functions are defined in the document, include the number within the `<SCRIPT>` tags, as in `LANGUAGE="JavaScript1.2."`

TIP

Add comments to your JavaScript to track what the script does. This is useful for future reference and helpful to people with whom you share your JavaScript functions. Add your name and the name of your JavaScript to the document source.

Adding a Little Excitement to the Page Load

Just as events can respond to a visitor's mouse actions, events can occur when the page loads or unloads. However, anything time consuming (such as playing a sound) or intrusive (such as displaying a welcome alert) can irritate visitors far more than impressing them with your technical skills.

We suggest that you perform actions with the onLoad or onUnload events only if visitors will expect it in the context of the page or for other reasons.

See Chapter 12 for more information about adding sounds.

Swapping Images

You can use the onMouseOver and onMouseOut event handlers to change linked images when the mouse cursor moves over them.

WARNING

Unfortunately, this technique works only with Netscape Navigator 3 or later and Internet Explorer 4 or later. Older browsers don't recognize images as objects.

To change an image when the mouse moves over it, you need an anchor tag (<A HREF="...">) and two versions of the image—one is the standard presentation, and the other is the highlighted presentation. When the page initially loads, the standard image is visible. Then, when the mouse moves over the image, the highlighted image replaces the standard image. Finally, when the mouse cursor moves away again, the images change back. Conceptually, the process is the same as changing the status bar text in the preceding example; however, instead of changing the status bar, you swap images.

To set up images to swap, you first need a pair of images that are precisely the same size but visually different.

TIP

You'll find sample images in the examples/ch11 folder on the Companion CD.

Next, you need a link using an image in your document. The image tag must also have a NAME= attribute so that JavaScript can identify and refer to it. We'll use the following sample document:

```
<!DOCTYPE HTML PUBLIC "-//W3C//DTD HTML 4.0//EN">
<HTML>
<HEAD>
<TITLE>Image Swap</TITLE>
</HEAD>
<BODY BGCOLOR="FFFFFF" TEXT="000000" LINK="0000FF" VLINK="800080"
ALINK="FF0000">
<CENTER>
<A HREF="http://www.raycomm.com/"><IMG SRC="image1.gif" WIDTH="50"
HEIGHT="10" BORDER="0" NAME="catbtn"></A>
</CENTER>
</BODY>
</HTML>
```

Two images, cleverly titled image1.gif and image2.gif, are available to swap within the image tag, which is called catbtn. To identify the image, you refer to it by name (catbtn) and src, which is a property of the catbtn image tag. For example, to change the image (but not change it back), you can use a statement such as the following

```
onMouseOver="catbtn.src='image2.gif'; return true"
```

In the context of the <IMG> tag, the onMouseOver statement looks like this:

```
<A HREF="http://www.raycomm.com/" onMouseOver="catbtn.src='image2.gif';
return true">
<IMG SRC="image1.gif" WIDTH="50" HEIGHT="10" BORDER="0" NAME="catbtn"></A>
```

The catbtn.src changes the source property of the catbtn object to image2.gif; it had previously been set to image1.gif.

Similarly, to change the image back when the cursor moves away, use an onMouseOut statement with the opposite image setting, as shown here:

```
<A HREF="http://www.raycomm.com/" onMouseOver="catbtn.src='image2.gif';
return true" onMouseOut="catbtn.src='image1.gif'; return true">
<IMG SRC="image1.gif" WIDTH="50" HEIGHT="10" BORDER="0" NAME="catbtn"></A>
```

For a series of images, you use a series of if statements in a function to make the changes. Using if statements keeps your HTML code easier to read and makes it easier to change your script later. You can easily add more statements to reshuffle images in different contexts by using a function like this:

```
function switcher (place) {
```

```
if (place==1) document.catbtn.src="image2.gif";
if (place==2) document.catbtn.src="image1.gif"; }
```

The if statements check for the value of place and change the image accordingly. You call this function from the body of your document with code, as shown below. Instead of placing the full change function in the <A> tag, you place switcher() in the attribute value.

```
<A HREF="http://www.raycomm.com/">
<IMG SRC="image1.gif" ALIGN="" WIDTH="50" HEIGHT="10" BORDER="0"
onMouseOver="switcher(1)" ALT="" NAME="catbtn" onMouseOut="switcher(2)">
</A>
```

If your visitors use the newest versions of Netscape Navigator or Internet Explorer and you want to do more—such as change the image and change the status bar—you can use a switch statement, as shown here:

```
function switcher (place) {
switch (place) {
   case(1): document.catbtn.src="image2.gif";
      window.status="Second Image";
      break;
   case(2): document.catbtn.src="image1.gif";
      window.status="First Image";
      break; }}
```

Using this technique, you can list all the options. Like the if statements above, the switch statement lists each option and the action to take. In a switch statement, each option is a case.

In this example, the first line calls the function and includes the number for the variable *place*. You use *place* in the switch statement, which has two cases. If *place* is equal to one, use case(1). Therefore, case(1) sets the source property for the image named catbtn (catbtn.src) to image2.gif. When you place an image element, you insert an HTML tag just as you do for the IF statement:

```
<A HREF="http://www.raycomm.com/">
<IMG SRC="image1.gif" ALIGN="" WIDTH="50" HEIGHT="10" BORDER="0"
onMouseOver="switcher(1)" ALT="" NAME="catbtn" onMouseOut="switcher(2)">
</A>
```

You may have noticed that the switch from the if statement switcher function to the case statement switcher function requires no changes within your HTML code. When you place JavaScript functions in the document head, you can make changes without editing all the tags in your code.

PART

III

Moving Beyond
Pure HTML

Using *onClick* and *onChange* Event Handlers

In addition to onMouseOver and onMouseOut event handlers, you can use onClick and onChange event handlers, which are activated when visitors click an object or a button or change a form field. Including these event handlers is similar to using the onMouseOver and onMouseOut event handlers. You can use the onChange or the onClick event handler to set link destinations in forms, among other things.

Alerting Visitors with *onClick*

A handy use for the onClick event is an alert box (see Figure 11.3), which is a small dialog box that contains a message and an OK button. For example, an alert could be an expanded note about the object, such as "Come to this page for more news on this year's programs!"

FIGURE 11.3

Alert boxes are a handy way to give visitors information.

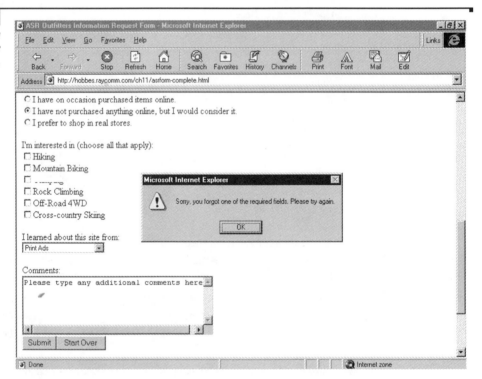

At its simplest, you can combine an event handler (to start the process) with an alert, like this:

```
<IMG SRC="infolink.jpg" onClick="alert('Visit RayComm!'); return true">
```

Visitors see the accompanying dialog box and must click OK to proceed. Alerts can be quite irritating, however, so use them only in conjunction with buttons or other actions so that visitors can make a conscious choice. For example, as shown in Figure 11.3, you can combine the alert with form validation information and base the alert pop-up on the visitor's form responses.

Setting Link Destinations in Forms

One of the handiest JavaScript functions is setting link destinations in forms to direct visitors to information based on their selections in the form. For example, if a form contains a Course Offered selection list, visitors can select courses that interest them, and you can programmatically set the destination of a jump to meet the needs of the selections. You can also use JavaScript to set destinations so that when your visitors click buttons or perform other actions on the page, the script opens new pages, just as a traditional link would. This technique can add visual interest to your pages as well as letting you interactively produce new pages for your visitors.

Minimally, to set destinations and activate links, use the onClick event handler, as shown here.

```
<FORM><INPUT TYPE="radio" NAME="lesson" VALUE="Lesson 1" CHECKED
onClick="self.location='lesson1.htm'">Lesson 1: Getting Started<BR></FORM>
```

The self.location='someurl.htm' entry opens the file someurl.htm in the same window when a visitor clicks the radio button. If you want the document to open in a separate window, the process is similar. For example, to open lesson1.htm in another frame, called main, you can use the following:

```
<INPUT TYPE="radio" NAME="lesson" VALUE="Lesson 1" CHECKED onClick="
parent.main.location='lesson1.htm'"> Lesson 1: Getting Started
```

NOTE

The parent.main.location object name refers to the parent document (in this example, that would be the frameset document, then the main object [frame] within it, then the location property of the frame).

PART

III

Moving Beyond
Pure HTML

A single jump can also lead to a variable destination—the document opened depends on the visitor's selection from a list. For example, your document contains catalog information, such as pictures, product descriptions, and prices. A visitor clicks a category to open the correct page of your catalog. Visitors might also select activities from a list such as this.

```
<FORM>
<SELECT NAME="Activity" onChange="setLink(this.selectedIndex)">
   <OPTION>Hiking
   <OPTION>Camping
   <OPTION SELECTED>Mountain
   <OPTION>Sailing
   <OPTION>Winter
</SELECT>
</FORM>
```

The onChange event handler passes information to a function called setLink. The selectedIndex property is the position in the list (starting with zero!) of the current selection in the list. So, this.selectedIndex is the numeric value that represents the position in the current list of the value selected.

A relatively simple function setLink, located in the document head, assigns the final URL to the page properties and loads the new URL:

```
<SCRIPT>
function setLink(num) {
   if (num == 0) {self.location="hiking.html"}
   if (num == 1) {self.location="camping.html"}
   if (num == 2) {self.location="mountain.html"}
   if (num == 3) {self.location="sailing.html"}
   if (num == 4) {self.location="winter.html"} }
</SCRIPT>
```

With this type of scripting, it's easier to figure out what's going on, it's easier to make changes later, and it's easier to accommodate unique, nonsequential names, such as newmountainbikes.html or augustactivities.html.

Using the *onSubmit* Event Handler

One of the most common uses for the onSubmit event handler is to validate form input. You can verify that visitors fill in required fields, that they make required selections, or that they fill in an appropriate combination of fields. Suppose you provide a form that lets visitors purchase a product—say, T-shirts. You can use JavaScript to verify that visitors include their mailing address, provide a credit card number, and specify a color. If you lack any of this input from visitors, you won't be able to complete the order.

The following examples, based on the ASR Outfitters general information form, show a couple of approaches to form validation. These example assume a form with NAME="survey". If your form is named differently, please adjust accordingly. You can also substitute form[0] for the name of the first form within your page.

You can use the following generic script to loop through your form and check for forgotten or omitted values:

```
<script language="JavaScript">
<!--
function checkOut() {
for (x=0; x<document.survey.elements.length; x++){
   if (document.survey.elements[x].value == "") {
       alert("Sorry, you forgot one of the required fields. Please
try again.")
       break;      }
       }
       return false;
    }
//-->
</script>
```

To check your form, use onSubmit="checkout(this.form) in your <FORM> tag. The script looks through each of the fields in your form to see if any are completely empty and then, if any are empty, flashes an alert with the text:

```
Sorry, you forgot one of the required fields. Please try again.
```

It then exits.

If some fields need to be filled and some don't or if you need to check specific values, you can do so. For example to ensure that the first name field (called firstname) is filled out and not too short (fewer than two characters), add the following IF statement to the script:

```
if (document.survey.firstname.value.length <= 2){
   alert("Please enter your first name.")
   return false}
```

PART

III

Moving Beyond
Pure HTML

The complete script would then look like this:

```
<script language="JavaScript">
<!--
function checkOut() {
for (x=0; x<document.survey.elements.length; x++){
   if (document.survey.elements[x].value == "") {
       alert("Sorry, you forgot one of the required fields. Please try
again.")
       break;      }
       }
       return false;
if (document.survey.firstname.value.length <= 2){
   alert("Please enter your full first name.")
   return false}
   }
//-->
</script>
```

You can continue adding other conditions in the same way.

One of the more complex validation problems involves e-mail addresses. Although more complex scripts are available, you'll probably find that a basic check to ensure that the address includes something, an @ sign, and something else will suffice:

```
<script language="JavaScript">
<!--
function checkOut() {
for (x=0; x<document.survey.elements.length; x++){
   if (document.survey.elements[x].value == "") {
       alert("Sorry, you forgot one of the required fields. Please try
again.")
       break;      }
       }
       return false;
if (document.survey.firstname.value.length <= 2){
   alert("Please enter your full first name.")
   return false}
if (document.survey.emailaddr.value.indexOf('@') == -1 ) {
   alert("Please correct your email address. It should look like
you@domain.com")
   return false}
   }
```

```
//-->
</script>
```

This addition verifies that the address contains an @ and that something after the @ exists. If you need more comprehensive validation, check out the scripts at the following Netscape site:

`developer.netscape.com/library/examples/javascript/formval/overview.html.`

Tracking Visitors Using Cookies

Cookies are little JavaScript programs that you can use to store information about visitors to your site. The JavaScript script leaves a cookie on a visitor's computer; when a visitor revisits your site, you can read the information and act on it. For example, if visitors fill out a form with their name the first time they visit a site, they might be greeted by name on the second visit.

Although the security risk to visitors is minimal, many people are (understandably) a little sensitive about having information stored about them and read by other computers. For that reason, browsers now offer visitors a lot of control over how cookies are handled. Early versions of Netscape Navigator simply accepted all cookies. Now, most browsers that recognize cookies warn visitors when a cookie is created and give visitors the option to accept or reject individual cookies.

Either way, the cookie information is not public property; the cookie stores information for you only, and not for public broadcast. It's like having a locker at the gym. Your locker may be in a room with other people's lockers, but only you have the key.

Cookies are not secret passageways into a visitor's computer, but rather a bookmark to identify where you and the visitor were in your adventure together. Creating a cookie is actually a bit of a cooperative venture in that the visitor answers prompts on the page and you save the information in a cookie.

Two main kinds of cookies exist:

- Session cookies, which endure only as long as a visitor is at a page
- Persistent cookies, which endure until the expiration date you set

Session Cookies

Suppose you want to keep some information about a visitor's browsing session, such as the pages browsed or the products purchased. You can do so using *session cookies*. The JavaScript script not only records the visitor's session information, but also sends a message to the visitor when he or she arrives at and exits your site.

NOTE

This example shows some of the capabilities and power of cookies. It's also likely to irritate many visitors. Even if they know that cookies can be set and used, they likely don't want to be reminded of it overtly.

To implement session cookies, first create an empty cookie when the page loads. Start with a functional HTML document, such as the following:

```
<!DOCTYPE HTML PUBLIC "-//W3C//DTD HTML 3.2//EN">
<HTML>
<HEAD>
<TITLE>ASR Outfitters Cookie Form</TITLE>
</HEAD>
Cookie Bearing Document
</BODY>
</HTML>
```

Now, follow these steps:

1. Add a function to the document <HEAD> that sets the document cookie to the local time and date:

```
<SCRIPT>
<!--
function homeMadeCookies () {
    var gotHere = new Date();
    document.cookie = gotHere.toLocaleString()}
// -->
</SCRIPT>
```

2. Initialize the cookie from the onLoad event handler, like this:

```
<BODY onLoad="homeMadeCookies()">
```

The onLoad event handler starts the function called homeMadeCookies, which creates and places a value into the variable *gotHere*. From that information, the next line converts the GMT time to local time and stores that in document.cookie.

By setting up a second function, you can display a message when the visitor leaves. The fareWell function looks like this:

```
fareWell () {
    var timedVisit = new Date();
    var tempTime = timedVisit.toLocaleString();
    alert("You got here at: " + document.cookie + " and now it's: " +
tempTime); }
```

Then, by adding an onUnload event handler to the <BODY> tag, you can display the farewell message:

```
<BODY onLoad="homeMadeCookies()" onUnload="fareWell()">
```

The fareWell entry uses an alert to display a brief—cookie-based—message thanking the visitor, as shown here:

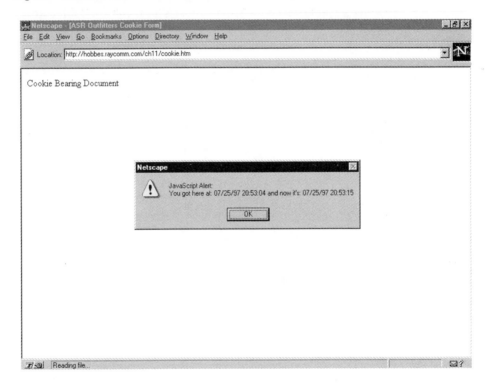

Persistent Cookies

You can also store information in cookies for a period of time. You use *persistent cookies* when you want to store information and use it in the future. For example, if a visitor fills out a form that includes his or her name and other personal information, you'd want to keep that information and use it when the visitor visits in the future.

Here are some facts you should know about persistent cookies:

- A browser retains a limited number of cookies. Netscape Navigator retains 300 cookies. Older cookies are discarded to make room for new ones.

- A cookie cannot be more than 4Kb.

- You can have only 20 cookies per domain. If you're working from a large ISP, you might not be able to set cookies for all visitors.

These restrictions may not seem limiting at first, but they become so when the demand for feedback increases.

Unlike session cookies, persistent cookies need an expiration date. After the cookie expires, a former visitor is treated as a new visitor.

More JavaScript Cookie Information

Bill Dortch of hIdaho Design (bdortch@hidaho.com) has created some outstanding scripts to manage cookies, and they are on the Companion CD in the examples/ch11 folder. See cookie.txt for the code to build and read cookies. Cookies.htm is a working version of the code.

We strongly recommend using Bill's scripts, rather than reinventing the wheel and developing your own.

Where to Go from Here

Whew! In this chapter, we introduced you to JavaScript and showed you some of the most basic (and useful!) JavaScript functions. As you can see, JavaScript offers a variety of useful applications and can help you create cutting-edge HTML documents.

From here, you can wander to several chapters. Here's what we recommend:

- Visit Chapter 6 to find out more about servers.

- See Chapter 12 to learn about including multimedia in your HTML documents.

- See Chapter 21 to learn to balance flashy elements with site usability.

Chapter

12

Including
Multimedia

Including Multimedia

In recent years, Web surfers have seen text-only pages transform into pages that bounce, shimmy, sing, and gyrate. Developers of public sites, in particular, are using flair and excitement in an effort to attract visitors and to keep them coming back again and again. Flashy elements don't always attract, however. Some visitors find them such a distraction that they don't browse the site, nor do they return to it. The key is to use glitz wisely and to carefully weigh its benefits and liabilities.

In this chapter, we'll show you how to include special effects—animated GIFs, sounds, videos, applets, and ActiveX controls—collectively known as multimedia. (We're defining multimedia as anything you can include in a Web page other than basic HTML code and static images.) We'll look at the pros and cons of various elements and discuss how to include them effectively, if you do choose to include them.

In the first part of this chapter, we'll show you how to include some elements that are HTML standard compliant and some that are not. Both types are compatible with most of the newer browsers on the market. Toward the end of the chapter, we'll show you how to include multimedia as designated by the HTML 4 specification. At the time of writing, these tags and attributes are not (yet!) widely supported, but you'll find that using them is very efficient.

TIP

The principles for including these effects apply to other elements you might discover. For example, if the engineers at your company want to publish their AutoCAD files on your corporate intranet, you can include them in Web pages, following the principles outlined in the "Adding Multimedia Using HTML 4" section in this chapter.

Deciding to Include Multimedia

Images, sounds, and video can make your pages come alive. And, done right, multimedia can give Web pages that "up with technology" look and feel. Before running off to gather multimedia elements, though, take heed. Multimedia poses several challenges, both for visitors and for the developer.

The Challenges for Visitors

Multimedia can bring your pages to a virtual halt as visitors sit and wait (and wait!) for the effects to download. Although some multimedia effects, such as an animated GIF image, can be as small as 2Kb, other effects, such as video, can easily grow to 5MB or more.

In addition, some multimedia effects—such as video, Shockwave animations, VRML (Virtual Reality Markup Language), and some sound files—require plug-ins (programs that visitors use to view effects that their browser(s) don't support). For example, if you include an MPEG movie file, visitors need the plug-in to view the effect.

QUICK LOOKUP

Shockwave animation is a special kind of animation file using technology developed by Macromedia.

Virtual Reality Markup Language provides simulated 3-D Web-browsing experiences.

What's really frustrating is that visitors must download and install a separate plug-in for each multimedia effect and for each company that provides the effect. For example, if you include an Envoy document, an IconAuthor multimedia presentation, and Corel CMX graphics in a Web page (you wouldn't do this, we hope), visitors would have to download and install three plug-ins just to see the multimedia you include. Will visitors take the time to do this? No way.

Visitors using Internet Explorer 3 or newer have it somewhat easier because Internet Explorer downloads plug-ins automatically after a visitor approves the installation. Visitors do still have to wait, wait, and wait to view the effect. Visitors using any version of Netscape Navigator, however, click to view the effect and then (in one vividly memorable example):

1. Are informed that they don't have the right plug-in.
2. Are taken to the Netscape Web page to get it.
3. Must click to download the plug-in.
4. Must fill out a form with personal information (name, address, type of business).
5. Submit the form.
6. Are taken back to the original site (different page).
7. Choose to download the plug-in.
8. Specify where it should be saved.
9. Wait for it to download (much longer than for Internet Explorer).
10. Browse to the downloaded file on the local hard drive.
11. Double-click the installation program to run it.
12. Accept the license agreement.
13. Approve the installation location.
14. Wait for the installation to finish.
15. Exit Netscape Navigator.
16. Restart Netscape Navigator.
17. Browse back to the original site.
18. View the effect (finally).

Eighteen steps and many minutes later, Netscape Navigator users get to see the multimedia effect. It wasn't worth it, by the way.

The Challenges for Developers

In addition to these resounding indictments of carefree multimedia use in Web pages, it gets worse. For you, the developer, obtaining relevant and useful multimedia objects is often difficult. Your first option is to create the effects yourself, which requires both raw materials (such as photographs, sounds, and video clips) and often special software that you must both purchase and learn to use. And, even if you're familiar with the software, developing effective multimedia objects can be especially time-consuming.

You can also browse the Web for multimedia elements. This is a less expensive and less time consuming option, but you may not find exactly what you want. Although tons of multimedia elements are available on the Web, they're likely to be inappropriate or not in the public domain.

TIP

You'll find some sound and graphics libraries as well as other multimedia files and development software on the Companion CD. Feel free to experiment with and use these in your Web pages.

Your goal is to carefully consider the advantages and disadvantages of each multimedia element *before* you include it. Start by asking these questions:

- Does the multimedia element add content that I cannot otherwise provide?
- Does the multimedia element clearly enhance or complement content?
- Do my visitors have browsers that support these elements?
- Do my visitors have fast Internet connections?
- Are my visitors likely to have the appropriate plug-ins or to have the time, inclination, and technical wherewithal to get and install them?
- Do I have the time and resources to develop or find multimedia elements?

If you answer yes to some or all these questions and you opt to include multimedia, the rest of this chapter is for you.

NOTE

Throughout this chapter, we point out that you can find multimedia elements on the Web. Remember, however, that most of what you find is not available for public use. Before you take a file and use it as your own, be sure that it's clearly labeled "for public use." If it's not, you can assume that it's not for you to take and use.

Considering Multimedia Usability

Before you commit to fully multimedia enhanced pages—or even to a single animated GIF on your home page—consider carefully what including multimedia will do to your site's usability. *Web Site Usability: A Designer's Guide*, by Spool et al., published by User Interface Engineering (www.uie.com), presents some alarming findings about the usability of Web pages that incorporate multimedia elements.

These authors conclude that "animation makes it considerably harder for users ..." and support that finding with observational research in which Web site visitors tried to scroll the page to move the animation out of sight, and, when that failed, they used their hands to cover up the distracting effects.

Although some sites were more problematic than others, and other studies show that animations are more effective than static images in advertisements, your site might well not benefit from any of these effects.

Using Animated GIFs

Perhaps the easiest multimedia element to include is an animated GIF, which is a file that, more or less, includes a bunch of images stacked together to give the illusion of movement. Animated GIFs are similar to those little cartoon booklets you had as a kid. When you quickly whirred through the pages, the cartoon seemed to move. Of course, the illusion of movement was nothing more than each individual cartoon drawing being slightly different. Animated GIFs work the same way.

The uses for animated GIFs vary considerably, from flashing commercial messages to elaborate mini-movies to small bullets or arrows that appear to grow or move. A common use is to help attract visitors' attention to a specific element, as shown in Figure 12.1.

If you're interested in developing your own animated GIFs, we recommend software such as Microsoft's Gif Animator for Windows (download it from www.microsoft.com and use it for free) or GifBuilder for the Macintosh. These packages provide the tools to combine individual images into an animated GIF. You can develop individual images with with any software that can creat GIF images, including Photoshop and PaintShop Pro. If you want to see what's available on the Web, go to www.yahoo.com or www.altavista.digital.com and search on gif animation. You will find lots of information, software, and software reviews.

FIGURE 12.1

*The ball beside
New! rolls toward
the item.*

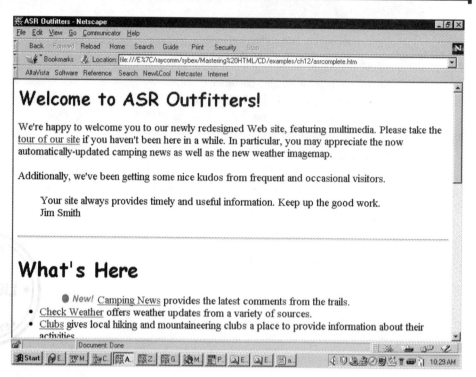

You'll find some sample animated GIFs on the Companion CD.

Animating Your Own GIFS

Developing an animated GIF often takes more time and effort than you expect. The process can become tedious, especially if you are working with longer animations or animations in which the illusion of smooth motion is needed (rather than simply presenting discrete panes of information, as in ad banners).

The first step is to generate the individual images that will eventually be each panel within the animated GIF. For a basic animated bullet—that appears to move from left to right—you might create a set of images like those shown here.

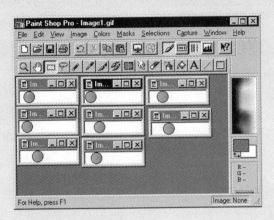

The easiest way to get smooth animation is to create a single image, select the object that changes or moves, move it into each successive position, and then save the image. In this example, after creating the small ball, we selected the ball, moved it two pixels to the right, saved the image, moved it again, and so forth. The more pixels between images, the jerkier the motion; the fewer pixels between images, the smoother the motion.

After you create the images, use a GIF animation program, such as Microsoft GIF Animator, shown here, to sequence the images and to set animation properties, such as how often to loop through the animation and how to redraw the images as the animation proceeds.

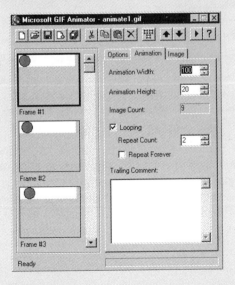

After you insert each of the frames and preview the image to your satisfaction, simply save it as a GIF.

PART

III

Moving Beyond
Pure HTML

Table 12.1 lists and describes the tags and attributes you use to include animated GIFs in your HTML documents. You can treat animated GIFs just like any other images. (See Chapter 7 for more information.)

TABLE 12.1: ANIMATED GIF TAGS AND ATTRIBUTES

Tag /Attribute	Description
<IMG>	Inserts an image in an HTML document.
SRC="..."	Specifies the location of the image file.
ALT="..."	Provides alternate text for visitors who don't view the image.

To include an animated GIF in your Web page, follow these steps:

1. Find or create an appropriate animated GIF image.

2. Place the image in your HTML document, with the regular image tags. You might have code like the following:

```
<IMG SRC="animate2.gif" WIDTH="99" HEIGHT="16" BORDER="0" ALT="*">
<A HREF="camping.html">Camping News</A> provides the latest comments
from the trails. <BR>
```

3. Enjoy the experience!

Testing Multimedia

If you're testing your pages either locally or over a direct Internet connection—say, through your network at the office, connected to the Internet with a dedicated line— take the time to test them with the slowest dial-up connection your visitors will be using. Check out what happens with both a 14.4 modem and a 28.8 modem. What's tolerable with a direct connection can seem interminable over a dial-up connection.

In ideal circumstances, a visitor using a 28.8 modem can download a maximum of 3.5Kb per second. In real life, that number decreases dramatically, depending on network traffic and a variety of intangibles. If your page contains 2Kb of text, a 4Kb bullet image, a 20Kb photograph, and a 9Kb logo, you're already talking about at least a 10-second download. Add a 60Kb animation or sound file, and you've just bumped that to 30 seconds—best case scenario. At this point, your visitor is off to greener pastures.

Adding Sounds

Adding audio can produce some fun effects, but if you surf the Web looking for sound, you'll find little of practical use. Generally speaking, Web page sounds come in two varieties:

- Sounds that play when visitors access the page
- Sounds that play when visitors click something

Sounds that play when visitors access a page are called *background sounds* and can be a short tune or one that plays the entire time a visitor is at the page. These mooing, beeping, crescendoing background sounds usually do nothing more than entertain.

TIP

Our take on the it-plays-the-whole-time-you're-visiting background sounds? If we want music to surf by, we'll put a CD in the computer.

Figure 12.2 includes a control box that visitors can click to play a sound. Although sounds accessed in this way are primarily for entertainment purposes, they could be of practical use. For example:

- If your car sounds like this <rumble>, you need a new muffler.
- If your car sounds like this <choke>, you might have bad gasoline.
- If your car sounds like this <kaChUNK> when you shift gears, your transmission is going out.

You get the idea. In lieu of adding the whole control box, however, you could just link directly to an audio file.

Some Disadvantages of Sounds

Many of the disadvantages associated with using multimedia elements in general are also associated with using sounds:

- Sound files are usually large and load slowly.
- Visitors need a sound card and speakers to hear sounds.
- Visitors in a corporate environment might not welcome a loud greeting from their computer.

PART

III

Moving Beyond
Pure HTML

FIGURE 12.2

The control box lets
visitors choose
whether to play the
sound.

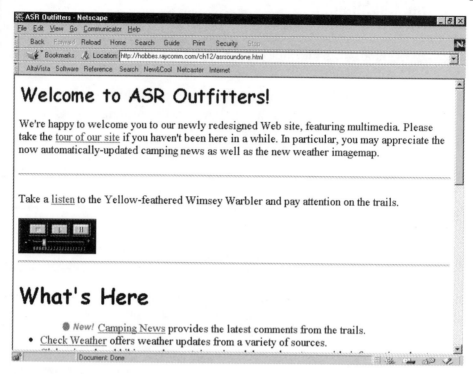

When choosing to add sound to your page, apply the guidelines we mentioned earlier about using multimedia elements in general. If an audio element does not enhance your message or provide content that is not possible in any other way, you're probably better off not to use it.

Sound File Formats

If you do decide to include a sound in your Web page, all you have to do is find a sound file in one of four formats (other formats are available, but are less common):

MIDI (Musical Instrument Digital Interface): A MIDI file contains synthesized music. If you can find or create one that meets your needs, MIDI is a great choice because the files are small. If you have a midi-capable musical instrument (such as a keyboard) and a little skill, you can play and record your own midi files.

AIFF (Audio Interchange File Format): An AIFF file contains a recorded sound sample, which can be music or a sound effect. This format is most common on Macintosh and usable on most other systems.

AU (or basic AUdio): An AU file also provides acceptable—but not great—quality sampled sound. These files are accessible on the widest range of browsers and computer systems.

WAV (as in WAVe): A WAV file provides very good quality sampled sound, but is usable almost exclusively on Windows computers.

If you have a sound card and a microphone, you can record your own sounds. The Companion CD contains some sound file libraries (look for the Earshot library), and you can find sound file libraries on the Web.

NOTE

Many—possibly most—of the sound files on the Web are not public domain, which means you can borrow them to experiment with and learn from, but not to publish as your own.

When you've found a sound file, use the HTML tags and attributes in Table 12.2 to add the file to your document.

TABLE 12.2 MULTIMEDIA FILE TAGS AND ATTRIBUTES

Tag/Attribute	Description
<EMBED>	Places an embedded object into a document.
ALIGN="{LEFT, RIGHT, CENTER, ABSBOTTOM, ABSMIDDLE, BASELINE, BOTTOM, TEXTTOP, TOP}"	Indicates how an embedded object is positioned relative to the document borders and surrounding contents.
HEIGHT="n"	Specifies the vertical dimension of the embedded object.
HIDDEN	Indicates that the embedded object should not be visible.
NAME="..."	Gives the object a name by which other objects can refer to it.
OPTIONAL PARAM="..."	Specifies additional parameters. For example, AVI movies accept the AUTOSTART attribute.
SRC="URL"	Indicates the relative or absolute location of the file containing the object you want to embed.

Continued ▶

PART

III

Moving Beyond
Pure HTML

TABLE 12.2: MULTIMEDIA FILE TAGS AND ATTRIBUTES (CONTINUED)

Tag/Attribute	Description
WIDTH="n"	Indicates the horizontal dimension of the embedded object.
AUTOSTART="…"	Specifies whether the sound file opens when the Web page is accessed or when a button is clicked. The value can be TRUE (automatically starts) or FALSE (visitors must do something).
HIDDEN="…"	Specifies whether the sound control box is visible in the Web page. The values TRUE and FALSE specify whether the control box is visible.
<BGSOUND>	Embeds a background sound file within documents. Use in the document <HEAD> of documents intended for visitors who use Internet Explorer.
LOOP="{n, INFINITE}"	Specifies the number of times a background sound file repeat. The value INFINITE is the default.
SRC="URL"	Indicates the absolute or relative location of the sound file.

To include sound files the easy and most user friendly way, link to them. For example, as you saw in Figure 12.2, earlier in this chapter, ASR Outfitters added a sound file of a bird call to one of its pages. You add a link to a sound file in the same way that you add a link to an image. The code looks like this:

```
Take a <A HREF="WEIRDBRD.AIF">listen</A> to the
Yellow-feathered Wimsey Warbler and pay attention on the trails.
```

If you use this option, visitors can choose whether to hear the sound, which is accessible from most browsers.

If you choose to inflict the sound on your visitors from the second they view your page, you'll need two tags—one for Internet Explorer and one for Netscape Navigator.

For Internet Explorer, follow these steps:

1. Start with an HTML document that at least has structure tags.

```
<!DOCTYPE HTML PUBLIC "-//W3C//DTD HTML 4.0//EN">
<HTML>
<HEAD>
<TITLE>ASR Outfitters</TITLE>
</HEAD>
<BODY>
```

2. Add the <BGSOUND> tag.

```
<TITLE>ASR Outfitters</TITLE>
<BGSOUND>
</HEAD>
<BODY>
```

3. Add the SRC= attribute and the file name.

```
<TITLE>ASR Outfitters</TITLE>
<BGSOUND SRC="wierdbrd.aif">
</HEAD>
<BODY>
```

4. Add the LOOP= attribute to specify how many times the sound should play.

```
<BGSOUND SRC="wierdbrd.aif" LOOP=1>
```

For Netscape Navigator, follow these steps:

1. Start with an HTML document that at least has structure tags.

```
<!DOCTYPE HTML PUBLIC "-//W3C//DTD HTML 4.0//EN">
<HTML>
<HEAD>
<TITLE>ASR Outfitters</TITLE>
</HEAD>
<BODY>
```

2. Add the <EMBED> tag.

```
<BODY>
<EMBED>
```

3. Add the SRC= attribute and the file name.

```
<BODY>
<EMBED SRC="wierdbrd.aif">
```

4. Add the AUTOSTART="TRUE" attribute to specify that the sound should play when the page is accessed. The TRUE value specifies that the sound start when the page is accessed. FALSE requires that visitors activate the sound file.

```
<BODY>
<EMBED SRC="wierdbrd.aif" AUTOSTART="TRUE">
```

5. Add the HIDDEN attribute to hide the control box.

```
<BODY>
<EMBED SRC="wierdbrd.aif" AUTOSTART="TRUE" HIDDEN>
```

PART

III

Moving Beyond
Pure HTML

Nothing appears in the page, but your visitors will hear the `wierdbrd.aif` sound as soon as they open the page.

Finally, you can also provide a classy little control in the Web page so that visitors can play the file right there. To do so, set the `AUTOSTART=` attribute to `FALSE`, and specify the dimensions of the control, like this:

```
<EMBED SRC="weirdbrd.aif" AUTOSTART="FALSE" HEIGHT="60" WIDTH="140">
```

TIP

See the "Adding Multimedia Using HTML 4" section at the end of this chapter to find out how version 4 makes this process even easier!

Adding Video

You'll find that video—in the right situation—is perhaps the most practical multimedia element. In one quick video clip, you can *show* visitors a concept or a process, rather than describing it in lengthy paragraphs or steps.

If you surf the Web, though, you'll find few videos. Despite its potential, Web-based video is virtually unusable in most situations. The only significant exception is for training on an intranet; most intranet users have high-speed connections. Video files are huge. Even a small, short, low-quality video is usually 2MB or more and takes several minutes to download over a dial-up connection.

In addition, visitors must have the right plug-in. And downloading a plug-in and the huge files to view a few seconds of video is not an attractive option.

Video File Formats

You can create your own video files or find them on the Web. Look for files in the following formats:

> **AVI (Audio Video Interleave):** This format, originally a Windows standard, is now somewhat more widely available. It's a good choice if your visitors will almost exclusively be using Windows.
>
> **MPEG (Motion Picture Experts Group):** This format is the most widely supported, and viewers are available for most platforms. Because it's highly compressed and usable, MPEG is the best universal choice.

QuickTime: This format, originally a Macintosh standard, is now available for Windows as well. It provides good quality if your visitors have the plug-in and use personal computers.

When you're ready to incorporate a video file, you use the tags and attributes described in Table 12.2, earlier in this chapter.

We recommend linking to video files, rather than embedding them in a Web page. The code looks like this:

```
Take a <A HREF="WEIRDBRD.MPG">look at video</A> of the
Yellow-feathered Wimsey Warbler and pay attention on the trails.
```

When video files are linked, visitors can choose whether to view them.

If you do choose to embed the video file—thereby forcing visitors to download it—follow these steps:

1. Start with an HTML document.

2. Add the <EMBED> tag.

```
<HR>
<EMBED>
<H2 ALIGN=CENTER>Happy Holiday!</H2>
```

3. Add the SRC= attribute and the file name.

```
<HR>
<EMBED SRC="firework.avi">
<H2 ALIGN=CENTER>Happy Holiday!</H2>
```

4. Specify the video size using the WIDTH= and HEIGHT= attributes.

```
<HR>
<EMBED SRC="firework.avi" WIDTH="250" HEIGHT="150">
<H2 ALIGN=CENTER>Happy Holiday!</H2>
```

5. Add the AUTOSTART="TRUE" attribute to specify that the video play when the page is accessed. Use FALSE to require visitors to activate the video file.

```
<HR>
<EMBED SRC="firework.avi" WIDTH="250" HEIGHT="150" AUTOSTART="true">
<H2 ALIGN=CENTER>Happy Holiday!</H2>
```

6. Add the LOOP= attribute to specify how many times the video plays.

```
<HR>
<EMBED SRC="firework.avi" WIDTH="250" HEIGHT="150" AUTOSTART="true"
LOOP="1">
<H2 ALIGN=CENTER>Happy Holiday!</H2>
```

PART

III

Moving Beyond
Pure HTML

7. If you want, add an ALIGN= attribute, such as ALIGN=LEFT.

```
<HR>
<EMBED SRC="firework.avi" WIDTH="250" HEIGHT="150" AUTOSTART="true"
LOOP="1" ALIGN="LEFT">
<H2 ALIGN=CENTER>Happy Holiday!</H2>
```

The resulting Web page—including the video from the Microsoft Clipart Gallery—looks like Figure 12.3.

FIGURE 12.3

Including video in Web pages is easy.

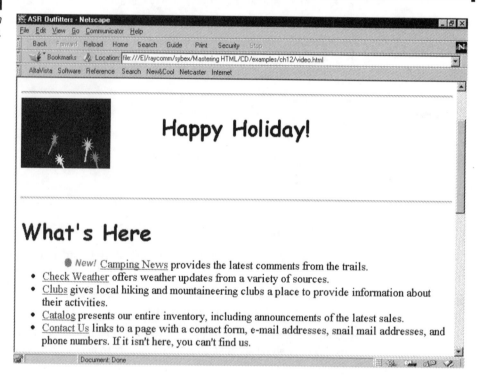

Including Java Applets

Applets, developed with the Java programming language, are mini-programs with which you can animate objects, scroll text, or add interactive components to your Web pages. Figure 12.4 shows the TicTacToe applet, and Figure 12.5 shows an applet that scrolls a welcome message across the top of a Web page.

FIGURE 12.4

This applet lets you play tic-tac-toe.

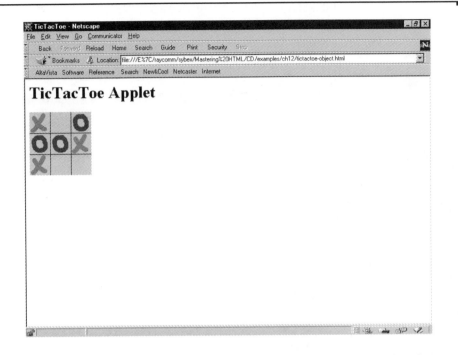

FIGURE 12.5

This applet scrolls a welcome message across the top of the page.

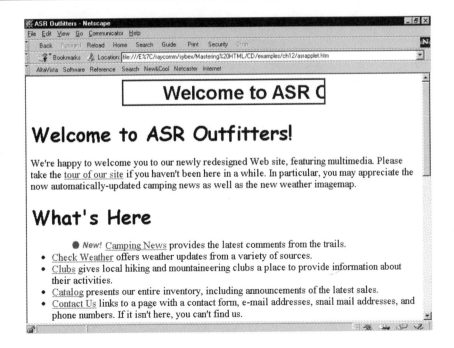

In addition, Java applets can organize and categorize topics on the Web. For example, AltaVista Search Public Service uses an applet to run the Refine feature, which lets visitors make choices and move categories around on the screen (see Figure 12.6).

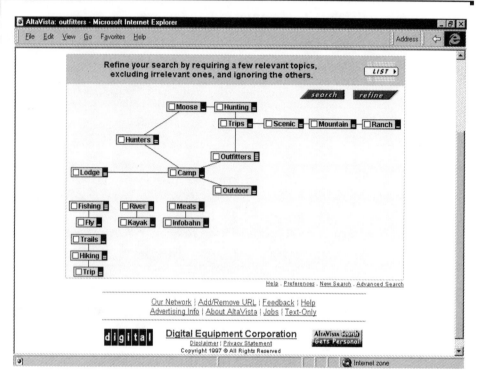

Java applets have the `class` file name extension. In the simplest cases, you need only the name of the applet to use it, for example, `TicTacToe.class`. With more complex applets, you must also provide *parameters*. In this section, we'll show you how to send those parameters to the applet, but you'll have to get the exact information to include in the parameter from the documentation that comes with applets.

The Java Developers Kit (JDK), available on the CD and from `www.sunsoft.com`, includes tools for developing applets. Unless you're a programmer or have some time on your hands, however, you'll be better off using prepackaged applets or tools that develop applets on the fly, such as Macromedia's Applet Ace, on the CD.

Applet files, like video files, are big and take up to a couple minutes to download. On the positive side, though, visitors with recent versions of Netscape Navigator or Internet Explorer can use applets without additional software.

Table 12.3 lists and describes the tags and attributes you use to include an applet in your Web pages.

TABLE 12.3: APPLET TAGS AND ATTRIBUTES

Tag /Attribute	Description
<APPLET>	Embeds a Java applet into an HTML document. You can include alternate text between <APPLET> tags. Browsers that support Java ignore all information between the <APPLET> tags.
ALIGN={LEFT, CENTER, RIGHT}	Specifies the horizontal alignment of the applet displayed.
ALT="..."	Displays a textual description of an applet, if necessary.
CODE="URL"	Specifies the relative or absolute location of the Java bytecode file on the server.
CODEBASE="URL"	Specifies the folder location of all necessary class files on the Web server.
HEIGHT="n"	Specifies the height (in pixels) of the applet object within the document.
HSPACE="n"	Specifies an amount of blank space (in pixels) to the left and right of the applet within the document.
NAME="..."	Assigns the applet a name so that other applets can identify it within the document.
TITLE="..."	Specifies a label assigned to the tag.
VSPACE="n"	Specifies the amount of vertical space (in pixels) above and below the applet.
WIDTH="n"	Specifies the width (in pixels) of the applet within the document.
<PARAM>	Specifies parameters passed to an embedded object.
NAME="..."	Indicates the name of the parameter passed to the embedded object.
VALUE="..."	Specifies the value associated with the parameter passed to the embedded object.

If you've found an applet to use and want to include it in your Web page, follow these steps. In this example, we'll show you how to add the TicTacToe applet.

1. Start with an HTML document.

PART

III

Moving Beyond
Pure HTML

2. Add some introductory text and perhaps a couple of horizontal rules to set off the applet from other page elements.

```
<H1>TicTacToe Game</H1>
<HR>
<HR>
```

3. Add the <APPLET> tags.

```
<H1>TicTacToe Game</H1>
<HR>
<APPLET>
</APPLET>
<HR>
```

4. Add the CODE= attribute along with the applet file name.

```
<H1>TicTacToe Game</H1>
<HR>
<APPLET CODE="TicTacToe.class">
</APPLET>
<HR>
```

5. Add the WIDTH= and HEIGHT= attributes to specify the size of the applet.

```
<H1>TicTacToe Game</H1>
<HR>
<APPLET CODE="TicTacToe.class" WIDTH="120" HEIGHT="120">
</APPLET>
<HR>
```

That's it! For this applet, which should look like Figure 12.4, earlier in this chapter, all you need is the applet.class file. To add an applet that requires parameters, such as the applet that scrolls the welcome banner, follow these steps (we used Macromedia's Applet Ace to create this banner and were able to simply copy and paste the parameters into our HTML document):

1. Start with an HTML document.

2. Add the <APPLET> tags.

```
<APPLET>
</APPLET>
```

3. Add the applet file.

```
<APPLET CODE="Banners.class">
</APPLET>
```

4. Add a <PARAM> tag that includes the parameter name and value.

```
<APPLET CODE="Banners.class"
<param name="bgColor" value="White">
</APPLET>
```

5. Continue adding parameters. We recommend adding one at a time to help elim-inate coding errors.

```
<applet code="Banners.class" width="400" height="50">
<param name="bgColor" value="White">
<param name="textColor" value="Black">
<param name="pause" value="1">
<param name="exit" value="scrollLeft">
<param name="align" value="Center">
<param name="fps" value="20">
<param name="repeat" value="1">
<param name="borderWidth" value="1">
<param name="bgExit" value="None">
<param name="messages" value="Welcome to ASR Outfitters!">
<param name="font" value="Helvetica">
<param name="cpf" value="2">
<param name="enter" value="scrollLeft">
<param name="bgEnter" value="None">
<param name="style" value="Bold">
<param name="borderColor" value="Black">
<param name="size" value="36">
</applet>
```

And that's it! This code displays a scrolling welcome, much like the one shown in Figure 12.5, earlier in this chapter.

Including ActiveX Controls

ActiveX controls are similar to Java applets—they're little programs that provide enhanced functionality to a Web page. For example, ActiveX controls can provide pop-up menus, the ability to view a Word document through a Web page, and almost all the pieces needed for Microsoft's HTML Help. These controls—developed by Microsoft and implemented with Internet Explorer 3—are powerful but Windows-centric. Although

PART

III

Moving Beyond
Pure HTML

CONTINUED

you can get a plug-in to view ActiveX controls in Netscape Navigator, you'll find the results are more reliable when you view ActiveX controls with Internet Explorer.

If you want to try out some controls—both free and licensed varieties—check out C|Net's ActiveX site at www.activex.com/ or Gamelan at www.gamelan.com. If you're so inclined, you can create ActiveX controls using popular Windows development packages, such as Visual Basic or Visual C++. You include ActiveX controls in a page just as you include multimedia elements. You use the <OBJECT> tag—as discussed in the next section.

Adding Multimedia Using HTML 4

So far in this chapter, we've shown you how to include multimedia elements using HTML 3.2–compliant tags and some HTML extensions. Now we're going to look at how HTML 4 approaches multimedia, which you'll find is different (and easier!).

The future of developing multimedia elements for the Web is clear: Instead of using several tags and attributes, you'll simply include the <OBJECT> tag and choose from attributes that support this tag (see Table 12.4). In this respect, the HTML 4 specification accommodates any kind of multimedia element. You need not specify that you're including a sound, a video, an applet, or whatever; you simply specify that you're including an object. And, you use only the HTML 4 tags and attributes listed in Table 12.4. You no longer need to code for both Netscape Navigator and Internet Explorer.

NOTE

Support for the <OBJECT> tag is a little sketchy, but improving with the release of each new browser.

TABLE 12.4: OBJECT TAGS AND ATTRIBUTES

Tag /Attribute	Description
<OBJECT>	Embeds a software object into a document.
ALIGN={LEFT, CENTER, RIGHT, TEXTTOP, MIDDLE, TEXTMIDDLE, BASELINE, TEXTBOTTOM, BASELINE}	Indicates how the embedded object lines up relative to the edges of the browser window and/or other elements within the browser window.

Continued ▶

TABLE 12.4: OBJECT TAGS AND ATTRIBUTES (CONTINUED)

Tag /Attribute	Description
BORDER=n	Indicates the width (in pixels) of a border around the embedded object. BORDER=0 indicates no border.
CODEBASE="..."	Specifies the absolute or relative location of the base directory in which the browser will look for data and other implementation files.
CODETYPE="..."	Specifies the MIME type for the embedded object's code.
CLASS="..."	Indicates which style class applies to the element.
CLASSID="..."	Specifies the location of an object resource, such as a Java applet. Use CLASSID="java:appletname.class" for Java applets.
DATA="URL"	Specifies the absolute or relative location of the embedded object's data.
DATAFLD="..."	Selects a column from a block of tabular data.
DATASRC="..."	Specifies the location of tabular data to be bound within the document.
HEIGHT=n	Specifies the vertical dimension (in pixels) of the embedded object.
HSPACE=n	Specifies the size of the margins (in pixels) to the left and right of the embedded object.
ID="..."	Indicates an identifier to associate with the embedded object.
NAME="..."	Specifies the name of the embedded object.
STANDBY="..."	Specifies a message that the browser displays while the object is loading.
TITLE="..."	Specifies a label assigned to the tag.
TYPE="..."	Indicates the MIME type of the embedded object.
VSPACE=n	Specifies the size of the margin (in pixels) at the top and bottom of the embedded object.
WIDTH=n	Indicates the horizontal dimension (in pixels) of the embedded object.

When objects require more information—for example, a Java applet needs specific settings to run—you pass data to the object with the <PARAM> tag. Table 12.5 lists and describes the <PARAM> tags and attributes.

PART

III

Moving Beyond
Pure HTML

TABLE 12.5: PARAMETER TAGS AND ATTRIBUTES	
Tag /Attribute	**Description**
<PARAM>	Specifies parameters passed to an embedded object. Use the <PARAM> tag within the <OBJECT> or <APPLET> tags.
NAME="..."	Indicates the name of the parameter passed to the embedded object.
TYPE="..."	Specifies the MIME type of the data found at the specified URL.
VALUE="..."	Specifies the value associated with the parameter passed to the embedded object.
VALUETYPE={REF, OBJECT, DATA}	Indicates the kind of value passed to the embedded object.

When you're developing for HTML 4–compliant browsers, you can use the <OBJECT> tag to include almost any kind of object. Let's start with the Java TicTacToe applet, which is on the Companion CD in the Java Developers Kit (JDK).

To add an applet using the <OBJECT> tag, follow these steps:

1. Start with a basic HTML document, like this:

```
<!DOCTYPE HTML PUBLIC "-//W3C//DTD HTML 4.0//EN">
<HTML>
<HEAD>
  <TITLE>TicTacToe</TITLE>
</HEAD>
<BODY BGCOLOR="FFFFFF" TEXT="000000" LINK="0000FF" VLINK="800080"
ALINK="FF0000">
<H1>TicTacToe Applet </H1>
</BODY>
</HTML>
```

2. Add the <OBJECT> tags.

```
<h1>TicTacToe Applet </h1>
<OBJECT>
</OBJECT>
```

3. Add alternate text between the <OBJECT> tags.

```
<h1>TicTacToe Applet </h1>
<OBJECT>
If your browser supported Java and objects, you could
be playing TicTacToe right now.
</OBJECT>
```

4. Add the CLASSID= attribute to indicate the name of the Java class file (program file). You use CLASSID= to incorporate programs, such as applets or ActiveX controls.

```
<h1>TicTacToe Applet </h1>
<OBJECT classid="java:TicTacToe.class">
If your browser supported Java and objects, you could
be playing TicTacToe right now.
</OBJECT>
```

5. Add the WIDTH= and HEIGHT= attributes. A square that is 120×120 pixels should be sufficient.

```
<h1>TicTacToe Applet </h1>
<OBJECT classid="java:TicTacToe.class" WIDTH=120 HEIGHT=120>
If your browser supported Java and objects, you could
be playing TicTacToe right now.
</OBJECT>
```

6. Save and test your document. In an HTML 4–compliant browser, you'll see the TicTacToe game, as shown here:

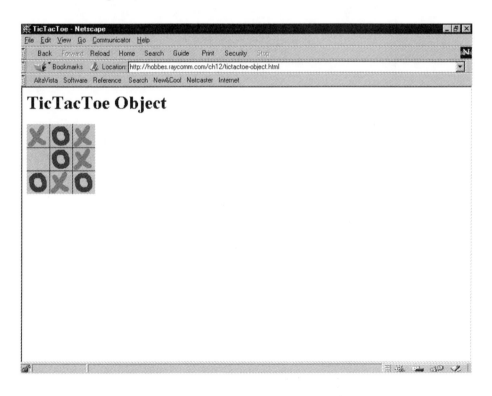

PART

III

Moving Beyond
Pure HTML

Visitors using browsers that don't support the <OBJECT> tag or don't support Java will see something like the following:

The process for adding video and sound is similar. The only difference is that you use the DATA= attribute instead of the CLASSID= attribute. Also, you add a TYPE= attribute to show the MIME type of the object. (You don't need the TYPE= when you're adding an applet because Java: precedes the name of the applet, making it clear what kind of object it is.)

To add a sound using the <OBJECT> tag, follow these steps:

1. Start with an HTML document.

2. Add the <OBJECT> tags.

   ```
   <OBJECT>
   </OBJECT>
   ```

3. Add the DATA= attribute along with the file name.

   ```
   <OBJECT DATA="weirdbrd.aif">
   </OBJECT>
   ```

4. Add the TYPE= attribute to specify the type of multimedia.

```
<OBJECT DATA="weirdbrd.aif" TYPE="audio/aiff">
</OBJECT>
```

5. Add the HEIGHT= and WIDTH= attributes to specify the object's size.

```
<OBJECT DATA="weirdbrd.aif" TYPE="audio/aiff" HEIGHT=50 WIDTH=100>
</OBJECT>
```

There you go! Your document should now look like Figure 12.2, shown earlier in this chapter.

Making It Sound Easy

If you're embedding sounds in your pages, consider using a regular link to the sound file rather than using the <OBJECT> tag to embed it. The only real advantage to using the <OBJECT> tag (or its Netscape-originated predecessor <EMBED>) is a neat little widget in the Web page that visitors can use to play the sound as if they were using a VCR. However, those neat little widgets aren't the same size in Internet Explorer and Netscape Navigator, so you end up with either a truncated object or one with loads of extra space around it.

We recommend using an icon or a text link to the sound file—it's much easier. Anyway, if the sound takes so long to play that your visitors have time to click Stop or Pause, the sound file is probably too big.

Where to Go from Here

This chapter showed you some of the more fun elements you can include in your HTML documents. Although multimedia files don't always have practical uses, they do make your pages more interesting and give them the "up with technology" look and feel. You also learned, however, that multimedia effects have a big disadvantage: The files are usually enormous, which slows download time considerably. Whether you choose to include the files using the HTML 3.2 tags and attributes or the HTML 4 tags and attributes depends on which browsers your visitors use.

From here, you can breeze through several related chapters:

- See Chapter 5 to learn about developing HTML Style Sheets, which let you add cool formatting to your documents.

PART

III

Moving Beyond
Pure HTML

- See Chapter 6 for more information about MIME types.
- See Chapter 11 to learn how JavaScript can also make your pages shimmy and shake.
- See Chapter 21 to learn how to balance flashy elements (such as multimedia) with usability.

Chapter

13

Bringing Pages to Life with Dynamic HTML

Bringing Pages to Life with Dynamic HTML

When you develop a Web page using Dynamic HTML (DHTML), your visitors can view new contents without reloading the page, change screen colors with a mouse click, and view animations without installing a plug-in. If this sounds like an exciting new world, it is; however, only browsers that support Style Sheets and JavaScript can support DHTML. As of this writing, that means only Internet Explorer 4 and Netscape Navigator 4.

In addition, you implement DHTML one way if you're developing for Internet Explorer and another way if you're developing for Netscape Navigator. If you develop a page using Internet Explorer technology, a visitor opening that page in Netscape Navigator will most likely see JavaScript error messages. If you develop a page using Netscape Navigator technology, a visitor opening that page in Internet Explorer will potentially see nothing special. As you can see, taking advantage of the latest and greatest can be disadvantageous.

That said, if you're developing for either of these cutting-edge browsers, you'll want to know about and use DHTML. In this chapter, we're going to introduce you to DHTML, look at some of the advantages and disadvantages associated with using it, and show you how to use DHTML in your documents—both the Netscape Navigator way and the Internet Explorer way. We'll then use DHTML to develop a practical application—collapsing pages.

TIP

We recommend that you have a firm understanding of Style Sheets and JavaScript before starting this chapter. For a quick review, flip back to chapters 5 and 11.

What Is Dynamic HTML?

Dynamic HTML expands on standard HTML by giving you the formatting control of Style Sheets combined with the interactive capabilities of scripting languages such as JavaScript—all rolled into one. When you develop pages with DHTML, visitors spend far less time accessing information because it's available directly within the browser, rather than having to retrieve the information from the server.

For example, suppose you have a table of contents page. If you develop it with standard HTML, visitors click an item; the browser then requests the document from the server and displays it when it arrives. If you develop the table of contents page with DHTML, however, the trip to the server is eliminated. Figures 13.1 and 13.2 show this process.

FIGURE 13.1

Visitors can click items in the table of contents and expand the information without reloading the file.

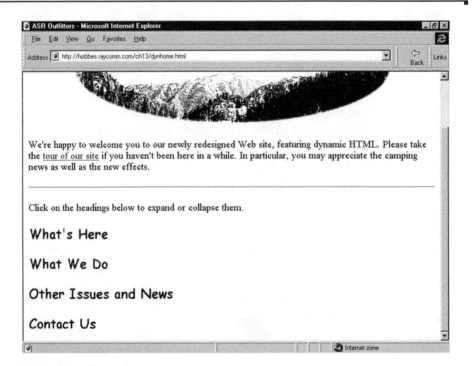

FIGURE 13.2

After selecting an item, the visitor can view the expanded content.

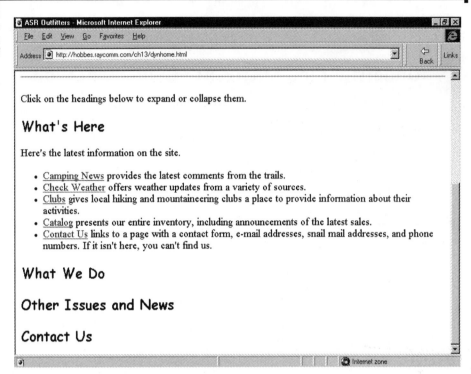

We show you how to create collapsible information in the section "Creating a Collapsible Document," later in this chapter.

Before you go sprinting off to add DHTML capabilities to your documents, you need to be familiar with Style Sheets and JavaScript. Within DHTML, Style Sheets tell browsers what elements should look like, and JavaScript functions change the properties set by Style Sheets. That's how page elements know to do something—blink, change colors, and so on.

You might recall from Chapter 11 that you can use JavaScript's onMouseOver event handler to change an image when a visitor moves the mouse over the image. Using Microsoft's implementation of DHTML and event handlers, you can do this with just about any page element. For example, you can change the color of text, increase the text size, or even make the text jump to a new location.

PART

III

Moving Beyond
Pure HTML

As you will see in the following section, Microsoft's implementation of DHTML uses mostly standard tags and attributes, an approach that offers wider support and better functionality and promises more in terms of long-range stability.

Understanding Microsoft's Implementation

Microsoft DHTML exposes all page elements to scripting; that is, each page element can be manipulated—recolored, scrolled, jiggled, and so on. If you can specify what the element is, you can format it with Style Sheets and then change the Style Sheets using a JavaScript script. For example, you can identify a heading, specify in the Style Sheet that the heading is red, and then specify in the JavaScript script that the red heading changes to green when a visitor passes the mouse over the heading.

If you haven't already done so, you might breeze through Chapters 5 and 11 before starting these examples. In particular, look closely at the ID= attribute description in Chapter 5, and check out the discussion of event handlers and functions in Chapter 11.

Let's take a look at the general process for adding DHTML capabilities to your HTML documents using Microsoft's implementation.

1. Start with a functional HTML document. The following code includes the HTML structural elements and Style Sheet elements:

```
<!DOCTYPE HTML PUBLIC "-//W3C//DTD HTML 4.0//EN">
<HTML>
<HEAD>
  <TITLE>Fix Colors</TITLE>
  <STYLE>
<!--
H1 { color : red }
-->
</STYLE>
</HEAD>
<BODY BGCOLOR="FFFFFF" TEXT="000000" LINK="0000FF" VLINK="800080"
ALINK="FF0000">
<H1>Need a Break?</H1>
<P>
If you'd like to change the color of the heading above
from red to black for better contrast and easier reading,
```

```
just click once anywhere in this paragraph.</A><P>
<P>
Click this paragraph to change it back.</A></P>
</BODY>
</HTML>
```

2. Add the ID= attribute for each instance that will be affected by a DHTML function. In this example, we'll change the heading color. Remember, ID= attributes must be unique in each instance.

```
<!DOCTYPE HTML PUBLIC "-//W3C//DTD HTML 4.0//EN">
<HTML>
<HEAD>
  <TITLE>Fix Colors</TITLE>
  <STYLE>
<!--
H1 { color : red }
-->
</STYLE>
</HEAD>
<BODY BGCOLOR="FFFFFF" TEXT="000000" LINK="0000FF" VLINK="800080"
ALINK="FF0000">
<H1 ID=firsthead>Need a Break?</H1>
<P>
If you'd like to change the color of the heading above
from red to black for better contrast and easier reading,
just click once anywhere in this paragraph.</A><P>
<P>
Click this paragraph to change it back.</A></P>
</BODY>
</HTML>
```

3. Add JavaScript event handlers. In this example, the event handlers each call a function (swapit() and revert()) to switch the color when a visitor clicks the text. Because Microsoft's DHTML technology exposes all elements to scripting and Style Sheets, you can add the event handlers directly to the <P> tag.

```
<H1 ID=firsthead>Need a Break?</H1>
<P onClick="swapit()">
If you'd like to change the color of the heading above
from red to black for better contrast and easier reading,
just click once anywhere in this paragraph.</A><P>
```

PART

III

Moving Beyond
Pure HTML

```
<P onClick="revert()">
Click this paragraph to change it back.</A></P>
</BODY>
</HTML>
```

4. Add the JavaScript functions, which actually change the colors on command from the event handlers. They each specify the color property of the firsthead element (identified with the ID= attribute) and set it to a specific color.

```
<!DOCTYPE HTML PUBLIC "-//W3C//DTD HTML 3.2//EN">
<HTML>
<HEAD>
  <TITLE>Fix Colors</TITLE>
  <STYLE>
<!--
H1 { color : red }
-->
</STYLE>
<SCRIPT>
<!-
function swapit() {this.document.all.firsthead.style.color="000000"}
function revert() {this.document.all.firsthead.style.color="FF0000"}
// ->
</SCRIPT>
</HEAD>
<BODY BGCOLOR="FFFFFF" TEXT="000000" LINK="0000FF" VLINK="800080"
ALINK="FF0000">
<H1 ID=firsthead>Need a Break?</H1>
<P onClick="swapit()">
If you'd like to change the color of the heading above
from red to black for better contrast and easier reading,
just click once anywhere in this paragraph.</A><P>
<P onClick="revert()">
Click this paragraph to change it back.</A></P>
</BODY>
</HTML>
```

In writing the function, you need to specify exactly which characteristics of which page element (technically, which *object*) the function applies to, and you do this using the full object name (think of it as an address). For example, the address in Step 4 identifies the color property of the `firsthead` element in the document. The resulting heading in the sample document changes color when a visitor clicks the paragraphs. Table 13.1 shows you other sample addresses.

TABLE 13.1: DYNAMIC HTML SAMPLE OBJECT AND PROPERTY IDENTIFIERS

This Sample Address	Does This
`this.document.body` `.style.color`	Specifies the color property of the style of the body of the document.
`this.document.all` `.otherstuff.style` `.display`	Specifies the display property of the style of the `otherstuff` ID section of this document.
`this.document.form(0)` `.style.background`	Specifies the background of the first form in this document

Understanding Netscape's Implementation

Rather than using standard HTML tags and attributes as Microsoft does, Netscape's version of DHTML introduces the <LAYER> tag and special JavaScript Style Sheets. Because all page elements are not exposed to JavaScript functions, you have to apply the <LAYER> tag to identify special sections and then apply a script to those sections. This solution does not seamlessly add or hide information.

For example, glance back at Figures 13.1 and 13.2, which show a collapsible table of contents—developed with Microsoft's implementation of HTML. You'll notice that when the topics expand and collapse, they move up and down on the page, depending on how much space the expanded topic needs. The same page developed with Netscape's implementation of DHTML, however, leaves space on the page for the expanded topic, but doesn't hide that extra space when the topic is collapsed, as shown in Figure 13.3.

If your visitors use Netscape Navigator 4, you *can* do some useful and interesting things with the Netscape version of DHTML—including moving objects around on the page, using animations, or providing information just when visitors need it. At the time of writing, however, it is unlikely that Netscape's implementation will become widely accepted, simply because it's a move away from, not toward, HTML standards.

FIGURE 13.3

A page developed with Netscape's implementation of DHTML doesn't hide the extra space.

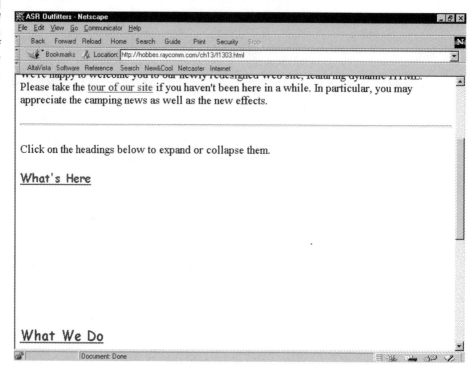

Table 13.2 lists and describes a few of the Netscape-specific DHTML tags and attributes. See the Master's Reference for a complete listing.

TABLE 13.2: NETSCAPE-SPECIFIC DYNAMIC HTML TAGS AND ATTRIBUTES	
Tab/Attribute	**Description**
`<LAYER>`	Sets up a layer—a section of the document that can be addressed or manipulated.
`<ILAYER>`	Sets up an inline layer—a section of the document that reserves space for its content and can be addressed or manipulated.
`NAME=`	Provides an identifying label for the `<LAYER>` or `<ILAYER>` tag so that the layers can be addressed by Style Sheets.
`VISIBILITY=` `{SHOW, HIDE}`	Sets the layer to be either visible or hidden.

Compared with the rather simple steps that the Microsoft implementation of DHTML requires, the steps that Netscape's implementation requires are more complex. To show you how this works, we'll change the background color of the first document heading we worked with in the previous section. (Netscape's implementation of DHTML won't let you change just the heading color.)

1. Start with a functional HTML document. The following code includes the HTML structural elements and Style Sheet elements:

```
<!DOCTYPE HTML PUBLIC "-//W3C//DTD HTML 4.0//EN">
<HTML>
<HEAD>
  <TITLE>Fix Colors</TITLE>
 <STYLE>
<!--
H1 { color : red }
-->
</STYLE>
</HEAD>


<BODY BGCOLOR="FFFFFF" TEXT="000000" LINK="0000FF" VLINK="800080"
ALINK="FF0000">
<H1>Need a Break?</H1>
<P>
If you'd like to change the background color of the heading above
for better contrast and easier reading,
just click here to change color.
<P>
Just click here to change it back.</P>
</BODY>
</HTML>
```

2. Add <ILAYER> tags around the element you'll be changing.

```
<!DOCTYPE HTML PUBLIC "-//W3C//DTD HTML 4.0//EN">
<HTML>
<HEAD>
  <TITLE>Fix Colors</TITLE>
 <STYLE>
<!--
H1 { color : red }
-->
</STYLE>
```

PART

III

Moving Beyond
Pure HTML

```
</HEAD>

<BODY BGCOLOR="FFFFFF" TEXT="000000" LINK="0000FF" VLINK="800080"
ALINK="FF0000">
<ILAYER><H1>Need a Break?</H1></ILAYER>
<P>
If you'd like to change the background color of the heading above
for better contrast and easier reading,
just click here to change color.
<P>
Just click here to change it back.</A></P>
</BODY>
</HTML>
```

3. Add a NAME= attribute to the <ILAYER> tag. We'll call it firsthead.

```
<!DOCTYPE HTML PUBLIC "-//W3C//DTD HTML 4.0//EN">
<HTML>
<HEAD>
  <TITLE>Fix Colors</TITLE>
  <STYLE>
<!--
H1 { color : red }
-->
</STYLE>
</HEAD>
<BODY BGCOLOR="FFFFFF" TEXT="000000" LINK="0000FF" VLINK="800080"
ALINK="FF0000">
<ILAYER NAME="firsthead"><H1>Need a Break?</H1></ILAYER>
<P>
If you'd like to change the background color of the heading above
for better contrast and easier reading,
just click here to change color.
<P>
Just click here to change it back.</P>
</BODY>
</HTML>
```

4. Add event handlers to change the color and change it back. Because the elements are not individually addressable, you have to add <A> tags.

```
<!DOCTYPE HTML PUBLIC "-//W3C//DTD HTML 4.0//EN">
<HTML>
```

```
<HEAD>
  <TITLE>Fix Colors</TITLE>
 <STYLE>
<!--
H1 { color : red }
-->
</STYLE>
</HEAD>

<BODY BGCOLOR="FFFFFF" TEXT="000000" LINK="0000FF" VLINK="800080"
ALINK="FF0000">
<ILAYER NAME="firsthead"><H1>Need a Break?</H1></ILAYER>
<P>
If you'd like to change the background color of the heading above
for better contrast and easier reading,
just click <A HREF="javascript:swapit()">here</A> to change color.
<P>
Just click <A HREF="javascript:revert()">here</A> to change change it
back.</A></P>
</BODY>
</HTML>
```

5. Add JavaScript functions (that the event handlers you just added refer to) that change the document.layers.firsthead.bgColor attribute (yes, it's case sensitive).

```
<!DOCTYPE HTML PUBLIC "-//W3C//DTD HTML 4.0//EN">
<HTML>
<HEAD>
  <TITLE>Fix Colors</TITLE>
 <STYLE>
<!--
H1 { color : red }
-->
</STYLE>
<SCRIPT>
<!--
function swapit() { document.layers.firsthead.bgColor="yellow" ; }
function revert() { document.layers.firsthead.bgColor="white" ; }
// -->
</SCRIPT>
```

PART III

Moving Beyond Pure HTML

```
</HEAD>

<BODY BGCOLOR="FFFFFF" TEXT="000000" LINK="0000FF" VLINK="800080"
ALINK="FF0000">
<ILAYER NAME="firsthead"><H1>Need a Break?</H1></ILAYER>
<P>
If you'd like to change the background color of the heading above
for better contrast and easier reading,
just click <A HREF="javascript:swapit()">here</A> to change color.
<P>
Just click <A HREF="javascript:revert()">here</A> to change it
back.</A></P>
</BODY>
</HTML>
```

When you try this document in Netscape Navigator 4, you'll see something similar to Figure 13.4.

FIGURE 13.4

The resulting heading now appears with a colored background.

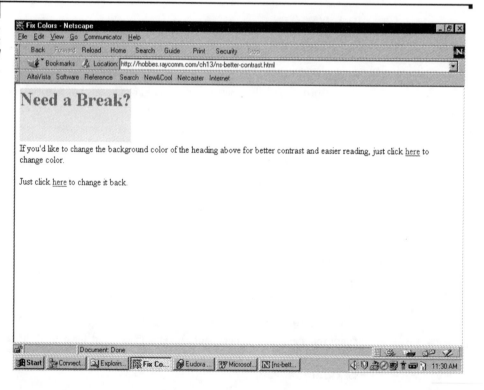

For more information about layers, check out the Master's Reference. For documentation from Netscape, visit `developer.netscape.com/library/documentation/index.html`.

Creating a Collapsible Document

One of the most useful DHTML capabilities is providing collapsible information, such as the table of contents you saw earlier. We chose this capability not only because it's handy, but because it illustrates the differences in the Microsoft and Netscape implementations of DHTML.

Collapsing a Document the Microsoft Way

To create a collapsible document, like the document shown in Figure 13.1, earlier in this chapter, follow these steps:

You'll find the code for these steps on the Companion CD in the `/examples/ch13` folder.

1. Start with a basic HTML document.

```
<!DOCTYPE HTML PUBLIC "-//W3C//DTD HTML 4.0//EN">
<HTML>
<HEAD>
<TITLE>ASR Outfitters</TITLE>
<STYLE TYPE="text/css">
<!--
BODY { font-size : 110% }
H1, H2, H3 { font-family : "Comic Sans MS" ; }
H1 { font-size : 180% ;  font-weight : bold }
-->
</STYLE>
</HEAD>
<BODY>
<CENTER>
```

PART

III

Moving Beyond
Pure HTML

```
<IMG SRC="asrlogo.gif">
</CENTER>
<P >We're happy to welcome you to our newly redesigned Web site,
featuring dynamic HTML. Please take the <A HREF="tour.html">tour of our
site</A> if you haven't been here in a while. In particular, you may
appreciate the camping news as well as the new effects. </P>
<HR>
<P>Click on the headings below to expand or collapse them.</P>
<H2>What's Here</A></H2>
<P>Here's the latest information on the site.</P>
<UL>
<LI>
<A HREF="camping.html">Camping News</A> provides the latest comments
    from the trails. <BR>
<LI><A HREF="weather.html">Check Weather</A> offers weather updates from
    a variety of sources.<BR>
<LI><A HREF="clubs.html">Clubs</A> gives local hiking and mountaineering
clubs
    a place to provide information about their activities.<BR>
<LI><A HREF="catalog.html">Catalog</A> presents our entire inventory,
    including announcements of the latest sales.<BR>
<LI><A HREF="contact.html">Contact Us</A> links to a page with a contact
    form, e-mail addresses, snail mail addresses, and phone numbers.
    If it isn't here, you can't find us. <BR>
</UL>
<H2>What We Do</H2>
<P>In addition to providing the latest camping and outdoor activities
news, we do
also provide mountaineering and hiking equipment nationwide via mail
order as well as through our stores in the Rocky Mountains.
Please take a few minutes to look through our <A
HREF="catalog.html">online offerings</A>.</P>
<H2>Other Issues and News</H2>
<UL>
<LI>As you may know, our URL was misprinted in the latest <I>Hiking
News</I>. Please
tell your hiking friends that the correct URL is
<TT>http://www.asroutfitters.com/</TT>.
<LI>To collect a $1000 reward, turn in the name of the person who set
the
```

```
fire in the Bear Lake area last weekend.
<OL>
<LI>Call 888-555-1212.
<LI>Leave the name on the recording.
<LI>Provide contact information so we can send you the reward.
</OL>
</UL>
<H2>Contact Us</H2>
<P>If you have suggestions or comments about the site or other
information
we could provide, we'd love to know about it. Drop us an e-mail at
<A
HREF="mailto:asroutfitters@raycomm.com">asroutfitters@raycomm.com</A>.
Of course, you could also contact us more traditionally at the following
address: </P>
<ADDRESS>ASR Outfitters
<BR>
4700 N. Center <BR>
South Logan, UT 87654<BR>
801-555-3422</ADDRESS>
</BODY>
</HTML>
```

2. Add <DIV> tags around each of the elements that should individually expand or collapse. Add a unique ID= attribute to each. You'll use the ID= attribute to specify the name for later reference from scripts. Also add a STYLE="display=none" attribute so that all elements start out hidden.

```
<H2>What's Here</H2>
<DIV ID="whathere" STYLE="display=none">
<P>Here's the latest information on the site.</P>
<UL>
<LI>
<A HREF="camping.html">Camping News</A> provides the latest comments
    from the trails. <BR>
<LI><A HREF="weather.html">Check Weather</A> offers weather updates from
    a variety of sources.<BR>
<LI><A HREF="clubs.html">Clubs</A> gives local hiking and mountaineering
clubs
    a place to provide information about their activities.<BR>
<LI><A HREF="catalog.html">Catalog</A> presents our entire inventory,
    including announcements of the latest sales.<BR>
```

```
<LI><A HREF="contact.html">Contact Us</A> links to a page with a contact
   form, e-mail addresses, snail mail addresses, and phone numbers.
   If it isn't here, you can't find us. <BR>
</UL>
</DIV>
<H2>What We Do</H2>
<DIV ID="whatwedo" STYLE="display=none">
<P>In addition to providing the latest camping and outdoor activities
news, we do
also provide mountaineering and hiking equipment nationwide via mail
order as well as through our stores in the Rocky Mountains.
Please take a few minutes to look through our <A
HREF="catalog.html">online offerings</A>.</P>
</DIV>
<H2>Other Issues and News</H2>
<DIV ID="otherstuff"  STYLE="display=none">
<UL>
<LI>As you may know, our URL was misprinted in the latest <I>Hiking
News</I>. Please
tell your hiking friends that the correct URL is
<TT>http://www.asroutfitters.com/</TT>.
<LI>To collect a $1000 reward, turn in the name of the person who set
the
fire in the Bear Lake area last weekend.
<OL>
<LI>Call 888-555-1212.
<LI>Leave the name on the recording.
<LI>Provide contact information so we can send you the reward.
</OL>
</UL>
</DIV>
<H2>Contact Us</H2>
<DIV ID="contactus"  STYLE="display=none">
<P>If you have suggestions or comments about the site or other
information
we could provide, we'd love to know about it. Drop us an e-mail at
<A
HREF="mailto:asroutfitters@raycomm.com">asroutfitters@raycomm.com</A>.
Of course, you could also contact us more traditionally at the following
address: </P>
```

```
<ADDRESS>ASR Outfitters<BR>
4700 N. Center <BR>
South Logan, UT 87654<BR>
801-555-3422</ADDRESS>
</DIV>
</BODY>
</HTML>
```

3. Add the event handlers to invoke scripts to make the changes.

```
<P>Click on the headings below to expand or collapse them.</P>
<H2 onClick="whathere()">What's Here</A></H2>
<DIV ID="whathere" STYLE="display=none">
<P>Here's the latest information on the site.</P>
<UL>
<LI>
<A HREF="camping.html">Camping News</A> provides the latest comments
    from the trails. <BR>
<LI><A HREF="weather.html">Check Weather</A> offers weather updates from
    a variety of sources.<BR>
<LI><A HREF="clubs.html">Clubs</A> gives local hiking and mountaineering
clubs
    a place to provide information about their activities.<BR>
<LI><A HREF="catalog.html">Catalog</A> presents our entire inventory,
    including announcements of the latest sales.<BR>
<LI><A HREF="contact.html">Contact Us</A> links to a page with a contact
    form, e-mail addresses, snail mail addresses, and phone numbers.
    If it isn't here, you can't find us. <BR>
</UL>
</DIV>
<H2 onClick="whatwedo()">What We Do</H2>
<DIV ID="whatwedo" STYLE="display=none">
<P>In addition to providing the latest camping and outdoor activities
news, we do
also provide mountaineering and hiking equipment nationwide via mail
order as well as through our stores in the Rocky Mountains.
Please take a few minutes to look through our <A
HREF="catalog.html">online offerings</A>.</P>
</DIV>
<H2 onClick="otherstuff()">Other Issues and News</H2>
<DIV ID="otherstuff"  STYLE="display=none">
<UL>
```

```
<LI>As you may know, our URL was misprinted in the latest <I>Hiking
News</I>. Please
tell your hiking friends that the correct URL is
<TT>http://www.asroutfitters.com/</TT>.
<LI>To collect a $1000 reward, turn in the name of the person who set
the
fire in the Bear Lake area last weekend.
<OL>
<LI>Call 888-555-1212.
<LI>Leave the name on the recording.
<LI>Provide contact information so we can send you the reward.
</OL>
</UL>
</DIV>
<H2 onClick="contactus()">Contact Us</H2>
<DIV ID="contactus"  STYLE="display=none">
<P>If you have suggestions or comments about the site or other
information
we could provide, we'd love to know about it. Drop us an e-mail at
<A
HREF="mailto:asroutfitters@raycomm.com">asroutfitters@raycomm.com</A>.
Of course, you could also contact us more traditionally at the following
address: </P>
<ADDRESS>ASR Outfitters
<BR>
4700 N. Center <BR>
South Logan, UT 87654<BR>
801-555-3422</ADDRESS>
</DIV>
</BODY>
</HTML>
```

4. Add the script at the top that controls all this. The four functions—one for each collapsible element—check to see if the element is hidden (DISPLAY=none) and set it to display as a block element (DISPLAY=block) if it started out hidden. If it started out visible, the function sets it to display as hidden. This function allows visitors to toggle the headings to collapse and expand with each click.

```
<SCRIPT>
<!--
function contactus() { if
(this.document.all.contactus.style.display=="none")
```

```
                    (this.document.all.contactus.style.display="block") ;
                    else (this.document.all.contactus.style.display="none")   ; }
        function otherstuff() { if
        (this.document.all.otherstuff.style.display=="none")
                    (this.document.all.otherstuff.style.display="block") ;
                    else (this.document.all.otherstuff.style.display="none")   ; }
        function whatwedo() { if
        (this.document.all.whatwedo.style.display=="none")
                    (this.document.all.whatwedo.style.display="block") ;
                    else (this.document.all.whatwedo.style.display="none")   ; }
        function whathere() { if
        (this.document.all.whathere.style.display=="none")
                    (this.document.all.whathere.style.display="block") ;
                    else (this.document.all.whathere.style.display="none")   ; }
        // -->
        </SCRIPT>
```

The resulting collapsible document should look like that in Figure 13.5.

FIGURE 13.5

Here's Microsoft's version of the collapsible document.

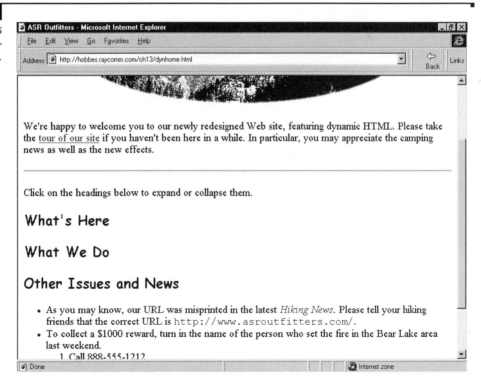

Implementing Browser Detection

If you plan to include DHTML capabilities in your HTML documents, consider implementing a JavaScript script to detect which browser your visitors are using. Remember, if visitors are not using the browser for which the documents were developed, they'll get error messages.

Your best bet is to let visitors first access a page that does not include DHTML capabilities and provide access to a page that does. Visitors who have DHTML-capable browsers can access the cool effects, and visitors who don't won't be bothered with those pesky JavaScript error messages.

You can use the following code in the beginning of your document to identify visitors using Internet Explorer 4 and shuffle them off automatically into dynhtml.html so they can get the full flavor. Other visitors who will get the content of the current document—presumably not dynamic, but certainly useful.

```
<!DOCTYPE HTML PUBLIC "-//W3C//DTD HTML 4.0//EN">
<HTML><HEAD><TITLE>Browser Redirect</TITLE>
<SCRIPT LANGUAGE="JavaScript">
<!--
browsName = navigator.appName;
browsVer = parseInt(navigator.appVersion);
if (browsName == "Microsoft Internet Explorer" &&
   browsVer >=4) {
   window.location = "dynhome.html" }
// -->
</SCRIPT>
</HEAD>
<BODY>
```

Then, within the document body, provide the content for the browsers that the script will not send away.

You can add extra detection clauses to identify other visitors and send them away too. For example, to also identify users of Netscape Navigator 4 and Internet Explorer 3—for example, to point them to documents using Style Sheets—add a couple more clauses right before the //--> end of the script:

```
if (browsName == "Microsoft Internet Explorer" &&
   browsVer >=3) {
```

CONTINUED

```
        window.location = "styleshome.html" }
  if (browsName == "Netscape" &&
     browsVer >=4) {
     window.location = "styleshome.html" }
```

Browser detection scripts can be useful whenever you have content that not all browsers can see.

Collapsing a Document the Netscape Way

To do it the Netscape way, you place menu items together in a line and then include the text below. If you leave it all lined up, you'll have gross holes in the page, as shown in Figure 13.2, earlier in this chapter. Follow these steps:

1. Start with a basic HTML document.

```
<!DOCTYPE HTML PUBLIC "-//W3C//DTD HTML 4.0//EN">
<HTML>
<HEAD>
<TITLE>ASR Outfitters</TITLE>
<STYLE TYPE="text/css">
<!--
BODY { font-size : 110% }
H1, H2, H3 { font-family : "Comic Sans MS" ; }
H1 { font-size : 180% ;  font-weight : bold }
-->
</STYLE>
</HEAD>
<BODY>
<CENTER>
<IMG SRC="asrlogo.gif">
</CENTER>
<P >We're happy to welcome you to our newly redesigned Web site,
featuring dynamic HTML. Please take the <A HREF="tour.html">tour of our
site</A> if you haven't been here in a while. In particular, you may
appreciate the camping news as well as the new effects. </P>
<HR>
```

PART

III

Moving Beyond
Pure HTML

```
<P>Click on the headings below to expand or collapse them.</P>
<H2>What's Here |
What We Do |
Other Issues and News |
Contact Us |
Collapse All </H2>

<P>Here's the latest information on the site.</P>
<UL>
<LI><A HREF="camping.html">Camping News</A> provides the latest comments
    from the trails. <BR>
<LI><A HREF="weather.html">Check Weather</A> offers weather updates from
    a variety of sources.<BR>
<LI><A HREF="clubs.html">Clubs</A> gives local hiking and mountaineering
clubs
    a place to provide information about their activities.<BR>
<LI><A HREF="catalog.html">Catalog</A> presents our entire inventory,
    including announcements of the latest sales.<BR>
<LI><A HREF="contact.html">Contact Us</A> links to a page with a contact
    form, e-mail addresses, snail mail addresses, and phone numbers.
    If it isn't here, you can't find us. <BR>
</UL>

<P>In addition to providing the latest camping and outdoor activities
news, we do
also provide mountaineering and hiking equipment nationwide via mail
order as well as through our stores in the Rocky Mountains.
Please take a few minutes to look through our <A
HREF="catalog.html">online offerings</A>.</P>

<UL>
<LI>As you may know, our URL was misprinted in the latest <I>Hiking
News</I>. Please
tell your hiking friends that the correct URL is
<TT>http://www.asroutfitters.com/</TT>.
<LI>To collect a $1000 reward, turn in the name of the person who set
the
fire in the Bear Lake area last weekend.
<OL>
```

```
<LI>Call 888-555-1212.
<LI>Leave the name on the recording.
<LI>Provide contact information so we can send you the reward.
</OL>
</UL>
<P>If you have suggestions or comments about the site or other
information
we could provide, we'd love to know about it. Drop us an e-mail at
<A
HREF="mailto:asroutfitters@raycomm.com">asroutfitters@raycomm.com</A>.
Of course, you could also contact us more traditionally at the following
address: </P>
<ADDRESS>ASR Outfitters<BR>
4700 N. Center <BR>
South Logan, UT 87654<BR>
801-555-3422</ADDRESS>
</BODY>
</HTML>
```

2. Add layer tags around each of the sections that will individually appear or disappear. Include in each the VISIBILITY attribute, set to HIDE. The name attributes for each of the layers must be unique—they're how the layers will be referred to from the functions you set up in the next steps.

```
<LAYER NAME="nswhathere" VISIBILITY="HIDE">
<P>Here's the latest information on the site.</P>
<UL>
<LI>
<A HREF="camping.html">Camping News</A> provides the latest comments
    from the trails. <BR>
<LI><A HREF="weather.html">Check Weather</A> offers weather updates from
    a variety of sources.<BR>
<LI><A HREF="clubs.html">Clubs</A> gives local hiking and mountaineering
clubs
    a place to provide information about their activities.<BR>
<LI><A HREF="catalog.html">Catalog</A> presents our entire inventory,
    including announcements of the latest sales.<BR>
<LI><A HREF="contact.html">Contact Us</A> links to a page with a contact
    form, e-mail addresses, snail mail addresses, and phone numbers.
    If it isn't here, you can't find us. <BR>
```

PART

III

Moving Beyond
Pure HTML

```
</UL>
</LAYER>

<LAYER NAME="nswhatwedo" VISIBILITY="HIDE">
<P>In addition to providing the latest camping and outdoor activities
news, we do
also provide mountaineering and hiking equipment nationwide via mail
order as well as through our stores in the Rocky Mountains.
Please take a few minutes to look through our <A
HREF="catalog.html">online offerings</A>.</P>
</LAYER>

<LAYER NAME="nsotherstuff" VISIBILITY="HIDE">
<UL>
<LI>As you may know, our URL was misprinted in the latest <I>Hiking
News</I>. Please
tell your hiking friends that the correct URL is
<TT>http://www.asroutfitters.com/</TT>.
<LI>To collect a $1000 reward, turn in the name of the person who set
the
fire in the Bear Lake area last weekend.
<OL>
<LI>Call 888-555-1212.
<LI>Leave the name on the recording.
<LI>Provide contact information so we can send you the reward.
</OL>
</UL>
</LAYER>

<LAYER NAME="nscontactus" VISIBILITY="HIDE">
<P>If you have suggestions or comments about the site or other
information
we could provide, we'd love to know about it. Drop us an e-mail at
<A
HREF="mailto:asroutfitters@raycomm.com">asroutfitters@raycomm.com</A>.
Of course, you could also contact us more traditionally at the following
address: </P>
<ADDRESS>ASR Outfitters<BR>
4700 N. Center <BR>
```

```
South Logan, UT 87654<BR>
801-555-3422</ADDRESS>
</LAYER>
```

3. Add anchor tags (<A>) with links to JavaScript event handlers to the menu at the top of the page. Each uses an anchor tag to call a JavaScript function (that you'll define in the next step).

```
<H2>
<A HREF="javascript:nswhathere()">What's Here</A> |
<A HREF="javascript:nswhatwedo()">What We Do</A> |
<A HREF="javascript:nsotherstuff()">Other Issues and News</A> |
<A HREF="javascript:nscontactus()">Contact Us</A> |
<A HREF="javascript:clearall()">Collapse All</A> </H2>
```

4. Add the scripts to the top of the page. The clearall() function sets all the layers to hidden. Each other function calls this function to clear the previous text before showing the new text. Otherwise, it would all overlap. The individual functions set the individual sections (named in the individual layer tags) to show.

```
<SCRIPT>
<!--
function clearall() {
    document.layers.nswhathere.visibility="hide" ;
    document.layers.nscontactus.visibility="hide" ;
    document.layers.nswhatwedo.visibility="hide" ;
    document.layers.nsotherstuff.visibility="hide" ; }

function nswhathere() { clearall() ;
        document.layers.nswhathere.visibility="show" ; }
function nscontactus() { clearall() ;
        document.layers.nscontactus.visibility="show" ; }
function nswhatwedo() { clearall() ;
        document.layers.nswhatwedo.visibility="show" ; }
function nsotherstuff() { clearall() ;
        document.layers.nsotherstuff.visibility="show" ; }
// -->
</SCRIPT>
</HEAD>
<BODY>
```

The resulting document looks like that in Figure 13.6.

PART

III

Moving Beyond
Pure HTML

FIGURE 13.6

Netscape's layers create the collapsible document.

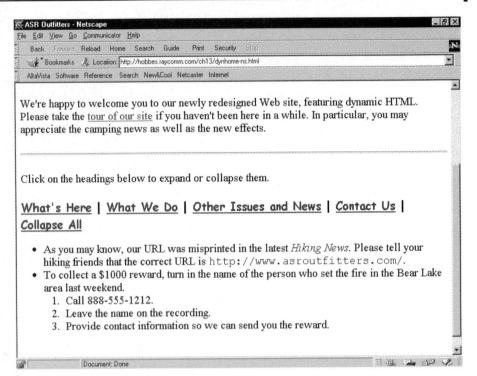

Where to Go from Here

As you learned in this chapter, Dynamic HTML offers loads of potential for making your pages leap off the screen. Though this chapter covered only the basics, you can combine any Style Sheet characteristic with a JavaScript function to make your pages flash, change, and move.

If you feel confident using Style Sheets and JavaScript, we recommend that you experiment with combining these two HTML aspects. You'll find a complete Style Sheet reference and JavaScript reference in the Master's Reference. Or, if you're not quite up to speed with these two topics, we recommend visiting the following chapters:

- See Chapter 5 for information about developing and applying Style Sheets.

- See Chapter 11 to learn how to use JavaScript scripts in your HTML documents.

- Check out Chapter 14 for information about push technologies.

Chapter

14

Implementing Push Technologies

Implementing Push Technologies

You start your browser…type in a URL…click Submit…and…wow (or ho-hum)…there's a Web page. This is the essence of *pull* technologies in which you (the browser user) request and receive information from a server. Now, you can also use *push* technologies, in which you don't have to access and request information from a server. The server brings it to you. What's more, you can set up your Web site so that other people can use these technologies to get information fed to them from your site automatically. Hmmm. This has some potential.

In this chapter, we'll introduce you to push technologies, show you what you can do with them, and show you how to set up your Web site so that visitors can access it with push technologies. Microsoft and Netscape have their own ideas about how push technologies should work. Microsoft's Webcasting technology is based on the CDF (Channel Definition Format), which is an early implementation of XML. Netscape's technology is Netcaster—augmented with Marimba's Castanet transmitter and channel technology to enhance plain Web page push.

XML is an abbreviation for Extensible Markup Language, which provides a middle ground between the simple but limited capabilities of HTML and the virtually unlimited capabilities and complexity of SGML. XML, as currently specified in a draft W3C specification, works with both HTML and SGML.

CDF is an abbreviation for Channel Definition Format, which is an extension of XML used for Microsoft's push technology.

Both CDF and XML are based at least in part on traditional HTML; however, Netscape offers a proprietary push technology solution as another part of its overall Netcaster product. This proprietary technology (Castanet) is not part of a published standard nor is it strictly HTML—it's also somewhat beyond the scope of this book. Therefore, in this chapter, we'll focus mainly on HTML-based push and Microsoft's approach, which is also supported by Netcaster and is relatively inexpensive.

What Are Push Technologies?

Every time you access a page, follow a link, or refresh your browser window you *pull* information from a Web server. With *push* technology, the server simply brings the information to you.

With true push technologies, server-side software accesses information and sends it to your computer. The push technologies we'll discuss in this chapter are more like "scheduled pull technologies." Rather than your directly accessing a Web page and getting information from it, your browser wanders to the server, collects specified information, and then brings it to you—on a schedule that you specify. It's kind of like most e-mail software: The software accesses the server at a specified interval and delivers messages to your mailbox.

In using push technologies, you're actually *subscribing* to a Web site (or *channel*, as it's known) or to information that a Web site provides in much the same way that you subscribe to a newspaper (only you don't have to pay anything). When you subscribe to a newspaper, it's delivered to you at regularly scheduled intervals—probably at the same time each day. Subscriptions to Web channels work the same way. You subscribe to a Web site, and you receive information from that Web site at intervals you specify or whenever new information becomes available. Rather than going out and surfing the Web for updated information, you can use push technologies to access and open a Web page every so often, receive notification whenever updated information is available, or get that updated information sent directly to your computer.

When the push program checks out the pages you've subscribed to, it "crawls" from the page to which you subscribed through (by default) two or three levels. That is, it finds all the pages within two or three links of the subscribed page (which is probably the home page). If content is buried farther down in the site, it's not likely to be retrieved unless you make special provisions, which we'll discuss later in this chapter.

Additionally, after the pages have been crawled, they're stored on your computer, and you can look at them at your convenience, even if you're not connected to the Web. In this respect, push technology gives you a Web browser for use when you're not actually connected to the Web.

What's more, using push technologies is a cinch, both from the information provider and Web site visitor perspectives. After you set up the subscription, all you do is click a button from a subscription menu. Take a look at Figure 14.1, which shows you some of the channels that come preconfigured for Internet Explorer.

FIGURE 14.1

You use push technologies to subscribe to Web sites and automatically get information from them.

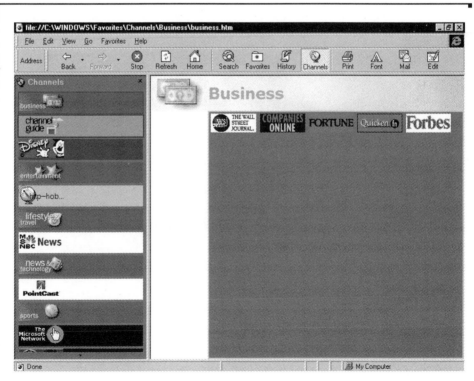

PART

III

Moving Beyond
Pure HTML

Subscribing to Channels

You can subscribe to any Web site using either Internet Explorer or Netscape's Netcaster—regardless of whether the developers made any special arrangements for push technology. For example, as shown in Figure 14.1 earlier in this chapter, you can subscribe to any number of Web sites that, by nature, provide regularly updated information. You can get information such as news, weather, sports, and entertainment delivered right to your computer. Many of these sites are set up explicitly as channels so that visitors can most efficiently access them.

You can also subscribe to sites that are not officially set up as channels. From the visitor's perspective, there's little difference between the two—possibly the official "channels" will be more usable or more structured, but the differences are not likely to be substantial.

To subscribe to a site using Internet Explorer (version 4, remember), simply follow these steps, in which we subscribe to the RayComm site:

1. Choose Favorites ➤ Subscriptions ➤ Subscribe to open the Subscribe dialog box, as shown in Figure 14.2.

FIGURE 14.2

The Internet Explorer Subscribe dialog box

2. Click Customize to start the Web Site Subscription Wizard and specify your options. If you don't want to review the options, simply click OK instead of Customize.

That's all there is to it.

To subscribe using Netcaster, follow these steps. Again in this example, we'll subscribe to the RayComm site.

1. In any Communicator component (Navigator, Composer, and so on), choose Communicator ➤ Netcaster to open the welcome screen:

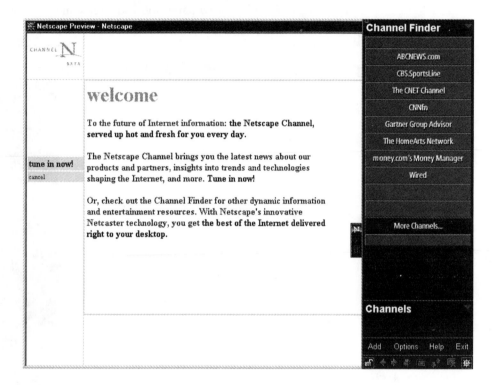

2. Click Add to open the Channel Properties dialog box:

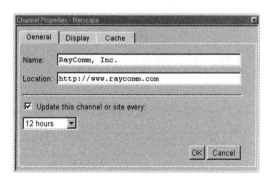

3. Enter a title and the URL of the site in the Name and Location boxes. You can also specify how often you want to receive new information in the Update This Channel or Site drop-down menu.

4. Click OK.

5. Click Channels in the Netcaster pane, and you'll see something like Figure 14.3.

FIGURE 14.3

Your channel is now on the list.

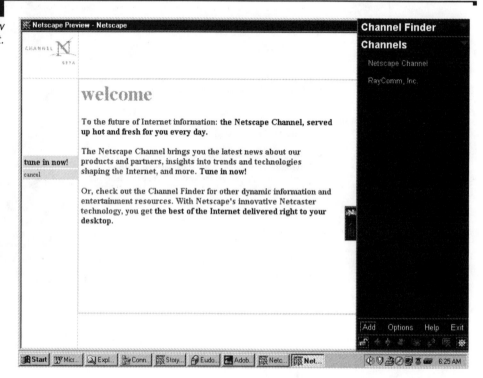

Setting Up Your Site As a Channel

Although anyone using Internet Explorer or Netcaster can subscribe to your site, if you take a few minutes to "officially" make your site accessible as a channel, you'll be able to better control your visitors' experience.

NOTE

Keep in mind that browsers only crawl down two or three levels by default, so you must place the most important content to be retrieved within two or three links of the home page.

Setting up a site as a channel requires only that you create one additional document (a CDF file) and upload it to the Web server with the rest of your site. Then, as long as one of your Web pages—probably the home page—links to the CDF file, Internet Explorer's crawling technology will find it and the instructions it contains.

The special CDF file looks very much like an HTML document, but a little different in terms of tags and content. Here's the sample document created for the ASR Outfitters site.

```
<?XML version="1.0"?>
<CHANNEL HREF="http://hobbes.raycomm.com/ch14/asrhome.htm">
<LOGO HREF="http://hobbes.raycomm.com/ch14/pushicon.gif" STYLE="icon" />
<LOGO HREF="http://hobbes.raycomm.com/ch14/pushasr.gif" STYLE="image" />

<ITEM HREF="http://hobbes.raycomm.com/ch14/asrcomplete.htm">
<TITLE>ASR Outfitters Home Page</TITLE>
<ABSTRACT>The latest announcements and information from ASR
Outfitters</ABSTRACT>
</ITEM>

<ITEM HREF="http://hobbes.raycomm.com/ch14/camping.html">
<TITLE>ASR Outfitters Camping Information</TITLE>
<ABSTRACT>The latest ASR Outfitters Camping news</ABSTRACT>
</ITEM>
</CHANNEL>
```

The first line functions as the <!DOCTYPE> tag for the CDF file—specifying the kind of document.

The next three lines give general information about the channel—the URL for the main page and the addresses for the logo and icon files. The logo is an 80×32 pixel GIF file, and the icon is a 16×16 GIF file. (By the way, the closing tag actually does have a /> at the end—this is not a typo.)

PART

III

Moving Beyond
Pure HTML

The following two sets of tags provide the basics about each item in the channel—the URL, the title, and a brief description in between the abstract tags. You can include as many or as few items in your channel as you want.

To create your own CDF file, simply fill in the title, URL, and abstract for the channel you're creating. Easy! After you finish the file and save it as a CDF document, include a link to it, as shown in the following code:

```
<A HREF="asr.cdf"><IMG SRC="pushasr.gif" ALIGN="" WIDTH="80" HEIGHT="32"
BORDER="0" ALT="">Click to Subscribe to the ASR Channel</A>
```

Now, anyone can view your site, click the icon, and subscribe, as shown here:

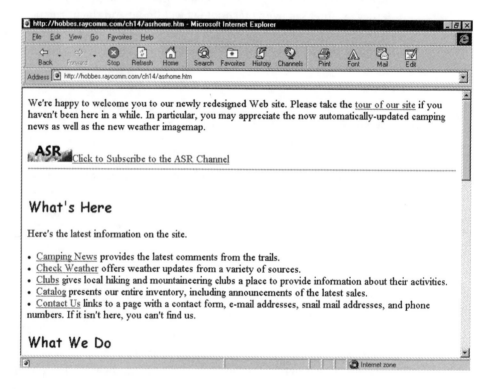

Where to Go from Here

Neat stuff! In this chapter, you got a taste of push technologies and the benefits they offer you and your visitors. As you can see, subscribing to and creating channels is a cinch. By subscribing to channels, you can easily and regularly get information without having to manually access a Web site. And, by pushing information, you can extend the same benefit to your visitors.

Let's venture to some of these other chapters:

- Visit Chapter 13 for information about Dynamic HTML.
- See Chapter 20 to learn how to create a coherent Web site.
- Take a look at Chapter 21 to find out specifics for creating public, personal, and intranet sites.

PART

III

Moving Beyond
Pure HTML

PART IV

More Tools for the HTML Pro

- *Choose HTML development tools*

- *Convert existing documents to HTML*

- *Validate HTML code*

- *Generate HTML from a database*

- *Create searchable HTML*

Chapter

15

Choosing HTML
Development Tools

FEATURING

Choosing HTML Development Tools

Choosing the HTML development tools that are right for you can be a daunting task. You'll find tons of software out there—both for developing HTML documents and for developing and editing images.

In this chapter, we'll examine the options and take a look at some specific tools. We'll discuss what each has to offer, point out any drawbacks, and recommend some tools. We can't tell you which to choose, but we can give you some information that will help you determine which are best for your needs. Let's take a look.

Choosing an Editing Tool

In general, there is no "right" kind of tool or "right" approach to developing HTML documents. It depends on you—your needs, preference, and budget. In the following sections, we'll examine the three categories of development tools:

- Text editors
- WYSIWYG editors
- High-end editors

Text Editors

You use a text editor when you want to manually enter HTML tags and attributes. If you've been following the sample code in this book and entering tags and attributes, you've been using a text editor.

Although hand-coding HTML is somewhat time consuming and requires careful proofreading, doing so gives you much more flexibility and control over the documents you create. For example, when the HTML 4 specification became available, developers using text editors could immediately incorporate the latest HTML effects—all they had to do was enter version 4–compliant tags and attributes. Developers using WYSIWYG editors could not immediately use version 4–compliant effects; they had to wait for the software to catch up with the latest specification.

Also, as we pointed in Chapter 3, by hand-coding you can add HTML extensions, such as JavaScript or Style Sheets, which you can't do (or easily do) using most WYSIWYG editors. If you want to add these advanced effects to your documents, using a text editor is the way to go.

Text editors come in two varieties:

- Plain text

- Enhanced

Plain text editors, such as Notepad (Windows), Simple Text (Macintosh), and vi (Unix), offer nothing more than text-editing capabilities. Figure 15.1 shows a basic HTML document in Notepad.

Enhanced editors, such as HotDog or HTMLpad, give you editing capabilities and automated commands that let you add code with a click of the mouse. Figure 15.2 shows HotDog in action.

Whether you use a plain text editor or an enhanced editor depends on your specific needs. If you want some help in entering tags and attributes, use an enhanced editor. If you don't mind doing all the typing yourself or if you simply prefer a smaller, faster editor, you'll probably choose a plain text editor.

WYSIWYG Editors

A WYSIWYG (What You See Is What You Get) editor lets you see roughly how the HTML document will look in a browser as you're creating it. Rather than entering tags and attributes and then viewing the results in a browser, you can preview documents as you create them. Most WYSIWYG editors display only the actual text, not the HTML code. Figure 15.3 shows how this works in Netscape Composer.

FIGURE 15.1

Plain text editors, such as Notepad, basically give you a blank screen in which to create an HTML document.

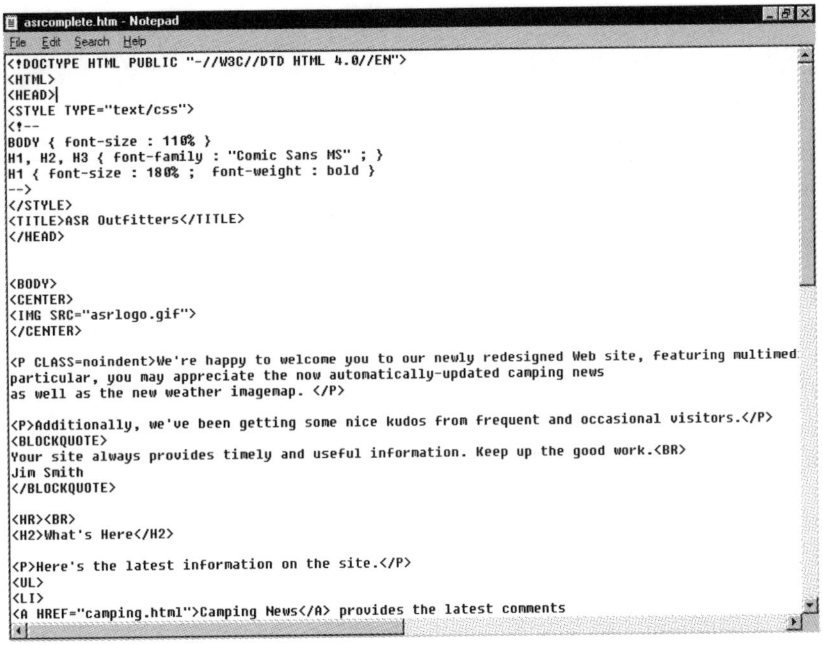

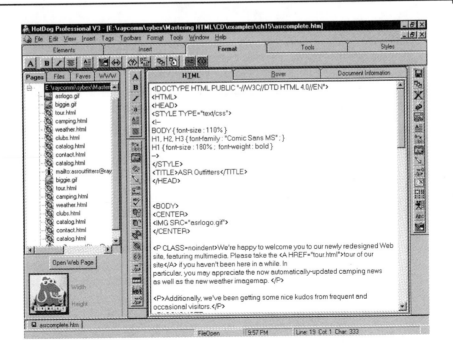

FIGURE 15.2

Some editors, such as HotDog, provide space to enter code and buttons and menu options that add code for you.

FIGURE 15.3

Most WYSIWYG editors, such as Netscape Composer, display no code—only an approximation of what the page will look like in a browser.

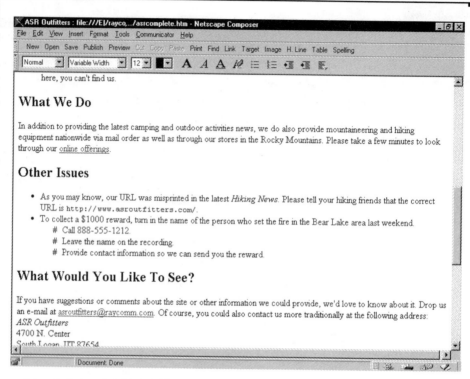

Some text editors, such as HomeSite (shown in Figure 15.4) and HotDog, offer a preview mode that mimics WYSIWYG. The difference between these and true WYSIWYG editors is that you cannot make any editing changes in the preview mode.

WYSIWYG editors offer you a middle ground between ease of use and the ability to do exactly what you want with your Web pages. With a WYSIWYG editor, you can quickly develop acceptable Web pages; you can create HTML documents about as fast as you can type. You can add HTML effects just by clicking a button or by choosing an option from a drop-down menu. Also, because you see the text and formatting, and not the code, it's easier to concentrate on the content.

Some drawbacks are associated with WYSIWYG editors, however. The biggest is that the WYSIWYG aspect is somewhat misleading. As we've mentioned throughout this book, the exact results of HTML code can vary significantly from browser to browser and from computer to computer. If you compare the WYSIWYG preview in any of these editors with the results in an actual browser, you'll likely find that the display is somewhat different, as shown in Figures 15.5 and 15.6.

FIGURE 15.4

*Some text editors,
such as HomeSite,
display previews of
the results.*

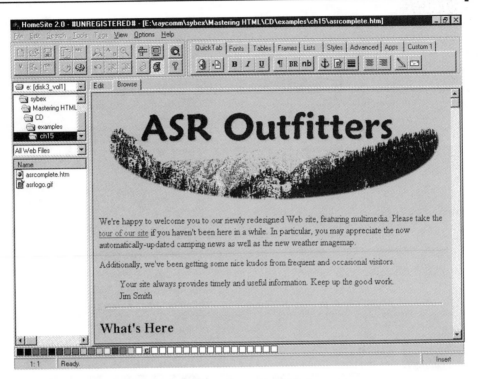

Another drawback is that WYSIWYG editors commonly produce nonstandard code in order to provide the effects most users expect. For example, using Netscape Composer you can indent page elements simply by clicking the Indent button. Although the ability to indent elements might be handy, the HTML specification doesn't provide any sort of tag or attribute for indention. So, in this example, Composer produces nonstandard code—and relies heavily on luck to work in most browsers.

Check out Chapter 17 to find out how to validate HTML code and avoid the nonstandard code that WYSIWYG editors sometimes produce.

A third drawback is that you can't use WYSIWYG editors to add the latest and greatest HTML effects, such as Style Sheets and Frames in HTML 4. The software companies must develop the application after the latest HTML specification becomes available.

FIGURE 15.5

An HTML document
previewed in
HotDog

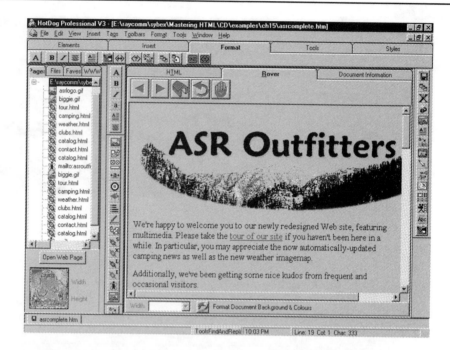

FIGURE 15.6

The same HTML
document viewed in
Netscape Navigator

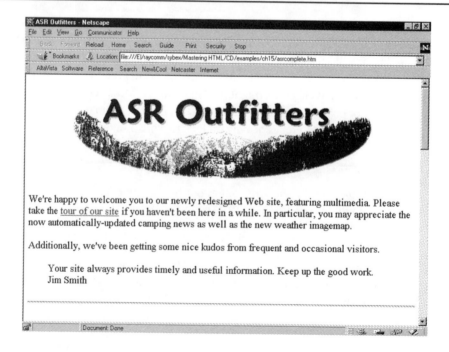

A final drawback to WYSIWYG editors is that they often don't provide a way (or an easy way) to add JavaScript or multimedia effects. For example, it's technically possible—according to the documentation—to use Netscape Composer to add JavaScript to your documents. To do so, however, you have to access a dialog box for each line of JavaScript you want to add, a tedious process. Furthermore, the editor "helpfully" tweaks the code, often causing existing code not to work properly. In this case, a text editor is definitely a better choice.

High-End WYSIWYG Editors

Finally, if you want to easily put together and maintain a complete Web site, you might look into high-end WYSIWYG editors such as NetObjects Fusion or Microsoft FrontPage. Although these editors are rather expensive, they give you great control over formatting and can help you develop really spiffy Web pages.

High-end WYSIWYG editors treat page elements as objects, meaning that you can click and drag elements around on the page and place them where you want. In doing so, you can create interesting layouts that will look fairly consistent from browser to browser.

 TIP

If you're a Quark Xpress or PageMaker user, you'll probably find these products the most useful and least frustrating of all the options.

In addition, high-end WYSIWYG editors provide site management services, which help you see how pages in the site connect and relate to each other. For example, take a look at Figure 15.7, which shows Microsoft FrontPage. Each time you create a page, FrontPage automatically adds the page to the overall structure. All you have to do is name the page and add content to it.

Many high-end WYSIWYG editors include templates. For example, using the Front-Page Wizard, you can choose from several templates, dozens of page options, and various color and background options. Similarly, in NetObjects Fusion, most templates include a banner, link buttons, bullets, and other formatting options. Templates come in a range of styles, from fun, as shown in Figure 15.8, to the more practical. And, if you want, you can pick and choose elements from the templates or start from scratch and create your own.

FIGURE 15.7

High-end WYSIWYG editors, such as FrontPage, help you manage your site.

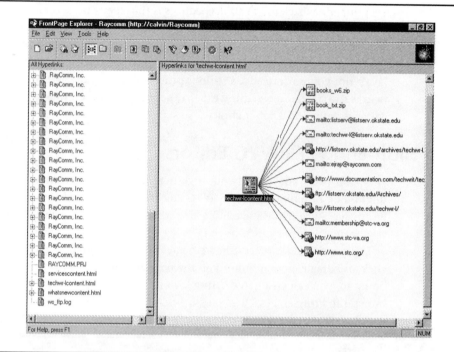

FIGURE 15.8

Fusion templates provide formatting for all the basic page elements.

Choosing an Image-Editing Tool

Just as there's no "right" tool to generate HTML, there's also no one image-editing tool that will meet every need for every person. Which one you choose is up to you, your needs, and your budget. Here are some of the more popular image-editing tools:

Paint Shop Pro offers a wide range of capabilities, it's easy to use, and it's affordable. In fact, we used Paint Shop Pro to create the images used in the sample Web sites throughout this book. For more information, visit www.jasc.com.

Photoshop is a more expensive tool, but you can literally do anything with it. Take a look around at any book or magazine cover—most were created with Photoshop. Unless you have very sophisticated image-editing needs or are already experienced with high-end image editing, this product might offer more than you need. However, it's *the* tool if you're looking for power. For more information, check out www.adobe.com.

Image Composer offers a new paradigm. Rather than working with bitmapped images, you can move and manipulate parts of images—just as you can using drawing capabilities in Microsoft Word or PowerPoint. If you're already familiar or proficient with Photoshop or similar products, you might find the paradigm shift a little challenging, but if you're starting from scratch, this is likely to be both easy and fun to learn. Find more information about Image Composer at www.microsoft.com.

Where to Go from Here

So, those are your basic choices, folks! In this chapter, you saw the advantages and disadvantages of using text editors, WYSIWYG editors, and high-end WYSIWYG editors. You also got an idea of the image-editing tools you can use. Exactly which tools you choose depends on your specific needs.

On from here!

- Visit Chapter 7 to learn how to include images in your HTML documents.
- Take a look at Chapter 16 to learn about conversion tools.
- Go to Chapter 17 to learn about validation services.
- See Chapters 20 and 21 to learn how to develop coherent public, personal, and intranet sites.

Chapter

16

Converting
Documents to HTML

FEATURING

Converting Documents to HTML

Company A's Vice President in Charge of Changing Stuff recently announced that she thinks that they should convert all hardcopy product documentation to online documentation—all 1473 pages of it. Starting from scratch, a team of developers created a bunch of HTML documents. Five months and hundreds of hours later, they have online documentation.

Company B's Vice President in Charge of Changing Stuff announced that she thinks that they should convert all hardcopy product documentation to online documentation—all 1547 pages of it. Company B chose to use HTML conversion tools. A few days later, and—voilà!—it has online documentation.

What's the difference? Technique!

In this chapter, we look at *conversion*, the process by which you take existing documents and turn them into HTML documents. We'll tell you why this is useful, show you its limitations, and introduce you to some conversion tools. Although conversion is not a panacea, you'll find that it can save you loads of time.

Why Convert?

For years, companies and organizations have developed marketing materials, policies and procedures, and documentation for hardcopy distribution. As the Web and intranets became popular, however, many companies moved this information online, spending thousand of hours regenerating it.

Thanks to fairly new and sophisticated conversion tools, taking existing documents and turning them into HTML documents has never been easier. No more are the days of re-creating hardcopy documents from scratch. Using conversion tools, such as those built into your word-processing software or special software, you can convert existing documents to HTML with little hassle and in a short time.

Conversion tools are particularly helpful when you are developing legacy documents and documents for multiple uses and when many people, such as everyone in an organization, are turning hardcopy into HTML. Legacy documents are simply those that have been around a long time but that are important to your organization. Personnel procedures and company policies are common examples, as are documentation for existing (and unchanging) products, and any kind of information that floats around the company in binders for common use. These documents are usually lengthy, and reformatting them from scratch for online use would take considerable time. Using a conversion tool, you can quickly reformat them for an intranet, for example.

A conversion tool is also handy when you are developing documents for multiple uses. For example, suppose you're developing documentation that you'll publish in hardcopy, place on the company's intranet, and make available on CD. In this case, you can develop documents primarily for one format—probably hardcopy—and then convert that to the other formats. Because HTML is not the primary format, you use a conversion tool to make the HTML format available.

If many people in an organization need to convert hardcopy documents, using a single conversion tool is much faster and more accurate than training everyone to code HTML. In addition, the result will be documents that are uniform in appearance.

Conversion tools, however, are not the perfect solution for converting documents to HTML. Although conversion tools convert the material to HTML, they don't reformat the material so that it's usable and readable online.

As a rule, good online documents have shorter paragraphs, shorter chunks of information, and more bulleted lists than hardcopy documents—all in an effort to make documents easier to read on the screen. Figures 16.1 and 16.2 show how good hardcopy and online formatting differ. With this in mind, you might use a conversion tool as a starting point and then manually reformat.

FIGURE 16.1

Hardcopy documents can have longer paragraphs and sections.

INTRODUCTION¶

Writing instructions for computer users continues to challenge technical communicators, as it apparently has for several years, based on the steady flow of new publications about computer documentation. The ever-increasing complexity of computer software, coupled with the near-impossibility of targeting with focus and precision the needs of a heterogeneous audience, leads to continued discussion and recommendations of the best or most usable or highest quality documentation; yet the literature yields few new solutions for the technical communication community. ¶

Much research and publication in the technical communication field continues to focus, as it has for the past several years, on how to provide "effective documentation" — whatever that might be — to computer users, including both novice users and others who need to use computers as a tool to accomplish specific tasks. Books, anthologies, periodicals, and articles about writing procedures, user's manuals, and usable

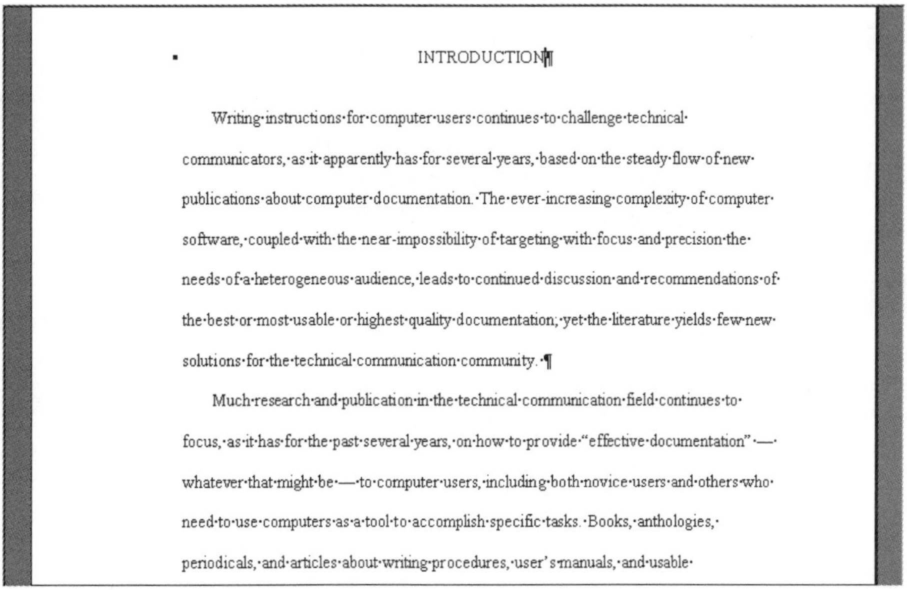

FIGURE 16.2

Online documents require short paragraphs, short sections, frequent headings, and bulleted lists.

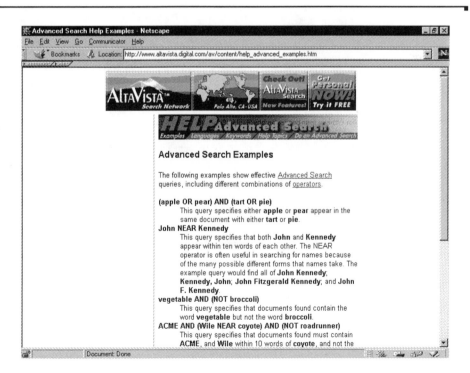

See Chapters 20 and 21 for some tips that will help improve the usability of your site.

So what exactly do the converted results look like? Of course, it varies from document to document and from software to software. Figure 16.3 shows how one document appears when converted with HTML Transit.

FIGURE 16.3

A converted document viewed in Internet Explorer

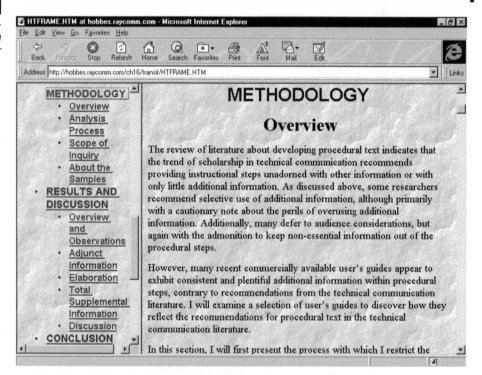

Selecting and Using Conversion Tools

The quality of the resulting HTML document depends on the conversion tools you use. You can use a word-processing program or conversion software. Which you choose depends on the originating document and the quality of HTML document you need. Let's take a look at your options.

Using Word-Processing Software

Using most newer word-processing programs, you can save documents as HTML with just a few mouse clicks. For example, Microsoft Word 2 and 6 can both save a document in HTML with the help of the Internet Assistant, which is available at the Microsoft site (www.microsoft.com). Microsoft Word 97 has a built-in Save As HTML option.

Using Microsoft Word (or similar word-processing programs) is ideal if:

- You are converting only a few documents.

- You are converting short documents.

- The resulting HTML documents don't need special or interesting formatting.

To convert a document with Word 97, simply open it, choose File ➤ Save As HTML, and specify a file name. This conversion will produce an HTML document that most browsers can read; however, as Figure 16.4 shows, the results are often—well—plain.

FIGURE 16.4

The Microsoft Word conversion is cheap and expedient, but the quality suffices only for basic applications.

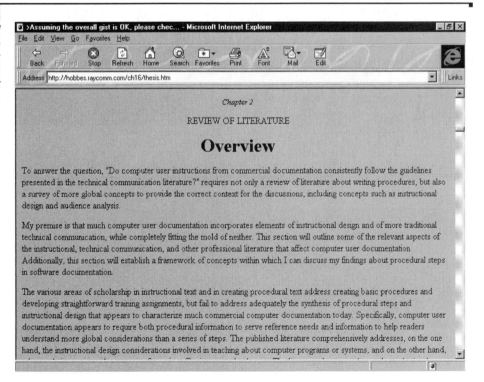

If you decide to use this option, you must use *styles* (predefined formats) throughout your documents. For example, to create a heading in a Word document, you can select the word, click the Bold button, and make the text a few point sizes bigger. (We don't recommend this, but you could do it.) A better solution is to select the text and then select a heading style from the drop-down menu in the formatting toolbar.

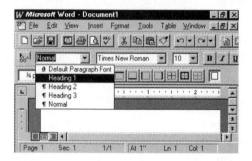

Heading styles are only one example of the styles you can apply. In applying styles throughout your documents—to paragraphs, captions, tables of contents, and so on— you prepare your document for conversion to HTML. Word essentially looks at each style and generates the HTML equivalent. For example, take a look back at Figure 16.3 earlier in this chapter. Notice how the headings are of different sizes—corresponding to different HTML heading levels. These HTML headings are correct because the Word document included styles for each element.

Using Conversion Software

Using conversion software—such as HTML Transit, WebMaker, or WebWorks—gives you much more flexibility in converting documents than using word-processing software. Consider conversion software if:

- You are converting many documents.
- You are converting long documents.
- You are converting intricately formatted documents.

You'll find demo versions of some of this software, including HTML Transit, on the Companion CD.

Conversion software offers you capabilities you simply don't get in word-processing software. For example, you can break long documents into shorter ones or automatically generate a table of contents. You can easily set up document formats, navigation structures, icons, and page layouts. In the long run, you save time and have to do very little manual formatting once the documents are converted.

Another big advantage of conversion software is that you can create a template and reuse it. You set up the template one time and create lots of HTML documents that look similar without having to manually format or set up the conversion for each document—similar documents convert similarly.

Also, you don't absolutely have to use styles throughout the original document—although the results will be better if you do. Some conversion software can recognize text patterns in your documents and convert to HTML tags based on those patterns.

Although the specific steps vary from software to software, the general process is the same. Here are the steps for doing so with HTML Transit:

1. Develop and save the original document with the software of your choice—Word, WordPerfect, FrameMaker, or whatever.

2. Reference the documents from HTML Transit.

3. Develop a template, adjusting the HTML Transit formatting settings so that the HTML documents appear as you want. Most conversion software offers a variety of formatting options and icons, as shown here:

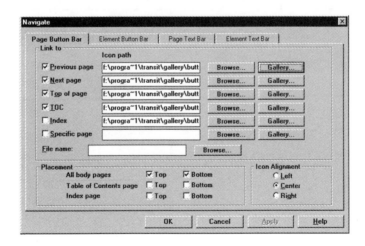

4. Save the template.

5. Click the Translate Publication button:

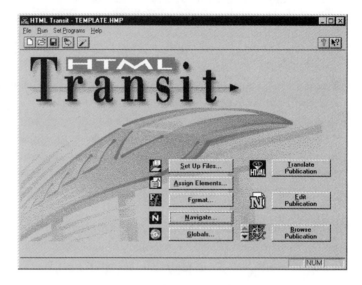

The resulting HTML document—a sample is shown in Figure 16.5—includes the formatting you specify.

Conversion software produces spiffy HTML documents.

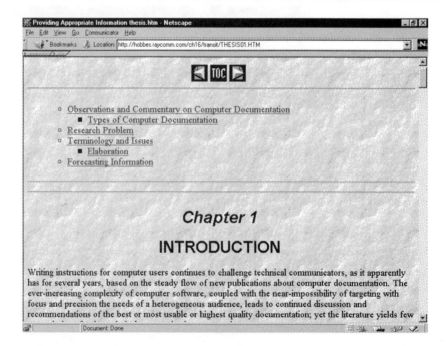

Where to Go from Here

In this chapter, we showed you how converting documents to HTML can save you loads of time and effort, and we showed you how different tools meet different conversion needs. You'll find that converting documents isn't nearly as hard as it sounds, using either existing tools or specialized applications.

From here, we recommend a visit to one of several chapters:

- See Chapter 2 to learn more about readability and usability.

- Breeze through Chapter 20 to learn more about developing effective online documents.

- Go to Chapter 21 for information about developing public, personal, and intranet sites.

Chapter

17

Using Validation Services

f you've been working through this book, you've probably encountered at least one case in which you tested your documents in a browser and they just didn't work right or didn't work at all. Maybe you forgot a closing tag...maybe you had extra spaces in a tag...or maybe you used a Netscape Navigator extension, which won't work in Internet Explorer...or maybe....

Regardless of the problem, you ended up troubleshooting and fixing it—that is, if you could find it. In this chapter, we'll show you how validation services can do a lot of your troubleshooting for you. Using validation services, you can ensure that your HTML code and structure comply with the HTML specification of your choice—or even work with a particular HTML extension or a particular browser. Additionally, you can use services on the Web (or software on your own computer) to ensure that your links work and to assess overall document style, accessibility, and likely download time.

In this chapter, we'll explain why validating HTML documents is important, introduce you to some validation tools, and demonstrate what they can do for you. At the end of the chapter, we'll show you how different validation services catch different problems so that you can see how to most effectively use services and choose those that best meet your needs.

Why Use Validation Services?

A validation service is a fancy term for a computer program that checks your HTML document—it verifies that the code you've entered is accurate and complete. The biggest advantage to using a validation service is that it can save you loads of time in troubleshooting problems in your HTML code. For example, particularly in long documents, you might spend a lot of time looking for a missing slash (/) in a closing tag, a typo in code (oops!), or a missing quotation mark (").

These types of errors might cause your document to appear odd, result in unexpected effects, or cause referenced files, such as an image file, not to appear. A bigger concern, though, is that documents with these errors might display just fine in your browser but not display properly (or at all) in your visitors' browsers. Browsers such as Netscape Navigator and Internet Explorer tend to tolerate a certain amount of coding errors. For example, the code shown in Figure 17.1 has a minor error in it, which Internet Explorer overlooks—it displays the page just fine. When NCSA Mosaic 3 displays the same HTML document, the bullets are missing, as you can see in Figure 17.2.

FIGURE 17.1

Some browsers overlook (or just let you get away with) this minor error— missing <UL> tags around a set of <LI> list items.

```
<HR><BR>
<H2>What's Here</H2 >
<P>Here's the latest information on the site.</P>


<LI><A HREF="camping.html">Camping News</A> provides the latest comments
    from the trails. <BR>
<LI><A HREF="weather.html">Check Weather</A> offers weather updates from
    a variety of sources.<BR>
<LI><A HREF="clubs.html">Clubs</A> gives local hiking and mountaineering clubs
    a place to provide information about their activities.<BR>
<LI><A HREF="catalog.html">Catalog</A> presents our entire inventory,
    including announcements of the latest sales.<BR>
<LI><A HREF="contact.html">Contact Us</A> links to a page with a contact
    form, e-mail addresses, snail mail addresses, and phone numbers.
    If it isn't here, you can't find us. <BR>


<H2>What We Do</H2>
<P>In addition to providing the latest camping and outdoor activities news, we do
also provide mountaineering and hiking equipment nationwide via mail order as well as
through our stores in the Rocky Mountains.
Please take a few minutes to look through our <A HREF="catalog.html">online
offerings</A>.</P>

<H2>Other Issues</H2>
<UL>
<LI>As you may know, our URL was misprinted in the latest <I>Hiking News</I>. Please
tell your hiking friends that the correct URL is
```

FIGURE 17.2

Other browsers won't overlook minor coding problems.

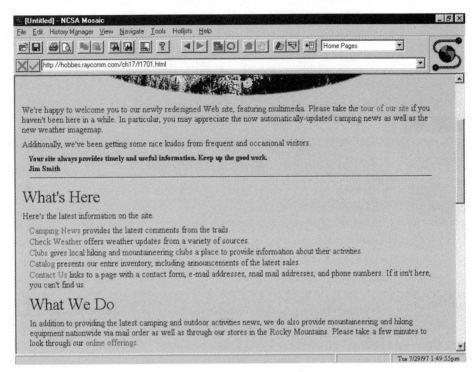

But, you say, nobody uses NCSA Mosaic 3 any more. To a certain extent, you're right—most people surfing the Web use either Internet Explorer or Netscape Navigator. You don't know, though, which other browsers might also have a problem with your faulty code, nor do you know who might be using those browsers. In particular, aural browsers, used by people with visual impairments, can often have problems with nonstandard code because these browsers essentially read the pages aloud.

Another advantage of using validation services is that you can verify that the code you used complies with an HTML standard. For example, if your document complies with the 3.2 or 4 standard, you can be sure that 3.2 or 4.0–compliant browsers will display your documents without a glitch.

Validation services also point out where you've deviated from an HTML standard—say, if you've used Netscape Navigator or Internet Explorer extensions. If you're developing HTML documents for an intranet and everyone uses Internet Explorer, you can safely use Internet Explorer extensions. If you're developing documents for a public site, however, you might at least want to know when you deviate from the HTML standard so that you can adjust for effects that browsers might not display consistently.

Finally, validation services can help you clean up your code. If you've made lots of changes to an HTML document, chances are you've probably left dangling tags or attributes that no longer belong in the document—tags that you're likely to overlook but that validation services will snag in a snap. As easy to use as WYSIWYG editors are, they don't always produce good or standard, compliant HTML code, as shown in Figure 17.3.

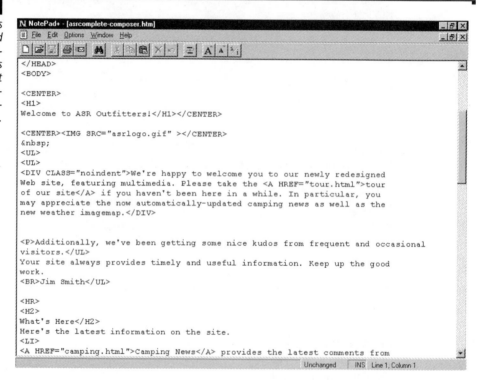

That said, validating your HTML code does not guarantee that your document is well formatted or complete. Documents that validate properly can easily be ugly and unusable. For example, a 17-page document with only three paragraphs and no headings could validate just fine—but it would be a rare visitor that managed to slog through it. Validation is a matter of knowing what your code looks like and how it works. A document that validates is not an accomplishment if all your other goals—including readability and usability—aren't met.

What Constitutes "Valid" HTML?

Back in Chapter 1, we talked about HTML standards and the World Wide Web Consortium (W3C), which develops the standards. HTML is a specific subset of SGML (Standard Generalized Markup Language). As such, it offers a neat little thing called a Document Type Definition (DTD), which expresses how documents must be structured in computer terms. In addition to the plain language specification published as the HTML standard, the consortium also publishes HTML DTDs.

These DTDs are the technical definitions of "proper" HTML. You can use validation services to compare your document with how the document "should" look, based on the <!DOCTYPE> tag at the top of your document or based on the type of HTML with which you claim compliance.

In addition to the "standard" DTDs, many validation services create specialized DTDs to validate your document for compliance with various Netscape- or Microsoft-specific standards. The proprietary extensions you use are checked to see whether you used them correctly, rather than being rejected because they're not standard (heck, you knew they weren't standard when you put them in, right?).

Using Related Services

In addition to validation services that verify you've entered code correctly and conformed to a specific HTML version, you can also use special validation services to check things like links, style, and usability.

Using Link Checkers

Link checkers resemble validation software in that they do automatically and quickly what you could do slowly and methodically—click on each and every link in every one of your pages and be sure that they all work. As with validation, these programs don't do anything you can't do yourself, but why not let the computer do it for you?

Even though you might check links and find them working just fine, link validation services can help keep your links current. For example, if you include links to pages outside your site, chances are at some point you'll end up with broken links. Remember that information on the Web changes constantly, and pages that you link to could change, move, or be deleted entirely. Although a link checker can't tell you if a page's content changes, it can tell you that the link itself no longer works—and more quickly than you or your visitors can do so.

Similarly, link checkers can help you track links within your own site. Particularly as your site grows, it's easy to accidentally break a link with a typo or by moving or renaming a page and forgetting to change some or all the pages that link to it. Link checkers tell you when you've broken a link.

TIP

Check links while you're developing your site *and* after you've uploaded your site to the server.

Using Style and Analysis Tools

Style and analysis tools check your documents for stylistic and usability problems. Many of these tools closely resemble—or are integrated into—other tools. In addition to the strict analysis, you also get editorial comments on the structure of your document. Rather than checking for strict compliance with HTML specifications or for compliance with browser-specific extensions, these tools analyze accessibility, check for optional—but recommended—tags such as ALT= attributes in <IMG> tags, and comment if you used "click here" for anchor links.

If you have specific other validation needs, check out some of the search engines on the Internet. Even spell checkers (www.goldendome.net/Tools/WebSter/, among others) are available to help you develop accurate, readable, and usable HTML documents.

Finding and Using Validation Services

You can find validation services in several places—on the Web, within software, or in separate validation software. Perhaps the easiest services to use are those you'll find on the Web. In most cases, all you have to do is paste your URL (or even plain HTML code) into a form on the Web site, as shown in Figure 17.4, and the validation service checks out your code. Easy!

For a variety of HTML validation services, check out these Web sites:

WebTechs (www.webtechs.com/html-val-svc/) offers a variety of options, from strict HTML 2 checking through checking for compliance with Netscape Navigator or Internet Explorer proprietary tags. You paste your HTML code in the WebTechs form, and it is checked. When you use validation services that offer only checking based on a URL, you have to upload your document to a Web site, then check it, then fix it, then upload it again to check the revised version—far more time consuming and tedious than just copying and pasting the code to check it.

FIGURE 17.4

*Simply type
your URL or
paste your
code sample into
the WebTechs form.*

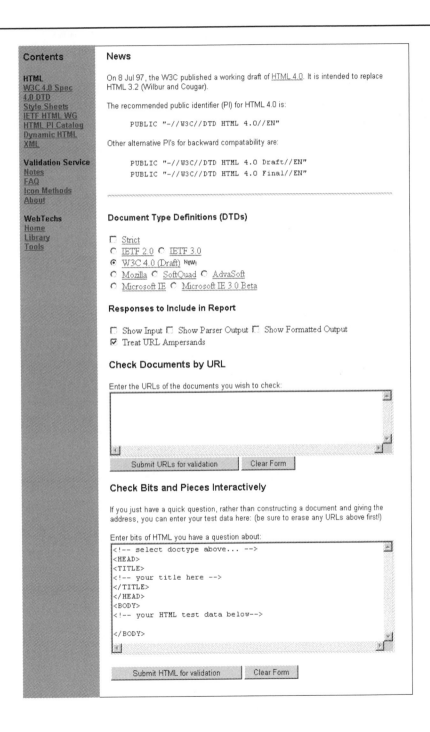

Contents

HTML
W3C 4.0 Spec
4.0 DTD
Style Sheets
IETF HTML WG
HTML PI Catalog
Dynamic HTML
XML

Validation Service
Notes
FAQ
Icon Methods
About

WebTechs
Home
Library
Tools

News

On 8 Jul 97, the W3C published a working draft of HTML 4.0. It is intended to replace
HTML 3.2 (Wilbur and Cougar).

The recommended public identifier (PI) for HTML 4.0 is:

```
PUBLIC "-//W3C//DTD HTML 4.0//EN"
```

Other alternative PI's for backward compatability are:

```
PUBLIC "-//W3C//DTD HTML 4.0 Draft//EN"
PUBLIC "-//W3C//DTD HTML 4.0 Final//EN"
```

Document Type Definitions (DTDs)

☐ Strict
○ IETF 2.0 ○ IETF 3.0
◉ W3C 4.0 (Draft) New!
○ Mozilla ○ SoftQuad ○ AdvaSoft
○ Microsoft IE ○ Microsoft IE 3.0 Beta

Responses to Include in Report

☐ Show Input ☐ Show Parser Output ☐ Show Formatted Output
☑ Treat URL Ampersands

Check Documents by URL

Enter the URLs of the documents you wish to check:

```
[                                        ]
```

    Submit URLs for validation   Clear Form

Check Bits and Pieces Interactively

If you just have a quick question, rather than constructing a document and giving the
address, you can enter your test data here: (be sure to erase any URLs above first!)

Enter bits of HTML you have a question about:

```
<!-- select doctype above... -->
<HEAD>
<TITLE>
<!-- your title here -->
</TITLE>
</HEAD>
<BODY>
<!-- your HTML test data below-->

</BODY>
```

    Submit HTML for validation   Clear Form

WebLint (www.cen.uiuc.edu/cgi-bin/weblint) offers several levels of HTML standard compliance checking. This program boasts that it identifies lint (errors) in your documents so that you can "pluck" it off.

Bobby (www.flfsoft.com/bobby/) lets you check your page for compliance with specific HTML levels (not yet version 4, though) as well as perform a style analysis. For example, it checks for compatibility with specific browsers and for universal access. If your page would be difficult for an aural or a text-only browser to parse, Bobby will tell you. In case you're wondering, the name *Bobby* refers to British police officers, not to anyone in particular.

NetMechanic (www.netmechanic.com) checks both HTML standard compliance and links to ensure that they all work.

Doctor HTML (www2.imagiware.com/RxHTML/) checks only one page at a time (for free, at least), but provides a lot of useful style analysis information, including time to load and other settings that you could make to help your page load or look better. Doctor HTML also checks out the page structure. The emphasis is on usability, not just HTML compliance. With a subscription, it will analyze your entire site at once.

Other Validation Services

Linkbot is a stand-alone software package, and you'll find it on the Companion CD. You will also find a number of Perl script-based solutions on the Internet.

You can also use validation services that are built into HTML editing software. For example, HotMetal (also available in an evaluation version on the CD) has a setting that keeps you from entering any invalid HTML code.

To show you the range of validation services available, we introduced some errors into an HTML document and submitted it to several validation services. We found that the results varied greatly from service to service. Listing 17.1 shows part of the code we used for the test.

Listing 17.1

```
<!DOCTYPE HTML PUBLIC "-//W3C//DTD HTML 4.0//EN">
<HTML>
<HEAD>
```

```
<STYLE TYPE="text/css">
<!--
BODY { font-size : 110% }
H1, H2, H3 { font-family : "Comic Sans MS" ; }
H1 { font-size : 180% ;  font-weight : bold }
-->
</STYLE>
</HEAD>

<BODY>
<CENTER>
<H1>Welcome to ASR Outfitters!</H1>
<IMG SRC="asrlogo.gif">
</CENTER>
<P CLASS=noindent>We're happy to welcome you to our newly redesigned Web
site, featuring multimedia. Please take the <A HREF="tour.html">tour of our
site</A> if you haven't been here in a while. In
particular, you may appreciate the now automatically updated camping news
as well as the new weather imagemap. </P>

<P>Additionally, we've been getting some nice kudos from frequent and
occasional visitors.</P>
<BLOCKQUOTE>
<FONT FACE="Comic Sans MS>
Your site always provides timely and useful information. Keep up the good
work.<BR>
Jim Smith </BLOCKQUOTE>
</FACE>

<HR><BR>
<H2>What's Here</H2 >
<P>Here's the latest information on the site.</P>

<LI><A HREF="camping.html"><IMG SRC="camping.gif"></A>
<A HREF="camping.html">Camping News</A> provides the latest comments from
the trails. <BR>
<LI><A HREF="weather.html">Check Weather</A> offers weather updates from a
variety of sources.<BR>
```

```
<LI><A HREF="clubs.html">Clubs</A> gives local hiking and mountaineering
clubs a place to provide information about their activities.<BR>
<LI><A HREF="catalog.html">Catalog</A> presents our entire inventory,
including announcements of the latest sales.<BR>
<LI><A HREF="contact.html">Contact Us</A> links to a page with a contact
form, e-mail addresses, snail mail addresses, and phone numbers. If it isn't
here, you can't find us. <BR>

...


</BODY>
</HTML>
```

A WebLint gateway provided fairly terse feedback, line by line, so you can track down the errors easily.

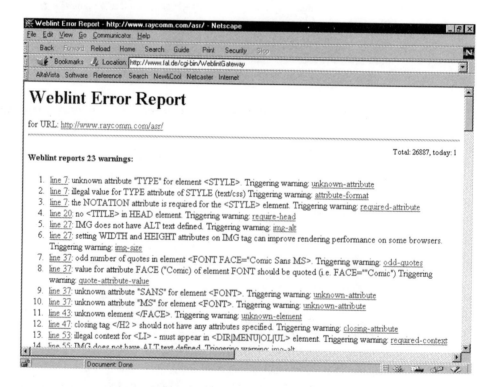

On the other hand, Bobby provided small icons superimposed over the checked page and hyperlinks to the problems and description—much friendlier.

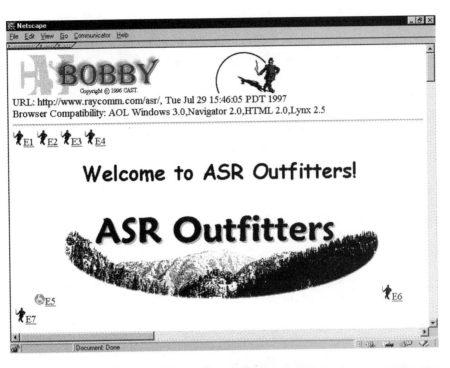

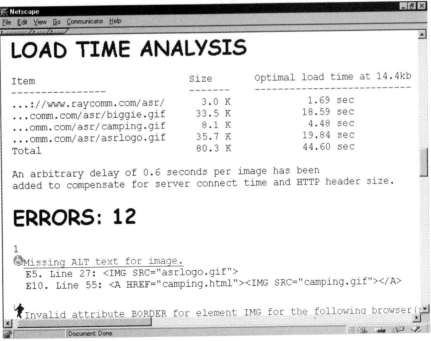

We recommend trying several of the services we've mentioned in this chapter. See which you like best, which are the most comprehensive, and which offer the most assistance in refining the structure of your page.

Where to Go from Here

In this chapter, you learned how validation services can help improve your HTML documents. In particular, they can ensure that your code is clean and that it complies with an HTML standard. They can also point out where your code deviates from a standard, ensure that links work, and even help make your documents readable and usable. Neat stuff!

If you're looking for a good chapter to visit next, try one of these:

- See Chapter 15 to find out about HTML development tools.
- Breeze through Chapter 16 to learn to convert existing documents to HTML.
- See Chapters 20 and 21 to learn how to develop coherent public, personal, and intranet sites.

Chapter

18

Generating HTML
from a Database

Generating HTML from a Database

A database is simply a collection of information arranged so that you can easily access and use it. A phone directory, a catalog, and a mailing list are examples of databases you've probably used.

In a way, the World Wide Web is a database—the world's largest. It's a collection of information that anyone connected to the Internet can access and use. The Yahoo! site (at www.yahoo.com), which is a collection of information about Web sites, including descriptions and URLs, is another database within the larger World Wide Web database.

As an HTML guru (you are one by now if you've made it to this chapter), you might need to move information from a database into a format that you can publish in an HTML document. In this chapter, we'll show you how to convert database information into HTML documents, look at a range of database tools, and show you a general process for generating HTML from a database.

Why Generate HTML from a Database?

Although it sounds complicated (it's not too bad, actually), generating HTML from a database saves a tremendous amount of time. For example, suppose you work for a company that manufactures nuts and bolts. Management decides to make the enormous product catalog—which includes thousands of items—available on the corporate Web site. You could spend weeks doing the data entry, or you could spend almost as much time moving pages from the catalog into and out of your favorite HTML tools.

Your best bet is to develop the online catalog by pulling information directly from a database. Even developing a new database specifically for online information is a better choice than entering information into an HTML document from scratch. Why? A computerized database is a dynamic entity, meaning that you can constantly add, change, and remove information. If you use database software to create the online catalog, updating your HTML documents is almost automatic—and a snap. The alternative is to find and manually edit each and every affected Web page every time some itty-bitty scrap of information changes.

When you generate HTML from a database, you can also provide online information in any number of segments. For example, you can list products by size, weight, color, or whatever, and you can fairly easily change how you present information once you have a database in place.

Generating HTML from a database is a good solution for the company that manufactures nuts and bolts; however, a database is not an ideal solution in all cases, particularly if the cost of setting up and maintaining the database outweighs the benefits. For example, if your company manufactures only one or two products, you might just as easily—perhaps more easily—develop an online catalog by simply creating a few HTML documents.

Exploring Your Options

How you generate HTML from a database depends on your specific needs and resources, which vary according to the size of your company and the size of the database. We're going to look briefly at the options for a very large company and for a small company. Most situations, however, fall somewhere in between, and so we'll focus on that scenario. The basic principles apply in any situation.

The Large Company Scenario

If you work for a large organization that has company-wide database solutions in place, you're probably using Oracle, Sybase, or Informix software. You probably also have programming resources at your disposal or have access to high-end (and fairly expensive) software such as Cold Fusion or Live Wire that automatically generate HTML documents from your database.

If you have programming resources and can create a custom database solution, that's your most sophisticated and flexible option. Your goal, regardless of resources, is to develop a database that's suitable for Web publication, and you need an expedient solution to push the data onto the Web. Most of the solutions discussed in this chapter will work for you.

The Small Company Scenario

On the other hand, if you work for a small company that uses server space from an ISP, you're likely to be locked into the ISP's tools, and you probably won't be able to link directly from your actual database (that you use in the office daily) into the Web.

If you must offer a live database to your visitors—so that they can run queries and possibly even change the data in real time—you'll have to use a generic solution: Perl scripts. Although the process for including a Perl script is beyond the scope of this chapter, we have provided some basic instructions and sample Perl code in the `examples/ch18 folder` on the Companion CD. If you choose to use a Perl script, this is a good place to start.

If you can settle for an expedient solution, read on. The in-between solution—discussed in the next section—lets you use the tools provided in most desktop database applications to save different "views" of the database in HTML and then simply link to those pages from the rest of your site.

The In-Between Scenario

In this situation, you generate HTML from a database using tools that are moderately priced and easily accessible, yet give you a broad range of capabilities. We assume that you have access to a Windows (95 or NT) Web server, have access to the data (either from a high-end database or from a desktop database), and need to get the information out to the Internet (or out to an intranet).

Deciding to Use a Database

If you do not yet have a database in place—and, therefore, don't know whether generating information from a database will best meet your needs—here are some questions to ask:

- Do you have a variety and/or large quantity of information?

- Does the data change frequently or require regular updates or maintenance?
- Do you realistically have the technical and financial resources to create a database?

If you answered yes to the first or second of these questions, you probably have some need for a database. If you also answered no to the third, reassess your needs before you jump into it—this isn't a one-day project.

ASR Outfitters decided to use a database for part of its site because of the variety of its products and their ever-changing availability. Rather than editing every product page every time prices, products, or availability changes, ASR Outfitters developers want to update the master database and then quickly and easily make that information available through the Web.

Deciding Which Information Should Go on the Web

At some point in this process, you'll need to decide which information within your database you should publish on the Web. You might want to publish all the information—that's certainly an option. If not, here are some considerations:

- Which information will visitors find most useful? ASR Outfitters wants visitors to see all the available product information, so they publish it all.
- Which information will visitors not need? Aside from internal documentation, pricing, and marketing information (which is all kept in different databases), ASR decided that publishing nearly all product information was appropriate.
- Which information can you not provide to the public? Because its product database is separate from confidential information, ASR did not have to contend with this problem. Management chose not to make cryptic acronyms and abbreviations available. This was not for security purposes but was an effort to reduce visitors' confusion.

You don't have to answer these questions now, but keep them in mind as you're working through the remaining sections in this chapter.

Choosing Software

You need to select software that matches your budget, platform, and database size. Although we can't tell you exactly what you need (there are simply too many variables), we can tell you what your options are. Here are some of the database software choices:

- Microsoft FoxPro
- Microsoft Access
- Lotus Approach
- Most other Macintosh or Windows database applications

Each of these applications can easily save HTML documents, and most can exchange data through a server, thereby making them reasonable candidates for almost any database you'd want to create. You'll find that these software packages are flexible and easy to use. You can provide your database information as HTML with a couple of mouse clicks.

Using these software packages, you can create two types of database views:

Static database view: Visitors click links to access information on predefined pages that you supply. You generate HTML documents regularly (weekly, perhaps), and visitors simply view those documents. For example, ASR could create a static database view to show its products and their availability. This solution works with all Web servers and in nearly all situations—it just takes time to regularly create and re-create the views.

Live database view: Visitors search the database and view information they want to see, rather than choosing from a list. For example, ASR could let visitors search for hiking boots, rather than browsing for the hiking boots entry. This solution not only requires database software, but also a Web server (on a Windows computer, in our example), full-time network access, and a tool to tie the pieces together. You use the database software just as you would for the static database view; however, you use the server, network access, and additional tools to enable the database and server to communicate.

ASR Outfitters chose to use Microsoft Access, simply because the company is standardized on Microsoft Office products; the consistent interface was a driving force. Also, Access gives them the option of easily creating either a static or a live database view.

TIP

In the following sections, we show you how ASR Outfitters developed both a static and a live database view and show you how to generate HTML from each type.

Generating Static HTML from Databases

If you decide to create a static database view, generating HTML from it is a cinch. Exactly how you do this depends on the software you're using, but the general process is that shown in Figure 18.1.

Generating HTML from a static database takes data straight from the database to HTML documents.

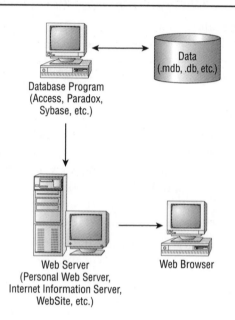

Here are the steps ASR followed to generate HTML from its static database:

1. Set up a template document, containing ASR Outfitters header and footer information, plus a special comment tag so that Access would know where to put the information.

2. In Access, set up the report (view of the data) that visitors will see.

3. Save the document as HTML (File ➤ Save As HTML) and use the Wizard to:
   - Select a template
   - Select a report

- Select a location
- Save the settings

At the end of the process, ASR Outfitters had something similar to Figure 18.2.

FIGURE 18.2

ASR Outfitters publishes static database views because of the ease and simplicity.

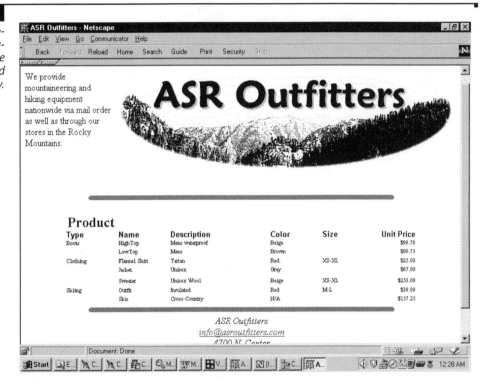

Generating HTML from Live Databases

If you decide to create a live database view, you'll find that the process is a bit more complicated, but certainly doable. Rather than publishing data directly from a database, as you can with static databases, you have to provide a way for the server (where your Web pages are published) to communicate with the database software, as shown in Figure 18.3.

FIGURE 18.3

Live databases require communication between the server and the database software.

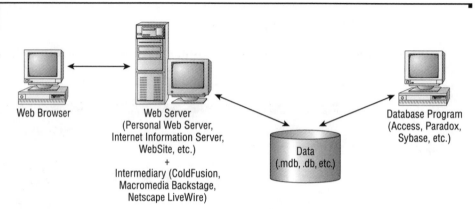

The software that allows this communication resides on the same computer system as the Web server, and it links the Web server to the data sources. Here are some of your options:

ColdFusion (www.allaire.com) is flexible, powerful, and easy to use. It allows you to connect to a variety of Microsoft and Oracle databases and lets you use nearly any Windows Web server.

Netscape LiveWire (home.netscape.com/) is a set of applications that are integrated into the Netscape Web Servers and allow connectivity to most major databases, including Oracle, Sybase, and Informix. Netscape LiveWire indirectly supports most Windows desktop database packages. It works with simple HTML administration pages that allow you to create pages from your database and maintain your site without writing your own scripts or programs.

Microsoft Internet Information Server or Personal Web Server in Conjunction with Access (www.microsoft.com) allows you to save database views as Active Server Pages, which these Microsoft Web servers can connect to the actual database files.

Microsoft BackOffice (backoffice.microsoft.com/) database products require somewhat more development effort than other solutions we mention here. If you are using a Microsoft database product, however, BackOffice lets you easily generate HTML from your database.

Macromedia Backstage (www.macromedia.com/) supports Oracle, Sybase, Informix, and Microsoft database packages, as well as desktop databases. Although it works with many Windows Web servers, it comes with the WebSite server from O'Reilly and Associates, a fully featured Web server.

Exactly how you generate HTML from a database depends on the software you choose; however, the general process is similar to that shown in Figure 18.4.

FIGURE 18.4

Setting up software to communicate with both a database and with a Web server rapidly grows complex.

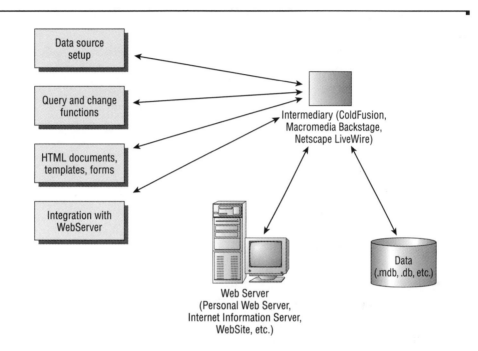

You can address these items in any order, but ASR found the following process effective:

1. Set up the data source. If you already have the data in a database—anything from Access to Oracle—this part is done.

2. Set up the intermediary software (Cold Fusion, in this case) to communicate with the database and with the Web server. The intermediary software usually connects directly to the database (the information) itself, and not to the data via the program used to create the data.

3. Set up query and change forms to get information out of and put information into HTML documents.

4. Edit the documents to fit into the overall site appearance.

ASR chose ColdFusion because it is easy to use and because developers could quickly get up to speed with it. They used the Web Application Wizard to select information to display, to select fields to search on, and to select additional data to present on request. The result was a simple HTML form in which visitors can enter search terms.

Developing the form—linked to the data—is as simple as choosing options from menus, as shown here.

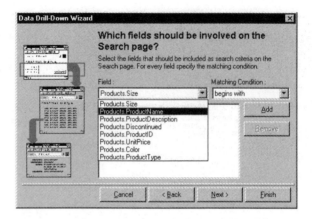

Furthermore, in addition to the plain text box shown in Figure 18.5, visitors can choose drop-down lists, checkboxes, or radio buttons.

FIGURE 18.5

A simple and easily generated ColdFusion search form

The HTML code, as shown in Figure 18.6, has the CFM extension. You'll find it easy to edit manually or with any HTML editing application.

HTML code that creates the ColdFusion search form.

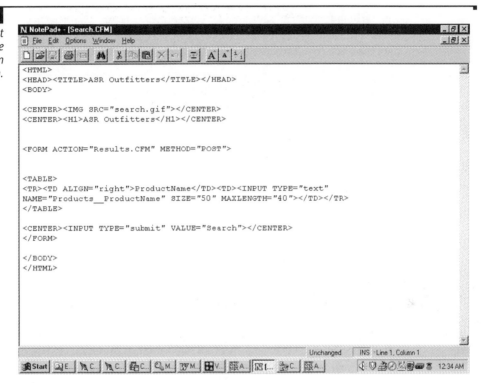

Maintaining Pages Generated from a Database

After you generate HTML from a database, you need to keep the pages current—just because they're automatically generated does not mean that they require no maintenance. Unlike maintaining regular HTML documents, maintaining database-generated documents involves both the data and the presentation.

You'll most likely update the data using the software in which you developed the database. You can also set up additional forms (such as a query form) to update the database directly from the Web. However, relatively few database applications lend themselves to online updating because of the potential security risks. Additionally, if you're providing, say, product information, few of your visitors are likely to be able to accurately and consistently update the product information.

Maintaining the presentation of database-generated documents is the easy part. You need edit only one or two documents, and the changes are reflected in all your pages.

Using Predefined Searches

One technique than can save time for you and your visitors is a *predefined search*. Instead of visitors typing in the search terms or even selecting terms from a list, they might simply click a link to automatically search in ways you define.

The easiest way to establish these searches is to go to the search form and run the query. Then, copy and paste the URL from the location line in the browser into the HTML editing program. For example, at the ASR site a detailed view of information about skis is at

```
http://calvin.raycomm.com/ASROutfitters/Detail.CFM?Products__ProductID=6
```

Adding this URL to the <A> tag,

```
<A HREF="
http://calvin.raycomm.com/ASROutfitters/Detail.CFM?Products__ProductID=6"
>Ski Information, Detailed</A>
```

makes it much easier for your visitors to find information.

Where to Go from Here

In this chapter, we showed you how generating HTML from a database can be useful, which tools you have at your disposal, which kinds of databases you can create, and—finally—how to generate HTML from a database. Knowing how to integrate databases into your Web site can save hundreds of hours of writing HTML pages plus add a whole new world of functionality to your site. Whether you're at a big company or organization, a small one, or somewhere in between, generating HTML from a database offers you a powerful tool for giving visitors easy-to-use information.

Where to now?

- Chapter 19 shows you how to make your entire site searchable.
- Chapter 6 gives you more information about Web servers.
- Chapter 9 covers HTML forms.
- Chapter 16 shows you how to convert existing documents for use on the Web.

Chapter

19

Making Your Web Site Searchable

Making Your Web Site Searchable

When you make your Web site searchable, you give visitors much more flexibility: They can jump immediately to the information they've come to get without necessarily following your predefined path. In this chapter, we're going to look at the techniques and tools you can use to add a searching capability to your site.

First, we'll discuss the pros and cons of making your site searchable (doing so is not for every site), and then we'll talk about which search tools, known as search engines, are available and how to use them. Although some of this information gets into advanced concepts, your comfort level will be fine if you've read Chapter 6, which is about understanding and using Web servers, and if you have a good grasp of the issues involved in HTML coding.

Choosing to Let Visitors Search Your Site

One of the most important decisions that you as a Web developer must make is how to present navigation choices to your visitors. Some sites are carefully mapped to guide visitors through every step from point A to point B. Other sites use common navigation shortcuts, such as headers and footers or navigation frames, to allow visitors to jump to specific points. Still other sites use database searches, and, of course, some sites combine any or all of these methods.

In addition to these methods, you have a more general tool for helping visitors to find their way around your site: a search engine. A *search engine* is a tool that visitors can use to find words or phrases within any or all of your Web pages.

NOTE

If you've spent any time on the Internet, you may have already used a search engine. For example, you may have tried AltaVista (www.altavista.digital.com) or Excite (www.excite.com), which provide an expedient way to search the Internet. All you do is enter a search query; the search engine plugs and churns for a second or two and provides a list of results containing documents that match your query.

Of course, as with everything, there are benefits and liabilities to adding a search engine to your site. Let's look at the benefits first.

The Benefits of Adding a Search Engine

A search engine helps visitors quickly determine whether your site has the information they want and helps them retrieve it. If visitors can enter the word *hiking* and instantly receive a listing of every single page on the ASR Outfitters site that contains that word, they can retrieve the information they need with much greater speed than by clicking through page after page of menus.

A search engine also helps visitors navigate from one part of the site to another, which can frequently be difficult. Visitors often have to find their way back to the home page of the site and then start over. With a search engine, they can search for what they want and immediately receive a link to it.

In addition, a search engine helps visitors view the sections of your site in a unified manner. At many sites, sections do not have a lot in common. Even though the information in all the sections may be useful, moving from one to another can be difficult, and a visitor may not even know that another section exists. A search engine helps visitors to get at this information.

The Liabilities of a Search Engine

As useful as a search engine is, there are some good reasons for *not* making your site searchable. For starters, adding a search engine can eat up significant resources (time and money). And, once your site is searchable, you have to keep it current. Before you make your site searchable, be absolutely sure that you have the resources to maintain it. A search engine that returns outdated information or dead links is a sure way to drive visitors from your site.

Privacy may also be a concern if your site contains sensitive documents. When dealing with search engines, there is no such thing as "security by obscurity." Be sure that you index only those pages that you want to be searchable, or, perhaps better still, don't add a search engine to your site. (See the sidebar "A Word about Indexing" for information about how this works.)

Yet another concern is site coherency. If you site has a clear predefined path that you want visitors to traverse, adding a search engine may defeat the purpose of the predefined path. In your planning process, consider the type of site you are building and whether a search engine fits with the scheme.

A Word About Indexing

The terms *index, indexing,* and *indexer* appear often in this chapter, and their use in this electronic context is similar to their traditional use. In the index at the back of this book, important words appear in alphabetic order along with the number of the page on which they are located. The purpose of an index is to help readers quickly locate a topic of interest.

The purpose of a computer index is much the same. All or most of the words in a group of files are listed along with their locations. If you want a specific word or concept, you can simply look it up in the index.

Once the index exists, special programs called *search front-ends* allow visitors to search the index for relevant documents. The programs that create the index are called *indexers* and include applications such as Glimpse, WAIS, WebIndex, Netscape's Catalog Server, and Microsoft's Index Server.

Using Low-Tech Alternatives

If you think a search engine may not be the best solution for your Web site but you would still like to add some searching functionality, you might consider some of the following alternatives. These approaches don't involve the overhead or resource drain associated with adding and maintaining a search engine.

Taking the "Guided Tour" Approach

This approach is basically a series of HTML pages with, at the extreme, only one link on each page: the link to the next page. This is probably the simplest and the least-flexible solution. Most sites that use this approach usually also provide links to the previous page and to the home page. It all amounts to the same thing, however— the visitor travels a set path and is not encouraged to deviate.

Whether this approach will work for you depends on the type of site you're creating. This approach works well, for example, in the context of an online book, which might include links only to the next page, to the previous page, and to the table of contents. The Jargon Guide, shown in Figure 19.1 (find it at `beast.cc.emory.edu/Jargon30/`) is a slightly enhanced version of this type of site. From any definition, visitors can go to the next definition, the previous definition, the index for the current letter, or the main page of the site. By also including links to other words, however, this site is also a version of the next approach.

Taking the "Everything Is a Link" Approach

At a site that uses this approach, each page links to all other relevant pages on (or off) the site for any word that visitors might associate with such a link. You'll recognize these sites because many or most of the words in the site link to something. Here's how it works. If you have the following text:

```
The quick brown fox jumps over the lazy dog.
```

you might have the following links:

- *The* links to a dictionary definition of the word *the*.
- *Quick* links to a page listing the relative velocities of land animals.
- *Brown* links to a page discussing pigmentation in mammal fur.
- *Fox* links to a page describing the animal.

And so on. You get the point.

Using Hierarchical Menus

Shortly before the advent of the Web, another method of information distribution became popular: Gopher. *Gopher* is a predominantly text-based series of menus, similar to the one shown in Figure 19.2, that consist of links to either files or other menus (which may be on the same server or another).

Although the World Wide Web stole Gopher's glory, Gopher sites still exist, and you can view them with any major Web browser. Many of the first Web sites looked just like Gopher sites. Of course, the documents were more attractive because HTML could do what plain text never could, but the interface was still a series of hierarchical menus leading to a file.

If you want simplicity and ease of use, consider using heirarchical menus —built with HTML, though—at your site. Visitors are familiar with menu structures and know how to use them. But, let's face it: Menus are boring when compared with the many visually appealing approaches.

FIGURE 19.1

The Jargon Guide

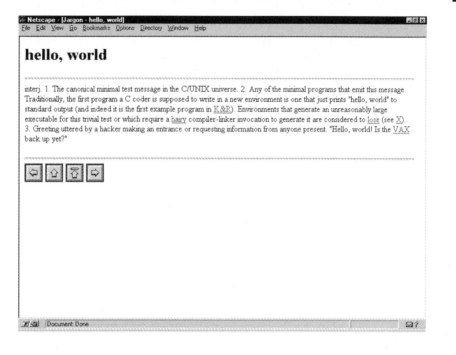

FIGURE 19.2

A Gopher menu site

Most of the best sites on the Internet use a combination of the three approaches we've just described, along with some unique twist. As you can see, it is possible to create an easily navigable site without resorting to a search engine.

Adding a Site Map

Even if you've lived in the same neighborhood your entire life, you probably need a map to get around the rest of the city. And when you visit a city for the first time, you most definitely need a map to find your way around.

The same is true when you visit sites on the Web. After you've visited a site several times, you usually know where to find what you want, but on your first visit (especially if you arrive via a link), you may have no idea where you've landed or what else is at the site.

One solution to this problem is a *site map*, a page that includes a structural overview of the site. It could take the form of a traditional map, a tree, or simply a list of pages and their locations. From a site map, visitors can gauge the breadth and depth of the site, determine where they are within the site, and figure out how to go to another section.

The simplest site map is a directory listing of all the files at the site. This solution is not necessarily ideal (or fascinating), but it can be effective. On the other hand, a site map can be completely graphical, giving visitors an instant visual sense of what the site contains. You can create an animated, interactive site map using Java or similar technology.

NOTE

A graphical site map is normally more difficult to create and to maintain than a textual one.

Figure 19.3 shows yet another solution, a site map automatically generated by a program that analyzes the directory structure of a site. Yahoo! (find it at www.yahoo.com) is also an example of this type of site map; the site is the entire World Wide Web. The site map shown in Figure 19.3 was generated with the program in Listing 19.1, a Perl script.

TIP

You can find this example, as well as the other program listings in this chapter, on the Companion CD. In this case, to use the program as is, simply copy it from the CD onto your Web site. You may need to modify some of the other examples before you can use them. In these cases, copy the program from the CD to your computer and edit it using the text editor of your choice.

FIGURE 19.3

*A site map
generated with
a Perl script*

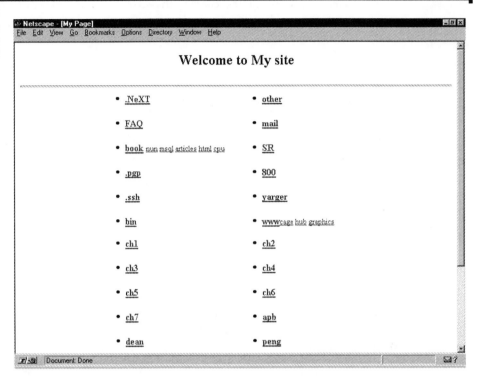

Listing 19.1

```perl
#!/usr/bin/perl -w ## Put the path to your Perl here.
# dir-it.pl
# Copyright 1997, Robert Niles - rniles@selah.net
#
# Permission to use as desired is granted as long as
# all Copyright information remains intact.
#
print "Content-type: text/html\n\n";


# Edit the sections, html_top and html_bottom as you please


# This is the path to the top level directory that
# will be checked and listed.
$top_dir = ".";
```

```perl
## Change directory to the current directory
chdir($top_dir);

## Initialize a counter
$count=1;

## Run the html_top function which prints a custom header
## For the HTML page.
&html_top;

## Start printing the site listing. Everything between here
## And the next HTML line is plain HTML code and can be edited
## as such.
print <<HTML;
<CENTER>
<TABLE WIDTH=480 border=0>
HTML

## Run the mainlist function which prints the main part of the
## site list
&mainlist;

## Start print HTML again.
print <<HTML;

</TABLE>
</center>
HTML

## Run the html_bottom function which prints footer to the HTML.
&html_bottom;
sub mainlist {
        opendir(DIR, ".") or die;
        @listing = readdir(DIR);
        foreach $list (@listing) {
```

```
    $stat = $list;
    stat($stat);
    if (-d _) {
            if ($list ne "." && $list ne "..") {
                    if ($count==1) {
                            print <<HTML;
<tr><td width=50% valign=top><UL><LI><b><a
href="$top_dir/$list">$list</a></b>
HTML
                            &subdir;
                            print "</td>";
                    }
                    if ($count==2) {
                            print <<HTML;
<td width=50% valign=top><UL><LI><b><a href="$top_dir/$list">$list</a></b>
HTML
                            &subdir;
                            print "</UL></td></tr>\n";
                    }
                    if ($count==1) {$count++;}
                    else {$count-;}
            }
    }
}
                    closedir(DIR);
}

sub subdir {
                    chdir($list) or return;
                    opendir(SUBDIR, ".");
                    @sub_listing = readdir(SUBDIR);
                    foreach $sub_list (@sub_listing) {
    $sub_stat = $sub_list;
    stat($sub_stat);
```

```
   if (-d _) {
        print "<font size=-1>";
        print
         qq%<a href="$top_dir/$list/$sub_list">$sub_list</a> %
              if $sub_list ne "." && $sub_list ne "..";
        print "</font>";
 }
            }
            $back = "..";
            chdir($back);
            closedir(SUBDIR);
}


sub html_top {
            print <<HTML;
<HTML>
<HEAD><TITLE>My Web Site</TITLE></HEAD>
<BASE HREF="http://my.isp.com/~me/">
<BODY BGCOLOR=#FFFFFF>
<center>
<TABLE WIDTH=580 BORDER=0>
<TR>
<TD align=center><h2>Welcome to my Web site</h2>
</TR>
</TABLE>
</center>
<HR>
HTML
}


sub html_bottom {
            print <<HTML;
</BODY>
</HTML>
HTML
}


exit(0);
```

Examining Perl Scripts

The first line in all these scripts is:

```
#!/usr/bin/perl -w ## Put the path to your Perl here.
```

Replace /usr/bin/perl with the location of the Perl program on your Web server. On a Unix machine the path is often /usr/bin/perl or /usr/local/bin/perl. On a Windows machine it will look something like C:\PERL\PERL.EXE.

The last half of the first line, Put the path to your Perl here, is simply a note to the reader called a comment. In Perl, a comment is anything that follows the # symbol (except for the # at the beginning of the script, which has a special meaning). Often, several # symbols appear in a row to make the comment easy to notice. You may even see something like this in a Perl script:

```
###################################################################
###################################################################
############### This next part is very important! ##################
###################################################################
###################################################################
```

In this way, whoever is reading the script will not miss whatever message the programmer has included.

Whenever the program sends actual HTML code to the visitor on the other end, it uses print commands. A small piece of code can be sent like this:

```
print "<h1>This is a small bit of HTML</h1>";
```

In contrast, a larger block generally looks like this:

```
print <<HTML;
<HTML><HEAD><TITLE>My Page</TITLE></HEAD>
<BODY>
<H1>My Page</H1>
<P>This is an entire HTML page.
</BODY></HTML>
HTML
```

Everything between the initial print <<HTM; and the final HTML line is simple HTML text. You can edit this text as you wish. Watch for words that begin with the $ character. These are usually the places where the Perl program inserts special values. For example, in the line print 'My name is $name'; the entry $name will probably be replaced by a name in the final output. If you are changing the HTML part of a script, edit or remove these entries only if you are sure that is what you want.

The script in Listing 19.1 originally came from the CGI Collection (find it at www.selah.net/cgi.html), a large number of CGI scripts covering many tasks commonly encountered by CGI programmers. There are many such collections on the Web, including the Selena Sol collection and Matt's Script Archive, both of which are included on the Companion CD.

You can probably use this script without modification. Simply copy it into your Web site as sitemap.cgi in whichever directory you would like your site map to begin. If you name the file index.cgi, the site map will be the default page for the directory. If you place a copy of the script as index.cgi in every directory on your site, you will have a directory-by-directory site map with multiple pages.

TIP

> You may need to check with your system administrator or get some special instructions to use this script, depending on the policies, procedures, and system configuration on the Web server you use.

Of course, using this script is only one way to implement a site map. Many commercial Web servers (such as Suite Spot from Netscape) come with tools that allow you to easily generate graphical site maps. In addition, NetObject's Fusion and the Website web server from O'Reilly and Associates (included on the accompanying CD as part of the Macromedia Backstage package) includes the site mapping programs. These programs do not generate site map HTML pages for the public, but rather generate site maps for your use. With these, you can add and modify pages and move them around the hierarchy of your site (among many other things).

Enabling Visitors to Search within Your Site

If you have examined all the options and have decided that adding a search engine to your site is worth the effort, the next step is to decide how to enable visitors to search within your site. Before you index your first page, answer the two questions in the following sections.

How Much of Your Site Will Be Indexed?

If you are absolutely confident that you want everyone to be able to hunt down every word on your site, the answer to this question is easy: Index the entire site.

For most people, however, there are gray areas, and this question requires a great deal of thought. Here are some sections of your site that probably should not be indexed:

- Pages that exist only to help you maintain the site
- Any password-protected pages (or index them on a separate search engine that is accessible only from the password-protected area)

NOTE

You want password-protected information hidden from the public. Also, you don't want to annoy visitors by letting them link to a blocked area that they are then forbidden to access.

Before you bring your search engine online, go through each page on your site (or each section, if you have a large site) and decide whether you want to allow it on the search engine. If other people have a stake in the content of your site, be sure you have a consensus before bringing a search engine online. Do not assume that a page should be on a search engine just because it is publicly available.

Who Can Access Your Search Engine?

As with the first question, if you want your site available to all visitors, this answer is easy: everybody. You may, however, want to restrict access to the search engine to a selected group of people or keep a selected group of people out.

The easiest way to do this is to place the CGI program within a password-protected area of your site. With most search engines, you can create separate indexes for different parts of your site. In this way, you can restrict access on a section-by-section basis.

As we mentioned earlier, be sure that it is not possible to retrieve a reference to a page that is password protected from an area of your Web site that is publicly available. Your visitors will not appreciate being shown a link to page to which they have no access.

Once you choose the parts of your site to index and decide who will have access to the index, make a list of all the directories that you will index. Almost all search engines index by directory. If you have a directory in which you want some files to be indexed and others not, you will probably have to split the directory into two directories, only one of which will be searchable. Once you have a list of all the directories and files on your server, select the directories you want to index.

If your Web server is on a Unix machine, run the command `ls -lR` from the root of your Web site to produce a list of all files within the site (not counting pages in user directories). From a Windows machine, use `dir /s` at a DOS prompt. On a Macintosh machine, use the system utilities to view a directory tree.

Finding and Implementing Search Engines

Choosing the right search engine depends on your equipment and resources. The search engine choices for a Unix server are different from those for a Windows or Macintosh system. One commonality, however, is the need for power. Search engines are, in general, resource heavy. Large amounts of hard disk space (often in the tens of gigabytes range) are needed to store the site index, and fast CPUs with lots of RAM are needed to run the front end for the searches. As in most cases, trade-offs are possible, and you can run a functional search engine with modest hardware. Still, if you want the performance of, for example, AltaVista (in which a large portion of the entire Web is indexed but searches can still seem instantaneous), you have to pay for AltaVista-level hardware, which is expensive.

Unix Solutions

If you are running a Web server based on Unix, you have a wide range of choices. Unlike the Windows world, few Unix solutions depend on a specific Web server. Some of these products are based on a scripting language such as Perl, in which case you need the language interpreter on your Web server machine. Still other products are distributed in source-code-only form. In such cases, you need a C compiler on your Web server machine.

If special software is needed, we've noted the requirement in the descriptions that follow.

Isite

Isite is a search engine/text indexer created by the Clearinghouse for Networked Information Discovery and Retrieval (CNIDR). This is a complete but fairly complicated system that can take even an experienced programmer several weeks to fully master. However, the rewards include having one of the most sophisticated searching mechanisms under the sun, which can allow just about any type of custom search imaginable (if, that is, you can find someone who can program it for you).

Find Isite at `vinca.cnidr.org/software/Isite/Isite.html`.

Glimpse

The University of Arizona created Glimpse as a kinder, gentler text-searching mechanism. Glimpse includes a text indexer and searching program with myriad simple, easy-to-use options for creating powerful searches. Additionally, an offshoot project called WebGlimpse makes an entire site searchable.

Find Glimpse at `glimpse.cs.arizona.edu:1994/`.

ht://Dig

San Diego State University created ht://Dig to index its (then small) campus Web site. Designed for small sites and intranets, ht://Dig is fast and easy to use. It is not limited to a single server and can index pages from several related Web servers. It includes many features not found in larger search engines such as *fuzzy searching* (searching for words using phonetic sounds or synonyms).

You can find this search engine at `htdig.sdsu.edu/`.

Htgrep

For really bargain basement (in terms of resources at least) searches, Htgrep is the ticket. Oscar Nierstrasz wrote Htgrep as a simple Perl solution to Web searching. Htgrep does not do any actual indexing. Instead, it takes the visitor's query and searches all the files on the site, one by one. For small sites, this can be effective, and it is the simplest to use of all the search engines. For sites of any appreciable size, however, this method is too slow.

Find Htgrep at iamwww.unibe.ch/~scg/Src/Doc/htgrep.html.

WAIS

In many ways, WAIS (Wide Area Information Search) is the grandfather of the modern crop of search engines such as SWISH (see below), Glimpse, and the like. The official WAIS is a commercial product and has passed through several owners in the past few years, but there are a couple of freely available offshoots of WAIS, such as freeWAIS and freeWAIS-sf. All versions of WAIS are robust and include many types of searches and even different ways of searching. Depending on the version you are using, however, creating a search interface can range from moderately tricky to downright impossible.

You can find WAIS at www.wais.com/.

SWISH

SWISH is a combination indexing/searching solution that you can also use as a searching-only front end to the WAIS indexer. SWISH was developed by Kevin Hughes of EIT as a WAIS-like indexing program and has many of the features of that system. SWISH has the advantage of small index files (generally about 1 to 5 percent of the total files you are indexing) and fast response time.

You can find SWISH at www.eit.com/software/swish/swish.html.

Windows Solutions

In the world of Microsoft Windows, the type of search engine you use for your Web site depends largely on the Web server you are running. Few third-party search engine front-ends and fewer still Web indexers are available for Windows. Luckily, almost all the major commercial Web servers for Windows come with tools that allow you to index your site and make it searchable.

WebSite

WebSite, by O'Reilly and Associates, is one of the most affordable and feature-filled Web servers available for Windows. WebSite contains several additional programs to help you administer your Web site. One of these is WebIndex, a fully functional text-indexing and searching application. WebIndex has a simple, easy-to-use interface with which you can browse the files on your site and add them to a list of files to index. The program does all the work for you from there, including adding search boxes to all pages. Of course, if you want, you can manually add, change, or remove any of the search boxes.

Netscape Catalog Server

Netscape bills its search engine solution as an entirely separate server called the Catalog Server. The Catalog Server is available only as a part of the SuiteSpot bundle, which includes most of Netscape's server products. Catalog Server can index information other than HTML and text files. It also provides a custom interface that allows visitors to not only search the information but also to browse through it in a logical fashion. Catalog Server also automatically updates the selected files, keeping the index current. Figure 19.4 shows Catalog Server in action.

FIGURE 19.4

*The Netscape
Catalog Server*

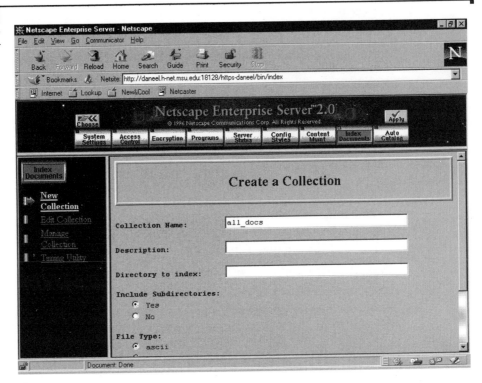

Microsoft Index Server

Index Server is a search application, included with Windows NT Server 4 as part of Internet Information Server. It can search and index ASCII text files, HTML files, and files created by the Microsoft Office and BackOffice suites of products. It can also search for document properties and HTML tags. It requires that Internet Information Server or Peer Web Server run continuously. Once set up, however, all index updates, optimization, and even crash recovery are automatic.

TIP

You can find more information on Index Server at www.microsoft.com/ntserver/search.

Search Engine Solutions

Many super search engines are at work on the Web today, including the following:

- AltaVista
- Lycos
- Web Crawler
- Excite

Versions of both AltaVista and Excite are available for individual sites.

Excite

Excite for Web Servers (EWS) was one of the first personal search engines provided by a major Internet indexer. The current support and development status of EWS is not clear, but a freely downloadable version for Unix or Windows NT is available at:

www.excite.com/navigate/

AltaVista

AltaVista Intranet Search Private Extension (PX) is a recent product created by Digital Equipment Corporation. It contains searching and indexing capabilities for an entire intranet, and you can find it at:

www.altavista.digital.com/search/products/

The AltaVista search engine works from a central server that may or may not be one of your Web servers. Because AltaVista Intranet Search PX is available only for Windows NT (on the DEC Alpha) and for Digital Unix, this can be important. Many sites that use AltaVista buy a separate server just to index their intranet. (Since AltaVista Intranet Search PX can cost upward of $60,000, buying a server just for its use is not too outlandish.)

After installing AltaVista, you simply tell it which Web server to index and let it loose. It will go to each Web server periodically and index everything it finds. The indexer is powerful and allows many types of queries that are not available on other search engines (unless you write them yourself).

For example, you can search just for images of boats on your site by typing `image: boat`, or you can find all the pages on your site that reference a specific page by typing `link:mypage.html`. A good way to test the AltaVista searching options is to use the global Web search interface, found at:

`www.altavista.digital.com/`

All the searches that you can do with this interface are also available in the Intranet Search PX edition.

Recommendations for Searching Solutions

Once you have investigated all the search engine options, you must select what is best for your site. In doing so, you'll want to consider the following:

- The size of your site
- The number of visitors
- Your technical support resources

If You Have a Moderately Sized Unix Site

Perhaps the most common type of Web site found throughout the Internet is medium sized and powered by a Unix-based (usually a free Unix such as Linux or FreeBSD) server running the Apache Web server. Because of the power and affordability of free Unix derivatives, as well as the decreasing costs of a permanent Internet connection, almost anyone can set up a Web server. Sometimes it seems as if almost everyone has.

Creating a search engine for a site like this usually involves some programming, but the result can be effective. A free indexing system such as Glimpse is usually a good choice in this situation. You can then use either WebGlimpse or SWISH as a search front-end, but, in most cases, if you have the programming help available, the best bet is to create your own search front-end that allows customized searches. We'll discuss a simple example of this shortly.

Sample Search: A Medium-Sized, Unix Solution

H-Net, Humanites OnLine (www.h-net.msu.edu/) is a prototypical example of the medium-sized, Unix system that forms the bulk of the Web. Its main search page (at www.h-net.msu.edu/cgi-bin/search) includes many options:

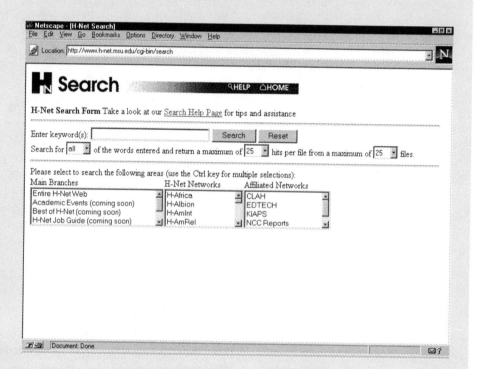

Visitors can search one or more of the site's sections or the entire site. In addition, many individual pages include search forms that allow searches automatically restricted to the current site. The searching capabilities of the site are driven by a Glimpse index and a custom front-end (written in Perl) that is loosely based on WWWWais by Kevin Hughes of EIT.

If You Have a Large Windows Site

The next largest (and fastest growing) segment of the Web server population consists of corporate sites that use Windows NT Server. Most of these sites run Netscape Suite Spot or the Microsoft Internet Information Server.

Creating a search engine for either of these servers is a simple matter of using the indexing tools that come with the server. Netscape Catalog Server and Microsoft Index Server are almost identical in form and function. They both allow you to easily select the areas of your site that you want to index. They both then automatically update the index. Both provide front-ends and allow most common searches. With either, you can create a custom front-end, but neither make it easy, and it is usually more trouble than it is worth.

If You Have a Small Windows Site

If you are like most people, you have access to a Windows 95 machine running on a Pentium processor. If that's the case, the Companion CD contains all the software you need to create a fully functional and searchable Web site. Within the Macromedia Backstage package is the WebSite Web server from O'Reilly and Associates. This Web server runs on both Windows 95 and Windows NT and matches the features of the more expensive servers from Netscape and Microsoft.

Within the WebSite package is a program called WebIndex, which easily creates a searchable index of the files on your Web site. Tools are provided to make search front ends, including a Search Wizard, which creates searchable pages with a couple of mouse clicks. In addition, the WebIndex search engine uses a standard CGI interface, so it is relatively easy to create your own custom search front ends.

Leveraging the Work of Internet Search Engines

In addition to the methods we've discussed so far, there is one other way to allow visitors to search your site. It is completely free and requires no modification to your existing setup. This technique involves "piggybacking" off of an existing search engine such as AltaVista, Lycos, WebCrawler, and so on.

These super search engines index as much of the Web as they can, which can be a *lot* (at the time of writing, AltaVista's index includes 31 million individual Web pages from more than a half million servers). If your site has been indexed by one of these search engines, anyone on the Internet can find your site through the search engine. The trick is to cull your site from the thousands of other sites that could be returned for a particular search query.

If AltaVista has indexed enough of your pages, you can use a special search function to create a custom search engine for your site at no cost. To get a preferential list of pages from your site, use the following in your search term:

```
host:www.myhost.com
```

If you want only pages from, say, the Sybex site returned (see Figure 19.5), include `+host:www.sybex.com` in your search term (notice the + symbol).

FIGURE 19.5

Searching a single host with AltaVista

Search the Web ▾ in any language ▾ and Display in Standard Form ▾

`+host:www.sybex.com`   Submit

Tip: Do not use AND or OR to combine words, simply type a few words or phrases.

Documents 1-10 of 25 matching the query, in no particular order.

Would you like to summarize the 25 documents?
Way-cool topics map! -- *for Java-enabled browsers*
Tables -- *for JavaScript-enabled browsers*
Text-only -- *any browser, really any browser*
Help -- User Survey -- *thanks for all the feedback!*

THE SYBEX HOME PAGE
   Use this virtual desktop as your guide. | Home | | Ordering & Services | | Catalog | | Authors | | Feedback | | New | | Jobs | | Updates | | Downloads.
   http://www.sybex.com/ - size 3K - 20.May.97 - English

SYBEX JOBS
   Sybex, the leading independent computer book publisher, with offices in Alameda, Paris, Düsseldorf, and Soest, offers opportunities for growth and...
   http://www.sybex.com/jobs.html - size 11K - 20.May.97 - English

THE SYBEX CATALOG
   THE HOT NEW SERIES: Practical skills for today's job market ! ELECTRONIC EDITIONS (This symbol indicates the availability of a fully searchable,...
   http://www.sybex.com/books.html - size 4K - 20.May.97 - English

ABOUT SYBEX: HISTORY
   A SHORT HISTORY OF SYBEX. Sybex was founded in 1976 by Rodnay Zaks at the same time as software giants like Apple, Microsoft, Digital Research, and...
   http://www.sybex.com/about/history.html - size 7K - 14.Feb.97 - English

THE SYBEX EMAIL PAGE
   EMAIL PAGE. info@sybex.com. for general questions and information. order@sybex.com. for questions and concerns about an existing or pending order....
   http://www.sybex.com/services/email_page.html - size 4K - 14.Feb.97 - English

SYBEX - FAQ PAGE
   THE F AQ PAGE. General Information. Technical Support. Authors/Proposals. General Information. Can I obtain the companion software or text updates for...
   http://www.sybex.com/services/faq.html - size 11K - 14.Feb.97 - English

SYBEX - TECHNICAL SUPPORT
   TECHNICAL SUPPORT. Sybex supports the software we provide on disk or CD-ROM with our books. The Sybex Technical Support department will help you...
   http://www.sybex.com/services/techsup.html - size 3K - 14.Feb.97 - English

SYBEX NEW
   New Books & Series. Press. Book Reviews. Sybex Newsletters--> New Books & Series. ABCs: A New Style of Beginner's Guide New MCSE study guide...
   http://www.sybex.com/new.html - size 4K - 20.May.97 - English

THE NETWORK PRESS NEWSLETTER
   NETWORK PRESS NEWSLETTER. A Publication of Sybex Computer Books Summer 1996. ARTICLE 1: THE NETWORK WARS: BIG-STAKES GAMES ARTICLE 2: NETWORK PRESS...
   http://www.sybex.com/new/ntwkS96.html - size 10K - 14.Feb.97 - English

SYBEX BOOK REVIEWS
   REVIEWS. CorelDRAW Design Workshop Source: Corel Magazine Date: April 1996 Column: Book Reviews/David Dean How to Lie with Charts Source: San Diego...
   http://www.sybex.com/new/review.html - size 5K - 9.May.97 - English

p. **1** 2 3 [Next]

More Tools for the
HTML Pro

Search Sample: A Sophisticated AltaVista Solution

AltaVista at Michigan State University (altavista.msu.edu), right across the street from H-Net, is the Computer Center that houses MSU's AltaVista machine. Except for the green and white logo at the top of the page, this site could easily be mistaken for AltaVista's main page. It provides a complete AltaVista style search of every major server on campus (including H-Net's). MSU's AltaVista is powered by the AltaVista Intranet Search Private Extension running on a DEC Alpha with Digital Unix.

By including +host:www.myhost.com in your query, you are guaranteed to be searching only your site (assuming your site is named www.myhost.com, that is). Because AltaVista uses simple HTML forms to interface with its search engine, it is possible to replicate an AltaVista search form on any or all of your HTML pages. You can thus add a search capability to any of your pages. A simple form to allow an AltaVista search might look like this:

```
<FORM method=POST action="http://altavista.digital.com/cgi-bin/query">
<INPUT TYPE=hidden NAME=pg VALUE=q>
Search the Web: <INPUT NAME=q size=55 maxlength=200 VALUE="">
<INPUT TYPE=submit VALUE=Submit>
</FORM>
```

You can also choose between searching the Web and searching Usenet newsgroups, and you can display the results in one of three forms of varying detail.

Use your favorite Web browser to view the source of the AltaVista home page (www.altavista.digital.com/) to get some more ideas.

To restrict the search to your specific site, filter the query through a CGI program that adds +host:www.myserver.com to the query and then forwards it to AltaVista for the results. The form on the Web page would be almost identical, except for a couple of small changes:

```
<FORM method=POST action="http://www.myserver.com/~me/av.cgi">
<INPUT TYPE=hidden NAME=addon1 VALUE="+host:www.myserver.com">
```

```
Search the Web: <INPUT NAME=q size=55 maxlength=200 VALUE="">
<INPUT TYPE=submit VALUE=Submit>
</FORM>
```

The form no longer refers to the AltaVista CGI program (www.altavista.digital
.com/cgi-bin/query), but rather to a custom-made CGI program on your server. This
CGI program simply adds the extra information to the query and sends it to AltaVista
for processing. You can do this in just a few lines of Perl:

```perl
#!/usr/bin/perl -w ## Your Perl Goes Here

use CGI; ## Require the CGI.pm module
$output = new CGI; ## Get all of the CGI information

$query = $output->param('q');

$i = 1;
while ($addon = $output->param("addon$i") ) {
    $q .= " $addon";
    $i++;
}

print "Location: http://www.altavista.digital.com/cgi-bin/query?pg=q&q=$q\n\n";
```

NOTE

This script will run without any modification on your Web server provided Perl
is installed. In addition, this script uses the CGI.pm Perl module, which provides
easy-to-use CGI related functions. This module is not a standard part of Perl, but
can be downloaded from the Comprehensive Perl Archive Network (CPAN) at
http://www.perl.com/CPAN/.

Even though it is only ten lines, the above script is actually somewhat more complicated than it needs to be. That's because Alta Vista added a little extra feature that
makes your site searches even more powerful.

In addition to the `host:www.myhost.com` feature, AltaVista provides another search enhancement. If you add `url:mypage.html` to an AltaVista search, pages that contain `mypage.html` in the URL will be given precedence in the result. As above, `+url:mypage .html` returns only those pages that contain `mypage.html`.

This is useful for two reasons. First, suppose that your site is not the only site on your server, and instead of a base URL such as `www.myhost.com`, your base URL is more like `www.myisp.com/~me`. Adding `+host:www.myisp.com` restricts the search to `www.myisp.com`, but that may return more hits than just your specific site. However, adding `+url:~me` along with `+host:www.myisp.com` guarantees that only pages from your specific branch of the server will return from the search.

Second, you can use this feature to limit the search to a specific page or section of pages within your site. Suppose you want to restrict your search to the `archives` directory. Along with the `+host:www.myisp.com`, add `+url:~me/archives`; only pages from the `archives` directory of your specific site will be found.

With this script in place, you can use the following HTML form to search any part of your Web site:

```
<FORM method=POST action="http://www.myisp.com/~me/av.cgi">
<INPUT TYPE=hidden NAME=addon1 VALUE="+host:www.myisp.com">
<INPUT TYPE=hidden NAME=addon2 VALUE="+url:~me/archives">
Search the Web: <INPUT NAME=q size=55 maxlength=200 VALUE="">
<INPUT TYPE=submit VALUE=Submit>
</FORM>
```

You can add as many hidden fields with `addon1`, `addon2`, `addon3`, and so on as you like, and the script aligns them and sends them with the visitor's query to AltaVista.

You may have noticed that this script does not display any HTML of its own. It simply forwards the request to AltaVista. This means that the page will not be in the same style as the rest of your site, but rather it will be an AltaVista search results page. AltaVista currently forbids the modification of its search results pages in any way, unless you have a special deal with Digital Equipment Corporation. Sending your visitors to the standard AltaVista search page is the price you have to pay for using a maintenance-free, cost-free solution for Web searching, as shown in Figure 19.6

FIGURE 19.6

The AltaVista Search Results page

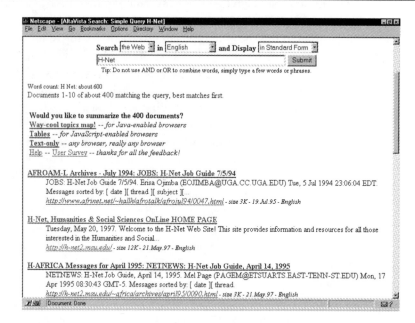

Indexing Your Site

Although many of the solutions for creating a site-wide search engine effectively do all the dirty work for you (especially the Windows applications), there is usually some configuration involved and possibly even some programming to create a really effective searching tool.

Windows

The WebIndex program, included with O'Reilly and Associates WebSite (included with Macromedia Backstage on the Companion CD) is typical of Windows indexing programs. Although it does not have all the bells and whistles of a Netscape Catalog Server or Microsoft Index Server, WebIndex is extremely robust and produces fast and efficient indexes.

Once you start the WebIndex application, the program immediately finds all files and directories that your server can access. A window then appears that lists all the found directories (indexing is currently limited to a by-directory basis). You can then choose any or all of the directories to include in the index list. You can create multiple indexes if you want certain files available to certain visitors. Once you are ready, click OK, and the program automatically indexes all the files in the selected directories, as shown in Figure 19.7.

FIGURE 19.7

Using WebIndex

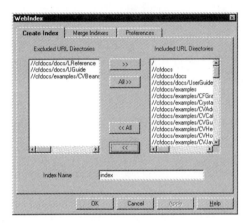

Creating a search front end is almost as simple as indexing. You can use WebSite, an application provided with WebView, to view and administer your entire site quickly and easily. Within WebView are several Wizards that help you create common pages for your site. The WebFind Form Wizard automatically creates an HTML page containing a form that allows for the searching of your site. The form is extremely customizable and allows for several special types of searches (including only the head or only the body of an HTML document).

Unix

From a Unix standpoint, creating the index and making it available on the Web is a more hands-on experience. To do so, you can use Glimpse and WebGlimpse.

Glimpse uses the glimpseindex program. Configuration is done with a pair of files: glimpse_include and glimpse_exclude. As you might guess, these files tell the indexing programs which files to include or exclude from the index. The glimpse_include file has precedence over glimpse_exclude. Therefore, if you want to index a limited portion of your site, you can place an asterisk (*) in the glimpse_exclude file, telling glimpseindex to ignore all files and then add the files and directories you want to include in the glimpse_include file.

You have many options for running glimpseindex, and many of them can add a great deal of functionality to your searches. For simplicity sake, however, you can run glimpseindex by itself with no options to index all files in the current directory and downward and to create the index files in the current directory.

Once you create your Glimpse index, you need to provide a front-end to allow visitors to search the index. Fortunately, you can use WebGlimpse to do just that. WebGlimpse is an application that, when run, starts at the current directory and works downward, "glimpsifying" all HTML files it encounters. WebGlimpse creates a copy of each HTML page that includes a search box, which allows a visitor to choose a number of items. Many of the features provided by the default WebGlimpse form cannot be found on other search engines. For instance, WebGlimpse includes a spelling error count that enables visitors to allow for a certain number of spelling errors when searching for their word.

Searching Sample: The Mnemonic Web Browser Project

The Mnemonic Web Browser Project (`oloon.student.utwente.nl/~mnemonic/search/index.html`) is an extremely high-end endeavor aimed at creating a Web browser than can compete with Netscape Navigator or Internet Explorer and yet be completely free. The search engine is a SWISH-based system, shown below, that allows an astounding number of options, some of which are hard to find elsewhere. For instance, you can search only in the emphasized (bolded or italicized) part of a document. The searches are also fast, which is what you would expect from EIT's SWISH.

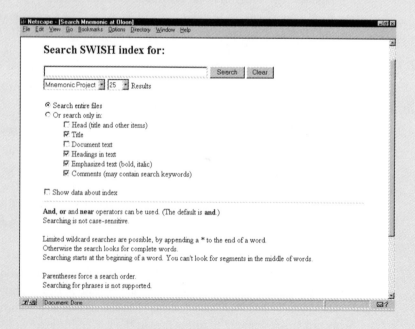

CONTINUED

For comparison, look at Microsoft's Search Page (www.microsoft.com/search/). At first glance, the main search page looks rather plain. The only selectable option is which area of the site you want to search (and you can select only one at a time). However, a little digging shows that you can perform an amazing number of search tricks on the query line. An advanced search help page exists (at www.microsoft.com/search/qrylang .htm), but is not directly accessible from the main search page. This page describes how to use options on the query line to emulate many of the Mnemonic site's advanced features. A quick glance at this large and arcane page shows the usefulness of the simple checkbox format of the Mnemonic project.

Where to Go from Here

In this chapter, we explored the world of interactive search engines. We looked at the various styles of site navigation and the benefits of each. We examined many of the most popular searching and indexing tools and discussed how to index your site and provide a searchable interface. Adding a search engine to your site provides an valuable service to your visitors.

Where to now?

- See Chapter 18 to find out how to use databases to provide other types of searches to your site.

- Chapter 6 explains how to set up and maintain your own Web server.

- Chapter 9 explains the HTML forms that present your database to others.

- In Chapter 10, find out how to use frames to provide navigation shortcuts to your visitors.

PART V

Developing Web Sites

LEARN TO:

- *Implement a coherent Web site*

- *Develop public, personal, and intranet sites*

- *Create HTML Help files*

Chapter

20

Implementing a
Coherent Web Site

FEATURING

Implementing a
Coherent Web Site

When you or your company prepares materials for written correspondence, you generally choose a paper type and color, emblazon it with a logo, and then send the correspondence in matching envelopes with, perhaps, matching business cards. The result is that you improve the overall appearance of each component and your message (and your company image) appears complete and professional.

Your challenge as a Web developer is to do the same for your Web site. In this chapter, we'll show you how to unite individual HTML documents to develop a coherent, easy-to-use Web site. In particular, we'll discuss how *theme-bearing elements* (items that consistently appear from page to page) and navigation menus can enhance your site and improve its usability. Also, we'll show you how to balance flash with functionality, which is important for making a visually interesting site that's easy to use. This is harder than it looks, but we'll give you numerous examples and illustrations.

Including Theme-Bearing Elements

Theme-bearing elements are Web page components that help unite multiple pages into a cohesive unit. Your visitors might not notice that you've included theme-bearing elements, but they will certainly notice if you haven't, or have used them inconsistently from page to page. In this sense, theme-bearing elements set up visitors' (probably subconscious) expectations. If your visitors browse through several pages that contain a logo, they'll begin to expect to see the same logo in the same place on each page. They may not consciously notice that it's there, but they'll certainly notice if it's missing or in a different location, just as you never pay attention to that broken-down car at the house on the corner—until it's gone.

Used correctly, theme-bearing elements make your site appear complete and professional, and they also help visitors know that they are in *your* site as they link from page to page. A visitor can view only one page at a time, so be sure that each page obviously belongs to the rest of the site and not to a page outside your site.

The following sections describe the theme-bearing elements you can use to unify pages in your site. You may have already included some of them, such as backgrounds and colors, but in addition we'll take a look at how you can use logos, icons, and buttons as theme-bearing elements.

Adding Backgrounds

Using consistent backgrounds—colors or images—is one of the easiest and most effective ways to unify Web pages, just as using the same color and style paper for multipage written correspondence identifies the material as a single package. Using a different background for each Web page can lead to some unwanted results. Visitors might think they've somehow linked outside your site, or they might pay more attention to the differences in design than to your content.

NOTE

Have you ever received business correspondence in which the first page is on heavy, cream-colored, linen-textured, letterhead, and the second page is on cheap 20-pound copier paper? Using different backgrounds for Web pages produces a similar effect.

Whether you use a solid color or an image depends on the effect you want to achieve. Background colors are less obtrusive and can effectively mark pages as belonging to a specific site. Take a look at Figures 20.1 and 20.2, which show you how background colors and images create different effects.

FIGURE 20.1

Colors are simple backgrounds, but they can create a theme between and among your pages.

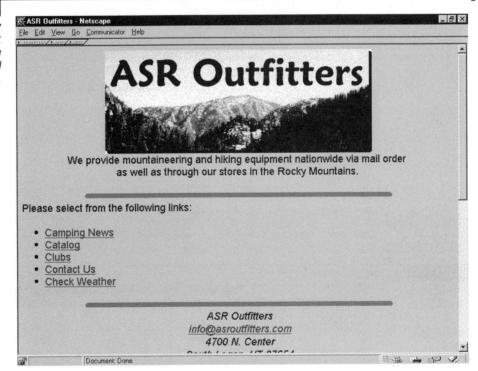

The solid color in Figure 20.1 adequately contrasts the page elements and helps unify the other page elements without attracting attention to itself. The textured background in Figure 20.2, however, doesn't unify the page elements but becomes a visually interesting part of the page. Although the image background isn't overwhelming in itself, it does make reading more difficult.

Some Web sites combine colors and images by using a mostly solid color but adding a small repeating graphic, such as the logo shown in Figure 20.3.

FIGURE 20.2

Images create backgrounds that are more visually complex, yet they can complement—not overbear—page elements.

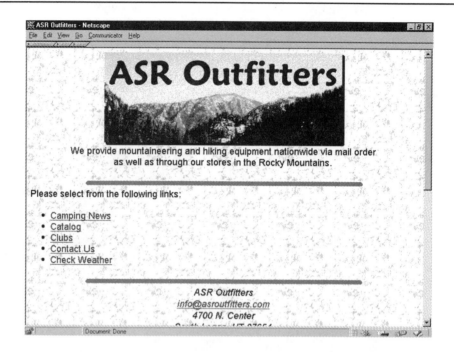

FIGURE 20.3

You can combine colors and images (or text) to create a subtle background.

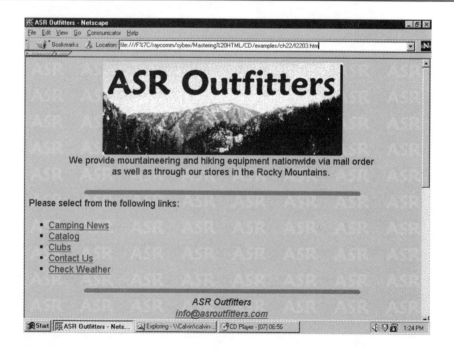

In using a small logo—which, in Figure 20.3, appears more like a watermark than an image—the image is less apparent and fades into the background. This is a great way to include a logo without significantly increasing download time or taking up valuable page space.

Regardless of whether you choose a color or an image background, follow these guidelines:

- Be sure that the background adequately contrasts with the text. Remember that online reading is inherently difficult because of monitor size and quality, resolution, lighting, and screen glare. If you use dark text, use a light background; if you use light text, use a dark background. If you have any doubt about whether the background contrasts adequately, it doesn't.

- Be sure that the background complements—not competes with—other elements such as images. For example, if you include images, be sure that the background doesn't overwhelm them. Many times placing a busy or colorful background under equally busy or colorful images makes online reading more difficult.

- Be sure that the background matches the style and tone of the Web site content. A solid black background makes an impression, but doesn't necessarily soothe and calm the visitor. It's not a good choice, for example, for the ASR Outfitters pages because it's quite obtrusive.

- Be sure that the foreground text is large and bold enough to be easily read against the background. Use the <FONT> tag—or, better yet, Style Sheets—to increase the size and, optionally, set a font to help your visitors easily read text. A slightly increased font size can overcome the visual distractions of a textured or patterned background. (You'll find more information about changing fonts and font sizes in Chapter 3.)

- Be sure to choose a nondithering color (one that appears solid and nonsplotchy in Web browsers). Because backgrounds span the entire browser window, the colors you choose make a big difference in how the background integrates with the page elements. If, for example, you use a dithering color as a background, the resulting splotches may be more apparent than the page's content. Your best bet is to choose one of the 216 safe colors listed in the Master's Reference.

- Be sure you view your Web pages in multiple browsers and with varying color settings—particularly if you use an image background or don't choose from the 216 safe colors. A good background test includes changing your computer settings to 256 colors, then viewing all your pages again. Reducing the computer system's color depth may also degrade the quality of the background.

You'll find information about how to include background colors in Chapter 3 and how to add background images in Chapter 7.

Choosing Colors

In most Web sites these days, colors abound—you see them in text, links, images, buttons, icons, and of course, backgrounds. The key is to use color to enhance your Web pages and identify a theme from page to page.

When developing a color scheme, consider which elements you want to color—text (regular text as well as links, active links, visited links), logos, buttons, bullets, background, and so on. For smaller color areas—text or links—you can choose any color you can imagine. For larger color areas, such as panes or backgrounds, stick to one of the 216 safe colors listed in the Master's Reference. The goal is to choose the colors you'll use for each element and use them consistently.

Most Web-development software, from Netscape Composer to Microsoft FrontPage, comes with prepared color schemes. If you're not good with colors—if your significant other occasionally mocks your color choices when you get dressed—consider using these prematched colors. Because color is the primary visual element in your pages, problematic color choice will be woefully apparent to all visitors.

The colors you choose should match the site's content. For example, if you're developing a marketing site for a high-tech company, you'll likely choose small areas of bright, fast-paced colors (reds, bright greens, or yellows) that correspond to the site's purpose of catching and holding visitors' attention. If you're developing an intranet site, you'd likely choose mellow colors, such as beige and blue or dark green, because the site's purpose is to inform visitors, not dazzle them.

If you choose particularly vivid colors, use them in small areas. As the old commercial goes, a little dab will do ya! A small expanse of red, for example, can attract attention and hold visitors to the page. A broad expanse of red—such as a background—will likely scare them off or at least discourage them from hanging around.

Including Logos

If you're developing a corporate Web site, consider using a logo on each page. In doing so, you not only help establish a theme, but you explicitly provide readers with the name of your company or organization throughout the site. Logos often include multiple theme-bearing elements: the logo itself, its colors, and the fonts or emphasis of the letters. Take a look at Figure 20.4, which shows a sample logo used on the ASR Outfitters page.

FIGURE 20.4

ASR Outfitters Home Page uses a non-scrolling logo as a theme-bearing element.

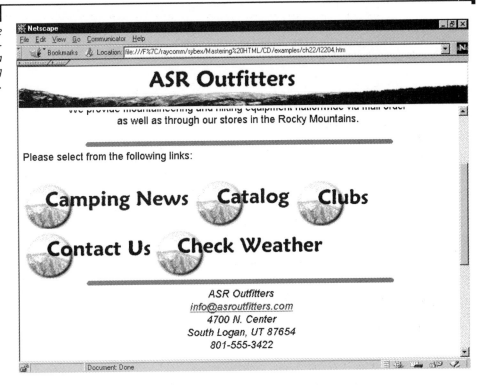

The logo helps set up other page elements. For example, the font appears in other places on the page, the colors are consistent throughout the page, and the image used as the foundation for the logo conveys the appropriate impression.

You may have no control over the logo you use—sometimes you're required to use your company's logo, for example. If you can develop a logo or enhance an existing logo, do so. Logos used online, particularly in Web sites, must carry more information about the company or organization and its style than a logo designed primarily for hard copy. A traditional logo includes paper choice, paper texture, and other elements establishing the organization's image—often, an online logo stands nearly alone without the help of other images or background images.

Where you place the logo depends on its emphasis. Many sites use a fairly large logo on the home page and a smaller version on subsequent pages. The logo thus appears on all pages, yet more space on subsequent pages is reserved for content.

An effective presentation is to combine small, classy logos with a clever arrangement of frames. For example, as shown in Figure 20.4, earlier in this chapter, a logo can reside in a small frame at the top of a page that does not scroll, remaining visible throughout the time that the visitors are at the site. Because it does not have to be reloaded, other pages load more quickly.

Incorporating Other Graphical Elements

Other theme-bearing elements include buttons, graphical links, icons, and bullets. These elements, even more than colors and logos, add interest to your pages because they combine color and shape. What's more, these can be (and should be) small; you can include them throughout a page, adding a splash of color with each use. Take a look back at Figure 20.4, a Web page that's a good example of how to employ a few graphical elements. Even in this black-and-white figure, the small graphical elements enhance the page.

 **TIP**

You can also enhance a page with animated GIF images, which add visual attraction without increasing load time. See Chapter 12 for more information about animated GIF images.

Making Your Site Navigable

As mentioned back in Chapter 2, part of what makes a Web site usable is how easily visitors can access it, browse through it, and find the information they want. Most visitors access your site through a home page, which is typically a single HTML document that provides links to the other pages in the site. However, not all your visitors will drop in using the home page. For instance, they might go directly to a page they've viewed before, or they might access your site through a search engine and go straight to a specific page. In either case, you have little control over how visitors move through your site.

To ensure that your visitors can link to the information they're looking for and to encourage them to browse your site, you need to make your site easily navigable—that is, make accessing, browsing, and finding information intuitive and inviting. You can do this by using *navigation menus*, which are sets of links that appear from page to page.

Navigation menus come in two varieties:

- Textual, which is a set of text links
- Graphical, which is a set of images (or icons) used as links

Textual Navigation

Textual navigation is simply text that links visitors to other information in the Web site. As shown in Figure 20.5, a textual navigation menu doesn't offer glitz, but effectively conveys what information resides at the other end of the link.

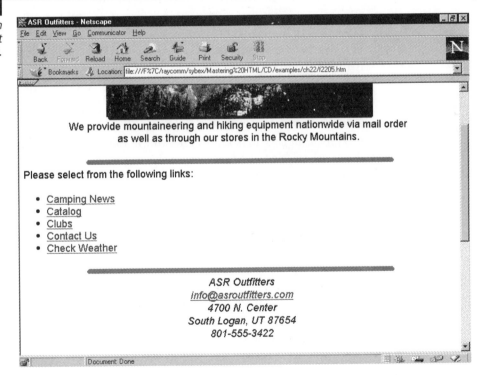

FIGURE 20.5

Textual navigation is often the most informative.

PART

V

Developing Web Sites

Textual navigation, though somewhat unglamorous, offers several advantages over graphical navigation. Textual navigation is more descriptive than graphical navigation because, done right, the text clearly tells visitors about the information in the site. Textual navigation links can be as long as necessary to describe the information at the end of the link; the description is not limited by the size of a button. The smaller (thus faster to download) the button, the less text you can fit on it.

Textual navigation is also more reliable than graphical navigation because the link itself is part of the HTML document, not a referenced element, such as navigation buttons.

Finally, text links download much faster than graphical navigation. The links download as part of the page, without the delays associated with images.

If you're considering using textual navigation, follow these guidelines:

- If your textual navigation menu appears as a vertical list, place the most important or most accessed links at the top.

- Make the text informative. Rather than calling links, "More Information," "Contact Information," and "Related Information," add specific summaries. For example, call these links "Product Specs," "Contact Us!," and "Other Sportswear Vendors." Whatever you do, don't use instructions such as "Click Here," which is uninformative and wastes valuable space. Additionally, words such as *Information* rarely do anything but take up space. After all, what would be at the other end of the link besides information?

- Provide the same menu—or at least a similar one—on each page. As your visitors link from page to page, they become familiar with the setup and location of the menu and actually (unconsciously) begin to expect that it contain certain information in a certain place.

- Customize the menu on each page so that the current page is listed, but not as a link. This helps visitors actually "see" where they are within the site; it also keeps menu locations consistent.

Graphical Navigation

Graphical navigation is a set of images that link to other information in the site. Most commonly, graphical navigation appears in the form of images with text on them, as shown in Figure 20.6. Graphical navigation can also be images that are pictures (called *icons*) representing what the buttons link to.

FIGURE 20.6

These navigation buttons include both text and images.

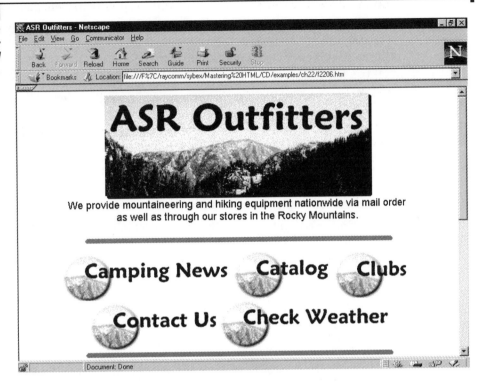

Graphical navigation has the distinct advantage of being visually more interesting than textual navigation. For example, because buttons and icons can include colors or patterns and can be almost any shape you can imagine, they are outstanding theme-bearing elements.

As colorful and interesting as graphical navigation might be, however, it has a few drawbacks. Primarily, it takes longer—sometimes much longer—to download than textual navigation. The download time depends on the file size and your visitor's connection speed, among other not-in-your-control variables.

Chapter 7 provides information about resizing images and making images quick to download.

Graphical navigation also tends be less informative than textual navigation. For example, if you're using buttons with text on them, you might be limited by the size of the button. The text can be difficult to read, depending on the size of the button and the resolution of the visitor's computer.

If you want to use graphical navigation, consider these guidelines:

- Be sure that button text is easily readable. Sometimes, when images used to create buttons are made smaller to fit within a navigation menu, the text becomes too small to read or the letters get pushed together. Your best bet is to try several button sizes to get a feel for which size is most effective.

- Be sure that the navigation menu integrates well with the other page elements. Images—including graphical navigation—are visually weighty page elements and often make other elements less apparent.

- Plan the navigation menu before you actually create it. Graphical navigation takes longer to develop than textual navigation, and it's much more difficult to change once it's in place. Even if all the pages aren't in place (or fully planned yet), at least create a placeholder for the navigation menu so that you don't have to revise the menu as you develop new content.

- Provide the same menu—or as close as possible—on every page. As with textual menus, visitors link from page to page and expect to see the same menu options in the same location on each page. Also, developing only one menu that you can use from page to page saves you time; you create it once and reuse it on each page.

Rather than creating several navigation buttons, you can create one image that includes several links. This single image with multiple links is called an image map. See Chapter 7 for more information.

Placing Navigation Menus

After you determine which kind of navigation menu to use, decide where to place the menu on your Web pages. Regardless of whether you use textual or graphical navigation, be sure to place menus where visitors are most likely to use them.

Because navigation menus, particularly graphical ones, often take up a lot of valuable page space, be sure to choose menu location(s) that don't interfere with other page elements. Here are some considerations when choosing a location for navigation menus:

Top of the page: Locating a navigation menu at the top of pages is particularly useful because it is easy to find and access. Visitors who are casually surfing your pages can easily link in and out, and those who link to a page in error can easily get out of the page. The big advantage to using the top of the page (from the visitor's perspective) is that he or she isn't forced to wade through information to access the menu.

Middle of the page: This location is effective in long pages because visitors can read through some of the information, but are not forced to return to the top or scroll to the bottom just to leave of the page.

Bottom of the page: This location works well in a couple of situations. For example, you can put the navigation menu at the bottom when you want visitors to read the material that precedes it. Keep in mind that visitors don't want to be forced to read information they're not interested in, but they don't mind browsing through a short page to get to a navigation menu at the bottom. Bottom navigation also works well on pages that already include many elements at the top, such as logos or descriptions; in this case, adding a navigation menu would crowd other important information.

Multiple locations: For most Web sites, you'll likely use a combination of these three locations, which is fine, as long as you use at least one consistently. You could, for example, place a menu at the top of all pages and place an additional menu at the bottom on longer pages. Or you might combine top and middle (or top, middle, and bottom) navigation locations for particularly long pages.

Balancing Flash with Usability

One of the most important principles of developing a Web site—particularly public and personal sites—is to balance flashy elements (ones that "dazzle" your visitors) with usability (which makes your site easy to use). If you've spent any time at all surfing the Web, you've probably noticed some really spectacular sites—ones that flash and make sounds and have moving pictures; however, you've probably also noticed that these flashing, beeping, moving sites have one significant drawback: They usually take forever to download. The result is that you end up waiting for the dazzling stuff, when all you were really looking for was the content.

PART

V

Developing
Web Sites

An Alternative Menu Location

If you use a framed Web site, place navigation menus separate from other Web page elements. Visually separating the menu from other page elements enhances your Web site. Many Web sites display the navigation menu on the left side of the browser window, but the bottom can often be more effective, as shown here:

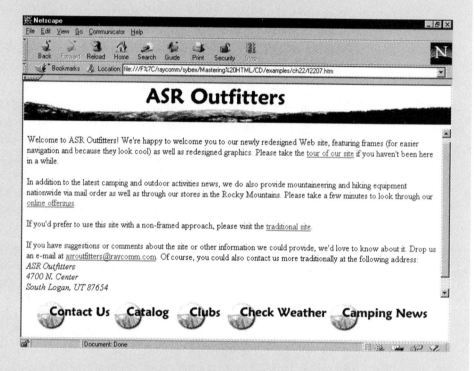

A menu at the left creates a two-column page appearance, which in many cases, makes the page visually interesting. It can also shorten the width of the right column, which helps readability.

Placing a navigation menu on the left can be less intrusive than placing it throughout the document. The menu, rather than being integrated with page elements, stands alone and can complement—not compete with—other page elements.

Finally, if the navigation menu appears in a separate frame, it can remain onscreen at all times, regardless of which pages visitors link to or how far they scroll down a page.

You'll find more information about frames and how to implement them in Chapter 10.

Every other Web surfer—including those who will surf your site—has had this experience. In a sense, glitz and flash have transformed Web surfing into Web waiting.

The key is to balance the number and kind of flashy elements you include with usability, which, you may recall from Chapter 2, refers to how easily your visitors can get to the information throughout your Web site. Yes—absolutely—flashy elements attract visitors, similar to the way that color and creativity in printed marketing materials help lure in customers and keep them glued to every word. But if you include too many elements that slow download time, visitors will get frustrated, leave your site, and probably won't return. Your goal is to make your site attractive and interesting but not to make visitors wait too long to access the information they want.

Sites that balance flash and usability include enhancements that download quickly and that are quickly available to most of your visitors. In balancing these, you'll find the following:

- Visitors spend more time in a balanced site than in one that lacks flash or usability.

- Visitors return to a balanced site more often than one that's difficult to use.

- Visitors spend more time in and return to a site that doesn't exclude some visitors from the effects. For instance, you're not likely to get many repeat visits from those using Internet Explorer if you've included only Netscape Navigator–supported effects or if you continually remind your visitors that the site was designed expressly for users of other browsers.

WARNING

Just because you *can* provide an effect doesn't mean you should. If the effect doesn't help convey information, improve your visitor's overall experience, or help project your public image, don't include it.

How to balance flash and usability? Consider which effects give you the flash, weigh the effects against download time, and consider the availability of the effects through different browsers. We can't tell you exactly how long each takes to download—too many variables exist such as file size, the type and the speed of the visitor's Internet connection, and the visitor's browser capability and computer resources. Table 20.1 summarizes the flashy effects you can add, the impact each can have on download time, and the availability in browsers.

TABLE 20.1: A SUMMARY OF WEB PAGE ENHANCEMENTS		
Enhancement	**Description**	**Availability**
Images	These are the most common enhancements included in Web pages because they add color and flash, yet they're fairly easy to obtain or create. For this reason, they're probably the biggest culprit of worldwide waiting because image files can grow to enormous sizes. You can, though, modify images and image files so that they take minimal time to download. Chapter 7 shows you how.	All graphical browsers.
Frames	These can slow things down slightly initially, but if used carefully can speed overall performance considerably because only new information must be downloaded with every new page, leaving logos and other elements in place in adjacent frames.	Available on most versions of Netscape Navigator and Internet Explorer.
Java applets	These slow down pages considerably, particularly for Netscape Navigator users. They can add power—both in terms of visual interest and through functional programs embedded in Web pages—but at a high cost.	Available on most versions of Internet Explorer and Netscape Navigator, and several other browsers.
JavaScript	This slows pages only slightly and can add attractive flash and glitz. However, many JavaScript effects are so overused as to be completely kitschy.	Available on most versions of Internet Explorer and Netscape Navigator. Some effects are less widely available.
ActiveX controls	These slow down pages, as do Java applets, but provide useful functionality.	Available on newer versions of Internet Explorer, and on Netscape Navigator with the proper plug-in.

Continued ▶

■ TABLE 20.1 CONTINUED: A SUMMARY OF WEB PAGE ENHANCEMENTS		
Enhancement	**Description**	**Availability**
Multimedia	Sounds, video, virtual reality worlds, and all the rest of the real flash slows pages nearly to a standstill. If you're adding important information or if you segregate the flash so that only people who really want it will get it, it's okay, but use with extreme caution.	Available on newer browsers with the proper plug-ins or controls.

Beware that some of these effects require visitors to have plug-ins installed on their computers. A plug-in, discussed in detail in Chapter 12, is an extra program used to view effects within browsers that don't typically support the effect. If you decide to include a Shockwave animation, for example, visitors need to have the appropriate plug-in to view it. If they don't have the plug-in and want to view the animation, they're forced to download the plug-in off the Internet and install it one time for every browser they use.

Is this a hassle? Yes, without a doubt. Most of your visitors won't take the time to download and install plug-ins just to view your site, unless the information provided through the plug-in is essential. Of course, if your information is that important and can be conveyed without the plug-in, include it using a completely hassle-free method. Also, you can be fairly certain that your visitors won't open a page in Netscape Navigator and then reopen the same page in Internet Explorer just to view nifty effects.

Where to Go from Here

In this chapter, you learned how using theme-bearing elements and navigation menus can enhance your site's usability, and you learned how balancing flash with usability can make sites inviting for your visitors. From here, you have several chapters at your fingertips that will add to the topics discussed in this chapter:

- Chapter 2 provides a thorough discussion about Web site usability. You might also check out this chapter for discussions about providing appropriate information in your Web pages.

- Chapter 7 shows you how to include images in your Web pages.

- Chapter 10 discusses the advantages and disadvantages of using frames and shows you how to implement a framed site.

- Chapter 21 provides tips and advice for developing specific types of sites—public, personal, or intranet.

- The Master's Reference provides a list of the 216 safe colors to use in Web sites.

Chapter

21

Tips for Web Sites: Public, Personal, and Intranet

Tips for Specific Web Sites: Public, Personal, and Intranet

Throughout this book, we've talked about how to add tags and attributes to create various Web page effects. In this chapter, we'll go a step further and discuss issues specific to the type of Web site you're developing. Broadly speaking, we can classify sites into three types:

- Public
- Personal
- Intranet

A public site usually focuses on a company or an organization, for example, AltaVista, your local Humane Society, or our business, RayComm, Inc. A personal site is a type of public site, but it focuses on an individual. Both types reside on the World Wide Web. An intranet, however, is a different animal altogether; it provides information about a company, but it makes the information available only to that company's employees.

Developing Public Sites

Public sites can address practically any topic, describe individuals, products, or services, and be published on any public Web server in the world. Public sites are those you find on the Internet. Presumably, if you've invested the time and resources to develop a Web site, you have a reason for wanting people to visit it. Although some visitors may happen upon it, you need to publicize your site to be sure that you reach the visitors you intend to reach.

Publicizing Your Site

Your primary option is to publicize by submitting information about your site to directories and indexes. A *directory* is a categorized, hierarchical list. For example, as you can see in Figure 21.1, Yahoo!, one of the oldest and best established directories, categorizes sites by subject. (Find Yahoo! at www.yahoo.com.)

FIGURE 21.1

The Yahoo! home page organizes information hierarchically.

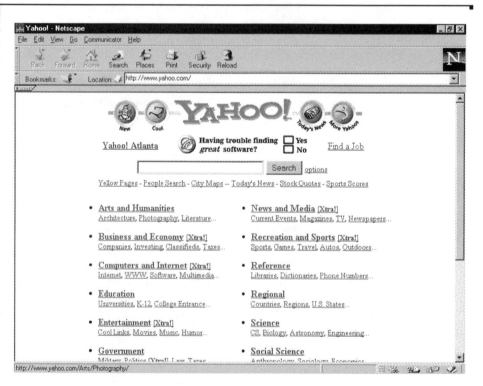

Indexes (also called *search services*) use computer programs that roam the Internet and record every page they find. The site information, including titles, descriptions, and modification dates, is then fed into a huge database that anyone on the Internet can search. AltaVista (`www.altavista.digital.com`), shown in Figure 21.2, is a well-known search service.

FIGURE 21.2

The AltaVista home page provides search options.

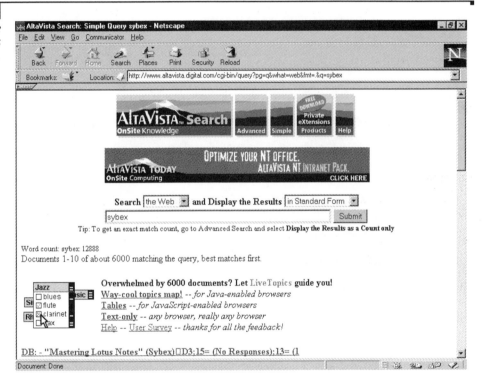

PART

V

Developing Web Sites

TIP

You can use the publicizing options discussed in the next few sections to publicize your personal site too!

Submitting Documents Yourself

You can easily submit HTML documents to directories and indexes by accessing their sites and completing online forms. For example, to submit your address to Lycos, a search service at Carnegie Mellon University, follow these steps:

1. Go to the Lycos Web site at:

   www.lycos.com

2. Choose Add Your Site to Lycos.

3. Fill out the online form, as shown in Figure 21.3.

4. Click Send.

FIGURE 21.3

An online form used to submit information to Lycos

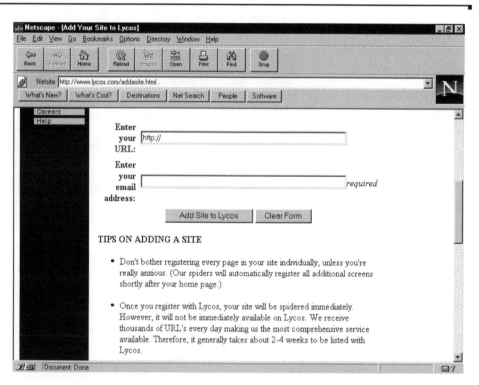

Other services may use slightly different procedures, but the basic process is the same. When your site is listed with these services, potential visitors can find you.

Figure 21.4 shows a sample page from Yahoo!, which includes a list of Web addresses and descriptions about what you'd find at each site.

FIGURE 21.4

Most directories and search engines display search results in the form of brief site descriptions.

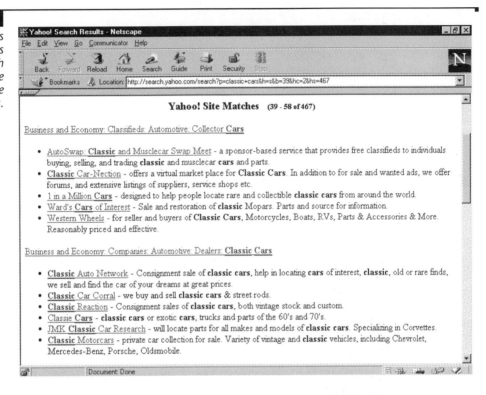

Your potential visitors determine which sites to visit based on these descriptions, so you need to make them informative. Unfortunately, not all services cull descriptions from the same place. For the most part, directories use information that you provide when you submit your site.

Providing Enticing Descriptions in Directories   Most directory services require—or at least request—a brief description about your site as part of the submission process. Figure 21.5 shows the submission page with a blank for the description.

PART

V

Developing Web Sites

Yahoo! is one of several services that require you to provide a description.

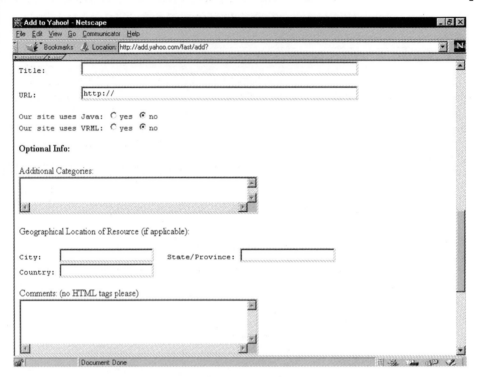

To draw people to your site, include the description and make it enticing and accurate. Even in this brief space, you can summarize your site and lure potential visitors into clicking the link to your site. Here are a few suggestions:

- Include key words. Rather than saying, "Use this site to find tax information," include specific words and phrases, such as, "Find small-business tax tips, tax forms, and tax-filing guidelines."

- Start your description with active verbs that describe what visitors would do with the information. For example, begin your description with words such as *find, create,* or *develop.*

- Include only major categories. Don't ramble on about obscure or tangential topics.

- Announce freebie files. Many times, potential visitors are looking for images or sounds that they can use in their own HTML documents. If you have any sort of freebies for them, let them know!

• Announce that you've included updated, cutting-edge, or timely information. Many potential visitors are looking for the latest information on a topic and will breeze past Web sites that seem to include old news.

Helping Search Services Find Your Site   Generally, search services display the first several words of the document body as the site description, regardless of whether the words are headings, paragraphs, or even JavaScript code. For example, the results shown in Figure 21.6 list the site addresses and a variety of descriptions.

FIGURE 21.6

*Search services—
such as AltaVista,
shown here—display
descriptions culled
from the HTML doc-
ument body.*

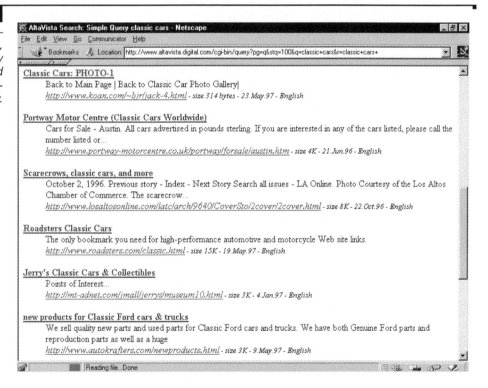

PART

V

Developing Web
Sites

You'll notice that descriptions vary considerably. Some sound like an introduction; others have nothing but jumbled information. Still others seem to summarize the document content, which is what potential visitors find most useful.

You can ensure that search services display an enticing description by including a <META> tag in the head of your HTML document that specifies the description. Here's the process:

1. Open the HTML document in a text editor.

2. In the document head (between the <HEAD> tags), add a <META> tag, like this:

```
<HEAD>
<TITLE>ASR Outfitters Home Page</TITLE>
<META>
</HEAD>
```

3. Add the NAME="Description" attribute to the tag.

```
<META NAME="Description">
```

4. Add the CONTENT="…" attribute to the tag, filling in the "…" with a concise, clear description of your page content. Stick to a line or so, and be sure that the description accurately and effectively portrays your site.

```
<META NAME="Description" CONTENT="ASR Outfitters provides hiking and
mountaineering equipment through direct sales and mail order throughout
the continental USA.">
```

5. Save and close your document.

When search engines—such as AltaVista or Lycos—find your page, they display the description found within the <META> tag along with your site address, as shown here.

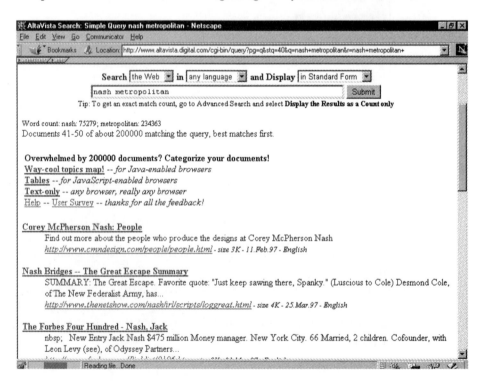

In addition to using the text of your site, you can include keywords to help identify matches for visitor searches. *Keywords* provide synonyms for common words that might not appear in the actual text of the Web site. For example, ASR Outfitters might use keywords such as the following:

climbing	camping	backpack
hiking	tent	dried food
biking	sleeping bag	affordable

To include keywords, simply add another <META> tag. Follow these steps:

1. Open the HTML document.

2. In the document head (between the <HEAD>tags), add a <META> tag, as shown here. If you included a description <META> tag, you can place this one above or below it.

   ```
   <HEAD>
   <TITLE>ASR Outfitters Home Page</TITLE>
   <META>
   </HEAD>
   ```

3. Add the NAME="keywords" attribute to the tag.

   ```
   <META NAME="keywords">
   ```

4. Add the CONTENT="..." attribute to the tag, filling in the "..." with a list of all the likely terms someone might use. Don't include punctuation between the terms.

   ```
   <META NAME="keywords" CONTENT="climbing hiking biking camping tent
   sleeping bag backpack dried food affordable">
   ```

5. Save and close your document.

Hiding Pages and Folders from Search Engines

If you've created a public site, you probably want robots or spiders to find your site and incorporate your pages into Internet-wide indexes such as AltaVista and Lycos. You might also have specific pages or folders on your server that you want to exclude. For example, at one time the www.raycomm.com/ server had a folder full of test documents and miscellaneous junk in the folder named /temp. Because that folder needed to stay on the server for testing purposes, we decided to exclude it from all search engines and indexes so that visitors wouldn't access it.

CONTINUED

Fortunately, you can keep automated visitors from accessing specified pages and folders through an agreement called the *Robots Exclusion Standard*. Just put a plain text document in the root folder of your Web server called robots.txt. In that file, use the following format to specify which robots to exclude and which folders to exclude them from. (All the lines that start with # are comments for you to read—they're disregarded by the robots.)

To keep robots out of your entire site, use a robots.txt file at your server root containing the following.

```
User-Agent: *
# The * specifies all agents or robots
Disallow: /
# The / indicates all documents under the server root.
```

To keep all robots out of the /temp folder, use a robots.txt file containing the following:

```
User-Agent: *
# The * specifies all agents or robots
Disallow: /temp
# The / indicates that all folders immediately under the server root
# starting with /temp should be excluded, including temp and temporary
```

Using Services to Submit Pages

Literally dozens of site submission services exist to relieve you of submitting your site manually. Some are free, and others charge a fee. Most free services submit your site to somewhere between 20 and 50 sites, including most of the popular ones, such as Alta-Vista, Yahoo!, and Lycos. For a fee, they'll submit your site to many more sites—up to a couple of hundred.

Is it worth your time to have your site submitted for free to several dozen sites? You bet it is. Check out www.submit-it.com/ for just one example.

Is it worth the cost to have your site submitted for a fee to a few hundred directories and search engines? Possibly, but probably not. First, the 20 to 50 directories and search engines to which most services submit include those that your visitors are likely to use. Second, if your information is so precisely targeted that it wouldn't be adequately listed with the major directory and index services, you can probably market it more effectively through other channels. For example, you might consider posting the information to listservs, newsgroups, or electronic magazines (*e-zines*), where you can target specific markets. Or, you might submit a press release about your site to a newsletter, magazine, or journal that targets specific markets.

Other Publicizing Methods

Because of the overwhelming number of new sites that appear on the Internet every day, simply adding your site to existing search engines and directories won't necessarily result in a flood of traffic.

Consider some of the following ways to publicize your new site:

- Include a brief announcement and URL in your e-mail signature.
- Write an article about your site and submit it to newsletters or journals in your field.
- Send an e-mail message announcing your site to people in your field.

Making Visitors Want to Browse Your Site

Think of your public Web site as being a retail store. The longer customers browse, the greater the chance that they'll buy something, even if they didn't go into the store intending to purchase anything. You want visitors to linger in your site for similar reasons. Longer visits likely mean that visitors will gather more information, notice more products and services, gain a better understanding of your organization, and purchase more merchandise (if you provide that option). Even if your public site serves more as a central clearinghouse for information—mostly providing links to information on the Web—you'll want visitors to spend time in your site and use the information you provide.

You can use several techniques to help keep visitors in your site longer. You'll find that you can easily combine these according to the site's purpose.

- Minimize how long visitors have to wait to download pages, and be sure that your site loads quickly. Check out Chapter 20 for information about balancing flashy elements with usability.
- Use informative links. Visitors won't spend much time in your site if you make them guess what information resides at the end of a link.

- Provide links that go to real information. Visitors tire easily of linking to pages that say, "This page under construction." At the very least, provide a date they can expect the information to be available—then do it.

- Make the most useful information and links easily accessible. If you know the site includes information that visitors frequently access, make that information easily accessible. Though you could force visitors to scroll through text to get to the information or links, be careful. Visitors will tolerate some amount of scrolling, but they're likely to move on to another site if they can't reach information quickly.

- Provide services and information to make visiting worthwhile. Offer free samples or added information about whatever you do.

- Provide services that visitors can use while visiting your site. For example, depending on your products or services, include an online mortgage amortization calculator, retirement planning advice, virtual coloring books, or relocation calculator.

Making Visitors Yearn to Return

After visitors complete their business in your Web site, make them want to return to it. Here are some ideas to try:

- Provide new information regularly and often. Visitors won't return to a site that provides the same information time after time.

- Provide accessible and complete contact information. Many visitors use the Web as an enormous phone book; rather than looking up your company's phone number, they head to your Web site to find out how to contact you.

- Update existing information, particularly product and service descriptions, to reflect the current availability of your products and services, and make it clear that you've recently updated the information.

- Include summaries of hot-off-the-press information that is related to your Web site.

- Include links to related information. Make your site a central information resource. For instance, we don't search for articles about the latest developments in browser technology; instead, we usually access reliable and current Web sites and link to articles from there.

- Let your visitors register for e-mail notification of changes to the site. You could collect addresses using a form on your site and send e-mail whenever you make

substantive changes, or you could use a service such as Net Minder (www
.netmind.com) to automatically notify your registered visitors of changes.

Notifying Visitors When You Change or Update Information

Net Minder is a service that monitors Web pages, notices when they change, and then
sends notification to anyone who requests it.

For example, by adding a little HTML code to its page, ASR Outfitters can provide a
small registration form, as shown here.

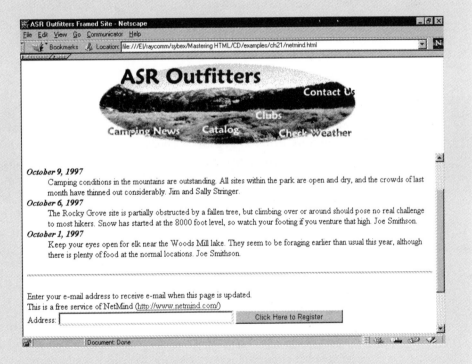

Visitors can type in their e-mail addresses, click the Click Here to Register button, and
then receive an e-mail message whenever the page changes.

CONTINUED

You can use the following code sample in your HTML document to include a mini form:

```
<FORM METHOD="GET" ACTION="http://www.netmind.com/cgi-bin/uncgi/url-mind">
Enter your e-mail address to receive e-mail when this page is
updated.<BR>
Your Internet e-mail address:<br>
<INPUT TYPE=TEXT SIZE=40 NAME="required-email"><br>
<INPUT TYPE=HIDDEN VALUE="http://www.you.com" NAME="url">
<INPUT TYPE=SUBMIT VALUE=" Click Here to Register ">
</FORM>
```

Just remember to replace http://www.you.com with the absolute URL of the page. See Chapter 4 for more information about absolute URLs.

Maintaining Public Sites

When you're running a public site, you'll probably have a steady stream of visitors. You'll build visitors' expectations for "if I need to know about thus and so, I can just go to the thus and so Web site." Problems crop up when you're updating the site— you will update the site, won't you? Your goal is to develop a maintenance plan that eliminates downtime and provides visitors with uninterrupted service. You want to eliminate even the shortest downtime stints—resulting, for example, from uploading files or encountering connectivity problems. If your Web site is occasionally down for maintenance, visitors will not rely on it as an information resource.

You can avoid these problems if you follow these suggestions:

- Keep backups of your site! And be sure that your ISP and server administrator do the same.

- Test the backups and confirm that you can restore the files in a reasonable amount of time. If you house your site at your ISP, be sure that you understand under which circumstances it is willing to restore the backup.

- Provide for redundant network connections (recommended for larger Web sites) to assure that visitors access your site if a network connection goes down.

- Find out what action your ISP takes if it has technical difficulties, such as hard disk crashes, system problems, power outages, network disruptions, hackers, and so on. While you—as a content provider—may not have to deal with these issues, you must take responsibility for ensuring that the Web site is adequately covered for all contingencies.

- Use a *test environment* that duplicates your real server as nearly as possible, with the same software, the same physical platform, and the same configuration. Viewing your site in a test environment gives you a good idea of what it will look like when you upload it to the server. See Chapter 6 for more information.

Putting Ads on Your Site

After developing a public site, consider selling ad space on your pages. You might think about using some margins of your pages to promote related products or to advertise other, complementary sites. If your situation is typical, you probably won't make a fortune (or even a mini fortune); even high-traffic sites such as Yahoo! don't yield high returns. Either selling ads directly or working with a reciprocal ad exchange service, though, can have some benefits.

If you're sure you want to sell ads and do it all yourself, you'll need to use specialized, and possibly custom, software to track hits. For a starting point, check into Selena Sol's Public Domain Script Archive and Matt's Script Archive, available on the Companion CD. Both have custom applications to help manage ads and to track hits.

A better option overall is to participate in a link exchange service, such as the Internet Link Exchange (find it at www.linkexchange.com/). This and other link exchanges find homes for your ads while placing ads on your site. After you visit the link exchange site and register, you receive some HTML code to put in your page—that code automatically displays the ad. You then also submit a GIF image for your ad banner. The service counts the number of ads that you show, which is essentially the number of hits to your site. For every two hits to your site, your ad appears somewhere else once.

Trying Online Commerce

If you represent a company or an organization that's moving toward online sales of products, work with your ISP to secure transactions so that visitors cannot steal credit card numbers. The script archives on the Companion CD have some shopping software, or you could outsource the whole mess to commercial services that will set up and run the shopping facilities, relieving you of the need to process orders and mail products. Check out your favorite search engine and search for e-commerce to get the latest services and software.

Developing Personal Sites

A personal site is a special type of public Web site that focuses on an individual. Though you can use personal sites to publish general information about yourself, such as your hobbies and interests, you can also use personal sites to market your skills or publish information you've researched or developed—which is what the next few sections show you how to do.

Marketing Your Skills

You can use a personal Web site to market your skills through a Web-based résumé, letter of introduction, or personal brochure. Most commonly, you'll market your skills to get a job (or a better job), although you could also use this vehicle to gain contract employment or to let companies know that you exist and are available. With one thoughtfully developed Web site, you can market yourself to millions of people around the world without the hassles or expense of traditional mailings.

Personal Web sites represent your skills, experience, and creativity in much the same way that traditional résumés and letters of application do. When you're applying for a job, you generally develop a résumé and a letter of application, and you probably pay particular attention to your personal appearance when you go to the interview. You create a package—one that informs a potential employer about your skills, shows your attention to detail and creativity, and projects some information about your personality. Your personal Web site should do the same.

Providing this information on the Web has several advantages over traditional job application materials. For example, your Web page résumé can't get buried on someone's desk, and multiple pages can't get separated or lost in the shuffle. Also, you can provide more details and examples on the Web than you could ever get away with in a traditional résumé.

Developing a Web Résumé

In developing a Web résumé, you have the same options as you do in developing a paper résumé—you can focus on experience or education, skills or training, or other aspects that might appeal to a future employer. The approaches break down into essentially two types: functional and skills-based, as shown in Figure 21.7.

FIGURE 21.7

Functional résumés focus on places of employment and educational institutions; skills-based résumés focus on your skills.

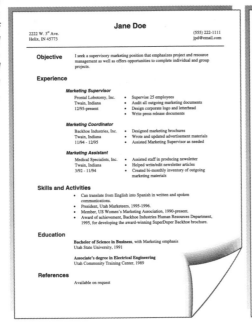

Functional Résumé

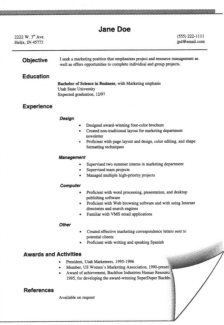

Skills-Based Résumé

Both types include basically the same sections—contact information, objective, education, employment, activities, and references. They differ only in emphasis.

When developing a Web résumé, use either of these types or some combination of the two. Tables 21.1 and 21.2 summarize the advantages and purposes for each.

TABLE 21.1: FUNCTIONAL RÉSUMÉS	
Purpose	To provide information about places you worked and/or educational institutions you attended.
Advantages	Lets you announce prestigious job titles, company names, university names, and degrees.
Focus	Places you've worked or education.
Categories	Objective, Education, Employment, Special Skills or Activities, References

TABLE 21.2: SKILLS-BASED RÉSUMÉS	
Purpose	To provide information about skills you've developed or coursework you've completed.
Advantages	Lets you downplay multiple jobs, unfinished degrees, or positions in which you learned a lot without adequate compensation or title.
Focus	Skills
Categories	Objective, Skills, Education, Activities, References

As we mentioned, you'll probably combine features of both types. For example, you may have worked for companies with well-recognized names and have held jobs with prestigious titles, but you also want to emphasize your specific skills. In this case, you primarily use a skills-based résumé but add an employment history page listing your previous employers. Or, perhaps you want to show your steady employment history and promotions through each job change. In this case, you want to primarily use a functional résumé but include a separate skills page.

Organizing Web résumés is tricky because you must accommodate both a nonlinear read, in which visitors select topics, and a linear read, in which visitors start at the top and read sequentially. Many typical Web site visitors expect your pages to look flashy and provide information quickly. In this case, provide multiple, shorter documents with links between and among them. In doing so, you provide pages that download quickly and display information that's easy to find.

TIP

See Chapter 20 for more information about balancing flashy elements with quick download time.

Other visitors, however, might want to print your documents, and you could spend a lot of time printing multiple pages from a site. For this reason, provide the complete résumé visitors can read linearly and print easily.

Essentially, you develop two complete résumé packages—one broken into chunks and the other flowed together into one document. In this way, you accommodate virtually any visitor (think potential employer!). These folks can easily view the information or print it, depending on their needs.

To meet both these structural needs, do two things. First, provide each of the résumé categories in separate HTML documents, as shown in Figure 21.8.

FIGURE 21.8

Put each résumé category in a document of its own.

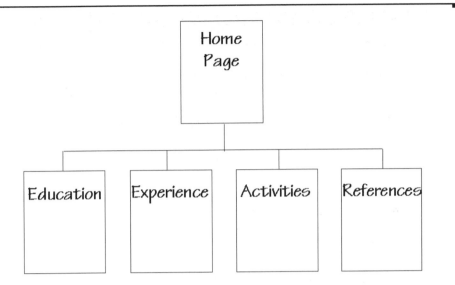

Why do this? You might recall from Chapter 2 that online reading produces some difficulties for visitors. For instance, visitors face obstacles such as computer resolution, small monitors, and screen glare, all of which make reading online difficult. The result is that visitors (or more specifically, their eyes) tire quickly, and they tend to gloss over information rather than read it thoroughly. By using multiple shorter documents, as shown in Figure 21.8, you improve the chances that visitors take the time to browse. These shorter documents are more inviting because the pages don't appear so difficult to wade through, and very short HTML documents virtually leap onto the screen, with little wait. Also, visitors can choose which information they access and in what order. The result is that visitors spend more time browsing your site and—essentially—more time considering you as a possible applicant.

Next, provide a link pointing to a single HTML document that includes the full résumé package. As shown in Figure 21.9, you can easily include a link from the home page and let visitors view a longer single document (as opposed to multiple shorter documents).

WARNING

Resist the temptation to use all the fanciest formatting options in your résumé. Your résumé should indeed look nice, but keep it quick to download and simply formatted.

FIGURE 21.9

Provide a link to both multiple short documents and a single longer document.

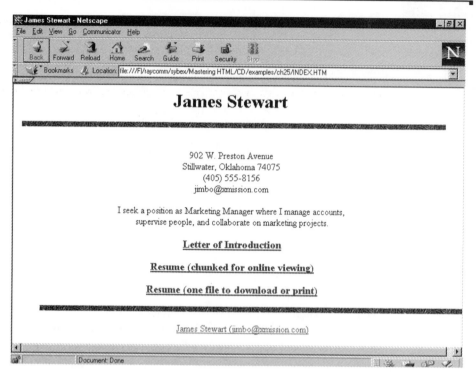

Developing a Web Résumé Home Page   Many Web résumés start on a home page, which is the most important page in the site because it's usually the first page that visitors access. Typically, it states your employment objective and includes links to each category of information, as shown in Figure 21.10.

Don't overlook the *employment objective*, which actually plays a big role in luring visitors to link to other pages in the résumé or deters them from going further. Focus your objective on the skills you can offer a company. For example, rather than saying, "I seek a position in which I can use my existing skills and learn new ones," state the specific skills you want to use, like this: "I seek a position as Marketing Manager so that I can manage accounts, supervise people, and collaborate on marketing projects." Focus on what you offer the company, rather than on what you want from them.

When developing your résumé home page, remember the following guidelines:

- Provide concise information about how, when, and where potential employers can contact you.

- Make browsing inviting—that is, minimize download time, provide links in a useful location, and provide informative link names.

FIGURE 21.10

Your résumé home page should state your objective and provide links to other information.

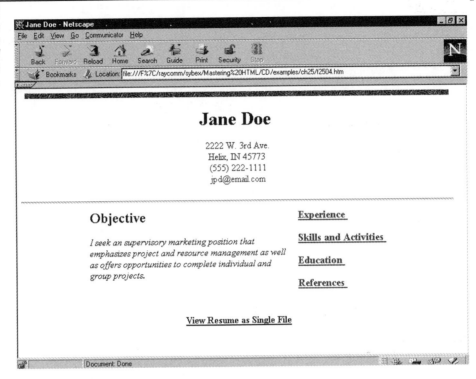

- Be sure your home page portrays the image you want to present. Use colors and layout that express your professionalism and personality and align with those used by your target market. See Chapters 3 and 5 for information about applying formatting effectively.

- Be sure that visitors can easily link to other pages from the home page. If you provide a list of links, place the most important or most frequently accessed information at the top of it.

- Be sure the information at the end of links is complete. Never provide a link in a résumé home page that goes to incomplete or unavailable information.

- Provide a link that goes to a full-length résumé in addition to the Web résumé that's chunked into smaller pieces. That way, visitors can easily print your résumé and have it on hand.

- Include only original information, images, or files. Don't "borrow" materials from other sites and use them as your own.

Developing Subsequent Résumé Pages   Subsequent pages in the résumé should reflect the topics that you announce in the home page. For example, if your home page announces categories such as work history, education, and references, develop a single HTML document for each category.

When creating these subsequent pages, use the same background, fonts, and color scheme that appear on the home page. This unites pages into a cohesive unit and provides visitors with visual cues that the pages are part of your site.

See Chapter 20 for information about including theme-bearing elements throughout your Web site.

Here are a few tips to remember when developing subsequent pages:

- Include your contact information on *every* page.

- Provide navigation menus so that visitors can access other main pages in the site easily and quickly.

- Be concise and clear. If you're tempted to go on to a second or third screen, move the less important information to a different page and provide a link to it.

Including a Letter of Introduction   Within your Web résumé, you can include a link to a letter of introduction, which provides information that complements—not repeats—your résumé. For example, your résumé might indicate that you were a team leader on the AlphaDoowhichie project. The letter of introduction can supplement this information by telling visitors about your specific role in the project, discussing the project's success, or detailing how the company benefited from your performance. Letters of introduction give you the opportunity to highlight your successes and provide the details that aren't always appropriate in résumés.

Here are some guidelines about letters of introduction you might find useful:

- Make the application visitor-oriented—that is, not only give details about your successes, but also specify how these successes have prepared you to fill the position.

- Limit the letter to three or four paragraphs—long enough to highlight the main points, but not so long that you bore visitors.

- Provide your contact information.

Incorporating Your Web Résumé into an Existing Personal Site

If you're developing a Web résumé as part of your personal site, consider that the personal site itself becomes part of the résumé. In this case, a potential employer might visit your personal pages plus the résumé-related pages.

Because of this, we recommend that you take some precautions:

- Make the personal pages as professional as possible.
- Store any potentially offensive documents in a subfolder without links to it. For example, we might use www.xmission.com/~ejray/ourstuff/ (but we don't). Send the complete URL only to the friends and family you want to be able to see it.
- Use the robots.txt file to keep spiders and robots out of your personal stuff, as discussed in "Publicizing Your Site" earlier in this chapter.
- Consider password protecting your personal pages. Anything from church activities to hunting to humor in arguably poor taste could offend some potential employers.

Publishing Your Résumé in Other Formats   Another option is to provide a link from your Web résumé (probably from the home page) to your résumé saved in other formats. Using RTF (Rich Text Format) and Adobe Acrobat formats, you overcome some difficulties inherent in Web pages—the biggest being that you have no control over how your résumé appears in your visitors' browsers. These files are not actually part of your HTML document—you link to them just as you link to any other files. Instead of automatically appearing in a visitor's Web browser as HTML documents do, the RTF or Acrobat documents download to the visitor's computer and are saved to the hard drive or loaded in an appropriate viewing program (a word processor for RTF files, Acrobat Reader if available for Acrobat files).

Your easiest and cheapest option is to provide a link to your résumé saved as an RTF file. RTF is a standard word-processing format that, in this context, lets your visitors view your résumé in the word processor of their choice. Most formatting remains intact in RTF documents, and you can create them from the Save As menu of most word-processing programs.

A few drawbacks are associated with using an RTF document, however:

- Visitors must take an extra step to download the file and open it in a word processor.

- Conversion problems can occur in the downloading process.
- Visitors can easily alter an RTF file.

A better, but more expensive, option is providing a link to an Adobe Acrobat version of your résumé. Acrobat format (also referred to as *PDF format* because files use the PDF file extension) is a technology designed to facilitate document sharing and remote printing—keeping all fonts and formatting intact and making it impossible to change the document. Think of it as putting a fax copy of your résumé on the Web— visitors view the document you created, complete with the layout and formatting you specified.

A few drawbacks are also associated with using Acrobat files. You, the résumé provider, have to purchase Acrobat Exchange or have it available through your company. Acrobat files are big, meaning that they take a while to download. Also, visitors must have an Acrobat reader or download and install one before they can view your résumé.

Check out Adobe's Acrobat Exchange at www.adobe.com for more information about Acrobat and purchasing information.

Self-Publishing Information

You might also develop a personal site is to *self-publish* information you've researched or developed. For example, you might publish genealogical information, your in-progress soon-to-be-hit novel, short stories, class projects, research papers, recommendations, or advice. Whatever the topic, you can self-publish on the Web easily and inexpensively, which is the main reason self-publishing has become so popular.

Before you self-publish, though, consider some of the downsides. First, most discerning readers are skeptical about the quality and reliability of self-published information, and your information may be perceived as unworthy. Assure visitors that the information you provide is reliable, researched, reviewed, or cross-referenced to other sources that support your claims. For example, include a bibliography, a works cited list, or a list of experts with whom you consulted. Also, consider providing links to other information on the Web that supports your claims.

Second, Web surfers, whether they realize it or not, tend to take self-published information and use it as their own. Most folks don't realize that they're "stealing" your information; self-published information that lacks an official (and highly visible) copyright or statement of ownership appears available for public use. To ensure that your information stays your own, always provide a copyright statement or state that the information is available for reference, but not to be taken and subsumed into other people's work.

Finally, if you're publishing information that's been published elsewhere—in magazines, journals, newspapers, and so on—be sure that you're not inadvertently plagiarizing. For example, if you're a Dilbert fan and want to put your 10 favorite Dilbert cartoons on your Web page, remember that someone else holds the copyright to those cartoons. Although most people who publish on the Web (or post information to the Internet on newsgroups or in other forums) don't have lawyers watching for copyright infringements, it's still wrong to take other people's stuff.

If you're publishing information about people, be sure that they want information published about them.

Has Information Been Taken from Your Site?

If you publish on the Web and you want to find out whether visitors have taken information and used it as their own, you can. Simply visit AltaVista, HotBot, or another full-text search engine and do the following:

- Search for keywords that appear in your documents.
- Search for unique phrases.
- Search for typing or spelling errors that you find in your pages. For example, a search for "accomodates your needs" will get poor spellers as well as anyone who copied the misspelled text directly.

When visitors access self-published research documents, their intent is usually to gather information so that they can learn from it or apply it to their own projects. Visitors might actually read the information from start to finish, or they might print it.

For these reasons, consider presenting the information as one long page, rather than as sections in separate, shorter documents with links between and among them. One long document is easier to read and to print.

Also, because these documents tend to be more than a screen or two, provide multiple navigation menus throughout the document, as shown in Figure 21.11. Place menus at the top and bottom of documents as well as throughout the body.

FIGURE 21.11

Placing navigation menus within long documents helps visitors wade through information.

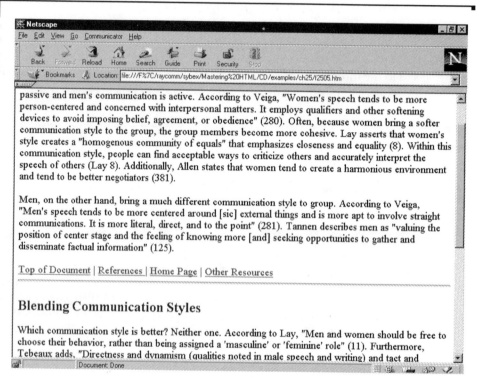

Blending Communication Styles

Developing Intranet Sites

Intranet sites are enterprise-wide Web sites accessible only by people within an organization. Intranets came about as a result of the need for improved corporate communications. As companies expand geographically, they face the challenges of providing company-wide information quickly and inexpensively—a feat not possible using traditional communication methods such as mailings, memorandums, faxes, or bulletin boards. Using an intranet, however, companies make information immediately accessible to all employees, regardless of their geographic location, and eliminate or significantly reduce the need for other forms of communication.

Although individuals or small groups generally develop and maintain public sites, employees often contribute content for intranets. For example, the Information Services Department might actually run the intranet, but one or more employees in each department within an organization might assume responsibility for providing and updating pages pertaining to that department.

The result can be a hodgepodge of information that doesn't generally fit into a coherent information resource. Your goal as an information coordinator—whether you're the company owner, the head of information services, or the person who also develops and maintains the company's public site—is to ensure that the intranet is a valuable, uniform, usable information resource.

In the following sections, we'll look at how to coordinate content from contributors, suggest some ways that you can put out the word about what's new or updated on your intranet, and introduce intranet discussion groups. The "you" in these sections is the content coordinator for an intranet, and the "visitors" are employees or members of an organization that uses an intranet.

Determining Intranet Content

Intranets provide substantial, company-specific information that helps employees do their jobs, automates processes, and provides updates or news. If your intranet is part of a corporate environment, a good starting point for content is the human resources department, where you're likely to find company policy manuals, training schedules, safety guidelines, evacuation plans, and much more.

You can also use an intranet to publish product or service descriptions. For example, when you place boilerplate (standardized) information about your products and services on your intranet, visitors can easily access it and use it in marketing materials, documentation, or whatever.

You might also publish information that's not pertinent to employees' jobs, but that employees would find useful:

- The cafeteria menu
- The company newsletter
- New contract announcements
- Annual budgets
- Company and retirement fund stock quotes

And if you intranet is connected to the Internet, you can also include links to industry news or to sister-company Web sites.

Your next step is to talk with employees about the information that they provide, distribute, and update to other groups within the company and about the information that they need and might (or might not) get from other departments. Ask about the following:

- Forms
- Reports
- Budgets
- Schedules
- Guidelines
- Procedures
- Policies
- Legacy documents

You can probably obtain some of this information using existing materials such as human resources handbooks, marketing brochures, company white papers, and so on.

Accommodating Visitor Needs

Visitors to intranet sites generally have one thing in mind: They're looking for information necessary to do their jobs. They might, for example, use the information to write a report, develop marketing materials, plan their schedules, and so on. For this reason, make absolutely certain that the information you provide is accurate and timely.

Visitors also expect you to provide accessible information—information they can find consistently from day to day. As a starting point, develop the overall site organization, taking into account all categories of information you will provide. Be sure to leave room for growth—adding new categories and expanding existing categories. For example, in developing a navigation menu, include all the categories of information that you'll eventually need. If you end up including links that don't yet have content, provide a statement about the information coming soon, or better yet, specify a date when you'll provide the information. You can also include contact information for people who can answer questions in the interim.

Finally, visitors don't expect an intranet site to be flashy. After all, they're accessing the site because they need information, not because they expect to be dazzled. Plan a site design that is visually appealing, but don't go overboard with sounds, colors, and other special effects. Consider including your company's logo and using its color scheme, but beyond that, think functional, not fancy.

Helping Others Contribute

As you saw in the previous sections, intranets are not usually the work of one person. Although you may be in charge of developing the site, others will actually provide and update the content. And not all contributors will have the same HTML proficiency; some will be novices, others will be experts. Striking a balance between consistency and creativity can be challenging. Here are some ideas that may help.

Provide Templates and Examples

If you maintain a consistent look and feel, your intranet will appear more established and polished than it actually is. Relying on information providers to care as much as you do about a consistent appearance is likely too much to hope for, so make it easy for them: Provide templates.

Templates include all the structure tags and other tags that set up the general document format. You can provide templates for departmental home pages, for contact information, for current projects, or for any other pages that are common to several department. You might also provide references to company-specific graphics and symbols. Using a template complete with these items, contributors can copy and paste the code into their documents and fill in the specific content. Figures 21.12 and 21.13 show a sample template and the resulting document format.

PART
V

Developing Web Sites

FIGURE 21.12

This short template can save contributors time and effort.

```
template.htm - Notepad
File  Edit  Search  Help
<!DOCTYPE HTML PUBLIC "-//W3C//DTD HTML 3.2//EN">
<HTML>
<HEAD>
  <TITLE>ASR Intranet</TITLE>
</HEAD>
<BODY BGCOLOR="FFFFFF" TEXT="000000" LINK="0000FF" VLINK="800080" ALINK="FF0000">
<CENTER><IMG SRC="asrintra.jpg" ALIGN="CENTER" BORDER="0" ALT="ASR Intranet Logo"></CENTER>

<!--Please do not change anything above this line except the title.-->

<H1 ALIGN=CENTER>Put Your Department Name Here</H1>

<P>Provide content here. </P>
<P>And here.</P>
<P>And here.</P>

<UL>
 <LI>List links here.
 <LI>And here.
 <LI>And here.
</UL>

<!--Replace department@intranet.asroutfitters.com in the following lines with your own
    email address.-->

<P>Send all questions to <A HREF="mailto:department@intranet.asroutfitters.com">
department@intranet.asroutfitters.com</A>.

<!--Please do not change anything below this line. The following
    command applies the document footer with the navigational toolbar
    and related information.-->

<!--#include virtual="/boilerplate/footer.htm"-->

</BODY>
</HTML>
```

FIGURE 21.13

The same template viewed in a browser, before being customized for specific departmental use.

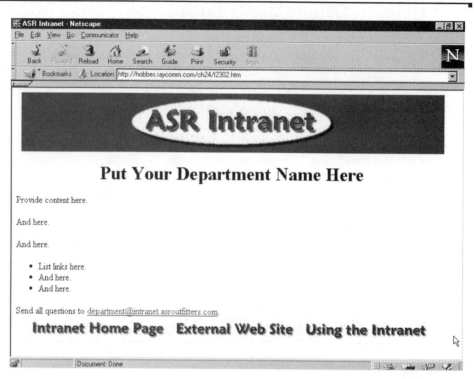

You can also provide templates for word-processing software such as Microsoft Word or WordPerfect. Contributors can then develop content in the word processor of their choice and easily save as HTML.

If your company has standardized on Netscape Navigator or Internet Explorer 4, consider providing Style Sheets to contributors. By supplying a Style Sheet, you help contributors concentrate on content and ensure a more consistent appearance throughout the site. (See Chapter 5 for more information about Style Sheets.)

Providing Access to Images

An alternative to referencing image files is to store them in a folder that contributors can access. The easiest way is to put them all in a folder immediately off the server root, such as /graphics, and provide copy-and-paste text, like this:

```
<IMG SRC="/graphics/corplogo.gif" ALT="ASR Corporate Logo" ALIGN=LEFT
HEIGHT=100 WIDTH=250>
```

Moving further into the copy-and-paste realm, you can also include copy-and-paste snippets of code to automatically include document headers and footers by using server-side includes.

```
<!--#include virtual="/includes/header.htm"-->
```

You provide the header, including anything that belongs at the top of the document such as the corporate logo, copyright, confidentiality information, and anything else your company requires. The contributor includes the single line in the document, and, when it appears on the Web, all the header information appears in place of the include tag. (See Chapter 6 for more about server-side includes.)

Publish Instructions and Guidelines

Publish—on the intranet, of course—instructions and guidelines for providing information on the intranet:

- Documentation for publishing information
- Acceptable versions of HTML (HTML 4, all Internet Explorer extensions, frames, or whatever)
- Formats for organizing and structuring the information
- Tools (and where to get them)
- Documentation for using tools
- HTML resources (this book, right?)
- Acceptable enhancements—images, applets, JavaScript, and so on

Also, specify that contributors include their contact information on each page so that content questions will go to them, not you. Make it clear that the "contact the Webmaster" links are only for visitors having technical difficulties. Contributors need to give visitors a way to contact them—during and after hours.

Provide Conversion Services

Offer to convert existing documents to intranet pages. Most departments have pages of information that could easily be converted to HTML.

If you offer this service, you could be overwhelmed with documents to convert. We strongly recommend providing one-time conversion services to help departments get material out on the intranet, but rather than assuming the responsibility for ongoing document conversion, take the time to train the contributors thoroughly so that departments can support themselves.

You'll find more information about converting documents and conversion tools in Chapter 16.

Remind Contributors as Necessary

Most content providers contribute information to the intranet in addition to their regular duties. You can help them manage their sections of the intranet by sending them e-mail reminders. Include information about how frequently visitors access their information, which information is not accessed, and so on, which you (or the system administrator) can get from the access logs. If visitors aren't accessing certain pages, help find out why. Is the information outdated, hard to find, not needed? With this information, you can help weed out information that isn't being used and make room for more.

Automating Processes

If you have programming resources available, consider automating some of the processes discussed in this chapter. For example, you can:

- Generate What's New lists
- Remind content providers of pages that haven't been updated in a specific amount of time
- Consolidate and summarize access logs, changes to pages, and new sections for reports to management
- Check incoming documents for compliance with corporate style, the correct version of HTML, and functional links

For more information, consult with your system administrator or internal programmers.

Announcing New or Updated Information

Visitors value new information, so be sure to notify them when the site is updated, and do so consistently. Even if visitors don't immediately need the information, making them aware that it's available might save them time later. Here are some ways to do so:

- Develop a What's New template that departments can use to feature new or updated information.

- Create New and Updated icons that contributors can include on their pages.

- E-mail employees regularly—say, weekly—and tell them what's new and updated.

- E-mail managers regularly about new and updated information, and request that they pass along the information to their employees.

Setting Up a Discussion Forum

In a real-time discussion forum, visitors can interact, regardless of time zones or schedules, using the intranet as the communications medium. For example, visitors can hold informal meetings, chat about projects, or even get live feedback about a document draft—all from their offices at their convenience.

You can choose from several forum options, based on the software you implement. For example, you can use Matt's Script Archive or Selena's Public Domain Script Archive, both available on the Companion CD, and adapt discussion forums from the scripts.

If you choose a more advanced software package, such as Ceilidh (pronounced kay-lee), also available on the CD, visitors can post HTML documents and request that other people edit and comment—right there online. The result is that visitors can open forums to large groups and get immediate feedback. Other visitors can monitor discussions for developments or news pertaining to their projects. By conducting meetings online through an intranet, companies move toward a newer, more open approach to communication. A discussion in progress looks like Figure 21.14.

Figure 21.15 shows the form used to respond to a posting about the highly ficti-tious Baumgartner proposal.

FIGURE 21.14

An ongoing discussion in Ceilidh

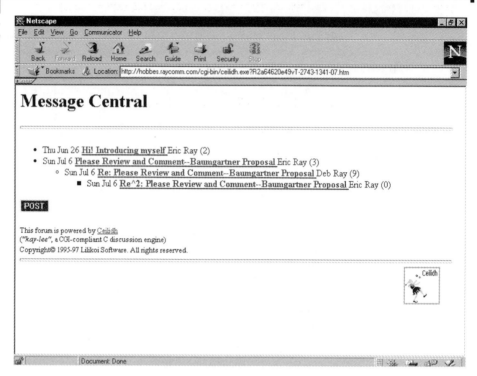

Installing Ceilidh is straightforward, but varies depending on the platform. Refer to the documentation in the Ceilidh folder on the CD for more information.

When using scripts and server-side programs, such as Matt's Script Archive or Selena's Public Domain Script Archive available on the CD, you may need assistance from your system administrator to implement and debug them. Documentation, when available, is included with the scripts or embedded in the code.

FIGURE 21.15

Responding to ongoing discussions is easy and fast.

Message Central

Title:

```
Re^2: Please Review and Comment--Baumgartner Proposal
```

Your name:

```
Eric Ray
```

Expire in: ⦿ 1 week   ○ 1 month   ○ 3 months

```
On Sun Jul 6, Deb Ray wrote:
---------------------------
>On Sun Jul 6, Eric Ray wrote:
>---------------------------
>>We should offer them everything they want at all costs.
>>We want this account.

>A very strong proposal--well supported. Might consider providing more
>details in the introduction to really lure them in. For example,

Like what kind of details? Can you be more specific? Can't
give them costs--if we do that, they don't need us.

include a mini cost analysis breakdown so that they can see up front
that it's gonna cost them next to nothin'. Good luck!
```

Submission type: ⦿ Regular   ○ Express

Express mail bypasses message verification but can not include HTML tags.

[CLEAR]   [SUBMIT]

Ceilidh is copyright © 1995-97 Lilikoi Software, http://www.lilikoi.com. All rights reserved.

PART

V

Developing Web Sites

Where to Go from Here

Armed with the information in this chapter, you have a running start on developing public, personal, or intranet sites. In fact, you'll likely be one step ahead of the Joneses if you follow the guidelines we provided.

From here, you can follow up with a visit to several chapters:

- See Chapter 20 for tips and advice that apply to all Web sites.
- Check out Chapter 6 if you're interested in more information about servers.
- See Chapter 2 for more information about the HTML document development process, which applies to public, personal, and intranet sites.

Chapter

22

Developing Help
Files with HTML

Developing Help Files with HTML

I f you have ever struggled with developing help files for multiple computer platforms, this chapter is for you. The days of developing help files for each platform from scratch are history. You can now take advantage of HTML and the latest developments from Netscape or Microsoft to create context-sensitive and searchable help files that you can use, with some constraints, on Windows, Macs, and Unix platforms. No muss, no fuss. (Well, maybe just a little.)

This chapter introduces you to HTML as a tool for developing online help files. We'll tell you a bit about Netscape's NetHelp and Microsoft's HTML Help—the two main technologies—discuss some of the tools that support these technologies, and show you how one company has successfully used NetHelp to meet cross-platform online help needs.

Understanding Help Files

Help files, like online documentation, provide information about a software product. Help files, however, differ significantly from online documentation. The primary difference is that help files give users context-sensitive information; users can click Help and link to a screen that provides information about the task at hand. As a rule, when users access Help (as opposed to online documentation), they're looking for just enough information to get over their current hurdle—they don't want to know the whys and wherefores of the application.

Another big difference is that help files often allow users to search for information on a specific topic, either by entering keywords or searching a database.

Online documentation is separate from the application, but help files link to the application. Although industrious users can browse help files, as a rule, help files are designed to provide help when needed, not to comprehensively document how the application works.

Help files also differ from online documentation in the way they're structured. Online documentation usually includes longer documents with explanations and descriptions of how the software works. Help files are typically short, include just enough information to get users through the task at hand, and usually have multiple links to related information. For example, as shown in Figure 22.1, Netscape Communicator's online help addresses a specific task and provides links to specific topics.

FIGURE 22.1

This Netscape Communicator help screen provides essential information and links to related information.

You can structure the help file as one long document with targeted links, which might be easier than managing and linking multiple files. The effect is the same, though. Users can link directly to the help information, without wading through several pages.

Additionally, many kinds of help files—particularly Windows Help (WinHelp)—offer you, the developer, a way to provide information that users cannot readily alter. WinHelp files are compiled into an unchangeable form before they can be used. On the other hand, you can easily change most HTML documents with a text editor.

If you want to put documentation online, but have no need to give users access to context-sensitive help, you can simply create an HTML document, as discussed throughout many other chapters in this book.

Developing Help Files

Developing platform-specific help files requires separate help file systems, different software, and varying approaches to presentation for each platform. Essentially, you must develop a help package from scratch for each platform you support, which is time-consuming and costly.

There are, however, some definite advantages associated with platform-specific help files:

Speed: Platform-specific help generally takes full advantage of specific system capabilities and runs quickly. The viewing software also generally loads and runs quickly—unlike a bulky and bloated Web browser.

Familiarity: Platform-specific help on most systems looks just like all the other help files and other applications on the system. Therefore, most users generally know what to expect when they click Help.

Stability: Platform-specific help is usually robust, typically running without glitches or crashes. This stems, in part, from help file tools having a much slower development cycle than Web browsers.

Consistency: In particular, Windows Help is seemingly everywhere, running on approximately 80 million computers around the world. Most Windows users are familiar and reasonably comfortable with the interface. (Macintosh and Unix Help are somewhat less common, and Unix Help is also not particularly user friendly.)

You'll notice that all these advantages focus on the user. Not one of them mentions that developing platform-specific help files is easy or fast. The process involves time, specialized software, and money—and has to be repeated for each supported platform.

If you're developing help for a single platform, platform-specific help is probably your best choice—you develop one set of help files and give users the benefit of speed and familiarity. If you're developing help files for multiple platforms, though, you might find HTML help a better choice.

Although HTML help doesn't offer users the speed or familiarity of platform-specific help, it eases the authoring process for the following reasons:

- You can author a single help file that is—in theory, at least—equally accessible on Windows, Macs, and Unix.

- You can easily create and link to online updates and corrections so that Internet or intranet users can easily access the latest information.

Understanding HTML Help Technologies

Although HTML help is the latest technology for developing online help files, at the time of writing, it offers more potential and promise than actual demonstrated strengths. Both Netscape and Microsoft are vying to perfect this technology, but thus far neither of their approaches gives users the stability or speed inherent in single-platform applications.

Netscape's NetHelp

Netscape's NetHelp is the only truly cross-platform solution in the HTML help arena. Although NetHelp lacks some of the more sophisticated features introduced in Microsoft's HTML Help, NetHelp does provide all the basic components of context-sensitive help and works well on multiple platforms.

Netscape used widely available solutions (such as JavaScript) to provide the searchability and context-sensitivity required by help applications. For this reason, NetHelp closely resembles traditional HTML.

NetHelp comes as a set of instructions along with HTML components that you are invited to adopt, adapt, and use. You'll find the NetHelp Software Developers Kit (SDK) at:

```
developer.netscape.com/one/nethelp/index.html
```

This kit includes all the tools you need to link to your software plus some code for navigation buttons and framesets. Figure 22.2 shows the NetHelp interface. Notice that the interface consists of little more than a couple of frames, a few navigation buttons for Contents and Index, and some (unseen, obviously) JavaScript tying it all together.

PART

V

Developing Web Sites

FIGURE 22.2

The basic NetHelp 1 interface offers bare bones functionality.

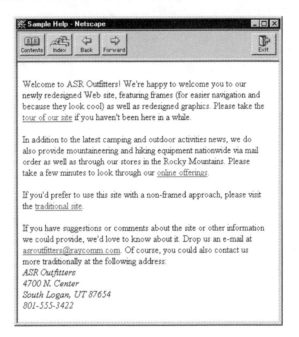

Microsoft HTML Help

Microsoft HTML Help uses HTML as the basic building block and equals or exceeds the power and capabilities of WinHelp (Microsoft's seasoned platform-specific help product). Unfortunately, these additional capabilities come in the form of ActiveX controls, platform-specific software code, and programs and add-ins that require Internet Explorer.

Microsoft provides the latest information about HTML Help and a basic authoring kit in the form of the Microsoft HTML Help Workshop. You can download it from:

`www.microsoft.com/workshop/author/htmlhelp/`

At the time of writing, HTML Help is fully functional only on Windows 95 and Windows NT and works properly only through Internet Explorer. Microsoft, however, has announced that it will support cross-platform capabilities in the near future. Figure 22.3 shows you the HTML Help interface.

FIGURE 22.3

The HTML Help interface is more sophisticated and attractive than that of NetHelp.

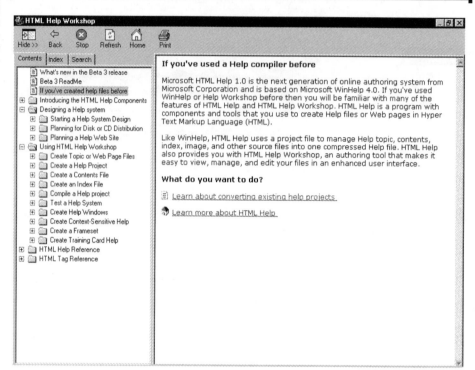

Using HTML Help-Authoring Tools

You use an authoring tool in conjunction with an application such as Microsoft Word to create HTML help files or to convert existing help files to HTML. These tools were originally developed to help create Windows Help (WinHelp). Some of them require that you first create a traditional WinHelp file (or at least create the RTF document file that can be compiled into a WinHelp file) before you develop the actual HTML help file.

If you're in the market for an authoring tool, you might consider those listed below. All work somewhat differently.

Doc-to-Help: Created by WexTech, Inc., Doc-to-Help lets you create a Word document that you can print as a manual or automatically turn into a WinHelp file or an HTML Help (Microsoft flavor) file. For more information, visit www.wextech.com.

RoboHelp: Based on Microsoft Word, RoboHelp takes a more online-focused approach. Although you cannot readily use a RoboHelp file for a printed manual, RoboHelp makes creating WinHelp, and then HTML help, quite straightforward. After creating the initial WinHelp file, you can recompile your file in either HTML Help or NetHelp format. For more information, visit www.blue-sky.com.

ForeHelp: A stand-alone help-authoring system, ForeHelp lets you produce either WinHelp or HTML Help (either NetHelp or HTML Help flavors) easily from scratch. Additional components let you convert WinHelp to HTML and back. Check out www.ff.com for more information.

HelpBreeze: Also based on Microsoft Word, HelpBreeze allows you to create WinHelp as well as pure HTML documents and HTML Help (the Microsoft variety). For more information, go to www.solutionsoft.com.

Case Study: NetHelp

In this section, we'll show you how one company, Computerized Medical Systems, Inc. (CMS), used NetHelp to develop HTML help files. We'll look at the company's help file needs, discuss why they chose HTML help, and show you how they actually implemented NetHelp.

CMS develops, sells, and supports Radiation Treatment Planning (RTP) systems. RTP systems, costing several hundred thousand dollars, can be found in hospitals and clinics worldwide, wherever cancer patients are receiving radiation treatment. CMS was looking for a better way to document its flagship product, the FOCUS 3-D Radiation Treatment Planning (RTP) system.

The Problem: Unwieldy, Unused Documentation

Originally, the FOCUS product shipped with a two-volume *Tutorial* and a seven-volume *Reference Guide*. CMS updated the software and the documentation as frequently as four times each year and shipped documentation update packages with each release.

Unfortunately, this solution met few people's needs. For example, customers complained about the size of the documentation and the difficulty in finding information. In fact, CMS found out through a survey that few customers actually referred to the documentation because they found it easier to call CMS customer support.

Additionally, CMS management found the cost of maintaining the documentation set prohibitive.

The Solution: Move It Online

After comparing the costs of print and online documentation, CMS decided to move the documentation online. Because the existing documentation was so voluminous and designed for paper presentation, CMS faced several challenges.

First, because the FOCUS application did not include the code necessary to allow online documentation to be context sensitive, additional development resources were required.

Second, sections of the paper documentation were long and included many graphics. Also, the content was reference-based, not how-to or action oriented, which is not the best organizational structure for online help.

CMS opted to break the project into two phases:

- Create online documentation. This included implementing the online and context-sensitive hooks in the software, converting the documentation to HTML, and establishing links within and between documents.

- Turn the current documentation into an online help or electronic performance support system. This phase included rewriting the existing material for online use, creating the procedures necessary to complete tasks, and identifying and creating multimedia tutorials.

The Requirements

As part of the planning process, CMS outlined the following requirements for the system they would develop:

- It had to run on the platforms used in house (HP-UX, SGI IRIX, MS Windows).

- It had to run on the platforms on which the product runs (HP-UX, SGI IRIX).

- It had to be readily converted to run on different platforms or ideally be platform independent.

- It had to be available now, rather than being merely a promise of to-be-implemented functionality.

Other, somewhat less critical, requirements included the following:

- Some level of context-sensitivity within the application.

- Minimal impact on system resources. Any decrease in performance would reduce the product speed, thereby undermining a significant product advantage.

- Minimal cost impact and within the timeframe of normal system development.

The only reasonable solution seemed to be HTML help. The developers considered both Netscape's NetHelp and Microsoft's HTML Help and came up with the pros and cons shown in Tables 22.1 and 22.2.

TABLE 22.1: PROS AND CONS OF NETHELP

Pros	Cons
Cross-platform	New technology; still under development; still do not know all the ramifications.
Based on standard HTML	Does not contain all the Windows Help features. Full-text search and index capabilities not yet available for evaluation.
Comparable to Windows Help in appearance and functionality	May be difficult to keep up with new versions/releases, especially if a development war takes place (with Microsoft).
Uses all available Netscape plug-ins, JavaScript, CGI, and so on	Requires the Netscape browser; browser licensing and configuration.
Easy to internationalize (no recompiling or juggling of file names)	Unknown effort required to incorporate into development.
No compiling required; simply replace files that change	Ability of users to edit the HTML files could be a problem.

TABLE 22.2: PROS AND CONS OF HTML HELP

Pros	Cons
Closest to the WinHelp look and feel	Not available for Unix platforms; no indication of when it will be available.
Many more features than NetHelp (especially compressed HTML and full-text search)	

CMS decided that Netscape's NetHelp would best meet their needs, primarily because HTML Help is not available for Unix. The absence of currently available—as opposed to promised—cross-platform support made HTML Help an impossible choice. To go along with this decision, they adopted the Netscape browser.

The NetHelp Application

To implement online help, CMS used Microsoft FrontPage and Netscape Navigator Gold, plus a variety of shareware code-based text editors. They determined that the cost and learning curve of a help-authoring tool would not justify the results—particularly given the relative simplicity of NetHelp. The resulting help screens are similar to that shown in Figure 22.4.

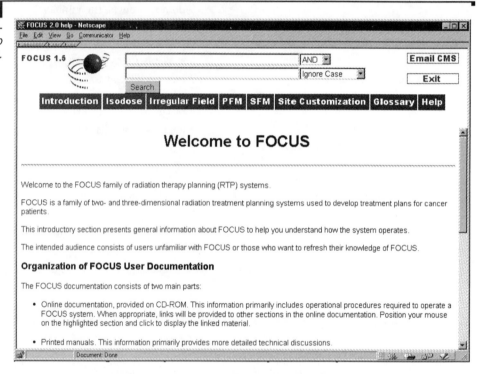

Along with the help interface, CMS used JavaScript to develop a search engine in FOCUS help. Because of the scope of the documentation, some sort of search capability was essential. The search engine takes the terms from two text input boxes and then compares them with every entry in a keyword array. It then creates a page that includes a link to every page that matches the keywords for that page.

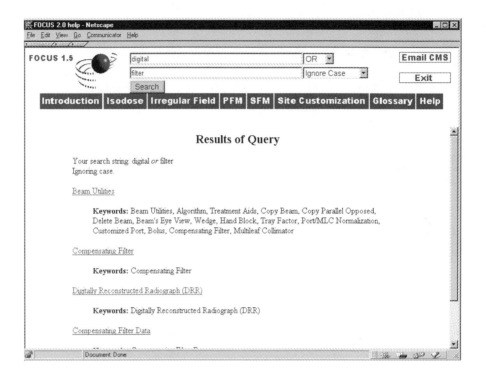

The programming staff linked the software to the help files by embedding specific URLs in the code. When users invoke help, the application sends a URL to the Netscape NetHelp program (API, technically), opens the Netscape browser, and then opens the associated topic.

Where to Go from Here

In this chapter, we looked at the emerging HTML help technologies. In particular, we showed you how Netscape and Microsoft implement the technology and briefly introduced you to some authoring tools. Though these technologies are not yet mature, you can expect to see them evolve and become more widely used in the near future.

From here, we suggest the following chapters:

- See Chapter 11 to find out more about JavaScript.
- Read Chapter 15 for information about other HTML tools.
- See Chapter 18 for information about generating HTML from a database.
- Look in Chapter 19 to find out how to create searchable HTML.

PART

V

Developing Web Sites

Master's Reference
Part 1

HTML TAGS AND ATTRIBUTES

T his section is a comprehensive reference guide to all HTML tags, including standard tags and those introduced by Netscape Navigator and Microsoft Internet Explorer. For each tag, we've provided sample code and indicated the following:

- The version of HTML with which the tag is associated
- Whether browsers widely support the tag
- Whether to pair the tag with a closing tag

For each tag's attributes, we've provided sample code and indicated the following:

- The version of HTML with which the attribute is associated
- Whether browsers widely support the attribute

If tags and attributes appear in the HTML 4 standard, in the HTML 3.2 standard, or in the HTML 2 standard, the version number appears next to Standard. We indicate tags or attributes that are specific to a browser, such as Internet Explorer. In general, a variety of browsers recognize technology-specific tags, such as those for frames, and other browsers rarely recognize browser-specific tags. HTML 2 was the first official HTML standard. The number of tags that this standard defined is small compared with what is in use today. HTML 2 did not support tables, client-side image maps, or frames. You can safely use all HTML 2 tags and attributes.

HTML 3.2 remains backward compatible with HTML 2, but provides many new tags. Included in HTML 3.2 is support for tables, client-side image maps, embedded applets, and many new attributes that help control alignment of objects within documents. You can assume that most browsers support or soon will support all HTML 3.2 tags and attributes.

HTML 4 remains backward compatible with other versions of HTML and expands the capabilities to better address multiple languages and browser technologies such as speech or Braille. Additionally, most formatting tags and attributes are deprecated (strongly discouraged) in HTML 4 in favor of Style Sheets. At the time of writing, no production browsers completely supported HTML 4, although Microsoft claimed that Internet Explorer 4 would do so.

Specifying that a tag or an attribute is Common means that approximately 75 to 80 percent of browsers in common use accommodate the tag. All recent versions of both Internet Explorer and Netscape Navigator recognize Common tags and attributes.

We indicate variables as follows:

Variable	What You Substitute
n	A number (such as a size)
URL	Some form of address (as in a hyperlink)
#RRGGBB	A color value or a color name
...	Some other value, such as a title or a name

<!-- -->

Inserts comments into a document. Browsers do not display comments, although comments are visible in the document source.

Standard: HTML 2
Common: Yes
Paired: Yes
Sample:

```
<!-- Here is the picture of Fido -->
<IMG SRC="fidopic.jpg">
```

<!DOCTYPE>

Appears at the beginning of the document and indicates the HTML version of the document.

The HTML 2 standard is:

```
<!DOCTYPE HTML PUBLIC "-//IETF//DTD HTML 2
//EN">
```

The HTML 3.2 standard is:

```
<!DOCTYPE HTML PUBLIC "-//W3C//DTD/ HTML 3.2
Final//EN">
```

The HTML 4 standard is:

```
<!DOCTYPE HTML PUBLIC "-//W3C//DTD/ HTML 4
Final//EN">
```

Standard: HTML 2
Common: Yes
Paired: No
Sample:

```
<!DOCTYPE HTML PUBLIC "-//W3C//DTD/ HTML 4
Final//EN">
```

<A>

Also called the *anchor* tag, identifies a link or a location within a document. You commonly use this tag to create a hyperlink, using the HREF= attribute. You can also use the <A> tag to identify sections within a document, using the NAME= attribute.

Standard: HTML 2
Common: Yes
Paired: Yes
Sample:

```
<A HREF="http://www.raycomm.com/">Visit
RayComm</a>
```

Attribute Information

ACCESSKEY="..."

Assigns a key sequence to the element.

Standard: HTML 4
Common: No
Sample:

```
<A HREF="help.html" ACCESSKEY="H">
HELP</a>
```

CHARSET="..."

Specifies character encoding of the data designated by the link. Use the name of a character set defined in RFC2045. The default value for this attribute, appropriate for all Western languages, is "ISO-8859-1".

Standard: HTML 4
Common: No
Sample:

```
<A HREF="help.html" CHARSET="ISO-8859-1">
HELP</a>
```

CLASS="..."

Indicates the style class to apply to the <A> element.

Standard: HTML 4
Common: No
Sample:

```
<A HREF="next.html" CLASS="casual">
Next</A>
```

COORDS="x1, y1, x2, y2"

Identifies the coordinates that define a clickable area. Measure coordinates, in pixels, from the top left corner of the image.

Standard: HTML 4
Common: No
Sample:

```
<A SHAPE="RECT" COORDS="20,8,46,30"
HREF="food.html">
```

HREF="URL"

Specifies the relative or absolute location of a file to which you want to provide a hyperlink.

Standard: HTML 2
Common: Yes
Sample:

```
<A HREF="details.html">More Info</a>
```

ID="..."

Assigns a unique ID selector to an instance of the <A> tag. When you then assign a style to that ID selector, it affects only that one instance of the <A> tag.

Standard: HTML 4
Common: No
Sample:

```
<A HREF="next.html" ID="123">Next</A>
```

NAME="..."

Marks a location within the current document with a name. The browser can then quickly move to specific information within a document. You can link to existing named locations in a document by using a fragment URL, consisting of a pound sign (#) and the name (from within that document), or by using a more complete URL, including a pound sign and a name (from other documents or sites).

Standard: HTML 2
Common: Yes
Sample:

```
<A HREF="#ingredients">Ingredients</A><BR>
<A NAME="ingredients"><h1>Ingredients</H1>
```

REL="..."

Specifies relationship hyperlinks.

Standard: HTML 3.2
Common: No
Sample:

```
<A REV="made"
HREF="mailto:bob@company.com">
```

REV="..."

Specifies reverse relationship hyperlinks.

Standard: HTML 3.2
Common: No
Sample:

```
<A REV="Previous"
HREF="http://www.raycomm.com/firstdoc.htm">
```

SHAPE="{RECT, CIRCLE, POLY}"

Specifies the type of shape used to represent the clickable area. SHAPE=RECT indicates that the shape is rectangular. SHAPE=CIRCLE specifies that the shape is a circle. SHAPE=POLY indicates that the shape is a polygon represented by three or more points.

Standard:	HTML 4
Common:	No
Sample:	

```
<A SHAPE="RECT" COORDS="20,8,46,30"
HREF="food.html">
```

STYLE="..."

Specifies Style Sheet commands that apply to the contents within the <A> tags.

Standard:	HTML 4
Common:	No
Sample:	

```
<A STYLE="background: red"
HREF="page2.html">Page 2</A>
```

TABINDEX="n"

Indicates where the element appears in the tabbing order of the document.

Standard:	HTML 4
Common:	No
Sample:	

```
<A HREF="food.html" TABINDEX="4">Food</A>
```

TARGET="..."

Indicates the name of a specific frame into which you load the linked document. You establish frame names within the <FRAME> tag. The value of this attribute can be any single word.

Standard:	HTML 4
Common:	Yes
Sample:	

```
<A HREF="/frames/frame2.html"
TARGET="pages">Go to Page 2</a>
```

TITLE="..."

Specifies text assigned to the tag that you can use for context-sensitive help within the document. Browsers may use this to show tool tips over the hyperlink.

Standard:	HTML 4
Common:	Yes
Sample:	

```
<A HREF="page2.html"
TITLE="Go to the next page">
```

Other Attributes

This tag also accepts the lang, dir, onClick, onDblClick, onMouseDown, onMouseUp, onMouseOver, onMouseMove, onMouseOut, onKeyPress, onKeyDown, and onKeyUp attributes. See the "Element-Independent Attributes" section of this reference for definitions and examples.

<ACRONYM>

Indicates an acronym in a document.

Standard:	HTML 4
Common:	No
Paired:	Yes
Sample:	

```
<P><ACRONYM>HTTP</ACRONYM> stands for
HyperText Transfer Protocol</P>
```

Attribute Information

CLASS="..."

Indicates which style class applies to the <ACRONYM> element.

Standard:	HTML 4
Common:	No
Sample:	

```
<P><ACRONYM CLASS="casual">HTTP</ACRONYM>
stands for HyperText Transfer Protocol</P>
```

ID="..."

Assigns a unique ID selector to an instance of the <ACRONYM> tag. When you then assign a style to that ID selector, it affects only that one instance of the <ACRONYM> tag.

> **Standard**: HTML 4
> **Common**: No
> **Sample**:

```
<P><ACRONYM ID="123">HTTP</ACRONYM> stands
for HyperText Transfer Protocol</P>
```

STYLE="..."

Specifies Style Sheet commands that apply to the definition.

> **Standard**: HTML 4
> **Common**: No
> **Sample**:

```
<P><ACRONYM STYLE="background: blue;
color: white">ESP</ACRONYM> stands for
extra-sensory perception.</P>
```

TITLE="..."

Specifies text assigned to the tag. For the <ACRONYM> tag, use this to provide the expansion of the term. You might also use this attribute for context-sensitive help within the document. Browsers may use this to show tool tips over the text.

> **Standard**: HTML 4
> **Common**: No
> **Sample**:

```
<P><ACRONYM TITLE="HyperText Transfer
Protocol">HTTP</ACRONYM> stands for
HyperText Transfer Protocol</P>
```

Other Attributes

This tag also accepts the lang, dir, onClick, onDblClick, onMouseDown, onMouseUp, onMouseOver, onMouseMove, onMouseOut, onKeyPress, onKeyDown, and onKeyUp attributes. See the Element-Independent Attributes section of this reference for definitions and examples.

<ADDRESS>

In a document, distinguishes an address from normal document text.

> **Standard**: HTML 2
> **Common**: Yes
> **Paired**: Yes
> **Sample**:

```
I live at:
<ADDRESS>123 Nowhere Ave<BR>City, State
12345</ADDRESS>
```

Attribute Information

ALIGN={LEFT, RIGHT, CENTER}

Indicates how the address text is aligned within the document. ALIGN=LEFT positions the address text flush with the left side of the document. ALIGN=RIGHT positions the address text flush with the right side of the document. ALIGN=CENTER centers the address text between the left and right edges of the document.

> **Standard**: HTML 3.2; deprecated in favor of Style Sheets
> **Common**: Yes
> **Sample**:

```
<ADDRESS ALIGN="CENTER">123 Anywhere
St.</ADDRESS>
```

CLASS="..."

Indicates the style class to apply to the <ADDRESS> element.

> **Standard**: HTML 4
> **Common**: No
> **Sample**:

```
<ADDRESS CLASS="casual">
123 First Ave.</ADDRESS>
```

ID="..."

Assigns a unique ID selector to an instance of the <ADDRESS> tag. When you then assign a style to that ID selector, it affects only that one instance of the <ADDRESS> tag.

Standard:	HTML 4
Common:	No
Sample:	

```
<ADDRESS ID="123">1600 Pennsylvania
</ADDRESS>
```

STYLE="..."

Specifies Style Sheet commands that apply to
the contents within the <ADDRESS> tags.

Standard:	HTML 4
Common:	Yes
Sample:	

```
<ADDRESS STYLE="background: red">
```

TITLE="..."

Specifies text assigned to the tag. You might
use this attribute for context-sensitive help
within the document. Browsers may use this to
show tool tips over the address text.

Standard:	HTML 4
Common:	No
Sample:	

```
<ADDRESS TITLE="Address">
```

Other Attributes

This tag also accepts the lang, dir, onClick,
onDblClick, onMouseDown, onMouseUp,
onMouseOver, onMouseMove, onMouseOut,
onKeyPress, onKeyDown, and onKeyUp attributes.
See the Element-Independent Attributes section of this reference for definitions and
examples.

<APPLET>

Embeds a Java applet object into an HTML
document. Typically, items that appear inside
the <APPLET> tags allow browsers that do not
support Java applets to view alternative text.
Browsers that do support Java ignore all information between the <APPLET> tags.

Standard	HTML 3.2; deprecated in HTML 4 in favor of <OBJECT>

Common:	Yes
Paired:	Yes
Sample:	

```
<APPLET CODE="game.class">
It appears your browser does not
support Java. You're missing out on
a whole world of neat things!
</APPLET>
```

Attribute Information

ALIGN={LEFT, CENTER, RIGHT}

Specifies the horizontal alignment of the Java
applet displayed. For example, a value of CEN-
TER tells the browser to place the applet evenly
spaced between the left and right edges of the
browser window.

Standard:	HTML 3.2; deprecated in HTML 4 in favor of Style Sheets.
Common:	No
Sample:	

```
<APPLET ALIGN=CENTER
CODE=""http://www.raycomm.com/
checkers.class">
You lose. Would you like to play again?
Hit the RELOAD button.<BR>
</APPLET>
```

ALT="..."

Displays a textual description of a Java applet,
if necessary.

Standard:	HTML 3.2
Common:	No
Sample:	

```
<APPLET CODE=""http://www.raycomm.com/
checkers.class">ALT="A Game of checkers">
We could have had a relaxing game of
checkers if your browser supported
Java applets. I'll gladly play with
you if you enable Java applets or
upgrade to a browser that supports
Java.
</APPLET>
```

CODE="*URL*"

Specifies the relative or absolute location of the Java bytecode file on the server.

Standard: HTML 3.2
Common: No
Sample:

```
<APPLET CODE="http://www.raycomm.com/
checkers.class">
Dang! Your browser does not support
Java applets. You may want to consider
installing a newer web browser.
</APPLET>
```

CODEBASE="*URL*"

Specifies the directory where you can find all necessary Java class files on the WWW server. If you set this attribute, you need not use explicit URLs in other references to the class files. For example, you would not need an explicit reference in the CODE= attribute.

Standard: HTML 3.2
Common: No
Sample:

```
<APPLET
CODEBASE="http://www.raycomm.com/
checkers.class" CODE="checkers.html">
If your browser supported inline Java
applets, you'd be looking at a very
attractive checkerboard right now.
</APPLET>
```

HEIGHT="*n*"

Specifies the height (measured in pixels) of the Java applet object within the document.

Standard: HTML 3.2
Common: No
Sample:

```
<APPLET HEIGHT="200" CODE="checkers.class">
Since your browser does not support inline
Java applets, we won't be playing checkers
today. </APPLET>
```

HSPACE="*n*"

Specifies an amount of blank space (measured in pixels) to the left and right of the Java applet within the document.

Standard: HTML 3.2
Common: No
Sample:

```
<APPLET HSPACE="10"
CODE="/checkers.class">
Sorry. Due to the fact your browser
does not support embedded Java
applets, you'll have to play checkers
the old way today.
</APPLET>
```

NAME="..."

Assigns the applet instance a name so that other applets can identify it within the document.

Standard: Internet Explorer
Common: No
Sample:

```
<APPLET SRC="/checkers.class"
NAME="Checkers">
</APPLET>
```

PARAM *NAME*="..."

Passes program parameters to the Java applet.

Standard: HTML 3.2
Common: No
Sample:

```
<APPLET CODE="/checkers.class"
PARAM COLOR="red">
Since your browser does not support
inline Java applets, I win this game
of checkers by forfeit.
</APPLET>
```

TITLE="..."

Specifies text assigned to the tag. You might use this attribute for context-sensitive help within the document. Browsers may use this to show tool tips over the embedded applet.

Standard: HTML 4
Common: No
Sample:

```
<APPLET SRC="/java/thing.class"
TITLE="Thing">
```

VSPACE="n"

Specifies the amount of vertical space (measured in pixels) above and below the Java applet.

Standard: HTML 3.2
Common: No
Sample:

```
<APPLET VSPACE="10"
CODE="/checkers.class">
If you had a Java-capable browser, you
could be playing checkers!
</APPLET>
```

WIDTH="n"

Specifies the width (measured in pixels) of a Java applet within a document.

Standard: HTML 3.2
Common: No
Sample:

```
<APPLET WIDTH="350"
CODE="/checkers.class">
Checkers can be a lot of fun, but it's
more fun if your browser supports Java.
Sorry.
</APPLET>
```

Other Attributes

This tag also accepts the lang, dir, onClick, onDblClick, onMouseDown, onMouseUp, onMouseOver, onMouseMove, onMouseOut, onKeyPress, onKeyDown, and onKeyUp attributes. See the Element-Independent Attributes section of this reference for definitions and examples.

<AREA>

Defines an area within a client-side image map definition (see the <MAP> tag). It indicates an area where visitors can choose to link to another document.

Standard: HTML 3.2
Common: Yes
Paired: No
Sample:

```
<AREA SHAPE=RECT COORDS="20,8,46,30"
HREF="food.html">
```

Attribute Information

ALT="..."

Provides a textual description for visitors who have text-only browsers.

Standard: HTML 4
Common: Yes
Sample:

```
<AREA ALT="This blue rectangle links to
blue.html" HREF="blue.html">
```

CLASS="..."

Indicates the style class you want to apply to the <AREA> element.

Standard: HTML 4
Common: No
Sample:

```
<AREA CLASS="casual" SHAPE="RECT"
COORDS="20,8,46,30" HREF="food.html">
```

COORDS="x1, y1, x2, y2"

Identifies the coordinates within an image map that define the image map area. Measure coordinates, in pixels, from the top left corner of the image.

Standard: HTML 3.2
Common: Yes
Sample:

```
<AREA SHAPE="RECT" COORDS="20,8,46,30"
HREF="food.html">
```

HREF="*URL*"

Identifies the location of the document you want to load when the indicated image map area is selected.

> **Standard:** HTML 3.2
> **Common:** Yes
> **Sample:**

```
<AREA SHAPE="RECT" COORDS="20,8,46,30"
HREF="food.html">
```

ID="..."

Assigns a unique ID selector to an instance of the <AREA> tag. When you then assign a style to that ID selector, it affects this instance of the <AREA> tag.

> **Standard:** HTML 4
> **Common:** No
> **Sample:**

```
<AREA ID="123">
```

NOHREF

Defines an image map area that does not link to another document.

> **Standard:** HTML 3.2
> **Common:** Yes
> **Sample:**

```
<AREA SHAPE="RECT" COORDS="20,8,46,30"
NOHREF>
```

NOTAB

Excludes the image map area from the tab order.

> **Standard:** Internet Explorer
> **Common:** Yes
> **Sample:**

```
<AREA SHAPE="RECT" COORDS="20,8,46,30"
HREF="food.html" NOTAB>
```

SHAPE="{RECT, CIRCLE, POLY}"

Specifies the type of shape used to represent the image map area. SHAPE=RECT indicates that the shape of the image map area is rectangular. SHAPE=CIRCLE specifies that the shape of the image map area is a circle. SHAPE=POLY indicates that the shape of the image map area is a polygon represented by three or more points.

> **Standard:** HTML 3.2
> **Common:** Yes
> **Sample:**

```
<AREA SHAPE="RECT" COORDS="20,8,46,30"
HREF="food.html">
```

STYLE="..."

Specifies Style Sheet commands that apply to the image map area.

> **Standard:** HTML 4
> **Common:** No
> **Sample:**

```
<AREA SHAPE="RECT" COORDS="20,8,46,30"
HREF="food.html" STYLE="background: red">
```

TABINDEX="*n*"

Indicates where the image map area appears in the tabbing order of the document.

> **Standard:** HTML 4
> **Common:** Yes
> **Sample:**

```
<AREA SHAPE="RECT" COORDS="20,8,46,30"
HREF="food.html" TABINDEX=4>
```

TARGET="..."

Identifies which named frame the linked document selected should load. For example, when visitors select an area within an image map, the linked document may load in the same frame or in a different frame, specified by TARGET="...".

> **Standard:** HTML 4
> **Common:** Yes
> **Sample:**

```
<AREA SHAPE="RECT" COORDS="20,8,46,30"
HREF="food.html" TARGET="leftframe">
```

TITLE="..."

Specifies text assigned to the tag. You might use this attribute for context-sensitive help within the document. Browsers may use this to show tool tips over the image map area.

Standard: HTML 4
Common: No
Sample:

```
<AREA SHAPE="RECT" COORDS="20,8,46,30"
HREF="food.html" NAME="Food!">
```

Other Attributes

This tag also accepts the lang and dir attributes. See the Element-Independent Attributes section of this reference for definitions and examples.

<B>

Indicates text that should appear in boldface.

Standard: HTML 2
Common: Yes
Paired: Yes
Sample:

```
The afternoon was <B>so</B> hot!
```

Attribute Information

CLASS="..."

Indicates which style class applies to the <B> element.

Standard: HTML 4
Common: No
Sample:

```
<B CLASS="casual">Boom!</B>
```

ID="..."

Assigns a unique ID selector to an instance of the <B> tag. When you assign a style to that ID selector, it affects only that one instance of the <B> tag.

Standard: HTML 4
Common: No
Sample:

```
I work for <B ID="123">Widgets Inc.</B>
```

STYLE="..."

Specifies Style Sheet commands that apply to the contents within the <B> tags.

Standard: HTML 4
Common: No
Sample:

```
<B STYLE="background: red">
```

TITLE="..."

Specifies text assigned to the tag. You might use this attribute for context-sensitive help within the document. Browsers may use this to show tool tips over the boldface

Standard: HTML 4
Common: No
Sample:

```
<B TITLE="Species">Dog Species</B>
```

Other Attributes

This tag also accepts the lang, dir, onClick, onDblClick, onMouseDown, onMouseUp, onMouseOver, onMouseMove, onMouseOut, onKeyPress, onKeyDown, and onKeyUp attributes. See the Element-Independent Attributes section of this reference for definitions and examples.

<BASE>

Identifies the location where all relative URLs in your document originate.

Standard: HTML 2
Common: Yes
Paired: No
Sample:

```
<BASE HREF="http://www.raycomm.com/info/">
```

Attribute Information

HREF="*URL*"

Indicates the relative or absolute location of the base document.

Standard: HTML 2
Common: Yes
Sample:

```
<BASE HREF="http://www.raycomm.com/">
```

TARGET="..."

Identifies in which named frame you load a document (see the HREF= attribute).

Standard: HTML 4
Common: Yes
Sample:

```
<BASE HREF="http://www.raycomm.com/frames/"
TARGET="main">
```

<BASEFONT>

Provides a font setting for normal text within a document. Font settings (see the <FONT> tag) within the document are relative to settings specified with this tag. Use this tag in the document header (between the <HEAD> tags).

Standard: HTML 3.2; deprecated in HTML 4 in favor of Style Sheets
Common: Yes
Paired: No
Sample:

```
<BASEFONT SIZE="5">
```

Attribute Information

COLOR="#RRGGBB" or "..."

Sets the font color of normal text within a document. Color names may substitute for the explicit RGB hexadecimal values.

Standard: HTML 3.2; deprecated in HTML 4 in favor of Style Sheets
Common: Yes
Sample:

```
<BASEFONT SIZE="2" COLOR="#FF00CC">
```

FACE="...,..."

Specifies the font face of normal text within a document. You can set this attribute to a comma-separated list of font names. The browser selects the first name matching a font available.

Standard: HTML 3.2; deprecated in HTML 4 in favor of Style Sheets
Common: Yes
Sample:

```
<BASEFONT FACE="Avant Guard, Helvetica,
Arial">
```

SIZE="*n*"

Specifies the font size of normal text within a document. Valid values are integer numbers in the range 1 to 7 with 3 being the default setting.

Standard: HTML 3.2; deprecated in HTML 4 in favor of Style Sheets
Common: Yes
Sample:

```
<BASEFONT SIZE="5">
```

<BDO>

Indicates text that should appear with the direction (left to right or right to left) specified, overriding other language-specific settings.

Standard: HTML 4
Common: No
Paired: Yes
Sample:

```
<P LANG="IW" DIR="RTL">This Hebrew text
contains a number, <BDO="LTR">29381</BDO>,
that must appear left to right.</P>
```

Attribute Information

This tag accepts the `lang` and `dir` attributes. See the Element-Independent Attributes section of this reference for definitions and examples.

<BGSOUND>

Embeds a background sound file within documents. Use in the document head of documents intended for visitors who use Internet Explorer.

Standard: Internet Explorer
Common: Yes
Paired: No
Sample:

`<BGSOUND SRC="scream.wav">`

Attribute Information

LOOP="{n, INFINITE}"

Specifies the number of times a background sound file repeats. The value INFINITE is the default.

Standard: Internet Explorer
Common: No
Sample:

`<BGSOUND SRC="bugle.wav" LOOP="2">`

SRC="URL"

Indicates the explicit or relative location of the sound file.

Standard: Internet Explorer
Common: No
Sample:

`<BGSOUND SRC="wah.wav">`

<BIG>

Indicates that text display in a larger font.

Standard: HTML 3.2
Common: Yes
Paired: Yes
Sample:

`<BIG>Lunch</BIG>`
`<p>Lunch will be served at 2 p.m.`

Attribute Information

CLASS="..."

Indicates which style class applies to the <BIG> element.

Standard: HTML 4
Common: No
Sample:

`<BIG CLASS="casual">Instructions</BIG>`

ID="..."

Assigns a unique ID selector to an instance of the <BIG> tag. When you then assign a style to that ID selector, it affects only that one instance of the <BIG> tag.

Standard: HTML 4
Common: No
Sample:

`<BIG ID="123">REMINDER:</BIG>`
`Eat 5 servings of fruits and`
`vegetables every day!`

STYLE="..."

Specifies Style Sheet commands that apply to the contents within the <BIG> tags.

Standard: HTML 4
Common: No
Sample:

`<BIG STYLE="background: red">`

TITLE="..."

Specifies text assigned to the tag. You might use this attribute for context-sensitive help within the document. Browsers may use this to show tool tips over the text inside the <BIG> tags.

Standard: HTML 4
Common: No
Sample:

`<BIG TITLE="Bigger">`

Other Attributes

This tag also accepts the `lang`, `dir`, `onClick`, `onDblClick`, `onMouseDown`, `onMouseUp`, `onmouseover`, `onMouseMove`, `onMouseOut`, `onKeyPress`, `onKeyDown`, and `onKeyUp` attributes. See the

Element-Independent Attributes section of this reference for definitions and examples.

<BLINK>

A Netscape-specific tag that makes text blink on and off.

> **Standard**: Netscape Navigator; Style Sheets offer the same functionality in a more widely recognized syntax.
> **Common**: No
> **Paired**: Yes
> **Sample**:

```
<P><BLINK>NEW INFO</BLINK>: We moved!
```

Attribute Information

CLASS="..."

Indicates which style class applies to the <BLINK> element.

> **Standard**: HTML 4
> **Common**: No
> **Sample**:

```
<BLINK CLASS="casual">NEW INFORMATION
</BLINK>
```

ID="..."

Assigns a unique ID selector to an instance of the <BLINK> tag. When you then assign a style to that ID selector, it affects only that one instance of the <BLINK> tag.

> **Standard**: HTML 4
> **Common**: No
> **Sample**:

```
<BLINK ID="123">12 Hour Sale!</BLINK>
```

STYLE="..."

Specifies Style Sheet commands that apply to the contents within the <BLINK> tags.

> **Standard**: HTML 4
> **Common**: No
> **Sample**:

```
<BLINK STYLE="background: red">
```

<BLOCKQUOTE>

Provides left and right indention of affected text and is useful for quoting a direct source within a document. Use for indention is deprecated. Use <BLOCKQUOTE> to signify only a block quotation.

> **Standard**: HTML 2
> **Common**: Yes
> **Paired**: Yes
> **Sample**:

```
Dr. Henry's remarks are below:
<BLOCKQUOTE>I really like the procedure.
</BLOCKQUOTE>
```

Attribute Information

CITE="..."

Specifies a reference URL for the quotation.

> **Standard**: HTML 4
> **Common**: No
> **Sample**:

```
<BLOCKQUOTE
CITE="http://www.clement.moore.com/
xmas.html">
Twas the night...
</BLOCKQUOTE>
```

CLASS="..."

Indicates which style class applies to the <BLOCKQUOTE> element.

> **Standard**: HTML 4
> **Common**: No
> **Sample**:

```
<BLOCKQUOTE CLASS="casual">
Twas the night before Christmas...
</BLOCKQUOTE>
```

ID="..."

Assigns a unique ID selector to an instance of the <BLOCKQUOTE> tag. When you then assign a style to that ID selector, it affects only that one instance of the <BLOCKQUOTE> tag.

Standard:	HTML 4
Common:	No
Sample:	

```
On July 12, John wrote a profound
sentence in his diary:
<BLOCKQUOTE ID="123">I woke up this
morning at nine and it was raining.
</BLOCKQUOTE>
```

STYLE="..."

Specifies Style Sheet commands that apply to the contents within the <BLOCKQUOTE> tags.

Standard:	HTML 4
Common:	No
Sample:	

```
<BLOCKQUOTE STYLE="background: red">
```

TITLE="..."

Specifies text assigned to the tag. You might use this attribute for context-sensitive help within the document. Browsers may use this to show tool tips over the quoted text.

Standard:	HTML 4
Common:	No
Sample:	

```
<BLOCKQUOTE TITLE="Quotation">
```

Other Attributes

This tag also accepts the lang, dir, onClick, onDblClick, onMouseDown, onMouseUp, onMouseOver, onMouseMove, onMouseOut, onKeyPress, onKeyDown, and onKeyUp attributes. See the Element-Independent Attributes section of this reference for definitions and examples.

<BODY>

Acts as a container for the body of the document. It appears after the <HEAD> tag and is followed by the </HTML> tag. In HTML 3.2, the <BODY> tag also sets various color settings and background characteristics of the document; however, in HTML 4, those formatting attributes are deprecated in favor of Style Sheets.

Standard:	HTML 2
Common:	Yes
Paired:	Yes
Sample:	

```
<BODY>
<H1>HELLO!</H1>
</BODY>
```

Attribute Information

ALINK="#*RRGGBB*" or "..."

Indicates the color of hyperlink text while the text is selected. Color names can substitute for the RGB hexadecimal values.

Standard:	HTML 3.2; deprecated in HTML 4 in favor of Style Sheets
Common:	Yes
Sample:	

```
<BODY BGCOLOR="#000ABC" TEXT="#000000"
LINK="#FFFFFF" VLINK="#999999"
ALINK="#FF0000">
```

BACKGROUND="*URL*"

Specifies the relative or absolute location of an image file that tiles across the document's background.

Standard:	HTML 3.2; deprecated in HTML 4 in favor of Style Sheets
Common:	Yes
Sample:	

```
<BODY BACKGROUND="images/slimey.gif">
```

BGCOLOR="#*RRGGBB*" or "..."

Indicates the color of a document's background. Color names can substitute for the RGB hexadecimal values.

Standard:	HTML 3.2; deprecated in HTML 4 in favor of Style Sheets
Common:	Yes
Sample:	

```
<BODY BGCOLOR="#000ABC" TEXT="#000000"
LINK="#FFFFFF" VLINK="#999999"
ALINK="#FF0000">
```

BGPROPERTIES="FIXED"

Specifies the behavior of the background image (see the BACKGROUND attribute.) BGPROPERTIES= FIXED indicates that the background image remains in place as you scroll the document, creating a watermark effect.

Standard: Internet Explorer
Common: No
Sample:

```
<BODY BACKGROUND="waves.jpg"
BGPROPERTIES="FIXED">
```

CLASS="..."

Indicates which style class applies to the <BODY> element.

Standard: HTML 4
Common: No
Sample:

```
<BODY CLASS="casual">
```

ID="n"

Assigns a unique ID selector to the <BODY> tag.

Standard: HTML 4
Common: No
Sample:

```
<BODY ID="123">
```

LEFTMARGIN="n"

Specifies the width (in pixels) of a margin of white space along the left edge of the entire document.

Standard: Internet Explorer
Common: No
Sample:

```
<BODY LEFTMARGIN="30">
```

LINK="#RRGGBB" or "..."

Indicates the color of hyperlink text within the document, which corresponds to documents not already visited by the browser. Color names can substitute for the RGB hexadecimal values.

Standard: HTML 3.2; deprecated in HTML 4 in favor of Style Sheets
Common: Yes
Sample:

```
<BODY BGCOLOR="#000ABC" TEXT="#000000"
LINK="#FFFFFF" VLINK="#999999"
ALINK="#FF0000">
```

SCROLL="{YES, NO}"

Indicates whether scrolling is possible within the document body.

Standard: Internet Explorer 4
Common: No
Sample:

```
<BODY BGCOLOR="silver" SCROLL="NO">
```

STYLE="..."

Specifies Style Sheet commands that apply to the document body.

Standard: HTML 4
Common: No
Sample:

```
<BODY STYLE="background: red">
```

TEXT="#RRGGBB" or "..."

Indicates the color of normal text within the document. Color names can substitute for the RGB hexadecimal values.

Standard: HTML 3.2; deprecated in HTML 4 in favor of Style Sheets.
Common: Yes
Sample:

```
<BODY BGCOLOR="#000ABC" TEXT="#000000"
LINK="#FFFFFF" VLINK="#999999"
ALINK="#FF0000">
```

TITLE="..."

Specifies text assigned to the tag. You might use this attribute for context-sensitive help within the document. Browsers may use this to show tool tips.

Standard: HTML 4
Common: No
Sample:

```
<BODY TITLE="Document body">
```

TOPMARGIN="*n*"

Specifies the size (in pixels) of a margin of white space along the top edge of the entire document.

Standard: Internet Explorer
Common: No
Sample:

```
<BODY TOPMARGIN="10">
```

VLINK="*#RRGGBB*" or "..."

Indicates the color of hyperlink text within the document, which corresponds to documents already visited by the browser. Color names can substitute for the RGB hexadecimal values.

Standard: HTML 3.2; deprecated in HTML 4 in favor of Style Sheets
Common: Yes
Sample:

```
<BODY BGCOLOR="#000ABC" TEXT="#000000"
LINK="#FFFFFF" VLINK="#999999"
ALINK="#FF0000">
```

Other Attributes

This tag also accepts the lang, dir, onload, onunload, onClick, onDblClick, onMouseDown, onMouseUp, onMouseOver, onMouseMove, onMouseOut, onKeyPress, onKeyDown, and onKeyUp attributes. See the "Element-Independent Attributes" section of this reference for definitions and examples.

Breaks a line of continuous text and prevents text alignment around images.

Standard: HTML 2
Common: Yes
Paired: No
Sample:

```
I live at:
<P>123 Nowhere Ave<BR>
New York, NY 12345
```

Attribute Information

CLASS="..."

Indicates which style class applies to the element.

Standard: HTML 4
Common: No
Sample:

```
<BR CLASS="casual">
```

CLEAR="{ALL, LEFT, RIGHT, NONE}"

Discontinues alignment of text to inline graphic images. The sample demonstrates how you can force the text to appear after the image and not alongside it.

Standard: HTML 3.2
Common: Yes
Sample:

```
<IMG SRC="portrait.jpg" ALIGN="RIGHT">
<BR CLEAR="ALL">
<P>The above photo was taken when I was in
Florida.
```

ID="..."

Assigns a unique ID selector to an instance of the <BR> tag. When you then assign a style to that ID selector, it affects only that one instance of the <BR> tag.

Standard: HTML 4
Common: No
Sample:

```
<BR ID="123">
```

STYLE="..."

Specifies Style Sheet commands that apply to the <BR> tag.

Standard: HTML 4
Common: No
Sample:

```
<BR STYLE="background: red">
```

TITLE="..."

Specifies text assigned to the tag. You might use this attribute for context-sensitive help within the document. Browsers may use this to show tool tips.

> **Standard**: HTML 4
> **Common**: No
> **Sample**:

```
<BR CLEAR="ALL" TITLE="Stop image wrap">
```

<BUTTON>

Sets up a button to submit or reset a form as well as to activate a script. Use the <IMG> tag between the opening and closing <BUTTON> tags to specify a graphical button.

> **Standard:** HTML 4
> **Common:** No
> **Paired:** Yes
> **Sample:**

```
<BUTTON TYPE="BUTTON" VALUE="Run Program"
onclick(doit)>Click it</BUTTON>
```

Attribute Information

ACCESSKEY="..."

Associates a key sequence with the button.

> **Standard**: HTML 4
> **Common**: Yes
> **Sample**:

```
<BUTTON ACCESSKEY="B">Click Me!
</BUTTON>
```

CLASS="..."

Indicates which style class applies to the <BUTTON> element.

> **Standard**: HTML 4
> **Common**: No
> **Sample**:

```
<BUTTON CLASS="casual" TYPE="SUBMIT"
VALUE="Submit">
```

DISABLED

Denies access to the input method.

> **Standard**: HTML 4
> **Common**: No
> **Sample**:

```
<BUTTON TYPE="SUBMIT" NAME="Pass"
DISABLED>
```

ID="*n*"

Assigns a unique ID selector to an instance of the <INPUT> tag. When you then assign a style to that ID selector, it affects only that one instance of the <INPUT> tag.

> **Standard**: HTML 4
> **Common**: No
> **Sample**:

```
<BUTTON ID="123" TYPE="SUBMIT"
VALUE="Submit">
```

NAME="..."

Gives a name to the value you pass to the form processor.

> **Standard**: HTML 4
> **Common**: Yes
> **Sample**:

```
<BUTTON TYPE="BUTTON" NAME="RUNPROG"
VALUE="Click to Run">
```

STYLE="..."

Specifies Style Sheet commands that apply to the element.

> **Standard**: HTML 4
> **Common**: No
> **Sample**:

```
<BUTTON STYLE="background: red"
TYPE="BUTTON" NAME="RUNPROG"
VALUE="Click to Run">
```

TABINDEX="*n*"

Specifies where the input method appears in the tab order. For example, TABINDEX=3 places the cursor at the button element after the visitor presses the Tab key three times.

Standard: HTML 4
Common: No
Sample:

```
<BUTTON TYPE="BUTTON" NAME="RUNPROG"
VALUE="Click to Run" TABINDEX="3">
```

TITLE="..."

Specifies text assigned to the tag. You might use this attribute for context-sensitive help within the document. Browsers may use this to show tool tips over the input method.

Standard: HTML 4
Common: No
Sample:

```
<BUTTON TYPE="SUBMIT" NAME="cc"
VALUE="visa" TITLE="Visa">
```

TYPE="..."

Indicates the kind of button to create. SUBMIT produces a button that, when selected, submits all the name-value pairs to the form processor. RESET sets all the input methods to their empty or default settings. BUTTON creates a button with no specific behavior that can interact with scripts.

Standard: HTML 4
Common: Yes
Sample:

```
<BUTTON TYPE="BUTTON" VALUE="Send Data..."
onclick(verify())>
</FORM>
```

VALUE="..."

Sets the default value for the button face.

Standard: HTML 4
Common: No
Sample:

```
<BUTTON TYPE="BUTTON" NAME="id"
VALUE="Press Me">
```

Other Attributes

This tag also accepts the lang, dir, onfocus, onblur, onClick, onDblClick, onMouseDown,

onMouseUp, onMouseOver, onMouseMove, onMouseOut, onKeyPress, onKeyDown, and onKeyUp attributes. See the Element-Independent Attributes section of this reference for definitions and examples.

<CAPTION>

Used inside <TABLE> tags to specify a description for a table.

Standard: HTML 3.2
Common: Yes
Paired: Yes
Sample:

```
<TABLE>
  <CAPTION VALIGN="TOP" ALIGN="CENTER">
  Test Grades For COOKING 101
  </CAPTION>
  <TR>
    <TH>Student</TH><TH>Grade</TH>
  </TR>
  <TR>
    <TD>B. Smith</TD><TD>88</TD>
  </TR>
  <TR>
    <TD>J. Doe</TD><TD>45</TD>   </TR>
</TABLE>
```

Attribute Information

ALIGN="{TOP, BOTTOM, LEFT, RIGHT}"

Indicates whether the caption appears at the top, bottom, left, or right of the table.

Standard: HTML 3.2; LEFT and RIGHT added in HTML 4
Common: Yes
Sample:

```
<CAPTION ALIGN="TOP">
Seattle Staff Directory
</CAPTION>
```

CLASS="..."

Indicates which style class applies to the <CAPTION> element.

Standard: HTML 4
Common: No
Sample:

```
<CAPTION CLASS="casual">Hydrogen vs
Oxygen</CAPTION>
```

ID="..."

Assigns a unique ID selector to an instance of the <CAPTION> tag. When you then assign a style to that ID selector, it affects only that one instance of the <CAPTION> tag.

Standard: HTML 4
Common: No
Sample:

```
<TABLE>
  <CAPTION ID="123">Great
  Painters</CAPTION>
```

STYLE="..."

Specifies Style Sheet commands that apply to the contents of the <CAPTION> tags.

Standard: HTML 4
Common: No
Sample:

```
<CAPTION STYLE="background: red">
```

TITLE="..."

Specifies text assigned to the tag. You might use this attribute for context-sensitive help within the document. Browsers may use this to show tool tips over the caption.

Standard: HTML 4
Common: Yes
Sample:

```
<CAPTION TITLE="Table caption">
```

Other Attributes

This tag also accepts the lang, dir, onClick, onDblClick, onMouseDown, onMouseUp, onMouseOver, onMouseMove, onMouseOut, onKeyPress, onKeyDown, and onKeyUp attributes.

See the Element-Independent Attributes section of this reference for definitions and examples.

<CENTER>

Positions text an equal distance between the left and right edges of the document. This tag, now officially replaced by the <DIV ALIGN="CENTER"> attribute, was included in HTML 3.2 only because of its widespread use.

Standard: HTML 3.2; deprecated in HTML 4
Common: Yes
Paired: Yes
Sample:

```
<CENTER><BLINK><H1>ONE-DAY
SALE!</H1></BLINK></CENTER>
```

<CITE>

Provides an in-text citation of a proper title such as the title of a book. Most browsers display the text inside the <CITE> tags in italics.

Standard: HTML 2
Common: Yes
Paired: Yes
Sample:

```
I just finished reading <CITE>Being
Digital</CITE> by Nicholas Negroponte.
```

Attribute Information

CLASS="..."

Indicates which style class applies to the <CITE> element.

Standard: HTML 4
Common: No
Sample:

```
This came from <CITE CLASS="casual">
Emerson's Walden Pond</CITE>
```

ID="..."

Assigns a unique ID selector to an instance of the <CITE> tag. When you then assign a style to that ID selector, it affects only that one instance of the <CITE> tag.

> **Standard**: HTML 4
> **Common**: No
> **Sample**:

I read about this in <CITE ID="123"> World Weekly News</CITE>

STYLE="..."

Specifies Style Sheet commands that apply to the contents within the <CITE> tags.

> **Standard**: HTML 4
> **Common**: No
> **Sample**:

<CITE STYLE="background: red">

TITLE="..."

Specifies text assigned to the tag. You might use this attribute for context-sensitive help within the document. Browsers may use this to show tool tips over the cited text.

> **Standard**: HTML 4
> **Common**: No
> **Sample**:

<CITE TITLE="Citation">FDA Vegetable Pamphlet</CITE>

Other Attributes

This tag also accepts the lang, dir, onClick, onDblClick, onMouseDown, onMouseUp, onMouseOver, onMouseMove, onMouseOut, onKeyPress, onKeyDown, and onKeyUp attributes. See the Element-Independent Attributes section of this reference for definitions and examples.

<CODE>

Embeds excerpts of program source code into your document text. This is useful if you want to show program source code inline within a paragraph of normal text. For showing formatted segments of source code longer than one line, use the <PRE> tag.

> **Standard**: HTML 2
> **Common**: Yes
> **Paired**: Yes
> **Sample**:

To display the value of the cost variable use the <CODE>printf("%0.2f\n", cost); </CODE> function call.

Attribute Information

CLASS="..."

Indicates which style class applies to the <CODE> element.

> **Standard**: HTML 4
> **Common**: No
> **Sample**:

<CODE CLASS="casual">x++;</CODE>

ID="..."

Assigns a unique ID selector to an instance of the <CODE> tag. When you then assign a style to that ID selector, it affects only that one instance of the <CODE> tag.

> **Standard**: HTML 4
> **Common**: No
> **Sample**:

<CODE ID="123">while(x) x-;</CODE>

STYLE="..."

Specifies Style Sheet commands that apply to the contents within the <CODE> tags.

> **Standard**: HTML 4
> **Common**: No
> **Sample**:

<BODY STYLE="background: red">

TITLE="..."

Specifies text assigned to the tag. You might use this attribute for context-sensitive help within the document. Browsers may use this to show tool tips over the code text.

Standard: HTML 4
Common: No
Sample:

```
<CODE TITLE="C Code">exit(1);</CODE>
```

Other Attributes

This tag also accepts the lang, dir, onClick, onDblClick, onMouseDown, onMouseUp, onMouseOver, onMouseMove, onMouseOut, onKeyPress, onKeyDown, and onKeyUp attributes. See the Element-Independent Attributes section of this reference for definitions and examples.

<COL>

Specifies attributes for a table column.

Standard: HTML 4
Common: No
Paired: No
Sample:

```
<TABLE>
<COLGROUP>
  <COL ALIGN="RIGHT">
  <COL ALIGN="CENTER">
<TR>  <TD>This cell is aligned right</TD>
  <TD>This cell is centered</TD>
</TR>
</TABLE>
```

Attribute Information

ALIGN="{LEFT, RIGHT, CENTER, JUSTIFY, CHAR}"

Specifies how text within the table columns will line up with the edges of the table cells, or if ALIGN=CHAR, on a specific character (the decimal point).

Standard: HTML 4
Common: No
Sample:

```
<COL ALIGN="CENTER">
```

CHAR="..."

Specifies the character on which cell contents will align, if ALIGN="CHAR". If you omit CHAR=, the default value is the decimal point in the specified language.

Standard: HTML 4
Common: No
Sample:

```
<COL ALIGN="CHAR" CHAR=",">
```

CHAROFF="n"

Specifies the number of characters from the left at which the alignment character appears..

Standard: HTML 4
Common: No
Sample:

```
<COL ALIGN="CHAR" CHAR="," CHAROFF="7">
```

ID="..."

Assigns a unique ID selector to an instance of the <COL> tag. When you assign a style to that ID selector, it affects only that one instance of the <COL> tag.

Standard: HTML 4
Common: No
Sample:

```
<COL ID="123">
```

SPAN="n"

Indicates the number of columns in the group.

Standard: HTML 4
Common: No
Sample:

```
<COLGROUP>
  <COL ALIGN="RIGHT" SPAN="2">
```

STYLE="..."

Specifies Style Sheet commands that apply to the contents of the <COL> tags.

Standard: HTML 4
Common: No
Sample:

```
<COL STYLE="background: black">
```

TITLE="..."

Specifies text assigned to the tag. You might use this attribute for context-sensitive help within the document. Browsers may use this to show tool tips over the table column.

Standard: HTML 4
Common: No
Sample:

```
<COL TITLE="Table column">
```

WIDTH="*n*"

Specifies the horizontal dimension of a column (in pixels or as a percentage). Special values of "0*" force the column to the minimum required width, and "2*" requires that the column receive proportionately twice as much space as it otherwise would.

Standard: HTML 4
Common: No
Sample:

```
<COL WIDTH="100">
```

VALIGN="{TOP, BOTTOM, BASELINE, MIDDLE}"

Vertically positions the contents of the table column. VALIGN="TOP" positions the contents flush with the top of the column. VALIGN="BUTTON" positions the contents flush with the bottom. VALIGN="CENTER" positions the contents at the center of the column. VALIGN="BASELINE" aligns the contents with the baseline of the current text font.

Standard: HTML 4
Common: No
Sample:

```
<COL VALIGN="TOP">
```

Other Attributes

This tag also accepts the lang, dir, onClick, onDblClick, onMouseDown, onMouseUp, onMouseOver, onMouseMove, onMouseOut, onKeyPress, onKeyDown, and onKeyUp attributes. See the Element-Independent Attributes section of this reference for definitions and examples.

<COLGROUP>

Specifies characteristics for a group of table columns.

Standard: HTML 4
Common: No
Paired: Yes
Sample:

```
<TABLE>
<COLGROUP VALIGN="TOP">
  <COL ALIGN="RIGHT">
  <COL ALIGN="CENTER">
<TR>
  <TD>This cell is aligned top and
  right</TD>
  <TD>This cell is aligned top and
  centered</TD>
</TR>
</TABLE>
```

Attribute Information

ALIGN="{LEFT, RIGHT, CENTER, JUSTIFY, CHAR}"

Specifies how text within the table columns lines up with the edges of the table cells, or if ALIGN=CHAR, on a specific character (the decimal point).

Standard: HTML 4
Common: No
Sample:

```
<COLGROUP ALIGN="CENTER">
```

CHAR="..."

Specifies the character on which cell contents align, if ALIGN="CHAR". If you omit CHAR=, the default value is the decimal point in the specified language.

Standard: HTML 4
Common: No
Sample:

```
<COLGROUP ALIGN="CHAR" CHAR=",">
```

CHAROFF="*n*"

Specifies the number of characters from the left at which the alignment character appears.

Standard: HTML 4
Common: No
Sample:

```
<COLGROUP ALIGN="CHAR" CHAR=","
CHAROFF="7">
```

ID="..."

Assigns a unique ID selector to an instance of the tag. When you then assign a style to that ID selector, it affects only that one instance of the tag.

Standard: HTML 4
Common: No
Sample:

```
<COLGROUP ID="123">
```

SPAN="*n*"

Indicates how many consecutive columns exist in the column group and to which columns the specified attributes apply.

Standard: HTML 4
Common: No
Sample:

```
<COLGROUP>
  <COL ALIGN="RIGHT" SPAN="2">
```

STYLE="..."

Specifies Style Sheet commands that apply to the contents of the <COLGROUP> tags.

Standard: HTML 4
Common: No
Sample:

```
<COLGROUP STYLE="color: red">
```

TITLE="..."

Specifies text assigned to the tag. You might use this attribute for context-sensitive help within the document. Browsers may use this to show tool tips over the column group.

Standard: HTML 4
Common: No
Sample:

```
<COLGROUP TITLE="Column Group">
```

WIDTH="*n*"

Specifies the horizontal dimension of columns within the column group (in pixels or as a percentage). Special values of "0*" force the column to minimum required width, and "2*" requires that the column receive proportionately twice as much space as it otherwise would.

Standard: HTML 4
Common: No
Sample:

```
<COLGROUP WIDTH=100>
  <COL ALIGN="RIGHT">
```

VALIGN="{TOP, BOTTOM, BASELINE, MIDDLE}"

Vertically positions the contents of the table column. VALIGN="TOP" positions the contents flush with the top of the column. VALIGN="BOTTOM" positions the contents flush with the bottom. VALIGN="CENTER" positions the contents at the vertical center of the column. VALIGN="BASELINE" aligns the contents with the baseline of the current text font.

Standard: HTML 4
Common: No
Sample:

```
<COLGROUP VALIGN="TOP">
```

Other Attributes

This tag also accepts the lang, dir, onClick, onDblClick, onMouseDown, onMouseUp, onMouseOver, onMouseMove, onMouseOut, onKeyPress, onKeyDown, and onKeyUp attributes. See the Element-Independent Attributes section of this reference for definitions and examples.

<COMMENT>

Indicates an author comment. Because these tags are Netscape-specific, we encourage you to use the <!--...--> tags instead.

Standard:	Netscape Navigator
Common:	Yes
Paired:	Yes
Sample:	

```
<COMMENT>This document was created
September 19, 1997</COMMENT>
```

<DD>

Contains a definition in a definition list. Use this tag inside <DL> tags. This tag can contain block level elements.

Standard:	HTML 2
Common:	Yes
Paired:	Yes, optional
Sample:	

```
<DL><DT>Butter
<DD>Butter is a dairy product.
</DL>
```

Attribute Information

CLASS="..."

Indicates which style class applies to the <DD> element.

Standard:	HTML 4
Common:	No
Sample:	

```
<DL>
  <DT>HTML
  <DD CLASS="casual">Hypertext Markup
Language
</DD>
```

ID="..."

Assigns a unique ID selector to an instance of the <DD> tag. When you then assign a style to that ID selector, it affects only that one instance of the <DD> tag.

Standard:	HTML 4
Common:	No
Sample:	

```
<DL>
  <DT>RS-232C
  <DD ID="123">A standard for serial
  communication between computers.
</DL>
```

STYLE="..."

Specifies Style Sheet commands that apply to the definition.

Standard:	HTML 4
Common:	No
Sample:	

```
<DD STYLE="background: blue; color: white">
```

TITLE="..."

Specifies text assigned to the tag. You might use this attribute for context-sensitive help within the document. Browsers may use this to show tool tips over the definition.

Standard:	HTML 4
Common:	No
Sample:	

```
<DD TITLE="Definition">
```

Other Attributes

This tag also accepts the lang, dir, onClick, onDblClick, onMouseDown, onMouseUp, onMouseOver, onMouseMove, onMouseOut, onKeyPress, onKeyDown, and onKeyUp attributes. See the Element-Independent Attributes section of this reference for definitions and examples.

<DEL>

Indicates text marked for deletion in the document. May be either block-level or inline, as necessary.

> **Standard**: HTML 4
> **Common**: No
> **Paired**: Yes
> **Sample**:

```
<P>HTTP stands for HyperText
Transfer <DEL>Transport</DEL>Protocol</P>
```

Attribute Information

CITE="url"

Indicates address of reference (definitive source, for example) for deletion.

> **Standard**: HTML 4
> **Common**: No
> **Sample**:

```
<DEL CITE="http://www.w3.org/">HTML 3.0 was
used for 10 years.</DEL>
```

CLASS="..."

Indicates which style class applies to the <DEL> element.

> **Standard**: HTML 4
> **Common**: No
> **Sample**:
\
```
<DEL CLASS="casual">POP stands for Post
Office Protocol</DEL>
```

DATETIME="..."

Indicates the date and time in precisely this format: YYYY-MM-DDThh:mm:ssTZD. For example, 1997-07-14T08:30:00-07:00 indicates July 14, 1997, at 8:30 AM, in U.S. Mountain Time (7 hours from Greenwich time). This time could also be presented as 1997-07-14T08:30:00Z.

> **Standard**: HTML 4
> **Common**: No
> **Sample**:

```
<DEL DATETIME="1997-07-14T08:30:00Z">POP
stands for Post Office Protocol</DEL>
```

ID="..."

Assigns a unique ID selector to an instance of the tag. When you then assign a style to that ID selector, it affects only that one instance of the <DEL> tag.

> **Standard**: HTML 4
> **Common**: No
> **Sample**:

```
<DEL ID="123">WWW stands for World Wide
Web</DEL>
```

STYLE="..."

Specifies Style Sheet commands that apply to the deleted text.

> **Standard**: HTML 4
> **Common**: No
> **Sample**:

```
<DEL STYLE="background: blue;
color: white">ESP stands for
extra-sensory perception.</DEL>
```

TITLE="..."

Specifies text assigned to the tag. You might use this attribute for context-sensitive help within the document. Browsers may use this to show tool tips over the text.

> **Standard**: HTML 4
> **Common**: No
> **Sample**:

```
<DEL TITLE="Definition">
More deleted text.</DEL>
```

Other Attributes

This tag also accepts the lang, dir, onClick, onDblClick, onMouseDown, onMouseUp, onMouseOver, onMouseMove, onMouseOut, onKeyPress, onKeyDown, and onKeyUp attributes. See the Element-Independent Attributes section of this reference for definitions and examples.

<DFN>

Indicates the definition of a term in the document.

> **Standard**: HTML 3.2
> **Common**: No

Paired: Yes
Sample:

```
<DFN>HTTP stands for HyperText
Transfer Protocol</DFN>
```

Attribute Information

CLASS="..."

Indicates which style class applies to the <DFN> element.

Standard: HTML 4
Common: No
Sample:

```
<DFN CLASS="casual">POP stands for Post
Office Protocol</DFN>
```

ID="..."

Assigns a unique ID selector to an instance of the <DFN> tag. When you then assign a style to that ID selector, it affects only that one instance of the <DFN> tag.

Standard: HTML 4
Common: No
Sample:

```
<DFN ID="123">WWW stands for World Wide
Web</DFN>
```

STYLE="..."

Specifies Style Sheet commands that apply to the definition.

Standard: HTML 4
Common: No
Sample:

```
<DFN STYLE="background: blue;
color: white">ESP stands for
extra-sensory perception.</DFN>
```

TITLE="..."

Specifies text assigned to the tag. You might use this attribute for context-sensitive help within the document. Browsers may use this to show tool tips over the definition text.

Standard: HTML 4
Common: No
Sample:

```
<DFN TITLE="Definition">
```

Other Attributes

This tag also accepts the lang, dir, onClick, onDblClick, onMouseDown, onMouseUp, onMouseOver, onMouseMove, onMouseOut, onKeyPress, onKeyDown, and onKeyUp attributes. See the Element-Independent Attributes section of this reference for definitions and examples.

<DIR>

Contains a directory list. Use the <LI> tag to indicate list items within the list. Use <UL>, rather than this deprecated tag.

Standard: HTML 2; deprecated in HTML 4. Use <UL> instead.
Common: Yes
Paired: Yes
Sample:

```
Choose a music genre:<DIR>
   <LI><A HREF="rock/">Rock</A>
   <LI><A HREF="country/">Country</A>
   <LI><A HREF="na/">New Age</A>
</DIR>
```

Attribute Information

CLASS="..."

Indicates which style class applies to the <dir> element.

Standard: HTML 4
Common: No
Sample:

```
<DIR CLASS="casual">
   <LI>Apples
   <LI>Kiwis
   <LI>Mangos
   <LI>Oranges
</DIR>
```

COMPACT

Causes the list to appear in a compact format. This attribute probably will not affect the appearance of the list as most browsers do not present lists in more than one format.

> **Standard**: HTML 2; deprecated in HTML 4
> **Common**: No
> **Sample**:

```
<DIR COMPACT>...
</DIR>
```

ID="..."

Assigns a unique ID selector to an instance of the <dir> tag. When you then assign a style to that ID selector, it affects only that one instance of the <dir> tag.

> **Standard**: HTML 4
> **Common**: No
> **Sample**:

```
<DIR ID="123">
  <LI>Thingie 1
  <LI>Thingie 2
</DIR>
```

STYLE="..."

Specifies Style Sheet commands that apply to the <DIR> element.

> **Standard**: HTML 4
> **Common**: No
> **Sample**:

```
<DIR STYLE="background: blue;
color: white">
  <LI>Thingie 1
  <LI>Thingie 2
</DIR>
```

TITLE="..."

Specifies text assigned to the tag. You might use this attribute for context-sensitive help within the document. Browsers may use this to show tool tips over the directory list.

> **Standard**: HTML 4
> **Common**: No
> **Sample**:

```
<DIR TITLE="Directory List">
```

Other Attributes

This tag also accepts the lang, dir, onClick, onDblClick, onMouseDown, onMouseUp, onMouseOver, onMouseMove, onMouseOut, onKeyPress, onKeyDown, and onKeyUp attributes. See the Element-Independent Attributes section of this reference for definitions and examples.

<DIV>

Indicates logical divisions within a document. You can use these to apply alignment, line-wrapping, and particularly Style Sheet attributes to a section of your document. <DIV ALIGN=CENTER> is the official replacement for the <CENTER> tag.

> **Standard**: HTML 3.2
> **Common**: No
> **Paired**: Yes
> **Sample**:

```
<DIV ALIGN="CENTER" STYLE="background:
blue">
<FONT SIZE=+2>All About Formic
Acid</FONT>
</DIV>
```

Attribute Information

ALIGN="{LEFT, CENTER, RIGHT, JUSTIFY}"

Specifies whether the contents of the section align with the left or right margins (LEFT, RIGHT), are evenly spaced between them (CENTER), or if the text stretches between the left and right margins (JUSTIFY).

> **Standard**: HTML 3.2; deprecated in HTML 4 in favor of Style Sheets

Common: No
Sample:

```
<DIV ALIGN="RIGHT">
Look over here!</DIV>
<DIV ALIGN="LEFT">
Now, look over here!</DIV>
```

CLASS="..."

Indicates which style class applies to the `<DIV>`
element.

Standard: HTML 4
Common: No
Sample:

```
<DIV CLASS="casual">
```

DATAFLD="..."

Selects a column from a previously identified
source of tabulated data (see the DATASRC=
attribute).

Standard: Internet Explorer 4
Common: No
Sample:

```
<DIV DATASRC="#data_table">
<DIV DATAFLD="name"></DIV>
</DIV>
```

DATAFORMATAS="{TEXT, HTML, NONE}"

Indicates how tabulated data formats within
the `<DIV>` element.

Standard: Internet Explorer 4
Common: No
Sample:

```
<DIV DATAFORMATAS="HTML"
DATASRC="#data_table">
```

DATASRC="..."

Specifies the source of data for data binding.

Standard: Internet Explorer 4
Common: No
Sample:

```
<DIV DATASRC="#data_table">
```

ID="..."

Assigns a unique ID selector to an instance of
the `<DIV>` tag. When you then assign a style to
that ID selector, it affects only that one instance
of the `<DIV>` tag.

Standard: HTML 4
Common: No
Sample:

```
<DIV ID="123">
```

NOWRAP

Disables line-wrapping for the section.

Standard: Netscape Navigator
Common: No
Sample:

```
<HR>
<DIV ALIGN="LEFT" NOWRAP>
The contents of this section will not
automatically wrap as you size the window.
</DIV><HR>
```

STYLE="..."

Specifies Style Sheet commands that apply to
the contents within the `<DIV>` tags.

Standard: HTML 4
Common: No
Sample:

```
<DIV STYLE="background: red">
```

TITLE="..."

Specifies text assigned to the tag. You might use
this attribute for context-sensitive help within
the document. Browsers may use this to show
tool tips over the contents of the `<DIV>` tags.

Standard: HTML 4
Common: No
Sample:

```
<DIV TITLE="Title" CLASS="casual">
```

Other Attributes

This tag also accepts the lang, dir, onClick, onDblClick, onMouseDown, onMouseUp, onMouseOver, onMouseMove, onMouseOut, onKeyPress, onKeyDown, and onKeyUp attributes. See the Element-Independent Attributes section of this reference for definitions and examples.

<DL>

Contains the <DT> and <DD> tags that form the term and definition portions of a definition list.

Standard: HTML 2
Common: Yes
Paired: Yes
Sample:

<DL><DT>Hygiene
<DD>Always wash your hands before preparing meat.</DL>

Attribute Information

CLASS="..."

Indicates which style class applies to the <DL> element.

Standard: HTML 4
Common: No
Sample:

<DL CLASS="casual">
  <DT>RAM
  <DD>Random Access Memory
</DL>

COMPACT

Causes the definition list to appear in a compact format. This attribute probably will not affect the appearance of the list as most browsers do not present lists in more than one format.

Standard: HTML 2; deprecated in HTML 4

Common: No
Sample:

<DL COMPACT>...
</DL>

ID="..."

Assigns a unique ID selector to an instance of the <DD> tag. When you then assign a style to that ID selector, it affects only that one instance of the <DD> tag.

Standard: HTML 4
Common: No
Sample:

<DL ID="123">
  <DT>Food
  <DD>We will be eating 3 meals/day.
</DL>

STYLE="..."

Specifies Style Sheet commands that apply to contents within the <DL> tags.

Standard: HTML 4
Common: No
Sample:

<DL STYLE="background: red">

TITLE="..."

Specifies text assigned to the tag. You might use this attribute for context-sensitive help within the document. Browsers may use this to show tool tips over the definition list.

Standard: HTML 4
Common: No
Sample:

<DL TITLE="Definition List">

Other Attributes

This tag also accepts the lang, dir, onClick, onDblClick, onMouseDown, onMouseUp, onMouseOver, onMouseMove, onMouseOut, onKeyPress, onKeyDown, and onKeyUp attributes. See the Element-Independent Attributes section of this reference for definitions and examples.

<DT>

Contains the terms inside a definition list. Place the <DT> tags inside <DL> tags.

> **Standard**: HTML 2
> **Common**: Yes
> **Paired**: Yes, optional
> **Sample**:

```
<DL><DT>Hygiene
<DD>Always wash your hands before
preparing meat.</DL>
```

Attribute Information

CLASS="..."

Indicates which style class applies to the <DT> element.

> **Standard**: HTML 4
> **Common**: No
> **Sample**:

```
<DL>
 <DT CLASS="casual">CUL8R
 <DD>See You Later
</DL>
```

ID="..."

Assigns a unique ID selector to an instance of the <DT> tag. When you then assign a style to that ID selector, it affects only that one instance of the <DT> tag.

> **Standard**: HTML 4
> **Common**: No
> **Sample**:

```
<DL>
 <DT ID="123">Caffeine
 <DD>Avoid caffeine during the
 stress management course.
</DL>
```

STYLE="..."

Specifies Style Sheet commands that apply to the contents within the <DT> tags.

> **Standard**: HTML 4
> **Common**: No
> **Sample**:

```
<DT STYLE="background: red">
```

TITLE="..."

Specifies text assigned to the tag. You might use this attribute for context-sensitive help within the document. Browsers may use this to show tool tips over the definition term.

> **Standard**: HTML 4
> **Common**: No
> **Sample**:

```
<DT TITLE="Term">Programmer</DT>
<DD>A method for converting coffee into
applications.
```

Other Attributes

This tag also accepts the lang, dir, onClick, onDblClick, onMouseDown, onMouseUp, onMouseOver, onMouseMove, onMouseOut, onKeyPress, onKeyDown, and onKeyUp attributes. See the Element-Independent Attributes section of this reference for definitions and examples.

<EM>

Makes the text stand out. Browsers usually do this with italic or boldface.

> **Standard**: HTML 2
> **Common**: Yes
> **Paired**: Yes
> **Sample**:

```
It is <EM>very</EM> important to read
the instructions before beginning.
```

Attribute Information

CLASS="..."

Indicates which style class applies to the <EM> element.

> **Standard**: HTML 4

Common: No
Sample:

Did you say my house was on
<EM CLASS="casual">FIRE?!</EM>

ID="…"

Assigns a unique ID selector to an instance of the <EM> tag. When you then assign a style to that ID selector, it affects only that one instance of the <EM> tag.

Standard: HTML 4
Common: No
Sample:

I have complained <EM ID="123">ten</EM>
times about the leaking faucet.

STYLE="…"

Specifies Style Sheet commands that apply to the contents within the <EM> tags.

Standard: HTML 4
Common: No
Sample:

<EM STYLE="background: red">

TITLE="…"

Specifies text assigned to the tag. You might use this attribute for context-sensitive help within the document. Browsers may use this to show tool tips over the emphasized text.

Standard: HTML 4
Common: No
Sample:

<EM TITLE="Emphasis">

Other Attributes

This tag also accepts the lang, dir, onClick, onDblClick, onMouseDown, onMouseUp, onMouseOver, onMouseMove, onMouseOut, onKeyPress, onKeyDown, and onKeyUp attributes. See the Element-Independent Attributes section of this reference for definitions and examples.

<EMBED>

Places an embedded object into a document. Examples of embedded objects include MIDI files and digital video files. Because the <EMBED> tag is not standard, we suggest you use the <OBJECT> tag instead. If the browser does not have built-in support for an object, visitors will need a plug-in to use the object within the document.

Standard: Netscape Navigator, supported by Internet Explorer
Common: No
Paired: No
Sample:

<EMBED SRC="fur_elise.midi">

Attribute Information

ACCESSKEY="…"

Specifies a key sequence that binds to the embedded object.

Standard: Internet Explorer 4
Common: No
Sample:

<EMBED SRC="st.ocx" ACCESSKEY="E">

ALIGN="{LEFT, RIGHT, CENTER, ABSBOTTOM, ABSMIDDLE, BASELINE, BOTTOM, TEXTTOP, TOP}"

Indicates how an embedded object is positioned relative to the document borders and surrounding contents. ALIGN="LEFT", ALIGN="RIGHT", or ALIGN="CENTER" makes the embedded object float between the edges of the frame either to the left, right, or evenly between. The behavior is similar to that of the ALIGN= attribute of the <IMG> tag.

ALIGN="TEXTTOP" or ALIGN="TOP" lines up the top of the embedded object with the top of the current text font. ALIGN="ABSMIDDLE" lines up the middle of the embedded object with the middle of the current text font. ALIGN="ABSBOTTOM" lines up the bottom of the embedded object with the bottom of the current text font. `ALIGN="BASELINE"` or `ALIGN="BOTTOM"` lines up the bottom of the embedded object with the baseline of the current text font.

Standard: Internet Explorer 4
Common: No
Sample:

```
<EMBED SRC="song.mid" ALIGN="CENTER">
```

HEIGHT="*n*"

Specifies the vertical dimension of the embedded object. (See the `UNITS=` attribute for how to measure dimensions.)

Standard: Netscape Navigator
Common: No
Sample:

```
<EMBED SRC="rocket.avi" WIDTH="50"
HEIGHT="40">
```

HIDDEN

Indicates that the embedded object should not be visible.

Standard: Internet Explorer 4
Common: No
Sample:

```
<EMBED SRC="song.mid" HIDDEN>
```

NAME="..."

Gives the object a name by which other objects can refer to it.

Standard: Netscape Navigator
Common: No
Sample:

```
<EMBED SRC="running.avi" NAME="movie1">
```

OPTIONAL PARAM="..."

Indicates additional parameters. For example, AVI movies accept the `AUTOSTART` attribute.

Standard: Netscape Navigator
Common: No
Sample:

```
<EMBED SRC="explode.avi" AUTOSTART="true">
```

PALETTE="#*RRGGBB*|#*RRGGBB*"

Indicates the foreground and background colors for the embedded object. You can specify colors with hexadecimal RGB values or with color names.

Standard: Netscape Navigator
Common: No
Sample:

```
<EMBED SRC="flying.avi"
PALETTE="Red|Black">
```

SRC="*URL*"

Indicates the relative or absolute location of the file containing the object you want to embed.

Standard: Netscape Navigator
Common: No
Sample:

```
<EMBED SRC="beethoven_9.midi">
```

TITLE="..."

Specifies text assigned to the tag. You might use this attribute for context-sensitive help within the document. Browsers may use this to show tool tips over the embedded object.

Standard: Internet Explorer 4
Common: No
Sample:

```
<EMBED SRC="explode.avi" TITLE="movie">
```

UNITS="{PIXELS, EN}"

Modifies the behavior of the `HEIGHT=` and `WIDTH=` attributes. `UNITS=PIXELS` measures attributes in pixels. `UNITS=EN` measures dimensions in EN spaces.

Standard: Netscape Navigator
Common: No
Sample:

```
<EMBED SRC="rocket.avi" WIDTH="50"
HEIGHT="40">
```

WIDTH="*n*"

Indicates the horizontal dimension of the embedded object. (See the UNITS= attribute for how to measure dimensions.)

> **Standard**:   Netscape Navigator
> **Common**:   No
> **Sample**:

```
<EMBED SRC="cartoon.avi" WIDTH="50">
```

Other Attributes

This tag also accepts the lang, dir, onClick, onDblClick, onMouseDown, onMouseUp, onMouseOver, onMouseMove, onMouseOut, onKeyPress, onKeyDown, and onKeyUp attributes. See the Element-Independent Attributes section of this reference for definitions and examples.

F

<FIELDSET>

Groups related form elements.

> **Standard**:   HTML 4
> **Common**:   No
> **Paired**:   Yes
> **Sample**:

```
<FORM …>
<FIELDSET>
..logically related field elements…
</FIELDSET>
</FORM>
```

Attribute Information

CLASS="…"

Indicates which style class applies to the <FIELDSET> element.

> **Standard**:   HTML 4
> **Common**:   No
> **Sample**:

```
<FIELDSET CLASS="casual">
Group Rates</FIELDSET>
```

ID="…"

Assigns a unique ID selector to an instance of the <FIELDSET> tag. When you then assign a style to that ID selector, it affects only that one instance of the <FIELDSET> tag.

> **Standard**:   HTML 4
> **Common**:   No
> **Sample**:

```
<FIELDSET ID="123">now!</FIELDSET>
```

STYLE="…"

Specifies Style Sheet commands that apply to the contents within the <FIELDSET> tags.

> **Standard**:   HTML 4
> **Common**:   No
> **Sample**:

```
<FIELDSET STYLE="background: red">
```

TITLE="…"

Specifies text assigned to the tag. You might use this attribute for context-sensitive help within the document. Browsers may use this to show tool tips over the font text.

> **Standard**:   HTML 4
> **Common**:   No
> **Sample**:

```
<FIELDSET TITLE="Personal data fields">
```

Other Attributes

This tag also accepts the lang, dir, onClick, onDblClick, onMouseDown, onMouseUp, onMouseOver, onMouseMove, onMouseOut, onKeyPress, onKeyDown, and onKeyUp attributes. See the Element-Independent Attributes section of this reference for definitions and examples.

<FONT>

Alters or sets font characteristics of the font the browser uses to display text.

> **Standard**:   HTML 3.2; deprecated in HTML 4 in favor of Style Sheets

Common: Yes
Paired: Yes
Sample:

```
The cat was really
<FONT SIZE="+3">BIG!</FONT>
```

Attribute Information

COLOR="#RRGGBB" or "..."

Indicates the color the browser uses to display
text. Color names can substitute for the RGB
hexadecimal values.

    Standard: HTML 3.2; deprecated
            in HTML 4 in favor of
            Style Sheets.
    Common: Yes
    Sample:

```
<FONT COLOR=#FF0000><H2>Win A
Trip!</H2></FONT> <FONT COLOR=
"lightblue"><p>That's right!
A trip to Hawaii can be yours if you
scratch off the right number!</FONT>
```

FACE="...,..."

Specifies a comma-separated list of font names
the browser uses to render text. If the browser
does not have access to the first named font, it
tries the second, then the third, and so forth.

    Standard: Netscape Navigator and
            Internet Explorer, not intro-
            duced in standard HTML in
            favor of Style Sheets.
    Common: Yes
    Sample:

```
<FONT SIZE=+1 FACE="Avant Guard,
Helvetica, Lucida Sans, Arial">
```

SIZE=n

Specifies the size of the text affected by the
FONT tag. You can specify the size relative to the
base font size (see the <BASEFONT> tag) which is
normally 3. You can also specify the size as a
digit in the range 1 through 7.

    Standard: HTML 3.2; deprecated
            in HTML 4 in favor of
            Style Sheets.
    Common: Yes
    Sample:

```
<BASEFONT SIZE=4>
<FONT SIZE=+2>This is a font of size
6</FONT> <FONT SIZE=1>This is a font
of size 1</FONT>
```

<FORM>

Sets up a container for a form tag. Within the
<FORM> tags, you can place form input tags such
as <FIELDSET>, <INPUT>, <SELECT>, and
<TEXTAREA>.

    Standard: HTML 2
    Common: Yes
    Paired: Yes
    Sample:

```
<FORM METHOD=POST
ACTION="/cgi-bin/search.pl">
Search : <INPUT TYPE=TEXT NAME="name"
SIZE=20><BR>
<INPUT TYPE=SUBMIT VALUE="Start Search">
</FORM>
```

Attribute Information

ACCEPT-CHARSET="..."

Specifies the character encodings for input
data that the server processing the form must
accept. The value is a list of character sets as
defined in RFC2045, separated by commas.

    Standard: HTML 4
    Common: No
    Sample:

```
<FORM METHOD=POST
ACCEPT-CHARSET="ISO-8859-1"
ACTION="/stat-collector.cgi">
```

ACCEPT="..."

Specifies a list of MIME types, separated by commas, that the server processing the form will handle correctly.

Standard: HTML 4
Common: No
Sample:

```
<FORM METHOD=POST ACCEPT="image/gif,
image/jpeg "ACTION="/image-collector.cgi">
```

ACTION="*URL*"

Specifies the explicit or relative location of the form processing CGI application.

Standard: HTML 2
Common: Yes
Sample:

```
<FORM METHOD=POST
ACTION="/stat-collector.cgi">
```

CLASS="..."

Indicates which style class applies to the <FORM>.

Standard: HTML 4
Common: No
Sample:

```
<FORM METHOD=POST CLASS="casual"
ACTION="/stat-collector.cgi">
```

ENCTYPE="..."

Specifies the MIME type used to submit (post) the form to the server . The default value is "application/x-www-form-urlencoded". Use the value "multipart/form-data" when the returned document includes files.

Standard: HTML 4
Common: No
Sample:

```
<FORM METHOD=POST ENCTYPE="application/x-
www-form-urlencoded"
ACTION="/stat-collector.cgi">
```

ID="..."

Assigns a unique ID selector to an instance of the <FORM> tag. When you then assign a style to that ID selector, it affects only that one instance of the <FORM> tag.

Standard: HTML 4
Common: No
Sample:

```
<FORM ACTION="/cgi-bin/ttt.pl"
METHOD=GET ID="123">
```

METHOD={POST,GET}

Changes how form data is transmitted to the form processor. When you use METHOD=GET, the form data is given to the form processor in the form of an environment variable (*QUERY_STRING*). When you use METHOD=POST, the form data is given to the form processor as the standard input to the program.

Standard: HTML 2
Common: Yes
Sample:

```
<FORM METHOD=POST
ACTION="/cgi-bin/www-search">
Enter search keywords:
<INPUT TYPE=TEXT NAME="query" SIZE=20>
<INPUT TYPE=SUBMIT VALUE="Search">
</FORM>
```

NAME="..."

Assigns the form a name accessible by bookmark, script, and applet resources.

Standard: Internet Explorer
Common: No
Sample:

```
<FORM METHOD=POST ACTION="/cgi-bin/ff.pl"
NAME="ff">
```

STYLE="..."

Specifies Style Sheet commands that apply to the contents within the <FORM> tags.

Standard: HTML 4
Common: No
Sample:

```
<FORM  STYLE="background: red">
```

TARGET="..."

Identifies in which previously named frame the output from the form processor should appear.

Standard: HTML 4
Common: Yes
Sample:

```
<FORM TARGET="output" METHOD=GET
ACTION="/cgi-bin/thingie.sh">
```

TITLE="..."

Specifies text assigned to the tag. You might use this attribute for context-sensitive help within the document. Browsers may use this to show tool tips over the fill-out form.

Standard: HTML 4
Common: No
Sample:

```
<FORM METHOD=POST ACTION="/cgi-bin/ff.pl"
TITLE="Fill-out form">
```

Other Attributes

This tag also accepts the lang, dir, onsubmit, onreset, onClick, onDblClick, onMouseDown, onMouseUp, onMouseOver, onMouseMove, onMouseOut, onKeyPress, onKeyDown, and onKeyUp attributes. See the Element-Independent Attributes section of this reference for definitions and examples.

<FRAME>

Defines a frame within a frameset (see the <FRAMESET> tag). The <FRAME> tag specifies the source file and visual characteristics of a frame.

Standard: HTML 4
Common: Yes
Paired: No
Sample:

```
<FRAMESET ROWS="*,70">
  <FRAME SRC="frames/body.html"
NAME="body">
```

```
  <FRAME SRC="frames/buttons.html"
NAME="buttons" SCROLLING=NO NORESIZE>
</FRAMESET>
```

Attribute Information

BORDER="n"

Specifies the thickness of the border (in pixels) around a frame. Use BORDER=0 to specify a frame with no border.

Standard: Netscape Navigator
Common: Yes
Sample:

```
<FRAME SRC="hits.html" BORDER="2">
```

BORDERCOLOR="#RRGGBB" or "..."

Specifies the color of the border around the frame. Use the color's hexadecimal RGB values or the color name.

Standard: Internet Explorer, Netscape Navigator
Common: Yes
Sample:

```
<FRAME SRC="hits.html" BORDERCOLOR="red">
```

FRAMEBORDER={1,0}

Indicates whether the frame's border is visible. A value of 1 indicates that the border is visible, and a value of 0 indicates that it is not visible.

Standard: HTML 4
Common: No
Sample:

```
<FRAME SRC="weather.html" FRAMEBORDER=0>
```

MARGINHEIGHT="n"

Specifies the vertical dimension (in number of pixels) of the top and bottom margins in a frame.

Standard: HTML 4
Common: No
Sample:

```
<FRAME SRC="cats.html" MARGINHEIGHT=10>
```

MARGINWIDTH=*"n"*

Specifies the horizontal dimension (in pixels) of the left and right margins in a frame.

    Standard: HTML 4
    Common: No
    Sample:

```
<FRAME SRC="dogs.html" MARGINWIDTH=10>
```

NAME=*"..."*

Gives the frame you are defining a name. You can use this name later to load new documents into the frame (see the TARGET= attribute) and within scripts to control attributes of the frame. Reserved names with special meaning include _blank, _parent, _self, and _top.

    Standard: HTML 4
    Common: Yes
    Sample:

```
<FRAME SRC="/cgi-bin/weather.cgi"
NAME="weather">
```

NORESIZE

Makes a frame's dimensions unchangeable. Otherwise, if a frame's borders are visible, visitors can resize the frame by selecting a border and moving it with the mouse.

    Standard: HTML 4
    Common: Yes
    Sample:

```
<FRAME SRC="bottom.html" NAME="bottom"
NORESIZE SCROLLING=NO>
```

SCROLLING={YES, NO, AUTO}

Indicates whether a scrollbar is present within a frame when text dimensions exceed the dimensions of the frame. Set SCROLLING=NO when using a frame to display only an image.

    Standard: HTML 4
    Common: Yes
    Sample:

```
<FRAME NAME="titleimg" SRC="title.html"
SCROLLING=NO>
```

SRC=*"URL"*

Specifies the relative or absolute location of a document that you want to load within the defined frame.

    Standard: HTML 4
    Common: Yes
    Sample:

```
<FRAME NAME="main" SRC="intro.html">
```

<FRAMESET>

Contains frame definitions and specifies frame spacing, dimensions, and attributes. Place <FRAME> tags inside <FRAMESET> tags.

    Standard: HTML 4
    Common: Yes
    Paired: Yes
    Sample:

```
<FRAMESET COLS="*,70">
  <FRAME SRC="frames/body.html"
NAME="body">
  <FRAME SRC="frames/side.html"
NAME="side">
</FRAMESET>
```

Attribute Information

BORDER=*"n"*

Specifies the thickness of borders (in pixels) around frames defined within the frameset. You can also control border thickness with the <FRAME> tag.

    Standard: Netscape Navigator
    Common: No
    Sample:

```
<FRAMESET COLS="*,150" BORDER=5>
  <FRAME SRC="left.html" NAME="main">
  <FRAME SRC="side.html" NAME="side">
</FRAMESET>
```

BORDERCOLOR="#*RRGGBB*" or "..."

Sets the color of the frame borders. Color names can substitute for the hexadecimal RGB color values.

> **Standard**: Netscape Navigator, Internet Explorer
> **Common**: Yes
> **Sample**:

```
<FRAMESET BORDERCOLOR="Red"
ROWS="100,*">
  <FRAME SRC="top.html" NAME="title">
  <FRAME SRC="story.html" NAME="Story">
</FRAMESET>
```

COLS="..."

Specifies the number and dimensions of the vertical frames within the current frameset.

Set COLS= to a comma-separated list of numbers or percentages to indicate the width of each frame. Use the asterisk (*) to represent a variable width. A frame of variable width fills the space left over after the browser formats space for the other frames (<FRAMESET COLS="100,400,10% *">).

Setting COLS= with percentage values controls the ratio of frame horizontal space relative to the amount of space available within the browser (<FRAMESET COLS="10%,*">).

You cannot use COLS= and ROWS= in the same tag.

> **Standard**: HTML 4
> **Common**: Yes
> **Sample**:

```
<FRAMESET COLS="*,100,*">
  <FRAME SRC="left.html" NAME="left">
  <FRAME SRC="middle.html" NAME="middle">
  <FRAMESET ROWS=2>
    <FRAME SRC="top.html" NAME="top">
    <FRAME SRC="bottom.html"
NAME="bottom">
  </FRAMESET>
</FRAMESET>
```

FRAMESPACING="*n*"

Specifies the space (in pixels) between frames within the browser window.

> **Standard**: Internet Explorer
> **Common**: No
> **Sample**:

```
<FRAMESET ROWS="*,100" FRAMESPACING=10>
  <FRAME SRC="top.html" NAME="top">
  <FRAME SRC="middle.html" NAME="middle">
</FRAMESET>
```

ROWS="..."

Specifies the number and dimensions of the horizontal frames within the current frameset.

Set ROWS= to a comma-separated list of numbers or percentages to indicate the height of each frame. Use the asterisk (*) to represent a variable height. A frame of variable height fills the space remaining after the browser formats space for the other frames (<FRAMESET ROWS="100,400,*">).

Setting ROWS= to a comma-separated list of percentages allows you to control the ratio of frame vertical space relative to the space available within the browser (<FRAMESET ROWS="10%,*">).

You cannot use ROWS= and COLS= in the same tag.

> **Standard**: HTML 4
> **Common**: Yes
> **Sample**:

```
<FRAMESET ROWS="*,100,*">
  <FRAME SRC="top.html" NAME="top">
  <FRAME SRC="middle.html" NAME="middle">
  <FRAMESET COLS=2>
    <FRAME SRC="bottom1.html" NAME="left">
    <FRAME SRC="bottom2.html" NAME="right">
  </FRAMESET>
</FRAMESET>
```

Other Attributes

This tag also accepts the onload and onunload attributes. See the Element-Independent Attributes section of this reference for definitions and examples.

<H*n*>

Specifies headings in a document. Headings are numbered 1–6, with <H1> representing the heading for the main heading in the document and <H3> representing a heading for a nested subtopic. Generally, text inside heading tags appears in boldface and may be larger than normal document text.

> **Standard**: HTML 2
> **Common**: Yes
> **Paired**: Yes
> **Sample**:

```
<H1>Caring For Your Canary</H1>
This document explains how you should
take care of a canary. With proper
care, you and your new bird will have
a lasting, happy relationship.
<H2>Feeding</H2>
```

Attribute Information

ALIGN={LEFT, CENTER, RIGHT}

Positions the heading in the left, right, or center of a document.

> **Standard**: HTML 3.2; deprecated in HTML 4 in favor of Style Sheets
> **Common**: Yes
> **Sample**:

```
<H3 ALIGN=RIGHT>History Of The
Platypus</H3>
```

CLASS="..."

Indicates which style class applies to the <H*n*> element.

> **Standard**: HTML 4
> **Common**: No
> **Sample**:

```
<H1 CLASS="casual" ALIGN=LEFT>
River Tours</H1>
```

ID="..."

Assigns a unique ID selector to an instance of the <H*n*> tag. When you then assign a style to that ID selector, it affects only that one instance of the <H*n*> tag.

> **Standard**: HTML 4
> **Common**: No
> **Sample**:

```
<H2 ID="123">Paper Products</H2>
```

STYLE="..."

Specifies Style Sheet commands that apply to the heading.

> **Standard**: HTML 4
> **Common**: No
> **Sample**:

```
<H1 STYLE="background: red">
```

TITLE="..."

Specifies text assigned to the tag. You might use this attribute for context-sensitive help within the document. Browsers may use this to show tool tips over the heading.

> **Standard**: HTML 4
> **Common**: No
> **Sample**:

```
<H1 TITLE="Headline">
```

Other Attributes

This tag also accepts the lang, dir, onClick, onDblClick, onMouseDown, onMouseUp, onMouseOver, onMouseMove, onMouseOut, onKeyPress, onKeyDown, and onKeyUp attributes. See the Element-Independent Attributes section of this reference for definitions and examples.

<HEAD>

Contains document head information. You can place any of the following tags within the document head: <LINK>, <META>, <TITLE>, <SCRIPT>, <BASE>, and <STYLE>.

Standard: HTML 2
Common: Yes
Paired: Yes
Sample:

```
<HTML>
<HEAD>
<TITLE>Making a Peanut-Butter and
Jelly Sandwich</TITLE>
<LINK REL=Parent
HREF="sandwiches.html">
</HEAD>
```

Attribute Information

PROFILE="URL"

Specifies the address of data profiles. You might use this attribute to specify the location of, for example, <META> tag information.

Standard: HTML 4
Common: No
Sample:

```
<HEAD PROFILE="http://www.raycomm.com/
general.html">
</HEAD<
```

Other Attributes

This tag also accepts the lang and dir attributes. See the Element-Independent Attributes section of this reference for definitions and examples.

<HR>

Draws horizontal lines (rules) in your document. This is useful for visually separating document sections.

Standard: HTML 2
Common: Yes
Paired: No
Sample:

```
<H2>Birthday Colors</H2>
<HR ALIGN=LEFT WIDTH="60%">
```

```
<P>Birthdays are usually joyous
celebrations so we recommend bright
colors.
```

Attribute Information

ALIGN={LEFT, CENTER, RIGHT}

Positions the line flush left, flush right, or in the center of the document. These settings are irrelevant unless you use the WIDTH= attribute to make the line shorter than the width of the document.

Standard: HTML 3.2; deprecated in HTML 4 in favor of Style Sheets
Common: Yes
Sample:

```
<H2 ALIGN=LEFT>Shopping List</H2>
<HR WIDTH="40%" ALIGN=LEFT>
<UL TYPE=SQUARE>
<LI>Eggs
<LI>Butter
<LI>Bread
<LI>Milk
</UL>
```

CLASS="..."

Indicates which style class applies to the <HR> element.

Standard: HTML 4
Common: No
Sample:

```
<HR CLASS="casual" WIDTH="50%">
```

COLOR="#RRGGBB" or "..."

Specifies the color of the line. The color name can substitute for the hexadecimal RGB values.

Standard: Internet Explorer. Style Sheets provide equivalent functionality.
Common: No
Sample:

```
<HR COLOR=#09334C>
```

ID=*"n"*

Assigns a unique ID selector to an instance of the ‹HR› tag. When you then assign a style to that ID selector, it affects only that one instance of the ‹HR› tag.

> **Standard**: HTML 4
> **Common**: No
> **Sample**:

```
<HR ID="123">
```

NOSHADE

Specifies that the browser not shade the line.

> **Standard**: HTML 3.2
> **Common**: Yes
> **Sample**:

```
<HR NOSHADE ALIGN=CENTER WIDTH="50%">
<IMG SRC="Bobby.jpg" ALIGN=CENTER
BORDER=0 ALT="Bobby">
<BR CLEAR=ALL>
<HR NOSHADE ALIGN=CENTER WIDTH="50%">
```

SIZE=*"n"*

Specifies the thicknes of the line (in pixels).

> **Standard**: HTML 3.2; deprecated in HTML 4 in favor of Style Sheets
> **Common**: Yes
> **Sample**:

```
<HR SIZE=10>
```

STYLE=*"..."*

Specifies Style Sheet commands that apply to the horizontal rule.

> **Standard**: HTML 4
> **Common**: No
> **Sample**:

```
<HR WIDTH="50%" STYLE="color: red">
```

WIDTH=*"n"*

Specifies the length of the line. You can specify the value with an absolute number of pixels or as a percentage to indicate how much of the total width available is used.

> **Standard**: HTML 3.2; deprecated in HTML 4 in favor of Style Sheets
> **Common**: Yes
> **Sample**:

```
<H2 ALIGN=CENTER>The End!</H2>
<HR WIDTH="85%">
<P ALIGN=CENTER>
<A HREF="/index.html">Home</A> |
<A HREF="Story3.html">Next Story</A> |
<A HREF="Story1.html">Prev Story</A>
```

TITLE=*"..."*

Specifies text assigned to the tag. You might use this attribute for context-sensitive help within the document. Browsers may use this to show tool tips over the horizontal rule.

> **Standard**: HTML 4
> **Common**: No
> **Sample**:

```
<HR TITLE="A line">
```

Other Attributes

This tag also accepts the onClick, onDblClick, onMouseDown, onMouseUp, onMouseOver, onMouseMove, onMouseOut, onKeyPress, onKeyDown, and onKeyUp attributes. See the Element-Independent Attributes section of this reference for definitions and examples.

‹HTML›

Contains the entire document. Place these tags at the top and bottom of your HTML file.

> **Standard**: HTML 2
> **Common**: Yes
> **Paired**: Yes
> **Sample**:

```
<HTML>
<HEAD><TITLE>Test Page</TITLE></HEAD>
<BODY>
  <H1>Is this working?</H1>
</BODY>
</HTML>
```

Attribute Information

This tag accepts the lang and dir attributes. See the Element-Independent Attributes section of this reference for definitions and examples.

<I>

Italicizes text.

> **Standard**: HTML 2
> **Common**: Yes
> **Paired**: Yes
> **Sample**:

```
After this, Tom told me to read
<I>Mastering HTML</I>. I had
no choice but to do so.
```

Attribute Information

CLASS="..."

Indicates which style class applies to the <I> element.

> **Standard**: HTML 4
> **Common**: No
> **Sample**:

```
This mouse is <I CLASS="casual">
enhanced</I>
```

ID="..."

Assigns a unique ID selector to an instance of the <I> tag. When you then assign a style to that ID selector, it affects only that one instance of the <I> tag.

> **Standard**: HTML 4
> **Common**: No
> **Sample**:

```
He called it a <I ID="123">Doo-Dad</I>!
```

STYLE="..."

Specifies Style Sheet commands that apply to italicized text.

> **Standard**: HTML 4
> **Common**: No
> **Sample**:

```
<I STYLE="color: green">
```

TITLE="..."

Specifies text assigned to the tag. You might use this attribute for context-sensitive help within the document. Browsers may use this to show tool tips over the italicized text.

> **Standard**: HTML 4
> **Common**: No
> **Sample**:

```
<I TITLE="Italicized">
```

Other Attributes

This tag also accepts the lang, dir, onClick, onDblClick, onMouseDown, onMouseUp, onMouseOver, onMouseMove, onMouseOut, onKeyPress, onKeyDown, and onKeyUp attributes. See the Element-Independent Attributes section of this reference for definitions and examples.

<IFRAME>

Creates floating frames within a document. Floating frames differ from normal frames because they are independently manipulable elements within another HTML document.

> **Standard**: HTML 4
> **Common**: No
> **Paired**: Yes
> **Sample**:

```
<IFRAME NAME="new_win"
    SRC="http://www.raycomm.com">
</IFRAME>
```

Attribute Information

ALIGN={LEFT, CENTER, RIGHT}

Specifies how the floating frame lines up with respect to the left and right sides of the browser window.

> **Standard**: HTML 4; deprecated usage. Use Style Sheets instead.
> **Common**: No
> **Sample**:

```
<IFRAME ALIGN=LEFT SRC="goats.html"
NAME="g1">
```

BORDER=*"n"*

Indicates the thickness of a border around a floating frame (in pixels).

> **Standard**:   Internet Explorer 4
> **Common**:   No
> **Sample**:

```
<IFRAME SRC="joe.html" NAME="Joe"
BORDER=5>
```

BORDERCOLOR=*"#RRGGBB"* or *"..."*

Specifies (in hexadecimal RGB values or the color name) the color of the border around a floating frame.

> **Standard**:   Internet Explorer 4
> **Common**:   No
> **Sample**:

```
<IFRAME SRC="joe.html" NAME="Joe"
BORDERCOLOR=#5A3F2E>
```

FRAMEBORDER={0,1}

Indicates whether the floating frame has visible borders. A value of 0 indicates no border, and a value of 1 indicates a visible border.

> **Standard**:   HTML 4
> **Common**:   No
> **Sample**:

```
<IFRAME SRC="main.html" NAME="main"
FRAMEBORDER=0>
```

FRAMESPACING=*"n"*

Indicates the space (in pixels) between adjacent floating frames.

> **Standard**:   Internet Explorer 4
> **Common**:   No
> **Sample**:

```
<IFRAME SRC="joe.html" NAME="Joe"
FRAMESPACING=10>
```

HEIGHT=*"n"*

Specifies the vertical dimension (in pixels) of the floating frame.

> **Standard**:   HTML 4
> **Common**:   No
> **Sample**:

```
<IFRAME SRC="joe.html" NAME="Joe"
WIDTH=500 HEIGHT=200>
```

HSPACE=*"n"*

Indicates the size (in pixels) of left and right margins within the floating frame.

> **Standard**:   Internet Explorer 4
> **Common**:   No
> **Sample**:

```
<IFRAME SRC="joe.html" NAME="Joe"
HSPACE=10 VSPACE=10>
```

ID=*"..."*

Assigns a unique ID selector to an instance of the <IFRAME> tag. When you then assign a style to that ID selector, it affects only that one instance of the <IFRAME> tag.

> **Standard**:   HTML 4
> **Common**:   No
> **Sample**:

```
<IFRAME SRC="Joe.html" NAME="Joe"
ID="123">
```

MARGINHEIGHT=*"n"*

Specifies the size of the top and bottom margins (in pixels) within the floating frame.

> **Standard**:   HTML 4
> **Common**:   No
> **Sample**:

```
<IFRAME SRC="top.html" NAME="topbar"
MARGINHEIGHT=50>
```

MARGINWIDTH=*"n"*

Specifies the size of the left and right margins (in pixels) within the floating frame.

> **Standard**:   HTML 4
> **Common**:   No
> **Sample**:

```
<IFRAME SRC="body.html" NAME="body"
MARGINWIDTH=50>
```

NAME="..."

Assigns the frame a unique name. You can use this name within other frames to load new documents in the frame and to manipulate the attributes of the frame.

    Standard: HTML 4
    Common: No
    Sample:

```
<IFRAME SRC="joe.html" NAME="Joe"
WIDTH=500 HEIGHT=200>
```

NORESIZE

Specifies that the floating frame cannot resize. Because the HTML 4 specification forbids resizable inline frames, this attribute is only relevant to Internet Explorer.

    Standard: Internet Explorer
    Common: No
    Sample:

```
<IFRAME SRC="joe.html" NAME="Joe"
NORESIZE>
```

SCROLLING={YES, NO}

Indicates whether the floating frame has scrollbars.

    Standard: HTML 4
    Common: No
    Sample:

```
<IFRAME SRC="top.html" SCROLLING=NO>
```

SRC="URL"

Specifies the relative or absolute location of the document file to load in the floating frame.

    Standard: HTML 4
    Common: No
    Sample:

```
<IFRAME NAME="pics" SRC="pics/">
```

STYLE="..."

Specifies Style Sheet commands that apply to the floating frame.

    Standard: HTML 4
    Common: No
    Sample:

```
<IFRAME SRC="dots.html" NAME="dots"
STYLE="background: red">
```

WIDTH="n"

Specifies the horizontal dimension (in pixels) of the floating frame.

    Standard: HTML 4
    Common: No
    Sample:

```
<IFRAME SRC="joe.html" NAME="Joe"
WIDTH=500 HEIGHT=200>
```

VSPACE="n"

Indicates the size (in pixels) of top and bottom margins within the floating frame.

    Standard: Internet Explorer 4
    Common: No
    Sample:

```
<IFRAME SRC="joe.html" NAME="Joe"
HSPACE=10 VSPACE=10>
```

Other Attributes

This tag also accepts the lang, dir, onClick, onDblClick, onMouseDown, onMouseUp, onMouseOver, onMouseMove, onMouseOut, onKeyPress, onKeyDown, and onKeyUp attributes. See the Element-Independent Attributes section of this reference for definitions and examples.

<IMG>

Places an inline image in a document. You can use the attributes ISMAP= and USEMAP= with the <IMG> tag to implement image maps.

    Standard: HTML 2
    Common: Yes
    Paired: No
    Sample:

```
<IMG SRC="images/left_arrow.gif" ALT="<-">
```

Attribute Information

ALIGN={LEFT, RIGHT, TOP, MIDDLE, BOTTOM}

Specifies the appearance of text that is near an inline graphic image. For example, if you use RIGHT, the image appears flush to the right edge of the document, and the text appears to its left. Using LEFT produces the opposite effect.

HTML 2 mentions only attribute values of TOP, MIDDLE, and BOTTOM. TOP aligns the top of the first line of text after the <IMG> tag to the top of the image. BOTTOM (the default) aligns the bottom of the image to the baseline of the text. MIDDLE aligns the baseline of the first line of text with the middle of the image.

HTML 3.2 added LEFT and RIGHT to the list of attribute values.

You can use the <BR> tag to control specific points where text stops wrapping around an image and continues below the instance of the image.

Standard: HTML 2; deprecated in HTML 4 in favor of Style Sheets
Common: Yes
Sample:

```
<IMG SRC="red_icon.gif" ALIGN=LEFT>
It's about time for volunteers to
pitch in.<BR CLEAR=ALL>
```

ALT="…"

Provides a textual description of images, which is useful for visitors who have text-only browsers. Some browsers may also display the ALT= text as a floating message when the visitor places the mouse pointer over the image.

Standard: HTML 2
Common: Yes
Sample:

```
<IMG SRC="smiley.gif" ALT=":-)">
```

BORDER="n"

Specifies the width (in pixels) of a border around an image. The default value is usually 0 (no border). The border color is the color of normal text within your document.

Standard: HTML 3.2
Common: Yes
Sample:

```
<IMG SRC="portrait.jpg" BORDER=2>
```

CLASS="…"

Indicates which style class applies to the <IMG> element.

Standard: HTML 4
Common: No
Sample:

```
<IMG CLASS="casual" SRC="dots.gif">
```

CONTROLS

If the image is a video file, indicates the playback controls that appear below the image.

Standard: Internet Explorer 2
Common: No
Sample:

```
<IMG DYNSRC="foo.avi" CONTROLS>
```

DATAFLD="…"

Indicates a column in previously identified tabular data.

Standard: Internet Explorer 4
Common: No
Sample:

```
<IMG SRC="thing.gif" DATAFLD="color">
```

DATASRC="…"

Specifies the location of tabular data to be bound.

Standard: Internet Explorer 4
Common: No
Sample:

```
<IMG SRC="thing.gif" DATASRC="#data_table">
```

DYNSRC=*"URL"*

Specifies the relative or absolute location of a dynamic image (VRML, video file, and so on).

Standard: Internet Explorer 2
Common: No
Sample:

```
<IMG DYNSRC="foo.avi">
```

HEIGHT=*"n"*

Specifies the vertical dimension of the image (in pixels). If you don't use this attribute, the image appears in the default height. Use this attribute, along with the WIDTH= attribute, to fit an image within a space. You can fit a large image into a smaller space, and you can spread a smaller image. Some Web designers use the WIDTH= and HEIGHT= attributes to spread a single pixel image over a large space to produce the effect of a larger solid-color image.

Standard: HTML 3.2
Common: Yes
Sample:

```
<IMG SRC="images/smiley.jpg" WIDTH=50
HEIGHT=50>
```

HSPACE=*"n"*

Establishes a margin of white space (in pixels) to the left and right of a graphic image. (See the VSPACE= attribute for how to control the top and bottom margins around an image.)

Standard: HTML 3.2
Common: Yes
Sample:

```
<IMG SRC="pics/pinetree.jpg" HSPACE=20
VSPACE=15>
```

ID=*n*

Assigns a unique ID selector to an instance of the <IMG> tag. When you then assign a style to that ID selector, it affects only that one instance of the <IMG> tag.

Standard: HTML 4
Common: No
Sample:

```
<IMG SRC="grapes.jpg" ID="123">
```

ISMAP

Indicates that the graphic image functions as a clickable image map. The ISMAP= attribute instructs the browser to send the pixel coordinates to the server image map CGI application when a visitor selects the image with the mouse pointer. When HTML 2 established the ISMAP= attribute, image maps were implemented in a server-side fashion only. Now, client-side image maps are more popular (see the USEMAP= attribute).

Standard: HTML 2
Common: Yes
Sample:

```
<A HREF="/cgi-bin/image map/mymap">
<IMG ISMAP SRC="images/main.gif"></A>
```

LOWSRC=*"URL"*

Indicates the absolute or relative location of a lower resolution version of an image.

Standard: Netscape Navigator
Common: No
Sample:

```
<IMG SRC="bigpic.jpg" LOWSRC="lilpic.jpg">
```

LOOP={*n*, INFINITE}

Indicates the number of times a video file plays back.

Standard: Internet Explorer 2
Common: No
Sample:

```
<IMG DYNSRC="bar.avi" LOOP=INFINITE>
```

NAME=*"..."*

Specifies a name by which bookmarks, scripts, and applets can reference the image.

Standard: Internet Explorer 4
Common: No
Sample:

```
<IMG SRC="tweakie.jpg" NAME="img_1">
```

SRC="*URL*"

Specifies the relative or absolute location of a file that contains the graphic image you want to embed in a document.

Standard: HTML 2
Common: Yes
Sample:

```
<IMG SRC="images/left_arrow.gif"
ALT="<-">
```

START={FILEOPEN, MOUSEOVER}

Specifies the event that triggers the playback of a dynamic image. START=FILEOPEN starts playback when the browser has completely downloaded the file. START=MOUSEOVER starts playback when a visitor places the mouse pointer over the image.

Standard: Internet Explorer 2
Common: No
Sample:

```
<IMG DYNSRC="ship.vrm" START=MOUSOVER>
```

STYLE="..."

Specifies Style Sheet commands that apply to the inline image.

Standard: HTML 4
Common: No
Sample:

```
<IMG SRC="dots.gif" STYLE="background: red">
```

TITLE="..."

Specifies text assigned to the tag. You might use this attribute for context-sensitive help within the document. Browsers may use this to show tool tips over the image.

Standard: HTML 4
Common: No
Sample:

```
<IMG SRC="pics/jill.jpg"
TITLE="Image">
```

USEMAP="*URL*"

Specifies the location of the client-side image map data (see the <MAP> tag). Because the <MAP> tag gives the map data an anchor name, be sure to include the name with the URL of the document that contains the map data.

Standard: HTML 3.2
Common: Yes
Sample:

```
<IMG ISMAP SRC="map1.gif"
USEMAP="maps.html#map1">
```

VRML="..."

Specifies the absolute or relative location of a VRML world to embed in a document.

Standard: Internet Explorer 4
Common: No
Sample:

```
<IMG VRML="vr/myroom.vrml">
```

VSPACE="*n*"

Establishes a margin of white space (in pixels) above and below a graphic image. (See the HSPACE= attribute for how to control the left and right margins of an image.)

Standard: HTML 3.2
Common: Yes
Sample:

```
<IMG SRC="pics/pinetree.jpg" HSPACE=20
VSPACE=15>
```

WIDTH="*n*"

Specifies the horizontal dimension of the image (in pixels). If you don't use this attribute, the image appears in the default width. Use this attribute, along with the HEIGHT= attribute, to fit an image within a space. You can fit a large image into a smaller space, and you can spread a smaller image. Some Web designers use WIDTH= and HEIGHT= to spread a single pixel image over a large space to produce the effect of a larger solid-color image.

Standard: HTML 3.2
Common: Yes
Sample:

```
<IMG SRC="images/smiley.jpg" WIDTH=50
HEIGHT=50>
```

Other Attributes

This tag also accepts the lang, dir, onClick, onDblClick, onMouseDown, onMouseUp, onMouseOver, onMouseMove, onMouseOut, onKeyPress, onKeyDown, and onKeyUp attributes. See the Element-Independent Attributes section of this reference for definitions and examples.

<INPUT>

Identifies several input methods for forms. This tag must appear between the opening and closing <FORM> tags.

Standard: HTML 2
Common: Yes
Paired: No
Sample:

```
<FORM ACTION="/cgi-bin/order/" METHOD=POST>
<INPUT NAME="qty" TYPE="TEXT" SIZE=5>
<INPUT TYPE="submit" VALUE="Order">
</FORM>
```

Attribute Information

ALIGN={LEFT, CENTER, RIGHT}

Lines up a graphical submit button (TYPE= IMAGE). The behavior of this tag is identical to that of the ALIGN= attribute of the <IMG> tag.

Standard: HTML 3.2; deprecated in HTML 4 in favor of Style Sheets
Common: Yes
Sample:

```
<INPUT TYPE=IMAGE SRC="picture.gif"
ALIGN=RIGHT>
```

ACCEPT="..."

Specifies a list of acceptable MIME types for submitted files.

Standard: HTML 4
Common: No
Sample:

```
<INPUT TYPE=FILE ACCEPT="image/gif">
Please submit a GIF image.
```

CHECKED

Use with TYPE=RADIO or TYPE=CHECKBOX to set the default state of those input methods to True.

Standard: HTML 2
Common: Yes
Sample:

```
<INPUT TYPE=CHECKBOX CHECKED
NAME="foo" VALUE="1"><BR>
2 <INPUT TYPE=CHECKBOX NAME="foo"
VALUE="2"><BR>
```

CLASS="..."

Indicates which style class applies to the <INPUT> element.

Standard: HTML 4
Common: No
Sample:

```
<INPUT CLASS="casual" TYPE=TEXT
NAME="age">
```

DATAFLD="..."

Selects a column from previously identified tabular data.

Standard: Internet Explorer 4
Common: No
Sample:

```
<DIV DATASRC="#data_table">
<INPUT TYPE=TEXT NAME="color"
DATAFLD="colorvals">
```

DATASRC="…"

Specifies the location of tabular data to be bound.

Standard: Internet Explorer 4
Common: No
Sample:

```
<INPUT TYPE=TEXT DATASRC="#data_table"
DATAFLD="dataval1">
```

DISABLED="…"

Disables an instance of the input method so that data cannot be accepted or submitted.

Standard: HTML 4
Common: No
Sample:

```
<INPUT TYPE=PASSWORD NAME="Pass"
DISABLED>
```

ID="n"

Assigns a unique ID selector to an instance of the <INPUT> tag. When you then assign a style to that ID selector, it affects only that one instance of the <INPUT> tag.

Standard: HTML 4
Common: No
Sample:

```
Age:
<INPUT TYPE=TEXT NAME="age" ID="123">
```

MAXLENGTH="n"

Indicates the number of characters you can enter into a text input field and is only useful to input methods of type TEXT or PASSWORD. Contrary to the SIZE= attribute, MAXLENGTH= does not affect the size of the input field shown on the screen.

Standard: HTML 2
Common: Yes
Sample:

```
Phone: <INPUT TYPE=TEXT NAME="phone"
MAXLENGTH=11>
```

NAME="…"

Gives a name to the value you pass to the form processor. For example, if you collect a person's last name with an input method of type TEXT, you assign the NAME= attribute something like "lastname." This establishes a *name-value pair* for the form processor.

Standard: HTML 2
Common: Yes
Sample:

```
Enter your phone number: <INPUT TYPE="text"
NAME="phone" SIZE=10>
```

NOTAB

Removes the input element from the tab order.

Standard: Internet Explorer
Common: No
Sample:

```
Hair color:
<INPUT TYPE=TEXT NAME="hcolor" NOTAB>
```

READONLY

Indicates that changes to the input method data cannot occur.

Standard: HTML 4
Common: No
Sample:

```
<INPUT TYPE=TEXT NAME="desc"
VALUE="1/4 inch flange assy"
READONLY>
```

SIZE="n"

Specifies the width of the input method (in characters). This applies only to input methods of type TEXT or PASSWORD. HTML 4 specifies size measurements in pixels for all other input methods, but pixel size specification is little supported.

Standard: HTML 2
Common: Yes
Sample:

```
Your Age: <INPUT TYPE="text" NAME="Age"
SIZE=5><BR>
```

SRC="*URL*"

Implements a graphic image for a submit button. For this to work, indicate TYPE=IMAGE.

Standard: HTML 3.2
Common: Yes
Sample:

```
<INPUT TYPE=IMAGE SRC="/images/push-
button.gif">
```

STYLE="..."

Specifies Style Sheet commands that apply to the input element.

Standard: HTML 4
Common: No
Sample:

```
<INPUT TYPE=RADIO NAME="food"
VALUE="1" STYLE="background: red">
```

TABINDEX="*n*"

Specifies where the input method appears in the tab order. For example, TABINDEX=3 places the cursor at the input element after the visitor presses the Tab key three times.

Standard: Internet Explorer
Common: No
Sample:

```
Credit card number:
<INPUT TYPE=TEXT NAME="ccard"
TABINDEX=5>
```

TITLE="..."

Specifies text assigned to the tag. You might use this attribute for context-sensitive help within the document. Browsers may use this to show tool tips over the input method.

Standard: HTML 4
Common: No
Sample:

```
<INPUT TYPE=RADIO NAME="cc"
VALUE="visa" TITLE="Visa">
```

TYPE="..."

Indicates the kind of input method to use. Valid values are TEXT, PASSWORD, RADIO, CHECKBOX, SUBMIT, RESET, IMAGE, FILE, HIDDEN, and BUTTON.

TEXT produces a simple one-line text input field that is useful for obtaining simple data such as a person's name, a person's age, a dollar amount, and so on. To collect multiple lines of text, use the <TEXTAREA> tag.

PASSWORD gives the visitor a simple one-line text input field similar to the TEXT type. When visitors enter data into the field, however, they do not see what they type.

TYPE=RADIO produces a small radio button that can be turned on and off. Use radio buttons when you want a visitor to select only one of several items. For multiple-value selections, see the CHECKBOX type or the <SELECT> tag.

SUBMIT produces a button that, when selected, submits all the name-value pairs to the form processor.

RESET sets all the input methods to their empty or default settings.

TYPE=IMAGE replaces the submit button with an image. The behavior of this value is identical to that of the submit button, except that the x,y coordinates of the mouse position over the image when selected are also sent to the form processor.

BUTTON creates a button with no specific behavior that can interact with scripts.

Standard: HTML 2
Common: Yes
Sample:

```
<FORM METHOD=POST ACTION="/cgi-
bin/thingie">
Name: <INPUT TYPE=TEXT NAME="name"><BR>
Password: <INPUT TYPE=PASSWORD
NAME="pass"><BR>
```

```
Ice Cream:  Vanilla<INPUT TYPE=RADIO
VALUE="1" CHECKED NAME="ice_cream">
Chocolate<INPUT TYPE=RADIO VALUE="2"
NAME="ice_cream"><br>
<INPUT TYPE=SUBMIT VALUE="Send Data...">
</FORM>
```

USEMAP="*URL*"

Indicates the relative or absolute location of a client-side image map to use with the form.

> **Standard**: HTML 4
> **Common**: No
> **Sample**:

```
<INPUT SRC="mapimage.gif"
USEMAP="maps.html#map1">
```

VALUE="..."

Sets the default input value method. Required when <INPUT> is set to TYPE=RADIO or CHECKBOX.

> **Standard**: HTML 2
> **Common**: Yes
> **Sample**:

```
<INPUT TYPE=HIDDEN NAME="id"
VALUE="123">
```

Other Attributes

This tag also accepts the lang, dir, onfocus, onblur, onselect, onchange, onClick, onDblClick, onMouseDown, onMouseUp, onMouseOver, onMouseMove, onMouseOut, onKeyPress, onKeyDown, and onKeyUp attributes. See the Element-Independent Attributes section of this reference for definitions and examples.

<INS>

Indicates text to be inserted in the document. May be either block-level or inline, as necessary.

> **Standard**: HTML 4
> **Common**: No
> **Paired**: Yes
> **Sample**:

```
<P>HTTP stands for HyperText
<INS>Transfer</INS>Protocol</P>
```

Attribute Information

CITE="*URL*"

Indicates address of reference (definitive source, for example) for insertion.

> **Standard**: HTML 4
> **Common**: No
> **Sample**:

```
<INS CITE="http://www.w3.org/">HTML 2 was
used for 2 years.</INS>
```

CLASS="..."

Indicates which style class applies to the <INS> element.

> **Standard**: HTML 4
> **Common**: No
> **Sample**:

```
<INS CLASS="joeadd">POP stands for Post
Office Protocol</INS>
```

DATETIME="..."

Indicates the date and time in precisely this format: YYYY-MM-DDThh:mm:ssTZD. For example, 1997-07-14T08:30:00-07:00 indicates July 14, 1997, at 8:30 AM, in U.S. Mountain Time (7 hours from Greenwich time). This time could also be presented as 1997-07-14T08:30:00Z.

> **Standard**: HTML 4
> **Common**: No
> **Sample**:

```
<INS DATETIME="1997-07-14T08:30:00Z">POP
stands for Post
Office Protocol</INS>
```

ID="..."

Assigns a unique ID selector to an instance of the <INS> tag. When you then assign a style to that ID selector, it affects only that one instance of the <INS> tag.

> **Standard**: HTML 4
> **Common**: No
> **Sample**:

```
<INS ID="123">WWW stands for World Wide
Web</INS>
```

STYLE="..."

Specifies Style Sheet commands that apply to
the inserted text.

Standard: HTML 4
Common: No
Sample:

```
<INS STYLE="background: blue;
color: white">ESP stands for
extra-sensory perception.</INS>
```

TITLE="..."

Specifies text assigned to the tag. You might
use this attribute for context-sensitive help
within the document. Browsers may use this to
show tool tips over the inserted text.

Standard: HTML 4
Common: No
Sample:

```
<INS TITLE="Definition">More deleted
text.</INS>
```

Other Attributes

This tag also accepts the lang, dir, onClick,
onDblClick, onMouseDown, onMouseUp,
onMouseOver, onMouseMove, onMouseOut,
onKeyPress, onKeyDown, and onKeyUp attributes.
See the Element-Independent Attributes section
of this reference for definitions and examples.

<ISINDEX>

Inserts an input field into the document so
that visitors can enter search queries. The
queries then go to a CGI application indicated
by the ACTION= attribute.

Standard: HTML 2; deprecated in HTML
4 in favor of <FORM>
Common: Yes
Paired: No
Sample:

```
<ISINDEX PROMPT="Keyword Search"
ACTION="/cgi-bin/search.cgi">
```

Attribute Information

ACTION="*URL*"

Specifies the URL of the application that
processes the search query. If you don't include
ACTION=, the query goes to a URL formed from
the document base (see the <BASE> tag).

Standard: HTML 2
Common: Yes
Sample:

```
<ISINDEX ACTION="/cgi-bin/index-search">
```

PROMPT="..."

Changes the input prompt for keyword index
searches. If you don't specify PROMPT=, the
browser displays a default prompt.

Standard: HTML 3.2
Common: Yes
Sample:

```
<ISINDEX PROMPT="Search for something">
```

<KBD>

Specifies keyboard input within a document.

Standard: HTML 2
Common: Yes
Paired: Yes
Sample:

```
Press <KBD>CTRL+S</KBD> to save your
document.
```

Attribute Information

CLASS="..."

Indicates which style class applies to the <KBD>
element.

Standard: HTML 4
Common: No
Sample:

```
Now press the <KBD CLASS="casual">F4
</KBD> key!
```

ID="..."

Assigns a unique ID selector to an instance of the <KBD> tag. When you then assign a style to that ID selector, it affects only that one instance of the <KBD> tag.

> **Standard**: HTML 4
> **Common**: No
> **Sample**:

```
Press <KBD ID="123">F1</KBD> for help.
```

STYLE="..."

Specifies Style Sheet commands that apply to the text within the <KBD> tags.

> **Standard**: HTML 4
> **Common**: No
> **Sample**:

```
<KBD STYLE="background: red">F10</KBD>
```

TITLE="..."

Specifies text assigned to the tag. You might use this attribute for context-sensitive help within the document. Browsers may use this to show tool tips over the keyboard text.

> **Standard**: HTML 4
> **Common**: No
> **Sample**:

```
Now press the <KBD
TITLE="Keyboard stuff">F4</KBD> key.
```

Other Attributes

This tag also accepts the lang, dir, onClick, onDblClick, onMouseDown, onMouseUp, onMouseOver, onMouseMove, onMouseOut, onKeyPress, onKeyDown, and onKeyUp attributes. See the Element-Independent Attributes section of this reference for definitions and examples.

<LABEL>

Provides identifying text for a form widget.

> **Standard**: HTML 4
> **Common**: No
> **Paired**: Yes
> **Sample**:

```
<LABEL FOR="idname">First Name</LABEL>
<INPUT TYPE="TEXT" ID="idname">
```

Attribute Information

ACCESSKEY="..."

Assigns a keystroke to the element.

> **Standard**: HTML 4
> **Common**: No
> **Sample**:

```
<LABEL FOR="idname" ACCESSKEY=H>
```

CLASS="..."

Indicates which style class applies to the <INPUT> element.

> **Standard**: HTML 4
> **Common**: No
> **Sample**:

```
<LABEL FOR="idname" CLASS="short">First
Name</LABEL>
<INPUT TYPE="TEXT" ID="idname">
```

FOR="..."

Specifies the ID of the widget associated with the label.

> **Standard**: HTML 4
> **Common**: No
> **Sample**:

```
<LABEL FOR="idname">First Name</LABEL>
<INPUT TYPE="TEXT" ID="idname">
```

ID="*n*"

Assigns a unique ID selector to an instance of the <INPUT> tag. When you then assign a style to that ID selector, it affects only that one instance of the <INPUT> tag.

    Standard: HTML 4
    Common: No
    Sample:

```
<LABEL FOR="idname" ID="234">First
Name</LABEL>
<INPUT TYPE="TEXT" ID="idname">
```

STYLE="..."

Specifies Style Sheet commands that apply to the input element.

    Standard: HTML 4
    Common: No
    Sample:

```
<LABEL FOR="idname" STYLE="background :
red">First Name</LABEL>
<INPUT TYPE="TEXT" ID="idname">
```

TABINDEX="*n*"

Specifies where the input method appears in the tab order. For example, TABINDEX=3 places the cursor at the input element after the visitor presses the Tab key three times.

    Standard: HTML 4
    Common: No
    Sample:

```
Credit card number:
<INPUT TYPE=TEXT NAME="ccard"
TABINDEX=5>
```

TITLE="..."

Specifies text assigned to the tag. You might use this attribute for context-sensitive help within the document. Browsers may use this to show tool tips over the input method.

    Standard: HTML 4
    Common: No
    Sample:

```
<INPUT TYPE=RADIO NAME="cc"
VALUE="visa" TITLE="Visa">
```

Other Attributes

This tag also accepts the lang, dir, onfocus, onblur, onselect, onchange, onClick, onDblClick, onMouseDown, onMouseUp, onMouseOver, onMouseMove, onMouseOut, onKeyPress, onKeyDown, and onKeyUp attributes. See the Element-Independent Attributes section of this reference for definitions and examples.

<LAYER>

Defines a layer within a document, which you can than manipulate with JavaScript. Specify the layer's contents by placing HTML between the <LAYER> tags or by using the SRC= attribute.

    Standard: Netscape Navigator 4
    Common: No
    Paired: Yes
    Sample:

```
<LAYER SRC="top.html" HEIGHT=100
WIDTH=100 Z-INDEX=4 NAME="top"
VISIBILITY=SHOW>
</LAYER>
```

Attribute Information

ABOVE="..."

Specifies the name of a layer above which the current layer should appear.

    Standard: Netscape Navigator 4
    Common: No
    Sample:

```
<LAYER SRC="grass.gif" Z-INDEX=1
NAME="Grass" VISIBILITY=SHOW>
<LAYER SRC="dog.gif" ABOVE="Grass"
NAME="Dog">
```

BACKGROUND=*"URL"*

Specifies the relative or absolute location of an image file that the browser tiles as the background of the layer.

>**Standard**:   Netscape Navigator 4
>**Common**:   No
>**Sample**:

```
<LAYER Z-INDEX=5 NAME="info"
BACKGROUND="goo.gif">
<H1>Hi there</H1></LAYER>
```

BELOW=*"..."*

Specifies the name of a layer below which the current layer should appear.

>**Standard**:   Netscape Navigator 4
>**Common**:   No
>**Sample**:

```
<LAYER BACKGROUND="road.jpg"
NAME="Road" UNDER="Car">
</LAYER>
```

BGCOLOR=*"#RRGGBB"* or *"..."*

Specifies the background color of the layer. Use either the hexadecimal RGB values or the color name.

>**Standard**:   Netscape Navigator 4
>**Common**:   No
>**Sample**:

```
<LAYER BGCOLOR=#FF0011>
<DIV ALIGN=CENTER>
  <H1><BLINK>EAT AT JOES!</BLINK></H1>
</DIV>
</LAYER>
```

CLIP=*"x1, y1, x2, y2"*

Indicates the dimensions of a clipping rectangle that specifies which areas of the layer are visible. Areas outside this rectangle become transparent.

You can give the x and y coordinates in pixels or as percentages to indicate relative portions of the layer. You can omit *x1* and *y1* if you want to clip from the top left corner of the layer.

>**Standard**:   Netscape Navigator 4
>**Common**:   No
>**Sample**:

```
<LAYER SRC="hawk.jpg" CLIP="20%,20%">
</LAYER>
```

HEIGHT=*"n"*

Specifies the vertical dimension of the layer (in pixels or as a percentage of the browser window height).

>**Standard**:   Netscape Navigator 4
>**Common**:   No
>**Sample**:

```
<LAYER SRC="frame.gif" ABOVE="bg"
NAME="frame" WIDTH=200 HEIGHT=200>
```

LEFT=*"n"*

Specifies the layer's horizontal position (in pixels) relative to the left edge of the parent layer. Use the TOP= attribute for vertical positioning.

>**Standard**:   Netscape Navigator 4
>**Common**:   No
>**Sample**:

```
<LAYER LEFT=100 TOP=150>
This layer is at {100,150}
</LAYER>
```

NAME=*"..."*

Gives the layer a name by which other layer definitions and JavaScript code can reference it.

>**Standard**:   Netscape Navigator 4
>**Common**:   No
>**Sample**:

```
<LAYER SRC="car.gif" NAME="CarPic"
ABOVE="Road">
</LAYER>
```

SRC=*"URL"*

Specifies the relative or absolute location of the file containing the contents of the layer.

>**Standard**:   Netscape Navigator 4
>**Common**:   No
>**Sample**:

```
<LAYER SRC="ocean.jpg"></LAYER>
```

TOP="*n*"

Specifies the layer's vertical position (in pixels) relative to the top edge of the parent layer. Use the LEFT= attribute for horizontal positioning.

> **Standard**: Netscape Navigator 4
> **Common**: No
> **Sample**:

```
<LAYER LEFT=100 TOP=150>
This layer is at {100,150}
</LAYER>
```

VISIBILITY={SHOW, HIDE, INHERIT}

Indicates whether the layer is initially visible. VISIBILITY=SHOW indicates the layer is initially visible. VISIBILITY=HIDE indicates the layer is not initially visible. VISIBILITY=INHERIT indicates the layer has the same initial visibility attribute as its parent layer.

> **Standard**: Netscape Navigator 4
> **Common**: No
> **Sample**:

```
<LAYER SRC="grass.gif" Z-INDEX=1
NAME="Grass" VISIBILITY=SHOW>
```

WIDTH="*n*"

Specifies the horizontal dimension of the layer (in pixels or as a percentage of the browser window width).

> **Standard**: Netscape Navigator 4
> **Common**: No
> **Sample**:

```
<LAYER SRC="frame.gif" ABOVE="bg"
NAME="frame" WIDTH=200 HEIGHT=200>
```

Z-INDEX="*n*"

Specifies where the layer appears in the stack of layers. Higher values indicate a position closer to the top of the stack.

> **Standard**: Netscape Navigator 4
> **Common**: No
> **Sample**:

```
<LAYER Z-INDEX=0 NAME="Bottom">
You may never see this text if
other layers are above it.
</LAYER>
```

<LEGEND>

Specifies a description for a fieldset. Use inside <FIELDSET> tags.

> **Standard**: HTML 4
> **Common**: No
> **Paired**: Yes
> **Sample**:

```
<FORM><FIELDSET>
  <LEGEND VALIGN=TOP ALIGN=CENTER>
  Test Grades For COOKING 101
  </LEGEND>…
</FORM>
```

Attribute Information

ALIGN={TOP, BOTTOM, LEFT, RIGHT}

Indicates whether the legend appears at the top, bottom, left, or right of the fieldset.

> **Standard**: HTML 4
> **Common**: No
> **Sample**:

```
<LEGEND ALIGN=TOP>
Seattle Staff Directory
</LEGEND>
```

CLASS="..."

Indicates which style class applies to the <LEGEND> element.

> **Standard**: HTML 4
> **Common**: No
> **Sample**:

```
<LEGEND CLASS="casual">Hydrogen vs
Oxygen</LEGEND>
```

ID="..."

Assigns a unique ID selector to an instance of the <LEGEND> tag. When you then assign a style to that ID selector, it affects only that one instance of the <LEGEND> tag.

> **Standard**: HTML 4
> **Common**: No
> **Sample**:

```
<LEGEND ID="123">Great
Painters</LEGEND>
```

STYLE="..."

Specifies Style Sheet commands that apply to the contents of the <LEGEND> tags.

> **Standard**: HTML 4
> **Common**: No
> **Sample**:

```
<LEGEND STYLE="background: red">
```

TITLE="..."

Specifies text assigned to the tag. You might use this attribute for context-sensitive help within the document. Browsers may use this to show tool tips over the legend.

> **Standard**: HTML 4
> **Common**: Yes
> **Sample**:

```
<LEGEND TITLE="of Sleepy Hollow">
```

Other Attributes

This tag also accepts the lang, dir, onClick, onDblClick, onMouseDown, onMouseUp, onMouseOver, onMouseMove, onMouseOut, onKeyPress, onKeyDown, and onKeyUp attributes. See the Element-Independent Attributes section of this reference for definitions and examples.

<LI>

Places items into ordered (see the <OL> tag), menu (see the <MENU> tag), directory (see the <dir> tag), and unordered (see the <UL> tag) lists.

> **Standard**: HTML 2
> **Common**: Yes
> **Paired**: Yes, optional
> **Sample**:

```
My favorite foods are:<UL>
  <LI>Pepperoni Pizza
  <LI>Lasagna
  <LI>Taco Salad
  <LI>Bananas
</UL>
```

Attribute Information

CLASS="..."

Indicates which style class applies to the <LI> element.

> **Standard**: HTML 4
> **Common**: No
> **Sample**:

```
<LI CLASS="casual">Dogs
```

ID=n

Assigns a unique ID selector to an instance of the <LI> tag. When you then assign a style to that ID selector, it affects only that one instance of the <LI> tag.

> **Standard**: HTML 4
> **Common**: No
> **Sample**:

```
<LI ID="123">Bees</LI>
```

STYLE="..."

Specifies Style Sheet commands that apply to the list item.

> **Standard**: HTML 4
> **Common**: No
> **Sample**:

```
<LI STYLE="background: red">
```

TITLE="..."

Specifies text assigned to the tag. You might use this attribute for context-sensitive help within the document. Browsers may use this to show tool tips over the list item.

> **Standard**: HTML 4
> **Common**: No
> **Sample**:

```
<LI TITLE="List Item">Thingie
```

TYPE="..."

Specifies the bullets for each unordered list item (see the <UL> tag) or the numbering for each ordered list item (see the <OL> tag). If you omit the TYPE= attribute, the browser chooses a default type.

Valid TYPE values for unordered lists are DISC, SQUARE, and CIRCLE.

Valid TYPE values for ordered lists are 1 for arabic numbers, a for lowercase letters, A for uppercase letters, i for lowercase roman numerals, and I for uppercase roman numerals.

> **Standard**:   HTML 3.2
> **Common**:   Yes
> **Sample**:

```
<UL>
 <LI TYPE=SQUARE>Food
 <OL>
   <LI TYPE=1>Spaghetti
   <LI TYPE=1>Tossed Salad
 </OL>
</UL>
```

VALUE="…"

Sets a number in an ordered list. Use this attribute to continue a list after interrupting it with something else in your document. You can also set a number in an ordered list with the START= attribute of the <OL> tag.

Because unordered lists do not increment, the VALUE= attribute is meaningless when used with them.

> **Standard**:   HTML 3.2
> **Common**:   Yes
> **Sample**:

```
<OL TYPE=1>
   <LI VALUE=5>Watch
   <LI>Compass
</OL>
```

Other Attributes

This tag also accepts the lang, dir, onClick, onDblClick, onMouseDown, onMouseUp, onMouseOver, onMouseMove, onMouseOut, onKeyPress, onKeyDown, and onKeyUp attributes. See the Element-Independent Attributes section of this reference for definitions and examples.

<LINK>

Establishes relationships between the current document and other documents. Use this tag

within the <HEAD> section. For example, if you access the current document by choosing a hyperlink from the site's home page, you can establish a relationship between the current document and the site's home page (see the REL= attribute). At this time, however, most browsers don't use most of these relationships. You can place several <LINK> tags within the <HEAD> section of your document to define multiple relationships.

With newer implementations of HTML, you can also use the <LINK> tag to establish information about Cascading Style Sheets. Some other relationships that the <LINK> tag defines include the following:

CONTENTS: A table of contents.

INDEX: An index.

GLOSSARY: A glossary of terms.

COPYRIGHT: A copyright notice.

NEXT: The next document in a series (use with REL=).

PREVIOUS: The previous document in a series (use with REV=).

START: The first document in a series.

HELP: A document offering help or more information.

BOOKMARK: A bookmark links to a important entry point within a longer document.

STYLESHEET: An external Style Sheet.

ALTERNATE: Different versions of the same document. When used with lang, ALTERNATE implies a translated document; when used with MEDIA, it implies a version for a different medium.

> **Standard**:   HTML 2
> **Common**:   Yes
> **Paired**:   No
> **Sample**:

```
<HEAD>
<TITLE>Prices</TITLE>
<LINK REL=Top HREF=
"http://www.raycomm.com/">
<LINK REL=Search HREF=
"http://www.raycomm.com/search.html">
</HEAD>
```

Attribute Information

HREF="*URL*"

Indicates the relative or absolute location of the resource you are establishing a relationship to/from.

Standard: HTML 2
Common: Yes
Sample:

```
<LINK REL=Prev HREF="page1.html">
```

MEDIA="..."

Specifies the destination medium for style information. It may be a single type or a comma-separated list. Media types include the following:

Screen—for online viewing (default setting)
Print—for traditional printed material and for documents on screen viewed in print preview mode
Projection—for projectors
Braille—for Braille tactile feedback devices
Speech—for a speech synthesizer
All—applies to all devices

Standard: HTML 4
Common: No
Sample:

```
<LINK MEDIA=SCREEN REL="STYLESHEET"
HREF="/global.css">
```

NAME="..."

Specifies a name by which bookmarks, scripts, and applets can reference the relationship.

Standard: Internet Explorer 4
Common: No
Sample:

```
<LINK REL="Search" HREF="/search.html"
NAME="Search">
```

REL="..."

Defines the relationship you are establishing between the current document and another resource. The HTML 3.2 specification includes several standard values for the REL= attribute.

REL=Top defines the site home page or the top of the site hierarchy. REL=Contents usually defines the location of a resource that lists the contents of the site. REL=Index provides a link to an index of the site. REL=Glossary indicates the location of a glossary resource. REL=Copyright indicates the location of a copyright statement. REL=Next and REL=Previous establish relationships between documents or resources in a series. REL=Help indicates the location of a help resource. REL=Search specifies the location of a search resource. REL=Style Sheet specifies information about Style Sheets.

Standard: HTML 2
Common: Yes
Sample:

```
<LINK REL=Help HREF="/Help/index.html">
<LINK REL=Style Sheet HREF="sitehead.css">
</HEAD>
```

REV="..."

Establishes reverse relationships between the current document and other resources. One common use is REV="made", after which you can set the HREF= attribute to a mailto: URL to contact the author of the document.

Standard: HTML 2
Common: Yes
Sample:

```
<LINK REV=made
HREF="mailto:jdoe@somewhere.com">
```

TARGET="..."

Specifies the name of a frame in which the referenced link appears.

Standard: Internet Explorer 4
Common: No
Sample:

```
<LINK TARGET="_blank" REL="Home"
HREF="http://www.mememe.com/">
```

TITLE="..."

Specifies text assigned to the tag that can be used for context-sensitive help within the document. Browsers may use this to show tool tips.

Standard: HTML 4
Common: Yes
Sample:

```
<LINK REL=Top HREF="/index.html"
TITLE="Home Page">
```

TYPE="..."

Specifies the MIME type of a Style Sheet to import with the <LINK> tag.

Standard: HTML 4
Common: No
Sample:

```
<LINK REL=STYLESHEET TYPE="text/css"
HREF="/style/main.css">
```

Other Attributes

This tag also accepts the lang, dir, onfocus, onblur, onchange, onselect, onClick, onDblClick, onMouseDown, onMouseUp, onMouseOver, onMouseMove, onMouseOut, onKeyPress, onKeyDown, and onKeyUp attributes. See the Element-Independent Attributes section of this reference for definitions and examples.

<LISTING>

Specifies preformatted text to include within a document. Unlike the <PRE> tags, the browser does not interpret HTML tags within the <LISTING>tags. HTML 3.2 declared this tag obsolete, so use <PRE> instead.

Standard: Obsolete
Common: Yes
Paired: Yes
Sample:

```
The output from these reports is shown
below.
<LISTING>
Company     Q1    Q2    Q3    Q4
-------   ---   ---   ----  ----
Widget Inc. 4.5m   4.6m  6.2m  4.5m
Acme Widget 5.9m  10.2m  7.3m  6.6m
West Widget 2.2m   1.3m  3.1m  6.1m
</LISTING>
```

<MAP>

Specifies a container for client-side image map data. Inside the <MAP> container, you place instances of the <AREA> tag.

Standard: HTML 3.2
Common: Yes
Paired: Yes
Sample:

```
<MAP NAME="mainmap">  <AREA NOHREF
ALT="Home" SHAPE=RECT COORDS="0,0,100,100">
  <AREA HREF="yellow.html" ALT="Yellow"
SHAPE=RECT COORDS="100,0,200,100">
  <AREA HREF="blue.html" ALT="Blue"
SHAPE=RECT COORDS="0,100,100,200">
  <AREA HREF="red.html" ALT="Red"
SHAPE=RECT COORDS="100,100,200,200">
</MAP>
```

Attribute Information

CLASS="..."

Indicates which style class applies to the element.

Standard: HTML 4
Common: No
Sample:

```
<MAP CLASS="casual" NAME="simba">
```

ID="..."

Indicates an identifier to associate with the map. You can also use this to apply styles to the object.

Standard: HTML 4
Common: No
Sample:

```
<MAP ID="123" NAME="simba">
```

NAME="..."

Establishes a name for the map information you can later reference by the USEMAP= attribute of the <IMG> tag.

> **Standard**: HTML 3.2
> **Common**: Yes
> **Sample**:

```
<MAP NAME="housemap">
. . .
<IMG SRC="house.gif" USEMAP="#housemap"
BORDER=0 ALT="Map of House">
```

STYLE="..."

Specifies Style Sheet commands that apply to the contents within the <MAP> tags.

> **Standard**: HTML 4
> **Common**: No
> **Sample**:

```
<MAP STYLE="background: black">
```

TITLE="..."

Specifies text assigned to the tag. You might use this attribute for context-sensitive help within the document. Browsers may use this to show tool tips.

> **Standard**: HTML 4
> **Common**: No
> **Sample**:

```
<MAP TITLE="Image map spec">
```

<MARQUEE>

Displays a scrolling text message within a document. Only Internet Explorer recognizes this tag.

> **Standard**: Internet Explorer
> **Common**: No
> **Paired**: Yes
> **Sample**:

```
<MARQUEE DIRECTION=LEFT BEHAVIOR=SCROLL
SCROLLDELAY=250 SCROLLAMOUNT=10>
Big sale today on fuzzy wuzzy widgets!
</MARQUEE>
```

Attribute Information

ALIGN={LEFT, CENTER, RIGHT, TOP, BOTTOM}

Specifies the alignment of text outside the marquee.

> **Standard**: Internet Explorer
> **Common**: No
> **Sample**:

```
<MARQUEE WIDTH=200 HEIGHT=50
ALIGN=LEFT DIRECTION=LEFT>
How To Groom Your Dog</MARQUEE>
```

BEHAVIOR={SLIDE, SCROLL, ALTERNATE}

Indicates the type of scrolling. BEHAVIOR= SCROLL scrolls text from one side of the marquee, across, and off the opposite side. BEHAVIOR= SLIDE scrolls text from one side of the marquee, across, and stops when the text reaches the opposite side. BEHAVIOR=ALTERNATE bounces the marquee text from one side to the other.

> **Standard**: Internet Explorer
> **Common**: No
> **Sample**:

```
<MARQUEE DIRECTION=LEFT
BEHAVIOR=ALTERNATE>
GO BEARS! WIN WIN WIN!
</MARQUEE>
```

BGCOLOR="#*RRGGBB*" or "..."

Specifies the background color of the marquee. Use a hexadecimal RGB color value or a color name.

> **Standard**: Internet Explorer
> **Common**: No
> **Sample**:

```
<MARQUEE BGCOLOR="red" DIRECTION=LEFT>
Order opera tickets here!
</MARQUEE>
```

DATAFLD="..."

Selects a column from a block of tabular data.

> **Standard**: Internet Explorer 4
> **Common**: No
> **Sample**:

```
<MARQUEE DATASRC="#data_table"
DATAFLD="nitems">
```

DATAFORMATAS={TEXT, HTML, NONE}

Specifies how items selected from tabular data format within the document.

> **Standard**: Internet Explorer 4
> **Common**: No
> **Sample**:

```
<MARQUEE DATASRC="#data_table"
DATAFLD="nitems" DATAFORMATAS=HTML>
```

DATASRC="..."

Specifies the location of tabular data to be bound within the document.

> **Standard**: Internet Explorer 4
> **Common**: No
> **Sample**:

```
<MARQUEE DATASRC="#data_table"
DATAFLD="nitems">
```

DIRECTION={LEFT, RIGHT}

Indicates the direction in which the marquee text scrolls.

> **Standard**: Internet Explorer
> **Common**: No
> **Sample**:

```
<MARQUEE DIRECTION=LEFT>
Order opera tickets here!
</MARQUEE>
```

HEIGHT="n"

Specifies the vertical dimension of the marquee (in pixels).

> **Standard**: Internet Explorer
> **Common**: No
> **Sample**:

```
<MARQUEE WIDTH=300 HEIGHT=50>
GO BEARS!</MARQUEE>
```

HSPACE="n"

Specifies the size of the margins (in pixels) to the left and right of the marquee.

> **Standard**: Internet Explorer
> **Common**: No
> **Sample**:

```
<MARQUEE DIRECTION=LEFT HSPACE=25>
Check out our detailed product
descriptions!</MARQUEE>
```

ID="..."

Assigns a unique ID selector to an instance of the <MARQUEE> tag. When you then assign a style to that ID selector, it affects only that one instance of the <MARQUEE> tag.

> **Standard**: Internet Explorer 4
> **Common**: No
> **Sample**:

```
<MARQUEE ID="3d4">
```

LOOP={n, INFINITE}

Controls the appearance of the marquee text.

> **Standard**: Internet Explorer
> **Common**: No
> **Sample**:

```
<MARQUEE LOOP=5>
December 12 is our big, all-day sale!
</MARQUEE>
```

SCROLLAMOUNT="n"

Indicates how far (in pixels) the marquee text shifts between redraws. Decrease this value for a smoother (but slower) scroll; increase it for a faster (but bumpier) scroll.

> **Standard**: Internet Explorer
> **Common**: No
> **Sample**:

```
<MARQUEE SCROLLAMOUNT=10
SCROLLDELAY=40>Plant a tree for Arbor Day!
</MARQUEE>
```

SCROLLDELAY="n"

Indicates how often (in milliseconds) the marquee text redraws. Increase this value to slow the scrolling action; decrease it to speed the scrolling action.

Standard:	Internet Explorer
Common:	No
Sample:	

```
<MARQUEE DIRECTION=RIGHT
SCROLLDELAY=30>Eat at Joe's!</MARQUEE>
```

STYLE="..."

Specifies Style Sheet commands that apply to the text within the <MARQUEE> tags.

Standard:	Internet Explorer 4
Common:	No
Sample:	

```
<MARQUEE STYLE="background: red">
```

TITLE="..."

Specifies text assigned to the tag. You might use this attribute for context-sensitive help within the document. Browsers may use this to show tool tips over the marquee.

Standard:	Internet Explorer 4
Common:	No
Sample:	

```
<MARQUEE TITLE="Scrolling Marquee">
```

VSPACE="n"

Specifies the size of the margins (in pixels) at the top and bottom of the marquee.

Standard:	Internet Explorer
Common:	No
Sample:	

```
<MARQUEE DIRECTION=LEFT VSPACE=25>
Check out our detailed product
descriptions!</MARQUEE>
```

WIDTH="n"

Specifies the horizontal dimension (in pixels) of the marquee.

Standard:	Internet Explorer
Common:	No
Sample:	

```
<MARQUEE WIDTH=300>
Go Bears!</MARQUEE>
```

<MENU>

Defines a menu list. Use the <LI> tag to indicate list items. Use <UL> instead of this deprecated element.

Standard:	HTML 2; deprecated in HTML 4
Common:	No
Paired:	Yes
Sample:	

```
Now you can:<MENU>
  <LI>Eat the sandwich
  <LI>Place the sandwich in the fridge
  <LI>Feed the sandwich to the dog
</MENU>
```

Attribute Information

CLASS="..."

Indicates which style class applies to the <MENU> element.

Standard:	HTML 4
Common:	No
Sample:	

```
<MENU CLASS="casual">
  <LI>Information
  <LI>Members
  <LI>Guests
</MENU>
```

COMPACT

Specifies that the menu list appear in a space-saving form.

Standard:	HTML 2; deprecated in HTML 4
Common:	Yes
Sample:	

```
<H2>Drinks Available</H2>
<MENU COMPACT>
  <LI>Cola</LI>
  <LI>Fruit Drink</LI>
  <LI>Orange Juice</LI>
  <LI>Water</LI>
</MENU>
```

ID="..."

Assigns a unique ID selector to an instance of the <MENU> tag. When you then assign a style to that ID selector, it affects only that one instance of the <MENU> tag.

Standard: HTML 4
Common: No
Sample:

```
You'll need the following:
<MENU ID="123">
  <LI>Extra socks
  <LI>Snack crackers
  <LI>Towel
</MENU>
```

STYLE="..."

Specifies Style Sheet commands that apply to the menu list.

Standard: HTML 4
Common: Yes
Sample:

```
<MENU STYLE="background: black; color:
white">
```

TITLE="..."

Specifies text assigned to the tag. You might use this attribute for context-sensitive help within the document. Browsers may use this to show tool tips over the menu list.

Standard: HTML 4
Common: No
Sample:

```
<MENU TITLE="Menu List">
```

Other Attributes

This tag also accepts the lang, dir, onClick, onDblClick, onMouseDown, onMouseUp, onMouseOver, onMouseMove, onMouseOut, onKeyPress, onKeyDown, and onKeyUp attributes. See the Element-Independent Attributes section of this reference for definitions and examples.

<META>

Specifies information about the document to browsers, applications, and search engines. Place the <META> tag within the document head. For example, you can use the <META> tag to instruct the browser to load a new document after 10 seconds (client-pull), or you can specify keywords for search engines to associate with your document.

Standard: HTML 2
Common: Yes
Paired: No
Sample:

```
<HEAD>
<TITLE>Igneous Rocks In North America
</TITLE>
<META HTTP-EQUIV="Keywords"
CONTENT="Geology, Igneous, Volcanos">
</HEAD>
```

Attribute Information

CONTENT="..."

Assigns values to the HTTP header field. When using the REFRESH HTTP header, assign a number along with a URL to the CONTENT= attribute; the browser then loads the specified URL after the specified number of seconds.

Standard: HTML 2
Common: Yes
Sample:

```
<META HTTP-EQUIV="Refresh"
CONTENT="2; URL=nextpage.html">
```

HTTP-EQUIV="..."

Indicates the HTTP header value you want to define, such as Refresh, Expires, or Content-Language. Other header values are listed in RFC2068.

Standard: HTML 2
Common: Yes
Sample:

```
<META HTTP-EQUIV="Expires" CONTENT=
"Tue, 04 Aug 1997 22:39:22 GMT">
```

NAME="..."

Specifies the name of the association you are defining, such as Keywords or Description.

Standard: HTML 2
Common: Yes
Sample:

```
<META NAME="Keywords" CONTENT=
"travel,automobile">
<META NAME="Description" CONTENT="The Nash
Metro moves fast and goes beep beep.">
```

Other Attributes

This tag also accepts the lang and dir attributes. See the Element-Independent Attributes section of this reference for definitions and examples.

<MULTICOL>

Formats text into newspaper-style columns.

Standard: Netscape Navigator 4
Common: No
Paired: Yes
Sample:

```
<MULTICOL COLS=2 GUTTER=10>
. . .
</MULTICOL>
```

Attribute Information

COLS="n"

Indicates the number of columns.

Standard: Netscape Navigator 4
Common: No
Sample:

```
<MULTICOL COLS=4>
```

GUTTER="n"

Indicates the width of the space (in pixels) between multiple columns.

Standard: Netscape Navigator 4
Common: No
Sample:

```
<MULTICOL COLS=3 GUTTER=15>
```

WIDTH="n"

Indicates the horizontal dimension (in pixels or as a percentage of the total width available) of each column.

Standard: Netscape Navigator 4
Common: No
Sample:

```
<MULTICOL COLS=2 WIDTH="30%">
```

<NOBR>

Disables line-wrapping for a section of text. To force a word-break within a <NOBR> clause, use the <WBR> tag.

Standard: Netscape Navigator
Common: Yes
Paired: Yes
Sample:

```
<NOBR>This entire line of text will
remain on one single line in the
browser window until the closing
tag appears. That doesn't happen
until right now.</NOBR>
```

Attribute Information

CLASS="..."

Indicate which style class applies to the element.

Standard: Netscape Navigator
Common: No
Sample:

```
<NOBR CLASS="casual">
```

ID="..."

Assigns a unique ID selector to an instance of the <NOBR> tag. When you then assign a style to that ID selector, it affects only that one instance of the <NOBR> tag.

Standard: Netscape Navigator
Common: No
Sample:

You'll need the following:
`<NOBR ID="123">`

STYLE="..."

Specifies Style Sheet commands that apply to the nonbreaking text.

Standard: Netscape Navigator
Common: Yes
Sample:

`<NOBR STYLE="background: black">`

<NOFRAMES>

Provides HTML content for browsers that do not support frames or are configured not to present frames. You can include a `<BODY>` tag within the `<NOFRAMES>` section to provide additional formatting and Style Sheet features.

Standard: HTML 4
Common: Yes
Paired: Yes
Sample:

```
<FRAMESET COLS="*,70">
  <FRAME SRC="frames/body.html"
NAME="body">
  <FRAME SRC="frames/side.html"
NAME="side">
</FRAMESET>
<NOFRAMES>
  <p>Your browser doesn't support frames.
Please follow the links below for the rest
of the story.
  <p><a href="Prices.html">Prices</a> | <a
href="About.html">About Us</a> | <a
href="Contact.html">Contact Us</a>
</NOFRAMES>
```

Attribute Information

TITLE="..."

Specifies text assigned to the tag. You might use this attribute for context-sensitive help within the document. Browsers may use this to show tool tips.

Standard: HTML 4
Common: No
Sample:

`<NOFRAMES TITLE="HTML for nonframed browsers">`

<NOSCRIPT>

Provides HTML content for browsers that do not support scripts. Use the `<NOSCRIPT>` tags inside a script definition.

Standard: HTML 4
Common: No
Paired: Yes
Sample:

```
<NOSCRIPT>
Because you can see this, you can tell that
your browser will not run (or is set not to
run) scripts. </NOSCRIPT>
```

O

<OBJECT>

Embeds a software object into a document. The object can be an ActiveX object, a Quick-Time movie, or any other objects or data that a browser supports.

Use the `<PARAM>` tag to supply parameters to the embedded object. You can place messages and other tags between the `<OBJECT>` tags for browsers that do not support embedded objects.

Standard: HTML 4
Common: No
Paired: Yes
Sample:

```
<OBJECT CLASSID="/thingie.py">
  <PARAM NAME="thing" VALUE=1>
  Sorry. Your browser does not support
  embedded objects. If it supported these
  objects you would not see this message.
</OBJECT>
```

Attribute Information

ALIGN={LEFT, CENTER, RIGHT, TEXTTOP, MIDDLE, TEXTMIDDLE, BASELINE, TEXTBOTTOM, BASELINE}

Indicates how the embedded object lines up relative to the edges of the browser windows and/or other elements within the browser window.

Using `ALIGN=LEFT`, `ALIGN=RIGHT`, or `ALIGN=CENTER` will cause the embedded object to *float* between the edges of the window either to the left, right, or evenly between. The behavior is similar to that of the `ALIGN=` attribute of the `<IMG>` tag.

`ALIGN=TEXTTOP` aligns the top of the embedded object with the top of the surrounding text.

`ALIGN=TEXTMIDDLE` aligns the middle of the embedded object with the middle of the surrounding text.

`ALIGN=TEXTBOTTOM` aligns the bottom of the embedded object with the bottom of the surrounding text.

`ALIGN=BASELINE` aligns the bottom of the embedded object with the baseline of the surrounding text.

`ALIGN=MIDDLE` aligns the middle of the embedded object with the baseline of the surrounding text.

> **Standard**: HTML 4; deprecated in favor of Style Sheets
> **Common**: No
> **Sample**:

```
<OBJECT DATA="shocknew.dcr"
TYPE="application/director" WIDTH=288
HEIGHT=200 ALIGN=RIGHT>
```

BORDER="*n*"

Indicates the width (in pixels) of a border around the embedded object. `BORDER=0` indicates no border.

> **Standard**: HTML 4
> **Common**: No
> **Sample**:

```
<OBJECT DATA="shocknew.dcr"
TYPE="application/director" WIDTH=288
HEIGHT=200 BORDER=10>
```

CODEBASE="..."

Specifies the absolute or relative location of the base directory in which the browser will look for data and other implementation files.

> **Standard**: HTML 4
> **Common**: No
> **Sample**:

```
<OBJECT CODEBASE="/~fgm/code/">
</OBJECT>
```

CODETYPE="..."

Specifies the MIME type for the embedded object's code.

> **Standard**: HTML 4
> **Common**: No
> **Sample**:

```
<OBJECT
CODETYPE="application/x-msword">
</OBJECT>
```

CLASS="..."

Indicates which style class applies to the element.

> **Standard**: HTML 4
> **Common**: No
> **Sample**:

```
<OBJECT CLASS="casual"
 CODETYPE="application/x-msword">
</OBJECT>
```

CLASSID="..."

Specifies the URL of an object resource.

> **Standard**: HTML 4
> **Common**: No
> **Sample**:

```
<OBJECT
CLASSID="http://www.raycomm.com/
bogus.class">
```

DATA="*URL*"

Specifies the absolute or relative location of the embedded object's data.

Standard: HTML 4
Common: No
Sample:

```
<OBJECT DATA="/~fgm/goo.AVI">
</OBJECT>
```

DATAFLD="..."

Selects a column from a block of tabular data.

Standard: Internet Explorer 4
Common: No
Sample:

```
<OBJECT DATA="dataview.ocx"
DATASRC="#data_table"
DATAFLD="datafld1">
```

DATASRC="..."

Specifies the location of tabular data to be bound within the document.

Standard: Internet Explorer 4
Common: No
Sample:

```
<OBJECT DATA="dataview.ocx"
DATASRC="#data_table">
```

DECLARE

Defines the embedded object without actually loading it into the document.

Standard: HTML 4
Common: No
Sample:

```
<OBJECT CLASSID="clsid:99B42120-6EC7-11CF-
A6C7-00AA00A47DD3" DECLARE>
</OBJECT>
```

HEIGHT="*n*"

Specifies the vertical dimension (in pixels) of the embedded object.

Standard: HTML 4
Common: No

Sample:

```
<OBJECT DATA="shocknew.dcr"
TYPE="application/director" WIDTH=288
HEIGHT=200 VSPACE=10 HSPACE=10>
```

HSPACE="*n*"

Specifies the size of the margins (in pixels) to the left and right of the embedded object.

Standard: HTML 4
Common: No
Sample:

```
<OBJECT DATA="shocknew.dcr"
TYPE="application/director" WIDTH=288
HEIGHT=200 VSPACE=10 HSPACE=10>
```

ID="..."

Indicates an identifier to associate with the embedded object. You can also use this to apply styles to the object.

Standard: HTML 4
Common: No
Sample:

```
<OBJECT DATA="shocknew.dcr"
TYPE="application/director" WIDTH=288
HEIGHT=200 VSPACE=10 HSPACE=10
ID="swave2">
```

NAME="..."

Specifies the name of the embedded object.

Standard: HTML 4
Common: No
Sample:

```
<OBJECT CLASSID="clsid:99B42120-6EC7-11CF-
A6C7-00AA00A47DD3" NAME="Very Cool Thingie">
</OBJECT>
```

SHAPES

Indicates that the embedded object has shaped hyperlinks (that is, image maps).

Standard: HTML 4
Common: No
Sample:

```
<OBJECT DATA="navbar.gif" SHAPES>
```

STANDBY="..."

Specifies a message that the browser displays while the object is loading.

> **Standard**: HTML 4
> **Common**: No
> **Sample**:

```
<OBJECT
 STANDBY="Please wait. Movie loading."
WIDTH=100 HEIGHT=250>
 <PARAM NAME=SRC VALUE="TheEarth.AVI">
 <PARAM NAME=AUTOSTART VALUE=TRUE>
 <PARAM NAME=PLAYBACK VALUE=FALSE>
</OBJECT>
```

TABINDEX="n"

Indicates the place of the embedded object in the tabbing order.

> **Standard**: HTML 4
> **Common**: No
> **Sample**:

```
<OBJECT
CLASSID="clsid:99B42120-6EC7-11CF-A6C7-
00AA00A47DD3" TABINDEX=3>
</OBJECT>
```

TITLE="..."

Specifies text assigned to the tag. You might use this attribute for context-sensitive help within the document. Browsers may use this to show tool tips over the embedded object.

> **Standard**: HTML 4
> **Common**: No
> **Sample**:

```
<OBJECT
 TITLE="Earth Movie" WIDTH=100
HEIGHT=250>
 <PARAM NAME=SRC VALUE="TheEarth.AVI">
 <PARAM NAME=AUTOSTART VALUE=TRUE>
 <PARAM NAME=PLAYBACK VALUE=FALSE>
</OBJECT>
```

TYPE="..."

Indicates the MIME type of the embedded object.

> **Standard**: HTML 4
> **Common**: No
> **Sample**:

```
<OBJECT DATA="shocknew.dcr"
TYPE="application/x-director" WIDTH=288
HEIGHT=200 VSPACE=10 HSPACE=10>
```

USEMAP="URL"

Indicates the relative or absolute location of a client-side image map to use with the embedded object.

> **Standard**: HTML 4
> **Common**: No
> **Sample**:

```
<OBJECT USEMAP="maps.html#map1">
```

VSPACE="n"

Specifies the size of the margin (in pixels) at the top and bottom of the embedded object.

> **Standard**: HTML 4
> **Common**: No
> **Sample**:

```
<OBJECT DATA="shocknew.dcr"
TYPE="application/director" WIDTH=288
HEIGHT=200 VSPACE=10 HSPACE=10>
</OBJECT>
```

WIDTH="n"

Indicates the horizontal dimension (in pixels) of the embedded object.

> **Standard**: HTML 4
> **Common**: No
> **Sample**:

```
<OBJECT DATA="shocknew.dcr"
TYPE="application/director" WIDTH=288
HEIGHT=200 VSPACE=10 HSPACE=10>
```

Other Attributes

This tag also accepts the `lang`, `dir`, `onClick`, `onDblClick`, `onMouseDown`, `onMouseUp`, `onMouseOver`, `onMouseMove`, `onMouseOut`, `onKeyPress`, `onKeyDown`, and `onKeyUp` attributes. See the Element-Independent Attributes section of this reference for definitions and examples.

<OL>

Contains a numbered (ordered) list.

Standard:	HTML 2
Common:	Yes
Paired:	Yes
Sample:	

```
<OL TYPE=i>
  <LI>Introduction
  <LI>Part One
  <OL TYPE=A>
    <LI>Chapter 1
    <LI>Chapter 2
  </OL>
</OL>
```

Attribute Information

CLASS="..."

Indicates which style class applies to the <OL> element.

Standard:	HTML 4
Common:	No
Sample:	

```
<OL CLASS="casual">
  <LI>Check engine oil
  <LI>Check tire pressures
  <LI>Fill with gasoline
<OL>
```

COMPACT

Indicates that the ordered list appears in a compact format. This attribute may not affect the appearance of the list as most browsers do not present lists in more than one format.

Standard:	HTML 2, deprecated in HTML 4
Common:	No
Sample:	

```
<OL COMPACT>
```

ID="n"

Assigns a unique ID selector to an instance of the <OL> tag. When you then assign a style to that ID selector, it affects only that one instance of the <OL> tag.

Standard:	HTML 4
Common:	No
Sample:	

```
Recommended bicycle accessories:
<OL ID="123">
  <LI>Water bottle
  <LI>Helmet
  <LI>Tire pump
</OL>
```

START="..."

Specifies the value at which the ordered list should start.

Standard:	HTML 2
Common:	Yes
Sample:	

```
<OL TYPE=A START=F>
```

STYLE="..."

Specifies Style Sheet commands that apply to the ordered list.

Standard:	HTML 4
Common:	Yes
Sample:	

```
<OL STYLE="background: black; color:
white">
```

TITLE="..."

Specifies text assigned to the tag. You might use this attribute for context-sensitive help within the document. Browsers may use this to show tool tips over the ordered list.

Standard:	HTML 4
Common:	No
Sample:	

```
<OL TITLE="Ordered list">
```

TYPE="..."

Specifies the numbering style of the ordered list. Possible values are 1 for arabic numbers, i for lower case roman numerals, I for uppercase roman numerals, a for lowercase letters, and A for uppercase letters.

> **Standard**:   HTML 2
> **Common**:   Yes
> **Sample**:

```
<OL TYPE=a>
  <LI>Breakfast
  <LI>Mrs. Johnson will speak
  <LI>Demonstration
  <LI>Lunch
</OL>
```

Other Attributes

This tag also accepts the lang, dir, onClick, onDblClick, onMouseDown, onMouseUp, onMouseOver, onMouseMove, onMouseOut, onKeyPress, onKeyDown, and onKeyUp attributes. See the Element-Independent Attributes section of this reference for definitions and examples.

<OPTION>

Indicates items in a fill-out form selection list (see the <SELECT> tag).

> **Standard**:   HTML 2
> **Common**:   Yes
> **Paired**:   No
> **Sample**:

```
Select an artist from the 1970s:<SELECT
NAME="artists">
  <OPTION>Boston
  <OPTION SELECTED>Pink Floyd
  <OPTION>Reo Speedwagon
</SELECT>
```

Attribute Information

CLASS="..."

Indicate which style class applies to the element.

> **Standard**:   HTML 4
> **Common**:   No
> **Sample**:

```
<OPTION NAME="color" CLASS="casual">
```

DISABLED="..."

Denies access to the input method.

> **Standard**:   HTML 4
> **Common**:   No
> **Sample**:

```
<OPTION VALUE="Bogus" DISABLED>Nothing here
```

ID="*n*"

Assigns a unique ID selector to an instance of the <OPTION> tag. When you then assign a style to that ID selector, it affects only that one instance of the <OPTION> tag.

> **Standard**:   HTML 4
> **Common**:   No
> **Sample**:

```
<OPTION ID="123">Mastercard
```

SELECTED

Marks a selection list item as preselected.

> **Standard**:   HTML 2
> **Common**:   Yes
> **Sample**:

```
<OPTION SELECTED VALUE=1>Ice Cream
</OPTION>
```

TITLE="..."

Specifies text assigned to the tag. You might use this attribute for context-sensitive help within the document. Browsers may use this to show tool tips over the selection list option.

> **Standard**:   HTML 4
> **Common**:   No
> **Sample**:

```
<OPTION TITLE="Option">Thingie
```

VALUE="..."

Indicates which data is sent to the form processor if you choose the selection list item. If the VALUE= attribute is not present within the <OPTION> tag, the text between the <OPTION> tags is sent instead.

Standard: HTML 2
Common: Yes
Sample:

`<OPTION VALUE=2>Sandwiches</OPTION>`

Other Attributes

This tag also accepts the `lang`, `dir`, `onfocus`, `onblur`, `onchange`, `onselect`, `onClick`, `onDblClick`, `onMouseDown`, `onMouseUp`, `onMouseOver`, `onMouseMove`, `onMouseOut`, `onKeyPress`, `onKeyDown`, and `onKeyUp` attributes. See the Element-Independent Attributes section of this reference for definitions and examples.

<P>

Indicates a paragraph in a document.

Standard: HTML 2
Common: Yes
Paired: Yes, optional
Sample:

`<P >As soon as she left,`
`the phone began ringing. "Hello,"`
`I said after lifting the receiver.</P>`
`<P>"Is she gone yet?" said the voice`
`on the other end.</P>`

Attribute Information

ALIGN={LEFT, CENTER, RIGHT}

Aligns paragraph text flush left, flush right, or in the center of the document.

Standard: HTML 3.2; deprecated in HTML 4 in favor of Style Sheets
Common: Yes
Sample:

`<P ALIGN=CENTER>There will be fun and`
`games for everyone!`

CLASS="..."

Indicates which style class applies to the <P> element.

Standard: HTML 4
Common: No
Sample:

`<P CLASS="casual">Tom turned at the`
`next street and stopped.`

ID="*n*"

Assigns a unique ID selector to an instance of the <P> tag. When you then assign a style to that ID selector, it affects only that one instance of the <P> tag.

Standard: HTML 4
Common: No
Sample:

`<P ID="123">This paragraph is yellow on`
`black!`

STYLE="..."

Specifies Style Sheet commands that apply to the contents of the paragraph.

Standard: HTML 4
Common: No
Sample:

`<P STYLE="background: red;`
`color: white">`

TITLE="..."

Specifies text assigned to the tag. You might use this attribute for context-sensitive help within the document. Browsers may use this to show tool tips over the paragraph.

Standard: HTML 4
Common: No
Sample:

`<P TITLE="Paragraph">`

WIDTH="*n*"

Specifies the horizontal dimension of the paragraph (in pixels).

> **Standard**:   Internet Explorer 4
> **Common**:   No
> **Sample**:

```
<P WIDTH=250>
```

Other Attributes

This tag also accepts the `lang`, `dir`, `onClick`, `onDblClick`, `onMouseDown`, `onMouseUp`, `onMouseOver`, `onMouseMove`, `onMouseOut`, `onKeyPress`, `onKeyDown`, and `onKeyUp` attributes. See the Element-Independent Attributes section of this reference for definitions and examples.

<PARAM>

Specifies parameters passed to an embedded object. Use the <PARAM> tag within the <OBJECT> or <APPLET> tags.

> **Standard**:   HTML 4
> **Common**:   No
> **Paired**:   No
> **Sample**:

```
<OBJECT CLASSID="/thingie.py">
<PARAM NAME="thing" VALUE=1>
Sorry. Your browser does not support
embedded objects.
</OBJECT>
```

Attribute Information

DATAFLD="..."

Selects a column from a block of tabular data.

> **Standard**:   Internet Explorer 4
> **Common**:   No
> **Sample**:

```
<PARAM DATA="dataview.ocx"
DATASRC="#data_table"
DATAFLD="datafld1">
```

DATASRC="..."

Specifies the location of tabular data to be bound within the document.

> **Standard**:   Internet Explorer 4
> **Common**:   No
> **Sample**:

```
<PARAM DATA="dataview.ocx"
DATASRC="#data_table">
```

NAME="..."

Indicates the name of the parameter passed to the embedded object.

> **Standard**:   HTML 4
> **Common**:   No
> **Sample**:

```
<PARAM NAME="startyear" VALUE="1920">
```

TITLE="..."

Specifies text assigned to the tag. You might use this attribute for context-sensitive help within the document. Browsers may use this to show tool tips.

> **Standard**:   HTML 4
> **Common**:   No
> **Sample**:

```
<PARAM TITLE="Object parameter"
NAME="size" VALUE="0">
```

TYPE="..."

Specifies the MIME type of the data found at the specified URL. Use this attribute with the VALUETYPE=REF attribute.

> **Standard**:   HTML 44
> **Common**:   No
> **Sample**:

```
<PARAM NAME="data"
VALUE="/data/sim1.zip"
VALUETYPE=REF
TYPE="application/x-zip-compressed">
```

VALUE="..."

Specifies the value associated with the parameter passed to the embedded object.

> **Standard**:   HTML 4
> **Common**:   No
> **Sample**:

```
<PARAM NAME="startyear" VALUE="1920">
```

VALUETYPE={REF, OBJECT, DATA}

Indicates the kind of value passed to the embedded object. VALUETYPE=REF indicates a URL passed to the embedded object. VALUETYPE=OBJECT indicates that the VALUE attribute specifies the location of object data. VALUETYPE=DATA indicates that the VALUE= attribute is set to a plain text string. Use this for passing alphanumeric data to the embedded object.

Standard: Internet Explorer 3, HTML 4
Common: No
Sample:

```
<PARAM NAME="length" VALUE="9"
VALUETYPE=DATA>
```

\<PLAINTEXT\>

Specifies that text appears as preformatted. This tag is obsolete; the \<PRE\> tags has replaced it.

Standard: Obsolete
Common: No
Paired: Yes
Sample:

```
<PLAINTEXT>Now go to the store and buy:
Wrapping paper
Tape
Markers
</PLAINTEXT>
```

\<PRE\>

Contains preformatted plain text. This is useful for including computer program output or source code within your document.

Standard: HTML 2
Common: Yes
Paired: Yes
Sample:

```
Here's the source code:
<PRE>
#include <stdio.h>
void main()
{
   printf("Hello World!\n");
}
</PRE>
```

Attribute Information

CLASS="..."

Indicates which style class applies to the \<PRE\> element.

Standard: HTML 4
Common: No
Sample:

```
<PRE CLASS="casual">BBQ INFO</PRE>
```

ID="..."

Assigns a unique ID selector to an instance of the \<PRE\> tag. When you then assign a style to that ID selector, it affects only that one instance of the \<PRE\> tag.

Standard: HTML 4
Common: No
Sample:

```
An example of an emotion:
<PRE ID="123">
  :-)
</PRE>
```

STYLE="..."

Specifies Style Sheet commands that apply to the contents within the \<PRE\> tags.

Standard: HTML 4
Common: Yes
Sample:

```
<PRE STYLE="background : red">
```

TITLE="..."

Specifies text assigned to the tag. You might use this attribute for context-sensitive help within the document. Browsers may use this to show tool tips over the preformatted text.

Standard: HTML 4
Common: No
Sample:

```
<PRE TITLE="preformatted text">
```

WIDTH="*n*"

Specifies the horizontal dimension of the pre-formatted text (in pixels).

> **Standard**: HTML 4
> **Common**: No
> **Sample**:

```
<PRE WIDTH=80>
```

Other Attributes

This tag also accepts the lang, dir, onClick, onDblClick, onMouseDown, onMouseUp, onMouseOver, onMouseMove, onMouseOut, onKeyPress, onKeyDown, and onKeyUp attributes. See the Element-Independent Attributes section of this reference for definitions and examples.

<Q>

Quotes a direct source within a paragraph. Use <BLOCKQUOTE> to signify only a longer or block quotation.

> **Standard**: HTML 4
> **Common**: No
> **Paired**: Yes
> **Sample**:

```
Dr. Henry remarked
<Q>I really like the procedure.</Q>
```

Attribute Information

CITE="..."

Specifies a reference URL for a quotation.

> **Standard**: HTML 4
> **Common**: No
> **Sample**:

```
<BLOCKQUOTE
CITE="http://www.clement.moore.com/
xmas.html">
Twas the night..."
</BLOCKQUOTE>
```

CLASS="..."

Indicates which style class applies to the <BLOCKQUOTE> element.

> **Standard**: HTML 4
> **Common**: No
> **Sample**:

```
<BLOCKQUOTE CLASS="casual">
Twas the night before
Christmas...</BLOCKQUOTE>
```

ID="..."

Assigns a unique ID selector to an instance of the <BLOCKQUOTE> tag. When you then assign a style to that ID selector, it affects only that one instance of the <BLOCKQUOTE> tag.

> **Standard**: HTML 4
> **Common**: No
> **Sample**:

```
On July 12, John wrote a profound
sentence in his diary:
<BLOCKQUOTE ID="123">I woke up this
morning at nine and it was raining.
</BLOCKQUOTE>
```

STYLE="..."

Specifies Style Sheet commands that apply to the contents within the <BLOCKQUOTE> tags.

> **Standard**: HTML 4
> **Common**: No
> **Sample**:

```
<BLOCKQUOTE STYLE="background: red">
```

TITLE="..."

Specifies text assigned to the tag. You might use this attribute for context-sensitive help within the document. Browsers may use this to show tool tips over the quoted text.

> **Standard**: HTML 4
> **Common**: No
> **Sample**:

```
<BLOCKQUOTE TITLE="Quotation">
```

Other Attributes

This tag also accepts the lang, dir, onClick, onDblClick, onMouseDown, onMouseUp, onMouseOver, onMouseMove, onMouseOut, onKeyPress, onKeyDown, and onKeyUp attributes. See the Element-Independent Attributes section of this reference for definitions and examples.

<SAMP>

Indicates a sequence of literal characters.

Standard: HTML 2
Common: Yes
Paired: Yes
Sample:

An example of a palindrome is the word <SAMP>TOOT</SAMP>.

Attribute Information

CLASS="..."

Indicates which style class applies to the <SAMP> element.

Standard: HTML 4
Common: No
Sample:

The PC screen read:
<SAMP CLASS="casual">Command Not Found </SAMP>

ID="..."

Assigns a unique ID selector to an instance of the <SAMP> tag. When you then assign a style to that ID selector, it affects only that one instance of the <SAMP> tag.

Standard: HTML 4
Common: No
Sample:

Just for fun, think of how many words end with the letters <SAMP ID="123">ing</SAMP>.

STYLE="..."

Specifies Style Sheet commands that apply to the contents within the <SAMP> tags.

Standard: HTML 4
Common: Yes
Sample:

<SAMP STYLE="background: red">

TITLE="..."

Specifies text assigned to the tag. You might use this attribute for context-sensitive help within the document. Browsers may use this to show tool tips.

Standard: HTML 4
Common: No
Sample:

<SAMP TITLE="Sample">

Other Attributes

This tag also accepts the lang, dir, onClick, onDblClick, onMouseDown, onMouseUp, onMouseOver, onMouseMove, onMouseOut, onKeyPress, onKeyDown, and onKeyUp attributes. See the Element-Independent Attributes section of this reference for definitions and examples.

<SCRIPT>

Contains browser script code. Examples include JavaScript and VBScript. It is a good idea to place the actual script code within the comment tags so that browsers that don't support the <SCRIPT> tag code can ignore it.

Standard: HTML 3.2
Common: Yes
Paired: Yes
Sample:

```
<SCRIPT LANGUAGE="JavaScript">
<!- . . . ->
</SCRIPT>
```

Attribute Information

LANGUAGE="..."

Indicates the type of script.

> **Standard**: HTML 4, Internet Explorer
> **Common**: Yes
> **Sample**:

```
<SCRIPT LANGUAGE="JavaScript">
```

SRC="*URL*"

Specifies the relative or absolute location of a script to include in the document.

> **Standard**: HTML 4, Internet Explorer
> **Common**: Yes
> **Sample**:

```
<SCRIPT type="text/javascript"
SRC="http://www.some.com/sc/script.js">
</SCRIPT>
```

TYPE="..."

Indicates the MIME type of the script. This is an alternative to the langUAGE tag for declaring the type of scripting.

> **Standard**: HTML 3.2
> **Common**: Yes
> **Sample**:

```
<SCRIPT type="text/javascript">
 document.write ("<EM>Great!<\/EM>")
</SCRIPT>
```

<SELECT>

Specifies a selection list within a form. Use the <OPTION> tags to specify items in the selection list.

> **Standard**: HTML 2
> **Common**: Yes
> **Paired**: Yes
> **Sample**:

```
What do you use our product for?<BR>
<SELECT MULTIPLE NAME="use">
  <OPTION VALUE=1>Pest control
  <OPTION VALUE=2>Automotive lubricant
  <OPTION VALUE=3>Preparing pastries
  <OPTION SELECTED VALUE=4>Personal
hygiene
  <OPTION VALUE=5>Other
</SELECT>
```

Attribute Information

ACCESSKEY="..."

Indicates a keystroke sequence associated with the selection list.

> **Standard**: HTML 4
> **Common**: No
> **Sample**:

```
<SELECT NAME="size" ACCESSKEY=S>
```

CLASS="..."

Indicates which style class applies to the element.

> **Standard**: HTML 4
> **Common**: No
> **Sample**:

```
<SELECT NAME="color" CLASS="casual">
```

DATAFLD="..."

Indicates a column from previously identified tabular data.

> **Standard**: Internet Explorer 4
> **Common**: No
> **Sample**:

```
<SELECT NAME="color"
DATASRC="#data_table" DATAFLD="clr">
```

DISABLED

Denies access to the selection list.

> **Standard**: HTML 4
> **Common**: No
> **Sample**:

```
<SELECT NAME="color" DISABLED>
```

ID="..."

Assigns a unique ID selector to an instance of the <SELECT> tag. When you then assign a style to that ID selector, it affects only that one instance of the <SELECT> tag.

Standard:	Internet Explorer 4
Common:	No
Sample:	

```
<SELECT ID="123" NAME="salary">
```

MULTIPLE

Indicates that a visitor can select more than one selection list item at the same time.

Standard:	HTML 2
Common:	Yes
Sample:	

```
<SELECT MULTIPLE>
```

NAME="..."

Gives a name to the value you are passing to the form processor. This establishes a *name-value pair* with which the form processor application can work.

Standard:	HTML 2
Common:	Yes
Sample:	

```
What is your shoe size?
<SELECT SIZE=4 NAME="size">
  <OPTION>
  <OPTION>
  <OPTION>
  <OPTION>
  <OPTION>
  <OPTION>
</SELECT>
```

READONLY

Indicates that your visitor cannot modify values within the selection list.

Standard:	Internet Explorer 4
Common:	No
Sample:	

```
<SELECT NAME="color" READONLY>
```

SIZE="*n*"

Specifies the number of visible items in the selection list. If there are more items in the selection list than are visible, a scrollbar provides access to the other items.

Standard:	HTML 2
Common:	Yes
Sample:	

```
<SELECT SIZE=3>
```

STYLE="..."

Specifies Style Sheet commands that apply to the contents within the <SELECT> tags.

Standard:	HTML 4
Common:	Yes
Sample:	

```
<SELECT STYLE="background: red"
NAME="color">
```

TABINDEX="*n*"

Indicates where in the tabbing order the selection list is placed.

Standard:	HTML 4
Common:	No
Sample:	

```
<SELECT NAME="salary TABINDEX=3>
```

TITLE="..."

Specifies text assigned to the tag. You might use this attribute for context-sensitive help within the document. Browsers may use this to show tool tips over the selection list.

Standard:	HTML 4
Common:	No
Sample:	

```
<SELECT TITLE="Select List"
NAME="Car">
```

Other Attributes

This tag also accepts the lang, dir, onfocus, onblur, onchange, onselect, onClick, onDblClick, onMouseDown, onMouseUp, onMouseOver, onMouseMove, onMouseOut, onKeyPress, onKeyDown, and onKeyUp attributes. See the Element-Independent Attributes section of this reference for definitions and examples.

<SMALL>

Specifies text that should appear in a small font.

Standard:	HTML 3.2
Common:	Yes
Paired:	Yes
Sample:	

```
<P>Our lawyers said we need to include
some small print:
<P><SMALL>By reading this document,
you are breaking the rules and will
be assessed a $2000 fine.</SMALL>
```

Attribute Information

CLASS="..."

Indicates which style class applies to the <SMALL> element.

Standard:	HTML 4
Common:	No
Sample:	

```
<SMALL CLASS="casual">Void where
prohibited</SMALL>
```

ID="..."

Assigns a unique ID selector to an instance of the <SMALL> tag. When you then assign a style to that ID selector, it affects only that one instance of the <SMALL> tag.

Standard:	HTML 4
Common:	No
Sample:	

```
Most insects are <SMALL ID="123">
small</SMALL>.
```

STYLE="..."

Specifies Style Sheet commands that apply to the contents within the <SMALL> tags.

Standard:	HTML 4
Common:	Yes
Sample:	

```
<SMALL STYLE="background: red">
```

TITLE="..."

Specifies text assigned to the tag. You might use this attribute for context-sensitive help within the document. Browsers may use this to show tool tips over the text inside the <SMALL> tags.

Standard:	HTML 4
Common:	No
Sample:	

```
<SMALL TITLE="Legalese">Actually doing
any of this will subject you to
risk of criminal prosecution.</SMALL>
```

Other Attributes

This tag also accepts the lang, dir, onClick, onDblClick, onMouseDown, onMouseUp, onMouseOver, onMouseMove, onMouseOut, onKeyPress, onKeyDown, and onKeyUp attributes. See the Element-Independent Attributes section of this reference for definitions and examples.

<SPACER>

A Netscape-specific tag that specifies a blank space within the document. We recommend using Style Sheets or other formatting techniques unless you're developing documents exclusively for visitors using Netscape Navigator.

Standard:	Netscape Navigator 4
Common:	No
Paired:	No
Sample:	

```
<SPACER TYPE=HORIZONTAL SIZE=150>
Doctors Prefer MediWidget 4 to 1
```

Attribute Information

SIZE="n"

Specifies the dimension of the spacer (in pixels).

Standard:	Netscape Navigator 3
Common:	No
Sample:	

```
<SPACER TYPE=HORIZONTAL SIZE=50>
<IMG SRC="rosebush.jpg">
```

TYPE={HORIZONTAL, VERTICAL}

Indicates whether the spacer measures from left to right or from top to bottom.

Standard: Netscape Navigator 3
Common: No
Sample:

```
<P>After you've done this, take
a moment to review your work.
<SPACER TYPE=VERTICAL SIZE=400>
<P>Now, isn't that better?
```

<SPAN>

Defines an inline section of a document affected by Style Sheet attributes. Use <DIV> to apply styles at the block element level.

Standard: HTML 4
Common: No
Paired: Yes
Sample:

```
<SPAN STYLE="background: red">...</SPAN>
```

Attribute Information

CLASS="..."

Indicates which style class applies to the <SPAN> element.

Standard: HTML 4
Common: No
Sample:

```
<SPAN CLASS="casual">
```

DATAFLD="..."

Selects a column from a previously identified source of tabular data (see the DATASRC= attribute).

Standard: Internet Explorer 4
Common: No
Sample:

```
<SPAN DATASRC="#data_table">
  <SPAN DATAFLD="name"></SPAN>
</SPAN>
```

DATAFORMATAS={TEXT, HTML, NONE}

Indicates the format of tabular data within the <SPAN> element.

Standard: Internet Explorer 4
Common: No
Sample:

```
<SPAN DATAFORMATAS=HTML
DATASRC="#data_table">
```

DATASRC="..."

Specifies the source of data for data binding.

Standard: Internet Explorer 4
Common: No
Sample:

```
<SPAN DATASRC="#data_table">
```

ID="..."

Assigns a unique ID selector to an instance of the <SPAN> tag. When you then assign a style to that ID selector, it affects only that one instance of the <SPAN> tag.

Standard: HTML 4
Common: No
Sample:

```
<SPAN ID="123">
```

STYLE="..."

Specifies Style Sheet commands that apply to the contents within the <SPAN> tags.

Standard: HTML 4
Common: No
Sample:

```
<SPAN STYLE="background: red">
```

TITLE="..."

Specifies text assigned to the tag. You might use this attribute for context-sensitive help within the document. Browsers may use this to show tool tips.

Standard: HTML 4
Common: No
Sample:

```
<SPAN TITLE="Section"
STYLE="background: red">
```

Other Attributes

This tag also accepts the `lang`, `dir`, `onClick`, `onDblClick`, `onMouseDown`, `onMouseUp`, `onMouseOver`, `onMouseMove`, `onMouseOut`, `onKeyPress`, `onKeyDown`, and `onKeyUp` attributes. See the Element-Independent Attributes section of this reference for definitions and examples.

<STRIKE>, <S>

Indicate a strikethrough text style.

Standard: HTML 3.2; deprecated in HTML 4 in favor of Style Sheets
Common: Yes
Paired: Yes
Sample:

```
My junior high biology teacher was
<STRIKE>sorta</STRIKE> really smart.
```

Attribute Information

CLASS="..."

Indicates which style class applies to the <STRIKE> element.

Standard: HTML 4
Common: No
Sample:

```
<STRIKE CLASS="casual">Truman</STRIKE> lost.
```

ID="..."

Assigns a unique ID selector to an instance of the <STRIKE> tag. When you then assign a style to that ID selector, it affects only that one instance of the <STRIKE> tag.

Standard: HTML 4
Common: No
Sample:

```
Don <STRIKE ID="123">ain't</STRIKE>
isn't coming tonight.
```

STYLE="..."

Specifies Style Sheet commands that apply to the contents within the <STRIKE> tags.

Standard: HTML 4
Common: No
Sample:

```
<STRIKE STYLE="background: red">
```

TITLE="..."

Specifies text assigned to the tag. You might use this attribute for context-sensitive help within the document. Browsers may use this to show tool tips over the text.

Standard: HTML 4
Common: No
Sample:

```
He was <STRIKE TITLE="omit">Ambitious
</STRIKE><B>Enthusiastic</B>.
```

Other Attributes

This tag also accepts the `lang`, `dir`, `onClick`, `onDblClick`, `onMouseDown`, `onMouseUp`, `onMouseOver`, `onMouseMove`, `onMouseOut`, `onKeyPress`, `onKeyDown`, and `onKeyUp` attributes. See the Element-Independent Attributes section of this reference for definitions and examples.

<STRONG>

Indicates strong emphasis. The browser will probably display the text in a boldface font.

Standard: HTML 2
Common: Yes
Paired: Yes
Sample:

```
If you see a poisonous spider in the room
then <STRONG>Get out of there!</STRONG>
```

Attribute Information

CLASS="..."

Indicates which style class applies to the <STRONG> element.

Standard: HTML 4
Common: No
Sample:

```
Did you say my dog is
<STRONG CLASS="casual">DEAD?!</STRONG>
```

ID="…"

Assigns a unique ID selector to an instance of the <STRONG> tag. When you then assign a style to that ID selector, it affects only that one instance of the <STRONG> tag.

Standard: HTML 4
Common: No
Sample:

```
Sure, you can win at gambling. But
it's more likely you will
<STRONG ID="123">lose</STRONG>.
```

STYLE="…"

Specifies Style Sheet commands that apply to the contents within the <STRONG> tags.

Standard: HTML 4
Common: No
Sample:

```
<STRONG STYLE="background: red">
```

TITLE="…"

Specifies text assigned to the tag. You might use this attribute for context-sensitive help within the document. Browsers may use this to show tool tips over the emphasized text.

Standard: HTML 4
Common: No
Sample:

```
I mean it was <STRONG TITLE="emphasis">
HOT!</STRONG>
```

Other Attributes

This tag also accepts the lang, dir, onClick, onDblClick, onMouseDown, onMouseUp, onMouseOver, onMouseMove, onMouseOut, onKeyPress, onKeyDown, and onKeyUp attributes. See the Element-Independent Attributes section of this reference for definitions and examples.

<STYLE>

Contains Style Sheet definitions and appears in the document head (see the <HEAD> tag). Place Style Sheet data within the comment tags (<!--… -->) to accommodate browsers that do not support the <STYLE> tag.

Standard: HTML 3.2
Common: No
Paired: Yes
Sample:

```
<HTML>
<HEAD>
<TITLE>Edible Socks: Good or Bad?</TITLE>
<STYLE TYPE="text/css">
<!--
  @import url(http://www.raycomm.com/mhtml/
styles.css)
  H1 { background: black; color: yellow }
  LI DD { background: silver; color:
black }
-->
</STYLE>
</HEAD>
```

Attribute Information

MEDIA="…"

Specifies the destination medium for style information. It may be a single type or a comma-separated list. Media types include the following:

Screen—for online viewing (default setting).
Print—for traditional printed material and for documents on screen viewed in print preview mode.
Projection—for projectors.
Braille—for Braille tactile feedback devices
Speech—for a speech synthesizer.
All—applies to all devices.

Standard: HTML 4
Common: No
Sample:

```
<HEAD>
<TITLE>Washington DC Taverns</TITLE>
<STYLE TYPE="text/css" MEDIA="all">
<!--
```

```
   @import url(Error! Bookmark not defined.
   H1 { background: black; color: white}
   LI DD { background: silver; color:
darkgreen }
-->
</STYLE>
</HEAD>
```

TITLE="..."

Specifies text assigned to the tag. You might use this attribute for context-sensitive help within the document. Browsers may use this to show tool tips.

Standard:	HTML 4
Common:	No
Sample:	

```
<STYLE TITLE="Stylesheet 1"TYPE="text/css">
<!-- H1 { background: black; color:
yellow }
   LI DD { background: silver; color:
black }
-->
</SCRIPT>
```

TYPE="..."

Specifies the MIME type of the Style Sheet specification standard used.

Standard:	HTML 4
Common:	No
Sample:	

```
<HEAD>
<TITLE>Washington DC Taverns</TITLE>
<STYLE TYPE="text/css">
<!--
   @import url(Error! Bookmark not defined.
   H1 { background: black; color: white}
   LI DD { background: silver; color:
darkgreen }
-->
</STYLE>
</HEAD>
```

Other Attributes

This tag also accepts the lang and dir attributes. See the Element-Independent Attributes section of this reference for definitions and examples.

<SUB>

Indicates subscript text.

Standard:	HTML 3.2
Common:	Yes
Paired:	Yes
Sample:	

```
<P>Chemists refer to water as
H<SUB>2</SUB>O.
```

Attribute Information

CLASS="..."

Indicates which style class applies to the <SUB> element.

Standard:	HTML 4
Common:	No
Sample:	

```
<SUB CLASS="casual">2</SUB>
```

ID="..."

Assigns a unique ID selector to an instance of the <SUB> tag. When you then assign a style to that ID selector, it affects only that one instance of the <SUB> tag.

Standard:	HTML 4
Common:	No
Sample:	

```
. . . At the dentist I ask for lots of
NO<SUB ID="123">2</SUB>.
```

STYLE="..."

Specifies Style Sheet commands that apply to the contents within the <SUB> tags.

Standard:	HTML 4
Common:	No
Sample:	

```
<SUB STYLE="background: red">
```

TITLE="..."

Specifies text assigned to the tag. You might use this attribute for context-sensitive help within the document. Browsers may use this to show tool tips over the subscripted text.

Standard: HTML 4
Common: No
Sample:

```
Before he died, he uttered, "Groovy."
<SUB TITLE="Footnote">2</SUB>
```

Other Attributes

This tag also accepts the lang, dir, onClick, onDblClick, onMouseDown, onMouseUp, onMouseOver, onMouseMove, onMouseOut, onKeyPress, onKeyDown, and onKeyUp attributes. See the Element-Independent Attributes section of this reference for definitions and examples.

<SUP>

Indicates superscript text.

Standard: HTML 3.2
Common: Yes
Paired: Yes
Sample:

```
<P>Einstein's most famous equation is
probably E=mc<SUP>2</SUP>.
```

Attribute Information

CLASS="..."

Indicates which style class applies to the <SUP> element.

Standard: HTML 4
Common: No
Sample:

```
<STYLE>
<!--
  SUP.casual {background: black;
    color: yellow}
-->
</STYLE>
. . .
z<SUP CLASS="casual">2</SUP> =
x<SUP CLASS="casual">2</SUP> +
y<SUP CLASS="casual">2</SUP>
```

ID="..."

Assigns a unique ID selector to an instance of the <PRE> tag. When you then assign a style to that ID selector, it affects only that one instance of the <SUP> tag.

Standard: HTML 4
Common: No
Sample:

```
<STYLE>
<!--
  #123 {background: black;
    color: yellow}
-->
</STYLE>
. . . Pythagorean theorem says
z<SUP ID="123">2</SUP>=4+16.
```

STYLE="..."

Specifies Style Sheet commands that apply to the contents within the <SUP> tags.

Standard: HTML 4
Common: No
Sample:

```
<SUP STYLE="background: red">
```

TITLE="..."

Specifies text assigned to the tag. You might use this attribute for context-sensitive help within the document. Browsers may use this to show tool tips over the superscripted text.

Standard: HTML 4
Common: No
Sample:

```
x<SUP TITLE="Exponent">2</SUP>
```

Other Attributes

This tag also accepts the lang, dir, onClick, onDblClick, onMouseDown, onMouseUp, onMouseOver, onMouseMove, onMouseOut, onKeyPress, onKeyDown, and onKeyUp attributes. See the Element-Independent Attributes section of this reference for definitions and examples.

<TABLE>

Specifies a container for a table within your document. Inside these tags you can place <TR>, <TD>, <TH>, <CAPTION>, and other <TABLE> tags.

Standard: HTML 3.2
Common: Yes
Paired: Yes
Sample:

```
<TABLE BORDER=0>  <TR>
   <TD><IMG SRC="Pine.jpg"
BORDER=0 ALT="Pine"></TD>
   <TD VALIGN=MIDDLE><P>Pine trees
naturally grow at higher elevations.
   They require less water and do not shed
leaves in the fall.</TD>  </TR>
</TABLE>
```

Attribute Information

ALIGN={LEFT, CENTER, RIGHT}

Positions the table flush left, flush right, or in the center of the window.

Standard: HTML 3.2
Common: Yes
Sample:

```
<TABLE ALIGN=CENTER>
```

BACKGROUND="*URL*"

Specifies the relative or absolute location of a graphic image file loaded as a background image for the entire table.

Standard: Internet Explorer 3, Netscape Navigator 4
Common: No
Sample:

```
<TABLE BACKGROUND="paper.jpg">
```

BGCOLOR="#*RRGGBB*" or "..."

Specifies the background color within all table cells in the table. You can substitute color names for the hexadecimal RGB values.

Standard: Deprecated in HTML 4 in favor of Style Sheets
Common: No
Sample:

```
<TABLE BGCOLOR="Peach">
```

BORDER="*n*"

Specifies the thickness (in pixels) of borders around each table cell. Use a value of 0 to produce a table with no visible borders.

Standard: HTML 3.2
Common: Yes
Sample:

```
<TABLE BORDER=0>
```

BORDERCOLOR="#*RRGGBB*" or "..."

Specifies the color of the borders of all the table cells in the table. You can substitute color names for the hexadecimal RGB values.

Standard: Internet Explorer 3.0
Common: No
Sample:

```
<TABLE BORDERCOLOR=#3F9A11>
```

BORDERCOLORDARK="#*RRGGBB*" or "..."

Specifies the darker color used to draw 3-D borders around the table cells. You can substitute color names for the hexadecimal RGB values.

Standard: Internet Explorer 4
Common: No
Sample:

```
<TABLE BORDERCOLORDARK="silver">
```

BORDERCOLORLIGHT="#*RRGGBB*" or "..."

Specifies the lighter color used to draw 3-D borders around the table cells. You can substitute color names for the hexadecimal RGB values.

Standard: Internet Explorer 4
Common: No
Sample:

```
<TABLE BORDERCOLORDARK="white">
```

CELLPADDING="*n*"

Specifies the space (in pixels) between the edges of table cells and their contents.

Standard: HTML 3.2
Common: Yes
Sample:

```
<TABLE CELLPADDING=5>
```

CELLSPACING="*n*"

Specifies the space (in pixels) between the borders of table cells and the borders of adjacent cells.

Standard: HTML 3.2
Common: Yes
Sample:

```
<TABLE BORDER=2 CELLSPACING=5>
```

CLASS="..."

Indicates which style class applies to the <TABLE> element.

Standard: HTML 4
Common: No
Sample:

```
<TABLE CLASS="casual" BORDER=2>
```

COLS="*n*"

Specifies the number of columns in the table.

Standard: HTML 4
Common: No
Sample:

```
<TABLE BORDER=2 COLS=5>
```

FRAME={VOID, BORDER, ABOVE, BELOW, HSIDES, LHS, RHS, VSIDES, BOX}

Specifies the external border lines around the table. For the FRAME= attribute to work, set the BORDER= attribute with a non-zero value.

FRAME=VOID indicates no border lines.

FRAME=BOX or FRAME=BORDER indicates border lines around the entire table. This is the default.

FRAME=ABOVE specifies a border line along the top edge.

FRAME=BELOW draws a border line along the bottom edge.

FRAME=HSIDES draws border lines along the top and bottom edges.

FRAME=LHS indicates a border line along the left side.

FRAME=RHS draws a border line along the right edge.

FRAME=VSIDES draws border lines along the left and right edges.

Standard: HTML 4
Common: No
Sample:

```
<TABLE BORDER=2 RULES=ALL FRAME=VSIDES>
```

ID="*n*"

Assigns a unique ID selector to an instance of the <TABLE> tag. When you then assign a style to that ID selector, it affects only that one instance of the <TABLE> tag.

Standard: HTML 4
Common: No
Sample:

```
<TABLE ID="123">
```

RULES={NONE, ROWS, COLS, GROUPS, ALL}

Specifies where rule lines appear inside the table. For the RULES= attribute to work, set the BORDER= attribute.

RULES=NONE indicates no rule lines.

RULES=ROWS indicates rule lines between rows.

RULES=COLS draws rule lines between columns.

RULES=ALL draws all possible rule lines.

RULES=GROUPS specifies rule lines between the groups defined by the <TFOOT>, <THEAD>, <TBODY>, and <COLGROUP> tags.

> **Standard:** HTML 4
> **Common:** No
> **Sample:**

```
<TABLE BORDER=2 RULES=BASIC>
```

STYLE="..."

Specifies Style Sheet commands that apply to the contents of cells in the table.

> **Standard:** HTML 4
> **Common:** No
> **Sample:**

```
<TABLE STYLE="background: red">
```

TITLE="..."

Specifies text assigned to the tag. You might use this attribute for context-sensitive help within the document. Browsers may use this to show tool tips over the table.

> **Standard:** HTML 4
> **Common:** No
> **Sample:**

```
<TABLE TITLE="Table">
```

WIDTH="*n*"

Specifies the width of the table. You can set this value to an absolute number of pixels or to a percentage amount so that the table is proportionally as wide as the available space.

> **Standard:** HTML 3.2
> **Common:** Yes
> **Sample:**

```
<TABLE ALIGN=CENTER WIDTH="60%">
```

Other Attributes

This tag also accepts the lang, dir, onClick, onDblClick, onMouseDown, onMouseUp, onMouseOver, onMouseMove, onMouseOut, onKeyPress, onKeyDown, and onKeyUp attributes. See the Element-Independent Attributes section of this reference for definitions and examples.

<TBODY>

Defines the table body within a table. This tag must *follow* the <TFOOT> tag.

> **Standard:** HTML 4
> **Common:** No
> **Paired:** Yes
> **Sample:**

```
<TABLE>
<THEAD>...
 </THEAD>
<TFOOT>...
 </TFOOT>
 <TBODY>...
 </TBODY>
```

Attribute Information

ALIGN="{LEFT, RIGHT, CENTER, JUSTIFY, CHAR}"

Specifies how text within the table footer will line up with the edges of the table cells, or if ALIGN=CHAR, on a specific character (the decimal point).

> **Standard**: HTML 4
> **Common**: Yes
> **Sample**:

```
<TR>
 <THEAD>
  <TH><B>Television</B></TH>
  <TH>
  <IMG SRC="tv.gif" ALT="TV" BORDER="0">
  </TH>
 </THEAD>
</TR>
```

CHAR="..."

Specifies the character on which cell contents will align, if ALIGN="CHAR". If you omit CHAR=, the default value is the decimal point in the specified language.

> **Standard**: HTML 4
> **Common**: No
> **Sample**:

```
<THEAD ALIGN="CHAR" CHAR=",">
```

CHAROFF="*n*"

Specifies the number of characters from the left at which the alignment character appears.

Standard: HTML 4
Common: No
Sample:

```
<THEAD ALIGN="CHAR" CHAR="," CHAROFF="7">
```

CLASS="..."

Indicates which style class applies to the <TBODY> element.

Standard: HTML 4
Common: No
Sample:

```
<TBODY CLASS="casual">
```

ID="*n*"

Assigns a unique ID selector to an instance of the <TBODY> tag. When you then assign a style to that ID selector, it affects only that one instance of the <TBODY> tag.

Standard: HTML 4
Common: No
Sample:

```
<TBODY ID="123">
```

STYLE="..."

Specifies Style Sheet commands that apply to the contents between the <TBODY>tags.

Standard: HTML 4
Common: No
Sample:

```
<TBODY STYLE="background: red">
```

TITLE="..."

Specifies text assigned to the tag. You might use this attribute for context-sensitive help within the document. Browsers may use this to show tool tips over the table body.

Standard: HTML 4
Common: No
Sample:

```
<TBODY TITLE="Table Body">
```

VALIGN={TOP, BOTTOM, MIDDLE, BASE-LINE}

Specifies the vertical alignment of the contents of the table body.

Standard: Internet Explorer 4
Common: No
Sample:

```
<TBODY VALIGN=MIDDLE>
```

Other Attributes

This tag also accepts the lang, dir, onClick, onDblClick, onMouseDown, onMouseUp, onMouseOver, onMouseMove, onMouseOut, onKeyPress, onKeyDown, and onKeyUp attributes. See the Element-Independent Attributes section of this reference for definitions and examples.

<TD>

Contains a table cell. These tags go inside the <TR> tags.

Standard: HTML 3.2
Common: Yes
Paired: Yes
Sample:

```
<TR>
 <TD>Bob Jones</TD>
 <TD>555-1212</TD>
 <TD>Democrat</TD>
</TR>
```

Attribute Information

AXIS="..."

Specifies an abbreviated cell name.

Standard: HTML 4
Common: No
Sample:

```
<TD AXIS="TV"><B>Television</B></TD>
```

AXES="..."

Lists AXIS values that pertain to the cell.

    Standard: HTML 4
    Common: No
    Sample:

```
<TD AXES="TV,
Programs"><B>Television</B></TD>
```

ALIGN={LEFT, RIGHT, CENTER, JUSTIFY, CHAR}

Specifies how text within the table header will line up with the edges of the table cells, or if ALIGN=CHAR, on a specific character (the decimal point).

    Standard: HTML 4
    Common: Yes
    Sample:

```
<TR>
  <TD><B>Television</B></TD>
  <TD>
  <IMG SRC="tv.gif" ALT="TV" BORDER=0>
  </TD>
</TR>
```

CHAR="..."

Specifies the character on which cell contents will align, if ALIGN="CHAR". If you omit CHAR=, the default value is the decimal point in the specified language.

    Standard: HTML 4
    Common: No
    Sample:

```
<TD ALIGN="CHAR" CHAR=",">
```

CHAROFF="n"

Specifies the number of characters from the left at which the alignment character appears.

    Standard: HTML 4
    Common: No
    Sample:

```
<TD ALIGN="CHAR" CHAR="," CHAROFF="7">
```

CLASS="..."

Indicates which style class applies to the <TD> element.

    Standard: HTML 4
    Common: No
    Sample:

```
<TD CLASS="casual">Jobs Produced</TD>
```

COLSPAN="n"

Specifies that a table cell occupy one column more than the default of one. This is useful when you have a category name that applies to more than one column of data.

    Standard: HTML 3.2
    Common: Yes
    Sample:

```
<TR><TD COLSPAN=2>Students</TD></TR>
<TR><TD>Bob Smith</TDH>
<TD>John Doe</TD>
</TR>
```

BACKGROUND="URL"

Specifies the relative or absolute location of a graphic image file for the browser to load as a background graphic for the table cell.

    Standard: Internet Explorer, Netscape Navigator
    Common: No
    Sample:

```
<TD BACKGROUND="waves.gif">
```

BGCOLOR="#RRGGBB" or "..."

Specifies the background color inside a table cell. You can substitute the hexadecimal RGB values for the appropriate color names.

    Standard: Deprecated in HTML 4 in favor of Style Sheets
    Common: No
    Sample:

```
<TR><TD BGCOLOR="Pink">Course Number</TD>
<TD BGCOLOR="Blue">Time taught</TD></TR>
```

BORDERCOLOR="#*RRGGBB*" or "..."

Indicates the color of the border of the table cell. You can specify the color with hexadecimal RGB values or by the color name.

Standard: Internet Explorer 2
Common: No
Sample:

```
<TR><TD BORDERCOLOR="Blue">
```

BORDERCOLORDARK="#*RRGGBB*" or "..."

Indicates the darker color used to form 3-D borders around the table cell. You can specify the color with its hexadecimal RGB values or with its color name.

Standard: Internet Explorer 4
Common: No
Sample:

```
<TD BORDERCOLORLIGHT=#FFFFFF
BORDERCOLORDARK=#88AA2C>
```

BORDERCOLORLIGHT="#*RRGGBB*" or "..."

Indicates the lighter color used to form 3-D borders around the table cell. You can specify the color with its hexadecimal RGB values or with its color name.

Standard: Internet Explorer 4
Common: No
Sample:

```
<TD BORDERCOLORLIGHT=#FFFFFF
BORDERCOLORDARK=#88AA2C>
```

ID="*n*"

Assigns a unique ID selector to an instance of the <TD> tag. When you then assign a style to that ID selector, it affects only that one instance of the <TD> tag.

Standard: HTML 4
Common: No
Sample:

```
<TD ID="123">
```

NOWRAP

Disables the default word-wrapping within a table cell, thus maximizing the amount of the cell's horizontal space.

Standard: Deprecated in HTML 4 in favor of Style Sheets
Common: No
Sample:

```
<TD NOWRAP>The contents of
this cell will not wrap at all</TD>
```

ROWSPAN="*n*"

Specifies that a table cell occupy more rows than the default of 1. This is useful when several rows of information are related to one category.

Standard: HTML 3.2
Common: Yes
Sample:

```
<TR><TD VALIGN=MIDDLE ALIGN=RIGHT
ROWSPAN=3>Pie Entries</TD>
<TD>Banana Cream</TD>
<TD>Mrs. Robinson</TD></TR>
<TR><TD>Strawberry Cheesecake</TD>
<TD>Mrs. Barton</TD></TR>
<TR><TD>German Chocolate</TD>
<TD>Mrs. Larson</TD></TR>
```

STYLE="..."

Specifies Style Sheet commands that apply to the contents of the table cell.

Standard: HTML 4
Common: No
Sample:

```
<TD STYLE="background: red">
```

TITLE="..."

Specifies text assigned to the tag. You might use this attribute for context-sensitive help within the document. Browsers may use this to show tool tips over the table header.

Standard: HTML 4
Common: No
Sample:

```
<TD TITLE="Table Cell Heading">
```

VALIGN={TOP, MIDDLE, BOTTOM, BASELINE}

Aligns the contents of a cell with the top, bottom, baseline, or middle of the cell.

Standard: HTML 3.2
Common: Yes
Sample:

```
<TD VALIGN=TOP><IMG SRC="images/bud.gif
BORDER=0></TD>
```

WIDTH="*n*"

Specifies the horizontal dimension of the cell in pixels or as a percentage of the table width.

Standard: HTML 3.2; not listed
in HTML 4
Common: Yes
Sample:

```
<TD WIDTH=200 ALIGN=LEFT><H2>African
Species</H2></TD>
```

Other Attributes

This tag also accepts the lang, dir, onClick, onDblClick, onMouseDown, onMouseUp, onMouseOver, onMouseMove, onMouseOut, onKeyPress, onKeyDown, and onKeyUp attributes. See the Element-Independent Attributes section of this reference for definitions and examples.

<TEXTAREA>

Defines a multiple-line text input field within a form. Place the <TEXTAREA> tags inside the <FORM> tags. To specify a default value in a <TEXTAREA> field, place the text between the <TEXTAREA> tags.

Standard: HTML 2
Common: Yes
Paired: Yes
Sample:

```
Enter any comments here:
<TEXTAREA NAME="comments" COLS=40
ROWS=5>
No Comments.
</TEXTAREA>
```

Attribute Information

ACCESSKEY="..."

Assigns a keystroke sequence to the <TEXTAREA> element.

Standard: HTML 4
Common: No
Sample:

```
<TEXTAREA COLS=40 ROWS=10 NAME="Story"
ACCESSKEY=S>
```

CLASS="..."

Indicates which style class applies to the <TEXTAREA> element.

Standard: HTML 4
Common: No
Sample:

```
<TEXTAREA CLASS="casual">
```

COLS="*n*"

Indicates the width (in character widths) of the text input field.

Standard: HTML 2
Common: Yes
Sample:

```
<TEXTAREA NAME="desc" COLS=50
ROWS=3></TEXTAREA>
```

DATAFLD="..."

Selects a column from a previously identified source of tabular data (see the DATASRC= attribute).

Standard: Internet Explorer 4
Common: No
Sample:

```
<TEXTAREA DATASRC="#data_table"
DATAFLD="name" NAME="st1">
```

DATASRC="..."

Specifies the source of data for data binding.

Standard: Internet Explorer 4
Common: No
Sample:

```
<TEXTAREA DATASRC="#data_table"
DATAFLD="name" NAME="st1">
```

DISABLED

Denies access to the text input field.

Standard: HTML 4
Common: No
Sample:

```
<TEXTAREA ROWS=10 COLS=10
NAME="Comments" DISABLED>
```

ID="*n*"

Assigns a unique ID selector to an instance of the <TEXTAREA> tag. When you then assign a style to that ID selector, it affects only that one instance of the <TEXTAREA> tag.

Standard: HTML 4
Common: No
Sample:

```
<TEXTAREA ID="123">
```

NAME="..."

Names the value you pass to the form processor. For example, if you collect personal feedback, assign the NAME= attribute something like "comments". This establishes a *name-value pair* with which the form processor can work.

Standard: HTML 2
Common: Yes
Sample:

```
<TEXTAREA COLS=30 ROWS=10
NAME="recipe"></TEXTAREA>
```

READONLY

Specifies that the visitor cannot change the contents of the text input field.

Standard: HTML 4
Common: No
Sample:

```
<TEXTAREA ROWS=10 COLS=10
NAME="Notes" READONLY>
```

ROWS="*n*"

Indicates the height (in lines of text) of the text input field.

Standard: HTML 2
Common: Yes
Sample:

```
<TEXTAREA NAME="desc" COLS=50
ROWS=3></TEXTAREA>
```

STYLE="..."

Specifies Style Sheet commands that apply to the <TEXTAREA> tag.

Standard: HTML 4
Common: No
Sample:

```
<TEXTAREA STYLE="background: red">
```

TABINDEX=*n*

Indicates where <TEXTAREA> appears in the tabbing order.

Standard: HTML 4
Common: No
Sample:

```
<TEXTAREA ROWS=5 COLS=40 NAME="story"
TABINDEX=2>
```

TITLE="..."

Specifies text assigned to the tag. You might use this attribute for context-sensitive help within the document. Browsers may use this to show tool tips over the text entry input method.

Standard: HTML 4
Common: No
Sample:

```
<TEXTAREA COLS=10 ROWS=2 NAME="tt"
TITLE="Text Entry Box">
```

Other Attributes

This tag also accepts the `lang`, `dir`, `onfocus`, `onblur`, `onchange`, `onselect`, `onClick`, `onDblClick`, `onMouseDown`, `onMouseUp`, `onMouseOver`, `onMouseMove`, `onMouseOut`, `onKeyPress`, `onKeyDown`, and `onKeyUp` attributes. See the Element-Independent Attributes section of this reference for definitions and examples.

<TFOOT>

Defines a table footer within a table. It must *precede* the <TBODY> tag.

Standard: HTML 4
Common: No
Paired: Yes
Sample:

```
<TFOOT>
<TR>
<TD>Totals</TD><TD>$100.25</TD></TR>
</TFOOT>
</TABLE>
```

Attribute Information

ALIGN={LEFT, RIGHT, CENTER, JUSTIFY, CHAR}

Specifies how text within the table footer will line up with the edges of the table cells, or if ALIGN=CHAR, on a specific character (the decimal point).

Standard: HTML 4
Common: Yes
Sample:

```
<TR>
 <THEAD>
  <TH><B>Television</B></TH>
  <TH>
  <IMG SRC="tv.gif" ALT="TV" BORDER=0>
  </TH>
 </THEAD>
</TR>
```

CHAR="..."

Specifies the character on which cell contents will align, if ALIGN="CHAR". If you omit CHAR=, the default value is the decimal point in the specified language.

Standard: HTML 4
Common: No
Sample:

```
<THEAD ALIGN="CHAR" CHAR=",">
```

CHAROFF="*n*"

Specifies the number of characters from the left at which the alignment character appears.

Standard: HTML 4
Common: No
Sample:

```
<THEAD ALIGN="CHAR" CHAR="," CHAROFF="7">
```

CLASS="..."

Indicates which style class applies to the <TFOOT> element.

Standard: HTML 4
Common: No
Sample:

```
<TFOOT CLASS="casual">
```

ID="*n*"

Assigns a unique ID selector to an instance of the <TFOOT> tag. When you then assign a style to that ID selector, it affects only that one instance of the <TFOOT> tag.

Standard: HTML 4
Common: No
Sample:

```
<TFOOT ID="123">
```

STYLE="..."

Specifies Style Sheet commands that apply to the contents between the <TFOOT> tags.

Standard: HTML 4
Common: No
Sample:

```
<TFOOT STYLE="background: red">
```

TITLE="..."

Specifies text assigned to the tag. You might use this attribute for context-sensitive help within the document. Browsers may use this to show tool tips over the table footer.

Standard: HTML 4
Common: No
Sample:

```
<TFOOT TITLE="Table Footer">
```

VALIGN={TOP, BOTTOM, MIDDLE, BASELINE}

Aligns the contents of the table footer with the top, bottom, or middle of the footer container.

    Standard: Internet Explorer 4
    Common: No
    Sample:

```
<TFOOT ALIGN=CENTER VALIGN=TOP>
```

Other Attributes

This tag also accepts the `lang`, `dir`, `onClick`, `onDblClick`, `onMouseDown`, `onMouseUp`, `onMouseOver`, `onMouseMove`, `onMouseOut`, `onKeyPress`, `onKeyDown`, and `onKeyUp` attributes. See the Element-Independent Attributes section of this reference for definitions and examples.

<TH>

Contains table cell headings. The `<TH>` tags are identical to the `<TD>` tags except that text inside `<TH>` is usually emphasized with bold-face font and centered within the cell.

    Standard: HTML 3.2
    Common: Yes
    Paired: Yes, optional
    Sample:

```
<TABLE>
<TH>Name</TH><TH>Phone No</TH>
<TD>John Doe</TD><TD>555-1212</TD>
<TD>Bob Smith</TD><TD>555-2121</TD>
</TABLE>
```

Attribute Information

AXIS="..."

Specifies an abbreviated cell name.

    Standard: HTML 4
    Common: No
    Sample:

```
<TH AXIS="TV"><B>Television</B></TH>
```

AXES="..."

Lists AXIS values that pertain to the cell.

    Standard: HTML 4
    Common: No
    Sample:

```
<TH AXES="TV,
Programs"><B>Television</B></TH>
```

ALIGN={LEFT, RIGHT, CENTER, JUSTIFY, CHAR}

Specifies how text within the table header will line up with the edges of the table cells, or if `ALIGN=CHAR`, on a specific character (the decimal point).

    Standard: HTML 4
    Common: Yes
    Sample:

```
<TR>
  <TH><B>Television</B></TH>
  <TH>
  <IMG SRC="tv.gif" ALT="TV" BORDER=0>
  </TH>
</TR>
```

CHAR="..."

Specifies the character on which cell contents align, if `ALIGN="CHAR"`. If you omit `CHAR=`, the default value is the decimal point in the specified language.

    Standard: HTML 4
    Common: No
    Sample:

```
<TH ALIGN="CHAR" CHAR=",">
```

CHAROFF="*n*"

Specifies the number of characters from the left at which the alignment character appears.

    Standard: HTML 4
    Common: No
    Sample:

```
<TH ALIGN="CHAR" CHAR="," CHAROFF="7">
```

BACKGROUND="*URL*"

Specifies the relative or absolute location of a graphic image file for the browser to load as a background graphic for the table cell.

Standard: Internet Explorer, Netscape Navigator
Common: No
Sample:

```
<TH BACKGROUND="waves.gif">
```

BGCOLOR="*#RRGGBB*" or "..."

Specifies the background color inside a table cell. You can substitute the hexadecimal RGB values for the appropriate color names.

Standard: Deprecated in HTML 4 in favor of Style Sheets
Common: No
Sample:

```
<TR><TH BGCOLOR="Pink">Course Number</TH>
<TH BGCOLOR="Blue">Time taught</TH></TR>
```

BORDERCOLOR="*#RRGGBB*" or "..."

Indicates the color of the border of the table cell. You can specify the color with hexadecimal RGB values or by the color name.

Standard: Internet Explorer 2
Common: No
Sample:

```
<TR><TH BORDERCOLOR="Blue">
```

BORDERCOLORDARK="*#RRGGBB*" or "..."

Indicates the darker color used to form 3-D borders around the table cell. You can specify the color with its hexadecimal RGB values or with its color name.

Standard: Internet Explorer 4
Common: No
Sample:

```
<TH BORDERCOLORLIGHT=#FFFFFF
BORDERCOLORDARK=#88AA2C>
```

BORDERCOLORLIGHT="*#RRGGBB*" or "..."

Indicates the lighter color used to form 3-D borders around the table cell. You can specify the color with its hexadecimal RGB values or with its color name.

Standard: Internet Explorer 4
Common: No
Sample:

```
<TH BORDERCOLORLIGHT=#FFFFFF
BORDERCOLORDARK=#88AA2C>
```

CLASS="..."

Indicates which style class applies to the <TH> element.

Standard: HTML 4
Common: No
Sample:

```
<TH CLASS="casual">Jobs Produced</TH>
```

COLSPAN="*n*"

Specifies that a table cell occupy more columns than the default of one. This is useful if a category name applies to more than one column of data.

Standard: HTML 3.2
Common: Yes
Sample:

```
<TR><TH COLSPAN=2>Students</TH></TR>
<TR><TD>Bob Smith</TDH>
<TD>John Doe</TD>
</TR>
```

ID="*n*"

Assigns a unique ID selector to an instance of the <TH> tag. When you then assign a style to that ID selector, it affects only that one instance of the <TH> tag.

Standard: HTML 4
Common: No
Sample:

```
<TH ID="123">
```

NOWRAP

Disables default word-wrapping within a table cell, maximizing the the cell's horizontal space.

Standard: Deprecated in HTML 4 in favor of Style Sheets.
Common: No
Sample:

```
<TH NOWRAP>The contents of
this cell will not wrap at all</TH>
```

ROWSPAN="*n*"

Specifies that a table cell occupy more rows than the default of 1. This is useful if several rows of information relate to one category.

Standard: HTML 3.2
Common: Yes
Sample:

```
<TR><TH VALIGN=MIDDLE ALIGN=RIGHT
ROWSPAN=3>Pie Entries</TH>
<TD>Banana Cream</TD>
<TD>Mrs. Robinson</TD></TR>
<TR><TD>Strawberry Cheesecake</TD>
<TD>Mrs. Barton</TD></TR>
<TR><TD>German Chocolate</TD>
<TD>Mrs. Larson</TD></TR>
```

STYLE="..."

Specifies Style Sheet commands that apply to the contents of the table cell.

Standard: HTML 4
Common: No
Sample:

```
<TH STYLE="background: red">
```

TITLE="..."

Specifies text assigned to the tag. You might use this attribute for context-sensitive help within the document. Browsers may use this to show tool tips over the table header.

Standard: HTML 4
Common: No
Sample:

```
<TH TITLE="Table Cell Heading">
```

VALIGN={TOP, MIDDLE, BOTTOM, BASELINE}

Aligns the contents of a cell with the top, bottom, baseline, or middle of the cell.

Standard: HTML 3.2
Common: Yes
Sample:

```
<TH VALIGN=TOP><IMG SRC="images/bud.gif
BORDER=0></TH>
```

WIDTH="*n*"

Specifies the horizontal dimension of the cell in pixels or as a percentage of the table width.

Standard: HTML 3.2; not listed in HTML 4
Common: Yes
Sample:

```
<TH WIDTH=200 ALIGN=LEFT><H2>African
Species</H2></TH>
```

Other Attributes

This tag also accepts the lang, dir, onClick, onDblClick, onMouseDown, onMouseUp, onMouseOver, onMouseMove, onMouseOut, onKeyPress, onKeyDown, and onKeyUp attributes. See the Element-Independent Attributes section of this reference for definitions and examples.

<THEAD>

Defines a table header section. At least one table row must go within <THEAD>.

Standard: HTML 4
Common: No
Paired: Yes
Sample:

```
<TABLE RULES=ROWS>
 <THEAD>
 <TR><TD>Column 1
<TD>Column 2
 </THEAD>
```

Attribute Information

ALIGN={LEFT, RIGHT, CENTER, JUSTIFY, CHAR}

Specifies how text within the table header will line up with the edges of the table cells, or if ALIGN=CHAR, on a specific character (the decimal point).

> **Standard**: HTML 4
> **Common**: Yes
> **Sample**:

```
<TR>
 <THEAD>
  <TH><B>Television</B></TH>
  <TH>
  <IMG SRC="tv.gif" ALT="TV" BORDER=0>
  </TH>
 </THEAD>
</TR>
```

CHAR="..."

Specifies the character on which cell contents align, if ALIGN="CHAR". If you omit CHAR=, the default value is the decimal point in the specified language.

> **Standard**: HTML 4
> **Common**: No
> **Sample**:

```
<THEAD ALIGN="CHAR" CHAR=",">
```

CHAROFF="n"

Specifies the number of characters from the left at which the alignment character appears.

> **Standard**: HTML 4
> **Common**: No
> **Sample**:

```
<THEAD ALIGN="CHAR" CHAR="," CHAROFF="7">
```

CLASS="..."

Indicates which style class applies to the <THEAD> element.

> **Standard**: HTML 4
> **Common**: No
> **Sample**:

```
<THEAD CLASS="casual">
```

ID="n"

Assigns a unique ID selector to an instance of the <THEAD> tag. When you then assign a style to that ID selector, it affects only that one instance of the <THEAD> tag.

> **Standard**: HTML 4
> **Common**: No
> **Sample**:

```
<THEAD ID="123">
```

STYLE="..."

Specifies Style Sheet commands that apply to the contents between the <THEAD> tags.

> **Standard**: HTML 4
> **Common**: No
> **Sample**:

```
<THEAD STYLE="background: red">
```

TITLE="..."

Specifies text assigned to the tag. You might use this attribute for context-sensitive help within the document. Browsers may use this to show tool tips over the table head.

> **Standard**: HTML 4
> **Common**: No
> **Sample**:

```
<THEAD TITLE="Table Heading">
```

VALIGN={TOP, MIDDLE, BOTTOM, BASELINE}

Aligns the contents of the table header with respect to the top and bottom edges of the header container.

> **Standard**: HTML 4
> **Common**: No
> **Sample**:

```
<THEAD ALIGN=LEFT VALIGN=TOP>
```

Other Attributes

This tag also accepts the lang, dir, onClick, onDblClick, onMouseDown, onMouseUp, onMouseOver, onMouseMove, onMouseOut, onKeyPress, onKeyDown, and onKeyUp attributes. See the Element-Independent Attributes section of this reference for definitions and examples.

<TITLE>

Gives the document an official title. The
<TITLE> tags appear inside the document
header inside the <HEAD> tags.

Standard: HTML 2
Common: Yes
Paired: Yes
Sample:

```
<HTML>
<HEAD>
<TITLE>How To Build A Go-Cart</TITLE>
</HEAD>
```

Attribute Information

This tag also accepts the lang and dir attributes. See the Element-Independent Attributes
section of this reference for definitions and
examples.

<TR>

Contains a row of cells in a table. You must
place the <TR> tags inside the <TABLE> container, which can contain <TH> and <TD> tags.

Standard: HTML 3.2
Common: Yes
Paired: Yes, optional
Sample:

```
<TABLE>
<TR><TH COLSPAN=3>Test Scores</TH></TR>
<TR>
  <TD>Bob Smith</TD>
  <TD>78</TD>
  <TD>85</TD>
</TR>
<TR>
  <TD>John Doe</TD>
  <TD>87</TD>
  <TD>85</TD>
</TR>
</TABLE>
```

Attribute Information

ALIGN={LEFT, RIGHT, CENTER, JUSTIFY, CHAR}

Specifies how text within the table row will
line up with the edges of the table cells, or if
ALIGN=CHAR, on a specific character (the decimal point).

Standard: HTML 4
Common: Yes
Sample:

```
<TR ALIGN=CENTER >
  <TD><B>Television</B></TD>
  <TD>
  <IMG SRC="tv.gif" ALT="TV" BORDER=0>
  </TD>
</TR>
```

BGCOLOR="#RRGGBB" or "..."

Specifies the background color of table cells in
the row. You can substitute the color names
for the hexadecimal RGB values.

Standard: Deprecated in HTML 4 in
favor of Style Sheets
Common: No
Sample:

```
<TR BGCOLOR="Yellow">
  <TD><IMG SRC="Bob.jpg" ALT="Bob"
  BORDER=0></TD>
  <TD ALIGN=LEFT VALIGN=MIDDLE>Bob
  Smith sitting at his desk on a July
  afternoon.</TD>
</TR>
```

BORDERCOLOR="#RRGGBB" or "..."

Specifies the color of cell borders within the
row. Currently, only Internet Explorer accepts
this attribute. You can substitute color names
for the hexadecimal RGB values.

Standard: Internet Explorer 2
Common: No
Sample:

```
<TR BORDERCOLOR="#3F2A55">
  <TD ALIGN=RIGHT
  VALIGN=MIDDLE>Computers</TD>
  <TD><IMG SRC="Computers.jpg"></TD>
</TR>
```

BORDERCOLORDARK="#*RRGGBB*" or "..."

Indicates the darker color for the 3-D borders around the table row. You can specify the color with its hexadecimal RGB values or with its color name.

> **Standard:** Internet Explorer 4
> **Common:** No
> **Sample:**

```
<TR BORDERCOLORLIGHT="silver"
BORDERCOLORDARK="black">
```

BORDERCOLORLIGHT="#*RRGGBB*" or "..."

Indicates the lighter color for 3-D borders around the table row. You can specify the color with its hexadecimal RGB values or with its color name.

> **Standard:** Internet Explorer 4
> **Common:** No
> **Sample:**

```
<TR BORDERCOLORLIGHT="silver"
BORDERCOLORDARK="black">
```

CHAR="..."

Specifies the character on which cell contents align, if ALIGN="CHAR". If you omit CHAR=, the default value is the decimal point in the specified language.

> **Standard**: HTML 4
> **Common**: No
> **Sample**:

```
<TR ALIGN="CHAR" CHAR=",">
```

CHAROFF="*n*"

Specifies the number of characters from the left at which the alignment character appears.

> **Standard**: HTML 4
> **Common**: No
> **Sample**:

```
<TR ALIGN="CHAR" CHAR="," CHAROFF="7">
```

CLASS="..."

Indicates which style class applies to the <TR> element.

> **Standard:** HTML 4
> **Common:** No
> **Sample:**

```
<TR CLASS="casual">
  <TD>Uranium</TD>
  <TD>Plutonium</TD>
  <TD>Radon</TD>
</TR>
```

ID="*n*"

Assigns a unique ID selector to an instance of the <TR> tag. When you then assign a style to that ID selector, it affects only that one instance of the <TR> tag.

> **Standard:** HTML 4
> **Common:** No
> **Sample:**

```
<TR ID="123">
```

NOWRAP

Indicates that text within table cells in the row not wrap. This may cause the table to expand beyond the horizontal dimensions of the current document.

> **Standard:** Internet Explorer 3; deprecated in HTML 4 in favor of Style Sheets
> **Common:** No
> **Sample:**

```
<TR NOWRAP>
  <TD>In this table cell I'm going to
  type a lot of stuff.</TD>
  <TD>In this table cell I'm going to
  continue to type a lot of stuff.</TD>
</TR>
```

STYLE="..."

Specifies Style Sheet commands that apply to all cells in the table row.

> **Standard:** HTML 4
> **Common:** No
> **Sample:**

```
<TR STYLE="background: red">
```

TITLE="..."

Specifies text assigned to the tag. You might use this attribute for context-sensitive help within the document. Browsers may use this to show tool tips.

Standard: HTML 4
Common: No
Sample:

```
<TR TITLE="Table Row">
```

VALIGN={TOP, MIDDLE, BOTTOM, BASELINE}

Specifies the vertical alignment of the contents of all cells within the row.

Standard: HTML 3.2
Common: Yes
Sample:

```
<TR VALIGN=TOP>
  <TD ALIGN=CENTER>John Smith</TD>
  <TD ALIGN=CENTER>Bob Doe</TD>
</TR>
```

Other Attributes

This tag also accepts the `lang`, `dir`, `onClick`, `onDblClick`, `onMouseDown`, `onMouseUp`, `onMouseOver`, `onMouseMove`, `onMouseOut`, `onKeyPress`, `onKeyDown`, and `onKeyUp` attributes. See the Element-Independent Attributes section of this reference for definitions and examples.

<TT>

Displays text in a monospace font.

Standard: HTML 2
Common: Yes
Paired: Yes
Sample:

```
After I typed in help, the words
<TT>help: not found</TT> appeared
on my screen.
```

Attribute Information

CLASS="..."

Indicates which style class applies to the <TT> element.

Standard: HTML 4
Common: No
Sample:

```
I sat down and began to type.
<P><TT CLASS="casual">It was a dark
and stormy night.</TT>
```

ID="*n*"

Assigns a unique ID selector to an instance of the <TT> tag. When you then assign a style to that ID selector, it affects only that one instance of the <TT> tag.

Standard: HTML 4
Common: No
Sample:

```
<TT ID="123">
```

STYLE="..."

Specifies Style Sheet commands that apply to the contents within the <TT> tags.

Standard: HTML 4
Common: No
Sample:

```
<TT STYLE="background: red">
```

TITLE="..."

Specifies text assigned to the tag. You might use this attribute for context-sensitive help within the document. Browsers may use this to show tool tips over the text within the <TT> tags.

Standard: HTML 4
Common: No
Sample:

```
Now, type <TT TITLE="User Typing">
MAIL</TT> and hit the <KBD>ENTER</KBD> key.
```

Other Attributes

This tag also accepts the lang, dir, onClick, onDblClick, onMouseDown, onMouseUp, onMouseOver, onMouseMove, onMouseOut, onKeyPress, onKeyDown, and onKeyUp attributes. See the Element-Independent Attributes section of this reference for definitions and examples.

‹U›

Underlines text in a document. Use this tag with moderation since underlined text can confuse visitors accustomed to seeing hyperlinks as underlined text.

Standard:	HTML 2; deprecated in HTML 4 in favor of Style Sheets
Common:	Yes
Paired:	Yes
Sample:	

```
After waterskiing, I was
<U>really</U> tired.
```

Attribute Information

CLASS="..."

Indicates which style class applies to the ‹U› element.

Standard:	HTML 4
Common:	No
Sample:	

```
Have you seen <U CLASS="casual">True
Lies</U> yet?
```

ID="n"

Assigns a unique ID selector to an instance of the ‹U› tag. When you then assign a style to that ID selector, it affects only that one instance of the ‹U› tag.

Standard:	HTML 4

Common:	No
Sample:	

```
<U ID="123">
```

STYLE="..."

Specifies Style Sheet commands that apply to the contents within the ‹U› tags.

Standard:	HTML 4
Common:	No
Sample:	

```
<U STYLE="background: red">
```

TITLE="..."

Specifies text assigned to the tag. You might use this attribute for context-sensitive help within the document. Browsers may use this to show tool tips over the underlined text.

Standard:	HTML 4
Common:	No
Sample:	

```
Read the book <U TITLE="BookTitle">
Walden</U> and you'll be enlightened.
```

Other Attributes

This tag also accepts the lang, dir, onClick, onDblClick, onMouseDown, onMouseUp, onMouseOver, onMouseMove, onMouseOut, onKeyPress, onKeyDown, and onKeyUp attributes. See the Element-Independent Attributes section of this reference for definitions and examples.

‹UL›

Contains a bulleted (unordered) list. You can then use the ‹LI› (List Item) tag to add bulleted items to the list.

Standard:	HTML 2
Common:	Yes
Paired:	Yes
Sample:	

```
Before you can begin, you need:<UL>
  <LI>Circular saw
  <LI>Drill with phillips bit
  <LI>Wood screws
</UL>
```

Attribute Information

CLASS="..."

Indicates which style class applies to the <UL> element.

> **Standard:** HTML 4
> **Common:** No
> **Sample:**

```
<UL CLASS="casual">
  <LI>Hexagon</LI>
  <LI>Pentagon</LI>
  <LI>Octogon</LI>
</UL>
```

COMPACT

Indicates that the unordered list appears in a compact format. This attribute may not affect the appearance of the list as most browsers do not present lists in more than one format.

> **Standard:** HTML 2; deprecated in HTML 4
> **Common:** No
> **Sample:**

```
<UL COMPACT>
  <LI>Flour
  <LI>Sugar
  <LI>Wheat
  <LI>Raisins
</UL>
```

ID="n"

Assigns a unique ID selector to an instance of the <UL> tag. When you then assign a style to that ID selector, it affects only that one instance of the <UL> tag.

> **Standard:** HTML 4
> **Common:** No
> **Sample:**

```
<UL ID="123">
```

SRC="URL"

Specifies the relative or absolute location of an image file to use for the bullets in the unordered list. Style Sheets provide a browser-independent method that is equivalent to this attribute.

> **Standard:** Internet Explorer 4
> **Common:** No
> **Sample:**

```
<UL SRC="blueball.gif">
```

STYLE="..."

Specifies Style Sheet commands that apply to the contents of the unordered list.

> **Standard:** HTML 4
> **Common:** No
> **Sample:**

```
<UL STYLE="background: red">
```

TITLE="..."

Specifies text assigned to the tag. You might use this attribute for context-sensitive help within the document. Browsers may use this to show tool tips over the unordered list.

> **Standard:** HTML 4
> **Common:** No
> **Sample:**

```
<UL TITLE="Food List">
  <LI>Spaghetti
  <LI>Pizza
  <LI>Fettuccini Alfredo
</UL>
```

TYPE={SQUARE, CIRCLE, DISC}

Specifies the bullet type for each unordered list item. If you omit the TYPE= attribute, the browser chooses a default type.

> **Standard:** HTML 2
> **Common:** Yes
> **Sample:**

```
<UL TYPE=DISC>
  <LI>Spaghetti
  <UL TYPE=SQUARE>
    <LI>Noodles
    <LI>Sauce
    <LI>Cheese
  </UL>
</UL>
```

Other Attributes

This tag also accepts the `lang`, `dir`, `onClick`, `onDblClick`, `onMouseDown`, `onMouseUp`, `onMouseOver`, `onMouseMove`, `onMouseOut`, `onKeyPress`, `onKeyDown`, and `onKeyUp` attributes. See the Element-Independent Attributes section of this reference for definitions and examples.

V

<VAR>

Indicates a placeholder variable in document text. This is useful when describing commands for which the visitor must supply a parameter.

> **Standard:** HTML 2
> **Common:** Yes
> **Paired:** Yes
> **Sample:**

```
To copy a file in DOS type <SAMP>COPY
<VAR>file1</VAR> <VAR>file2</VAR></SAMP>
and press the ENTER key.
```

Attribute Information

CLASS="..."

Indicates which style class applies to the <VAR> element.

> **Standard:** HTML 4
> **Common:** No
> **Sample:**

```
I, <VAR CLASS="casual">your name</VAR>,
solemnly swear to tell the truth.
```

ID="n"

Assigns a unique ID selector to an instance of the <VAR> tag. When you then assign a style to that ID selector, it affects only that one instance of the <VAR> tag.

> **Standard:** HTML 4
> **Common:** No
> **Sample:**

```
<VAR ID="123">
```

STYLE="..."

Specifies Style Sheet commands that apply to the contents within the <VAR> tags.

> **Standard:** HTML 4
> **Common:** No
> **Sample:**

```
<VAR STYLE="background: red">
```

TITLE="..."

Specifies text assigned to the tag. You might use this attribute for context-sensitive help within the document. Browsers may use this to show tool tips over the text within the <VAR> tags.

> **Standard:** HTML 4
> **Common:** No
> **Sample:**

```
Use a H<VAR TITLE="Heading Level
Number">n</VAR> tag.
```

Other Attributes

This tag also accepts the `lang`, `dir`, `onClick`, `onDblClick`, `onMouseDown`, `onMouseUp`, `onMouseOver`, `onMouseMove`, `onMouseOut`, `onKeyPress`, `onKeyDown`, and `onKeyUp` attributes. See the Element-Independent Attributes section of this reference for definitions and examples.

W

<WBR>

Forces a word break. This is useful in combination with the <NOBR> tag to permit line-breaks where they could otherwise not occur.

> **Standard:** Netscape Navigator
> **Common:** No
> **Paired:** No
> **Sample:**

```
<NOBR>
This line would go on forever, except
that I have this neat tag called WBR
that does <WBR>this!</NOBR>
```

<XMP>

Includes preformatted text within a document. Unlike the <PRE> tag, the browser does not interpret HTML tags within the <XMP> tags. HTML 3.2 declared this tag obsolete; so use <PRE> instead.

Standard: Obsolete
Common: No
Paired: Yes
Sample:

```
The output from these reports is
shown below.
<XMP>
Company    Q1    Q2    Q3    Q4
------   ---   ---   ---   ---
Widget Inc  4.5m  4.6m  6.2m  4.5m
Acme Widget 5.9m 10.2m 7.3m  6.6m
West Widget 2.2m  1.3m  3.1m  6.1m
</XMP>
```

Element-Independent Attributes and Event Handlers

Many HTML elements accept the attributes and event handlers described in this section. See the cross-references from individual elements for specific support information.

Attributes

lang="..."

Specifies the language used within the section. This attribute is used most often within documents to override site-wide language specifications. Use standard codes for languages, such as DE for German, FR for French, IT for Italian, and IW for Hebrew. See ISO Specification 639 at

www.sil.org/sgml/iso639a.html

for more information about language codes.

Standard: HTML 4
Common: No
Sample:

```
<P>The following quote is in German.
<Q LANG="DE">Guten Tag!</Q></P>
```

dir="{LTR, RTL}"

Specifies the direction (left to right or right to left) for the text used within the section. This attribute is used most often within documents to override site-wide language direction specifications.

Standard: HTML 4
Common: No
Sample:

```
<P>The following quote is in Hebrew,
therefore written right to left, not left
to right. <Q LANG="IW" DIR="RTL">Hebrew
text goes here and is presented right to
left, not left to right. </Q></P>
```

Event Handlers

Each of the following event handlers helps link visitor actions to scripts. See the JavaScript reference for a fuller explanation of their use, and see Chapter 11 for JavaScript instructions.

onLoad="..."

Occurs when the browser finishes loading a window or all frames within a <FRAMESET>. This handler works with <BODY> and <FRAMESET> elements.

onUnload="..."

Occurs when the browser removes a document from a window or frame. This handler works with <BODY> and <FRAMESET> elements.

onClick="..."

Occurs when a visitor clicks the mouse over an element. This handler works with most elements.

onDblClick="..."

Occurs when a visitor double-clicks the mouse over an element. This handler works with most elements.

onMouseDown="..."

Occurs when a visitor presses the mouse button over an element. This handler works with most elements.

onMouseUp="..."

Occurs when a visitor releases the mouse button over an element. This handler works with most elements.

onMouseOver="..."

Occurs when a visitor moves the mouse over an element. This handler works with most elements.

onMouseMove="..."

Occurs when a visitor moves the mouse while still over an element. This handler works with most elements.

onMouseOut="..."

Occurs when a visitor moves the mouse away from an element. This handler works with most elements.

onFocus="..."

Occurs when a visitor moves the focus to an element either with the mouse or the tab key. This handler works with <LABEL>, <INPUT>, <SELECT>, <TEXTAREA>, and <BUTTON>.

onBlur="..."

Occurs when a visitor moves focus from an element either with the mouse or the tab key.

This handler works with <LABEL>, <INPUT>, <SELECT>, <TEXTAREA>, and <BUTTON>.

onKeyPress="..."

Occurs when a visitor presses and releases a key over an element. This handler works with most elements.

onKeyDown="..."

Occurs when a visitor presses a key over an element. This handler works with most elements.

onKeyUp="..."

Occurs when a visitor releases a key over an element. This handler works with most elements.

onSubmit="..."

Occurs when a visitor submits a form. This handler works only with <FORM>.

onReset="..."

Occurs when a visitor resets a form. This handler works only with <FORM>.

onSelect="..."

Occurs when a visitor selects text in a text field. This handler works with the <INPUT> and <TEXTAREA> elements.

onChange="..."

Occurs when a visitor modifies a field and moves the input focus to a different control. This handler works with <INPUT>, <SELECT>, and <TEXTAREA>.

Master's Reference
Part 2

CASCADING STYLE SHEETS REFERENCE

This reference lists all the properties that you can use to set up a Style Sheet or to introduce styles into a document. For a complete introduction to Style Sheets and their capabilities, including an introduction to some of the specialized terminology used in this reference section, see Chapter 5.

The properties are organized into the following categories:

- Font properties, which affect the style of the typeface

- Text properties, which control paragraph and line-spacing values

- Box padding, border, margin, and position properties, which place and format elements within boundaries on a page

- Color and background properties, which specify background colors and background images, not just for the whole page, but for each element individually

- Classification properties, which control the presentation (or lack thereof) of standard elements, including lists

Each entry in this reference includes a description of the property, a list of the property's values, notes about the use of the property, and examples of the properties used in statements.

NOTE

At the time of writing, the newest versions of Internet Explorer and Netscape Navigator supported most of these Style Sheet features, but not all. Be sure to test extensively in a variety of browsers before relying on the properties listed here.

Font Properties

The font properties control the display of text elements, such as headings and para- .
graphs. This is the most common type of formatting you'll use in Style Sheets. These
properties—particularly the font-family property—are also the most problematic,
because no standard exists for fonts. Therefore, what works on one system or one
platform may not work on another. Fortunately, you can specify alternate font families, as well as a generic font family.

The six font properties cover the font family (typeface), weight, and effects such as
small caps or italics. The first property, font, is a *shorthand* property, as explained
below.

font

Use this property as a shortcut to incorporate any or all of the other font properties.
If you use the font shorthand property, you can also set the line spacing, using the
line-height property (listed in the "Text Properties" section of this reference). You
can include one, many, or all of the font properties in this one property.

If you do not set font-style, font-variant, font-weight, or font-family, you
accept the document default values for these properties. Shorthand properties do
not have default settings; refer to entries for the individual properties for their default
values.

If you set the font properties for an element, these settings are used by inline elements (such as EM) and by all elements of that type unless a class definition overwrites
the settings.

Values

The possible values for the font property are the set of all possible values listed in the
individual property entries:

font-style	Sets the font to an oblique or italic face (optional).
font-variant	Sets the font to small caps (optional).
font-weight	Sets the font to lighter or bolder (optional).
font-size	Sets the size of the font (required).
line-height	Sets the line spacing for the font (optional).
font-family	Sets the font face or type used (required).

See the entries for the individual properties for more details about these values.

Notes

If you do not include a setting for a particular property (such as font-variant), the browser uses the parent value of that property.

The order of the properties in a statement is not important.

Examples

    H1 {font: Arial, Helvetica, sans-serif bold 14pt/18pt}

This statement uses values for the font-family, font-style, font-size, and line-height (in that order). For the font-family, three values are listed, telling the browser to use Arial, and if Arial is not available use, Helvetica, and if Helvetica is not available, use a generic sans-serif font. The font-style is bold. The font-size is 14 points, and the line-height is 18 points.

    H3 {font: 12pt/120% serif}

This statement sets the font-size, line-height, and font-family using a 12-point font, a line height of 120% (14.4 points), and a generic serif font family.

    BODY {font: italic Helvetica 100%/130% }

This statement sets the base class for the document; all other tags will default to these values. It sets the font-style to italic, the font-family to Helvetica, the font-size to normal (100% of the browser default), and the line-height to 130%.

font-family

Use this property to change only the font family for an HTML tag or element. You can set a list of font families and include a generic family at the end of the list. The browser works through the list until it finds a matching font family available on the visitor's system.

The font-family property defaults to the browser settings. These may be the browser preferences, the browser default Style Sheet, or the visitor's default Style Sheet. If the default is the browser preferences or Style Sheet, your settings take precedence, but if it is the visitor's Style Sheet, your settings are overridden by the visitor's Style Sheet.

Inline elements (such as EM) use this property, as do child elements and all elements of that type unless the settings are overwritten by a class definition.

NOTE

> A paragraph or heading tag is the child of the body tag; list items are the children of a list tag. Class definitions allow you to have more than one type or version of a tag for formatting. For example, a warning note could have its own class of paragraph tag, as discussed in Chapter 5.

Values

> `family` *name*   Sets a specific font family. Use any font name for the family name. For font names, check the list of fonts on your system.
>
> *generic family*   Sets a generic font family. Use one of the following for generic family names: `serif` for fonts such as Times or Palatino, `sans-serif` for fonts such as Helvetica, `cursive` for fonts such as Zapf-Chancery, `fantasy` for fonts such as Western or Circus, or `monospace` for fonts such as System or Courier.

You can list several choices for the font family and one choice for a generic family. Separate the list members with a comma.

Notes

With this property, you can list a series of alternatives separated by commas. End each list with a generic family name; the browser can then substitute an available font of the correct generic type when none of your specific family types are available. The browser works through the list from left to right until it finds a match on the visitor's system.

If a font name contains spaces, place that font name in quotation marks.

Examples

    H1 {font-family: "Comic Sans MS", Architecture, sans-serif}

In this statement, the font choices for heading 1 tags (H1) are Comic Sans MS, Architecture, and a generic sans-serif. If the visitor's system has Comic Sans MS, it will use that font. Notice that Comic Sans MS is enclosed in quotation marks, because it includes a space. If Comic Sans MS is not available, the browser looks for Architecture. If neither font family is available, the browser uses a generic sans-serif font.

    BODY {font-family: Arial, Helvetica, sans-serif}

This statement sets BODY, the base class for all text elements in your page, to Arial or Helvetica (in order of preference). If neither of these families is available, the browser uses a generic sans-serif font. Apply the properties you want as defaults for the page to the BODY tag.

font-size

Use this property to control the size of text using a variety of measurements. It is more flexible than the font tag in the HTML specification, which scales text only by reference to the default size.

Values

absolute size   Defines the font-size by using a table of computed font sizes. These values can be one of the following: xx-small, x-small, small, medium (the default), large, x-large, or xx-large. Different font families may have different table values; thus, a small in one family might not be exactly the same size as a small in another family.

relative size   Defines the font-size by using another table of values. For this type of sizing, you can use either larger or smaller. This is similar to the absolute size, but the resulting size is relative to the parent container font size rather than to the base browser font size.

length   Uses millimeter, centimeter, inch, point, pixel, pica, x-height (the height of the font's lowercase letter *x*), or em (the height of the font) units as measurements. This type of sizing forces a particular measurement to be used for the element, ignoring any browser settings. Specify the measurement after the number as follows: mm for millimeters, cm for centimeters, in for inches, pt for points, px for pixels, pc for picas, ex for x-height settings, or em for em settings. The em and ex settings generate a font size relative to the parent font.

percentage   Sets the font-size as a percentage of the parent element's font-size. Specify this value by including a % symbol after the number.

You can assign a single value for this property. If you use a keyword, such as x-large or larger, the browser recognizes the keyword and acts accordingly. If you use a numeric value, be sure to follow it with the appropriate measurement indicator, such as pt to indicate a point size or % to indicate a percentage.

Notes

When you use the absolute size value, the browser adjusts the font size according to the visitor's preferences. For example, if the default font size for the browser is 10 points, this corresponds to the medium value. The adjustment from medium is 1.5 for each increment in the list. So, if medium is 10 points, small is 6.7 points, and large is 15 points. Absolute size is the best choice for sizing fonts, because if the visitor changes the base font from 10 points to 14 points, your document scales with the change.

In terms of absolute size and relative size, the default is expressed as medium.

Length and percentage values do not use the absolute or relative tables of values. The font sizes are interpreted, and so they may appear different in different situations.

For length values, the default is taken from the browser or visitor settings. The em and ex values are interpreted as references to the parent font size. For example, 1.5em is equivalent to large, larger, and 150% for absolute, relative, and percentage font sizes.

Relative units set up the property in relation to the font and size properties. Use relative units wherever you can, because they scale more easily from situation to situation (for example, in different browsers and displays, or in the transition from display to printer). Relative units include em (1 em is equal to the font size), ex (the height of the lowercase letter *x* in a font), and px (screen pixels).

Absolute lengths are useful when the properties of the browser are well-known or when you want to set a particular font size to conform to a specification. Absolute units include inches, millimeters and centimeters, points (1 point = 1/72 inch), and picas (1 pica = 12 points). You cannot have a negative font size.

If the size is expressed as a percentage, the default is 100%. Any value less than 100% is smaller than the parent, and any value more than 100% is larger than the parent. For example, if the parent font is 12 points, and this property is set to 110%, the font size for this element is 13.2 points. If the font size is set to 80% of the 12-point parent, the element appears as 9.6 points.

Examples

```
BODY {font-size: 14pt}
```

This statement sets the base font-size to 14 points. This is useful when you want the presentation of text to be large, such as at a site for the visually impaired or for children.

```
P {font-size: 90%}
```

This statement uses a percentage value to make the font-size depend on the settings in the <BODY> tag. So, if this statement and the preceding one appear in the same Style Sheet, the font in the paragraph (P) will be 12.6 points.

```
ADDRESS {font-size: x-small}
```

This statement sets the font-size for the ADDRESS element using an absolute value. If this statement appears in the same Style Sheet as the first example, the font-size for the ADDRESS element will be 4 points.

font-style

Use this property to add emphasis with an oblique or italic version of the font. If the default setting inherited for a particular element is an italic style font, you can use the font-style property to set the current element to normal, sometimes called roman (or upright).

When you set the `font-style` for an element, inline elements (such as EM) and included block elements use this style. Also, if you set the `font-style` for a body or list container, all the elements within it use the setting.

Values

normal style   If you have set the default style to an oblique or italic style, the keyword `normal` sets the `font-style` to a roman or upright style.

italic style   If you want an italic `font-style`, the keyword depends on the font. Fonts with Italic, Cursive, or Kursiv in their names are usually listed as Italic in the browser's database.

oblique style   As with the italic style, the keyword for an oblique `font-style` depends on the font. Fonts with Oblique, Slanted, or Incline in their names are usually listed in the browser's database as Oblique fonts. The browser may also generate an oblique font from a family that does not have an oblique or italic style.

You can use one of the three values.

Notes

The browser maintains a list of the fonts available on the system, with the font name, font family, and values of the font such as oblique or italic.

Examples

```
BODY {font-style: oblique}
H1, H2, H3 {font-style: normal}
```

The first statement sets the base body (BODY) to an oblique version of the font. Because the heading levels 1, 2, and 3 (H1, H2, H3) inherit this from the BODY class, the second statement sets them to `normal`. If the base font is not oblique or italic, you do not need to set the `font-style` to `normal`.

```
BODY EM {font-style: italic}
```

This statement sets up the emphasis tag (EM) to be an italic `font-style`. This means that when you emphasize some inline text, it will be italicized automatically.

font-variant

Use this property to switch between normal and small-caps fonts. If you assign this property to an element, all included blocks and inline elements use the setting.

Values

normal variant   If the tag has inherited a small-caps setting from its parent, the keyword `normal` sets the `font-variant` to a regular font. This is the default.

small-caps variant   Sets the lowercase letters to display as uppercase letters in a smaller font size. Use the keyword `small-caps`.

Notes

In some cases, when a small-caps version of the font is not available to the browser, the browser creates small caps by using scaled uppercase letters.

Examples

```
H1 {font-variant: small-caps}
```

This statement sets the level 1 headings (H1) to a small-cap version of the default font.

```
ADDRESS {font-variant: small-caps}
```

This statement sets the contents of any <ADDRESS> tag to appear in small caps, using the default BODY font.

```
BODY EM {font-variant: small-caps}
```

This statement sets text in the inline element EM to use the small-caps version of the default font.

font-weight

Use this property to set the weight of a font, creating darker and lighter versions of the normal font. You can set the `font-weight` property as a relative weight or as a specific numeric value that represents a degree of darkness or heaviness for the font.

Values

normal weight   The keyword `normal` resets the font to its normal weight. This is the default.

relative weight   Sets the `font-weight` relative to the normal weight inherited by the element. These values can be one of the following: `bold`, `bolder`, `light`, or `lighter`.

gradient weight   Sets the `font-weight` as a degree of heaviness. These values can be one of the following: 100, 200, 300, 400 (same as `normal`), 500, 600, 700 (same as `bold`), 800, or 900.

You can use one value from the list.

Notes

When you set a `font-weight` value for an element, the child elements for that element inherit the weight of the font. This weight becomes their normal weight, and you can increase or decrease the weight based on the inherited weight. When you then set a child element's weight using a relative weight (for example, `bolder` or `lighter`), it is relative to the weight of the parent font.

The gradient weight value gives you greater control over the weight of the font. The numeric weight values must be stated exactly; partial numbers (such as 250) are not accepted.

There are no guarantees that the font family will include the full range of weight values. The browser will map the values you assign to those available for the font it uses. Fonts that have a weight lighter than normal are usually listed in the browser's database as Thinner, Light, or Extra-light.

Examples

```
P {font-weight: bold}
```

This statement makes the weight of the paragraph (P) font bold. Use this when your layout requires a heavier text presentation.

```
BODY {font-weight: 500}
```

This statement uses the numeric representation to set the base font weight to slightly heavier than normal. This will make the text for all the elements appear darker. All included and inline elements use this as their normal weight. If you then use the relative keywords, as in the next statement, the text is bolder (or lighter) than the 500 weight set in BODY.

```
H1 {font-weight: bolder}
```

This statement makes the H1 elements darker than the base font, regardless of what setting the base font has for its weight. If your base font were 900 in the <BODY> tag, however, there is no value that is bolder, and the browser would not be able to make the H1 text bolder.

```
BODY EM {font-weight: 400}
```

This statement controls the weight of emphasized text in the document. If the BODY weight is 500 or if you include emphasized text in a paragraph set to bold, as in the first statement in this section, the emphasized text would appear lighter.

Text Properties

Text properties control the layout or display of lines and words on a page and within a text element. These properties include the familiar values for spacing and aligning text within an area, as well as values for controlling text capitalization and effects (such as underlining and blinking). Combined with the font properties, the text properties give you control over the appearance of the text on your page. The font properties control the typeface; the text properties control the paragraph settings.

letter-spacing

Use this property to control the spacing between characters in words in a text element. The distance you set applies across the elements; you cannot insert larger and smaller spaces between characters. This property is useful if you want to add space between characters for an open-looking presentation.

This property defaults to the spacing set in the parent element or to the browser if no style is set. Inline and included block elements use the value set with the letter-spacing property.

Values

normal spacing   Resets the distance between characters to whatever is normal for the font and font size in use. Use the keyword normal. This is the default.

length   Sets a standard spacing length between characters. The value adds to the normal length inherited by the element from its parent, or reduces the normal length if you use a negative value.

Specify the measurement after the number as follows: mm for millimeters, cm for centimeters, in for inches, pt for points, px for pixels, pc for picas, ex for x-height settings, or em for em settings. The em and ex settings generate a font size relative to the parent font.

Notes

When you specify a length, relative units set up the property in relation to the font and size properties. Use relative units wherever you can, because they scale more easily from situation to situation (for example, in different browsers and displays, or in the transition from display to printer). Relative units include em (1 em is equal to the width of a capital *M* in a font), ex (the height of the lowercase letter *x* in a font), and px (screen pixels).

Absolute lengths are useful when the properties of the browser are well-known or when you want to set a particular letter spacing to conform to a specification.

Absolute units include inches, millimeters and centimeters, points (1 point = 1/72 inch), and picas (1 pica = 12 points).

When you use a length unit, you can use a positive or a negative number or a decimal number (for example, `0.4em` or `1.2em`). If you use a negative value, be sure that you don't make your text illegible with too small spacing between characters.

Examples

    H1 {letter-spacing: 2em}

This statement increases the character spacing in words found in the level 1 headings (H1) to twice the font size.

    P {letter-spacing: -0.5em}

This statement decreases the character spacing for paragraphs in the document to one-half the font size.

line-height

Use this property to set the distance (leading or spacing) between lines of text within an element. Elements inherit the settings for this property; if you change the settings in the child element, you change the inherited results. For example, if you set unordered lists (UL) to 2 (for double-spaced) and then set list-items (LI) to 1.5, you have effectively triple-spaced list items (2×1.5). In other words, the inheritance is cumulative, rather than a setting for a later element replacing the previous setting.

Values

normal height   Sets the spacing value to default to the browser-specific setting, which is usually 1 to 1.2 times the font size. Use the keyword `normal`. This is the default.

number   Sets the distance between the baselines of each line of text in the element to the font size multiplied by the specified number. For example, if the font size is 10 points and you set `line-height` to 2, the spacing will be 20 points.

length   Sets the spacing using one of the standard measurements. Some measurements are relative, and some are absolute. See the description of the length value for the `letter-spacing` property for valid measurements.

percentage   Sets the spacing to a percentage of the line's font size.

Notes

See the "Notes" section for the `letter-spacing` property for information about relative and absolute length settings.

When you use a length unit, you can use a positive or a negative number. If you use a negative number, you'll create overlapping text, which may make it illegible.

Using a percentage for the `line-height` property is a flexible way to set line spacing, because it adapts to the font and display of the browser. Child elements will inherit the result of this setting.

Examples

```
P {line-height: 1.2;
    font-size: 10pt}
P {line-height: 1.2em;
    font-size: 10pt}
P {line-height: 120%;
    font-size: 10pt}
```

These three statements produce the same result: The text will have 12 points between each line.

text-align

Use this property to arrange the text horizontally within the element box. This is useful for centering headings or creating effects with justification. You can set the alignment on any block-level element, such as P, H1, UL, and so on. The browser sets the property default (either from the browser properties, browser Style Sheet, or visitor Style Sheet). Inline and included block elements use the settings. For example, if you justify an unordered list (UL), the list items (which are included block elements) are justified.

Values

left alignment Aligns text along the left margin, for a ragged-right layout. Use the keyword `left`.

right alignment Aligns text along the right margin, for a ragged-left layout. Use the keyword `right`.

centered Places the text a uniform distance from the left and right margins. Use the keyword `center`.

justified   Creates uniform line lengths. The browser will use word spacing to create lines of text that abut both the left and right margins of the element box. Use the keyword `justify`.

Examples

```
H1, H2 {text-align: center}
```

This statement centers both level 1 (H1) and level 2 (H2) headings across the width of the page (however wide or narrow the display is).

```
P.EMERG {text-align: right;
    Background: url(exclaim.gif) no-repeat}
```

This statement aligns paragraphs of class EMERG (`P.EMERG`) with the right margin of the element box. `P.EMERG` also has an icon that appears once at the left margin of the element box.

text-decoration

Use this property to control the effects used on text elements. This property is particularly useful for drawing attention to text elements, such as notes and warnings.

The default is not to use any text decoration, and the property is not inherited, although some properties do continue throughout sections. For example, a P with underlining will be underlined throughout, even through sections with other formatting, such as boldface. The decoration uses the settings from the `color` property (listed in the "Background and Color Properties" section).

Values

no text decoration   Leaves the text plain (unadorned). Use the keyword `none`. This is the default.

underlined   Draws a single, thin line under the text. Use the keyword `underline`.

overlined   Draws a single, thin line above the text. Use the keyword `overline`.

lined through   Draws a single, thin line through the text, like strikeout. Use the keyword `line-through`.

blinking   Makes the text blink. Use the keyword `blink`.

You can combine `underline`, `overline`, `line-through`, and `blink` in a single statement.

Notes

If you apply the text-decoration to an element that has no text or is an empty element (such as BR), the property has no effect.

Examples

```
H1 {color: blue;
        text-decoration: underline}
```

This statement sets the level 1 headings (H1) to use the color blue and have an underline (it, too, will be blue).

```
P EM {text-decoration: blink}
```

This statement sets the emphasis in paragraphs (P EM) to blink. Because nothing else is set, the emphasis will use all the other paragraph (P) properties that you have set.

```
H1 EM {text-decoration: overline}
```

This statement sets the emphasized text in level 1 headings to have a line above it. If this statement appears in the same Style Sheet as the first statement in this section, this emphasized text will have a line above and a line below.

text-indent

Use this property to indent the first line of paragraphs. Traditionally, indented first lines compensated for a lack of space between paragraphs and acted as a visual cue for the reader. You can set the indent as an absolute or a relative measurement.

Elements use whatever setting the parent has, so if you set text-indent for BODY, all block elements, such as H1 and P, default to first-line indention. The default value is 0, for no indention.

Values

length Sets the size of the first-line indent to the specified measurement. Some measurements are relative, and some are absolute. See the description of the length value for the letter-spacing property for valid measurements.

percentage Sets the first-line indent to a percentage of the line length.

Notes

For most browsers, you can use negative values to create a hanging-indent format.

An indent is not added to the first line of the second text stream if the text within the element is separated by an inline element that breaks the line (such as BR).

See the "Notes" section for the `letter-spacing` property for information about relative and absolute length settings.

Examples

```
BODY {text-indent: 1%}
```

This statement creates a base class BODY with a first-line indent of 1% of the line length. Because a percentage is used, the ratio of indent to line length stays the same whether the browser window or font is sized larger or smaller.

```
H1 {text-indent: 3em}
```

In this statement, the indention for level 1 headings (H1) is also relative to the font size (em measurements are based on the font size). If this line appears in the same Style Sheet as the first statement, the indention is the base 1% plus an additional 3 ems.

```
P.WARN {text-indent: 2cm}
```

This statement specifies a 2-centimeter first-line indent. Since this is an absolute measurement, this setting can produce unexpected results on different machines.

text-transform

Use this property to set the capitalization standard for one or more elements. For example, if you want all uppercase letters for a warning or title case for all headings, you can set this property in one place and allow the browser to adjust the text. Child elements, including both block and inline elements, use the parent's setting for this property. The default is no transformation.

Values

no transformation   Does not change the case for any of the text. Use the keyword none. This is the default.

capitalized   Creates a title case element, capitalizing the first letter of each word in the element. Use the keyword `capitalize`.

uppercased   Sets all the text to uppercase. Use the keyword `uppercase`.

lowercased   Sets all the text to lowercase, eliminating any uppercase letters from the element. Use the keyword `lowercase`.

Examples

```
H1 {text-transform: capitalize}
```

This statement forces all the text in level 1 headings (H1) to use uppercase for the first letter of each word. This is a form of the title case.

```
P.HEADLINE {text-transform: uppercase}
```

In this statement, the paragraph class P.HEADLINE forces all the text into uppercase. This is not the same as setting a small-caps font (font-variant: small-caps), because no adjustment is made to the size of the lowercase letters.

vertical-align

Use this property to set inline text elements within a parent element to have different vertical alignment from the parent. The vertical-align property is an important layout tool for document designers. You could, for example, define a class for superscript or subscript text and apply it where required. This property is typically used to set the alignment between inline graphics (such as keycaps or toolbar icons) and the surrounding text. The default value is for alignment along the baselines of the elements. These settings are not used by any other elements.

Values

baseline alignment   Aligns the bottom of lowercase letters in the two elements. Use the keyword baseline. This is the default setting.

subscript alignment   Moves the inline element down below the baseline of the parent element. Use the keyword sub.

superscript alignment   Moves the inline element up from the baseline of the parent element. Use the keyword super.

top alignment   Similar to superscript, aligns the inline element with the highest part of the parent element. Use the keyword top. This works line by line. For example, if the line has no ascenders, top moves the inline text to the top of the x-height for the parent element.

text-top alignment   Aligns the inline element with the top of the ascender in the parent element. Use the keyword text-top.

middle alignment   Centers the inline text and the parent element text, aligning the mid-points of the two elements. Use the keyword middle. This may be required when you are using a large and small size for the two elements or when the inline element is an image.

bottom alignment   Aligns the inline element with the lowest part of the parent element on the same line. Use the keyword bottom. Use this with caution, because it may produce unexpected results.

text-bottom alignment Aligns the bottom of the inline element with the bottom of the parent font's descender. Use the keyword `text-bottom`. This is the preferable method for aligning inline elements with the bottom of a textual parent element.

percentage Raises or lowers (with negative values) the baseline of the inline element the given percentage above or below the baseline of the parent element. Use this in combination with the `line-height` property of the element.

Notes

If you use subscript (`sub`) or superscript (`super`) alignment, decrease the font size in relation to the parent element.

If you want to include inline images that replace words or letters in your text (such as toolbar buttons or keycaps), use a percentage value with the `vertical-align` property. This allows you to obtain precision in the placement of inline elements, such as images, that do not have a true baseline.

Examples

```
IMG.KEYCAP {vertical-align: -20%}
```

This statement creates an image class (`IMG`) called `KEYCAP`. Elements that you apply this class to will drop below the baseline of the parent text element; 20% of the image will be below the baseline of the parent element's text.

```
P.LOGRYTHM {vertical-align: super}
```

This statement creates a paragraph class called `LOGRYTHM` for superscripting. You could, for example, use this for the exponents in equations.

```
.REGMARK {vertical-align: text-top}
```

In this statement, a generic class, called `REGMARK`, aligns the inline element to the top of the parent font.

word-spacing

Use this property to control the spacing between words in a text element. As with the `letter-spacing` property, the distance you set applies across the elements; you cannot insert larger and smaller spaces between words, as in typesetting. This property is useful if you want to add space between words for an open-looking presentation.

This property assumes the settings for its parent element or the browser, and inline or included block elements use any changes you make in the `word-spacing` property.

Values

normal spacing   Resets the distance between words to whatever is normal for the font and font size in use. Use the keyword normal. This is the default.

length   Sets a standard spacing length between words. The value adds to the normal length inherited by the element from its parent, or reduces the normal length if you use a negative value. For example, if BODY sets the font size to 10pt and the word spacing to 1em, the child elements will use 10-point word spacing (1em = the point size). If you then add 0.4em to the word spacing, the child element has a wider word spacing than the parent. See the description of the length value for the letter-spacing property for valid measurements.

Notes

See the "Notes" section of the letter-spacing property for information about relative and absolute length settings.

When you use a length unit, you can use a positive or a negative number, as well as a decimal number (such as 0.4em). If you use a negative number, be careful that you do not eliminate the spaces between words, making your text unreadable.

Examples

```
H1 {word-spacing: 1em}
P {word-spacing: 0.4em}
```

In both these statements, the space between words in the elements will increase; the spacing in heading level 1 (H1) elements increases by 1 em, and paragraph (P) elements increase by 0.4 (4/10 of the font size).

Box Padding Properties

In the element box, the padding provides the distance between the element contents and the border. You can use the padding shorthand property to set the padding on all sides of the element or use the individual properties to set the padding on each side separately.

NOTE

With box properties, you can manipulate the layers around the element. These layers, from the element out, are padding, border, margin, and position. Each of these layers has its own set of properties, which are included in this reference in the order listed, beginning with box padding.

padding

Use this shorthand property to set the distance for all four padding directions (top, right, bottom, and left). This area uses the element's settings for background (such as color and image).

Padding is not inherited, so included and inline elements use the default of zero (0) rather than the settings from the parent element.

Values

length   Sets an absolute or a relative distance between the element contents and the inside of the box border. Specify the measurement after the number as follows: mm for millimeters, cm for centimeters, in for inches, pt for points, px for pixels, pc for picas, ex for x-height settings, or em for em settings. The em and ex settings generate a font size relative to the parent font.

percentage   Sets the distance between the element contents and the inside of the box border as a percentage of the parent element.

Use a single value to make the padding on each side equidistant. If you use two values, the browser uses the first one for the top and bottom padding, and the second one for the left and right padding. If you provide three values, the browser assigns them to the top padding, the left and right padding, and the bottom padding. If you provide all four values, the browser assigns them, in order, to the top, right, bottom, and left padding. You can mix value types—specifying padding in percentages for some and absolute measurements for other values.

Notes

You cannot have a negative padding value. You can use a decimal number, such as 0.4 or 1.2.

For length settings, relative units set up the property in relation to the font and size properties. Use relative units wherever you can because they scale more easily from situation to situation (for example, in different browsers and displays, or in the transition from display to printer). Relative units include em (1 em is equal to the width of a capital *M* in a font), ex (the height of the lowercase letter *x* in a font), and px (screen pixels).

Absolute lengths are useful when the properties of the browser are well-known or when you want to set a particular size to conform to a specification. Absolute units include inches, millimeters and centimeters, points (1 point = 1/72 inch), and picas (1 pica = 12 points).

Examples

```
H1 {font-size: 20pt;
     padding: 1em 0.5em}
H2 {font-size: 15pt;
     padding: 1em 0.5em}
```

If you include these two statements in a Style Sheet, the headings at levels 1 and 2 will have 20 and 15 points, respectively, between the content and the top and bottom borders. Heading 1 (H1) will have a left and right padding of 10 points; heading 2 (H2) will have a left and right padding of 7.5 points.

padding-bottom

Use this property to add space between the bottom of the contents and the border below. Padding is not inherited, so included and inline elements use the default of zero (0) rather than the settings from the parent element.

Values

length   Sets an absolute or relative distance between the bottom of the contents and the border below. See the description of the length value for the padding property for valid measurements.

percentage   Sets the bottom padding size to a percentage of the parent element.

Notes

See the "Notes" section for the padding property.

Examples

```
BODY {padding-bottom: 3em}
```

This statement sets the padding distance between the bottom of the page to 3 ems, which allows it to vary with the font size.

```
H1 {padding-bottom: 2pt}
```

This statement sets the distance for the bottom padding to 2 points for level 1 headings (H1). It will add a distance of 2 points to the space between the text of the heading and the location of the border, regardless of the font size of the heading.

```
P.CAP {padding-bottom: 0.5cm}
```

This statement sets up a paragraph class called CAP (P CLASS=CAP) in which the distance between the bottom of the element contents and the border location is an absolute value of $\frac{1}{2}$ centimeter.

padding-left

Use this property to add space between the left edge of the contents and the border location. Padding is not inherited, so included and inline elements use the default of zero (0) rather than the settings from the parent element.

Values

length   Sets an absolute or relative distance between the left edge of the contents and the border. See the description of the length value for the `padding` property for valid measurements.

percentage   Sets the left padding size to a percentage of the parent element.

Notes

See the "Notes" section for the `padding` property.

Examples

```
ADDRESS {padding-left: 10%}
```

This statement adds space to the left of the ADDRESS elements. Unlike the left margin space, this padding space shows the element background. This space is a relative space; the amount of the space depends on the size of the element.

padding-right

Use this property to add space between the right edge of the contents and the border location. Padding is not inherited, so included and inline elements use the default of zero (0) rather than the settings from the parent element.

Values

length   Sets an absolute or relative distance between the right edge of the contents and the border. See the description of the length value for the `padding` property for valid measurements.

percentage   Sets the right padding size to a percentage of the parent element.

Notes

See the "Notes" section for the `padding` property.

Examples

```
P {padding-left: 8px;
    padding-right: 8px}
P {padding: 0 8px}
```

These two statements produce the same result. The first uses the individual properties to set the left and right padding to 8 pixels. The second uses the shorthand `padding` property to set the top and bottom padding to zero and the left and right padding to 8 pixels.

padding-top

Use this property to add space between the top of the contents and the border location. Padding is not inherited, so included and inline elements use the default of zero (0) rather than the settings from the parent element.

Values

length   Sets an absolute or a relative distance between the top of the contents and the border. See the description of the length value for the `padding` property for valid measurements.

percentage   Sets the top padding size to a percentage of the parent element.

Notes

See the "Notes" section for the `padding` property.

Examples

```
ADDRESS {padding-top: 1cm}
```

This statement adds a centimeter above the element contents before placing the border. Using an absolute measurement like this is less browser-sensitive than the relative values.

Box Border Properties

Every container has a border. Element borders reside between the padding and margin in the element container. By default, borders have no style set (are not visible), regardless of color or width.

The default for the border is a medium-width line with no pattern that inherits the color (foreground) setting for the parent element.

You can use the `border` shorthand property to set all the border properties, or use the individual properties.

border

Use this shorthand property to set some or all of the border properties. You can set a single value for all four sides of the border.

Values

The possible values for the border property are the set of all possible values listed in the individual property entries:

border-width   Sets the border width for the border using a single value. This value can be one of the following: valuethin, medium, thick, or a length measurement.

border-style   Sets the pattern used to fill the border. You can set the style to any of the following: none, dotted, dashed, solid, double, groove, ridge, inset, or outset.

border-color   Sets the color for all sides of the border. This value can be one of the color names or RGB values.

See the entries for the individual properties for details about these values.

Notes

Unlike other shorthand properties, you can use only a single setting for each value you include. The property is applied evenly to all sides of the box border.

See the "Notes" section for the border-color, border-style, and border-color properties.

Examples

P.WARN {border: 2em double red}

This statement generates a border around the paragraph class element WARN (P CLASS=WARN). The border is a red, double-line border that is 2 ems wide.

P.NOTE {border: 2px ridge blue}

This statement generates borders around the paragraph class element NOTE (P CLASS=NOTE). The border is a ridged, blue border that is 2 pixels wide.

border-bottom

Use this shorthand property to set some or all of the border properties for the bottom border of the element container.

Values

border-width   Sets the width for the bottom border. This value can be one of the following: thin, medium, thick, or a length measurement.

border-style   Sets the pattern used to fill the bottom border. You can set the style to any of the following: none, dotted, dashed, solid, double, groove, ridge, inset, or outset.

> `border-color` Sets the color for the bottom border. This value can be one of the color names or RGB values.

You can use one setting for each of the values of `border-bottom` property. See the entries for the individual properties for more details about these values.

Notes

See the "Notes" section for the `border-color`, `border-style`, and `border-color` properties.

Examples

```
P.SECTEND {color: blue;
    border-bottom: 0.5em dashed #8A2BE2}
    /* #8A2BE2 is a blueviolet color */
```

This statement overrides the foreground color for the SECTEND class of paragraphs (P CLASS=SECTEND) and replaces it with an RGB value (`blueviolet`). If you use an RGB value, it is helpful to include a comment that indicates what color you expect. See the entry for the `border-color` property for more information about specifying border colors. SECTEND paragraph text will appear blue and concludes with a dashed, violet-blue line that is 0.5 em thick. The em thickness associates the width of the border with the font size for the paragraph.

```
P.NOTE {color: green;
    border-bottom: 5em groove}
```

This statement specifies that NOTE class paragraphs (P CLASS=NOTE) will use the color green for foreground objects (such as text and the border) and have a grooved, 5-em terminating line.

border-bottom-width

Use this property to set the thickness of the bottom border for an element. The border width is, by default, a medium thickness and is unaffected by any border settings for the parent element.

Values

> *thin width* Sets a thin line for the bottom border. Use the keyword `thin`.
>
> *medium width* Sets a medium line for the bottom border. Use the keyword `medium`. This is the default.
>
> *thick width* Sets a relatively thick line for the bottom border. Use the keyword `thick`.

length Sets the bottom border width using an absolute or a relative measurement. See the description of the length value for the `border-width` property for valid measurements.

You can use one of the values listed above to set the width of the bottom border.

Notes

See the "Notes" section for the `border-width` property.

Examples

```
P.UNDER {border-style: solid;
    border-bottom-width: 0.5cm;
    border-color: gray}
```

This creates a class of paragraph called UNDER (P CLASS=UNDER) in which the bottom border is ½ centimeter. This is an absolute setting, unaffected by the browser, page size, or element properties such as font.

```
H1 {border-style: solid;
    border-bottom-width: thin
    border-color: #F0F8FF}
```

This statement specifies the border as a standard, thin line.

border-color

Use this property to create a border using colors that are different from the foreground color for the element. The border color uses the foreground color of the element as a default setting. This shorthand property sets the visible border to the selected color(s).

Values

color Sets the color for the border. This value can be one of the color names or RGB values. See the "Notes" section for valid values.

If you specify a single color, all four borders will appear as that color. If you include two colors, the top and bottom borders use the first color, and the left and right borders use the second color. If you include three colors, the top border uses the first color, the left and right borders use the second color, and the bottom border uses the third color. To give each border a unique color, list four colors; the borders use them in the following order: top, right, bottom, left.

Notes

You can use either color keywords or RGB values to specify border colors. If you name a color, the keyword must be one that the browser will recognize; the RGB colors are recognized by more browsers.

Color keywords include the following:

aqua	gray	navy	silver
black	green	olive	teal
blue	lime	purple	white
fuchsia	maroon	red	yellow

These colors are taken from the Windows VGA palette.

For an RGB specification, use any one of the three variants listed in Table 2.1 to specify the color.

TABLE 2.1: THE RGB VALUES

Color	RGB Hex	RGB Integer	RGB Percent
Aqua	#00FFFF	rgb(0,255,255)	rgb(0%,100%,100%)
Black	#000000	rgb(0,0,0)	rgb(0%,0%,0%)
Blue	#0000FF	rgb(0,0,255)	rgb(0%,0%,100%)
Fuchsia	#FF00FF	rgb(255,0,255)	rgb(100%,0%,100%)
Gray	#808080	rgb(128,128,128)	rgb(50%,50%,50%)
Green	#008000	rgb(0,128,0)	rgb(0%,50%,0%)
Lime	#00FF00	rgb(0,255,0)	rgb(0%,100%,0%)
Maroon	#800000	rgb(128,0,0)	rgb(50%,0%,0%)
Navy	#000080	rgb(0,0,128)	rgb(0%,0%,50%)
Olive	#808000	rgb(128,128,0)	rgb(50%,50%,0%)
Purple	#800080	rgb(128,0,128)	rgb(50%,0%,50%)
Red	#FF0000	rgb(255,0,0)	rgb(100%,0%,0%)
Silver	#C0C0C0	rgb(192,192,192)	rgb(75%,75%,75%)
Teal	#008080	rgb(0,128,128)	rgb(0%,50%,50%)
White	#FFFFFF	rgb(255,255,255)	rgb(100%,100%,100%)
Yellow	#FFFF00	rgb(255,255,0)	rgb(100%,100%,0%)

For more information about choosing colors, refer to the list of 216 safe HTML colors in Part 5 of this Master's Reference.

Examples

```
P.WARN {border-color: #8B0000} /* dark red border */
```

This statement specifies that the paragraphs of class WARN (P CLASS=WARN) are outlined with a dark red border.

```
P.DANCING {border-color: #F0F8FF #F0FFFF blue #5F9EA0}
```

This statement sets the border on each side of the element to a different color. This creates a multi-hued line around paragraphs of class DANCING (P CLASS=DANCING). The top is aliceblue, the right is azure, the bottom is blue, and the left is cadetblue.

border-left

Use this shorthand property to set some or all of the border properties for the border on the left side of the element container.

Values

border-width   Sets the width for the left border. This value can be one of the following: thin, medium, thick, or a length measurement.

border-style   Sets the pattern used to fill the left border. You can set the style to any of the following: none, dotted, dashed, solid, double, groove, ridge, inset, or outset.

border-color   Sets the color for the left border. This value can be one of the color names or RGB values.

You can use one value for each of the values of the border-left property. See the entries for the individual properties for more details about these values.

Notes

See the "Notes" section for the border-color, border-style, and border-color properties.

Examples

```
P.INSERT {border-left: thin solid red}
```

This statement places a thin, red line next to the INSERT class paragraphs (P CLASS=INSERT). This is a useful way to create a class for all your elements that insert "change bars" (a line that shows that changes have been made in the text) in the left border.

2

border-left-width

Use this property to set the thickness of the border on the left side of an element. The border width is, by default, a medium thickness and is unaffected by any border settings for the parent element.

Values

thin width   Sets a thin line for the left border. Use the keyword `thin`.

medium width   Sets a medium line for the left border. Use the keyword `medium`. This is the default.

thick width   Sets a relatively thick line for the left border. Use the keyword `thick`.

length   Sets the left border width using an absolute or a relative measurement. See the description of the length value for the `border-width` property for valid measurements.

You can use one of the values listed above to set the width of the left border.

Notes

See the "Notes" section for the `border-width` property.

Examples

```
P.INSERT {border-style: dashed;
          border-left-width: 5em;
          border-color: red}
```

This statement creates a paragraph class called INSERT that uses a dashed, red line on the left border. The thickness of the line depends on the size of the paragraph font.

border-right

Use this shorthand property to set some or all of the border properties for the border to the right of the element contents.

Values

`border-width`   Sets the width for the right border. This value can be one of the following: `thin`, `medium`, `thick`, or a length measurement.

`border-style`   Sets the pattern used to fill the right border. You can set the style to any of the following: `none`, `dotted`, `dashed`, `solid`, `double`, `groove`, `ridge`, `inset`, or `outset`.

`border-color`   Sets the color for the right border. This value can be one of the color names or RGB values.

You can use one value for each of the values of the `border-left` property. See the entries for the individual properties for more details about these values.

Notes

See the "Notes" section for the `border-color`, `border-style`, and `border-color` properties.

Examples

```
P.NEWS {padding-right: 15em;
     border-right: thick dotted navy}
```

This creates a thick, dotted line that appears to the right of paragraphs of the class NEWS (P CLASS=NEWS). The line is navy blue and is 15 ems from the element contents.

```
H3.STRIKE {border-right: thick groove black}
```

This adds a thick, grooved, black line to the right of level 3 headings of the class STRIKE (H3 CLASS=STRIKE). This is a useful way to create a class that inserts an indicator that the information is out-of-date and about to be removed.

border-right-width

Use this property to set the thickness of the border on the right side of an element. The border width is, by default, a medium thickness and is unaffected by any border settings for the parent element.

Values

thin width   Sets a thin line for the right border. Use the keyword `thin`.

medium width   Sets a medium line for the right border. Use the keyword `medium`. This is the default.

thick width   Sets a relatively thick line for the right border. Use the keyword `thick`.

length   Sets the right border width using an absolute or a relative measurement. See the description of the length value for the `border-width` property for valid measurements.

You can use one of the values listed above to set the width of the right border.

Notes

See the "Notes" section for the `border-width` property.

Examples

```
P.STRIKE {border-style: dashed;
     border-right-width: 5px;
     border-color: blue}
```

This statement creates a paragraph class called STRIKE that uses a dashed, blue line on the right border of the element. The line is 5 pixels wide.

border-style

Use this property to display a border and specify a border style. You can create different effects by combining line styles with color and width. This property uses none as the default, not displaying the border at all, regardless of the color or width settings.

Values

no style   Prevents the display of one or more borders. Use the keyword none. This is the default.

dotted line   Sets the border as a dotted line, with spaces where the element background shows through. Use the keyword `dotted`.

dashed line   Sets the border as a series of dashes, alternating the element background and the border color. Use the keyword `dashed`.

solid line   Sets the border as a single, solid line in the border color or element foreground color. Use the keyword `solid`.

double lines   Sets the border as two solid lines in the border color or element foreground color. Use the keyword `double`.

grooved line   Sets the border as a 3-D rendering of a grooved line drawn in the border color. Use the keyword `groove`.

ridged line   Sets the border as a raised 3-D rendering peaking in the middle of the line, drawn in the border color. Use the keyword `ridge`.

inset border   Sets the border as a 3-D rendering creating the illusion that the inside of the element is sunken into the page. Use the keyword `inset`.

outset border   Sets the border as a 3-D rendering creating the illusion that the inside of the element is raised above the page. Use the keyword `outset`.

Use as many as four values from the list above to stylize the borders around an element. Since the initial setting for the `border-style` property is none, no borders are visible unless you set them up with a style plus a width.

Notes

Not all browsers can display the more esoteric styles, such as ridge, inset, and out-set. If the browser cannot interpret the style, it will substitute a solid line. Some browsers may simply render all borders as solid lines.

Examples

```
P.LOOKNEW {border-style: outset;
    border-width: 0.5cm;
    border-color: gray}
```

This statement creates the illusion that the LOOKNEW class paragraph elements (P CLASS=LOOKNEW) are set above the page in a raised box.

```
P.DANCING {border-style: groove ridge inset outset;
    border-color: #F0F8FF #F0FFFF blue #5F9EA0}
```

With these properties, each side of the paragraphs in the class DANCING (P CLASS=DANCING) are a different shade of blue and a different style.

border-top

Use this shorthand property to set some or all of the border properties for the top border of the element container.

Values

border-width   Sets the width for the top border. This value can be one of the following: thin, medium, thick, or a length measurement.

border-style   Sets the pattern used to fill the top border. You can set the style to any of the following: none, dotted, dashed, solid, double, groove, ridge, inset, or outset.

border-color   Sets the color for the top border. This value can be one of the color names or RGB values.

You can use one setting for each of the values of the border-top property. See the entries for the individual properties for more details about these values.

Notes

See the "Notes" section for the border-color, border-style, and border-color properties.

Examples

```
H1 {margin-top: 0.5in;
     color: red;
     background: white;
     padding: 9em;
     border-top: thin solid blue}
```

This statement creates level 1 headings (H1) that have red text on a white background and a thin, solid, blue line positioned 9 ems above the text. There is another line ½ inch above the heading. The 9-em padding is a relative value that depends on the font size and is equivalent to 9 blank lines above the heading.

border-top-width

Use this property to set the thickness of the border along the top of an element. The border width is, by default, a medium thickness and is unaffected by any border settings for the parent element.

Values

thin width   Sets a thin line for the top border. Use the keyword `thin`.

medium width   Sets a medium line for the top border. Use the keyword `medium`. This is the default.

thick width   Sets a relatively thick line for the top border. Use the keyword `thick`.

length   Sets the top border width using an absolute or a relative measurement. See the description of the length value for the `border-width` property for valid measurements.

You can use one of the values listed above to set the width of the top border.

Notes

See the "Notes" section for the `border-width` property.

Examples

```
H1, H2, H3 {font-size: 15pt;
     font-style: Futura, sans serif;
     border-style: solid;
     border-left-width: 1.5em}
```

This statement applies to the three levels of headings, giving each heading a solid line that is 1.5 ems. Since this is relative to the font, the line will be 22.5 points. The border color is not set, so the border uses the foreground color of the element.

border-width

Use this shorthand property to set the thickness of all the borders for an element. You can give the borders unique widths or use a single width for all the borders.

Values

thin width   Sets a thin line for the border. Use the keyword `thin`.

medium width   Sets a medium line for the border. Use the keyword `medium`. This is the default.

thick width   Sets a relatively thick line for the border. Use the keyword `thick`.

length   Sets the border width using an absolute or a relative measurement. Uses inch, millimeter, centimeter, point, pixel (the size according to the screen display), pica, x-height (the height of the font's lowercase letter *x*), or em (the width of a capital *M* in the font) units as measurements. This type of sizing forces a particular measurement to be used for the element, ignoring any browser's settings. Specify the measurement after the number as follows: `in` for inches, `mm` for millimeters, `cm` for centimeters, `pt` for points, `px` for pixels, `pc` for picas, `ex` for x-height settings, or `em` for em settings. With this property, the `em` and `ex` settings generate a border size relative to the parent font.

If you use one of the values above, it applies evenly to the borders on the four sides of the element. If you use two values, the browser applies the first to the top and bottom borders of the element, and the second to the left and right borders. If you include three values, the browser uses the first for the top border, the second for the left and right borders, and the last for the bottom border. If you use four values, the browser applies them in the following order: top, right, bottom, left.

Notes

The `thin` setting will always be less than or equal to the `medium` setting, which will always be less than or equal to the `thick` setting. The border widths do not depend on the element font or other settings. The `thick` setting, for example, is rendered in the same size wherever it occurs in a document. You can use the relative length values to produce variable (font-dependent) widths.

With a length setting, you cannot have a border with a negative width. You can use a decimal number, for example, 0.4 or 1.2.

Relative units set up the property in relation to the font and size properties. Use relative units wherever you can, because they scale more easily from situation to situation (for example, in different browsers and displays, or in the transition from display to printer). Relative units include em (1 em is equal to the width of a capital *M* in the font), ex (the height of the lowercase letter *x* in a font), and px (screen pixels).

Absolute lengths are useful when the properties of the browser are well-known or when you want to set a particular border size to conform to a specification. Absolute units include inches, millimeters and centimeters, points (1 point = 1/72 inch), and picas (1 pica = 12 points).

Examples

```
P.LOOKNEW {border-style: outset;
        border-width: 0.5cm;
        border-color: gray}
```

This statement sets all the borders for the paragraphs of class LOOKNEW (P CLASS=LOOKNEW) at ½ centimeter.

```
P.DANCING {border-style: groove ridge inset outset;
        border-width: thin thick medium 1cm;
        border-color: #F0F8FF #F0FFFF blue #5F9EA0}
```

This statement sets each border in the paragraphs of class DANCING (P CLASS= DANCING) at different widths. The top border is thin, the right border is thick, the bottom is medium, and the left border is 1 centimeter.

Box Margin Properties

Margins set the size of the box around an element. You measure margins from the border area to the edge of the box.

margin

Use this property as a shorthand to set up all the margins for an element's box. This measurement gives the browser the distance between the element border and the edge of the box. This area is always transparent, so you can view the underlying page background.

Values

length   Sets an absolute or a relative distance between the border and the box edge. See the border-width property in the "Box Border Properties" section for valid measurements.

percentage Sets the margin size as a percentage of the parent element's width.

automatic Use this optional value to set the margin to the browser's default. Use the keyword auto.

Use one of the values above. For length and percentage, you can use one, two, three, or four numbers. If you use one number, the browser applies it to all four margins (top, right, bottom, and left). If you use two numbers, the first number sets the top and bottom margin, and the second number sets the left and right margin. If you use three numbers, you are setting the top margin with the first, the right and left margins with the second, and the bottom margin with the third. You can mix length and percentage values.

Notes

You can use negative values for margins, but not all browsers will handle the settings correctly, and some may ignore the setting and substitute the default of zero (0) or use their own algorithm.

See the "Notes" section for the border-width property in the "Box Border Properties" section for information about relative and absolute length settings.

Examples

```
P.1 {margin: 5%}
```

This statement establishes paragraph margins, for paragraphs of class 1, to 5% each of the total width of the box.

```
P {margin: 2em 3pt}
```

This statement sets the paragraph elements' top and bottom margins to 2 ems (relative to the size of the font) and the left and right margins to 3 points.

```
P.NOTE {margin: 1em 3em 4em}
```

This statement sets the margins for paragraphs of class NOTE (P CLASS=NOTE). The top margin is 1 em (relative to the font size), the left and right margins are 3 ems, and the bottom margin is 4 ems. If the font size is 10 points, the top margin will be 10 points, the left and right margins will be 30 points, and the bottom margin will be 40 points.

margin-bottom

Use this property to set only the bottom margin of an element's box. The bottom margin is the distance between the bottom border and the bottom edge of the box. This generally defaults to zero (0) and is not used by included block or inline elements.

Values

> *length*   Sets an absolute or relative distance between the border and the box's bottom edge. See the `border-width` property in the "Box Border Properties" section for valid measurements.
>
> *percentage*   Sets the bottom margin size as a percentage of the parent element's width.
>
> *automatic*   Use this optional value to set the bottom margin to the browser's default. Use the keyword `auto`.

You can use one of the values above to set the bottom margin.

Notes

> See the "Notes" section for the `margin` property

Examples

```
P {margin-bottom: 4em}
```

This statement sets the bottom margin of all paragraphs to 4 ems. This is a relative measure, so the actual distance depends on the font. For example, if the font size is 10 points, the bottom margin will be the equivalent of 4 blank lines, or 40 points. This establishes a distance of 4 ems between the border and the box bottom.

```
H1 {margin-top:5em;
    margin-bottom: 1em}
```

This statement positions level 1 headings (H1) with the equivalent of five lines above and one line below. This creates a separation between the preceding topic and the heading and strengthens the association between the heading and its topic contents below.

margin-left

Use this property to set only the left margin of an element's box. The left margin is the distance between the border and the left edge of the box. You can use this to create indented text or other element placements. The default for the left margin is zero (0), or no space. The settings in one element are not used by its included or inline elements.

Values

> *length*   Sets an absolute or a relative distance between the border and the box's left edge. See the `border-width` property in the "Box Border Properties" section for valid measurements.

percentage   Sets the left margin size as a percentage of the parent element's width.

automatic   Use this optional value to set the left margin to the browser's default. Use the keyword `auto`.

You can use one of the values above to set the left margin.

Notes

See the "Notes" section for the `margin` property.

Examples

```
BODY {margin-left: 3%}
```

This statement sets up a basic left margin for the page using the <BODY> tag. The browser should display this margin as 3% of the width of the page. No element within the page will appear outside this margin. If the browser shows 640 × 480 pixels, the body margin (left) uses 18 pixels.

```
P {margin-left: 1cm}
```

This statement sets a left margin for paragraphs at the absolute value of 1 centimeter. With this, you can add a left gutter to your page.

```
P {margin-left: 4em}
```

This statement creates a variable gutter for the paragraphs on a page. The actual size of the 4-em margin depends on the font size used for the paragraphs.

margin-right

Use this property to set just the right margin of an element's box. The right margin is the distance between the border and the right edge of the box. You can use this to force the element away from the right edge of the page. This generally defaults to zero (0) and is not used by included block or inline elements.

Values

length   Sets an absolute or a relative distance between the border and the box's right edge. See the `border-width` property in the "Box Border Properties" section for valid measurements.

percentage   Sets the right margin size as a percentage of the parent element's width.

automatic   Use this optional value to set the right margin to the browser's default. Use the keyword `auto`.

You can use one of the values above to set the right margin.

Notes

See the "Notes" section for the `margin` property.

Examples

```
BODY {margin-right: 0.5in}
```

This statement creates a margin on your page that is a ½-inch wide. Nothing will appear in this margin area.

```
P {margin-right: 10%}
```

This statement establishes an outside gutter that is 10% of the paragraph width. The actual distance depends on the paragraph width.

```
H1 {margin-right: 15em}
```

This statement creates an outside gutter whose size depends on the heading font size. This inserts a distance equal to 1.5 times the heading font size. This means that if the level 1 heading uses a 15-point font, for example, the distance between the border and box edge is less than it would be with a 20-point font. If you want all headings to wrap before the edge of the box, but at the same place in the page, use percentage or absolute measurements.

margin-top

Use this property to set only the top margin of an element's box. The top margin is the distance between the border and the top of the box. You can use this to insert space above an element, perhaps to visually reinforce its relationship with the elements around it. This generally defaults to zero (0) and is not used by included block or inline elements.

Values

length   Sets an absolute or a relative distance between the border and the box's top edge. See the `border-width` property in the "Box Border Properties" section for valid measurements.

percentage   Sets the top margin size as a percentage of the parent element's width.

automatic   Use this optional value to set the top margin to the browser's default. Use the keyword `auto`.

You can use one of the values above to set the top margin.

Notes

See the "Notes" section for the `margin` property.

Examples

```
H1 {margin-top:5em;
    margin-bottom: 1em}
```

This statement positions level 1 headings (H1) with the equivalent of five lines above and one line below. This creates a separation between the preceding topic and the heading and strengthens the association between the heading and its topic contents below.

```
BODY {margin-top: 1em}
```

This statement adds the equivalent of one line to the margin of any element inside the body of the document. The actual distance depends on the font size for the element.

```
P {margin-top: 5%}
```

This statement adds a variable distance (5% of the height) to paragraph elements.

```
H1 {margin-top: 1cm}
```

This statement adds an absolute distance of 1 centimeter to the space between the box edge and the border of level 1 headings (H1). Whatever the environment, the browser tacks a centimeter of transparent margin to the element's box.

Box Position Properties

The box position properties control the arrangement of elements in relation to one another and the page, rather than within themselves. The float and clear properties control which elements can sit next to each other. The width and height properties set dimensions for elements, giving you more control of the page layout.

clear

Use this property to allow or disallow other elements, usually inline images, to float beside the element specified. You can allow floating elements on either side, both sides, or neither side. The default is to allow floating elements on both sides of the element (the none setting). This property is not used by inline and included elements.

Values

no restrictions   Allows floating elements on either side of this element. Use the keyword none. This is the default.

not on left   Moves the element below any floating elements on the left. Use the keyword left.

not on right   Moves the element below any floating elements on the right. Use the keyword `right`.

not on both   Does not allow floating elements on either side of this element. Use the keyword `both`.

Use one of these values to designate the position for floating elements in relation to a particular element.

Notes

This property indicates where floating elements are not allowed.

Examples

```
P.PRODNAME {clear: none}
```

This statement creates a paragraph class called PRODNAME (P CLASS=PRODNAME) that allows floating elements to appear on either side of it.

```
P {clear: right}
```

In this statement, the paragraph element allows floating elements on its left side, but not the right.

```
H1, H2, H3 {clear: both}
```

This statement prevents elements from appearing next to the headings in the document. All floating elements, usually images, are pushed up or down and appear above or below the headings.

float

Use this property to set an element in a position outside the rules of placement for the normal flow of elements. For example, the `float` property can raise an element from an inline element to a block element. This is usually used to place an image. The default, which is not an inherited value, is to display the element where it appears in the flow of the document (the `none` setting).

Values

no changes   Displays the element where it appears in the flow of the parent element. Use the keyword `none`. This is the default.

left float   Wraps other element contents to the right of the floating element. Use the keyword `left`.

right float   Wraps other element contents to the left of the floating element. Use the keyword `right`.

Notes

A floating element cannot overlap the margin in the parent element used for positioning. For example, an illustration that is a left-floating element (pushes other contents to the right of itself) cannot overlap the left margin of its parent container.

Examples

```
P {clear: none}
IMG.KEYCAP {float: none}
IMG.PRODLOGO {float: left}
```

These statements specify that if an image of class KEYCAP (IMG CLASS=KEYCAP) is inserted in the course of a paragraph, it appears within the flow of the text. If an image of class PRODLOGO (IMG CLASS=PRODLOGO) is inserted, it appears against the left margin of the parent element, and the text wraps on its right.

height

Use this property to set the height of an element on a page. Browsers will enforce the height, scaling the image to fit. This property will be familiar to anyone who has used the height and width values of an image on a Web page.

Values

length   Sets an absolute or a relative height for images in a particular element or class. Uses inch, centimeter, millimeter, point, pixel (the size according to the screen display values), pica, x-height (the height of the font's lowercase letter *x*), or em (the width of a capital *M* in the font) units as measurements. This type of sizing forces a particular measurement to be used for the element, ignoring any browser's settings. Specify the measurement after the number as follows: in for inches, cm for centimeters, mm for millimeters, pt for points, px for pixels, pc for picas, ex for x-height settings, or em for em settings. The em and ex settings generate a size relative to the parent font.

automatic   Allows the browser to either set the height to the actual image height or, if the width is set, preserve the aspect ratio of images. Use the keyword auto.

You can use one of these values for the height of elements.

Notes

Some browsers may not handle the height (or width) property if the element is not a replaced element (one that uses a pointer in the HTML source to indicate the file with the actual content).

Generally, replaced elements have their own, intrinsic, measurements. If you want to replace these dimensions with a height (and/or width) property setting, the browser tries to resize the replaced element to fit. To maintain the aspect ratio, you need to set one of the properties, height or width, to auto. To preserve the aspect ratio of images positioned with height, include the width property in the statement and set the width to auto. If you position an image with the width property, include the height property in the statement and set the height to auto.

If you need to set the size of an image, it's usually best to set it in proportion to the container element (using a relative setting); otherwise, leave these settings at auto, which allows the browser to use the image's original size.

You cannot use a negative value for the height or width of an element.

With a length setting, relative units set up the property in relation to the font and size properties. Use relative units wherever you can, because they scale more easily from situation to situation (for example, in different browsers and displays, or in the transition from display to printer). Relative units include em (1 em is equal to the width of a capital *M* in the font), ex (the height of the lowercase letter *x* in a font), and px (screen pixels).

Absolute units are useful when the properties of the browser are well-known or when you want to set a particular size to conform to a specification. Absolute units include inches, millimeters and centimeters, points (1 point = 1/72 inch), and picas (1 pica = 12 points).

Examples

```
IMG.KEYCAP {float: none;
    width: auto
    height: 1.2em;
    vertical-align: middle}
```

This statement creates an IMG class (IMG CLASS=KEYCAP) where the images appear in the text stream. These images have a controlled width and a height that is 1.2 ems. For example, in a stream of text with a font size of 12 points, the image will be 14.4 points. The statement also adjusts the vertical position of the image in relation to the line.

```
IMG.PRODLOGO {float: left;
    width: 2cm;
    height: auto}
```

In this statement, images of class PRODLOGO (IMG CLASS=PRODLOGO), which have the text wrap on the right around them, have a controlled width of 2 centimeters. However, it is better to avoid absolute measurements and use relative values or the image's own values (by setting width and height to auto).

width

Use this property to set the width of an element on a page. Browsers will enforce the width, scaling the image to fit.

Values

length Sets an absolute or relative width for images in a particular element or class. See the height property for valid measurements.

percentage Sets the image size as a percentage of the parent element's width.

automatic Allows the browser to either set the width to the actual image width or, if height is set, preserve the aspect ratio of images. Use the keyword auto.

You can use one of these values for the width of elements.

Notes

See the "Notes" section for the height property.

Examples

```
IMG.KEYCAP {float: none;
    width: auto
    height: 1.2em;
    vertical-align: middle}
```

In this statement, images of class KEYCAP (IMG CLASS=KEYCAP) will appear in the text stream aligned to the middle of the line of text where it appears. Its height is set to 1.2 ems and the width to auto, which allows the browser to position it properly (the height does not disturb the paragraph formatting around it, and the width is adjusted to fit).

```
IMG.PRODLOGO {float: left;
    width: 2cm;
    height: auto}
```

This statement creates an image class PRODLOGO (IMG CLASS=PRODLOGO) that forces the text to wrap on the right of it, is 2 centimeters wide, and has whatever height is proportionate to the 2-centimeter width.

Background and Color Properties

Color affects the foreground elements, such as text and borders, and background properties affect the surface on which the document elements appear. You can set these globally and locally for individual elements. When you paint the background for an element, you are layering on top of the document's background. If you do not set a background for an element, it defaults to transparent, allowing the document background to show. The `color` property inherits from the document body.

You can control a wide variety of properties for backgrounds, including the position, repetition, and scrolling. You can use the `background` shorthand property to set all the background properties, or use the individual properties. The background is set relative to the element's box properties.

background

Use this property as a shorthand to include the full collection of background values. The `background` property will be familiar to anyone who has changed the page color of a Web page or added a graphic as wallpaper. This property now extends to individual elements, allowing you to have a variety of backgrounds. It also allows more functionality in the background, including scrolling and repetitions.

Values

The possible values for background are the set of all possible values listed in the individual property entries:

`background-attachment`   Sets up a background that scrolls with the element.

`background-color`   Sets a background color for the page or elements on the page.

`background-image`   Sets an image behind the element.

`background-position`   Positions the background within the element's box.

`background-repeat`   Sets the number of times and direction that a background repeats.

See the entries for the individual properties for details about these values.

Notes

If you do not include a property (such as `background-repeat`), the browser uses the default. The order of the properties in a statement is not important.

Examples

```
BODY {background: url(sunshine.gif) blue repeat-y}
```

This statement sets up a background for the page using the <BODY> tag. If the browser cannot find the image, it uses a blue background. If needed, the background image repeats down the page (but not across the page).

```
HI {background: white}
```

This statement changes the background for level 1 headings (H1) to white using the color keyword. If this statement appears in the same Style Sheet as the first statement, the sunshine background is overlaid with a white box where the level 1 headings appear.

```
P EM {background: url(swirl.gif) yellow top left}
```

In this statement, paragraph emphasis (EM) is changed to a swirl GIF file that starts at the top-left corner of the element's box. If the GIF file cannot be found, the browser uses a yellow background.

background-attachment

Use this property to specify whether the background image of an element will scroll with the element or remain at a fixed location on the page. If the image is larger than the element box, visitors scrolling down the screen either see different parts of the background image (a fixed attachment) or a single part of the image (a scrolling attachment) that moves with the display of the element down the page.

The default, scroll, applies only to the element in the statement. Inline and included block elements do not inherit this property.

Values

scrolling   Moves the image with the element on the page so that the same part is visible when visitors scroll down the screen. Use the keyword scroll. This is the default.

fixed   Keeps the image fixed in relation to the page, so different parts are visible when visitors scroll down the screen. Use the keyword fixed.

Notes

Use this property in conjunction with the background-image property.

Examples

```
P { background-image: url(logo.gif);
    background-attachment: fixed}
```

This statement uses the image logo.gif as the background for the paragraphs in the document. The image is fixed to the page, not the contents of the paragraph.

background-color

Use this property to set the background color for the page or elements on the page. If you set the background for the base class BODY, your other tags will appear to inherit that color unless you change their background colors from transparent.

Values

color   Sets the color for the background. This value can be one of the color names or RGB values. See the border-color property in the "Box Border Properties" for color keywords and values.

transparent   Makes the page background the default for viewing. Use the keyword transparent.

Notes

This value sets the background color only. To set the background as an image, you need to use either the background property or the background-image property.

This property affects the box area owned by the element. This is set using the margins and padding properties, listed in the "Box Margin Properties" and "Box Padding Properties" sections.

When you set an element's background to transparent or don't set it at all, the page's background color or image appears in its place.

See the "Notes" section for the border-color property in the "Box Border Properties" section for information about color settings.

Examples

H1 {background-color: blue}

In this statement, the background color for level 1 headings (H1) is set to blue using the color keyword.

P.NOTE {background-color: #800000}

This statement creates a paragraph class called NOTE (P CLASS=NOTE) that has a background color of maroon using the RGB hexadecimal value for the color.

background-image

Use this property to define an image for the background. The browser will look for additional information about the image's position, repetition, and attachment (or association). If you accept the defaults for these properties, your background image will not repeat, will be attached to the page (not the element), and will have a starting position at the upper-left corner of the element's box.

Values

no image   Does not use an image for the background. Use the keyword none if you need to override a previous statement. This is the default.

image url   Cues the browser that you are going to provide a file name. Use the keyword url.

Notes

The images you use must be GIF or JPG image files to ensure that all graphical browsers can read them.

You may also want to include a background-color property in case the image you have selected is not available.

Examples

```
P {
        background-image: url(litelogo.jpg);
        background-repeat: no-repeat;
        background-attachment: fixed; }
```

This statement sets up the document paragraphs to have a background image (called litelogo.jpg) that does not repeat and is fixed to the document canvas rather than to the element.

background-position

Use this property to position the element background within its space, using the initial position as a mark. Every element has a box that describes the area it controls. The background-position property is useful when your image is not the same size as the element for which it provides a background. With this property, you can indicate the position of the image relative to the element box.

Values

length   Sets the starting point on the element's box edge, in an absolute or a relative measurement, and also gives the coordinates as measurements. Uses inch, centimeter, millimeter, point, pixel (the size according to the screen display values), pica, x-height (the height of the font's lowercase letter *x*), or em (the height of the font) units as measurements. Specify the measurement after the number as follows: in for inches, cm for centimeters, mm for millimeters, pt for points, px for pixels, pc for picas, ex for x-height settings, or em for em settings. The em and ex settings generate a size relative to the parent font.

percentage Indicates as a percentage where on the box edge the browser begins placing the image. You can repeat this value to give a vertical and horizontal starting point.

vertical position Sets the vertical starting position. Use the keyword top, center, or bottom. The browser determines the size of the element box and works from there.

horizontal position Sets the horizontal starting position. Use the keyword left, center, or right. The browser determines the width of the element box and works from there.

With the length and percentage settings, you can use two numbers to indicate the vertical and horizontal starting point. Unlike percentage, however, the length measurement does not apply to both the image and the element box in the same way. The length measurement indicates the coordinates inside the element box where the top-left corner of the image appears.

Notes

Using 0% 0% is synonymous with using top left. In the first case, the initial position of the image is determined this way; the upper-left corner of the image is considered 0% horizontal and 0% vertical, and the same is done with the element box. You could position an image using 50% 50%, and the browser would then begin at the middle of the element and the image. If the image is larger than the element box, you lose the edges that extend beyond the element box. Similarly, if your image is smaller than the element box, you will have an edge, inside your element box, with no image.

You can combine the percentage and length measures. It would be legal to set the property using 25% 2cm. This would start rendering the image at $\frac{1}{4}$ the way into the image at a $\frac{1}{4}$ the distance across the element box. The image would begin to appear 2 centimeters below the top of the element box.

The length measurements indicate the distance from the box border where the browser starts to render the image.

When you use a length unit, you can use a positive or a negative number. You can, in some cases, use a decimal number. Whichever system of measurement you choose to use must be communicated with the short form for the system (for example, cm or in).

Relative units set up the property in relation to the font and size properties. Use relative units wherever you can, because they scale more easily from situation to situation (for example, in different browsers and displays, or in the transition from display to printer). Relative units include em (1 em is equal to the width of a capital *M* in the font), ex (the height of the lowercase letter *x* in a font), and px (screen pixels).

Absolute lengths are useful when the properties of the browser are well-known or when you want to set a particular size to conform to a specification. Absolute units include the inches, millimeters and centimeters, points (1 point = 1/72 inch), and picas (1 pica = 12 points).

You can also use keywords to position the image within the element's box. Table 2.2 gives you some corresponding values to work with.

TABLE 2.2: KEYWORDS AND THEIR VALUES

Keyword	Percentage	Description
top left, left top	0% 0%	The top-left corner of the image starts at the top-left corner of the element box.
top, top center, center top	50% 0%	The horizontal middle of the image appears in the horizontal middle of the element box. The top of the image begins at the top of the element box.
right top, top right	100% 0%	The top-right corner of the image starts at the top-right corner of the element box.
left, left center, center left	0% 50%	The vertical middle of the image appears in the vertical middle of the element box. The left side of the image is flush against the left side of the element box.
center, center center	50% 50%	The absolute middle of the image positions over the absolute middle of the element box.
Right, right center, center right	100% 50%	The vertical middle of the image positions over the vertical middle of the element box. The right edge of the image is flush against the right side of the element box.
bottom left, left bottom	0% 100%	The bottom-left corner of the image is positioned at the bottom-left corner of the element box.
bottom center, center bottom	50% 100%	The horizontal centers of the image and element box appear together, and the bottom edges of each remain together.
bottom right, right bottom	100% 100%	The lower-right corner of the image positions in the lower-right corner of the element box.

Examples

```
BODY {background-image: url(litelogo.gif);
      background-position: 50% 50%}
```

This sets the base class, BODY, to position a background image centered on the page.

```
H1 {background-image: url(exclaim.gif);
    background-position: top left}
```

In this statement, an image has been assigned to the background of heading level 1 (H1) tags that starts rendering at the upper-left corner of the element box.

background-repeat

Use this property to control whether an image repeats horizontally, vertically, both, or neither. Images normally repeat both horizontally and vertically, filling in the area within the element's margins. By default, backgrounds repeat both horizontally and vertically.

Values

horizontal and vertical repeat   Sets horizontal and vertical repetitions of the image. Use the keyword repeat. This is the default.

horizontal repeat   Sets horizontal repetitions only. Use the keyword repeat-x.

vertical repeat   Sets vertical repetitions only. Use the keyword repeat-y.

no repeat   Prevents repeated copies of the image from displaying. Use the keyword no-repeat.

Notes

This property works in conjunction with the background-image and background-position properties. Combining these properties into a single statement enables you to create a pattern of background images that enhance the presentation of information.

Examples

```
P {background-image: url(logo1.gif);
   background-color: blue;
   background-position: top left;
   background-repeat: repeat-y}
```

This statement adds a background to your document paragraphs. The first copy of the image appears in the upper-left corner of the page and repeats down the page. If the image is not found, the browser uses a blue background.

color

Use this property to set the foreground, or element, color. If the element is text, you can set the color of the text with this property. Both inline (such as images) and included block elements (such as EM) use this property.

Values

color   Sets the color for the background. This value can be one of the color names or RGB values. See the border-color property in the "Box Border Properties" for color keywords and values.

Notes

You can set this property using one of the three systems of RGB or by using a color keyword. Although most browsers should recognize the color keyword, individual browser/system configurations may display the same color differently.

Choose the system that makes the most sense to you and stick with that. See Part 5 of this Master's Reference for color values and resources.

If you use RGB values, put a comment next to the line to help you remember what the color was supposed to be. Comments start with /* and end with */.

See the "Notes" section for the border-color property in the "Box Border Properties" section for more information about color settings.

Examples

```
BODY {color: black}
```

This statement uses the keyword black to set the default foreground color in the document to black.

```
P {color: #0000FF}
```

This statement changes the paragraph (P) foreground color to blue using the RGB hexadecimal value.

```
EM {color: rgb(75%,0%,0%)}
```

In this statement, emphasis (EM) is set to maroon using the RGB percentage value.

Classification Properties

This group of properties controls the presentation of some standard elements, such as the display and lists. The properties can change the type of an element from an inline to a block, from a list-item to an inline element, and so on. These properties also include controls for lists and list-items, giving you more control over the presentation of the bulleted lists on your page.

display

Use this property to change the display values of an element. You can change an element's type between inline, block, and list-item:

- An inline element does not start and stop on its own line, but is included in the flow of another element. A standard inline element is EM, for emphasis; you can also include images in the stream of text as an inline element.
- A block element starts on its own line and ends with another line break.
- A list-item is a subset of block elements, but is contained within a larger block element.

Every element has its own default value for display.

Values

no display   Prevents the display of the element. Use the keyword none.

block display   Sets the element with a line break before and after. Use the keyword block.

inline display   Removes the line breaks from an element and forces it into the flow of another element. Use the keyword inline.

list-item display   Sets the element as a line in a list. Use the keyword list-item.

Notes

You can use the display property values to create special elements such as run-in headings and running lists, as well as to force images into inline presentations.

Examples

```
H1 {display: inline}
```

This statement sets the browser not to force the level 1 headings (H1) onto a separate line. You could combine this with a line break (BR) before the heading, to start a new line, but let the contents of the section start right after the heading. You may want to extend the right margin of the heading to add some space between the heading and the content.

```
LI.INTEXT {display: inline}
```

Use this if you want to reformat your lists of the class INTEXT (LI CLASS=INTEXT) as a integral part of a paragraph. For example, you could list:

- block
- inline

- list-item
- none

Or you could list block, inline, list-item, none.

list-style

Use this shorthand property to set all the list properties in a single statement. If you set this property for a list element (as opposed to the list-item elements), the list-items use the settings you establish. You can override the list settings with individual list-item settings.

Values

The possible settings values for list-style are the set of all possible values listed in the individual property entries:

list-style-type Sets the type of bullet used in the list. You can set the style type to any of the following: disc, circle, square, decimal, lower-roman, upper-roman, lower-alpha, upper-alpha, or none.

list-style-position Sets a hanging outdent (outside), so that the bullet is not flush with the text of the list-item, or an indented bullet (inside), so that it is flush with the text of the list-items.

list-style-image Sets an image to use for a bullet. Use the keyword url.

See the entries for the individual properties for details about these values.

Notes

These values apply only to elements with a display characteristic of list-item. If you use the url keyword to specify an image, you don't need to set the type, because the bullet position will be occupied by the image.

Examples

OL.OUTLINE {list-style: lower-roman inside}

This creates a list class called OUTLINE (OL CLASS=OUTLINE), which numbers the list items.

LI.COMMENT {list-style: none}

If you use this statement in the same Style Sheet as the first statement, you can insert list-items that have no numbering.

list-style-image

Use this property to replace the standard bullet characters with an image of your choice. If you set this property for a list element (as opposed to the list-item elements), the list-items use the settings you establish. You can override the list settings with individual list-item settings.

Values

no image   Suppresses the image bullets that the element may have inherited.

image url   Identifies a specific image that you want to use for a bullet. Use the keyword url.

Notes

If you use an image, be sure it is a small image. Resize the image before assigning it as a bullet character.

If the browser cannot find the image identified in the url, it will default to list-style-type setting.

List-items use the settings from the lists. You can insert list-items with different settings, creating a series of effects (such as comments or highlights by using a different bullet or position).

Examples

```
LI.PRODICON {url (logo.gif)}
```

This replaces the bullet character for list-items of type PRODICON (LI CLASS= PRODICON) with an image called logo.gif.

list-style-position

Use this property to set an indent or outdent for the bullet. This property allows the bullet to stand out from the list contents (outside) or lays it flush with the list-items (inside). If you set this property for a list element (as opposed to the list-item elements), the list-items use the settings you establish. You can override the list settings with individual list-item settings

Values

indent   Aligns the bullet character with the left margin of the list-item contents. Use the keyword inside.

outdent   Creates a hanging-indent effect, with the bullet standing out from the left margin of the list-item contents. Use the keyword outside.

Notes

List-items use the settings from the lists. You can insert list-items with different settings, creating a series of effects (such as comments or highlights by using a different bullet or position).

Examples

```
UL {list-style-position: outside;
    list-style-type: circle}
LI.LEVEL2 {list-style-position: inside}
LI.PRODSTART {list-style-image: url (logolitl.gif)}
```

If you combine these three statements in a Style Sheet, your basic list-items in an unordered list will have a hollow circle that hangs outside the left margin of the list contents. You can add level 2 class list-items (LI CLASS=LEVEL2) that use the circle bullet but lay it flush to the list-item contents. This creates a visual effect where these list-items appear to be secondary. The third statement creates the effect of list headings by replacing the circle with a logo, and these list-items use the parent's list-style-position setting.

list-style-type

Use this property to indicate a style of bullet or numbering you want for your lists. You can create several list classes and list-item classes and then combine them to give your information navigational structure. If you set this property for a list element (as opposed to the list-item elements), the list-items use the settings you establish. You can override the list settings with individual list-item settings.

Values

no bullet   Suppresses the display of bullet characters. Use the keyword none.

disc bullet   Places a filled circle as the bullet. Use the keyword disc.

circle bullet   Places a hollow circle as the bullet. Use the keyword circle.

square bullet   Places a filled square as the bullet. Use the keyword square.

decimal bullet   Numbers the list-items using arabic numerals (1, 2, 3, ...). Use the keyword decimal.

lowercase-roman bullet   Numbers the list-items using lowercase roman numerals (i, ii, iii, ...). Use the keyword lower-roman.

uppercase-roman bullet   Numbers the list-items using uppercase roman numerals (I, II, III, ...). Use the keyword upper-roman.

lowercase-alpha bullet   Letters the list-items using lowercase letters (a, b, c, …).
Use the keyword `lower-alpha`.

uppercase-alpha bullet   Letters the list-items using uppercase letters (A, B, C, …).
Use the keyword `upper-alpha`.

Notes

If you use numbering or lettering, and you insert list-items with an alternate type, the
numbering includes the unnumbered list-items in its counts. For example:

```
A    full-featured
     WYSIWIG
     compliant
D    backward compatible
```

Examples

```
OL {list-style-type: lower-roman}
```

This statement sets up a numbering system for the ordered lists in the document
(OL). These lists will use i, ii, iii, and so on as a "bullet" for each list item.

```
LI.COMMENT {list-style-type: none}
```

You can override the list settings with a list-item setting. If you apply the list-item
class COMMENT (LI CLASS=COMMENT) to an item in a numbered list, the browser includes
it in the numbering, but does not display the number for the list-item.

white-space

Use this property to control the white space within an element. This setting controls
the wrapping of text within the element. You can use the default, which produces
results similar to what you see in Web pages already, or you can use the `pre` keyword
to indicate that the content is already formatted correctly and should be displayed "as
is." This property introduces a new value, `nowrap`, which relies on you to provide the
information about when to wrap a line using line breaks (BR).

Values

no changes   Keeps the default of wrapping lines at the browser page size. Use
the keyword `normal`. This is the default.

previous formatting   Assigns the formatting in the document source to the document display. Use the keyword `pre`.

no wrapping   Prevents the visitor from wrapping lines within an element. Use
the keyword `nowrap`.

Notes

When you want to control the line wrap in paragraphs or headings, you can do it with this property. If you select `normal`, it overrides the settings of a parent element since browsers default to this setting. If your element is a preformatted entity (such as sample code), you may want to use the `pre` keyword to force the browser to display it exactly as it occurs in the source text. Use the `nowrap` keyword to prevent the browser from ending the line without an explicit instruction, such as BR, in the source.

Some browsers may ignore this setting and retain their own defaults. Even though the default value for white-space is listed as `normal`, some browsers will have a default setting for all HTML elements.

Examples

```
PRE {white-space: pre}
```

This statement indicates that the text in the element is preformatted. The spacing between characters, words, and lines is set in the source, as are the line breaks.

```
P {white-space: normal}
```

This statement sets the spacing in the paragraph elements (P) to normal, which is how text is currently displayed.

```
H1 {white-space: nowrap}
```

This statement prevents the browser from wrapping the level 1 headings (H1). For these headings to break across more than one line, you will need to explicitly add BR tags at the break spots.

Master's Reference
Part 3

JavaScript

This section covers the JavaScript statement keywords, objects, method and functions, and properties. These are all the pieces that you need to build a JavaScript for your page. We've included some examples here, but look in Chapter 11 to find the details of how to write JavaScript. In our explanations of the examples, we have used the term *entry* (rather than parameter or operator) to refer to the various parts of the syntax.

This reference sorts entries by general purpose; the sections cover the constructs, operators, escape character, reserved words, objects, methods and functions, and properties. Constructs are statement types that you can use to control the flow of a script. Operators are the algebraic, logical, and bitwise symbols for working with values in your statements. Escape character allows you to insert a special character into your text. Reserved words are terms that JavaScript either currently uses or plans to use in the future. The objects are the containers in which properties reside and which affect methods and functions.

Constructs

Constructs are the structures that you use in a JavaScript to control the flow of the script. If the course of the script depends on input or circumstance, you use a construct to direct the processing of the script. For example, to display the answer to a test question after a visitor has tried unsuccessfully to respond correctly, you can use a construct called an `if` statement.

This section contains an alphabetic list of JavaScript constructs. Each entry describes a single construct and provides its syntax and an example.

break

A break statement ends a series of `while` or `for` statements. Sometimes you want a condition that ignores everything else and jumps out of the loop to carry on with the rest of the script. You do this with a break statement. The syntax for the `break` statement is:

```
break
```

Example:

```
function alphacount (x)
    {
    var count = 0
    while (var < 1000)
        {
        if (var >= 990)
            break
        var += (getUserNumber())
        }
    }
```

This example is a function, alphacount, that adds user input until at least 990, but it could conceivably go as high as 1000. If the value is between 990 and 1000, the break statement is triggered, and the while statement ends.

comment

You place comments within your scripts to help you recall what variables represent or which conditions that change over time may affect loops or other calls. A comment does not perform a function; it is simply a note to yourself or to future users of the script. The syntax of the comment statement is:

```
// comment text
```

Example:

```
readMe="" //set the readMe variable to null
bigNews=1 //set the bigNews variable to 1
if (readMe < bigNews)
    {
    bigNews += song
    // add song to bigNews, increments bigNews by a user variable
    getStory(readMe) // this function retrieves the user's guess
    }
```

In this example, the variable declarations and the if statement are documented with comments.

continue

Like the break statement, continue breaks out of a for or a while loop. Instead of going to the next set of instructions past the loop, the continue statement sends the script back to the condition in the while statement or to the update expression in a for loop. The syntax of the continue statement is:

```
continue
```

Example:

```
while (cows!="home") {
    if (barnDoor = "open") {
        cows = "home"
        continue }
    callCows() }
```

In this `while` loop, the condition checks the value of the variable *cows*. As long as the value is not equal to "home", the loop continues. Within the loop is an `if` statement that checks the state of the *barnDoor*; when the variable *barnDoor* is "open", the statement sets the value of *cows* to "home" and sends the script back up to the condition statement. Otherwise, the loop continues to run the function `callCows`.

for

The `for` statement repeats an action for a counted number of times. You give the script the starting conditions, ending conditions, and iteration information. A starting condition could be `month=1`, indicating the repetitions begin at January. The ending condition, in this case, could be `month=12`, indicating the repetitions continue through the months of the year. Inside this repetition, you include a series of statements that perform a function (such as display a result: In January our sales were $1500K). The increment would likely be `month++`, indicating that the value of `month` is increased by 1 as each repetition is completed. The syntax of the `for` statement is:

```
for ([initial expression]; [condition];[update expression]) {
    statements
}
```

The `initial expression` entry is the statement or variable declaration, `condition` is the boolean or comparison statement, and `update expression` is the incrementation scheme tied in with a variable in the condition.

Example:

```
horse = 100
for (cows=0, cows <= horse, horse++)
    { getCowCount(cows) }
```

This example simply repeats the function `getCowCount` until the number of cows is more than the number of horses. Each time the results of `getCowCount` is less than or equal to the number of horses (in the variable *horse*), the number of horses is incremented by 1. This loop could go on for a long time.

for in

The for in statement doesn't need counters to complete its repetitions. If, for example, you have a list of commands in objects that use the menu name (the File object contains all the menu items found under the File menu), you can iterate through the list, presenting them as part of a list of options. The benefit is that you can store the information in an object and update it once to use many times. When the list of menu items is complete, the script moves on to the next set of instructions. The syntax of the for in statement is:

```
for (variable in object) {
    statements }
```

The variable entry represents a value, and object is an array of object properties.

Example:

```
function house (rooms, location, floors, residents) {
    this.rooms = rooms
    this.location = location
    this.floors = floors
    this.residents = residents }
while (newHome != "no") {
    description = ""
    for (info in house) {
        description += house + "." + info + " = " + house[info] + "<BR>" }
    description += "<HR>"
    return description
    getNewHouse (newHome)
    }
```

In this example, the function house fills the information about the object house. The object house contains the properties: rooms, location, floors, and residents. The statement inside the for in loop generates a series of statements that fill the object. For example, if the user provided the following information, 10, London, 5, and 9, the variable description would end up being this series:

house.rooms = 10

house.location = London

house.floors = 5

house.residents = 9

function

This construct sets up a JavaScript function. The function makes some kind of calculation using information provided—words, numbers, or objects. With a function command you can fill an object with the selected information. For example, if you collect information from a visitor in several boxes, you can put this together into a single variable that you then use to address the visitor throughout the session. Define functions in the <HEAD> section of the Web page, because functions must be declared before they can be used. The syntax of the function statement is:

```
function name ([parameter} {,parameter] [..., parameter]) {
    statements }
```

Example:

```
// this function works out the grade for the test
function calc_pass_fail (ans_right, ans_wrong, ans_blank) {
    return ans_right / (ans_right + ans_wrong + ans_blank) }
```

In this example, the function calc_pass_fail reads in the variables *ans_right*, *ans_wrong*, and *ans_blank* to produce the person's percentage grade for the most recent test. Subsequent JavaScript scripts might control which page visitors see, depending on their grade.

if

The if statement works just like the spoken equivalent: *If this is true, do this*. Use this construct when you want the script to perform a task when the right conditions arise. For example, to include some information in a result page, use the if construct—if the user selects examples, include examples in the results page. The syntax of the if statement is:

```
if (condition) {
    statements }
```

Example:

```
if (tests = 0) {
    document.write("Take tests.")
    }
```

In this example, the if statement determines if the visitor has taken any tests. If the visitor has not taken any tests (tests = 0), "Take tests." appears on the screen.

if else

Like the if statement, this construct allows you to apply decision-making to the script: *If this is true, do this; otherwise, do this.* Use this construct when you have two alternatives that depend on the conditions. For example, suppose you want to display correct or incorrect notes next to the visitor's response in a test. If the visitor answers correctly, include a congratulations message; otherwise, show the correct answer. The syntax of the if else statement is:

```
if (condition) {
    statements }
else {
    statements }
```

Example:

```
if (tests != 0) {
    if (tests = 1) { document.write("lesson 2") }
    else {
        if (tests = 2) { document.write("lesson 3") }
        else {
            if (tests = 3) { document.write("lesson 4") }
        }
    }
}
else { document.write("lesson 1") }
```

In this example, the if statements check which test the visitor has completed and print the name of the next lesson. The first if statement simply tests whether the visitor has taken any tests; the test counter is incremented at the end of each test (not in this function or loop).

new

Use this construct to create a user-defined object. Creating an object is a process with two steps:

1. Define the object with a function.

2. Create an instance of the object with new.

The syntax of the new statement is:

```
objectName = new objectType ( parameter1 [, parameter2] [..., parameterN])
```

The objectName entry is the name of the new object; this is how you refer to it in later code. The objectType entry is the object type, a function call that defines the object. The parameter1 ... parameterN entries are the properties for the object.

Example:

```
function house (rooms, location, floors, residents) {
    this.rooms = rooms
    this.location = location
    this.floors = floors
    this.residents = residents }
newHouse new house (8, Praireville, 3, 4)
```

This example creates an object type called house and populates newHouse, which is of type house, with 8 rooms, a Praireville location, 3 floors, and 4 residents.

return

The return statement works in conjunction with the function statement. To display a calculated value, you include a return statement to bring the value back to the script. The syntax of the return statement is:

```
return
```

Example:

```
function square (x) {return x * x }
```

This simple example uses the return statement with the expression that generates the value that should be returned (the square of the number *x* passed to the function).

switch

The switch statement is similar to the if else statement, in that it presents the script with a series of alternate routes that depend on conditions found. The switch statement is cleaner than nesting a series of if else statements. The syntax of the switch statement is:

```
switch (expression) {
    case1: statement;
    break;
    case2: statement;
    break;
    default statement; }
```

Example:

```
switch (infoType) {
    case ("reference") : destination = "refchapt.html";
    break;
    case ("how-to") : destination = "instruct.html";
```

```
    break;
    case ("overview") : destination = "intro.html";
    default : destination = "toc.html"; }
```

This example takes the value in the variable *infoType* and compares it to a list of known values. If the value in *infoType* matches any of the stated cases (reference, how-to, or overview), the script stores a page name in the destination variable. If no match is found, the script sets the destination to the table of contents (toc.html).

this

The construct this refers to the object in focus. For example, when filling an object's array (list of properties), you would have a series of this statements (one for each property). The syntax of the this statement is:

```
this[.propertyName]
```

Example:

```
function house (rooms, location, floors, residents) {
    this.rooms = rooms
    this.location = location
    this.floors = floors
    this.residents = residents }
newHouse new house (8, Praireville, 3, 4)
```

This example creates an object type called house and populates newHouse, which is of type house, with 8 rooms, a Praireville location, 3 floors, and 4 residents.

var

This is a keyword that indicates the statement is performing an assignment to a variable. You use this to set the initial value of the variables (always a good idea!) outside the function. The syntax of the var keyword is:

```
var varName [= value] [..., varName [= value]}
```

The *varName* entry is the name of the variable, and value becomes the contents of the variable.

Example:

```
var cust_id = 0, reading = 0
```

In this simple statement, *customer id* (cust_id) and *usage* (reading) variables are set to zero. This is in preparation for a function in which a customer number is assigned and a variable that tracks session activities is launched.

while

The `while` statement is similar to the `if` statement. It also is like its spoken equivalent: *While I'm gone, clean the house*. The `while` statement is also like the `for` and `for in` statements; it creates a loop that repeats a set of statements as long as a condition is true. The syntax of the `while` statement is:

```
while (condition) {
    statement; }
```

Example:

```
copies = 0
original = 0
while (copies <5) {
    copies++
    while (original < 10) {
        original++ }
    }
```

In this example, the two values, `copies` and `original`, are set to zero before entering the `while` loop. The outside loop checks that the number of copies made is less than 5. If that condition is true, the number of copies is incremented by 1, and then a second `while` loop iterates through the pages in the original.

with

To use a series of statements from the same object, such as the Math object, place them inside a `with` statement. You then need not identify each function, method, or property as belonging to the Math object. Usually when you write a statement that uses a function from an object, you have to include the object in the statement. The `with` construct lets you group a series of statements and identifies the parent object for the functions, methods, and properties. The syntax of the `with` statement is:

```
with (object) {
    statements; }
```

Example:

```
with (Math) {
    a = PI * r * r
    x = r * cos(theta)
    y = r * sin(theta) }
```

In this example, the object Math is used to assign values to the properties a, x, and y.

Operators

An operator is a symbol that represents an action; the most familiar operators are the mathematic symbols for addition, subtraction, multiplication, and division. JavaScript includes these basic actions and some more complex operations, each with a special symbol. As is the case with those familiar mathematic symbols, an order of operation defines the precedence of each operator in an expression.

Table 3.1 defines the operators and presents them in their order of operation. You can use parentheses to control the order or precedence in a statement. In the table, operators of equal precedence are grouped together. For example, (), [], and . (period) have the same precedence in the order of operation.

Some of these operators work on the bits in your values. To work on the bits, JavaScript converts your values to bits, performs the operation, and converts the value back to its original type. This can lead to some interesting results, particularly if you are unfamiliar with the bit values or if you miscalculate. Table 3.2 lists the assignment operators.

TABLE 3.1: JAVASCRIPT OPERATORS

Operator	Description	What It Does
()	Function call or statement organizer	Organizes functions and forces a different order on the equations: x+2*y is the same as x+(2*y) because multiplication takes precedence over addition.
[]	Subscript	Use when you have a pointer and an element. For example, if you have an associative list (a variable that contains a set of values), you can use this to identify individual members in the list. These lists are called arrays.
.	Members	Use when you are using the methods and properties for an object. For example, Math.abs calls the absolute function from the Math object.
!	NOT	The boolean negation symbol. Use it when your expression is designed to include everything except the item marked with this NOT symbol. For example, for names in phone book, if name ! BOB, call. This calls everyone except Bob.

Continued ▶

Operator	Description	What It Does
~	Ones complement	The bitwise equivalent of the NOT operator. Using this changes a 0 (zero) to a 1 (one) and vice versa.
++	Increment	Use in front of or behind a variable to add one to its value. For example, RIGHT++ is the same as RIGHT+1.
—	Decrement	Use in front of or behind a variable to subtract one from its value. For example, SUBMIT-- is the same as SUBMITS-1.
*	Multiply	Use to multiply two numeric values. These must be numbers.
/	Divide	Use to divide two numeric values. If you use integers on both sides of the division expression, you'll not get any decimal values. For example, if IN and OUT are declared as integers, and IN is 12 and OUT is 7, IN/OUT=1.
%	Modulo	Modulo division returns the remainder from a division operation. For example, 7/2 as an integer division gives you a result of 3. 7%2 gives you 1.
+	Addition	Combines two values (numbers or words).
-	Subtraction	Takes one value (number or word) out of another.
<<	Bitwise left shift	Moves the contents of an object or element left. This works on the bits in the object, moving them left and filling in the right with spaces. This converts the object into bits and then shifts them. For example, 7<<2 becomes 111 (the binary representation of 7) shifted left 2 places (11100) which, when converted back to integer values, is 28.
>>	Bitwise right shift	Like the left shift above, this moves the bits to the right; unlike the left shift, the bits shifted right drop out of the value. So, using the same example above, 7>>2 becomes 1.

TABLE 3.1 CONTINUED: JAVASCRIPT OPERATORS

Continued ▶

TABLE 3.1 CONTINUED: JAVASCRIPT OPERATORS

Operator	Description	What It Does
>>>	Zero-fill right shift operator	This bitwise shift operator moves bits to the right and pads the left with zeros.
<	Less than	Compares two values. If the value on the right is larger than the value on the left, this operation returns True.
>	Greater than	Compares two values. If the value on the left is larger than the value on the right, this operation returns True.
<=	Less than or equal to	Compares two values. If the value on the right is equal to or larger than the value on the left, this operation returns True.
>=	Greater than or equal to	Compares two values. If the value on the left is equal to or larger than the value on the right, this operation returns True.
==	Equality	Compares two values. If they are equal, the operation returns True.
!=	Inequality	Compares two values. If they are not equal, the operation returns True.
&	Bitwise AND	Checks the bits of two values and determines where they are both the same. If the value is a multi-bit value, the operation checks each position. If the two values do not have a matching number of bits, the smaller value is left padded until the number of positions match. If they match, a 1 is returned. For example, 10&7 returns 2 because 1010 & 0111 only match in the second to last position, giving you 0010, which is 2.
^	Bitwise EOR (exclusive OR)	Returns True if one or the other of the values is 1. When the values match, it returns a 0. So, using the example above, 10^7 returns 1101 which is 13.
|	Bitwise OR	Returns true (1) if one value is 1. Unlike EOR, this operator returns True if both values are 1. So, the 10|7 expression returns 1111, which is 15.

Continued ▶

TABLE 3.1 CONTINUED: JAVASCRIPT OPERATORS

Operator	Description	What It Does
&&	Logical AND	Unlike bitwise operators, logical operators compare expression results. Use the logical operators to link boolean comparisons into a test for a branching statement. For example, if Bob is older than Ray, *and* Ray is not working today, send the package to Ray. The package is sent to Ray only if the two conditions are met.
||	Logical OR	Results in True if either expression is true. So, using the same example above, Ray would receive the package if *either* he was younger than Bob or was not working that day.
?:	If-else	This is the symbol for the `if else` construct, which is described in the Constructs section.
,	Comma	Separates values in a sequence, such as assignments to an object that contains an array.
operator=	Assignment	Creates assignments. Table 3.2 shows the range of possibilities.

TABLE 3.2: THE ASSIGNMENT OPERATORS

Operator	What It Does
=	Puts the value on the right into the variable on the left; any contents are replaced.
+=	Adds the value on the right to the variable on the left; the contents are augmented.
*=	Multiplies the variable on the left by the value on the right and places the result in the variable.
/+	Divides the variable on the left by the value on the right and places the result in the variable.
%=	Divides the variable on the left by the value on the right and places the difference in the variable.
<<=	Performs a bitwise shift on the variable on the left equal to the value on the right; the result is placed in the variable.

Continued ▶

	TABLE 3.2 CONTINUED: THE ASSIGNMENT OPERATORS
Operator	**What It Does**
>>=	Performs a bitwise shift on the variable on the left equal to the value on the right; the result is placed in the variable.
>>>=	Performs a bitwise shift on the variable on the left equal to the value on the right; the result is placed in the variable.
&=	Performs a bitwise AND on the variable and value; the result is placed in the variable.
^=	Performs a bitwise EOR on the variable and the value; the result is placed in the variable.
|=	Performs a bitwise OR on the variable and the value; the result is placed in the variable.

Escape Character

The backslash (\) is the escape character in JavaScript. An escape character tells the system that the next character in the sequence is either a special instruction or is a reserved character being used in quoted text. Table 3.3 lists the escape sequences that JavaScript uses.

	TABLE 3.3: THE JAVASCRIPT ESCAPE SEQUENCES
Character	**Function**
\b	Backspace
\n	New line
\t	Tab
\r	Carriage return
\f	Form feed
\\	Backslash (in text)
\'	Single quote (in text)
\"	Double quote (in text)
\ooo	Octal number
\hh	Hexadecimal number

Reserved Words

JavaScript has a number of reserved words, words that you cannot use for variables in your script. These words are either in use, for example, as functions, or are reserved for future use:

abstract	else	instanceof	super
boolean	extends	int	switch
break	false	interface	synchronized
byte	final	long	this
cse	finally	native	throw
catch	float	new	throws
char	for	null	transient
class	function	package	true
const	goto	private	try
continue	if	protected	var
default	implements	public	void
do	import	return	while
double	in	static	with

Objects

Objects are a simple way of referring to parts of a Web page. Using objects gives structure to your Web pages and JavaScript scripts. In general, you apply methods, functions, and properties to objects to achieve a result.

This section contains an alphabetic listing of the available JavaScript objects. Each entry describes the object, gives its format, and shows an example. Each entry also contains a list of the associated properties, methods, and event handlers.

Anchor

The anchor object is text on a page that represents a destination for a link. The anchor object can also be a link object. The browser creates an anchor array when it opens the page. This array contains information about each anchor object. You can access the anchors or their length from this array.

The anchor object has the following format:

```
<A [HREF=URL] NAME="anchorname" [TARGET="windowName"]> anchorText </A>
```

To access the anchors array:

```
document.anchors.length
document.anchors.[index]
```

The index entry is an integer representing an anchor in the document.

The anchor object has no properties or methods. The anchor array has the property length, which you can use to get the number of anchors on the page from the array.

There are no event handlers for the anchor object, which is a property of document.

Example:

```
<A NAME="reference_library"><H1>Books on JavaScripting<H1></A>
```

This statement establishes a target in a document. If, for example, that document is called JSIntro.html, you can use the following statement in an anchor object or a link object to jump to the location of the line above:

```
<A HREF="JSIntro.html#reference_library">Reference Books for Scripting</A>
```

button

This object is a pushbutton on a form. The browser sets the appearance of the button, but you control the text prompt on the button and the action it performs. The button object has the following format:

```
<INPUT
TYPE="button"
NAME="buttonName"
VALUE="buttonText"
[onClick="handlerText"]>
```

The buttonName entry is the name for the button, which is how you identify the button. Each button on the page needs a unique buttonName. The buttonText entry is the label that appears on the button.

The name property reflects the NAME= attribute. The value reflects the VALUE= attribute. The button uses the onClick method and the onClick event handler. It is the property of form.

Example:

```
<INPUT
    TYPE="button"
    NAME="goNow"
    VALUE="Let's GO!"
    onClick="buttonClick(this.form)" >
```

In this example, a Let's Go button appears on the form. When the visitor clicks the button, the event handler onClick runs the function that processes the form.

checkbox

A checkbox appears on a form to let visitors make selections (none, one, or more) from a list. The checkbox object has the following format:

```
<INPUT
TYPE="checkbox"
NAME="checkboxName"
VALUE="checkboxValue"
[CHECKED]
[onClick="handlerText"]>
textToDisplay
```

The checkboxName entry is the name property for the checkbox object; you identify the checkbox with this name if you reference it in your script. The checkboxValue entry is the return value when the checkbox is selected; this defaults to On. The CHECKED entry specifies that the checkbox appear as checked when the browser first displays it. The textToDisplay entry is the label, the option text next to the checkbox.

You can set the checkbox checked property, changing the state (on or off) of the checkbox. The defaultChecked property reflects the CHECKED attribute. The name property reflects the NAME= attribute, and the value property reflects the VALUE= attribute. The checkbox object uses the click method and the onClick event handler. It is the property of form.

Example:

```
<H3>Pick the modules that you want to study:</H3>
<BR><INPUT TYPE="checkbox" NAME="studymodul_newdocs" CHECKED> Creating a new
document
<BR><INPUT TYPE="checkbox" NAME="studymodul_trackdocs" CHECKED> Tracking
documents in the system
<BR><INPUT TYPE="checkbox" NMAE="studymodul_routedocs" CHECKED> Route
documents through the system
```

and so on...

In this example, you have a list of options; each option appears with its checkbox selected.

date

The date object lets you work with dates. It includes a large number of methods for getting date information, such as the calendar date or the time of day. Dates prior to 1970 are not allowed. The date object has the following format:

```
dateObjectName = new Date()
dateObjectName = new Date("month day, year hours: minutes: seconds")
```

```
dateObjectName = new Date(year, month, day)
dateObjectName = new Date(year, month, day, hours, minutes, seconds)
```

The new keyword generates a new object using the Date object. In the second statement, the properties month, day, year, hours, minutes, and seconds are string values. In the third and fourth statements, they are integers.

The date method has the following format:

```
dateObjectName.methodName(parameters)
```

The date object has no properties and uses the following methods:

getDate	getSeconds	setDate	setTime
getDay	getTime	setHours	setYear
getHours	getTimeZoneoffset	setMinutes	toGMTString
getMinutes	getYear	setMonth	toLocaleString
getMonth	parse	setSeconds	UTC

The date object has no event handlers because built-in objects have no event handlers. The date object is the property of no other object.

Example:

```
var logofftime= new Date();
logofftime=logofftime.getHours()+":"+logofftime.getMinutes()+":
"+logofftime.getSeconds();
```

In this example, the script creates a new date variable called *logofftime* and then populates that variable with the current time.

document

The document object is the container for the information on the current page. This object controls the display of HTML information for the visitor. The document object includes only the <BODY> sections of an HTML document and has the following format:

```
<BODY
    BACKGROUND="backgroundImage"
    BGCOLOR="backgroundColor"
    TEXT="foregroundColor"
    LINK="unusedLinkColor"
    ALINK="activeLinkColor"
    VLINK="followedLinkColor"
    [onLoad="handlerText"]
    [onUnload="handlerText"]>
</BODY>
```

Although onLoad and onUnload are included in the <BODY> tag, they are not document event handlers—they are window event handlers.

The document object has the properties shown in Table 3.4.

TABLE 3.4: THE PROPERTIES OF THE DOCUMENT OBJECT

Property	What It Does/Is
alinkColor	Reflects the active link color
anchors	An array containing a list of the anchors on the document
bgColor	Reflects the background color
cookie	Specifies a cookie (information about the user/session)
fgColor	Reflects the foreground color for text and other foreground elements such as borders or lines
forms	An array containing a list of the forms in the document
lastModified	Reflects the date the document was last changed
linkColor	Reflects the basic link color
links	Reflects the link attributes
location	Reflects the location (URL) of the document
referrer	Reflects the location (URL) of the parent or calling document
title	Reflects the contents of the <TITLE> tag
vlinkColor	Reflects the color of past links activity

The document object also uses five methods—clear, close, open, write, and writeln—but uses no event handlers. Although the onLoad and onUnload event handlers are included in the <BODY> tag, they are window events. The document object is the property of window.

Example:

```
function setMeUp() {
    document.alinkColor="darkcyan"
    document.linkColor="yellow"
    document.vlinkColor="white" }
…
<BODY onLoad="setMeUp()">
```

In this example, the settings for the link colors use the document properties. This is equivalent to the following <BODY> declaration:

```
<BODY
    ALINK="darkcyan"
    LINK="yellow"
    VLINK="white">
```

elements

The elements object is an array of the form objects in the order in which they occur in the source. This gives you an alternate access path to the individual form objects. You can also determine the number of form objects by using the length property. This is similar to the anchor array in that you can read from it, but not write to it. The elements object has the following format:

```
formName.elements[index]
formName.elements.length
```

The formName entry is either the name of the form or an element in the form's array. The index entry is an integer representing an object on a form.

The elements object uses the length property, which reflects the number of elements on a form. There are no methods and no event handlers for the elements object. It is the property of form.

Example:

```
userInfo.username.value
userInfo.elements[0].value
```

Both statements return the same value if the element username is the first item in the elements array.

form

This object defines the form with which users interact. It includes checkboxes, textareas, radio buttons, and so on. You use the form object to post data to a server. It has the following format:

```
<FORM
    NAME="formName"
    TARGET="windowName"
    ACTION="serverURL"
    METHOD=GET | POST
    ENCTYPE="encodingType"
    [onSubmit="handlerText"] >
</FORM>
```

The windowName entry is where form responses go. If you use this, the server responses are sent to a different window—another window, a frame, or a frame literal (such as _top). The serverURL is the location where the information from the form goes when it is posted. The GET | POST (GET or POST) commands specify how the information is sent to the server. With GET, which is the default, the information is appended to the receiving URL. With POST, the form sends the information in a data body that the server handles. The encodingType entry is the MIME encoding of the data sent. This defaults to application/x-www-form-urlencoded; you can also use multipart/form-data.

Here is the format for using the object's properties and methods:

```
formName.propertyName
formName.methodName(parameters)
forms[index].propertyName
forms[index].methodName(parameters)
```

The formName entry is the NAME= attribute of the form. The propertyName and methodName entries are one of the properties listed in Table 3.5. The index entry is an integer representing the form object within the array. Statements one and three are equivalent, as are statements two and four.

TABLE 3.5: THE PROPERTIES OF THE FORM OBJECT

Property	What It Does/Is
action	Reflects the server URL
elements	A list of the elements in the form
encoding	Reflects the ENCTYPE= attribute
length	The number of elements on the form
method	Indicates how the information is processed (GET or POST)
target	Reflects the window where forms go

The form object uses the submit method and the onSubmit event handler. It is the property of document.

Example:

```
function setCase (caseSpec){
if (caseSpec == "upper") {
    document.f1.userName.value=document.f1.userName.value.toUpperCase()
    document.f1.userPass.value=document.f1.userPass.value.toUpperCase()}
    else {
    document.f1.userName.value=document.f1.userName.value.toLowerCase()
    document.f1.userPass.value=document.f1.userPass.value.toLowerCase()}
}
</SCRIPT>
<BODY>
<FORM NAME="f1">
```

```
<P>Enter a name and password for the test page</P>
<B>Your name:</B>
<INPUT TYPE="text" NAME="userName" SIZE=20>
<BR><B>Your Password:</B>
<INPUT TYPE="text" NAME="userPass" SIZE=20>
<P>The system is case-sensitive, please choose an option below for how we
should save your name and password.</P>
<INPUT TYPE="radio" VALUE="off" NAME="upperRadio"
     onClick="setCase('upper')"
   "Set my info into uppercase letters.">
<INPUT TYPE="button" VALUE="on" NAME="lowerRadio"
     onClick="setCase('lower')"
   "Set my info to lowercase letters.">
</FORM>
```

In this example, the visitor enters his or her name and then can choose all uppercase or all lowercase for the information that gets saved.

frame

The frame object is a window within a window and has its own URL. A page can contain a series of frames. There is also a frames array that lists all the frames in your code. The frame object has the following format:

```
<FRAMESET
    ROWS="rowHeightList"
    COLS="columnWidthList"
    [onLoad="handlerText"]
    [onUnload="handlerText"] >
    [<FRAME SRC="locationOrURL" NAME="frameName">]
        [<NOFRAMES>
        [HTML tags and so on...
        for browsers that do not support frames]
        </NOFRAMES>
</FRAMESET>
```

The rowHeightList entry is a comma-separated list of values that set the row height of the frame. The default unit of measure is pixels. The columnWidthList is a comma-separated list of values that set the column width of the frame. The default unit of measure is pixels.

The `locationOrURL` entry is the location of the document to be displayed in the frame. This URL cannot include an anchor name. The `location` object describes the URL components. The `frameName` entry is the target for links.

To use the object's properties, follow this format:

```
[windowReference.]frameName.propertyName
[windowReference.]frames[index].propertyName
window.propertyName
self.propertyName
parent.propertyName
```

The *windowReference* entry is a variable from the window object definition or one of the synonyms: top or parent. The `frameName` entry is the value of the `NAME=` attribute in the `<FRAME>` tag. The `index` entry is an integer representing a frame object in the array, and the `PropertyName` entry is one of the properties listed in Table 3.6.

To use the object's array, follow this format:

```
[frameReference.]frames[index]
[frameReference.]frames.length
[windowReference.]frames[index]
[windowReference.]frames.length
```

TABLE 3.6: THE PROPERTIES OF THE FRAME OBJECT	
Property	**What It Does/Is**
frames	The array, or list, of frames in the document
name	Reflects the NAMES= attribute (as assigned in <FRAMESET>)
length	An integer that reflects the number of child frames within this frame
parent	The window or frame that contains this frame
self	The current frame
window	The current frame

The frames array has a `length` property that reflects the number of child frames within a frame. The `frame` object uses the `clearTimeout` and `setTimeout` methods.

The `frame` object does not use event handlers. Although the `onLoad` and `onUnload` event handlers appear within `<FRAMESET>`, they are event handlers for the `window` object. The `frame` object is a property of `window`. The frames array is a property of both `frame` and `window`.

Example:

This is a multipart example. The first piece of code sets up framed windows, which are structured the same (4 frames). The frameset comes after the `<HEAD>` tag and replaces the `<BODY>` tag.

3

```
<HTML>
<HEAD>
    <TITLE>Central Zoo: Front Entrance</TITLE>
</HEAD>
<FRAMESET COLS="40%, 60%" onLoad="alert('We\'re in like Flynn')">
<FRAME NAME="frame1" SRC="mainframe.html">
<FRAME NAME="frame2" SRC="littleframe.html">
</FRAMESET>
</HTML>
```

In this example, the form gives the visitor background color options that are controlled by pushbuttons. When a visitor selects a color, it is assigned to the background of the document in another frame. A visitor can also change the contents of the secondary frame. The calls in the first document (SRC=) populate the frames with the files.

hidden

The hidden object contains a text object that is suppressed, not displayed, on an HTML form. This object is used to pass information when the form is submitted. Although the visitor cannot change the value directly, the developer (you) can control the contents, changing it programmatically. The hidden object has the following format:

```
<INPUT
    TYPE="hidden"
    NAME="hiddenName"
    [VALUE="textValue"] >
```

The hiddenName entry is the name of the object, which allows you to access the object using the NAME= property. The TextValue entry is the initial value for the object.

The hidden object uses two properties—name and value. These reflect the object name and contents. The hidden object does not use any methods or event handlers. It is the property of form.

Example:

```
<FORM NAME="form1">
<INPUT  TYPE="hidden" NAME="hiddenPass">
<INPUT  TYPE="text" NAME="password" VALUE="" SIZE=5>
<INPUT  TYPE="button" NAME="test" VALUE="Test"
    onClick="document.form1.hiddenPass.value=document.form1.password.value;
    alert(document.form1.hiddenPass.value)">
</FORM>
```

This example reads in a password from a text object and stores it in the hidden object. As a test of the form, we've included a line that displays the hidden object in an alert, which is not something you would normally do.

history

The history object contains the list of visited URLs; this information is available in the history list of the browser. The history object has the following format:

```
history.length
history.methodName(parameters)
```

The length entry is an integer representing a position in the history list. The methodName entry is one of the methods listed below.

The history object uses the length property. There are three methods for the history object: back, forward, and go. Each of these navigate through the history list. The history object does not use event handlers. It is the property of document.

Example:

```
if (score < 65) { history.go(-2) }
```

The if statement checks the score against a satisfactory performance measure of 65. If the student scores less than 65 on the test, the browser goes back to the beginning of the lesson, two pages earlier.

```
<INPUT TYPE="button" NAME="reviewButton" VALUE="Look Again!"
    onClick=history.back() >
```

The reviewButton button performs the same function as the browser's back button.

link

A link object includes the text and images that contain the information for a hypertext jump. A link object is also an anchor object. When the jump is complete, the starting page location is stored in the destination document's referrer property. The link object has the following format:

```
<A HREF=locationOrURL
    [NAME="anchorName"]
    [TARGET="windowName"]
    [onClick="handlerText"]
    [onMouseOver="handlerText"] >
    linkText
</A>
```

The locationOrURL entry is the destination address. The anchorName entry is the current location within the jump-from page. The windowName is the window that the link is loaded into, if different from the current window. This can be an existing window, a frame, or a synonym such as _top or _self.

You can also define a link using the link method.

To use a link's properties, follow this format:

```
document.links[index].propertyName
```

The `index` entry is an integer representing the `link` object in the links array.

To use the links array, follow this format:

```
document.links[index]
document.links.length
```

You can read the links array, but you cannot write values to it.

Table 3.7 list the properties of the `link` object.

TABLE 3.7: THE PROPERTIES OF THE LINK OBJECT

Property	What It Does/Is
hash	Contains the anchor name in the URL
host	Contains the `hostname:port` portion of the URL
hostname	Contains the host and domain name or IP address of the network host
href	Includes the entire URL
pathname	Contains the URL-pathname (directory structure/location) part of the URL
port	Specifies the communication port on the server
protocol	Specifies the type of URL (for example, `http` or `ftp`)
search	Contains the page name (for example, `index.html`)
target	Reflects the TARGET= attribute

The `links` array uses the `length` property. The `link` object does not use any methods. The `link` object uses the `onClick` and `onMouseOver` event handlers. It is the property of document.

Example:

```
<SCRIPT>
    var there="http://www.raycomm.com/"
</SCRIPT>
</HEAD>
<BODY>
<FORM NAME="form1">
    <B>Choose a document, then click "Take me there" below.</B>
    <BR><INPUT TYPE="radio" NAME="destination" VALUE="Overview"
        onClick="there =
```

```
            'http://www.raycomm.com/intro.html'">
            Overview of JavaScripting
  <BR><INPUT TYPE="radio" NAME="destination" VALUE="HowTo"
            onClick="there =
            'http://www.raycomm.com/makeScript.html'">
            Learn to Make a Script
  <BR><INPUT TYPE="radio" NAME="destination" VALUE="Reference"
            onClick="there =
            'http://www.raycomm.com/refchapt.html'">
            JavaScript Reference Information
  <BR>
  <P><A HREF="" onClick="this.href=there"
            onMouseOver="self.status=there; return true;">
            <B>Take me there!</B>
  </A>
</FORM>
```

In this example, a form gives visitors access to the set of chapters. They can select a chapter/destination or go to the default destination.

location

The `location` object contains information about the current URL. It contains a series of properties that describe each part of the URL. A URL has the following structure:

```
protocol//hostname:port pathname search hash
```

The `protocol` specifies the type of URL (for example, `http` or `ftp`). The `hostname` contains the host and domain name or IP address of the network host. The `port` specifies the communication port on the server (not all addresses use this). The `pathname` is the directory structure/location on the server. The `search` value is the page name (for example, `index.html`). The `hash` value is preceded by the hash mark (#) and indicates a target anchor on the page.

Here are some common protocol types:

javascript	ftp	http	news
about	mailto	file	gopher

The `location` object has the following format:

```
[windowReference.]location.propertyName
```

The `location` object uses the same properties as the link object, as shown in Table 3.7 earlier. The `location` object does not use any methods or event handlers. It is a property of `document`.

Example:

```
window.location.href="http://javatutorial.writelivelihood.com/"
```
In this example, the URL of the current page is set to the JavaTutorial home page.
```
parent.frame3.location.href="http://javatutorial.writelivelihood.com/"
```
This example opens the JavaTutorial home page in frame3.
```
<SCRIPT>
var there="http://www.raycomm.com/"
var takeLesson=""
document.write ("Welcome to " + document.location + ". Not ever done!")
</SCRIPT>
```

This example displays a message at the top of the page that welcomes visitors to the current location.

Math

This is a built-in object that includes a large set of methods and properties for mathematic constants and operations. An example of a constant is *pi*, which is referenced as `Math.PI`. If you are using a series of expressions, you can use the `with` construct. In general, the `math` object has the following format:

```
varName = Math.propertyName [expression]
varName = Math.method()
```

The actual format will vary with the property in use. Check the property entries for the exact syntax.

The `math` object uses the following properties, each of which is described in the Properties section:

E	LN10	LOG2E	SQRT1_2
LN2	LOG10E	PI	SQRT2

The `math` object uses the following methods, each of which is described in the Methods and Functions section:

abs	atan	exp	max	sin
acos	ceil	floor	pow	sqrt
asin	cos	log	random	tan

The `math` object uses no event handlers since it is a built-in object. It is not a property of anything. See the entries for individual properties and methods for examples.

navigator

Use this object to determine a visitor's version of Netscape Navigator. It has the following format:

```
navigator.propertyName
```

Properties and Methods

The navigator object does not use any methods, and it contains the properties shown in Table 3.8. It does not use any event handlers, and it is not the property of anything.

TABLE 3.8: THE PROPERTIES OF THE NAVIGATOR OBJECT

Property	What It Does
appCodeName	Contains the internal code name of the browser
appName	Contains the external name of the browser
appVersion	Contains the version number of the browser
userAgent	Contains the user-agent header

Example:

```
var userBrowser = navigator.appName + " " + navigator.appVersion
```

The values for the navigator properties appName and appVersion are in a variable called userBrowser. You can use this later to test the browser's suitability for the functionality available on your page.

password

The password object is a text field that conceals its value and displays asterisks in place of typed characters. A password object is part of a form and must be defined within a <FORM> tag. This object has the following format:

```
<INPUT
    TYPE="password"
    NAME="passwordName"
    [VALUE="textValue"]
    SIZE=integer >
```

The passwordName entry is the name of the object. The textValue entry is a default value for the password, and size is the length of the password field.

To use the password properties and methods, follow this format:

```
passwordName.propertyName
passwordName.methodName(parameters)
```

```
formName.elements[index].propertyName
formName.elements[index].methodName(parameters)
```

The `passwordName` entry is the value of the `NAME=` attribute in the password object. The `formName` entry is the form container or an element in the forms array. The `propertyName` is one of the properties listed below, and `methodName` is one of the methods listed below. The first and third statements are equivalents, as are the second and fourth statements.

The `password` object uses the properties listed in Table 3.9 and uses the `focus`, `blur`, and `select` methods.

TABLE 3.9: THE PROPERTIES OF THE PASSWORD OBJECT

Property	What It Does
defaultValue	Reflects the VALUE= attribute
name	Reflects the NAME= attribute
value	Reflects the current contents of the password object's field

The `password` object does not use event handlers. It is a property of `form`.

Example:

```
<INPUT TYPE="password" NAME="password" VALUE="password.defaultValue" SIZE=8>
```

This is useful if the visitor has already visited the site and created a password or if you have assigned passwords to visitors.

radio

A radio button forces a single selection from a set of options. Similar to the checkbox, it is a part of a form; unlike the checkbox, only one radio button can be selected from the set. The `radio` object has the following format:

```
<INPUT
    TYPE="radio"
    NAME="radioName"
    VALUE="buttonValue"
    [CHECKED]
    [onClick="handlerText"] >
    textToDisplay
```

The `radioName` entry is the name of the object. This offers you one method for addressing the `radio` object in your script. The `buttonValue` entry is the value that is returned to the server when the button is selected. The default is On. You can access this value using the radio.value property. The CHECKED attribute sets the button to selected, and textToDisplay is the label displayed next to the radio button.

The radio button uses the click method and the properties shown in Table 3.10.

TABLE 3.10: THE PROPERTIES OF THE RADIO OBJECT

Property	What It Does/Is
checked	Lets you set the selection through your script (rather than visitor interaction); good for situations in which one choice automatically determines several others
defaultChecked	Reflects the settings for the CHECKED attribute
length	The number of radio buttons in the object
name	Reflects the NAME= attribute (radioName above)
value	Reflects the VALUE= attribute (buttonValue above)

The radio object uses the onClick event handler, and it is the property of form.

Example:

```
<SCRIPT>
var there="http://www.raycomm.com/"
function checkThis(){
    confirm("Thanks for registering")}
</SCRIPT>
</HEAD>
<BODY onLoad="window.alert('Welcome! You can register through this page. For
    future reference, this page is ' + '<P>' + document.location)">
    <FORM NAME="form1" onSubmit="checkThis()">
    <B>Choose a document, then click "Take me there" below.</B>
    <BR><INPUT TYPE="radio" NAME="destination" VALUE="Overview"
        onClick="there = 'http://www.raycomm.com/intro.html'">
        Overview of JavaScripting
    <BR><INPUT TYPE="radio" NAME="destination" VALUE="HowTo"
        onClick="there =
        'http://www.raycomm.com/makeScript.html'">
        Learn to Make a Script
    <BR><INPUT TYPE="radio" NAME="destination" VALUE="Reference"
        onClick="there =
        'http://www.raycomm.com/refchapt.html'">
        JavaScript Reference Information
    <BR>
```

```
    <P><A HREF="" onClick="this.href=there"
        onMouseOver="self.status=there; return true;">
        <B>Take me there!</B>
    </A>
    <P><INPUT TYPE="text" NAME="whoIs" VALUE="user" SIZE=15>
    <P><INPUT TYPE="radio" NAME="lesson" VALUE="Lesson 1" CHECKED
        onClick="takeLesson='lesson1.htm'"> Lesson 1: Getting Started
    <P><INPUT TYPE="radio" NAME="lesson" VALUE="Lesson 2"
        onClick="takeLesson='lesson2.htm'"> Lesson 2: Concepts and
        Operations
    <P><INPUT TYPE="radio" NAME="lesson" VALUE="Lesson 3"
        onClick="takeLesson='lesson3.htm'"> Lesson 3: Projects
    <P><INPUT TYPE="reset" VALUE="Defaults" NAME="resetToBasic">
    <INPUT TYPE="submit" VALUE="Send it in!" NAME="submit_form1">
    <HR>
  </FORM>
  </BODY>
```

This example creates two groups of radio buttons that set up the destination for the link/jump for the visitor or the course selections.

reset

This object is a reset button on a form. It clears the form fields of any visitor interaction/ entries and resets their values to the default. This is a form element and must be defined in the <FORM> tag. The onClick event handler cannot be canceled. Once the reset object is clicked, the form is reset, and all visitor entries are lost. The reset object has the following format:

```
<INPUT
    TYPE="reset"
    NAME="resetName"
    VALUE="buttonText"
    [onClick="handlerText"] >
```

The resetName entry is the name of the object. It allows you to access the object within your script. The buttonText entry is the label for the button.

To use the reset properties and methods, follow this format:

```
resetName.propertyName
resetName.methodName(parameters)
formName.elements[index].propertyName
formName.elements[index].methodName(parameters)
```

Statements one and three are equivalent, as are statements two and four.

The reset object has two properties. It uses the click method and the onClick event handler. It is a property of form.

Example:

```
<INPUT TYPE="reset" NAME="clearForm" VALUE="Start Over">
```

This statement places a reset button (this one says Start Over) that clears the current form when it is clicked.

```
<SCRIPT>
    var takeLesson=""
</SCRIPT>
</HEAD>
<BODY>
<FORM NAME="form1">
    <P><INPUT TYPE="text" NAME="whoIs" VALUE="user" SIZE=15>
    <P><INPUT TYPE="radio" NAME="lesson" VALUE="Lesson 1" CHECKED
onClick="takeLesson='lesson1.htm'"> Lesson 1: Getting Started
    <P><INPUT TYPE="radio" NAME="lesson" VALUE="Lesson 2"
onClick="takeLesson='lesson2.htm'"> Lesson 2: Concepts and Operations
    <P><INPUT TYPE="radio" NAME="lesson" VALUE="Lesson 3"
onClick="takeLesson='lesson3.htm'"> Lesson 3: Projects
    <P><INPUT TYPE="reset" VALUE="Defaults" NAME="resetToBasic">
    <P><INPUT TYPE="submit" NAME="launch_lessons" VALUE="Start the
    Learning!">
</FORM>
```

This example has a form on which visitors identify the kind of information they want (as in Getting Started, Concepts and Operations, Projects, and so on) and the lesson they want (selected from the list of radio buttons.) The reset statement clears any changes the visitor may have made and resets the form to Getting Started. The submit statement sends the selections to be processed according to the instructions (not seen) for the form.

select

The select object presents the visitor with a drop-down list of pre-set choices. It contains an options array. This is a form element and must be defined within a <FORM> tag. The select object has the following format:

```
<SELECT>
    NAME="selectName"
    [SIZE="integer"]
    [MULTIPLE]
```

```
    [onBlur="handlerText"]
    [onChange="handerText"]
    [onFocus="handerText"]
    <OPTION VALUE="optionValue" [SELECTED]> textToDisplay [… <OPTION>
textToDisplay
</SELECT>
```

The `selectName` entry is the name of the object; the `select` object contains the list. The `MULTIPLE` entry indicates that the object accepts multiple selections—such as checkboxes. If the list is not set to multiple, it is like a `radio` object, and only one choice, is available. The `OPTION` entry is a selection element in the list, and `optionValue` is the value returned to the system when the option is selected. The `SELECTED` entry indicates that the option is the default value for the list, and `textToDisplay` is the text shown in the list.

To select the object's properties and methods, follow this format:

```
selectName.propertyName
selectName.methodName(parameters)
formName.elements[index].propertyName
formName.elements[index].methodName(parameters)
```

To use an option's properties, follow this format:

```
selectName.options[index1].propertyName
formName.elements[index2].options[index1].propertyName
```

The `index1` entry is an integer representing the sequence of options in the list (the first option in the sequence is zero [0]), and `index2` is an integer representing the element in the form.

To use the options array, follow this format:

```
selectName.options
selectName.options[index]
selectName.options.length
```

The `selectName` entry is the value of the `NAME=` attribute in the select object. The `index` entry is an integer representing an option in the select object, and `length` is the number of options in the select object.

The elements in the options array are read-only. You can get the number of options from the list, but you cannot change the values in the list.

The `select` object uses the properties shown in Table 3.11.

TABLE 3.11: THE PROPERTIES OF THE SELECT OBJECT

Property	What It Does
length	Reflects the number of options
name	Reflects the NAME= attribute
options	Reflects the <OPTION> tags
selectedIndex	Reflects the position of the selected option in the list (or the first of multiple options)

The options array uses the properties listed in Table 3.12.

TABLE 3.12: THE PROPERTIES OF THE OPTIONS ARRAY

Property	What It Does
defaultSelected	Reflects the SELECTED= attribute indicating which option is the default selection for the list
index	Reflects the position of the option in the list (the list begins at zero)
length	Reflects the number of options
name	Reflects the NAME= attribute
selected	Lets you select an option from your script, rather than from visitor input
selectedIndex	Reflects the position of the selected option in the list
text	Reflects the textToDisplay for the option list item
value	Reflects the VALUE= attribute

The select object uses the blur and focus methods and the onBlur, onChange, and onFocus event handlers. The select object is a property of form. The options array is a property of select.

Example:

```
<SELECT NAME="lesson_list">
    <OPTION SELECTED> Introduction
    <OPTION>Installation
    <OPTION>Setting up an account
    <OPTION>Creating a document
    <OPTION>Filing a document
    <OPTION>Recovering a filed document
    <OPTION>Sending a document to the printer
</SELECT>
```

The form contains a list of chapters in a book, from which the visitor can select a single item.

string

A `string` object is a series of characters, such as a name, a phrase, or other information. It has the following format:

```
stringName.propertyName
stringName.methodName(parameters)
```

The `stringName` entry is the variable name (that owns the string). The `length` entry is the size of the string. This is a character count and includes spaces and special characters. The `methodName` entry is one of the methods listed below.

The `string` object has a single property, `length`, which is the number of characters in the string. The `string` object uses the following methods:

anchor	charAt	index	small	sup
big	fixed	italics	strike	toLowerCase
blink	fontcolor	lastIndexOf	sub	toUpperCase
bold	fontsize	link	substring	

Some of these methods will look familiar as they deal with the format of the text in the `string` object.

Because it is a built-in object, the `string` object does not use event handlers. It is not a property of anything.

Example:

```
var user_id new string()
user_id = getUserText.value
user_id.toUpperCase()
```

This simple example takes the contents of the text field `getUserText` and assigns it to a newly created string variable called `user_id`. The last statement shifts the contents of the variable to uppercase.

submit

This object is a button on a form that starts the processing of the form. The submission is controlled by the form's `action` property. The `submit` object has the following format:

```
<INPUT>
    TYPE="submit"
    NAME="submitName"
    VALUE="buttonText"
    [onClick="handlerText"] >
```

To use the submit object's properties and methods, follow this format:

```
submitName.propertyName
submitName.methodName(parameters)
formName.elements[index].propertyName
formName.elements[index].methodName(parameters)
```

The submit object uses two properties—name and value. It uses a single method, click, and the onClick event handler. It is a property of form.

Example:

```
<FORM NAME="form1">
    <B>Choose a document, then click "Take me there" below.</B>
    <BR><INPUT TYPE="radio" NAME="destination" VALUE="Overview"
        onClick="there =
        'http://www.raycomm.com/intro.html'">
        Overview of JavaScripting
    <BR><INPUT TYPE="radio" NAME="destination" VALUE="HowTo"
        onClick="there =
        'http://www.raycomm.com/makeScript.html'">
        Learn to Make a Script
    <BR><INPUT TYPE="radio" NAME="destination" VALUE="Reference"
        onClick="there =
        'http://www.raycomm.com/refchapt.html'">
        JavaScript Reference Information
    <BR>
    <P><INPUT TYPE="submit" NAME="goThere" VALUE="Take Me!"
        onClick="window.open(there)">
</FORM>
```

This example has a form on which a visitor identifies a lesson (selected from the list of radio buttons.) The submit statement opens the selected document in a new window.

text

The text object is a field on the form used to collect information from the visitor. The visitor can type short string sequences, such as a word, a phrase, or numbers, into the text object. Because the text object is a form element, it must be defined within a <FORM> tag. The text object has the following format:

```
<INPUT
    TYPE="text"
    NAME="textName"
```

```
VALUE="textValue"
SIZE=integer
[onBlur="handlerText"]
[onChange="handlerText"]
[onFocus="handlerText"]
[onSelect="handlerText"] >
```

The `textName` entry is the variable name for the object. The `textValue` entry is the initial value for the text object, and SIZE is the length of the box on the page.

To use the `text` object's properties and methods, follow this format:

```
textName.propertyName
textName.methodName(parameters)
formName.elements[index].propertyName
formName.elements[index].methodName(properties)
```

The `text` object has these three properties, shown in Table 3.13.

	TABLE 3.13: THE PROPERTIES OF THE TEXT OBJECT

Property	What It Does
defaultValue	Gets the default value setting
name	Reflects the variable's name
value	Contains the current contents of the text object

The `text` object uses these three methods: `focus`, `blur`, and `select`, and it uses the `onBlur`, `onChange`, `onFocus`, and `onSelect` event handlers. It is a property of `form`.

Example:

```
var userProfile="user"
<INPUT TYPE="text" NAME="userType" VALUE="user" SIZE="15" onChange=
"userProfile=this.value">
<INPUT TYPE="text" NAME="userGroup" VALUE="" SIZE="32" onChange=
"userProfile+=this.value">
```

These statements create a user profile by getting the text entries the visitor makes in the text objects' fields. The first statement sets the default for the variable *userProfile*. The next two statements change this variable only if the visitor changes the contents of the fields.

textarea

Like the text object, the textarea object offers a way for visitors to enter textual data. The textarea object is a multiline field, whereas the text object is a single line. The textarea object must also be defined within a <FORM> tag.

You can dynamically update the textarea object by setting the value property. The textarea object has the following format:

```
<TEXTAREA
    NAME="textareaName"
    ROWS="integer"
    COLS="integer"
    [onBlur="handlerText"]
    [onChange="handlerText"]
    [onFocus="handlerText"]
    [onSelect="handlerText"] >
    textToDisplay
</TEXTAREA>
```

The textareaName entry is the name of the object.

To use the properties and methods of the textarea object, follow this format:

```
textareaName.propertyName
textareaName.methodName(parameters)
formName.elements[index].propertyName
formName.elements[index].methodName(parameters)
```

The textarea object uses three properties—defaultValue, name, and value—and three methods: focus, blur, and select. It uses the onBlur, onChange, onFocus, and onSelect event handlers. It is a property of form.

Example:

```
<P>Decribe the FOLD function and give three examples of what you can do with
the FOLD function:</P>
<TEXTAREA NAME="foldEssay" ROWS=5 COLS=65
onChange="question3Essay=this.value">
</TEXTAREA>
```

This example gives the visitor a field in which to answer an essay question; the answer is stored in the variable *question3Essay*.

window

The `window` object is the topmost object for JavaScript's `document`, `location`, and `history` objects. The `self` and `window` properties are synonymous and refer to the current window. The keyword `top` refers to the uppermost window in the hierarchy, and `parent` refers to a window that contains one or more framesets. Because of its unique position, you do not have to address the properties of `window` in the same fashion as other objects: `close()` is the same as `window.close()` and `self.close()`.

The `window` object uses event handlers, but the calls to these handlers are put in the <BODY> and <FRAMESET> tags. It has the following format:

```
windowVar = window.open("URL", windowName" [,windowFeatures"])
```

The `windowVar` entry is the name of a new window, and `windowName` is the TARGET= attribute of the <FORM> and <A> tags.

To use a window's properties and methods, follow this format:

```
window.propertyName
window.methodName(parameters)
self.propertyName
self.methodName(parameters)
top.propertyName
top.methodName(parameters)
parent.propertyName
parent.methodName(parameters)
windowVar.propertyName
windowVar.methodName(parameters)
propertyName
methodName(parameters)
```

To define the `onLoad` or `onUnload` event handlers, include the statement in the <BODY> or <FRAMESET> tags.

```
<BODY
    [onLoad="handlerText"]
    [onUnload="handlerText"]
</BODY>
<FRAMESET
    [onLoad="handlerText"]
    [onUnload="handlerText"] >
</FRAMESET>
```

The `window` object contains the properties shown in Table 3.14.

TABLE 3.14: THE PROPERTIES OF THE WINDOW OBJECT

Property	What It Does/Is
defaultStatus	The default message for the window's status bar
frames	A list (array) of the window's child frames
length	The number of frames in a parent window
name	Reflects the *windowName* variable
parent	A synonym for *windowName* where the window contains a frameset
self	A synonym for the current *windowName*
status	Contains a priority or transient message for the status bar
top	A synonym for the topmost browser window
window	A synonym for the current *windowName*

The window object also uses these methods:

alert	confirm	prompt	clearTimeout
close	open	setTimeout	

The window object uses two event handlers—onLoad and onUnload. It is not a property of anything.

Example:

```
<SCRIPT>
function checkThis(){
    windowReply=window.open("reginfo.html", "answerWindow",
    "scrollbars=yes, width=100, height=200")
    document.form1.submit();
    confirm("Thanks for registering");
    self.close()}
</SCRIPT>
```

This example opens a window with the registration information.

Methods and Functions

You use methods and functions to manipulate containers, which are objects. If you think of the browser as a stage, the actors and the sets are objects; the lines spoken and the actions taken (according to the script) are the methods and functions applied to the objects.

This section is an alphabetic listing of the JavaScript methods and functions. Each entry describes a single method or function and includes syntax information and examples and identifies the object to which the method or function belongs or affects.

abs

The abs method belongs to the math object and returns the value as an unsigned number. It has the following syntax:

```
Math.abs(number)
```

The number entry is any numeric expression or a property of an object.

Example:

```
<SCRIPT>
function tryMe(baseVal){
var baseVal=Math.random()
showMe = window.open("")
    with (Math) {
        showMe.document.write("<P>" + round(baseVal*random()))
        showMe.document.write("<P>" + abs(round(baseVal*random())))
        //rounds number to the nearest integer
        showMe.document.write("<P>" + abs(baseVal/5))
        // return the absolute value
        showMe.alert("Close 'er up now, skip?")
        showMe.close()
} }
```

acos

The acos method belongs to the math object and returns the arc cosine of a number in radians. It has the following syntax:

```
Math.acos(number)
```

The number entry is any numeric expression or a property of an object.

Example:

```
    with (Math) {
        msgWindow.document.write(acos(random()))
        // find the arc cosine
```

alert

The alert method belongs to the window object and displays a small dialog box with a message string and an OK button. It has the following syntax:

```
alert("message")
```

The message is any string expression or a property of an object.

Example:

```
<BODY onLoad="window.alert('Welcome! You can register through this page. For
    future reference, this page is ' + '<P>' + document.location)">
// this loads a message that includes the page address through
// the document.location
```

This example uses the alert dialog box at the beginning of the page display.

anchor

The anchor method belongs to the string object and generates an HTML anchor for a hypertext target in a document. Use the anchor method with the write or writeln method. It has the following syntax:

```
text.anchor(nameAttribute)
```

The text and nameAttribute entries are any string or property of an object.

Example:

```
var intro="Welcome the JavaScripting Tutorial!"
tocWindow=window.open("","displayWindow")
tocWindow.document.write(intro.anchor("contents_anchor")
for (x=0; x < 5; x++) {
    switch(x){
    case[1]: if (c1 != "true") {
        tocWindow.document.write (c1 + c1.anchor("overviewtoC")
            break;
        case[2]: if (c2 != "true") {
            tocWindow.document.write (c2 + c2.anchor("ObjectstoC")
            break;
        case[3]: if (c3 != "true") {
            tocWindow.document.write (c3 + c3.anchor("structuretoC")
            break;
        case[4]: if (c4 != "true") {
            tocWindow.document.write (c4 + c4.anchor("f_m_ptoC")
            break;
        case[5]: if (c5 != "true") {
            tocWindow.document.write (c5 + c5.anchor("formstoC")
```

```
        break;
case[6]: if (c6 != "true") {
    tocWindow.document.write (c6 + c6.anchor("openwintoC")
    break;
case[7]: if (c7 != "true") {
    tocWindow.document.write (c7 + c7.anchor("cookietoC")
    break;
```

asin

The asin method belongs to the math object and returns the arc sine of a number in radians. It has the following syntax:

```
Math.asin(number)
```

The number entry is any numeric expression or a property of an object.

Example:

```
with (Math) {
    msgWindow.document.write(asin(random()))
    // find the arc sine
```

atan

The atan method belongs to the math object and returns the arc tangent of the number in radians. It has the following syntax:

```
Math.atan(number)
```

The number entry is any numeric expression or a property of an object.

Example:

```
with (Math) {
            msgWindow.document.write(atan(random()))
    // find the arc tangent
```

back

The back method belongs to the history object and uses the history list to return to the previous document. You can use this method to give visitors an alternative to the browser's back button. It has the following syntax:

```
history.back()
```

Example:

```
<P><INPUT TYPE="button" VALUE="Take Me Back!" onClick="history.back()">
<INPUT TYPE="button" VALUE="Let's Keep Going!" onClick="history.forward()">
```

This code puts two buttons beside each other on a line. The first button goes back to the last document; the second button is useful if the visitor has already moved back in the history list and is ready to go forward again.

big

The `big` method belongs to the string object and displays the associated string as a large font (as if the text were tagged with a `<BIG>` tag). It has the following syntax:

```
stringName.big()
```

The `stringName` entry is any string expression or a property of an object.

Example:

```
<SCRIPT>
var welcome="Welcome to our flashy new digs!"
document.write("<P>" + welcome.big())
alert("That's All Folks!")
</SCRIPT>
```

blink

The `blink` method belongs to the `string` object and displays the associated string as blinking, as if the text were tagged with a `<BLINK>` tag. It has the following syntax:

```
stringName.blink()
```

The `stringName` entry is any string expression or a property of an object.

Example:

```
<SCRIPT>
var welcome="Welcome to our flashy new digs!"
document.write("<P>" + welcome.blink())
alert("That's All Folks!")
</SCRIPT>
```

blur

The `blur` method belongs to the `password`, `select`, `text`, and `textarea` objects and is the programmatic way to move the focus off a form object such as a `text` object. It has the following syntax:

```
password.blur()
selectName.blur()
textName.blur()
textareaName.blur()
```

The password entry is either the NAME of a password object or an element in the elements array. The selectName entry is either the NAME of a select object or an element in the elements array. The textName entry is either the NAME of a text object or an element in the elements array. The textareaName entry is either the NAME of a textarea object or an element in the elements array.

Example:

```
<script>
var userPass=""
var userName=""
var formulate= new window()
    // set up the variables to be used later
    formulate.window.open()
    // open a window for the form
    document.formulate.userPass.focus()
    var timer=setTimeout("document.formulate.userPass.blur()", 8000)
    // put the focus onto the the password box for 8 secs
    clearTimeout(timer)
    document.formulate.userName.focus()
    timer=setTimeout("document.formulate.userName.blur()", 30000)
    // clear the timeout, put the focus on the username box for 30 secs
    document.formulate.userAuth.click()
    //force a selection in the userAuth checkbox
    clearTimeout(timer)
    msgWindow.window.close()
    // clear the timeout variable and close the window
</script>
...
    <form NAME="formulate">
    <input type="password" NAME="userPass" SIZE=5>tell us your secret
    <input type="text" name="userName" value="Name" size=15>
    <input type="checkbox" name="userAuth" value="Validate Me">
    authorize us to check this stuff out!
    </form>
```

bold

The bold method belongs to the string object and displays the associated string as bold, as if the text were tagged with a <BOLD> tag. It has the following syntax:

```
stringName.bold()
```

The `stringName` entry is any string expression or a property of an object.

Example:

```
<SCRIPT>
var welcome="Welcome to our flashy new digs!"
document.write("<P>" + welcome.bold())
alert("That's All Folks!")
</SCRIPT>
```

ceil

The `ceil` method belongs to the `math` object and returns the nearest integer that is equal to or greater than the given number. It has the following syntax:

```
Math.ceil(number)
```

The `number` entry is any numeric expression or a property of an object.

Example:

```
with (Math) {
    msgWindow.document.write(ceil(random()*baseVal))
    // return the integer nearest the number (greater or equal)
```

charAt

The `charAt` method belongs to the `string` object and returns the character found at the given `index` in the string. It has the following syntax:

```
stringName.charAt(index)
```

The `stringName` entry is any numeric expression or a property of an object.

Example:

```
<SCRIPT>
var welcome="Welcome to our flashy new digs!"
confirm(welcome)
for (var place=0; place < welcome.length; place++) {
    document.write("<P>" + welcome.charAt(place));}
    // this for loop actually puts out each letter on its own line
</SCRIPT>
```

clear

The `clear` method belongs to the `document` object and empties the contents of the document window. It has the following syntax:

```
document.clear()
```

Example:
```
alert("That's All Folks!")
self.clear()
```

clearTimeout

The `clearTimeout` method belongs to the `frame` and `window` objects and resets the variable for the `setTimeout` method. It has the following syntax:
```
clearTimeout(timeoutID)
```
The `timeoutID` entry is the name of the value returned by a previous call to `setTimeout`.

Example:
```
<script>
var userPass=""
var userName=""
var formulate= new window()
    // set up the variables to be used later
    formulate.window.open()
    // open a window for the form
    document.formulate.userPass.focus()
    var timer=setTimeout("document.formulate.userPass.blur()", 8000)
    // put the focus onto the the password box for 8 secs
    clearTimeout(timer)
    document.formulate.userName.focus()
    timer=setTimeout("document.formulate.userName.blur()", 30000)
    // clear the timeout, put the focus on the username box for 30 secs
    document.formulate.userAuth.click()
    //force a selection in the userAuth checkbox
    clearTimeout(timer)
    msgWindow.window.close()
    // clear the timeout variable and close the window
</script>
...
    <form NAME="formulate">
    <input type="password" NAME="userPass" SIZE=5>tell us your secret
    <input type="text" name="userName" value="Bobs your uncle" size=15>
    <input type="checkbox" name="userAuth" value="Validate Me">
    authorize us to check this stuff out!
    </form>
```

click

The click method belongs to the button, checkbox, radio, reset, and submit objects and simulates, programmatically, the visitor's click on a form object. It has the following syntax:

```
password.click()
selectName.click()
textName.click()
textareaName.click()
```

The password entry is either the NAME of a password object or an element in the elements array. The selectName entry is either the NAME of a select object or an element in the elements array. The textName entry is either the NAME of a text object or an element in the elements array. The textareaName is either the NAME of a textarea object or an element in the elements array.

Example:

```
<script>
var userPass=""
var userName=""
var formulate= new window()
    // set up the variables to be used later
    document.formulate.userAuth.click()
    //force a selection in the userAuth checkbox
    clearTimeout(timer)
    msgWindow.window.close()
    // clear the timeout variable and close the window
</script>

…

    <form NAME="formulate">
    <input type="password" NAME="userPass" SIZE=5>tell us your secret
    <input type="text" name="userName" value="Bobs your uncle" size=15>
    <input type="checkbox" name="userAuth" value="Validate Me">
    authorize us to check this stuff out!
    </form>
```

close

The close method belongs to the document object and closes the stream to an object and forces the layout. It has the following syntax:

```
document.close()
```

3

Example:

```
<script>
var userPass=""
var userName=""
var formulate= new window()
    // set up the variables to be used later
    clearTimeout(timer)
    msgWindow.window.close()
    // clear the timeout variable and close the window
</script>
...
    <form NAME="formulate">
    <input type="password" NAME="userPass" SIZE=5>tell us your secret
    <input type="text" name="userName" value="Name" size=15>
    <input type="checkbox" name="userAuth" value="Validate Me">
    authorize us to check this stuff out!
    </form>
```

close

The close method belongs to the window object and closes the given window. It has the following syntax:

```
windowReference.close()
```

The windowReference entry is any valid means of identifying a window object.

Example:

```
<SCRIPT>
alert("That's All Folks!")
self.close()
</SCRIPT>
```

confirm

The confirm method belongs to the window object and displays a small dialog box with the message string and two buttons, OK and Cancel. It has the following syntax:

```
confirm("message")
```

The message entry is a string expression or a property of an object.

Example:

```
<SCRIPT>
function checkThis(){
    windowReply=window.open("reginfo.html", "answerWindow",
```

```
        "scrollbars=yes, width=100, height=200")
        document.form1.submit();
        confirm("Thanks for registering");
        self.close()}
    </SCRIPT>
```

This example displays the confirmation message when the visitor clicks the submit button.

cos

The cos method belongs to the math object and returns the cosine of the number. It has the following syntax:

```
Math.cos(number)
```

The number entry is any numeric expression or a property of an object.

Example:

```
<SCRIPT>
function tryMe(baseVal){
var baseVal=Math.random()
showMe = window.open("")
    with (Math) {
        showMe.document.write("<P>" + cos(baseVal))
        showMe.document.write("<P>" + abs(cos(baseVal)))
        // return the cosine of the number
    } }
```

escape

The escape function returns the ASCII encoded value for the given string. It has the following syntax:

```
escape("string")
```

The string entry is a nonalphanumeric string that represents a reserved or unprintable character from the ISO Latin-1 character set. For example, escape(%26) returns &.

eval

The eval function runs a JavaScript expression, statement, function, or sequence of statements. The expression can include variables and object properties. It has the following syntax:

```
eval("string")
```

The string entry is a JavaScript expression, statement, function, or sequence of statements.

exp

The exp method belongs to the math object and returns the value equal to Euler's constant (e) raised to the power of the given number. It has the following syntax:

```
Math.exp(number)
```

The number entry is any numeric expression or a property of an object.

Example:

```
<SCRIPT>
function tryMe(baseVal){
var baseVal=Math.random()
showMe = window.open("")
    with (Math) {
        showMe.document.write("<P>" + exp(baseVal))
        showMe.document.write("<P>" + abs(exp(baseVal)))
        // return Euler's constant (e) to the power of the number given
} }
```

fixed

The fixed method belongs to the string object and displays the associated string as fixed width (monospaced), as if the text were tagged with a <TT> tag. It has the following syntax:

```
stringName.fixed()
```

The stringName entry is any string expression or a property of an object.

Example:

```
<SCRIPT>
var welcome="Welcome to our flashy new digs!"
document.write("<P>" + welcome.fixed())
</SCRIPT>
```

floor

The floor method belongs to the math object and returns the nearest integer that is equal to or less than the given number. It has the following syntax:

```
Math.floor(number)
```

The number entry is any numeric expression or a property of an object.

Example:

```
    with (Math) {
        msgWindow.document.write(random())
```

```
    // generate a random number
    msgWindow.document.write(floor(random()*baseVal))
    // return the integer nearest the number (less or equal)
```

focus

The focus method belongs to the password, select, text, and textarea objects and allows you to progammatically move the focus to a form object. This simulates the visitor's moving the cursor to the object. It has the following syntax:

```
password.focus()
selectName.focus()
textName.focus()
textareaName.focus()
```

The password entry is either the NAME of a password object or an element in the elements array. The selectName entry is either the NAME of a select object or an element in the elements array. The textName is either the NAME of a text object or an element in the elements array. The textareaName is either the NAME of a textarea object or an element in the elements array.

Example:

```
<script>
var userPass=""
var userName=""
var formulate= new window()
    // set up the variables to be used later
    formulate.window.open()
    // open a window for the form
    document.formulate.userPass.focus()
    var timer=setTimeout("document.formulate.userPass.blur()", 8000)
    // put the focus onto the the password box for 8 secs
    clearTimeout(timer)
    document.formulate.userName.focus()
    timer=setTimeout("document.formulate.userName.blur()", 30000)
    // clear the timeout, put the focus on the username box for 30 secs
    document.formulate.userAuth.click()
    //force a selection in the userAuth checkbox
    clearTimeout(timer)
    msgWindow.window.close()
    // clear the timeout variable and close the window
</script>
    ...
```

3

```
<form NAME="formulate">
<input type="password" NAME="userPass" SIZE=5>tell us your secret
<input type="text" name="userName" value="Name" size=15>
<input type="checkbox" name="userAuth" value="Validate Me">
authorize us to check this stuff out!
</form>
```

fontcolor

The `fontcolor` method belongs to the `string` object and displays the associated string in the given color, as if the text were tagged with a `<FONT COLOR="">` tag. It has the following syntax:

```
stringName.fontcolor(colorKeyword)
```

The `stringName` entry is any string expression or a property of an object.

Example:

```
<SCRIPT>
var welcome="Welcome to our flashy new digs!"
document.write("<P>" + welcome.fontcolor("crimson"))
</SCRIPT>
```

fontsize

The `fontsize` method belongs to the `string` object and displays the associated string at the given size, as if the text were tagged with a `<FONT SIZE="">` tag. It has the following syntax:

```
stringName.fontsize(size)
```

The `stringName` entry is any string expression or a property of an object.

Example:

```
<SCRIPT>
var welcome="Welcome to our flashy new digs!"
document.write("<P>" + welcome.fontsize(8))
</SCRIPT>
```

forward

The `forward` method belongs to the `history` object and uses the history list to recall a previously viewed document that the visitor has used the Back button or the back method to leave. You can use this method to give visitors an alternative to the browser's Forward button. You can also use the `history.go(1)` method to perform this action. It has the following syntax:

```
history.forward()
```

Example:

```
<P><INPUT TYPE="button" VALUE="Take Me Back!" onClick="history.back()">
<INPUT TYPE="button" VALUE="Let's Keep Going!" onClick="history.forward()">
```

This code puts two buttons beside each other on a line. The first button goes back to the last document. The second button is useful if the visitor has already moved back in the history list and is ready to go forward again.

getDate

The getDate method belongs to the date object and returns the day of the month (0–31) for the given date. It has the following syntax:

```
dateObjectName.getDate()
```

The datObjectName entry is any date object or a property of an object.

Example:

```
<SCRIPT>
function callMe(){
Xmas95 = new Date("December 25, 1995 23:15:00");
weekday = Xmas95.getDate();
confirm(weekday);
var who=1;
var docMod=document.lastModified
 switch (who) { // this switch has two streams
    case(1) :
        alert(docMod);
        chrono=new Date()
        alert(chrono.getDate());
        alert(chrono + " already?!");
        who++;
        break;
    case(2) :    docMod="";
        docMod.setDay(1);
        docMod.setMonth(6);
        docMod.setDate(30);
        docMod.setYear(1997);
        docMod.setTime(11, 59, 59);
        document.write("<P>" + chrono.fontcolor("darkmagenta"));
        who++;
        break;
    }
</SCRIPT>
```

getDay

The getDay method belongs to the date object and returns the day of the week (0–6) for the given date. It has the following syntax:

```
dateObjectName.getDay()
```

The getObjectName entry is any date object or a property of an object.

Example:

```
<SCRIPT>
function callMe(){
Xmas95 = new Date("December 25, 1995 23:15:00");
weekday = Xmas95.getDate();
confirm(weekday);
var who=1;
var docMod=document.lastModified
 switch (who) { // this switch has two streams
    case(1) :
        alert(docMod);
        chrono=new Date()
        alert(chrono.getDay());
        alert(chrono + " already?!");
        who++;
        break;
    case(2) :    docMod="";
        docMod.setDay(1);
        docMod.setMonth(6);
        docMod.setDate(30);
        docMod.setYear(1997);
        docMod.setTime(11, 59, 59);
        document.write("<P>" + chrono.fontcolor("darkmagenta"));
        who++;
        break;
    }
</SCRIPT>
```

getHours

The getHours method belongs to the date object and returns the hour (0–23) of the given date. It has the following syntax:

```
dateObjectName.getHours()
```

The datObjectName entry is any date object or a property of an object.

Example:

```
<SCRIPT>
function callMe(){
Xmas95 = new Date("December 25, 1995 23:15:00");
weekday = Xmas95.getDate();
confirm(weekday);
var docMod=document.lastModified
alert(docMod);
chrono=new Date()
alert(chrono.getHours());
alert(chrono + " already?!");
</SCRIPT>
```

getMinutes

The getMinutes method belongs to the date object and returns the minutes (0–59) for the given date. It has the following syntax:

```
dateObjectName.getMinutes()
```

The dateObjectName entry is any date object or a property of an object.

Example:

```
<SCRIPT>
function callMe(){
Xmas95 = new Date("December 25, 1995 23:15:00");
weekday = Xmas95.getDate();
confirm(weekday);
var docMod=document.lastModified
alert(docMod);
chrono=new Date()
alert(chrono.getMinutes());
alert(chrono + " already?!");
</SCRIPT>
```

getMonth

The getMonth method belongs to the date object and returns the month (0–11) of the given date. It has the following syntax:

```
dateObjectName.getMonth()
```

The dateObjectName entry is any date object or a property of an object.

Example:

```
<SCRIPT>
function callMe(){
Xmas95 = new Date("December 25, 1995 23:15:00");
weekday = Xmas95.getDate();
confirm(weekday);
var docMod=document.lastModified
alert(docMod);
chrono=new Date()
alert(chrono.getMonths());
alert(chrono + " already?!");
</SCRIPT>
```

getSeconds

The getSeconds method belongs to the date object and returns the seconds (0–59) of the given date. It has the following syntax:

```
dateObjectName.getSeconds()
```

The datObjectName entry is any date object or a property of an object.

Example:

```
<SCRIPT>
function callMe(){
Xmas95 = new Date("December 25, 1995 23:15:00");
weekday = Xmas95.getDate();
confirm(weekday);
var docMod=document.lastModified
alert(docMod);
chrono=new Date()
alert(chrono.getSeconds());
alert(chrono + " already?!");
</SCRIPT>
```

getTime

The getTime method belongs to the date object and returns the time (number of milliseconds since January 1, 1970 00:00:00) for the given date. It has the following syntax:

```
dateObjectName.getTime()
```

The dateObjectName entry is any date object or a property of an object.

Example:

```
<SCRIPT>
function callMe(){
Xmas95 = new Date("December 25, 1995 23:15:00");
weekday = Xmas95.getTime();
confirm(weekday);
var docMod=document.lastModified
alert(docMod);
chrono=new Date()
alert(chrono.getHours());
alert(chrono + " already?!");
</SCRIPT>
```

getTimezoneOffset

The getTimezoneOffset method belongs to the date object and returns the difference between local time and GMT in minutes. It has the following syntax:

```
dateObjectName.getTimezoneOffset()
```

The dateObjectName entry is any date object or a property of an object.

Example:

```
<SCRIPT>
function callMe(){
Xmas95 = new Date("December 25, 1995 23:15:00");
weekday = Xmas95.getDate();
confirm(weekday);
var docMod=document.lastModified
alert(docMod);
chrono=new Date()
alert(chrono.get.timezoneOffset());
alert(chrono);
</SCRIPT>
```

getYear

The getYear method belongs to the date object and returns the last two digits of the year of the given date. It has the following syntax:

```
dateObjectName.getYear()
```

The dateObjectName entry is any date object or a property of an object.

3

Example:

```
<SCRIPT>
function callMe(){
Xmas95 = new Date("December 25, 1995 23:15:00");
weekday = Xmas95.getDate();
confirm(weekday);
var docMod=document.lastModified
alert(docMod);
chrono=new Date()
alert(chrono.getYear());
alert(chrono + " already?!");
</SCRIPT>
```

go

The go method belongs to the `history` object and uses the history list to recall a previously viewed document. You can use this method to give visitors an alternative to the browser's Back and Forward buttons. You can also use the back and forward methods. The go method has the following syntax:

```
history.go(number)
```

The `number` entry is a positive or negative integer. A positive integer moves the visitor forward, and a negative integer moves the visitor back.

Example:

```
<P><INPUT TYPE="button" VALUE="Take Me Back!" onClick="history.back()">
<INPUT TYPE="button" VALUE="Let's Keep Going!" onClick="history.forward()">
```

This code places two buttons beside each other on a line. The first button goes back to the last document. The second button is useful if the visitor has already moved back in the history list and is ready to go forward again.

Using the go method, these lines would appear like this:

```
<P><INPUT TYPE="button" VALUE="Take Me Back!" onClick="history.go(-1)">
<INPUT TYPE="button" VALUE="Let's Keep Going!" onClick="history.go(1)">
```

indexOf

The `indexOf` method belongs to the `string` object and returns the position of the first occurrence of the search value starting from the position given. It has the following syntax:

```
stringName.indexOf("searchValue", [fromIndex])
```

The `stringName` entry is any string or object property. The `searchValue` is a string from within `stringName`. The `fromIndex` entry is the starting position for the search; the default is zero (first position).

Example:

```
var champion="We are the champions! We are the champions!"
champion.indexOf("are")
chamption.lastIndexOf("are)
```

This example returns the number 3 for the `indexOf` statement and 25 for the `lastIndexOf` statement.

isNaN

The `isNaN` function is Unix-based; it determines whether the value given is a number. It has the following syntax:

```
isNaN(testValue)
```

Example:

```
floatValue=parseFloat(toFloat)
if isNaN (floatValue) {
    not Float()
}else {
    isFloat()
}
```

This example generates the value and then evaluates it.

italics

The `italics` method belongs to the `string` object and displays the associated string as italics or oblique, as if the text were tagged with a <FONT STYLE=""> tag. It has the following syntax:

```
stringName.italics()
```

The `stringName` entry is any string expression or a property of an object.

Example:

```
<SCRIPT>
var welcome="Welcome to our flashy new digs!"
document.write("<P>" + welcome.italics())
</SCRIPT>
```

3

lastIndexOf

The lastIndexOf method belongs to the string object and returns the position of the last occurrence of the search value starting from the position given. It has the following syntax:

```
stringName.lastIndexOf("searchValue", [fromIndex])
```

The stringName entry is any string or object property. The searchValue entry is a string from within stringName. The fromIndex entry is the starting position for the search; the default is zero (first position).

Example:

```
var champion="We are the champions! We are the champions!"
champion.indexOf("are")
chamption.lastIndexOf("are)
```

This example returns the number 3 for the indexOf statement and 25 for the lastIndexOf statement.

link

The link method belongs to the anchor object and creates a jump to a URL. It has the following syntax:

```
linkText.link(hrefAttribute)
```

The linkText entry is a string or property that is used as the label for the link. The hrefAttribute entry is a valid URL for the destination.

Example:

```
var c1="JavaScripting Overview"
var c2="JavaScript Objects"
var c3="JavaScript Constructs"
...
document.write(c1.link("http://www.writelivelihood.com/JS/Courses/
js_overview.html")document.write(c2.link("http://www.writelivelihood.com/JS/
Courses/js_objects.html")
document.write(c3.link("http://www.writelivelihood.com/JS/
Courses/js_constructs.html")
```

You can use this example to build the table of contents for a dynamically selected course by including a selection form and a switch statement.

log

The `log` method belongs to the `math` object and returns the natural logarithm (base e) of the given number. It has the following syntax:

```
Math.log(number)
```

The `number` entry is any numeric expression or a property of an object.

Example:

```
with (Math) {
    msgWindow.document.write(log(baseVal))
    // return the natural logarithm (base of e) of the number
```

max

The `max` method belongs to the `math` object and returns the higher of two given numbers. It has the following syntax:

```
Math.max(number1, number2)
```

The `number1` and `number2` entries are any numeric expression or a property of an object.

Example

```
with (Math) {
    msgWindow.document.write(random())
    // generate a random number
    msgWindow.document.write(max(baseVal, (random()*3)))
    // return the highest value
```

min

The `min` method belongs to the `math` object and returns the lower of two given numbers. It has the following syntax:

```
Math.min(number1, number2)
```

The `number1` and `number2` entries are any numeric expression or a property of an object.

Example:

```
with (Math) {
    msgWindow.document.write(random())
    // generate a random number
    msgWindow.document.write(min(baseVal, (random()*3)))
    // return the lowest value
```

3

open (document object)

The open method for documents belongs to the window object and opens an output destination for the write and writeln statements. It has the following syntax:

```
document.open(["mimeType"])
```

The mimeType entry is any one of the following:

text/html	image/jpeg
text/plain	image/x-bitmap
image/gif	plugIn

Example:

```
<script>
var userPass=""
var userName=""
var formulate= new window()
    // set up the variables to be used later
    formulate.window.open()
</script>
```

open (window object)

The open method for window objects belongs to the window object and allows you to set up and open an instance of the browser for displaying information. It has the following syntax:

```
windowVar=window.open("URL", "windowName" [,"windowsFeatures"])
```

The windowVar entry is the name of the new window, and URL is the location of the document to be loaded into the new window. The windowName entry is used in the TARGET= attribute of the <FORM> and <A> tags. The windowsFeatures entry is a comma-separated list that can contain one or more of the following:

```
toolbar[=yes|no] | [=1|0]
location[=yes|no] | [=1|0]
directories[=yes|no] | [=1|0]
status[=yes|no] | [=1|0]
menubar[=yes|no] | [=1|0]
scrollbars[=yes|no] | [=1|0]
resizable[=yes|no] | [=1|0]
width=pixels
height=pixels
```

Example:

```
<script>
var userPass=""
var userName=""
var formulate= new window()
    // set up the variables to be used later
    formulate.window.open('http://www.raycomm.com'
                'titlebar=no,menubar=no,scrollbars=no')
```

parse

The parse method belongs to the date object and returns the number of milliseconds between a given date string and January 1, 1970 00:00:00 local time. It has the following syntax:

```
Date.parse(dateString)
```

The dateString entry is a date or an object property.

Example:

```
checkValue=Date.parse("1, 1, 99")
if isNaN (checkValue) {
    notGood()
}else {
    isGood()
}
```

This example generates the value and then evaluates it.

parseFloat

The parseFloat function determines if a value is a number and returns a floating point number for a string. It has the following syntax:

```
parseFloat(string)
```

The string entry is a string or object property.

Example:

```
toFloat="3.14"
floatValue=parseFloat(toFloat)
if isNaN (floatValue) {
    not Float()
}else {
    isFloat()
}
```

This example generates the value and then evaluates it.

parseInt

The `parseInt` function determines if a value is a number and returns an integer value of the given radix or base. It has the following syntax:

```
parseInt(string [,radix])
```

The `string` entry is a string or an object property, and the `radix` is an integer.

Example:

```
document.write(parseInt("F", 16))
    // the 16 indicates that the F is a hexidecimal number (base 16)
document.write(parseInt("1111", 2))
document.write(parseInt ("0xF"))
```

These examples return the same value, 15.

pow

The pow method belongs to the `math` object and returns the first number raised to the power of the second number. It has the following syntax:

```
Math.pow(base, exponent)
```

The base and exponent entries are any numeric expression or a property of an object.

Example:

```
with (Math) {
    msgWindow.document.write(random())
    // generate a random number

    msgWindow.document.write(pow(baseVal, random()))
    // raise the first number to the power of the second
number
```

prompt

The prompt method belongs to the `window` object and displays a dialog box with a message and an input field. Even though `prompt` is a `window` method, you do not have to include the `windowReference` in the statement. The prompt method has the following syntax:

```
prompt(message, [inputDefault])
```

The `message` entry is a text string or an object property, and `inputDefault` is a string, an integer, or an object property.

Example:

```
<script>
var userPass=""
var userName=""
var formulate= new window()
```

```
        prompt ("Are you done yet?" 1)
    </script>

    ...

        <form NAME="formulate">
        <input type="password" NAME="userPass" SIZE=5>tell us your secret
        <input type="text" name="userName" value="Name" size=15>
        <input type="checkbox" name="userAuth" value="Validate Me">
        authorize us to check this stuff out!
        </input>
        </form>
```

random

The random method belongs to the math object and generates a random number between 0 and 1. It has the following syntax:

```
Math.random()
```

Example:

```
<SCRIPT>
function tryMe(baseVal){
var baseVal=Math.random()
showMe = window.open("")
    with (Math) {
        var firstOne=(random())
        var secondOne=(abs(random()))
        showMe.document.write("<P>" + firstOne)
        showMe.document.write("<P>" + secondOne)
        // generate a random number
} }
```

round

The round method belongs to the math object and returns the value of the number given to the nearest integer. It has the following syntax:

```
Math.round(number)
```

The number entry is any numeric expression or a property of an object.

Example:

```
<SCRIPT>
function tryMe(baseVal){
var baseVal=Math.random()
showMe = window.open("")
    with (Math) {
```

```
            var firstOne=(random())
            var secondOne=(abs(random()))
            showMe.document.write("<P>" + firstOne)
            showMe.document.write("<P>" + secondOne)
            // generate a random number
            showMe.document.write("<P>" + round(baseVal*random()))
            showMe.document.write("<P>" + abs(round(baseVal*random())))
            //rounds number to the nearest integer
            showMe.alert("Close 'er up now, skip?")
            showMe.close()
    } }
```

select

Like the focus and blur methods, the select method performs an action programmatically. It belongs to the password, text, and textarea objects. The select method selects the input area of a given password, text, or textarea form object. It has the following syntax:

```
passwordName.select()
textName.select()
textareaName.select()
```

The passwordName entry is the NAME= attribute of the password object. The textName entry is the NAME= attribute of the text object, and textareaName is the NAME= attribute of the textarea object.

Example:

```
<script>
var userPass=""
var userName=""
var formulate= new window()
    // set up the variables to be used later
    document.formulate.userPass.select()
</script>
    …
    <form NAME="formulate">
    <input type="password" NAME="userPass" SIZE=5>tell us your secret
    <input type="text" name="userName" value="Name" size=15>
    <input type="checkbox" name="userAuth" value="Validate Me">
    authorize us to check this stuff out!
    </form>
```

setDate

The setDate method belongs to the date object and sets the day of the month for a given date. It has the following syntax:

```
dateObjectName.setDate(dayValue)
```

The dateObjectName entry is any date object or a property of an object. The dayValue is an integer between 1 and 31 or a property of an object representing the month.

Example:

```
<SCRIPT>
function callMe(){
Xmas95 = new Date("December 25, 1995 23:15:00");
weekday = Xmas95.getDate();
confirm(weekday);
var docMod=""
docMod.setDay(1);
docMod.setMonth(6);
docMod.setDate(30);
docMod.setYear(1997);
docMod.setTime(11, 59, 59);
alert(docMod);
</SCRIPT>
```

setHours

The setHours method belongs to the date object and sets the hour of the day for a given date. It has the following syntax:

```
dateObjectName.setHours(hoursValue)
```

The dateObjectName entry is any date object or a property of an object. The hoursValue entry is an integer between 0 and 23 or a property of an object representing the hour.

Example:

```
<SCRIPT>
function callMe(){
Xmas95 = new Date("December 25, 1995 23:15:00");
weekday = Xmas95.getDate();
confirm(weekday);
var docMod=""
docMod.setDay(1);
docMod.setMonth(6);
```

3

```
docMod.setDate(30);
docMod.setYear(1997);
docMod.setHours(11);
docMod.setMinutes(59);
docMod.setSeconds(59);
alert(docMod);
</SCRIPT>
```

setMinutes

The setMinutes method belongs to the date object and sets the minutes of the hour for a given date. It has the following syntax:

```
dateObjectName.setMinutes(minuteValue)
```

The dateObjectName entry is any date object or a property of an object. The minuteValue entry is an integer between 0 and 59 or a property of an object representing the minute.

Example:

```
<SCRIPT>
function callMe(){
Xmas95 = new Date("December 25, 1995 23:15:00");
weekday = Xmas95.getDate();
confirm(weekday);
var docMod=""
docMod.setDay(1);
docMod.setMonth(6);
docMod.setDate(30);
docMod.setYear(1997);
docMod.setHours(11);
docMod.setMinutes(59);
docMod.setSeconds(59);
alert(docMod);
</SCRIPT>
```

setMonth

The setMonth method belongs to the date object and sets the month of the year for a given date. It has the following syntax:

```
dateObjectName.setMonth(monthValue)
```

The dateObjectName entry is any date object or a property of an object. The monthValue is an integer between 0 and 11 or a property of an object representing the month. It has the following syntax:

Example:

```
<SCRIPT>
function callMe(){
Xmas95 = new Date("December 25, 1995 23:15:00");
weekday = Xmas95.getDate();
confirm(weekday);
var docMod=" "
docMod.setDay(1);
docMod.setMonth(6);
docMod.setDate(30);
docMod.setYear(1997);
docMod.setHours(11);
docMod.setMinutes(59);
docMod.setSeconds(59);
alert(docMod);
</SCRIPT>
```

setSeconds

The setSeconds method belongs to the date object and sets the seconds of the minute for a given date. It has the following syntax:

```
dateObjectName.setSeconds(secondsValue)
```

The dateObjectName entry is any date object or a property of an object. The secondValue entry is an integer between 0 and 59 or a property of an object representing the seconds.

Example:

```
<SCRIPT>
function callMe(){
Xmas95 = new Date("December 25, 1995 23:15:00");
weekday = Xmas95.getDate();
confirm(weekday);
var docMod=" "
docMod.setDay(1);
docMod.setMonth(6);
docMod.setDate(30);
docMod.setYear(1997);
```

3

```
docMod.setHours(11);
docMod.setMinutes(59);
docMod.setSeconds(59);
alert(docMod);
</SCRIPT>
```

setTime

The `setTime` method belongs to the `date` object and sets the number of milliseconds since January 1, 1970 00:00:00. It has the following syntax:

```
dateObjectName.setTime(timeValue)
```

The `dateObjectName` entry is any `date` object or a property of an object. The `timeValue` entry is an integer or a property of an object representing the number of milliseconds since the epoch.

Example:

```
<SCRIPT>
function callMe(){
Xmas95 = new Date("December 25, 1995 23:15:00");
weekday = Xmas95.getDate();
confirm(weekday);
var docMod=""
docMod.setDay(1);
docMod.setMonth(6);
docMod.setDate(30);
docMod.setYear(1997);
docMod.setTime(11, 59, 59);
alert(docMod);
</SCRIPT>
```

setTimeout

The `setTimeout` method belongs to the `frame` and `window` objects and evaluates an expression after the set number of milliseconds have past. It has the following syntax:

```
timeoutID=setTimeout(expression, msec)
```

The `timeoutID` entry is the identifer for the timeout variable; it is used later by the `clearTimeout` method. The `expression` entry is a string or a property of an object. The `msec` entry is a numeric value, a numeric string, or an object property representing the number of millisecond units for the timeout.

Example:

```
<script>
var userPass=""
var userName=""
var formulate= new window()
    // set up the variables to be used later
    formulate.window.open()
    // open a window for the form
    document.formulate.userPass.focus()
    var timer=setTimeout("document.formulate.userPass.blur()", 8000)
    // put the focus onto the the password box for 8 secs
    clearTimeout(timer)
    document.formulate.userName.focus()
    timer=setTimeout("document.formulate.userName.blur()", 30000)
    // clear the timeout, put the focus on the username box for 30 secs
    document.formulate.userAuth.click()
    //force a selection in the userAuth checkbox
    clearTimeout(timer)
    msgWindow.window.close()
    // clear the timeout variable and close the window
</script>
    <form NAME="formulate">
    <input type="password" NAME="userPass" SIZE=5>tell us your secret
    <input type="text" name="userName" value="Name" size=15>
    <input type="checkbox" name="userAuth" value="Validate Me">
    authorize us to check this stuff out!
    </form>
```

setYear

The setYear method belongs to the date object and sets the year for a given date. It has the following syntax:

```
dateObjectName.setYear(yearValue)
```

The dateObjectName entry is any date object or a property of an object. The yearValue entry is a two-digit integer or a property of an object representing the year (you can use only the years between 1900 and 2000).

Example:

```
<SCRIPT>
function callMe(){
```

3

```
Xmas95 = new Date("December 25, 1995 23:15:00");
weekday = Xmas95.getDate();
confirm(weekday);
var docMod=""
docMod.setDay(1);
docMod.setMonth(6);
docMod.setDate(30);
docMod.setYear(1997);
docMod.setTime(11, 59, 59);
alert(docMod);
</SCRIPT>
```

sin

The sin method belongs to the math object and returns the sine of the given number. It has the following syntax:

```
Math.sin(number)
```

The number entry is any numeric expression or a property of an object.

Example:

```
<SCRIPT>
function tryMe(baseVal){
var baseVal=Math.random()
showMe = window.open("")
    with (Math) {
        showMe.document.write("<P>" + sin(random()))
} }
```

small

The small method belongs to the string object and displays the associated string using a smaller font, as if the text were tagged with a <SMALL> tag. It has the following syntax:

```
stringName.small()
```

The stringName entry is any string expression or a property of an object.

Example:

```
<SCRIPT>
var welcome="Welcome to our flashy new digs!"
confirm(welcome)
    // this opens a small box with the text and an ok button
document.write("<P>" + welcome.small())
</SCRIPT>
```

sqrt

The sqrt method belongs to the math object and returns the square root of the given number. It has the following syntax:

```
Math.sqrt(number)
```

The number is any nonnegative numeric expression or a property of an object.

Example:

```
<SCRIPT>
function tryMe(baseVal){
var baseVal=Math.random()
showMe = window.open("")
    with (Math) {
        showMe.document.write("<P>" + sqrt(baseVal))
        showMe.document.write("<P>" + abs(sqrt(baseVal)))
        // return the square root of the number
} }
```

strike

The strike method belongs to the string object and displays the associated string with strikethrough. It has the following syntax:

```
stringName.strike()
```

The stringName entry is any string expression or a property of an object.

Example:

```
<SCRIPT>
var welcome="Welcome to our flashy new digs!"
confirm(welcome)
    // this opens a small box with the text and an ok button
document.write("<P>" + welcome.strike())
</SCRIPT>
```

sub

The sub method belongs to the string object and displays the associated string subscripted to the rest of the text. It has the following syntax:

```
stringName.sub()
```

The stringName entry is any string expression or a property of an object.

Example:

```
<SCRIPT>
var welcome="Welcome to our flashy new digs!"
```

```
confirm(welcome)
    // this opens a small box with the text and an ok button
document.write("<P>" + welcome.sub())
</SCRIPT>
```

submit

The submit method belongs to the form object and submits a form. It has the following syntax:

```
formName.submit()
```

The formName entry is the name of a form or an element in the forms array.

Example:

```
<SCRIPT>
function checkThis(){
    document.form1.submit();
    confirm("Thanks for registering");
    self.close()}


</SCRIPT>
</HEAD>

<BODY onLoad="window.alert('Welcome! You can register through this page. For
future reference, this page is ' + '<P>' +document.location)">
<FORM NAME="form1">
    <P><INPUT TYPE="text" NAME="whoIs" VALUE="user" SIZE=15>
    <P><INPUT TYPE="radio" NAME="lesson" VALUE="Lesson 1" CHECKED
onClick="takeLesson='lesson1.htm'"> Lesson 1: Getting Started
    <P><INPUT TYPE="radio" NAME="lesson" VALUE="Lesson 2"
onClick="takeLesson='lesson2.htm'"> Lesson 2: Concepts and Operations
    <P><INPUT TYPE="radio" NAME="lesson" VALUE="Lesson 3"
onClick="takeLesson='lesson3.htm'"> Lesson 3: Projects
    <P><INPUT TYPE="reset" VALUE="Defaults" NAME="resetToBasic">
    <INPUT TYPE="submit" VALUE="Send it in!" NAME="submit_form1"
onClick="checkThis()">
    <HR>

</FORM>
</BODY>
```

substring

The substring method belongs to the string object and returns a portion of a given string. It has the following syntax:

```
stringName.substring(index1, index2)
```

The stringName entry is the string or an object property. The index 1 entry is an integer representing the starting position of the substring within the string; this can be any integer from zero to stringName.length-1. The index 2 entry is an integer representing the ending position of the substring within the string; this can be any integer larger than index1 from zero to stringName.length-1.

Example:

```
var champion="We are the champions! We are the champions!"
document.write(champion.substring(11,19))
document.write(champion.substring(13,15))
```

This example returns "champions" and "amp".

sup

The sup method belongs to the string object and displays the associated string as a superscript to the surrounding text. It has the following syntax:

```
stringName.sup()
```

The stringName entry is any string expression or a property of an object.

Example:

```
<SCRIPT>
var welcome="Welcome to our flashy new digs!"
confirm(welcome)
    // this opens a small box with the text and an ok button
document.write("<P>" + welcome.sup())
alert("That's All Folks!")
self.close()
    // at the end, a box appears, with the message
    // That's All Folks! and an ok button
    // the next line closes the browser
</SCRIPT>
```

tan

The tan method belongs to the math object and returns the tangent of the given number. It has the following syntax:

```
Math.tan(number)
```

The number entry is any numeric expression or a property of an object that represents the size of an angle in radians.

Example:

```
with (Math) {
    msgWindow.document.write(tan(random()))
    //find the are tangent
```

toGMTString

The `toGMTString` method belongs to the `date` object and converts a date to a string, using the internet GMT conventions. The exact format varies according to the visitor's platform. It is generally more reliable to use the `getMonth`, `getDay`, and other such `date` methods to get the information if you plan to manipulate it at all. The `toGMTString` method has the following syntax:

```
dataGMT.toLocalString()
```

The `dateObjectName` is any date object or a property of an object.

Example:

```
function (showDate) {
    var docMod="";
    docMod.setDay(1);
    docMod.setMonth(6);
    docMod.setDate(30);
    docMod.setYear(1997);
    docMod.setTime(11, 59, 59);
    docMod.toLocaleString();
    document.write("<P>" + docMod.fontcolor("darkmagenta"));
    docMod.toGMTString();
    document.write("<P>" + docMod.fontcolor("darkmagenta")) }
```

This converts the contents of the date variable *docMod* first to local time and then to GMT time before displaying each value.

toLocaleString

The `toLocalString` method belongs to the `date` object and converts a date to a string, using the local conventions. It is generally more reliable to use the `getMonth`, `getDay`, and other such `date` methods to get the information if you plan to manipulate it at all. The `toLocalString` method has the following syntax:

```
dataObjectName.toLocalString()
```

The `dateObjectName` entry is any date object or a property of an object.

Example:

```
function (showDate) {
    var docMod="";
    docMod.setDay(1);
    docMod.setMonth(6);
    docMod.setDate(30);
    docMod.setYear(1997);
    docMod.setTime(11, 59, 59);
    docMod.toLocaleString();
    document.write("<P>" + docMod.fontcolor("darkmagenta"));
    docMod.toGMTString();
    document.write("<P>" + docMod.fontcolor("darkmagenta")) }
```

This converts the contents of the date variable docMod first to local time and then to GMT time before printing out each value.

toLowerCase

The toLowerCase method belongs to the string object and converts the contents of a text string to all lowercase letters. It has the following syntax:

```
stringName.toLowerCase()
```

The stringName entry is any string expression or a property of an object.

Example:

```
<SCRIPT>
    function upAndDown() {
        confirm(document.WhoAreYou.nameInfo.value.toUpperCase());
        confirm(document.WhoAreYou.FavFoodGroup.value.toLowerCase()); }
</SCRIPT>
</HEAD>
<BODY>
<form NAME="WhoAreYou">
    <input type="text" name="nameInfo" value="" size=30 maxlength=30>
    <input type="text" name="FavFoodGroup" size=15>
    <input type="submit" name="getGoing" value="Yumm!"
        onClick="upAndDown()">
</form>
```

toUpperCase

The toUpperCase method belongs to the string object and converts the contents of a text string to all uppercase letters. It has the following syntax:

```
stringName.toUpperCase()
```

The `stringName` is any string expression or a property of an object.

Example:

```
<SCRIPT>
    function upAndDown() {
        confirm(document.WhoAreYou.nameInfo.value.toUpperCase());
        confirm(document.WhoAreYou.FavFoodGroup.value.toLowerCase()); }
</SCRIPT>
</HEAD>

<BODY>
<form NAME="WhoAreYou">
    <input type="text" name="nameInfo" value="" size=30 maxlength=30>
    <input type="text" name="FavFoodGroup" size=15>
    <input type="submit" name="getGoing" value="Yumm!"
        onClick="upAndDown()">
</form>
```

unescape

Like the `escape` function, the `unescape` function converts an ASCII value. The `unescape` function takes the integer or hexadecimal value of the character and returns the ASCII character. It has the following syntax:

```
unescape("string")
```

The `string` entry is either an integer ("%integer") or a hexadecimal value ("hex").

UTC

The `UTC` method belongs to the `date` object and returns the number of milliseconds between the contents of a date object and the epoch (January 1, 1970 00:00:00, Universal Coordinated Time [GMT]). It has the following syntax:

```
Date.UTC(year, month, day [,hrs] [,min] [,sec])
```

The year entry is a two-digit representation of a year between 1900 and 2000. The month entry is a number between zero and 12 representing the month of the year. The day entry is a number between zero and 31 representing the day of the month. The hrs entry is a two-digit number between 00 and 23 representing the hour of the day. The min entry is a two-digit number between 00 and 59 representing the minute of the hour, and sec is a two-digit number between 00 and 59 representing the second of the minute.

Example:

```
<SCRIPT>
var welcome="Welcome to our flashy new digs!"
confirm(welcome)
    // this opens a small box with the text and an ok button
 var chrono=new Date()
var docMod=document.lastModified
var fakeBD=new Date("July 1, 1977 00:00:00")
var otherDisp= Date.UTC(fake BD)
    // create some new Date variables
</SCRIPT>
```

write

The write method belongs to the document object and sends expressions to the document as encoded HTML strings. It has the following syntax:

```
write(expression1 [,expression2] [..., expression N])
```

The expression1 through expressionN entries are any JavaScript expression or a property of an object.

Example:

```
<SCRIPT>
var welcome="Welcome to our flashy new digs!"
confirm(welcome)
    // this opens a small box with the text and an ok button
document.write("<P>" + welcome.small())
document.write("<P>" + welcome.big())
document.write("<P>" + welcome.blink())
document.write("<P>" + welcome.bold())
document.write("<P>")
document.write("<P>" + welcome.fixed())
    // these write out the contents of welcome using a number of
    // text attributes
</SCRIPT>
```

writeln

Like the write method, the writeln method belongs to the document object and sends expressions to the document as encoded HTML strings. The writeln method generates a newline character (hard return). HTML ignores the newline character excecpt within tags such as <PRE>. The writeIn method has the following syntax:

```
writeln(expression1 [,expression2] [..., expression N])
```

The `expression1` through `expressionN` entries are any JavaScript expression or a property of an object.

Example:

```
<SCRIPT>
var welcome="Welcome to our flashy new digs!"
confirm(welcome)
    // this opens a small box with the text and an ok button
document.writeln(welcome.small())
document.writeln(welcome.big())
document.writeln(welcome.blink())
document.writeln(welcome.bold())
document.writeln("<P>" + welcome.fixed())
</SCRIPT>
```

Event Handlers

When users interact with your Web page through JavaScript scripts, you need event handlers to recognize the event and communicate back to your script. These event handlers help manage the interaction between your visitors and your JavaScript objects by providing the information in the visitor response to the JavaScript for later use.

This section is an alphabetic listing of the JavaScript event handlers. Each entry describes a single event handler, includes examples, and identifies the objects for which the event handler works. The syntax for these event handlers can be seen in the corresponding object listings.

onBlur

A blur occurs when the focus moves from one object to another on the page. The object that was in focus loses focus and is blurred.

Example:

```
onBlur="document.login.submit()"
```

When the visitor leaves the field, the system submits the information for logging into the next page.

The `onBlur` event handler works for the `select`, `text`, and `textarea` objects.

onChange

A change occurs when the visitor alters the contents of an object and then moves the focus from the object. The object is changed. Use the `onChange` event handler to validate the information submitted by visitors.

Example:

```
onChange="testName(this.value)"
```

This example sends the contents of the field to the `testName` function when the visitor changes information and leaves the field.

The `onChange` event handler works for the `select`, `text`, and `textarea` objects.

onClick

A click occurs when the visitor clicks an object on the page with the mouse. This event could lead to a selection or a change or could launch a piece of JavaScript code.

Example:

```
onClick="compute(this.form)"
```

When the visitor clicks the object, the script runs the `compute` function and sends the form contents.

This event handler has been updated to not act if the event handler returns false when it is employed by a `checkbox`, `radio`, `submit`, or `reset` object.

The `onClick` event handler works for the `document`, `button`, `checkbox`, `radio`, `link`, `reset`, and `submit` objects.

onDblClick

A double-click occurs when the visitor clicks twice quickly on an object on the page.

Example:

```
<a href="seeMyFamily.html" onDblClick="this.href='theFastTour'">
```

This example loads a different page if the visitor double-clicks a link.

This event is new in JavaScript 1.2, so it will not work with versions of Netscape Navigator 3 or earlier or with Internet Explorer 3 or earlier. The `onDblClick` event handler is not implemented in the Macintosh versions of the Netscape Navigator browser.

The `onDblClick` event handler works for the `document`, `area` (in an image map), and `link` objects.

onDragDrop

A drag-and-drop occurs when the visitor drops an object, such as a file, onto the browser window.

Example:

```
onDragDrop="send(newInfo)"
```

This passes the dropped object to a function called `send`. This could be preformatted data that the visitor can mail to you by dropping the file onto the web page.

3

This event is new in JavaScript 1.2, so it will not work with versions of Netscape Navigator 3 or earlier or with Internet Explorer 3 or earlier.

The onDragDrop event handler works for the window object.

onFocus

The focus on a page is selected when the visitor either tabs or clicks a field or an object on the page. Selecting within a field does not create a focus event; rather, it generates a select event.

Example:

```
onFocus="msgWindow.document.write('tell me what you want!')"
```

When the visitor clicks in the field object, the script writes out the phrase "tell me what you want!"

The onFocus event handler works for the select, text, and textarea objects.

onKeyDown

A key down occurs as the visitor presses a keyboard key. This event precedes the keyPress event.

Example:

```
onKeyDown="msgWindow.document.write('tell me what you want!')"
```

When the visitor presses the key, the script writes out the phrase "tell me what you want!"

This event is new in JavaScript 1.2, so it will not work with versions of Netscape Navigator 3 or earlier or with Internet Explorer 3 or earlier.

The onKeyDown event handler works for the document, image, link, and textarea objects.

onKeyPress

A key press occurs when the visitor presses or holds a keyboard key. You can use this in combination with fromCharCode and charCodeAt methods to determine which key was pressed. This is useful when you prompt the visitor to type **y** for yes and any other key for no.

Example:

```
onKeyPress="msgWindow.document.write('tell me what you want!')"
```

When the visitor presses the key, the script writes out the phrase "tell me what you want!"

The onKeyPress event handler works for the document, image, link, and textarea objects.

This event is new in JavaScript 1.2, so it will not work with versions of Netscape Navigator 3 or earlier or with Internet Explorer 3 or earlier.

onKeyUp

A key up occurs when the visitor releases the keyboard key. You can use this to clear the results of the onKeyPress or onKeyDown event handlers.

Example:

```
onKeyUp="msgWindow.document.write('tell me what you want!')"
```

When the visitor releases the key, the script writes out the phrase "tell me what you want!"

The onKeyUp event handler works for the document, image, link, and textarea objects.

This event is new in JavaScript 1.2, so it will not work with versions of Netscape Navigator 3 or earlier or with Internet Explorer 3 or earlier.

onLoad

A load event occurs when the browser receives all the page information, including framesets, and displays it. Locate the onLoad event handler inside the <BODY> or <FRAMESET> tags.

Example:

```
<BODY onLoad="window.alert("Current as of " + document.lastModified + "!")">
```

This example opens an alert window after the page is loaded and displays a message that includes the lastModified property. This gives the visitor the document's modification date.

The onLoad event handler works for the window object.

onMouseDown

A mouse button down occurs when the visitor presses one of the mouse buttons. You can use the event properties to determine which button was pressed.

Example:

```
onMouseDown="msgWindow.document.write('tell me what you want!')"
```

When the visitor moves the mouse button down, the script writes out the phrase "tell me what you want!"

The onMouseDown event handler works for the button, document, and link objects.

This event is new in JavaScript 1.2, so will not work with versions of Netscape Navigator 3 or earlier or with Internet Explorer 3 or earlier.

onMouseMove

A mouse movement occurs when the visitor moves the mouse over any point on the page. This is not an event handler that works for any particular object, but can be evoked if an object requests the event.

Example:

```
onMouseMove="msgWindow.document.write('tell me what you want!')"
```

When the visitor moves the mouse, the script writes out the phrase, "tell me what you want!"

This event is new in JavaScript 1.2, so it will not work with versions of Netscape Navigator 3 or earlier or with Internet Explorer 3 or earlier.

onMouseOut

An onMouseOut event occurs when the visitor moves the mouse point off an object on the page. This event handler defines what should happen when the visitor removes the mouse from an object such as a link.

Example:

```
<a href="myFamily.html" onMouseOut="alert('Hey, we've got great pics down
this way, come back!')">Meet my Family</a>
```

When the visitor's mouse passes off the link (Meet my Family), an alert box appears with this message:

```
Hey, we've got great pics down this way, come back!
```

This event is new in JavaScript 1.2, so it will not work with versions of Netscape Navigator 3 or earlier or with Internet Explorer 3 or earlier.

The onMouseOut event handler works for the area, layer, and link objects.

onMouseOver

An onMouseOver event occurs when the visitor passes the mouse pointer over an object on the page. You must return True within the event handler if you want to set the status or defaultStatus properties.

Example:

```
onMouseOver="window.status="Come on in!"; return true"
```

The onMouseOver event handler works for the area, layer, and link objects.

onMouseUp

A mouse button up event occurs when the visitor releases the mouse button.

```
<a href="myFamily.html" onMouseUp="alert('Hey, we've got great pics down
this way, come back!')">Meet my Family</a>
```

When the visitor's mouse button moves back up while over the link (Meet my Family), an alert box appears with this message:

```
Hey, we've got great pics down this way, come back!
```

This event is new in JavaScript 1.2, so will not work with versions of Netscape Navigator 3 or earlier or with Internet Explorer 3 or earlier.

The onMouseUp event handler works for the button, document, and link objects.

onMove

A move occurs when a visitor or a browser-driven script moves a window or a frame.

```
onMove="window.status='Come on in!' "
```

When the window moves, the message "Come on in!" appears in the status line.

This event is new in JavaScript 1.2, so it will not work with versions of Netscape Navigator 3 or earlier or with Internet Explorer 3 or earlier.

The onMove event handler works for the window and frame objects.

onSelect

A select event occurs when the visitor highlights text inside a text or textarea field.

Example:

```
onSelect="document.bgColor=blue"
```

The background color of the document changes to blue when the visitor selects text from the field.

The onSelect event handler works for the text and textarea objects.

onResize

A resize occurs when a visitor or a browser-driven script changes the size of the window or frame.

```
onMove="window.status='Stop that!'"
```

When the window is resized, the message "Stop that!" appears in the status line.

This event is new in JavaScript 1.2, so will not work with versions of Netscape Navigator 3 or earlier or with Internet Explorer 3 or earlier.

The onResize event handler works for the window and frame objects.

OnReset

Use the onReset event handler to act when the form is reset.

Example:

```
<BODY>
<form onReset="alert('Please try again!) … >
<INPUT TYPE="text" NAME="newInTown" VALUE="" SIZE=100 MAXLENGTH=25>
<INPUT TYPE="Reset" NAME="Reset" VALUE="Reset">
</form>
```

This example prints a "Please try again!" alert box when the visitor resets the form.

The onReset event handler works for the form object.

3

onSubmit

When the document is one or more forms, use the onSubmit event handler to validate the contents of the form.

Example:

```
<SCRIPT>
    function hotelGuys (checksOut) {
        if (checksOut == "false") {
            alert("Please fill in all fields.")}
        else {
            document.forms[0].submit();
            alert("We came here Jasper");}}
</SCRIPT>

...

<BODY>
<form onSubmit="hotelGuys(checksOut='true')">
<INPUT TYPE="text" NAME="newInTown" VALUE="" SIZE=100 MAXLENGTH=25>
<INPUT TYPE="submit" NAME="register" VALUE="">
</form>
```

This example uses an if else statement either to request more information from the visitor or to submit the form. Normally, you wouldn't set the state in the call. You would call another function that would test the entries, and that function would then call hotelGuys.

The onSubmit event handler works for the form object.

onUnload

The unload event occurs when the browser leaves a page. One good use for the onUnload event handler is to clear any function variables you may have set into motion with the onLoad or other event handlers.

Example:

```
<BODY onLoad="CountOn(4)" onUnload="ClearCount()">
```

A counter starts when the page begins loading. You can use this to display a splash-screen for a limited time. When the visitor leaves the page, the counter is reset to zero by the ClearCount function.

The onUnload event handler works for the window object.

Properties

Properties affect objects; unlike methods and functions, which do something within an object, properties assign attributes, such as appearance or size.

This section is an alphabetic listing of the JavaScript properties. Each entry describes a single property, includes syntax information and examples, and identifies which object the property affects.

action

The `action` property is part of the `form` object and contains the URL to which the `<FORM>` is submitted. You can set this property at any time. It has the following syntax:

```
formName.action=formActionText
```

The `formName` entry is either the form or an element from the forms array.

Example:

```
document.lesson3.action=http://www.raycomm.con/lesson3results.htm
```

This example loads the URL `http://www.raycomm.com/lesson3results.htm` into the action property for the form `lesson3`.

alinkColor

The `alinkColor` property is part of the `document` object and sets the color for an active link. Once the layout of the HTML code is complete, this becomes a read-only property of the `document` object, so you cannot change the `alinkColor` property. The color is expressed in hexadecimal (three sets of double hex digits) or as one of the color keywords. Place the code that sets this property before any `<BODY>` tags, and do not use the `<BODY ALINK="…">` attribute. The `alinkColor` property has the following syntax:

```
document.alinkColor="colorLiteral"
document.alinkColor="colorRGB"
```

Example:

```
document.alinkColor="green"
document.alinkColor="008000"
```

The two statements are equivalent. The first statement sets the `alinkColor` using the keyword green, which is 008000 in hex.

anchors

The `anchors` property is part of the `anchor` object and is the array of objects listing the named anchors in the source. The array lists the anchors in the order in which they appear in the document. The `anchors` property has the following syntax:

```
document.anchors[index]
document.anchors.length
```

The index entry is an integer that represents the anchor's position in the list; length returns the number of items in the array.

Example:

```
var visitor=document.anchors.length
document.write("there are " + visitor + " links to other pages... can you
visit them all?")
```

The script stores the number of anchors in the variable *visitor* and uses that in a statement written out for the visitor.

appCodeName

The appCodeName property is a read-only part of the navigator object. It has the following syntax:

```
navigator.appCodeName
```

Example:

```
var whoAreYou=navigator.appCodeName
if (whoAreYou !="Mozilla") {
    document.write("Good job, carry on!")
```

This example gets the code name of the browser and, if it's not Mozilla, writes a note to the visitor.

appName

The appName property is a read-only part of the navigator object. It has the following syntax:

```
navigator.appName
```

Example:

```
var whoAreYou=navigator.appName
document.write("Hey! Good thing you're using " + whoAreYou + "!")
```

This example puts the application name into the variable *whoAreYou* and includes it in a statement displayed for the visitor.

appVersion

The appVersion property is a read-only part of the navigator object. It has the following syntax:

```
navigator.appVersion
```

The version is in the following format:

```
releaseNumber (platform; country)
```

Example:

```
document.write("You're checking us out with " + navigator.appVersion)
```

This statement displays a result similar to this:

```
You're checking us out with 2.0 (Win95, I)
```

bgColor

The bgColor property is part of the document object and reflects the BGCOLOR= attribute of the <BODY> tag, but can be changed at any time. The default for bgColor is in the visitor's browser preferences. The bgColor property has the following syntax:

```
document.bgColor="colorLiteral"
document.bgColor="colorRGB"
```

Example:

```
document.bgColor="darkblue"
document.bgColor="00008B"
```

These statements are equivalent. Both set the background color to dark blue; one through the keyword, and the other through the hex value for the color.

checked

The checked property is a boolean value representing the state of a radio or checkbox object. True or 1 is checked; false or 0 is cleared. The checked property has the following syntax:

```
checkboxName.checked
radioName[index].checked
```

The checkboxName entry is the NAME= attribute of a checkbox object. The radioName entry is the NAME= attribute of a radio object. The index entry represents the radio button with the radio object.

Example:

```
<INPUT TYPE="radio" NAME="=courseOption1" VALUE="courseOption"
onClick="techComm.checked='1'" >
```

This example sets the checkbox for the techComm value of courseOption1 to checked when the visitor selects the courseOption1 radio button.

cookie

A cookie is information stored by the browser. The cookie property is part of a document object that you can read using the substring, charAt, indexOf, and lastIndexOf methods. You can also write information to a cookie. The cookie property has the following syntax:

```
document.cookie
```

3

Example:

```
document.cookie="expires in " + counter + " days"
```

This example assigns the string that reads "expires in n days"; *n* is the number of days remaining and is set with counter.

defaultChecked

The defaultChecked property is part of the checkbox and radio objects. It indicates the default state (checked or not checked) of a checkbox or a radio button. You can read or set the property at any time. The defaultChecked property has the following syntax:

```
checkboxName.defaultChecked
radioName.[index].defaultChecked
```

Example:

```
document.chartForm.dataFocus[i].defaultChecked=true
```

The statement sets the radio button at position i in the array to the default for the dataFocus group of buttons.

defaultSelected

This property is similar to the defaultChecked property; it indicates whether the option in a select object is the default selection. Only MULTIPLE select objects can have more than a single item selected. The defaultSelected property is part of the options array and has the following syntax:

```
selectName.options[index].defaultSelected
```

The selectName entry refers to the select object either by the NAME= attribute or as an element within an array. The index entry is an integer representing an option in a select object.

Example:

```
<SCRIPT>
    function backAgain () {
        alert(document.javajive.lessonList.length);
        for (var a = 0; a < document.javajive.lessonList.length; a++) {
    if (document.javajive.lessonList.options[a].defaultSelected == true) {
        document.javajive.lessonList.options[a].selected=true }
        }
    }
</SCRIPT>
</HEAD>
```

```
<BODY>
<FORM NAME="javajive" onSubmit="backAgain ()">
<SELECT NAME="lessonList">
    <OPTION SELECTED> Introduction
    <OPTION>Installation
    <OPTION>Setting up an account
    <OPTION>Creating a document
    <OPTION>Filing a document
    <OPTION>Recovering a filed document
    <OPTION>Sending a document to the printer
</SELECT>
<INPUT TYPE="submit" NAME="getchathere" VALUE="Submit">
</form>
```

In this example, the form contains a list of chapters in a book, from which the visitor can select a single item. The backAgain function cycles through the list of options to find which one(s) should be selected by default and resets the default.

defaultStatus

This property is part of the window object and contains the default message displayed in the status bar. You can set the defaultStatus property at any time. If you plan to use the status bar for an onMouseOver event handler statement, you must return True. The defaultStatus property has the following syntax:

```
windowReference.defaultStatus
```

The windowReference entry is one of the available window identifiers (such as self).

Example:

```
window.defaultStatus = "Finish the modules in less than a week!"
```

The default contents for the status bar display are set to a phrase that complements the purpose of the site.

defaultValue

This property is part of the hidden, password, text, and textarea objects. It contains the default information for a password, text, or textarea object. If the object is a password, the initial value is null, regardless of the defaultValue. For a text object, the defaultValue reflects the VALUE= attribute. For textarea objects, it is the contents of the object found between the <TEXTAREA> tags. If you set defaultValue through a script, it overrides the initial value. The immediate display value of the object is not changed when you change the defaultValue through your script; if you later run a function that resets the defaults, your change appears.

The defaultValue property has the following syntax:

```
passwordName.defaultValue
textName.defaultValue
textareaName.defaultValue
```

Example:

```
document.javajive.lessonLeader.defaultValue="ee cummings"

...

<INPUT TYPE="reset" NAME="resetScoreCard" VALUE="Reset the Scores" >
```

A line in your script changes the default value of the lessonLeader text object, and later in the script, the default values are reset. When this second line is executed, the contents of the lessonLeader text object is updated with ee cummings.

E

This read-only math property is approximately 2.718, which is Euler's constant, the base of natural logarithms. It is part of the math object and has the following syntax:

```
Math.E
```

Example:

```
document.write("The base of natural logarithms is Euler's contant which is:
" + Math.E)
```

This statement displays the phrase followed by the value stored in the E property.

elements

The elements property is an array of the items in a form such as checkbox, radio, and text objects. These items are listed in the array, in the order in which they occur.

encoding

The encoding property is part of the form object and contains the MIME-encoding format information for the form. You can set the encoding property at any time; the initial value is the ENCTYPE= attribute of the <FORM> tag. The various encoding types may require specific values; check the specifications for the encoding type. The encoding property has the following syntax:

```
formName.encoding
```

Example:

```
function formEncode() (
    return document.javajive.encoding }
```

The formEncode function gets the MIME-encoding information from the form.

fgColor

This property is part of the document object and specifies the foreground color of the text. You can express the color using one of the color keywords or the hexadecimal RGB value. This property uses the browser preference settings as its initial value. You can change this value either by setting the COLOR= attribute of the <FONT> tag or by using the fontcolor method. The fgColor property has the following syntax:

```
document.fgColor
```

Example:

```
document.fgColor="darkred"
document.fgColor="8B0000"
```

These two statements are equivalent. The first uses the color keyword, and the second uses the hexadecimal RGB value for the same color.

forms

The forms property is an array that lists the objects in a form, in the order in which they occur in the code.

frames

The frames property is an array that lists the child frames within a frame.

hash

The hash property is part of the URL, and it identifies an anchor on the destination page. It is part of the link and location objects and has the following syntax:

```
location.hash
```

(See the examples for the anchor object and the href proeprty.)

host

The host property is part of the URL, and it identifies the hostname:port for the page. This property is a concatenation of the hostname and port properties. You can set the host property; it is better to set the href property, however, if you want to change a location. The host property is part of the link and location objects and has the following syntax:

```
links[index].host
location.host
```

(See the examples for the link and location objects.)

hostname

The hostname property is part of the URL and identifies the host server by its DNS or IP address. If the port property is null, the hostname and host properties are the same. The hostname property is part of the link and location objects and has the following syntax:

```
links[index].hostname
location.hostname
```

(See the examples for the link and location objects.)

href

The href property is part of the link and location objects and contains the full URL. The protocol, host, port, pathname, search, and hash properties are substrings within the href property, which has the following syntax:

```
links[index].href
location.href
```

Example:

```
<script>
var question1="false"
var question2="false"
var question3="false"

function roundTheClock() {
    for (var x=0; x<6; x++) {
    switch(x){
        case(1): if (question1 != "true") {
            win1= new window.open (answer1.location.href) }
            break;
        case(2): if (question2 != "true") {
            win2= new window.open (answer2.location.href) }
            break;
        case(3): if (question3 != "true") {
            win3=new window.open (answer3.location.href) }
            break;
} } }

</script>
```

In this example, the loop opens a series of windows with the answers to questions that the visitor anwered incorrectly.

index

The index property is part of the options array. It is an integer value that gives the position of an object within the options array of a select object. The index property has the following syntax:

```
selectName.options[indexValue].index
```

The selectName entry is the name of the select object or element in the elements array. The indexValue entry is an integer representing the option in a select object.

Example:

```
for (var x=0; x < document.jivejingle.courseSelect.length; x++) {
    document.write (document.jivejingle.courseSelect.options[x].index) }
```

This example displays the contents of the list of courseSelect.

lastModified

The lastModified property is part of the document object. It is a read-only date string indicating when the document was last changed or updated and has the following syntax:

```
document.lastModified
```

Example:

```
<SCRIPT>
    document.write ("Welcome, this course description is current as of " +
document.lastModified)
</SCRIPT>
```

This script keeps the date current without manual intervention.

length

The length property works with objects and arrays; you can use it to get the number of elements within the object or array. It has the following syntax:

```
formName.length
```

Returns the number of elements on a form.

```
frameReference.length
```

Returns the number of frames within a frame.

```
history.length
```

Returns the number of entries in the history object.

```
radioName.length
```

Returns the number of buttons within a radio object.

3

```
select.Name.length
```
Returns the number of objects in a `select` list object.
```
stringName.length
```
Returns the number of character spaces in a `string`.
```
windowReference.length
```
Returns the number of frames in a parent window.
```
anchors.length
elements.length
forms.length
frameReference.frames.length
windowReference.frames.length
links.length
selectName.options.length
```
Returns the number of entries in the array.

Example:
```
var visitor=document.anchors.length
document.write("there are " + visitor + " links to other pages... can you
visit them all?")
```
In this example, the script stores the number of anchors in the variable *visitor* and uses that in a statement displayed to the visitor.

The length property is found in the following objects:

frame	select
history	string
radio	window

And within the following arrays:

anchors	frames
elements	links
forms	options

linkColor

The `linkColor` property is part of the `document` object. It contains the setting for the inactive and unused links in a document. This property reflects the setting in the <BODY> tag of a document. After the layout, this is a read-only property. To set this property in a script, place the code before any <BODY> tags, and do not use the <BODY LINK="..."> attribute. The `linkColor` property has the following syntax:
```
document.linkColor
```

Example:

```
document.write ("The " + document.linkColor + " jumps are places you've
never been!")
```

This statement displays the link color for the visitor.

links

The links property is an array of document links listed in source order.

LN2

The LN2 property is part of the built-in math object. It is a read-only constant that represents the natural logarithm of two (approximately 0.693) and has the following syntax:

```
Math.LN2
```

Example:

```
document.write ("Bob says your chances of winning are: " + longShot + " in "
+ longShot/Math.LN2)
```

This example computes a value and displays the results in a statement for the visitor.

LN10

The LN10 property is part of the built-in math object. It is a read-only constant that represents the natural logarithm of 10 (approximately 2.302) and has the following syntax:

```
Math.LN10
```

Example:

```
document.write ("Bob says your chances of winning are: " + longShot + " in "
+ longShot*Math.LN10)
```

This example computes a value and displays the results in a statement for the visitor.

location

The location property is part of the document object. It contains the complete URL of the document. Unlike the location object, you cannot change the document's location property. The location property has the following syntax:

```
document.location
```

Example:

```
<SCRIPT>
    var there="http://www.raycomm.com/"
    var takeLesson=""
    function weAre() {
```

```
        self.status='Welcome, this is ' + document.location + '
        our site is NEVER done!'}
    function checkThis(){
        alert("Thanks for registering")}
</SCRIPT>
</HEAD>
<BODY onLoad="window.alert('Welcome!'); weAre()">
```

This displays a notice to the visitor, including the document's location, in in the status line of the window.

LOG2E

The LOG2E property is part of the built-in math object. It is a read-only constant that represents the base 2 logarithm of E (approximately 1.442). It has the following syntax:

```
Math.LOG2E
```

Example:

```
document.write ("Bob says your chances of winning are: " + longShot + " in "
+ longShot*Math.LOG2E)
```

This example computes a value and displays the results in a statement for the visitor.

LOG10E

The LOG10E property is part of the built-in math object. It is a read-only constant that represents the base 10 logarithm of E (approximately 0.434). It has the following syntax:

```
Math.LOG10E
```

Example:

```
document.write ("Bob says your chances of winning are: " + longShot + " in "
+ longShot/Math.LOG2E)
```

This example computes a value and displays the results in a statement for the visitor.

method

The method property is part of the form object. It indicates how a form is sent to the server when it is submitted. This reflects the contents of the METHOD= attribute of the <FORM> tag. This property contains either GET or POST. You can set this property at any time. The method property has the following syntax:

```
formName.method
```

Example:

```
if (document.javajive.method == "GET") {
    document.write("The server will get your answers now.")
else { document.write("Your answers will be posted to the server now.") } }
```

This example displays different text depending on the method.

name

This property is used to identify the objects and elements contained by a number of objects and arrays. For window objects, this is a read-only property; you can set the name of other objects.

In a window object, the name reflects the windowName attribute. In other objects, it reflects the NAME= attribute. The name property is the same for all radio buttons in a radio object.

The name property differs from the label used for the button, reset, and submit objects. The name property is not displayed; it is an internal, programmatic reference.

If a frame object contains several elements or objects with the same name, the browser creates an array using the name and listing the objects as they occur in the frame source.

The name property has the following syntax for window objects:

```
windowReference.name
window.Reference.frames.name
```

The name property has the following syntax for other objects:

```
objectName.name
frameReference.name
frameReference.frames.name
radioName[index].name
selectName.options.name
```

For a select object, objectName.name and selectName.options.name produce the same result.

For a frame object, objectName.name, frameReference.name, and frameReference.frames.name produce the same result.

Example:

```
newWindow=window.open("http://www.webwonders.net/testone.htm")
function whatYouBuilt () {
    for (var counter=0, counter<document.elements.length, counter++) {
        msgWindow.document.write(document.sample.elements[counter].name +
"<BR>") } }
```

In this example, the function loops through the loaded document and displays a list of the elements.

The name property is found in the following objects and arrays:

button	hidden	reset	text	options array
checkbox	password	select	textarea	
frame	radio	submit	window	

options

The options property is an array that contains a list of the options in a select object.

parent

The parent property is one of the synonyms available for referencing a window that contains the current frame. This is a read-only property for the window and frame objects. You can use this property when referencing one frame from another within a window or parent frame. It has the following syntax:

```
parent.propertyName
parent.methodName
top.frameName
top.frames[index]
```

The propertyName entry is the defaultStatus, status, length, name, or parent property. This could also be the length, name, or parent property when the reference is from a parent to a frame. The methodName entry is any method associated with the window object. (See the window object entry for more information about the available methods.) The frameName and frames[index] entries reference individual frames by either their NAME value or their position in an array of frames.

Example:

```
<INPUT TYPE="button" NAME="doItButton" VALUE="Make it so!"
    onClick="parent.frames[2].document.bgColor=colorChoice">
```

This example is part of the frame object example. In this statement, the background color of the sibling (index value2) of the current frame is set to the user's color choice.

pathname

The pathname property is part of the link and location objects. It is the part of the URL that indicates the directory location for the page on the server. You can set the pathname at any time, but if you need to change the document pathname, it is safer to use the href property. The pathname property has the following syntax:

```
location.pathname
```

(See the examples for the location object.)

PI

The PI property is part of the built-in `math` object. It is a read-only constant that represents the ratio of circle circumference to diameter (approximately 3.14159). The PI property has the following syntax:

```
Math.PI
```

Example:

```
document.write ("Bob says your chances of winning are: " + longShot + " in "
+ longShot*Math.PI)
```

This example computes a value and displays the results in a statement for the visitor.

port

The `port` property is part of the `link` and `location` objects. It is the `port` element in the URL and identifies the port, if any, used on the server. If this property is null, the `host` and `hostname` properties are the same. The `port` property has the following syntax:

```
location.port
```

(See the example for the `location` object.)

protocol

The `protocol` property is part of the `link` and `location` objects. It is part of the URL and uses the following protocols:

file: accesses a local file system

ftp: uses the FTP protocol (File Transfer Protocol)

gopher: uses the Gopher protocol

http: uses the HTTP protocol (HyperText Transfer Protocol)

mailto: uses the SMTP protocol (Standard Mail Transfer Protocol)

news: uses the NNTP protocol (Network News Transfer Protocol)

snews: uses the secure NNTP protocol

https: uses the secure HTTP protocol

telnet: uses the Telnet protocol

tn3270: uses the 3270 Telenet protocol

The `port` property has the following syntax:

```
location.protocol
```

(See the examples for the `link` and `location` objects.)

referrer

The `referrer` property is part of the `document` object. It is a read-only property of the `document` object that contains the originating document URL when a visitor jumps from an originating document to a destination document. The `referrer` property has the following syntax:

```
document.referrer
```

Example:

```
document.write("welcome, I see you joined us from " + document.referrer + ".
How's the weather back there?")
```

This statement displays a message for the visitor that includes the location URL of the original document.

search

The `search` property is found in the `link` and `location` objects. It is part of the URL; although you can change this property at any time, it is best to use the `href` property to change `location` attributes. The `search` property has the following syntax:

```
location.search
```

Example:

```
newWindow=window.open
    ("http://www.raycomm.com/Look/scripts?qt=property=elements")
with (document) {
    write("the href property is " + newWindow.location.href + "<P>")
    write("the protocol property is " + newWindow.location.protocol + "<P>")
    write("the host property is " + newWindow.location.host + "<P>")
    write("the host name is " + newWindow.location.hostName + "<P>")
    write("the port property is " + newWindow.location.port + "<P>")
    write("the pathname property is" + newWindow.location.pathname + "<P>")
    write("the search property is " + newWindow.location.search + "<P>")
    write("the hash property is " + newWindow.location.hash + "<P>")
    close() }
```

Which displays the following:

```
the href property is
http://www.raycomm.com/Look/scripts?qt=property=elements
the protocol property is http:
the host property is www.raycomm.com
the host name is www.raycomm.com
```

```
the port property is
the pathname property is /Look/scripts
the search property is ?qt=property=elements
the hash property is
```

selected

The `selected` property is part of the `options` array. It contains a boolean value that indicates whether the `option` in a `select` object is currently selected. For selected options, this property is True. You can set this property programmatically. It has the following syntax:

```
selectName.options[index].selected
```

Example:

```
for (x=document.saleForm.buyTheseThings.length, x > 0, x-) {
    if (document.saleForm.buyTheseThings.options[x].selected = "true") {
        document.saleForm.buyTheseThings.options[x].selected = "false"
    else {
        document.saleForm.buyTheseThings.options[x].selected = "true" }
    } }
```

In this example, the `for` loop traverses the list of options altering the selections. The result is an inversion of the visitor's selections.

selectedIndex

The `selectedIndex` property is part of the `select` object and the `options` array. It contains information about the order in which a `select` object was defined. You can set the `selectedIndex` property at any time, and the displayed information is updated. The `selectedIndex` property works well with `select` objects that are not MULTIPLE select objects. It has the following syntax:

```
selectName.selectedIndex
selectName.options.selectedIndex
```

Example:

```
function (whatSelection) () {
    return document.saleForm.giveAwayOptions.selectedIndex }
```

This simple function brings back the selection from the list of options.

self

The `self` property is part of the `window` object. This property is a synonym for the current window or `frame` object. Use this read-only property to help keep your code clear. It has the following syntax:

```
self.propertyName
self.methodName
```

Example:

```
self.javatest.whichIsFunction.index[x]
document.javatest.whichIsFunction.index[x]
```

These two statements are equivalent.

SQRT1_2

The SQRT1_2 property is part of the built-in math object. It is a read-only constant that represents the square root of $\frac{1}{2}$ (approximately 0.707). It has the following syntax:

```
Math.SQRT1_2
```

Example:

```
document.write ("Bob says your chances of winning are: " + longShot + " in "
+ longShot/Math.SQRT1_2)
```

This example computes a value and displays the results in a statement for the visitor.

SQRT2

The SQRT2 property is part of the built-in math object. It is a read-only constant that represents the square root of 2 (approximately 1.414). It has the following syntax:

```
Math.SQRT2
```

Example:

```
document.write ("Bob says your chances of winning are: " + longShot + " in "
+ longShot*Math.SQRT2)
```

This example computes a value and displays the results in a statement for the visitor.

status

The status property is part of the window object. It contains a priority or transient message that is displayed in the status bar of the window. It has the following syntax:

```
windowReference.status
```

Example:

```
self.status="Welcome to our little home away from home!"
```

This example puts the message onto the window's status line.

target

The target property is part of the form, link, and location objects. It works for the link and location and the form objects slightly differently. For the link and location objects, the target property contains the window name for a jump. For the form object, it contains the destination for form submissions. Although you can set the `target` property at any time, it cannot assume the value of an expression or a variable (meaning you can't build those fancy statements such as `document.write`). The `target` property has the following syntax:

```
formName.target
linkName.target
```

Example:

```
self.status("When you submit your request, the information will appear in "
+ self.buyTheseThings.target + ".")
```

This statement displays a message in the window status bar telling visitors where their selections will appear. This is useful if you want to confirm the request before displaying the information.

text

The `text` property is part of the `options` array. It is the displayed value in an options list. If you change the `text` property for an option list, the display character, initially set in the `<OPTION>` tag, does not change, but the internal information does change. The `text` property has the following syntax:

```
selectName.options[index].text
```

Example:

```
for (x=0, x < self.javajive.pickMe.length, x++) {
    if (self.javajive.pickMe.option[x].select == true) {
        document.write(self.javajive.pickMe.option[x].text) }
    }
```

This example tests to see if the option has been selected; if it has, it displays the option text. If you change the `text` property programmatically, the resulting list is different from the list of options the visitor sees and selects from.

title

The `title` property is part of the `document` object. It reflects the value between the `<TITLE>`, and you cannot change this value. The `title` property has the following syntax:

```
document.title
```

Example:

```
self.status(self.title)
```

top

The top property is part of the window object. It is a read-only synonym for the top-most window and has the following syntax:

```
top.propertyName
top.methodName
top.frameName
top.frames[index]
```

The propertyName entry is defaultStatus, status, or length. The methodName entry is any window method. The frameName and frames[index] entries are frame references for frames within the window.

Example:

```
top.close()
```

This closes the topmost window.

```
for (x=0, x<top.length, x++) {
    top.frame[x].close() }
```

This closes the frames on a page.

userAgent

The userAgent property is part of the navigator object. It is part of the HTTP protocol information. Servers use this property to identify the client browser. The userAgent property has the following syntax:

```
navigator.userAgent
```

Example:

```
document.write("You're using " + navigator.userAgent)
```

This displays the browser information, as in:

```
You're using Mozilla/2.0 (win16; I)
```

value

The value property differs for the various objects. In all cases, it reflects the VALUE= attribute of the object.

For hidden, password, text, and textarea objects or for an item in the options array, you can programmatically change the property. If you change it for the text and textarea objects, the display updates immediately. If you change it for the password object, security could give you some pause. If you evaluate your changes, you'll get the current value back; if a visitor changes it, security will not pass the changes. For the options array, the VALUE= attribute is not displayed, but is an internal representation.

For the button, reset, and submit objects, the value property is a read-only reflection of the text on the face of the button.

For checkbox and radio objects, the value property is returned to the server when the checkbox or radio button is selected. It is not the value of the selection; it is simply On or Off.

The value property has the following syntax:

```
objectName.value
radioName[index].value
selectName.options.[index].value
```

(For examples of the value property, see the appropriate object entry.

The value property is part of the following objects and arrays:

button	password	submit	options (array)
checkbox	radio	text	
hidden	reset	textarea	

vLinkColor

The vLinkColor is a part of the document object. It contains the color settings for the links on the page that have been visited. To set this value programmatically, place your script ahead of the <BODY> tag; once the layout has been done, this becomes a read-only property. If you do set the property in a script, do not use the <BODY VLINK="..." attribute. To set the color, use either the color keyword or a hexadecimal RGB number (three double digits). The vLinkColor has the following syntax:

```
document.vLinkColor="colorLiteral"
document.vLinkColor="colorRGB"
```

Example:

```
document.write("To determine where you've been,
check the color of your inks!
<BR>If the link is " + document.linkColor + ", you haven't gone there.
<BR>Could be a whole new world waiting for you!<BR>If the link is "
 + document.vLinkColor +
", you've followed that lead... where did it take you?")
```

In a document that contains linkColor=blue and document.vLinkColor=red, the result of this write statement is:

```
To determine where you've been, check the color of your links!
If the link is blue, you haven't gone there.
Could be a whole new world waiting for you!
If the link is red, you've followed that lead... Where did it take you?
```

window

The `window` property is part of the `frame` and `window` objects. It is a synonym for the current window. Although you can use the `window` property to refer to the current frame, it is better to use the `self` property in that situation. This property is read-only and has the following syntax:

```
window.propertyName
window.methodName(parameters)
```

Example:

```
window.status="Welcome to our humble home away from home!"
```

This example displays the message in the status bar.

Master's Reference
Part 4

HTML Special Characters

Standard HTML Characters

The characters in Table 4.1 were included in HTML 2 and HTML 3.2 and are also included in the current HTML 4 specification. Most browsers should display these characters, based on the mnemonic or numeric representation.

TABLE 4.1: STANDARD HTML CHARACTERS

Symbol	Mnemonic Representation	Numeric Representation	Description
			No-break space
¡	&iexcl;	&#161;	Inverted exclamation mark
¢	&cent;	&#162;	Cent
£	&pound;	&#163;	Pound sterling
¤	&curren;	&#164;	General currency
¥	&yen;	&#165;	Yen
¦	&brvbar;	&#166;	Broken (vertical) bar
§	&sect;	&#167;	Section
¨	&uml;	&#168;	Umlaut (diaeresis)
©	&copy;	&#169;	Copyright sign
ª	&ordf;	&#170;	Ordinal indicator, feminine
«	&laquo;	&#171;	Angle quotation mark, left
¬	&not;	&#172;	Not
	&shy;	&#173;	Soft hyphen
®	&reg;	&#174;	Registered
¯	&macr;	&#175;	Macron
°	&deg;	&#176;	Degree
±	&plusmn;	&#177;	Plus-or-minus
²	&sup2;	&#178;	Superscript two
³	&sup3;	&#179;	Superscript three
´	&acute;	&#180;	Acute accent
µ	&micro;	&#181;	Micro
¶	&para;	&#182;	Pilcrow (paragraph)
·	&middot;	&#183;	Middle dot
¸	&cedil;	&#184;	Cedilla
¹	&sup1;	&#185;	Superscript one
¼	&frac14;	&#188;	Fraction one-quarter

TABLE D.1 CONTINUED: STANDARD HTML CHARACTERS

Symbol	Mnemonic Representation	Numeric Representation	Description
º	&ordm;	&#186;	Ordinal indicator, masculine
»	&raquo;	&#187;	Angle quotation mark, right
½	&frac12;	&#189;	Fraction one-half
¾	&frac34;	&#190;	Fraction three-quarters
¿	&iquest;	&#191;	Inverted question mark
À	&Agrave;	&#192;	Uppercase A, grave accent
Á	&Aacute;	&#193;	Uppercase A, acute accent
Â	&Acirc;	&#194;	Uppercase A, circumflex
Ã	&Atilde;	&#195;	Uppercase A, tilde
Ä	&Auml;	&#196;	Uppercase A, diaeresis or umlaut mark
Å	&Aring;	&#197;	Uppercase A, angstrom
Æ	&AElig;	&#198;	Uppercase AE diphthong (ligature)
Ç	&Ccedil;	&#199;	Uppercase C, cedilla
È	&Egrave;	&#200;	Uppercase E, grave accent
É	&Eacute;	&#201;	Uppercase E, acute accent
Ê	&Ecirc;	&#202;	Uppercase E, circumflex
Ë	&Euml;	&#203;	Uppercase E, umlaut (diaeresis)
Ì	&Igrave;	&#204;	Uppercase I, grave accent
Í	&Iacute;	&#205;	Uppercase I, acute accent
Î	&Icirc;	&#206;	Uppercase I, circumflex
Ï	&Iuml;	&#207;	Uppercase I, umlaut (diaresis)
Ð	&ETH;	&#208;	Uppercase Eth, Icelandic
Ñ	&Ntilde;	&#209;	Uppercase N, tilde
Ò	&Ograve;	&#210;	Uppercase O, grave accent
Ó	&Oacute;	&#211;	Uppercase O, acute accent
Ô	&Ocirc;	&#212;	Uppercase O, circumflex
Õ	&Otilde;	&#213;	Uppercase O, tilde
Ö	&Ouml;	&#214;	Uppercase O, umlaut (diaresis)
×	&times;	&#215;	Multiplication
Ø	&Oslash;	&#216;	Uppercase O, slash
Ù	&Ugrave;	&#217;	Uppercase U, grave accent
Ú	&Uacute;	&#218;	Uppercase U, acute accent
Û	&Ucirc;	&#219;	Uppercase U, circumflex

Continued ▶

TABLE 4.1 CONTINUED: STANDARD HTML CHARACTERS

Symbol	Mnemonic Representation	Numeric Representation	Description
Ü	Ü	Ü	Uppercase U, umlaut (diaresis)
Ý	Ý	Ý	Uppercase Y, acute accent
þ	Þ	Þ	Uppercase THORN, Icelandic
ß	ß	ß	small sharp s, German
à	à	à	Lowercase a, grave accent
á	á	á	Lowercase a, acute accent
â	â	â	Lowercase a, circumflex
ã	ã	ã	Lowercase a, tilde
ä	ä	ä	Lowercase a, umlaut (diaresis)
å	å	å	Lowercase a, angstrom
æ	æ	æ	Lowercase ae diphthong (ligature)
ç	ç	ç	Lowercase c, cedilla
è	è	è	Lowercase e, grave accent
é	é	é	Lowercase e, acute accent
ê	ê	ê	Lowercase e, circumflex
ë	ë	ë	Lowercase e, umlaut (diaresis)
ì	ì	ì	Lowercase i, grave accent
í	í	í	Lowercase i, acute accent
î	î	î	Lowercase i, circumflex
ï	ï	ï	Lowercase i, umlaut (diaresis)
ð	ð	ð	Lowercase eth, Icelandic
ñ	ñ	ñ	Lowercase n, tilde
ò	ò	ò	Lowercase o, grave accent
ó	ó	ó	Lowercase o, acute accent
ô	ô	ô	Lowercase o, circumflex
õ	õ	õ	Lowercase o, tilde
ö	ö	ö	Lowercase o, umlaut (diaresis)
÷	÷	÷	Division
ø	ø	ø	Lowercase o, slash
ù	ù	ù	Lowercase u, grave accent
ú	ú	ú	Lowercase u, acute accent
û	û	û	Lowercase u, circumflex

TABLE 4.1 CONTINUED: STANDARD HTML CHARACTERS			
Symbol	**Mnemonic Representation**	**Numeric Representation**	**Description**
ü	&uuml;	&#252;	Lowercase u, umlaut (diaresis)
ý	&yacute;	&#253;	Lowercase y, acute accent
þ	&thorn;	&#254;	Lowrcase thorn, Icelandic
ÿ	&yuml;	&#255;	Lowercase y, umlaut (diaresis)

Portions © International Organization for Standardization 1986: Permission to copy in any form is granted for use with conforming SGML systems and applications as defined in ISO 8879, provided this notice is included in all copies.

Extended HTML Characters

Most of the extended HTML characters (see Table 4.2) are new in HTML 4, and at the time of writing, relatively few browsers supported them. New browser versions are expected to support them.

TABLE 4.2: EXTENDED HTML CHARACTERS			
Symbol	**Mnemonic Representation**	**Numeric Representation**	**Description**
Œ	&OElig;	&#338;	Latin uppercase ligature Œ
œ	&oelig;	&#339;	Latin lowercase ligature œ
Š	&Scaron;	&#352;	Latin uppercase S with caron
š	&scaron;	&#353;	Latin lowercase s with caron
Ÿ	&Yuml;	&#376;	Latin uppercase Y with umlaut
ƒ	&fnof;	&#402;	Latin lowercase f with hook
ˆ	&circ;	&#710;	Modifier letter circumflex
˜	&tilde;	&#732;	Small tilde
Α	&Alpha;	&#913;	Greek uppercase alpha
Β	&Beta;	&#914;	Greek uppercase beta
Γ	&Gamma;	&#915;	Greek uppercase gamma

Continued ▶

	TABLE 4.2 CONTINUED: EXTENDED HTML CHARACTERS		
Symbol	Mnemonic Representation	Numeric Representation	Description
Δ	&Delta;	&#916;	Greek uppercase delta
E	&Epsilon;	&#917;	Greek uppercase epsilon
Z	&Zeta;	&#918;	Greek uppercase zeta
H	&Eta;	&#919;	Greek uppercase eta
Θ	&Theta;	&#920;	Greek uppercase theta
I	&Iota;	&#921;	Greek uppercase iota
K	&Kappa;	&#922;	Greek uppercase kappa
Λ	&Lambda;	&#923;	Greek uppercase lambda
M	&Mu;	&#924;	Greek uppercase mu
N	&Nu;	&#925;	Greek uppercase nu
Ξ	&Xi;	&#926;	Greek uppercase xi
O	&Omicron;	&#927;	Greek uppercase omicron
Π	&Pi;	&#928;	Greek uppercase pi
P	&Rho;	&#929;	Greek uppercase rho
Σ	&Sigma;	&#931;	Greek uppercase sigma
T	&Tau;	&#932;	Greek uppercase tau
Y	&Upsilon;	&#933;	Greek uppercase upsilon
Φ	&Phi;	&#934;	Greek uppercase phi
X	&Chi;	&#935;	Greek uppercase chi
Ψ	&Psi;	&#936;	Greek uppercase psi
Ω	&Omega;	&#937;	Greek uppercase omega
α	&alpha;	&#945;	Greek lowercase alpha
β	&beta;	&#946;	Greek lowercase beta
λ	&gamma;	&#947;	Greek lowercase gamma
δ	&delta;	&#948;	Greek lowercase delta
ε	&epsilon;	&#949;	Greek lowercase epsilon
ζ	&zeta;	&#950;	Greek lowercase zeta
η	&eta;	&#951;	Greek lowercase eta
ϑ	&theta;	&#952;	Greek lowercase theta
ι	&iota;	&#953;	Greek lowercase iota
κ	&kappa;	&#954;	Greek lowercase kappa
λ	&lambda;	&#955;	Greek lowercase lambda
μ	&mu;	&#956;	Greek lowercase mu
ν	&nu;	&#957;	Greek lowercase nu
ξ	&xi;	&#958;	Greek lowercase xi
o	&omicron;	&#959;	Greek lowercase omicron
π	&pi;	&#960;	Greek lowercase pi

	TABLE 4.2 CONTINUED: EXTENDED HTML CHARACTERS		
Symbol	**Mnemonic Representation**	**Numeric Representation**	**Description**
ρ	&rho;	&#961;	Greek lowercase rho
ς	&sigmaf;	&#962;	Greek lowercase final sigma
σ	&sigma;	&#963;	Greek lowercase sigma
τ	&tau;	&#964;	Greek lowercase tau
υ	&upsilon;	&#965;	Greek lowercase upsilon
φ	&phi;	&#966;	Greek lowercase phi
χ	&chi;	&#967;	Greek lowercase chi
ψ	&psi;	&#968;	Greek lowercase psi
ω	&omega;	&#969;	Greek lowercase omega
θ	&thetasym;	&#977;	Greek lowercase theta symbol
ϒ	&upsih;	&#978;	Greek upsilon with hook symbol
π	&piv;	&#982;	Greek pi
			En space
			Em space
			Thin space
–	&ndash;	&#8211;	En dash
—	&mdash;	&#8212;	Em dash
'	&lsquo;	&#8216;	left single quotation mark
'	&rsquo;	&#8217;	right single quotation mark
‚	&sbquo;	&#8218;	Single low-9 quotation mark
"	&ldquo;	&#8220;	Left double quotation mark
"	&rdquo;	&#8221;	Right double quotation mark
„	&bdquo;	&#8222;	double low-9 quotation mark
†	&dagger;	&#8224;	Dagger
‡	&Dagger;	&#8225;	Double dagger
•	&bull;	&#8226;	Bullet (black small circle)
…	&hellip;	&#8230;	Horizontal ellipsis (three-dot leader)
‰	&permil;	&#8240;	Per mille sign
'	&prime;	&#8242;	Prime (minutes or feet)
"	&Prime;	&#8243;	Double prime (seconds or inches)
‹	&lsaquo;	&#8249;	Single left-pointing angle quotation mark

Continued ▶

TABLE 4.2 CONTINUED: EXTENDED HTML CHARACTERS

Symbol	Mnemonic Representation	Numeric Representation	Description
›	›	›	Single right-pointing angle quotation mark
—	‾	‾	Overline (spacing overscore)
/	⁄	⁄	Fraction slash
ℑ	ℑ	ℑ	Blackletter Uppercase I (imaginary part)
℘	℘	℘	Script Uppercase P (power set or Weierstrass p)
ℜ	ℜ	ℜ	Blackletter Uppercase R (real part symbol)
™	™	™	Trademark
ℵ	ℵ	ℵ	Alef (first transfinite cardinal)
←	←	←	left arrow
↑	↑	↑	Up arrow
→	→	→	Right arrow
↓	↓	↓	Down arrow
↔	↔	↔	Left-right arrow
↵	↵	↵	Down arrow with corner Left (carriage return)
⇐	⇐	⇐	Left double arrow
⇑	⇑	⇑	Up double arrow
⇒	⇒	⇒	Right double arrow
⇓	⇓	⇓	Down double arrow
⇔	⇔	⇔	Left-right double arrow
∀	∀	∀	For all
∂	∂	∂	Partial differential
∃	∃	∃	There exists
∅	∅	∅	Empty set (null set or diameter)
∇	∇	∇	Nabla (backward difference)
∈	∈	∈	Element of
∉	∉	∉	Not an element of
∋	∋	∋	Contains as member
∏	∏	∏	n-ary product (product sign)
Σ	∑	∑	N-ary sumation
-	−	−	Minus

4

TABLE 4.2 CONTINUED: EXTENDED HTML CHARACTERS

Symbol	Mnemonic Representation	Numeric Representation	Description
*	&lowast;	&#8727;	Asterisk operator
√	&radic;	&#8730;	Square root (radical)
∝	&prop;	&#8733;	Proportional to
∞	&infin;	&#8734;	Infinity
∠	&ang;	&#8736;	Angle
∩	&cap;	&#8745;	Intersection (cap)
∪	&cup;	&#8746;	Union (cup)
∫	&int;	&#8747;	Integral
∴	&there4;	&#8756;	Therefore
~	&sim;	&#8764;	Tilde operator (varies with or similar to)
≈	&cong;	&#8773;	Approximately equal to
≅	&asymp;	&#8776;	Almost equal to (asymptotic to)
≠	&ne;	&#8800;	Not equal to
	&equiv;	&#8801;	Identical to
≤	&le;	&#8804;	Less-than or equal to
≥	&ge;	&#8805;	Greater-than or equal to
⊂	&sub;	&#8834;	Subset of
⊃	&sup;	&#8835;	Superset of
⊄	&nsub;	&#8836;	Not a subset of
⊅	&sube;	&#8838;	Subset of or equal to
⊇	&supe;	&#8839;	Superset of or equal to
⊕	&oplus;	&#8853;	Circled plus (direct sum)
⊗	&otimes;	&#8855;	Circled times (vector product)
∧	&and;	&#8869;	Logical and (wedge)
⊥	&perp;	&#8869;	Up tack (orthogonal to or perpendicular)
∨	&or;	&#8870;	Logical or (vee)
.	&sdot;	&#8901;	Dot operator
	&lceil;	&#8968;	Left ceiling (apl upstile)
⌉	&rceil;	&#8969;	Right ceiling
⌊	&lfloor;	&#8970;	Left floor (apl downstile)
⌋	&rfloor;	&#8971;	Right floor
〈	&lang;	&#9001;	Left-pointing angle bracket
〉	&rang;	&#9002;	Right-pointing angle bracket

Continued ▶

TABLE 4.2 CONTINUED: EXTENDED HTML CHARACTERS			
Symbol	**Mnemonic Representation**	**Numeric Representation**	**Description**
◊	&loz;	&#9674;	lozenge
♠	&spades;	&#9824;	Spade
♣	&clubs;	&#9827;	Club (shamrock)
♥	&hearts;	&#9829;	Heart (valentine)
♦	&diams;	&#9830;	Diamond

Portions © International Organization for Standardization 1986: Permission to copy in any form is granted for use with conforming SGML systems and applications as defined in ISO 8879, provided this notice is included in all copies.

Master's
Reference
Part 5

HTML Color Codes

As we mentioned throughout the book, certain colors provide more uniform results than others. These listings present a variety of color codes for use in HTML documents, including the 216 safe colors. See Chapter 7 for more information about selecting colors for HTML documents, and check out the Mastering HTML Web site to see the colors in action.

In this section, you'll find the 216 safe colors, 16 basic (standard) color names, Netscape's color names, and finally a chart combining both the safe and the named colors, for ease of reference.

Safe Colors

Below is a list of all 216 "safe" colors that look consistently good in most situations, including backgrounds and broad expanses of color. Color names are not listed because the best colors (depicted here as a list of RRGGBB codes) do not necessarily correspond directly to named colors.

#000000	#0033CC	#009966
#000033	#0033FF	#009999
#000066	#006600	#0099CC
#000099	#006633	#0099FF
#0000CC	#006666	#00CC00
#0000FF	#006699	#00CC33
#003300	#0066CC	#00CC66
#003333	#0066FF	#00CC99
#003366	#009900	#00CCCC
#003399	#009933	#00CCFF

#00FF00	#33CC66	#6699CC
#00FF33	#33CC99	#6699FF
#00FF66	#33CCCC	#66CC00
#00FF99	#33CCFF	#66CC33
#00FFCC	#33FF00	#66CC66
#00FFFF	#33FF33	#66CC99
#330000	#33FF66	#66CCCC
#330033	#33FF99	#66CCFF
#330066	#33FFCC	#66FF00
#330099	#33FFFF	#66FF33
#3300CC	#660000	#66FF66
#3300FF	#660033	#66FF99
#333300	#660066	#66FFCC
#333333	#660099	#66FFFF
#333366	#6600CC	#990000
#333399	#6600FF	#990033
#3333CC	#663300	#990066
#3333FF	#663333	#990099
#336600	#663366	#9900CC
#336633	#663399	#9900FF
#336666	#6633CC	#993300
#336699	#6633FF	#993333
#3366CC	#666600	#993366
#3366FF	#666633	#993399
#339900	#666666	#9933CC
#339933	#666699	#9933FF
#339966	#6666CC	#996600
#339999	#6666FF	#996633
#3399CC	#669900	#996666
#3399FF	#669933	#996699
#33CC00	#669966	#9966CC
#33CC33	#669999	#9966FF

#999900	#CC6600	#FF3300
#999933	#CC6633	#FF3333
#999966	#CC6666	#FF3366
#999999	#CC6699	#FF3399
#9999CC	#CC66CC	#FF33CC
#9999FF	#CC66FF	#FF33FF
#99CC00	#CC9900	#FF6600
#99CC33	#CC9933	#FF6633
#99CC66	#CC9966	#FF6666
#99CC99	#CC9999	#FF6699
#99CCCC	#CC99CC	#FF66CC
#99CCFF	#CC99FF	#FF66FF
#99FF00	#CCCC00	#FF9900
#99FF33	#CCCC33	#FF9933
#99FF66	#CCCC66	#FF9966
#99FF99	#CCCC99	#FF9999
#99FFCC	#CCCCCC	#FF99CC
#99FFFF	#CCCCFF	#FF99FF
#CC0000	#CCFF00	#FFCC00
#CC0033	#CCFF33	#FFCC33
#CC0066	#CCFF66	#FFCC66
#CC0099	#CCFF99	#FFCC99
#CC00CC	#CCFFCC	#FFCCCC
#CC00FF	#CCFFFF	#FFCCFF
#CC3300	#FF0000	#FFFF00
#CC3333	#FF0033	#FFFF33
#CC3366	#FF0066	#FFFF66
#CC3399	#FF0099	#FFFF99
#CC33CC	#FF00CC	#FFFFCC
#CC33FF	#FF00FF	#FFFFFF

The color names and RGB values in Table 5.1 are the 16 colors from the basic Windows VGA color palette. These color names are standard within the HTML 4 specification, and most browsers recognize their names. These colors look consistently clear—if often garish—on Windows computers.

TABLE 5.1: BASIC COLORS AND NAMES	
Color Name	**RRGGBB Value**
Aqua	#00FFFF
Black	#000000
Blue	#0000FF
Fuchsia	#FF00FF
Gray	#808080
Green	#008000
Lime	#00FF00
Maroon	#800000
Navy	#000080
Olive	#808000
Purple	#800080
Red	#FF0000
Silver	#C0C0C0
Teal	#008080
White	#FFFFFF
Yellow	#FFFF00

Named Colors

Table 5.2 presents color names supported by Netscape Navigator (version 3 and later). These colors are not necessarily recommended for backgrounds, because they may not look their best in all visitors' browsers at all resolutions, but they are easy to remember and use. To accommodate all browsers that support colors, however, you must use the color code given in the second column rather than the name.

TABLE 5.2: COLOR NAMES SUPPORTED BY NETSCAPE NAVIGATOR					
Name	**Code**	**Name**	**Code**	**Name**	**Code**
Aliceblue	#F0F8FF	Antiquewhite	#FAEBD7	Aqua	#00FFFF
Aquamarine	#7FFFD4	Azure	#F0FFFF	Beige	#F5F5DC

Continued ▶

TABLE 5.2: (CONTINUED) COLOR NAMES SUPPORTED BY NETSCAPE NAVIGATOR					
Name	**Code**	**Name**	**Code**	**Name**	**Code**
Bisque	#FFE4C4	Black	#000000	Blanched-almond	#FFEBCD
Blue	#0000FF	Blueviolet	#8A2BE2	Brown	#A52A2A
Burlywood	#DEB887	Cadetblue	#5F9EA0	Chartreuse	#7FFF00
Chocolate	#D2691E	Coral	#FF7F50	Cornflower-blue	#6495ED
Cornsilk	#FFF8DC	Crimson	#DC143C	Cyan	#00FFFF
Darkblue	#00008B	Darkcyan	#008B8B	Dark-goldenrod	#B8860B
Darkgray	#A9A9A9	Darkgreen	#006400	Darkkhaki	#BDB76B
Darkmagenta	#8B008B	Color Name	Color code	Darkolive-green	#556B2F
Darkorange	#FF8C00	Darkorchid	#9932CC	Darkred	#8B0000
Darksalmon	#E9967A	Darkseagreen	#8FBC8F	Darkslateblue	#483D8B
Darkslategray	#2F4F4F	Darkturquoise	#00CED1	Darkviolet	#9400D3
Deeppink	#FF1493	Deepskyblue	#00BFFF	Dimgray	#696969
Dodgerblue	#1E90FF	Firebrick	#B22222	Floralwhite	#FFFAF0
Forestgreen	#228B22	Fuchsia	#FF00FF	Gainsboro	#DCDCDC
Ghostwhite	#F8F8FF	Gold	#FFD700	Goldenrod	#DAA520
Gray	#808080	Green	#008000	Greenyellow	#ADFF2F
Honeydew	#F0FFF0	Hotpink	#FF69B4	Indianred	#CD5C5C
Indigo	#4B0082	Ivory	#FFFFF0	Khaki	#F0E68C
Lavender	#E6E6FA	Lavender-blush	#FFF0F5	Lawngreen	#7CFC00
◌ Lemonchiffon	#FFFACD	Lightblue	#ADD8E6	Lightcoral	#F08080
Lightcyan	#E0FFFF	Light-goldenrodyellow	#FAFAD2	Lightgreen	#90EE90
Lightgrey	#D3D3D3	Lightpink	#FFB6C1	Lightsalmon	#FFA07A
Lightseagreen	#20B2AA	Lightskyblue	#87CEFA	Lightslategray	#778899
Lightsteelblue	#B0C4DE	Lightyellow	#FFFFE0	Lime	#00FF00
Limegreen	#32CD32	Linen	#FAF0E6	Magenta	#FF00FF
Maroon	#800000	Medium-aquamarine	#66CDAA	Mediumblue	#0000CD
Medium-orchid	#BA55D3	Medium-purple	#9370DB	Medium-seagreen	#3CB371
Medium-slateblue	#7B68EE	Medium-springgreen	#00FA9A	Medium-turquoise	#48D1CC

Continued ▶

TABLE 5.2: (CONTINUED) COLOR NAMES SUPPORTED BY NETSCAPE NAVIGATOR

Name	Code	Name	Code	Name	Code
Medium-violetred	#C71585	Midnightblue	#191970	Mintcream	#F5FFFA
Mistyrose	#FFE4E1	Moccasin	#FFE4B5	Navajowhite	#FFDEAD
Navy	#000080	Oldlace	#FDF5E6	Olive	#808000
Olivedrab	#6B8E23	Orange	#FFA500	Orangered	#FF4500
Orchid	#DA70D6	Pale-goldenrod	#EEE8AA	Palegreen	#98FB98
Paleturquoise	#AFEEEE	Palevioletred	#DB7093	Papayawhip	#FFEFD5
Peachpuff	#FFDAB9	Peru	#CD853F	Pink	#FFC0CB
Plum	#DDA0DD	Powderblue	#B0E0E6	Purple	#800080
Red	#FF0000	Rosybrown	#BC8F8F	Royalblue	#4169E1
Saddlebrown	#8B4513	Salmon	#FA8072	Sandybrown	#F4A460
Seagreen	#2E8B57	Seashell	#FFF5EE	Sienna	#A0522D
Silver	#C0C0C0	Skyblue	#87CEEB	Slateblue	#6A5ACD
Slategray	#708090	Snow	#FFFAFA	Springgreen	#00FF7F
Steelblue	#4682B4	Tan	#D2B48C	Teal	#008080
Thistle	#D8BFD8	Tomato	#FF6347	Turquoise	#40E0D0
Violet	#EE82EE	Wheat	#F5DEB3	White	#FFFFFF
Whitesmoke	#F5F5F5	Yellow	#FFFF00	Yellowgreen	#9ACD32

Table 5.3 presents the named colors and "safe" colors together in a list. The numbered safe colors between named colors represent colors in the spectrum between those two points. For example, if you want to use a safe dark blue color, choose from the two "safe" colors—#000099 and #0000CC—that are between dark blue and medium blue in the table.

TABLE 5.3: THE NAMED COLORS AND THE SAFE COLORS

Name	Code	Name	Code	Name	Code
Black	#000000	Darkblue	#000099		#003300
	#000033		#0000CC		#003333
	#000066	Mediumblue	#0000CD		#003366
Navy	#000080	Blue	#0000FF		#003399
Darkblue	#00008B		#0000FF		#0033CC

Continued ▶

TABLE 5.3: THE NAMED COLORS AND THE SAFE COLORS

Name	Code	Name	Code	Name	Code
Blue	#0033FF	Midnightblue	#191970	Limegreen	#33FF00
Darkgreen	#006400	Dodgerblue	#1E90FF		#33FF33
	#006600	Lightseagreen	#20B2AA		#33FF66
	#006633	Forestgreen	#228B22		#33FF99
	#006666	Seagreen	#2E8B57		#33FFCC
	#006699	Darkslategray	#2F4F4F		#33FFFF
	#0066CC	Limegreen	#32CD32	Medium-	#3CB371
	#0066FF		#330000	Turquoise	#40E0D0
Green	#008000		#330033	seagreen	
Teal	#008080		#330066	Royalblue	#4169E1
Darkcyan	#008B8B		#330099	Steelblue	#4682B4
	#009900		#3300CC	Darkslateblue	#483D8B
	#009933		#3300FF	Medium-	#48D1CC
	#009966		#333300	turquoise	
	#009999		#333333	Indigo	#4B0082
	#0099CC		#333366	Darkolivegreen	#556B2F
	#0099FF		#333399	Cadetblue	#5F9EA0
Deepskyblue	#00BFFF		#3333CC	Cornflower-	#6495ED
	#00CC00		#3333FF	blue	
	#00CC33		#336600		#660000
	#00CC66		#336633		#660033
	#00CC99		#336666		#660066
	#00CCCC		#336699		#660099
	#00CCFF		#3366CC		#6600CC
Darkturquoise	#00CED1		#3366FF		#6600FF
Medium-	#00FA9A		#339900		#663300
springgreen			#339933		#663333
Lime	#00FF00		#339966		#663366
	#00FF00		#339999		#663399
	#00FF33		#3399CC		#6633CC
	#00FF66		#3399FF		#6633FF
Springgreen	#00FF7F		#33CC00		#666600
	#00FF99		#33CC33		#666633
	#00FFCC		#33CC66		#666666
Aqua	#00FFFF		#33CC99		#666699
Cyan	#00FFFF		#33CCCC		#6666CC
	#00FFFF		#33CCFF		#6666FF

Continued

TABLE 5.3: THE NAMED COLORS AND THE SAFE COLORS

Name	Code	Name	Code	Name	Code
Cornflower-blue	#669900	Lightskyblue	#87CEFA	Darkorchid	#99CC33
		Blueviolet	#8A2BE2		#99CC66
	#669933	Darkred	#8B0000		#99CC99
	#669966	Darkmagenta	#8B008B		#99CCCC
	#669999	Saddlebrown	#8B4513		#99CCFF
	#6699CC	Darkseagreen	#8FBC8F		#99FF00
	#6699FF	Lightgreen	#90EE90		#99FF33
	#66CC00	Mediumpurple	#9370DB		#99FF66
	#66CC33				#99FF99
	#66CC66	Darkviolet	#9400D3		#99FFCC
	#66CC99	Palegreen	#98FB98		#99FFFF
	#66CCCC		#990000	Yellowgreen	#9ACD32
Cornflower-blue	#66CCFF		#990033	Sienna	#A0522D
			#990066	Brown	#A52A2A
Medium-aquamarine	#66CDAA		#990099	Darkgray	#A9A9A9
			#9900CC	Lightblue	#ADD8E6
	#66FF00		#9900FF	Greenyellow	#ADFF2F
	#66FF33	Darkorchid	#9932CC	Paleturquoise	#AFEEEE
	#66FF66		#993300	Lightsteelblue	#B0C4DE
	#66FF99		#993333	Powderblue	#B0E0E6
	#66FFCC		#993366	Firebrick	#B22222
	#66FFFF		#993399	Dark-goldenrod	#B8860B
Dimgray	#696969		#9933CC		
Slateblue	#6A5ACD		#9933FF	Medium-orchid	#BA55D3
Olivedrab	#6B8E23		#996600		
Slategray	#708090		#996633	Rosybrown	#BC8F8F
Lightslategray	#778899		#996666	Darkkhaki	#BDB76B
Medium-slateblue	#7B68EE		#996699	Silver	#C0C0C0
			#9966CC	Medium-violetred	#C71585
Lawngreen	#7CFC00		#9966FF		
Chartreuse	#7FFF00		#999900		#CC0000
Aquamarine	#7FFFD4		#999933		#CC0033
Maroon	#800000		#999966		#CC0066
Purple	#800080		#999999		#CC0099
Olive	#808000		#9999CC		#CC00CC
Gray	#808080		#9999FF		#CC00FF
Skyblue	#87CEEB		#99CC00		#CC3300

Continued ▶

TABLE 5.3: THE NAMED COLORS AND THE SAFE COLORS

Name	Code	Name	Code	Name	Code
Medium-violetred	#CC3333	Goldenrod	#DAA520	Deeppink	#FF1493
		Palevioletred	#DB7093		#FF3300
	#CC3366	Crimson	#DC143C		#FF3333
	#CC3399	Gainsboro	#DCDCDC		#FF3366
	#CC33CC	Plum	#DDA0DD		#FF3399
	#CC33FF	Burlywood	#DEB887	Deeppink	#FF33CC
	#CC6600	Lightcyan	#E0FFFF		#FF33FF
	#CC6633	Lavender	#E6E6FA	Orangered	#FF4500
	#CC6666	Darksalmon	#E9967A	Tomato	#FF6347
	#CC6699	Violet	#EE82EE		#FF6600
	#CC66CC	Palegoldenrod	#EEE8AA		#FF6633
	#CC66FF	Lightcoral	#F08080		#FF6666
	#CC9900	Khaki	#F0E68C	Tomato	#FF6699
	#CC9933	Aliceblue	#F0F8FF		#FF66CC
	#CC9966	Honeydew	#F0FFF0		#FF66FF
	#CC9999	Azure	#F0FFFF	Hotpink	#FF69B4
	#CC99CC	Sandybrown	#F4A460	Coral	#FF7F50
	#CC99FF	Wheat	#F5DEB3	Darkorange	#FF8C00
	#CCCC00	Beige	#F5F5DC		#FF9900
	#CCCC33	Whitesmoke	#F5F5F5		#FF9933
	#CCCC66	Mintcream	#F5FFFA		#FF9966
	#CCCC99	Ghostwhite	#F8F8FF	Darkorange	#FF9999
	#CCCCCC	Salmon	#FA8072		#FF99CC
	#CCCCFF	Antiquewhite	#FAEBD7		#FF99FF
	#CCFF00	Linen	#FAF0E6	Lightsalmon	#FFA07A
	#CCFF33	Lightgolden-rodyellow	#FAFAD2	Orange	#FFA500
	#CCFF66			Lightpink	#FFB6C1
	#CCFF99	Oldlace	#FDF5E6	Pink	#FFC0CB
	#CCFFCC	Red	#FF0000		#FFCC00
	#CCFFFF		#FF0000		#FFCC33
Indianred	#CD5C5C		#FF0033		#FFCC66
Peru	#CD853F		#FF0066		#FFCC99
Chocolate	#D2691E		#FF0099		#FFCCCC
Tan	#D2B48C		#FF00CC		#FFCCFF
Lightgrey	#D3D3D3	Fuchsia	#FF00FF	Gold	#FFD700
Thistle	#D8BFD8	Magenta	#FF00FF	Peachpuff	#FFDAB9
Orchid	#DA70D6		#FF00FF	Navajowhite	#FFDEAD

Continued ▶

TABLE 5.3: THE NAMED COLORS AND THE SAFE COLORS

Name	Code	Name	Code	Name	Code
Moccasin	#FFE4B5	Seashell	#FFF5EE		#FFFF66
Bisque	#FFE4C4	Cornsilk	#FFF8DC		#FFFF99
Mistyrose	#FFE4E1	Lemonchiffon	#FFFACD		#FFFFCC
Blanched-almond	#FFEBCD	Floralwhite	#FFFAF0	Lightyellow	#FFFFE0
		Snow	#FFFAFA	Ivory	#FFFFF0
Papayawhip	#FFEFD5	Yellow	#FFFF00	White	#FFFFFF
Lavender blush	#FFF0F5	Yellow	#FFFF00		
			#FFFF33		

INDEX

Note to the Reader: Throughout this index **boldfaced** page numbers indicate primary discussions of a topic. *Italicized* page numbers indicate illustrations.

B

C

double quotes ("), identifying specific location of
name anchors, 113-114
<DT> tag, for definition
terms, 83, 685-686
DTD (Document Type
Definition) element, 63,
527
Dynamic HTML (DHTML).
See also HTML documents;
Style Sheets
creating collapsible
documents
the Microsoft way,
469-477
the Netscape Navigator
way, 477-482
described, 457-460
Microsoft's implementa-
tion, 460-463
Netscape Navigator's
implementation,
463-469
sample object and prop-
erty identifiers, 463
specifying functions for
objects, 462-463
dynamic information, 48, 49

—E—

E read-only math property,
JavaScript, 913
e-commerce, 619
elements object, JavaScript,
839
elements property,
JavaScript, 913
<EM> tag, for emphasis, 74
e-mail
links, 115
responses, for forms, 333
templates, 337-339
<EMBED> tag, 437, 438,
686-688
embedding
JavaScript, 397-402
Style Sheets, 121-124,
141-142
embedding JavaScript,
397-402
employment objective, on
Web résumés, 624
encoding property,
JavaScript, 913
enhanced text editors, 500
enterprise-wide Web sites.
See intranets

—T—

Java™ Development Kit Version 1.1.3 Binary Code License

This binary code license ("License") contains rights and restrictions associated with use of the accompanying software and documentation ("Software"). Read the License carefully before installing the Software. By installing the Software you agree to the terms and conditions of this License.

1. **Limited License Grant**. Sun grants to you ("Licensee") a non-exclusive, non-transferable limited license to use the Software without fee for evaluation of the Software and for development of Java™ compatible applets and applications. Licensee may make one archival copy of the Software and may re-distribute complete, unmodified copies of the Software to software developers within Licensee's organization to avoid unnecessary download time, provided that this License conspicuously appear with all copies of the Software. Except for the foregoing, Licensee may not re-distribute the Software in whole or in part, either separately or included with a product. Refer to the Java Runtime Environment Version 1.1.1 binary code license http://java.sun.com/products/JDK/1.1.1/index.html) for the availability of runtime code which may be distributed with Java compatible applets and applications.

2. **Java Platform Interface**. Licensee may not modify the Java Platform Interface ("JPI", identified as classes contained within the "java" package or any subpackages of the "java" package), by creating additional classes within the JPI or otherwise causing the addition to or modification of the classes in the JPI. In the event that Licensee creates any Java-related API and distributes such API to others for applet or application development, Licensee must promptly publish an accurate specification for such API for free use by all developers of Java-based software.

3. Restrictions. Software is confidential copyrighted information of Sun and title to all copies is retained by Sun and/or its licensors. Licensee shall not modify, decompile, disassemble, decrypt, extract, or otherwise reverse engineer Software. Software may not be leased, assigned, or sublicensed, in whole or in part. **Software is not designed or intended for use in on-line control of aircraft, air traffic, aircraft navigation or aircraft communications; or in the design, construction, operation or maintenance of any nuclear facility. Licensee warrants that it will not use or redistribute the Software for such purposes.**

4. Trademarks and Logos. This License does not authorize Licensee to use any Sun name, trademark or logo. Licensee acknowledges that Sun owns the Java trademark and all Java-related trademarks, logos and icons including the Coffee Cup and Duke ("Java Marks") and agrees to: (i) to comply with the Java Trademark Guidelines at http://java.sun.com/trademarks.html; (ii) not do anything harmful to or inconsistent with Sun's rights in the Java Marks; and (iii) assist Sun in protecting those rights, including assigning to Sun any rights acquired by Licensee in any Java Mark.

5. Disclaimer of Warranty. Software is provided "AS IS," without a warranty of any kind. ALL EXPRESS OR IMPLIED REPRESENTATIONS AND WARRANTIES, INCLUDING ANY IMPLIED WARRANTY OF MERCHANTABILITY, FITNESS FOR A PARTICULAR PURPOSE OR NON-INFRINGEMENT, ARE HEREBY EXCLUDED.

6. Limitation of Liability. SUN AND ITS LICENSORS SHALL NOT BE LIABLE FOR ANY DAMAGES SUFFERED BY LICENSEE OR ANY THIRD PARTY AS A RESULT OF USING OR DISTRIBUTING SOFTWARE. IN NO EVENT WILL SUN OR ITS LICENSORS BE LIABLE FOR ANY LOST REVENUE, PROFIT OR DATA, OR FOR DIRECT, INDIRECT, SPECIAL, CONSEQUENTIAL, INCIDENTAL OR PUNITIVE DAMAGES, HOWEVER CAUSED AND REGARDLESS OF THE THEORY OF LIABILITY, ARISING OUT OF THE USE OF OR INABILITY TO USE SOFTWARE, EVEN IF SUN HAS BEEN ADVISED OF THE POSSIBILITY OF SUCH DAMAGES.

7. **Termination**. Licensee may terminate this License at any time by destroying all copies of Software. This License will terminate immediately without notice from Sun if Licensee fails to comply with any provision of this License. Upon such termination, Licensee must destroy all copies of Software.

8. **Export Regulations**. Software, including technical data, is subject to U.S. export control laws, including the U.S. Export Administration Act and its associated regulations, and may be subject to export or import regulations in other countries. Licensee agrees to comply strictly with all such regulations and acknowledges that it has the responsibility to obtain licenses to export, re-export, or import Software. Software may not be downloaded, or otherwise exported or re-exported (i) into, or to a national or resident of, Cuba, Iraq, Iran, North Korea, Libya, Sudan, Syria or any country to which the U.S. has embargoed goods; or (ii) to anyone on the U.S. Treasury Department's list of Specially Designated Nations or the U.S. Commerce Department's Table of Denial Orders.

9. **Restricted Rights**. Use, duplication or disclosure by the United States government is subject to the restrictions as set forth in the Rights in Technical Data and Computer Software Clauses in DFARS 252.227-7013(c) (1) (ii) and FAR 52.227-19(c) (2) as applicable.

10. **Governing Law**. Any action related to this License will be governed by California law and controlling U.S. federal law. No choice of law rules of any jurisdiction will apply.

11. **Severability**. If any of the above provisions are held to be in violation of applicable law, void, or unenforceable in any jurisdiction, then such provisions are herewith waived to the extent necessary for the License to be otherwise enforceable in such jurisdiction. However, if in Sun's opinion deletion of any provisions of the License by operation of this paragraph unreasonably compromises the rights or increase the liabilities of Sun or its licensors, Sun reserves the right to terminate the License and refund the fee paid by Licensee, if any, as Licensee's sole and exclusive remedy.

What's on the CD

This Companion CD-ROM contains the code and images from most examples in this book, several clip media libraries, and a variety of freeware, shareware, and evaluation versions of tools to help you develop HTML documents easily.

Examples   These files, taken from the book, show how to apply various HTML effects. You can work with them, see how they're put together, and use them as learning tools.

Graphics Tools   This collection includes Windows utilities that you can use to develop and modify images and to create animated GIFs. Try out the GIF Construction Set from Alchemy Mindworks, Inc., and PaintShop Pro from JASC, Inc.

Scripts   Use these scripts on a Web server to enhance the functionality of all your Web pages. Check out Selena Sol's Script Archive, by Selena Sol and Gunther Birznieks; Matt's Script Archive, from Matt Wright; cgiemail from MIT; and Ceilidh, from Lilikoi Software, Inc.

HTML Authoring Tools   These evaluation versions of high-end Web and HTML development tools provide sophisticated capabilities. See Macromedia, Inc.'s Backstage Director and Flash demos; the 30-day trial version of NetObjects Fusion 2.0 from NetObjects, Inc.; Drumbeat from Elemental Software; and HTML Transit from InfoAccess, Inc.

Clip Media   These archives are a starting point for your development efforts. Try the Artbeats Webtools Demo, from Artbeats Software, Inc.; the Buttonhut Collection from AfterHours Communications Corp.; the Iconographics Sampler from Iconographics; the 4inPrint Sampler from InPrint Advertising, Inc.; 20 Krazy Kids Clipart from Havana Street; and the Earshot sound sampler from DXM Productions.

Help Development Tools   These demos show you how to use help and HTML-based help development software. Take a look at HelpBreeze 2 from Solutionsoft; ForeHelp Demo from ForeFront, Inc.; WexTech's Documentation Studio Demo; and the WinHELP Office 4 demo from Blue Sky Software Corporation.

Other HTML Tools   A range of other HTML tools includes everything from HTML editing to link checking to easy conversion from Word to HTML. See HTMLPad from Intermania Software; GrabNet, WebWhacker, and WebSeeker from ForeFront, Inc.; CD2HTML from Falk Petro; LinkBot from Tetranet Software; HTML Power Tools from OppoSite Software; Opera from Opera Software A/S; WordtoWeb from Solutionsoft; and ActiveX Control Pad from Microsoft, Inc.

Other Utilities   To round out the CD, we've garnered a variety of other utilities from Aladdin Development Technology (Stuffit), Apple Computer (QuickTime), Adobe Corporation (Acrobat Reader), Ipswitch, Inc. (WS-FTP), Nico Mak Computing (WinZip), and JavaSoft (the Java Developer's Kit), among others.